Readings
in Motor Learning

Readings
in Motor Learning

Edited by ROBERT N. SINGER
Florida State University

Lea & Febiger
Philadelphia · *1972*

Health Education,
Physical Education, and
Recreation Series

Ruth Abernathy, Ph.D., Editorial Adviser
Director, School of Physical and Health Education
University of Washington, Seattle, Washington 98105

ISBN 0-8121-0350-5

Library of Congress Catalog Card Number 79-146033

Printed in the United States of America

PREFACE

Ask anyone for a definition of the word "learning" and see how many varied responses are offered. Preface that with "motor," "psychomotor," "perceptual-motor," or a similar term and the concept becomes more confused yet since "motor learning" implies different ideas to different people. Many researchers, practitioners, and laymen are concerned with learning in the psychomotor domain, but in dissimilar ways. The person's background and his field of interest will influence his conception of it. Thus, the engineering psychologist, the experimental psychologist, the military psychologist, the industrial psychologist, the physical educator, the special educator, the neuropsychologist, and the social psychologist all approach motor learning from different points of view so that their terminology, theories, practices, and research strategies also differ. In fields of study such as physical education, upper-level and graduate courses dealing with motor learning are being added at an enthusiastic rate in various universities throughout the country. Several psychology departments now offer a course in human motor performance. The content of all these courses leads to better teaching methodologies, indepth theory analyses, and more sophisticated research undertakings on the part of the students.

Although some texts are available for students interested in motor learning, very rarely are articles which contribute to a basic understanding of the field selectively designated as mandatory readings. Nevertheless, the more concerned and sophisticated student of motor learning needs to go beyond the summaries and interpretations of various articles found in the typical texts on the subject. He desires to obtain more precise knowledge about all aspects of learning. It stands to reason, then, that a book of such readings in the area of motor learning would be of value.

The body of knowledge on motor learning is extensive, but without a common thread. This book attempts to organize the research in a meaningful way for the student. The examination and analysis of "classical" articles dealing with topics related to the learning process pose a challenge. The readings should reflect the efforts of representatives of the various disciplines and interest groups. Many apparent differences can be resolved by replacing unfamiliar terms with familiar ones, and analogies to skills of concern can be drawn. A major difficulty in the preparation of the book was identifying the parameters surrounding motor learning, and then, forming unified sections of the book. Another problem was in the selection of meritorious articles— no simple task. With many good ones from which to choose, those ultimately incorporated in this book are indicative of my subjective estimate of quality work. The judgment one employs in selecting such readings is, at the least, open to question. The readings in this collection were included according to various criteria. One, the articles represented authoritative material in the areas related to motor learning. Two, they were, for the most part, indicative of more recent probings on a given topic. Three, they were neither too simple nor too sophisticated with regard to the nature of the material covered and the manner in which it was reported. For example, articles containing extensive descriptions of instrumentation, extremely sophisticated statistics, and highly theoretical issues and conceptual terms were omitted from the collection. And four, the articles were chosen for their clarity in handling material and the interest generated by the author's writing style. Adequate coverage of the basic topics related to the learning of motor skills was of prime concern. Perhaps some areas of investigation were inadvertently omitted, but certainly no offense was intended. In summary, the articles selected for the book describe many aspects of and considerations in motor performance. They made important contributions to the literature: in theory, in research directions, and in practical applications. Most of the articles are of recent vintage. Hopefully, they will suggest topics, experimental designs, theoretical frameworks, and practical implications for all those interested in and concerned with any aspect of the acquisition of motor skills. When the student has assimilated the ideas in these readings, he should have acquired a perspective of the scope and direction of the research and writings in this area.

Historically, research on motor skills has not made too much of an impact on the public or educational institutions. Work in the cognitive domain has been much more impressive. During World War II and the Korean War, psychologists were called upon to contribute to the understanding of human performance in military tasks. Training research was supported fairly intensively by the government. In the 1960's, man's quest for the mastery of space resulted in further inquiries into man's motor behavior under unusual circumstances. Industrial technologists, vocational researchers, and physical educators have always been concerned with motor learning, and their contributions to the research literature have increased tremendously in recent years.

Although "motor learning" is a convenient descriptive term to use in order to distinguish it from cognitive and affective learning, the concept should by no means be considered in isolation of these other factors. Cognitive and affective elements interact with movement behaviors to influence skill proficiency. The range of variables and considerations involved in the acquisition of skills becomes apparent with each succeeding reading. It is exciting to view motor learning as a relatively untapped field of study. Perhaps this book will indicate the present state of our knowledge of this area, and at the same time, demonstrate the need for more research on all skilled types of behavior, recreational, occupational, and routine.

This book of readings may be used as a textbook for a course in motor learnings or as a supplement to a standard text. Many of the readings may also complement discussions in teaching methods, foundations, or courses in basic principles as well. Each section or chapter of the book is preceded by introductory material to familiarize the student with the nature of the given topic. An overview of each article is also included to emphasize further its major points and values. Hopefully, this book of readings will encourage the student to examine other literature, especially in a topical area that stirs his interest.

Appreciation is extended to the many authors and publishers who made the book possible. The influence of these scholars on our instructional techniques and future research can in no way be measured. Collectively, the advances in knowledge resulting from their efforts reflect the scientific foundations of the study of human motor behavior.

Robert N. Singer
Tallahassee, Florida

CONTENTS

PART 5. *Development and Aging*

PART 6. *Emotions*

PART 7. *Performance Variables*

PART 8. *Practice*

Chapter 12: *During-Practice Considerations*

PART 9. *Social Influence*

PART 1

MOTOR LEARNING AND SKILL

Terminologies and Descriptions

The definition, nature, and conditions of learning have been extensively discussed in many scholarly publications, but they are still disputed because so many of the issues related to learning have not been resolved. Learning, especially the area of study called motor learning, has been defined in various ways. Each explanation is acceptable to those whose theoretical orientation coincides with a particular interpretation. Generally speaking, though, learning that is *primarily* demonstrated through movement-oriented behavior has been termed motor learning. Learning is typically demonstrated through measures of performance. With the acquisition of skill in motor tasks, performances are elevated and they become more predictably consistent. Thus, skill is the word employed to describe high standards of performance, either in a relative sense or on the basis of absolute standards. In many cases, one of the primary goals in motor learning, if not the sole one, is the attainment of proficiency in the task at hand. Whether the act is athletic, occupational, recreational, secretarial, aviational, industrial, or something else, skill can only be realized after numerous practice sessions.

Just as learning and motor learning have been described in various ways, the term skill also has different implications. There are superficial and sophisticated ways of analyzing skilled performance. Any student of motor learning should be aware of the human qualities and practice conditions that contribute to the acquisition of skill. The word skill also refers to an act, task, or measure. Further understanding of motor learning is afforded to the student who is cognizant of the different possible categories of skills. Each may require unique human qualities and/or practice techniques to reach the ultimate objective.

The purpose of this first chapter of readings, then, is to familiarize the student with the terminology and concepts used in similar and dissimilar ways, but all associated with the label, motor learning. Historical developments in motor learning research are then briefly discussed to provide an overview. Finally, the nature of performance proficiency, or the skilled act, is presented in two position papers.

Chapter 1

THE NATURE OF MOTOR LEARNING AND SKILL

What's in a Name?*

AILEENE LOCKHART

THIS first paper helps to explain the application of "labels." If the student of motor skill learning is confused because of the various names associated with the same process or task, he has a right to be. It would surely be easier to make sense of the research reports if agreed-upon definitions and descriptions were in use. Fortunately, Lockhart recognizes the problem that exists with labeling, and explains the breadth of the area of motor learning. From a discussion of the terminologies and relationships, the reader becomes more aware of the nature of the literature encompassed under the rubric, motor learning.

When we ask such questions as "How does man learn gross motor skills?" "What factors affect learning and performance?" "Under what conditions does he perform with greatest efficiency and effectiveness?" or "What are the dimensions of human physical skills and abilities?" we pose questions of fundamental concern to all whose business is human motion. Systematic efforts to unravel the mysteries of how patterned motion is accomplished are seen in studies which go by different names: motor learning, sensory-motor learning (sensori-motor, sensori-neuromotor); psycho-motor learning (psychomotor); menti-motor learning (ideo-motor); neuro-muscular learning (neuromotor); perceptual-motor learning (perceptuo-motor, visuo-motor, tactual-motor). There are others, but so far kinesthetico-motor or proprioceptor-motor have escaped the attention of this writer!

What do all of these terms imply? Definitions, when given at all, are usually so diverse, contradictory, and imbricated as to render them confusing. Why so many names? Should they be discriminated among or are they synonymous? Why does one writer discuss "sensory-motor learning" and another "psycho-

* From *Quest,* 1964, Monograph II, pp. 9-13. Reprinted with permission of the author and publisher.

motor learning" when each is referring to the same phenomenon? How can we explain what a writer means who, when discussing the classic Pavlovian experiment, indicates that an automatic reflex is an example of a perceptual-motor skill? Is it not confusing to find in a section labelled "Concepts of Psychomotor Organization" the concluding question, "What is the nature of perceptual-motor integration?"

Perhaps there are many explanations. One may be that investigators naturally communicate in language familiar to them. The behavioristic psychologist concerned with motor learning might be expected to use the term psycho-motor. The experimenter interested primarily in the functioning of the sense organs performs sensory-motor investigations. Those concerned with perceptually guided, non-verbal behavior often refer to perceptual-motor learnings.

Sometimes a specific label is quite precisely and descriptively chosen, thus visuo-motor refers to motion guided specifically by the sense of vision. On the other hand, we do not need to look far to find instances of at least semicareless usage. There are many examples too where terms seem to have been chosen because they are *not* definitive or limiting; they thus allow wide generality and so protect the authors from too precise limitation and finely-precise identification. A fear of misunderstanding perhaps prompts other choices of labels. Though the uncomplicated term "motor learning," for example, is widely employed and rather universally understood, many—fearful that this term alone might imply a disembodied mind, merely a constellation of muscles—prefer to tack on a prefix of some sort.

We cannot rule out the probability that some use a hyphenated title because it sounds original or academically oriented or learned. Perhaps such titles are the result of unintended pretense but they leave the impression that we know more than we do about the complex, mysterious phenomenon of learning; the entity of learning cannot be analyzed into such precise, identifiable categories and sub-categories. The variety of terms no doubt also reflects the fact that as yet we have more unanswered than answered questions regarding how the learning of motor skills is accomplished. Much of our "Knowledge" is inferential; many of our hypotheses stem not only from varied bits but varied qualities of evidence.

Learning about the nature, characteristics and conditions of skill learning and successful performance is a responsibility of the physical educator. That we have become extremely aware of this again is shown in the nature of much of the research now being conducted and by the numerous many-titled courses on this aspect of our discipline which are offered to professional students.

Proud Titles—Modest Gains

Most physical educators are holistic in point of view but many do damage to our profession by using dualistic terms. Though more and more people are now less disturbed by dualism than in former years, it seems wise for physical educators to avoid any hint of mind-body dichotomy.

We might profit from experiences in other fields and keep our terminology well within the limits of careful research. We could then take pride in our labels. The number of different terms which are used in a semicareless manner in a great number of current investigations leads to confusion. We can and should attempt to avoid their indiscriminate use, and meaningless expressions also should be dropped.

An effort to distinguish among some commonly used terms is made below. No claim is made that the distinctions drawn are necessarily correct. The writer's purpose is merely to encourage and stimulate discussion and, hopefully, to speed the day when final agreement regarding their meaning may arrive.

Sensory-Motor: As currently viewed by most psychologists, what we know comes to us first through the sensory systems for it is the receptors which signal impingements to the central nervous system. It is through the senses that we are informed about both the internal and external environment. All activity depends first upon sensory input. While it is widely understood that the nature of man is holistic, investigations in which the *primary* problem focuses on sensory discrimination (though the results are studied by motor responses) might properly be called "sensory-motor." Studies the chief purpose of which is to investigate the function of sensing or detecting (such as auditory capacities, visual capabilities, vestibular sensitivity) appear to be appropriately designated as sensory-motor.

Psycho-Motor: It is possible for an experienced diver to learn to perform a new dive or stunt purely through conceptualization but it is difficult to know that the "half-gainer" has been learned until it has been performed, at which time it becomes a motor skill. According to some current Russian studies, the formation of a motor skill does not begin when physical practice starts, but *before,* with the creation of the idea. Thus it is advantageous to "mentally fulfill" or rehearse idea-feelings and memories of skills before attempting them. These theories resemble those of the Gestaltists and differ markedly from Pavlovian concepts.

Some classify all human abilities into two types, the cognitive (where the chief outcomes are facts and concepts) and the psychomotor (where principal outcomes are motor sets and skills). In this case, fundamental psychomotor abilities would include such physical factors as strength, speed, precision, and coordination. This appears to be a defensible classification. The term psycho-motor, however, implies an unfortunate dualism to many persons and therefore is avoided today.

Menti-Motor: Though there are cortical aspects in voluntary action and in motion regulation, this term traditionally contrasts the mental factor with the physical, physiological, somatic. Some authors (Hetherington, for example) used the term, however, for quite different purposes—to emphasize the connectedness of mind and soma. It seems wise though to use this label only when the mental aspects are the *primary* considerations under investigation, the motor being merely the method of measuring results and inferring relationships. The term is now practically obsolete for it strongly suggests through historical and philosophical use an obvious mentalistic concept with the implication that the mind and body are not only separate but even antagonistic. Such ideas currently are shunned completely.

Neuro-Muscular: Little can be learned without neuromuscular involvement. Nevertheless this term seems to limit investigation merely to motor responses, for it too suggests the unhappy doctrine of physical-mental opposition. Though cortical activity leads to motor response, though physical coordination involves cortical control, regulation and integration, the term neuro-muscular appears too restrictive to include the complex interplay of all the sensory, perceptual, ideational, and psychological variables which must be simultaneously involved in gross motor learning and highly skilled performance. The term appears to cut off learning at the level of the spinal cord.

Perceptual-Motor: An individual reacts as he sees the world. He has a general operational scheme of life, with past experiences providing him with a coherent plan or framework through which he makes relationships. This idea is in tune with reigning Gestalt psychology and accounts for the present popularity of the term "perceptual-motor." It is not at present, in the views held by a good many psychologists and physical educators, tainted with dualistic notions. Some maintain, indeed, that perception and motion are not two separately identifiable entities at all; that, in fact, it is impossible to consider motor responses separate from perceptual stimuli. The term refers to the learning of overt motor responses which result from *primarily* non-verbal stimuli. Of the terms discussed so far, perceptual-motor appears to be the best choice for characterizing the kind of studies which are of great interest to physical educators.

How About Motor Learning?

As presently envisioned by most psychologists and physiologists, this term refers to action instigated through the sense receptors, integrated through the nervous system, and modulated through the response mechanisms into controlled motor behavior. This name emphasizes organized motion, the executive expression of organismic activity (the end-result, not the means of getting there). It is rarely used with a dualistic intent. There are many kinds of learnings; the term motor learning simply designates the type of learning we are talking about: that manifested by controlled movement.

The term motor learning does not suggest any one explanation of learning nor a single method of exploration. It is not restricted by the limitations and exclusions implied by the nomenclature of "sensory-motor," "neuro-muscular," "psycho-motor," or "menti-motor." It should be pointed out that it does not rule out the involvement of each of these factors in the total heuristic process of acquiring motor skills. It simply describes chiefly the motor factor rather than other factors, all of which are most certainly simultaneously operative in the single holistic function of learning. It refers most specifically to the outcome (the task) in which physical educators are primarily interested: those learnings in which overt muscularly controlled responses predominate.

The player may run almost automatically without conscious control (sensory-motor), but when he makes a broken-field run toward an opponent's goal his responses are perceptually cued (perceptual-motor), are affected by psychical processes (psycho-motor) and ought to be directed toward a definite plan (ideo-motor). In learning to serve a tennis ball a player must control motion, but having learned the specific pattern he serves semi-automatically, relegating the perceptual motor to the sensory-motor, and is thus left free to concentrate on the strategy appropriate for use against his opponent.

Seldom is there pure sensory-motor learning, pure perceptual-motor learning, pure any kind of learning. On the basis of present knowledge, the mechanism for learning appears essentially the same, no matter what the specific primary outcome is. This should be argument enough against any assumption of dualism. Dualistic concepts are of our own making, within the personality, theoretical abstractions; no basis for them resides in the functioning of the human body.

It is suggested throughout the preceding discussion that when investigations are made which are highly specific and as far as possible restricted chiefly to one aspect of the learning process the term chosen be one which emphasizes *the primary factor* under consideration and that it be descriptive of the task, not explanatory. To follow this suggestion it seems to the writer that the term "motor learning" would include all studies aimed at understanding primarily those factors which have specific relevance to the motor function. (It is important to note the word "primarily.") This term—motor learning—seems restrictive enough to indicate the *primary task,* but open enough to admit all the constellation of complex inputs, integrations, and interactions that most certainly are involved in the learning and performance of complex gross motor activities. What's in a name? Regardless of the one chosen, those who would understand learning of any sort must remember that so far as is presently known *the ingredients of learning are intricate, multi-dimensional, delicately integrated, and basically inseparable.*

Historical Introduction*

ARTHUR L. IRION

THE history of motor skills research is prepared by Irion, with an analysis of the major contributions to "the movement" from the end of the nineteenth century to the present time. Trends in research are interesting to view. It is probable, though, that in his analysis of skills research, Irion has omitted research reported in physical education journals and related areas. Being an experimental psychologist, his concerns lie in the skills typically analyzed by military, industrial, and experimental psychologists. Although his interpretation of the literature concerned with skills indicates a decline in number in recent published research, a casual glance at the volumes of *The Research Quarterly,* published by the American Association for Health, Physical Education, and Recreation from the first publication in 1930 to today, would probably reveal a major swing to research concerned with the acquisition of motor skills. It is recommended that the serious student read the entire publication cited below for its valuable contribution to knowledge on skilled performance. Numerous outstanding researchers have reported material in that book.

The history of research in the area of motor skills extends from the very end of the last century to the present day. Although it is difficult to identify a first experiment, the best-known early investigations were those of Bryan and Harter (1897, 1899) on the learning of telegraphic language. These papers were preceded by an earlier study of Bryan's (1892) and a paper by Dresslar (1891-1892). However, there does not appear to have been a "founder" of this area of research in the sense that Pavlov founded the work in conditioned response learning or Ebbinghaus founded the field of verbal rote learning. Recently, Noble (1968) has nominated Woodworth as a candidate for foundership on the basis of his book, *Le Mouvement* (1903). However, neither this work nor Woodworth's earlier monograph (1899) on the accuracy of voluntary movement appears to have been referred to by a significant number of subsequent authors until Ammons (1958) pointed to the importance of Woodworth's contributions.

While it is undeniably true that here, as in other situations, want of identifiable ancestry can be an embarrassment, it is also true that the field of motor

* From "Historical Introduction," in E. A. Bilodeau and Ina McD. Bilodeau (editors), *Principles of Skill Acquisition,* N. Y.: Academic Press, 1969, pp. 1-4. Abridged and reprinted with permission of the author and publisher.

skills probably owes some of its vitality to just that deficiency. A founder tends to define the field of discourse, to set the methods of investigation, to identify the problems to be solved, and, all too often, to bequeath a legacy of sterility as well. Too frequently, the dead hand of the founder continues to rest on the helm of the ship, the weight of the tradition he has established serving to limit the scope and imaginativeness of the work of those who have followed. The field of motor skills does not suffer from a lack of variety or imaginativeness. Indeed, the approaches are so extremely various that there is some difficulty in defining just what the field of motor skills is. The diverse skeins of interest and activity in the skills area tend to overlap with the whole remaining field of experimental psychology to such an extent that an argument could be made in support of the proposition that the history of skills research *is* a miniature version of the total history of experimental psychology. The traditional experimental areas of learning, sensation, perception, cognition, work phenomena, physiological correlates of behavior, motivation, and psychometrics have all been represented in the research on skills.

While part of the difficulty of defining the area of skills may stem from the lack of a founding father, the lack of a serviceable basic concept is probably a more significant deficiency. Other areas of investigation have been more fortunate in this respect. The concept of the *idea,* developed so thoroughly by the associationists, proved to have great value for the workers in the field of rote learning. The concept that was the obvious analog to the idea and that should have been useful to the workers in the skills area, the Cartesian reflex, turned out to be not so very useful, after all, in the skills context. Quite evidently, the concept of the reflex has been much more valuable to the physiological psychologists and to the Pavlovians than it has been to the workers in the skills area. The difficulty is that while the idea and the reflex are excellent concepts for describing behaviors that naturally break into discrete units, they are not nearly as satisfactory for describing behaviors that are essentially continuous. It is true that some motor performances may be considered as a series of discrete events, and it is also true that the exigencies of the laboratory have forced workers to consider some other motor events in the conceptual framework of discrete events whether or not this could be accomplished with realism. While it cannot be denied that, because of the former circumstance and in spite of the latter one, considerable advances have been made in understanding skills in terms of a model for discrete events, it is also possible that the use of this kind of model may, in the long run, prove to be more harmful than beneficial.

In their excellent review, E. A. Bilodeau and Bilodeau (1961) offer a "deliberately naive" definition that differentiates the motor-skills field from other areas in terms of the relative importance of the hand, the tongue, and the eye. Although their definition turns out—particularly when one considers the restrictions they place upon it—to be considerably more deliberate than naive, a somewhat more precise definition of coordination has been offered by Fitts (1964), to wit: "By a skilled response I shall mean one in which receptor-effector-feedback processes are highly organized, both spatially and temporally. The central problem for the study of skill learning is how such organizations or patterning comes about" (Fitts, 1964, p. 244).

The history of skills research can be broken into two rather obvious segments, and each of these, in turn, can be split into two smaller divisions. The major shift or break in the history appears to have occurred about 1945. The causes appear to be multiple. First, there was the publication of the very influential book, *Principles of Behavior,* by Hull (1943). Second, at the close of World War II there existed a considerable number of young experimental psychologists who had been exposed to skills problems in the research and aircrew selection programs of the Army Air Corps (in Great Britain a similar influence was exerted by the program sponsored by the RAF and directed by Sir Frederic Bartlett). Then, too, following the war there was a considerable amount of federal support for research in the area of skills. Finally, and most significantly, the immediate postwar period saw the introduction of new statistical techniques for handling skills data. One who gives more than a cursory glance at the pre-1945 skills literature is struck by the fact that the investigators seem to have been handcuffed by their inability to treat their data in meaningful ways. Occasionally quantitative data were presented in the form of means with their probable errors and/or with appended critical ratios for pairs of conditions. More often, the investigator presented his data in the form of learning curves. The great preoccupation that the early experimenters exhibited with respect to learning curves probably reflects, as much as anything else, the want of a technique for treating their data in any other meaningful way. The lack of analytical power also had another influence. Since the research worker was more or less limited to the drawing of one or more curves and letting the reader come to his own conclusions, the experimenter was virtually forced to confine his investigations to variables that produced large effects. Lacking the tools for analyzing even large differences, he did not dare to venture into the investigation of variables that produced more subtle effects.

If the major break in the character of skills research is accepted as having occurred, the further subdivision of each of the two resulting historical periods may be suggested. These subdivisions must be proposed in a more tentative fashion. However, it does appear that the pre-1945 period exhibits a change of emphasis that took place between 1925 and 1935. Before 1925, much of the work was exploratory in character—or, at least, it seems so when examined in retrospect. After 1935 a greater degree of theoretical orientation can be observed. If a definite date is desired for the dividing point, perhaps the appearance of McGeoch's (1927) review of the skills literature could serve as a reference date. The post-1945 era also appears to be divisible into two segments. The first of these was marked by extremely high research productivity in the skills area while the more recent period is marked by a turning away from some of the traditional core problems (distribution of practice and reminiscence, for example) and by the exploration of new theoretical approaches to the study of skills. There has also been a modest decrease in research productivity during this fourth period. If a dividing event to separate the third from the fourth period is wanted, the closing down of the Air Force Personnel Training and Research Center in 1957 might be suggested.

We are left, then, with four periods: 1890-1927, 1927-1945, 1945-1957, and 1957 to the present time. The first period was a time of definition and exploration. The second was marked by an increase in the sophistication of experimental work, by the borrowing of techniques and concepts from other areas of psychology, and, particularly, by the emergence of several theoretical formulations that gave structure to the work of the period. The third period was marked by enormous productivity. Although the time occupied by the third period (12 years) is short, very nearly half of all the published research in the field was produced during this time. It is more difficult to describe the characteristics of the fourth period since we are still in it. Certainly some changes of theoretical orientation are to be seen, but such changes are to be found throughout the history of research on skills and particularly during the two previous transition periods.

The contribution of each era to the total literature of the skills field can be estimated only approximately since the estimates must reflect a judgment as to what should be, and should not be, counted as skills research. For what it may be worth, such an estimate is offered. It would seem that the first era contributed about 7% of the total published research; the second era contributed about 16%; the third era about 47%; and the fourth era (to the present) about 30%...

References

Ammons, R. B. "Le mouvement." In G. S. Seward & J. P. Seward (Eds.), *Current psychological issues: Essays in honor of Robert S. Woodworth.* New York: Holt, 1958. pp. 146-183.

Bilodeau, E. A., & Bilodeau, I. McD. Motor-skills learning. *Annual Review of Psychology,* 1961, *12,* 243-280.

Bryan, W. L. On the development of voluntary motor ability. *American Journal of Psychology,* 1892, *5,* 125-204.

Bryan, W. L., & Harter, N. Studies in the physiology and psychology of the telegraphic language. *Psychological Review,* 1897, *4,* 27-53.

Bryan, W. L., & Harter, N. Studies on the telegraphic language: The acquisition of a hierarchy of habits. *Psychological Review,* 1899, *6,* 345-375.

Dresslar, F. B. Some influences which affect the rapidity of voluntary movements. *American Journal of Psychology,* 1891-1892, *4,* 514-527.

Fitts, P. M. Perceptual-motor skill learning. In A. W. Melton (Ed.), *Categories of human learning.* New York: Academic Press, 1964. pp. 243-285.

Hull, C. L. *Principles of behavior.* New York: Appleton-Century, 1943.

McGeoch, J. A. The acquisition of skill. *Psychological Bulletin,* 1927, *24,* 437-466.

Noble, C. E. The learning of psychomotor skills. *Annual Review of Psychology,* 1968, *19,* 203-250.

Woodworth, R. S. The accuracy of voluntary movement. *Psychological Review,* 1899 (Monograph Suppl., Whole No. 13).

Woodworth, R. S. *Le mouvement.* Paris: Doin, 1903.

Skill = Speed × Accuracy × Form × Adaptability*

HARRY W. JOHNSON

Often the meaning of a term is more readily drawn from a humorous illustration. Johnson's attempt at identifying the dimensions of skill should not be underrated because of the lack of sophisticated commentary and the use of a fable in his article. Although it is true he oversimplifies the nature of skill, the article serves to encompass generally the definition, dimensions, and training techniques associated with skills. It provides an introduction for an understanding of the area as well as the more penetrating readings that follow.

The heart of this little article lies in a fable called "The Woodchoppers' Ball." Perhaps you would do best to turn to that first.

This is an age of change. In industry, especially, every day brings new developments. And each new product, each new process, each new package

* Abridged and reprinted with permission of author and publisher: Johnson, H. W. Skill = speed × accuracy × form × adaptability. PERCEPTUAL AND MOTOR SKILLS, 1961, *13,* 163-170.

is likely to bring with it the necessity for new skills. Manifestly, it behooves the leaders in industry to search for (a) means of selecting people capable of learning new skills readily, and (b) means of teaching new skills efficiently.

Even the briefest contemplation of the teaching of skills brings to mind another need—(c) means of determining the amount of a new skill acquired.

But what do we mean by "skills?" As Maier (1) pointed out, a psychologist entering a shop would be likely to find that the "unskilled workers" there possessed a higher degree of what he considered skill than the "skilled workers." But the skill of the latter, he would find, was backed up by understanding and knowledge, and so our definition of skill must be carefully framed: *Skill is the ability to execute a pattern of behavioral elements in proper relation to a certain environment.* The environment may include a wrench or a tennis racket. It will most certainly include the floor or ground. In sports it often includes a ball. And the elements may be simultaneous or in a sequence. The definition, it is to be hoped, is sufficiently broad to include all "skills" as the term is ordinarily used, only excluding those abilities commonly subsumed under the headings of understanding and knowledge.

But this definition has no particular value until we consider the dimensions of the skill. When these dimensions have been clarified, we can see how to measure a skill or develop a skill. We can even make a beginning in evaluating aptitude for a skill. And the dimensions are probably most readily made apparent by the following foolish little fable.

The Woodchoppers' Ball

Once upon a time there lived in the Great North Woods two lumbermen. One was a Swede and one was a Finn, and both of them were experts with the axe. All the Swedes in the Great North Woods thought that the Swede was the greatest axeman in the world. All of the Finns in the Great North Woods thought that the Finn was the greatest axeman in the world. Nobody else in the Great North Woods, if there *was* anyone else in the Great North Woods, really mattered.

Naturally, this division of opinion led to arguments. Frequently, especially on weekends, these arguments led to fights. Since none of these seemed to settle the point, someone, more intelligent than the rest, suggested that a contest be staged. It was further suggested that the contest be followed by a party with a dance and that the entire affair be called the Woodchoppers' Ball.

Elaborate plans for the Woodchoppers' Ball were made. A huge hall with a stage was engaged. A judge was chosen who happened to be half Swede and half Finn and was trusted by everyone. A band was hired to play for the dance. And loads and loads of wood were brought for the use of the contestants.

Meanwhile, all over the Great North Woods, wagers were made on the outcome of the contest. People who had money bet money. People who had principles, or who simply didn't have money, put up all sorts of personal possessions or agreed to do things that were dangerous or ridiculous or difficult or tedious if their protagonist lost. As the time of the Woodchoppers' Ball approached, feeling was running very high.

When the great day came, the Judge got up on the platform and called the meeting to order, "Ladies and Gentlemen," he shouted in a very loud voice. "This here is a contest to decide which of these two men is the better man with an axe. This is not a contest of luck, and it is not a contest of popularity. It is a contest of skill. We are here tonight to decide which of these two men is the most skillful axeman in the world."

"That being the case," he went on, maintaining his remarkable volume, "my assistants and I have spared no effort to keep things fair. These chopping blocks you see before you are standard in size and shape and absolutely identical. On either side of the stage, and carefully guarded, you will see two tremendous piles of wood which have been perfectly matched, stick by individual stick. And the lights for the positions of the two contestants are as nearly identical as we can make them. We will now flip a coin to see who gets the east end of the stage and who gets the west end, and then the contest can get under way."

The coin was flipped, positions were taken, and the contestants were ready to begin. Each contestant was given ten cords of wood, specifications which the men must meet in chopping the wood were carefully explained, and the Judge raised the starting gun. The crowd went quiet, waiting for the signal to begin.

When the Judge fired the starting gun, the Swede and the Finn began to chop and the audience began to yell. The more the men chopped, the more the people shouted, especially since it became increasingly evident that the finish would be very close. In fact, as nearly as anyone in the audience could tell, the two men struck their last blows at exactly the same time, and the crowd hushed tensely, waiting for the Judge's decision. There was considerable delay while the Judge consulted with the people who had planned the party, but finally he bravely stepped forward to the edge of the platform, and announced, "Ladies and Gentlemen: I hereby declare the contest you have just witnessed to have ended in a draw!"

The first reaction to this was a moan of disappointment, but, as the full import of the decision sank in, this swiftly gave way to manifestations of indignation. The murmur of the crowd grew louder, and several angry remarks were shouted. The Judge raised his hands for silence. "We knew you'd feel this way," he said loudly, "so me and the committee has decided to do something about it." His judgemanship, leadership, and diplomacy were much better than his grammar. After all, English was a third language. "We have plenty of wood, and skill ain't all speed. We're going to test the *accuracy* of these two men and decide who the skillful one is that way."

So, the axemen competed in splitting matches and they competed in splitting straws. They competed in hitting pencil marks and they competed in hitting bird shot. In short, they competed in about every test of accuracy the Judge could devise. But anything the Swede could do the Finn could do likewise, and anything the Finn could do, the Swede could do as well. In accuracy, it gradually became clear, the Swede and the Finn were as evenly matched as they were in speed.

Finally, an old man with a long white beard whispered something lengthy in the Judge's ear, and the Judge made the following announcement: "Ladies and Gentlemen," he said, although by this time nobody was either, "Since this ain't gettin nowhere, I'd like to ask your opinion of a suggestion that's just been made. These men are obviously equal in speed and they're just as equal in accuracy. But there's still a side to chopping wood that we haven't tested. The more skill an axeman has, the less effort he'll use to get the job done. These two men are of an age and of a size. We propose that they be given all the wood they want and both chop until one of them drops. If that's agreeable to the contestants and agreeable to the audience we'll test their skill by that." The two heroes glanced at each other grimly and nodded their heads. The crowd shouted its approval.

But they didn't know what they had let themselves in for. At the end of an hour, the men were still chopping, and keeping up the required cords per hour. At the end of two hours, they were chopping yet, and many of the spectators had found entertainment of their own. To make a long story short, some time later, ninety-nine per cent of the crowd was mightily surprised by a loud thud and a louder silence which signified that both contestants had dropped to the floor.

This third tie, showing the Swede and the Finn to be equal in "form" as well as in speed and accuracy, was almost too much. The contest had just about lost an audience. But the old man with the beard stepped up to the Judge once more. This time he didn't consult so long, but he gestured quite a bit. When the Judge stepped forward this time he had a proposal that, as it turned out, let the gamblers settle their bets and the dancing begin. "We've compared these men in speed, we've compared them in accuracy, and we've compared them in what you might call smoothness. But in all this, they've worked on standard chopping blocks and they've used their own axes. Now, let's see how adaptable they are. They will now be asked to chop wood of various heights. They'll chop under various conditions and they'll chop with various axes."

At this suggestion, the Finn grew pale and gripped his axe. However, he gamely entered this strange new kind of battle. But the truth was quickly out. The Swede could chop any wood under any conditions that the Judge saw fit to impose. Moreover, he chopped on any block and he chopped with any axe. Without his own axe and block, the Finlander was an ordinary man. In terms of adaptability, the Swede was easily superior, and nobody argued, although half of them were sad, when the Judge declared the Swede the Most Skillful Woodchopper in the World.

And so the story is ended. But one word remains to be said. The writer hastens to take this opportunity to assure the fair-minded reader that the outcome of this contest is unrelated to the writer's nationality.

So, skill has four dimensions: speed, accuracy, form, and adaptability. Do these dimensions apply to skills other than chopping wood? Further clarification may be afforded by considering a supremely simple skill—the ability to push a certain button when a light flashes red. Speed is easily observed by noting the time from the flashing of the light to the completion of the act. Accuracy can be checked as precisely as instruments will allow. Form will be good as it approaches a minimum of effort expended. And adaptability will be demonstrated by the variety of conditions and circumstances under which the button can be pushed on signal. . . .

References

1. Maier, N. R. F. *Psychology in industry: a psychological approach to industrial problems.* (2nd ed.) Boston: Houghton Mifflin, 1955.
2. Tiffin, J., & McCormick, E. J. *Industrial psychology.* (4th ed.) New York: Prentice-Hall, 1958.

The Experimental Study of Skill*

FREDERIC BARTLETT

If ever a name is to be associated with contributing to our knowledge on skill, it should be Bartlett's. In this particular paper, he concentrates

* From *Research, 4,* 217-221, 1951. Reprinted with permission of the author and publisher.

on problems primarily associated with industrial, man-operated machine tasks, although many of the statements are pertinent to all types of skills. Such terms as "display," "load," and "ceiling" are incorporated in the discussion and help us to examine the nature of skill more fruitfully. A plea is made for "carefully controlled experimental research into the basic character and requirements of human skill." Without well-controlled experimentation on all aspects of skill, the product, process, and function of learning will be only superficially understood. Bartlett identifies some problematical areas and suggests points to consider when dealing with the acquisition of skill.

Everybody now recognizes that no large human group can achieve and hold any important position in the modern world unless it provides for the development in its population of a great variety of skills, many of them highly specialized, and also arranges conditions for their exercise which avoid undue physical and mental strain. Probably the majority of the skills now demanded have to do with the design, operation or maintenance of machines. There are others, however, more concerned with the use of evidence, made available in many different ways, so as to arrive at decisions directly affecting the behaviour of other persons.

It seems often to be supposed that if the populations concerned can be kept contented, by some process, maybe, of joint conference or consultation, by an "understanding" type of management, and by the lavish provision of amenities which lie outside the skills themselves, human skill behaviour can be left to take whatever form natural development and technical invention may dictate. Or again it is assumed that no matter what may be the form of skill required, there will always be plenty of people in any large population who will be equal to its demands. Such people, it is thought, will find their proper places either by natural or by directed selection.

There is truth in both of these assumptions. Each omits some vital considerations. The human body and mind are, in fact, so built that they can do some things easily and well, with great likelihood of contentment, keeping intact their normal reserve of strength, and with good health. If the same tasks have to be done in different ways, performance will be difficult and relatively ineffective, and there is almost certain to be wide discontent, fatigue and ill health. Whatever else may be done in the interests of studies of so-called human or personal relations, there remains a great need for carefully controlled experimental research into the basic character and requirements of human skill. Not only has such work an important bearing upon some of the most pressing practical problems of the day, but it also raises fundamental issues of a theoretical kind which possess deep interest and significance.

Problems of Equipment Design

All skill is obviously a joint result of immediate environmental conditions and the capacities and range of capacities of the performer. Among the first group of determinants those which have until lately received the least systematic attention—and even now they appear to be little known outside certain groups of experimental psychologists—have to do with equipment design. Consider two simple and direct illustrations.

Many machines must be provided with recording devices to tell the operator whether he is working within prescribed limits of speed, direction and pressure, what stage of completion his task has reached, and to give him other information relevant to his performance. The commonest form of such recording devices is that in which a moving indicator automatically varies its position on a horizontal, or vertical, or circular scale. It is easy to demonstrate experimentally that in many cases a moving indicator of this type is far less easy to interpret accurately and quickly than a direct counter recorder. This is especially the case where multiple dial recorders are needed, or where single scales have multiple indicators. Well-designed counter recording devices will then not only make more work and more accurate work possible in the same time, with machine tools like lathes, jig borers, drills and the like, but, what is much more important, they will reduce strain and irritation to a marked degree.

The general problem is: what kind and what amount of evidence can the human operator deal with best? Here is another instance which offers a rather more complex field for analysis, because it brings in the kind of evidence which comes from skilled movements themselves. There are many forms of operations in which positional directional changes have to be effected, with appropriate timing, in order to keep contact with signals that appear now in one place and now in another. All forms of tracking require this, and so does the operation of machines like cranes, television cameras, and in one way or another nearly all types of transport and navigation control. Usually changes of directional control are brought about by the operation of levers, wheels and other devices depending upon voluntary movement, often of a considerable amount. There is, however, accumulating and convincing evidence that in general, in such cases, a type of control depending principally on variation of pressure, with minimal limb movement, is vastly easier to learn and also to maintain accurately and without fatigue.

No basic explanation of this is as yet well established. It does seem clear, however, that the computing mechanism, which is somewhere in, or perhaps more accurately *is,* the central nervous system of the performer, can just as easily be supplied with too much evidence as with too little. If anybody is set to listen to a message that is coming to him in several different languages at once he is less likely to be as quick, sure and accurate, or, to use language of social significance, as good humoured and contented, as he will be if the message is all in one mode of communication and the items are simple and unambiguous. Whatever may be the correct explanation, the principles involved in an enquiry of this kind, although they are admirably adapted to scientific study, have received exceedingly little systematic attention from the design engineer, for they are generally held to lie beyond his accepted range.

Both these illustrations concern detail in equipment design, and a large number of other examples could already be given. The details have innumerable applications and for these the collaboration of the engineer, the physicist, the physiologist, of other scientists and of the technical experts is required. The experimental psychologist should be able to tackle the principles, but in general he cannot and should not go further.

Two conclusions of general methodological significance begin to emerge. The first is that in the sphere of human behaviour there are a large number of concrete problems which, although they do not immediately appear to raise issues of wide social importance, must be studied first if the larger social problems are to be successfully attacked. They can be studied so as to yield warrantable evidence, and it is likely that the methods which they successfully exploit can then, step by step, be developed in wider fields. The second conclusion is that while all such problems are likely to have multiple applications, requiring field investigation and specialized technical knowledge, they are also bound to be concerned with fundamental hypotheses and principles which are the proper sphere of the laboratory scientist.

At this point it is desirable to consider briefly some of these principles as they can be seen in operation in the internal mechanism of human skill.

Basic Characters and Conditions of Human Skilled Performance

It is impossible to understand anything important about skill behaviour if the only measures we have are of the amount of any kind of production achieved, or of the overall quantity of energy expended in such achievement. It is also illusory to suppose that if we analyse any bodily skill into what are regarded as constituent parts, and time such parts when they are considered to be efficiently performed, we can derive anything important about the whole skill by a simple combination of our separate measures. If we begin making allowances for normal rests, for fatigue, for the piling up or for the lack of work material, we introduce a large number of highly unstable variables and learn nothing new about the nature of skill itself.

Bodily skill consists essentially of a sequence, very often a repeated sequence, or cycle, of movements, in which each item grows out of preceding and leads to succeeding movements. When we take the item, or even a group of items, out of the sequence and measure it by itself we can get very misleading ideas about its character and properties within the skill. We have to learn how to record, in such a way that quantitative treatment becomes possible, the constituent items within a sequence, perhaps within several cycles of a sequence, together with the associated amount of whatever is regarded as the product of the skill. The key characters to which we have to pay attention are the number of constituent items, the time at which each constituent begins and finishes, and particularly the interval between the completion of one constituent and the scanning of the next. Ways in which this can be done are now available, and have been several times described,* although outside of experimental psychology they are not nearly as well known as they could be. It will be clear that the common stopwatch method, or any variation which is confined in the main to the recording of reaction times, is utterly inadequate.

There is another vital preliminary consideration. The movements involved in bodily skill are almost always, perhaps always, initiated by stimuli belonging to the environment, which must be noticed and interpreted through the exteroceptive senses, especially those of sight and hearing, though sometimes by smell, taste and touch. We have therefore to include a record of the sequence, and the characters in sequence, of these signals; and in the case of bodily skills this usually sets a much simpler recording problem. It is this consideration which makes matters of "display," the spacing and emphasizing of signals for action, an important part of the general skill problem; how to arrange the signals in such ways that all normal sensory equipment can deal with them readily and accurately.

It would seem as if a third kind of running record ought to be made. For as soon as a skill performance begins new signals, coming from the muscles, joints, tendons and skin will tell the performer's brain something about what is going on. These are very much more difficult to record, but fortunately a detailed record is less necessary in this case. For the muscles and all the rest of the internal bodily response mechanisms can play the parts they do only because they are extremely flexible and so to speak "willing to be led." The leads must be taken by the senses which can tell us about the external signals,

* See especially references 1, 3, 6.

and provided we can get a recording of the signals and the corresponding movements, it is reasonably safe to infer the parts played by the sensory "feedback" from the movements themselves.

When we have achieved a running record of this kind it can be experimentally demonstrated that the key points to study carefully are, on the display side, the ways in which the signals are grouped relatively to the skilled movements; on the "control" side the "timing" of the movements.

The grouping of signals is usually studied as a function of what is called "receptor organization"; that is, of the building together of the objective signs for action through the special senses of the performer which they stimulate. The most important objective characters of any set of signals are their number, position, size, shape, rate of change, and whenever the change involves movement, the direction and speed of movement. To this must be added whatever forms of contrast make ready identification of particular signals, or classes of signals, easy and certain.

On the control side by far the most important single function is "timing," that is to say, the application of a required movement within those limits of time at which it will produce its maximum effect, and fit best into the course of preceding and succeeding movements. Notable irregularities in a pattern of control movements are the surest evidence of awkwardness in skill, and are usually the first sign of any break up of skill as a result of unsatisfactory working conditions. "Timing" as a character of skill must be carefully distinguished from "reaction time," as a character of isolated response, or of groups of responses. The same overall time for a group of responses is consistent with considerable variations of internal timing, and some of these variations become of overriding importance when the performance is one which has to be maintained in continuous exercise. Again, the absolute maximum speed of single response usually, and very likely always, lies well inside the limits of its speed required in any realistic skill performance.

If we can arrange a recording which allows us to deal with these properties of display and control definitely and quantitatively we shall then find that our basic problems tend to cluster in three large groups, concerned with a speed, b load and c ceiling, or tolerance limits.

Speed. Speed is defined as the rate at which signals and associated movements succeed one another in the sequence which makes up the cycle or group of cycles of performance with which we are concerned. Speaking generally it is found that variations of speed alone make no important differences to timing provided they lie within certain limits. But outside those limits slowing down and speeding up both produce adverse effects disproportionately greater compared with the absolute variation of speed involved; they are very powerful sources of irritation, discontent, fatigue and of the symptoms of ill health.

Load. This is defined as the number and distribution of distinguishable sources or positions from which signals required to be dealt with simultaneously or in very rapid succession reach the operator. This condition demands specially careful experimental study, for equal loads may not produce equivalent effects if the items of load are differently distributed. At present the evidence suggests that within fairly wide limits, load is related to effective performance in a more directly proportionate way than speed. But we cannot yet be quite sure that this is always the case, and we know still less about why, in many instances studied, it has been found to occur.

The most important problems, both in theory and for practice, concern concurrent variation of speed and load. This is extremely apt to happen, especially in machine-controlled skill. When the economic rate at which machines will run is increased—a matter of frequent occurrence nowadays—

there is a tendency, with or without a closer grouping of machines, or of machine display, to increase the load. If this runs into trouble, as it constantly does, there is a "commonsense" supposition that an increase in one can be countered by a proportionate decrease in the other. Whatever may be the truth this, certainly, never is.

There is one particularly troublesome form of increase of load. The rapid spread of automatic controls, which has become possible mainly as a result of electronic developments, often leads the machine designer to say "Now that the operator does not need to be bothered by this and that we can give him something else to do." This would be sound enough provided the automatic devices were wholly "fool proof." They practically never are. The operator's manifest load remains the same, but his latent load is increased. There is nothing like a latent load for piling up cumulative fatigue.

Ceiling, or Tolerance Limits. That condition of organized human performance known as "ceiling" or "tolerance limits" raises a number of fascinating theoretical problems. Apart from these it has a practical significance which has been very much neglected. If we take any important set of external or internal conditions under which skilled behaviour may be required, such, for instance, as temperature and humidity, or range of variability in any of the leading aspects of display or control, or length of exercise, or speed and load, we find that they can change within limits, without necessarily involving any important change in the effective performance and maintenance of the actions required. But if we step outside those limits in any direction, even by a small amount, marked changes of performance at once appear. These "tolerance limits" have no known consistent relationship to minimal discriminable differences in the conditions concerned, and so no measure of them can be achieved in terms of any of the well-established methods for determining sensory or other thresholds. In any healthy and reasonably expert population they remain quite remarkably consistent. For example, in a temperate climate such as our own, a very wide range of skills begin to deteriorate decisively at an effective temperature of about 83° to 88°F (28° to 31°C). Once the tolerance limit is reached for any of the determining conditions of skill, nothing whatever in the way of permanent gain can be produced by any known form of extra reward or punishment. These may indeed set up spurts, but at such a cost that, except in a crisis which has only a very short duration, the policy is wasteful from every point of view.

The Transfer of Skill

One of the most extraordinary characters of human skill is its capacity to get narrowly tied up with the particular conditions under which it is learned. In an age of rapid practical scientific invention this can become a very serious matter. For alleged economic reasons learners are very often trained on equipment that is already obsolete or obsolescent. When they are transferred to current operational equipment it has appeared again and again that they are in a worse position than they would have been if they had never practised the required skill at all. To counter this we have to look into the fundamental principles of synthetic training. Methods of synthetic training have been exploited widely in the Fighting Services, though often with inadequate guidance, but they are used far less than they might well be for training in industry and other fields.

Four main principles, all closely related, appear to need consideration; the form they may have to take in special instances must of course be directed by appropriate technical knowledge.

1. Equipment and method of teaching must be designed rather to show what the skill is required to effect than how the effect is produced.

2. Very generally there is more positive transfer from the relatively difficult to the relatively easy than from the relatively easy to the relatively difficult. Training should not normally begin with lines of least resistance.

3. So far as machine-directed bodily skills are concerned it appears that the greatest difficulties in the way of effective transfer all have to do with *a* timing and *b* directional relations between display and control. While therefore design must preserve as much consistency as possible in these, because complete uniformity cannot be achieved, training must go as far as it can to prepare learners at an early stage for variability.

4. Efficient learning and the normal range of its exercise are largely functions of aging. It must not be asserted that those methods which are best for the adolescent or young adult will also be best for people who are approaching, or in, or beyond their middle age.

Some General Conclusions

This article has attempted no more than to raise, in a broad and general way, a few of the problems which are now attracting the attention of the experimental psychologist, or, to use the phrase which now has considerable vogue, especially in the United States, of the human engineer. To appreciate the full force and scope of the methods of investigation which are involved, they must be seen in active demonstration in the laboratory and in the field. No community which hopes to build or maintain an effective position, and to meet the fierce demands of contemporary civilization, can afford to neglect them. All over the world people are today well aware that beneath all problems that are concerned with the control of natural forces lie human problems the answers to which are hardly known at all in warrantable or demonstrable terms.

The forms in which such problems most frequently present themselves to all thoughtful people appear to be directly social. They seem to be concerned with the interrelations of groups that have become larger and larger as the ease and effectiveness of all forms of communication have increased. To many ardent minds it seems as if the only hope is to establish quickly a direct "science of human relations." But in their immediate social forms these problems are so vast and so complicated that we cannot find methods in any of the other fields in which science has proved its worth which are applicable to them. And so we are left with a hodge-podge of empirical enquiry and a welter of opinions which cannot get beyond a stage of dispute. Even when some brilliant intuitive mind proclaims a solution to a complex social problem, nobody can tell whether, or to what extent, it is correct or incorrect until the events which it may forecast have actually occurred.

It is high time that in this field also those directions and developments of method which have won scientific victories in other realms should be given a fair trial, and that, building slowly upon the study of simpler and more controllable problems, we should advance step by step to the more complex. If this is to be done it demands a degree of scientific cooperation and mutual understanding which has rarely been achieved in the past, and above all the provision of those opportunities which will attract a few of the very best scientific minds to a study of human behaviour.

Bibliography

The methods referred to in the foregoing article are more fully illustrated and discussed in the following:

1. Mackworth, N. H. The Measurement of Human Performance *Medical Research Council Special Report No. 268.* London, 1949.

2. Bartlett, F. C. and Mackworth, N. H. Planned Seeing *R.A.F. Publication No. 3139B*. London, 1950.

Many of the basic characters of skill and methods available for their study are considered in:

3. Welford, A. T. *et alii, Skill and Age—An Experimental Approach*. Oxford, 1951.

For additional detail about speed, load and tolerance limits see:

4. Conrad, R. Speed and Load Stress in a Sensori-Motor Skill. *Brit. J. industr. Med.* 8 (1951) 1.

5. Bartlett, F. C. Human Tolerance Limits. *Acta Psycholog.* 7 (1950) 133.

For a general and somewhat popular introduction to the whole field see:

6. Bartlett, F. C. *The Mind at Work and Play*. London, 1951.

PART 2

ORGANIZATION OF THE PSYCHOMOTOR DOMAIN

Taxonomies, Systems, and Classifications

The psychomotor domain encompasses a broad spectrum of movement behaviors, and one of the obvious concerns is motor learning. In order to synthesize, organize, and make meaning of extensive research findings, taxonomies are formed. As will be seen in the readings in this section of the book, taxonomies may serve to structure different aspects of a domain. And, in fact, taxonomies, classifications, and systems have been proposed for psychomotor educational objectives, abilities, responses, and tasks.

These efforts serve to present "the big picture," or at least, a major scholarly thrust in the area. Each represents a unification of a number of research outcomes as well as a theoretical or directly applicable formulation. The individual experimental studies reported in other chapters can be analyzed in part according to any of the suggested frameworks included here. The findings may be understood better, they may support or refute a taxonomy, or they may lead to new theoretical formations. At any rate, orderliness is the goal for which to strive. Organizational plans in the form of theories, taxonomies, classifications, and systems are directed to this objective. Based as they are on fact and logic, such developments in the psychomotor domain help us to understand more effectively the learning process.

Readings in Part II illustrate very recent attempts to structure the psychomotor domain. Educational objectives, well received in the cognitive and affective domains, are also being developed in the psychomotor area. The first selection that follows briefly indicates one effort in the latter direction. Human attributes underlying motor performance and contributing to proficiency are discussed in the next two articles. Fleishman is noted for his work in factor analysis, and his paper is a milestone in attempting to identify primary abilities associated with achievement in motor skills.

Since there are so many tasks that comprise acts that are primarily motor, a system or theory that would structure them is a necessity. Thus, an attempt at such an endeavor is included here. Finally, responses too are many and varied in the psychomotor domain, and an analysis and unification of them is made in one of the readings.

The papers included in this part range from the highly theoretical or speculative to the very obvious (taken directly from research evidence). They should be recognized, for the most part, as ventures into heretofore unexplored areas to give the theoretical depth which applied areas usually lack. These papers yield challenging ideas, new research directions, and findings applicable to those concerned with motor skills.

Chapter 2

EDUCATIONAL OBJECTIVES, ABILITIES, RESPONSES, AND TASKS

Physical Education and the Classification of Educational Objectives: Psychomotor Domain*

MARVIN I. CLEIN and WILLIAM J. STONE

THE classification of primary organizational categories in the learning of motor skills related to educational objectives is an arduous task, but it has overwhelming redeeming benefits. Bloom's *Taxonomy of Educational Objectives: The Cognitive Domain* and Krathwohl's *Taxonomy of Educational Objectives: The Affective Domain* demonstrate rewarding ventures into the taxonomic area. In the article that follows, the authors briefly report the efforts of Simpson to develop a taxonomy in the psychomotor domain. The nature of the taxonomy is outlined and its potential uses for physical educators are listed. The reader is directed to Simpson's own work for detail and greater perspective of the effort and its potential consequences for all who teach psychomotor skills.

In the summer of 1965 preliminary investigations began at the University of Illinois toward developing a system for classifying educational goals, or objectives, related to the learning of motor skills. In order for this classification system to be most useful its developers felt that the organizational pattern must follow taxonomic form—that is, a classification into major categories according to motor learning principles: specifically, listing major categories which would indicate the step-by-step progression of how individuals learn to perform motor tasks. The fact that motor activities involve mental as well as attitudinal aspects added to the difficulty of the undertaking.

* From *The Physical Educator*, 1970, 27, 34-35. Reprinted with permission of the authors and publisher.

The guiding principles of earlier taxonomies[1,3] in other areas served to direct the work of this project. These principles suggested a classification that:

1. made a major distinction between categories of behavior in motor learning.
2. provided categories of behavior that would follow a logical order.
3. provided an understanding of how individuals learn a motor skill.
4. allowed for realistic and "ordered" educational goals which could be developed with the learner.

The first project report was published during May, 1966 by project chairman E. J. Simpson[4] and her co-workers. It is the purpose here to provide a brief description of their work and make a preliminary application for the physical education profession.

Educational objectives are placed into three categories, often referred to as domains. These domains include: the cognitive (intellectual skills), the affective (interests, attitudes, appreciations, and desires), and the psychomotor (motor skills). Although the learning of a motor skill may involve all three areas, a taxonomy of educational objectives in the psychomotor domain has important implications for physical educators. The usefulness of such a taxonomy may include:

1. the development of the types of objectives that may be used in the physical education curriculum.
2. an evaluation device for physical education curriculums.
3. the evaluation of stated objectives for both the learner and teacher.
4. a guideline for test making as well as for other evaluation methods (i.e., practice teaching observation).
5. providing a theoretical base for research.
6. evaluating methods and procedures of teaching.
7. developing materials for class use.

The authors have made extensive use of this taxonomy in the teaching of methods courses as: (a) a suggested guideline for students to follow in preparing for a teaching assignment and (b) as a means of evaluating the students' teaching procedure. It should be emphasized, however, that in reviewing the taxonomy which follows, one should keep in mind that the work in this area is still tentative and perhaps incomplete. The present form does, nevertheless, provide a stepping off point for needed further research. Although earlier and more complete taxonomies in each of the cognitive and affective domains have received wide use among educators, there has been little attention given to the psychomotor domain. The classification system will be incomplete until the psychomotor domain is included.

The procedures followed in the development of the taxonomy of educational objectives in the psychomotor domain were outlined in the project report.[4] These procedures took the following form:

1. a comprehensive review of related literature, especially of any that described ways of classifying psychomotor activities, and, hence, suggested possibilities for classifying the educational objectives of this domain.
2. collecting and analyzing the behavioral objectives of this domain as one way of gaining insight regarding a possible classification system.
3. laboratory analyses of certain tasks to discover by observation and introspection the nature of the psychomotor activity involved. These analyses were carried out by the research assistants on the project who had read widely in the area before attempting analyses.
4. conferences with scholars who have specialized knowledge of the nature

of psychomotor activity, development of classification systems for educational objectives, and of the areas of study where educational objectives in the psychomotor domain are of paramount concern.

The results of the above procedures led to the development of a tentative classification system in the psychomotor domain. This classification system follows:

Classification of Educational Objectives, Psychomotor Domain

The major organization principle is that of complexity, i.e., moving from the lowest to the highest order of complexity. The educational objectives are illustrated by the desired behavior of the performer, in this case a student learning the skill of *batting*.

1.0 *Perception*—This is the process of becoming aware and attaching meaning to objects, events, or situations. It is interpretation, and the first link in the chain leading to motor activity. There are three subcategories indicating different levels with respect to the perceptual process.

1.1 *Sensory stimulation*—This is impingement of a stimulus upon one or more of the sensory organs. The varieties of sensory stimulation are not listed in any particular order of importance. Examples are given only for those which are commonly associated with motor activity.

1.11 *Auditory*—Stimulation occurring through the sense organs of hearing. The student listens to the instructor explain how to bat.

1.12 *Visual*—Images obtained through the eyes. The student observes a demonstration of batting, either through live performance, motion picture, or still pictures. Vision is the dominant sensory apparatus for many individuals.

1.13 *Tactile*—Stimulation pertaining to the sense of touch. The student is encouraged to hold the bat and feel the size, shape, and texture.

1.14 *Taste*—Stimulation of the taste buds, eliciting flavor in the mouth.

1.15 *Smell*—To perceive by excitation of the olfactory nerves.

1.16 *Kinesthetic*—Sensations arising in a variety of receptors located in the joints, muscles, and tendons. The learner gets the "feel" of swinging a bat. As with the preceding stimuli, kinesthetic sensations occur throughout the learning process, and are apparent in the most complex stage, automatic performance (5.2).

1.2 *Cue selection*—The process of selecting the appropriate cues to which one must respond in order to complete the task. The batter must sort out the distracting cues issued by the pitcher and "watch the ball."

1.3 *Translation*—The process of relating perception to action both during and after performing a motor act. The batter is mentally relating his movement to results and is aided in this process by feedback, especially visual and kinesthetic feedback.

2.0 *Set*—The preparatory stage or readiness to respond. This stage is best illustrated by the batter in baseball as he gets "set" for the pitch.

2.1 *Mental set*—The mental readiness to perform the task, thus mentally concentrating on the task of batting.

2.2 *Physical set*—Physically ready to perform the task by assuming the optimum posture or body position. The batter concentrates on his stance and the position of his bat prior to the pitch.

2.3 *Emotional set*—A favorable commitment toward performance; hence, the batter has a desire to bat skillfully.

3.0 *Guided response*—The initial response in the development of skill is illustrated as the student swings the bat for the first time at a thrown ball. The student may or may not receive manual guidance from the instructor.

3.1 *Imitation*—Performing an act as a direct response to the perception of another person performing it. The young batter swings the bat as he perceives the way in which the instructor demonstrated.

3.2 *Trial and error*—The performer responds in various ways, gradually refining his performance until the appropriate response is achieved. The batter eliminates extraneous movements and rejects inadequate responses until he can meet the ball with the bat.

4.0 *Mechanism*—The learned response has become habitual and the performer can now hit the ball consistently with confidence and some degree of skill. This stage assumes more complexity than the previous level and may include batting in a game situation.

5.0 *Complex overt response*—At this level the performer can accomplish a complex motor act with a high degree of skill, i.e., smoothly and efficiently. The skilled batter in athletic competition presents the best example.

5.1 *Resolution of uncertainty*—The task can be accomplished without resorting to a prior mental picture of task sequence, hence the batter can step into the batter's box and be prepared to hit without the necessity of having a mental image of the process.

5.2 *Automatic performance*—The individual can perform a finely coordinated motor skill with a great deal of ease and muscle control. The batter can now hit the ball with ease under far more complex conditions, such as variations in the speed, direction, height, and spin of the oncoming ball.

Selected References

1. Bloom, Benjamin S., et al., *Taxonomy of Educational Objectives, Handbook I, Cognitive Domain.* David McKay Company, Inc., New York, 1956.
2. Cratty, Bryant J., *Movement Behavior and Motor Learning.* 2nd Edition, Lea & Febiger, Philadelphia, 1967.
3. Krathwohl, David R., et al., *Taxonomy of Educational Objectives, Handbook II: Affective Domain.* David McKay Company, Inc., New York, 1964.
4. Simpson, Elizabeth J., *The Classification of Educational Objectives: Psychomotor Domain.* Urbana: University of Illinois Press, 1966.

*Performance Assessment on an Empirically Derived Task Taxonomy**

EDWIN A. FLEISHMAN

ANOTHER type of taxonomy is reported by Fleishman. Since he has been a major contributor of research on many aspects of learning skills for a number of years, it is only fitting that an article of his that attempts to synthesize and organize many of his findings be included here. Through factor analysis and correlational analysis, the human requirements for success in various motor tasks are indicated. It should be emphasized that the tasks typically studied by him are (a) laboratory-oriented and required

* From *Human Factors,* 1967, *9,* 349-366. Abridged and reprinted with permission of the author and publisher.

apparatus, or else (b) fall into the classification of physical fitness tests. Therefore, the abilities derived are a function of the tasks measured, and the tasks measured are by no means all-inclusive in the field of motor skills. Nevertheless, the student will be impressed with the sophistication and extent of Fleishman's research. The implications for performers and instructors of any kind of skills are apparent, for the identification of unique motor abilities and physical proficiency items provides a needed system of task requirements.

In this presentation I want to review some questions felt to be critical to the problem of assessing operator performance capability. I will pay particular attention to three key issues. These are (1) the need to identify the classes of behavior that should be assessed; (2) the need to develop measures diagnostic of these classes of behavior; and (3) the need to develop appropriate experimental and statistical methodology for predicting from these measures to complex tasks.

I want to describe the research program we have carried out on the identification of classes of behavior and on the development of diagnostic measures for use in laboratory and field settings. I will also describe some applications of this work to some specific problems and will review some unanswered questions and possible future directions.

The Need for A Task Taxonomy

For many years psychologists have studied learning and performance, often in applied contexts, under numerous task and environmental conditions, and have accumulated vast quantities of data. And yet, as new systems are conceived for the exploration of space, for defense, for command and control, it appears that accumulated data and experience of the past are largely inapplicable and that the problems of skill identification, training and performance must be restudied almost from scratch. Why is this the case? Why such a waste of prior findings?

Superficially, each new system differs from other systems with respect to application, mission, and technology and apparently in its task demands on its human operators. No two task analyses are ever quite the same. No two systems ever have identical job requirements. No training device or simulator ever quite seems to fit the requirements of any system except the one for which it was developed. Is it reasonable to conclude that the tasks of men in systems are so varied that there are no common dimensions with respect to the basic abilities required, the types of training needed for job proficiency, or the degradation of skilled behavior under given environmental conditions?

Our present lack of a set of unifying dimensions underlying skilled behavior would appear to require one to answer the question in the affirmative. Why else have so many prominent psychologists (e.g., Melton, Fitts, Gagné, Miller) called so often for so long for a method for classifying human tasks—for a "task taxonomy?"

The problem is not only one of finding ways to generalize principles from one operational system to another. It also involves the generalization of findings from the laboratory to operational tasks. One reason why much of current research in the experimental laboratory appears so sterile to those who try to apply it to real-life training situations is the lack of concern by learning and other psychologists for the problem of task dimensions. This, of course, is often true for laboratory studies of the effects of environmental factors, the effects of motivational variables, the effects of drugs, etc. on human performance. It is not too long ago that a favorite distinction was between "motor" and "mental" tasks and between "cognitive" and "non-cognitive" tasks. Such distinctions are clearly not very helpful in generalizing results to new situations, which involve a complex array of tasks and skills not adequately described by such all-inclusive terms. Tasks selected in laboratory research are not often based on any clear rationale about the class of task or skill represented. Most learning theory is devoid of any concern about task dimensions and it is this deficiency which, many of us feel, makes it so difficult to apply these theories in the real world of tasks and people. What we need is a learning and performance theory which ascribes task dimensions a central role.

At the other extreme, we find task descriptions, often developed by job and systems analysts, which are highly detailed and highly specific. These are extremely useful and necessary for a variety of purposes, but their very specificity limits the kinds of generalizations we can make to new classes of skills and tasks.

Categories which conceive of man-task interactions in terms of classes of functions certainly would seem to be steps in the right direction. Thus, Gagné (1964) tends to use categories like discrimination, identification, sequence learning, problem solving; and Robert Miller (1965) uses terms like scanning, identification of cues, interpretation, short-term and long-term memory, decision-making, etc. Psychologists working with other approaches (e.g., Alluisi, 1965) use dimensions like tracking, vigilance, arithmetic, and pattern comparison.

These categories may turn out to be highly useful in both (1) organizing psychological data into categories of consistent principles, or (2) allowing more dependable predictions from laboratory to operations and from one operation to another. The demonstration, of course, still needs to be made. One needs to recognize, of course, that these approaches are initially armchair, rational descriptive approaches. And there is nothing wrong with this, provided the necessary experimental-predictive work is carried out to test the utility of these systems. However, I am skeptical that any small number of categories is going to be successful. For example, one of the most systematic approaches is that developed by Alluisi in his extension of the Lockheed-Aerospace Medical Research Laboratories approach. I am sure that this work represents a major step forward in task standardization and that we will learn much from it. However, the basic battery will consist of from 6 to 8 tests covering categories such as vigilance processes, memory functions, communication functions, intellectual functions, procedural functions, etc. My own feeling is that everything we know about the correlations among human performances indicates a greater degree of specificity than this and considerable diversity of functions within each sub-area; we probably cannot generalize too far within each area. We will just have to admit that human performance is complex and consists of many components. The problem is to simplify our description as far as we can, seeking all the while to find the limits and generality of the categories developed. The selection of measures diagnostic and representative of these categories is an empirical rather than an armchair question.

The point that needs to be made is that there are empirical-experimental approaches to developing task taxonomies and that these represent alternative ways of going about it. It is my feeling that we already know quite a bit about task dimensions from experimental-correlational studies already completed, and that these allow us to be much more specific about task dimensions than do the more general categorical terms previously described. And

I believe that combinations of experimental and correlational methods can develop a taxonomy of human performance which is applicable to a large variety of tasks and situations. Furthermore, such an approach yields empirical indices for diagnostic measures of the categories developed.

Conceptual and Methodological Framework

I find it useful to distinguish between the concepts of ability and skill. As we use the term, *ability* refers to a more general trait of the individual which has been inferred from certain response consistencies (e.g., correlations) on certain kinds of tasks. These are fairly enduring traits, which in the adult are more difficult to change. Many of these abilities are, of course, themselves a product of learning, and develop at different rates, mainly during childhood and adolescence. Some abilities (e.g., color vision) depend more on genetic than learning factors, but most abilities depend on both to some degree. In any case, at a given stage of life, they represent traits or organismic factors which the individual brings with him when he begins to learn a new task. These abilities are related to performances in a variety of human tasks. For example, the fact that spatial-visualization has been found related to performance on such diverse tasks as aerial navigation, blue-print reading, and dentistry, makes this ability somehow more basic.

The term *skill* refers to the level of proficiency on a specific task or limited group of tasks. As we use the term skill, it is task-oriented. When we talk about proficiency in flying an airplane, in operating a turret lathe, or in playing basketball, we are talking about a specific skill. Thus, when we speak of acquiring the skill of operating a turret lathe, we mean that this person has acquired the sequence of responses required by this specific task. The assumption is that the skills involved in complex activities can be described in terms of the more basic abilities. For example, the level of performance a man can attain on a turret lathe may depend on his basic abilities of manual dexterity and motor coordination. However, these same basic abilities may be important to proficiency in other skills as well. Thus, manual dexterity is needed in assembling electrical components and motor coordination is needed to fly an airplane.

Implicit in the previous analysis is the important relation between abilities and learning. Thus individuals with high manual dexterity may more readily learn the specific skill of lathe operation. The mechanism of transfer of training probably operates here. Some abilities may transfer to the learning of a greater variety of specific tasks than others. In our culture, *verbal* abilities are more important in a greater variety of tasks than are some other types of abilities. The individual who has a great many highly developed basic abilities can become proficient at a great variety of specific tasks.

Elsewhere (Fleishman, 1964; Gagné & Fleishman, 1959) we have elaborated our analysis of the development of basic abilities. This included a discussion of their physiological bases, the role of learning, environmental and cultural factors, and evidence on the rate of ability development during the life span. We have also interpreted abilities in terms of an information processing model of human performance, where abilities can be thought of as "capacities for utilizing different kinds of information" (Fleishman & Rich, 1963). With this much conceptualization in mind, we can say that in much of our previous work one objective has been to describe certain skills in terms of these more general ability requirements.

The original impetus for this program was a very applied problem. While we were with the Air Force Personnel and Training Research Center, one of our missions was to build better psychomotor tests for the prediction of pilot success. The wartime Air Force program had been highly successful in developing such tests. For example, the Complex Coordination Test had consistent validity for pilots. This seems not surprising, since the test seemed to be a "job sample" of aspects of the pilot's job. The pilot does manipulate stick and rudder controls. But there were many tests which had substantial validity, but did not at all "resemble" the pilot's job. Cases in point are the Rotary Pursuit and Two Hand Coordination Tests. So it seemed to me that the first step was to discover the sources of validity in these tests. What ability factors were there in common to psychomotor tests which were common to pilot performance?

Perhaps a not too extreme statement is that most of the categorization of human skills, which is empirically based, comes from correlational and factor analysis studies. Many of these studies in the literature are ill-designed or not designed at all. This does not rule out the fact that properly designed, systematic programmatic correlational research can yield highly useful data about general skill dimensions. We can think of such categories as representing empirically derived patterns of *response consistencies* to task requirements varied in systematic ways. In a sense this approach describes tasks in terms of the common abilities required to perform them. The fact that individuals who do well on task A also do well on tasks B and C but not on tasks D, E, and F indicates, inferentially, a common process involved in performing the first three tasks distinct from the processes involved in the latter three. To account for the observed consistencies, an ability is postulated. Once this has been achieved, further experimental-correlational studies are conducted to sharpen and define the limits and generality of this particular ability.

As an example, let us take the term tracking, a frequent behavioral category employed by laboratory and systems psychologist alike. But we can all think of a wide variety of different tasks in which some kinds of tracking are involved. Can we assume that the behavioral category of tracking is useful in helping us generalize results from one such situation to another? Is there a general tracking ability? Are individuals who are good at compensatory tracking also the ones who are good at pursuit tracking? Do people who are good at positional tracking also do well with velocity or acceleration controls? What happens to the correlations between performances as a function of such variations? It is to these kinds of questions that our own program was directed.

Some Previous Research

In subsequent years we have conducted a whole series of interlocking experimental-factor analytic studies, attempting to isolate and identify the common variance in a wide range of perceptual-motor performances. Essentially this is laboratory research in which tasks are specifically designed or selected to test certain hypotheses about the organization of abilities in a certain range of tasks. Subsequent studies tend to introduce task variations aimed at sharpening or limiting our ability to factor definitions. The purpose is to define the fewest independent ability categories which might be most useful and meaningful in describing performance in the widest variety of tasks.

Our studies generally start with some gross area of human performance. Thus, we have conducted studies of fine manipulative performances (Fleishman & Hempel, 1954a; Fleishman & Ellison, 1962), gross physical proficiency (Hempel & Fleishman, 1955; Fleishman, 1963; Fleishman, 1964), positioning movements and static reactions (Fleishman, 1958a), and movement reactions (Fleishman & Hempel, 1956; Fleishman, 1958b).

Thus far, we have investigated more than 200 different tasks administered to thousands of subjects in a series of interlocking studies. From the patterns of correlations obtained, we have been able to account for performance on this wide range of tasks in terms of a relatively small number of abilities. In subsequent studies, our definitions of these abilities and their distinctions from one another are becoming more clearly delineated. Furthermore, it is now possible to specify the tasks which should provide the best measure of each of the abilities identified.

There are about 11 psychomotor factors and 9 factors in the area of physical proficiency which consistently appear to account for the common variance in such tasks. These are defined as follows. (For more details on their definition and the devices which best measure them, the reader is referred to Fleishman, 1960b; Fleishman, 1962; Fleishman, 1964.)

Control Precision. This factor is common to tasks which require fine, highly controlled, but not overcontrolled, muscular adjustments, primarily where larger muscle groups are involved (Fleishman, 1958b; Fleishman & Hempel, 1956; Parker & Fleishman, 1960). This ability extends to arm-hand as well as to leg movements. It is most critical where such adjustments must be rapid, but precise.

Multilimb Coordination. This is the ability to coordinate the movements of a number of limbs simultaneously, and is best measured by devices involving multiple controls (Fleishman, 1958b; Fleishman & Hempel, 1956; Parker & Fleishman, 1960). The factor has been found general to tasks requiring coordination of the two feet (e.g., the Rudder Control Test), two hands (e.g., the Two Hand Pursuit and Two Hand Coordination Tests), and hands and feet (e.g., the Plane Control and Complex Coordination Tests).

Response Orientation. This ability factor has been found general to visual discrimination reaction psychomotor tasks involving rapid directional discrimination and orientation of movement patterns (Fleishman, 1957a; Fleishman, 1957b; Fleishman, 1958b; Fleishman & Hempel, 1956; Parker and Fleishman, 1960). It appears to involve the ability to *select* the correct movement in relation to the correct stimulus, especially under highly speeded conditions.

Reaction Time. This represents simply the speed with which the individual is able to respond to a stimulus when it appears (Fleishman, 1954; Fleishman, 1958b; Fleishman & Hempel, 1955; Parker & Fleishman, 1960). There are consistent indications that individual differences in this ability are independent of whether the stimulus is auditory or visual and are also independent of the type of response which is required. However, once the stimulus situation or the response situation is complicated to involve alternate choices, reaction time is not the primary factor that is measured.

Speed of Arm Movement. This represents simply the speed with which an individual can make a gross, discrete arm movement where accuracy is not the requirement (Fleishman & Hempel, 1954b; Fleishman & Hempel, 1955; Fleishman, 1958b; Parker & Fleishman, 1960). There is ample evidence that this factor is independent of the reaction time factor.

Rate Control. This ability involves the timing of continuous anticipatory motor adjustments relative to changes in speed and direction of a continuously moving target or object (Fleishman & Hempel, 1955; Fleishman & Hempel, 1956; Fleishman, 1958b). This factor is general to tasks involving compensatory movements as well as following pursuit, and extends to tasks involving responses to change in rate. Our research has shown that adequate measurement of this ability requires an actual response in relation to the changing direction and speed of the stimulus object, and not simply judging the rate of the stimulus alone.

Manual Dexterity. This ability involves skillful, well-directed arm-hand movements in manipulating fairly large objects under speed conditions (Fleishman, 1953b; Fleishman, 1954; Fleishman & Hempel, 1954b; Hempel & Fleishman, 1955; Parker & Fleishman, 1960; Fleishman and Ellison, 1962).

Finger Dexterity. This is the ability to make skillful, controlled manipulations of tiny objects involving, primarily, the fingers (Fleishman, 1953; Fleishman, 1954; Fleishman & Hempel, 1954a; Hempel and Fleishman, 1955; Parker & Fleishman, 1960; Fleishman & Ellison, 1962).

Arm-Hand Steadiness. This is the ability to make precise arm-hand positioning movements where strength and speed are minimized; the critical feature, as the name implies, is the steadiness with which such movements can be made (Fleishman, 1953b; Fleishman, 1954; Fleishman, 1958a; Fleishman, 1958b; Hempel & Fleishman, 1955; Parker & Fleishman, 1960). The ability extends to tasks in which a steady arm or hand position is to be maintained.

Wrist, Finger Speed. This ability has been called "tapping" in many previous studies through the years (Fleishman, 1953b). It has been used in a variety of different studies, primarily because these are in the form of printed tests which are quick and easy to administer. However, our research shows that this factor is highly restricted in scope and does not extend to many tasks in which apparatus is used (Fleishman, 1954; Fleishman & Hempel, 1954a; Fleishman and Ellison, 1962). It has been found that the factor is best measured by printed tests requiring rapid tapping of the pencil in relatively large areas.

Aiming. This ability appears to be measured by printed tests which provide the subject with very small circles to be dotted in, where there are a large number of circles and when the test is highly speeded (Fleishman, 1953b; Fleishman, 1954; Hempel & Fleishman, 1955; Fleishman and Ellison, 1962). The subject typically goes from circle to circle placing one dot in each circle as rapidly as possible. This factor has not been found to extend to apparatus tests and, hence, the naming of this factor as "aiming" or as other investigators have called it, "eye-hand coordination," seems much too broad.

Before closing our discussion of the classification of motor abilities, we should refer to the area of motor performance often called *physical proficiency.* Our experimental-factor analytical work indicates that the following factors account for performance in more than sixty different physical fitness tasks. (For details, see Fleishman, 1964; this reference also indicates the tasks most diagnostic of each factor.)

Extent Flexibility. Ability to flex or stretch the trunk and back muscles as far as possible in either a forward, lateral, or backward direction.

Dynamic Flexibility. The ability to make repeated, *rapid* flexing movements in which the resiliency of the muscles in *recovery* from strain or distortion is critical.

Explosive Strength. The ability to expend a maximum of energy in one or a series of explosive acts. This factor is distinguished from other strength factors in requiring mobilization of *energy* for a burst of effort rather than continuous strain, stress, or repeated exertion of muscles.

Static Strength. The maximum *force* which a subject can exert, for a brief period, where the force is exerted continuously up to this maximum. In contrast to other strength factors, this is the force which can be exerted against external objects (e.g., lifting heavy weights, pulling against a dynamometer), rather than in supporting or propelling the body's own weight.

Dynamic Strength. The ability to exert muscular force repeatedly or continuously over time. It represents muscular endurance and emphasizes the resistance of the muscles to fatigue. The common emphasis of tests measuring this factor is on the power of the muscles to propel, support, or move the body repeatedly or to support it for prolonged periods.

Trunk Strength. This is a second, more limited, dynamic strength factor specific to the trunk muscles, particularly the abdominal muscles.

Gross Body Coordination. Ability to coordinate the simultaneous actions of different parts of the body while making gross body movements.

Gross Body Equilibrium. The ability of an individual to maintain his equilibrium, despite forces pulling him off balance, where he has to depend mainly on non-visual (e.g., vestibular and kinesthetic) cues. Although also measured by balance tests where the eyes are kept open, it is best measured by balance tests conducted with the eyes closed.

Stamina. The capacity to continue maximum effort requiring prolonged exertion over time. This factor has the alternate name of "cardiovascular endurance."

More detailed descriptions of the operations involved in each of the perceptual motor and physical proficiency categories given above are presented elsewhere (Fleishman, 1960b; Fleishman, 1962; Fleishman, 1964; Fleishman, 1966a; Fleishman, 1966b). Some ability categories are more general in scope than others. But it is important to know, for example, that it is not too useful to talk about strength as a dimension; that in terms of what tasks the same people can do well, it is more useful to talk in terms of at least three general strength categories which may be differentially involved in a variety of physical tasks.

Perhaps it might be useful to provide some examples of how one examines the generality of an ability category and how one defines its limits. The specification of an ability category is an arduous task. The definition of the Rate Control factor may provide an illustration. In early studies it was found that this factor was common to compensatory as well as following pursuit tasks. To test its generality, tasks were developed to emphasize rate control, which were not conventional tracking tasks (e.g., controlling a ball rolling through a series of alleyways). The factor was found to extend to such tasks. Later studies attempted to discover if emphasis on this ability is in judging the rate of the stimulus as distinguished from ability to respond at the appropriate rate. A task was developed involving only the timing of button-pressing in response to judgments of moving stimuli. Performance on this task did *not* correlate with other rate control tasks. Finally, several motion picture tasks were adapted in which the subject was required to extrapolate the course of a plane moving across a screen. The only response required was on an IBM answer sheet. These tasks did not relate to the core of tasks previously found to measure "rate control." Thus, our definition of this ability was expanded to include measures beyond pursuit tasks, but restricted to tasks requiring the timing of a muscular adjustment to the stimulus change.

A similar history can be sketched for each ability variable identified. Thus, we know that the subject must have a feedback indicator of how well he is coordinating before the Multilimb Coordination factor is measured; we know that by complicating a simple reaction time apparatus, by providing additional choice reactions, we measure not reaction time but a separate factor (Response Orientation). However, varying the stimulus modality involved in a simple reaction-task does not result in measurement of a separate factor.

The development of stable and reliable measures of individual difference variables will continue to be a difficult task, requiring systematic programmatic work.

Of course, we do not present these factors as any kind of final list of perceptual-motor ability categories. But they do provide our current best evidence on recurrent ability factors and we have not been able to add to this list in our later studies of task intercorrelations. In other words, these factors continue to account for variance in a wide range of tasks.

A legitimate question here concerns the proportion of common variance we are able to account for in terms of the relatively small number of abilities identified. It does appear, in the perceptual-motor domain, as I have tried to describe, that a relatively small number are very useful in organizing quite meaningfully a wide variety of performances. This does not mean that there are no more factors to discover. And, it does not mean the factors identified account for a large proportion of the variance in every psychomotor task. There is much specificity, but the pursuit of the common variance is one of the primary tasks of the psychologist. . . .

Need for A Massive Research Effort on Task Taxonomy

Thus far, we have described some developments in establishing a task taxonomy. . . . However, we need a much more concerted, programmatic effort than has been mounted so far.

We have developed a rationale and approach to such an effort of which only the general outlines can be presented here.[1] This approach to the development, empirical study, and verification of a behavior taxonomy might include the following major phases.

1. The Rational Analysis of Real Tasks to reduce the mass of tasks involved in a broad spectrum of jobs to a set of generalized task categories. These categories will comprehensively cover the identifiable skills in the original jobs, but with obvious duplication eliminated.

2. The Synthesis and Testing of "Naturalistic" Tasks to translate general task and skill categories into direct analogs for laboratory measurement. The analysis of performance on these naturalistic (in the sense that they are direct analogs of real or "natural" tasks) laboratory tasks would be directed primarily at an identification of general, homogeneous behavior categories.

3. The Definition of Behavior Categories based on the analysis of correlations among performances on naturalistic laboratory tasks varied in systematic ways. New dimensions would be added to the definitions by rational analysis and description of conditions that may influence the establishment of performance levels for each type of behavior. The nature and extent of effect that variations in conditions of establishment have on performance in each behavior class would be determined through laboratory experimentation and mathematical-statistical analysis.

4. Performance Forecasting based on sets of equations derived from: (a) the original laboratory testing on naturalistic tasks, (b) the detailed experimentation with variables affecting performance within each behavior class, (c) assumptions concerning the manner in which performance of different types of behavior combines in complex tasks, and (d) experimentation with various combinations of behavioral classes. Forecasting equations need to be verified and improved on the basis of measurements of performance on both laboratory and real tasks. Accurate performance forecasting would not only be potentially useful in its own right, but it will also verify the isomorphism of the behavior taxonomy to a specified segment of the population of "real-world" tasks.

Figure 1 presents a further refinement and possible work-flow diagram of major phases oriented toward military systems problems and principal sub-

[1] The writer is indebted to his colleagues at A. I. R., Drs. Robert Gagné, James Altman, and Harold Van Cott, and earlier Robert Miller, for their contributions to these developments.

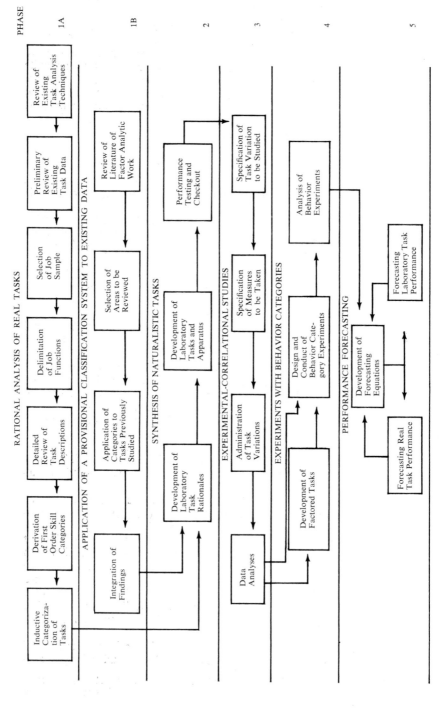

Figure 1. Work-Flow Diagram for Development, Study, and Verification of a Behavior Taxonomy.

phases of such a research program. Actually we have developed detailed procedures about what needs to be done within each block of the diagram.

Concluding Statement

The centrality of the taxonomy problem is critical to military psychology, to problems of assessing complex performance, and to so many questions of generalizing from system to system. The "state of the art" questions raised here have implications for psychology as a science and to the kinds of generalizations that can be made from research to field situations. I feel that there is a need for research along at least these parallel lines. These include:

1. An integrative literature review using a consistent set of performance categories to develop principles of what kinds of performances are affected by what kinds of treatments, environmental factors, procedures, etc. This review would utilize the kinds of categories described in this paper, categories derived from experimental-correlational studies of human tasks. The review would examine results with laboratory tasks, simulators, on-the-job performance, etc., from diverse fields. The key is the use of a common task descriptive framework to see if this provides greater consistency in establishing principles which relate treatments (e.g., effects of environmental factors, stress, drugs, etc.) to classes of human performance.

2. The development of interim standard performance testing facilities using currently available data about task dimensions rather than the usual armchair categories, and the validation of such facilities against operational performance. One approach has been described in this paper. As these and other approaches are tried we will learn much about their relative utility.

3. A long-range experimental program concerned with developing a behavioral-task taxonomy by systematic, programmatic task manipulations.

I would like to close with a quote from the (1960) *Annual Review of Psychology* article on engineering psychology:

> It is clear to those working in the area of engineering psychology, and it should become clear to others, that this vigorous and expanding universe of knowledge has semantic and taxonomic problems which have not been overcome. Nor can they be overcome in any stable way by the ingenuity of organizers of its literature. The roots of these difficulties are many, not the least being the semantic and taxonomic problems of experimental psychology. . . . Foremost among deficiencies of this type is the lack of taxonomies of tasks or of skills (Melton & Briggs, 1960, 89-90).

Although we have come some small distance, what was true in 1960 is no less true today.

References

Alluisi, E. A. & Thurmond, J. B. Behavioral effects of infectious diseases: Annual Progress Report. Louisville, Kentucky: University of Louisville, Perf. Res. Lab. Rep. No. PR-65-3, 1965.

Fleishman, E. A. Testing for psychomotor abilities by means of apparatus tests. *Psychol. Bull.*, 1953, *50*, 241-262. (b)

Fleishman, E. A. A comparative study of aptitude patterns in unskilled and skilled psychomotor performances. *J. appl. Psychol.*, 1957, *41*, 263-272. (a)

Fleishman, E. A. Factor structure in relation to task difficulty in psychomotor performance. *Educational and Psychol. Measmt*, 1957, *17*, 522-532. (b)

Fleishman, E. A. An analysis of positioning movements and static reactions. *J exp. Psychol.*, 1958, *55*, 12-24. (a)

Fleishman, E. A. Dimensional analysis of movement reactions. *J. exp. Psychol.*, 1958, *55*, 438-453. (b)

Fleishman, E. A. Psychomotor tests in drug research. J. G. Miller and L. Uhr (Eds.) *Drugs and behavior.* New York: Wiley, 1960. (b)

Fleishman, E. A. The description and prediction of perceptual-motor skill learning. In R. Glaser (Ed.) *Training research and education.* Pittsburgh: University of Pittsburgh Press, 1962.

Fleishman, E. A. Factor analyses of physical fitness tests. *Educational and Psychol. Measmt,* 1963, *23,* 647-661.

Fleishman, E. A. *The structure and measurement of physical fitness.* Englewood Cliffs, New Jersey: Prentice-Hall, 1964.

Fleishman, E. A. Human abilities and the acquisition of skill. In E. A. Bilodeau (Ed.) *Acquisition of Skill.* New York: Academic Press, 1966. (a)

Fleishman, E. A. & Ellison, G. D. A factor analysis of fine manipulative performance. *J. appl. Psychol.,* 1962, *46,* 96-105.

Fleishman, E. A. & Hempel, W. E. A factor analysis of dexterity tests. *Personnel Psychology,* 1954, *7,* 15-32. (a)

Fleishman, E. A. & Hempel, W. E. Changes in factor structure of a complex psychomotor test as a function of practice. *Psychometrika,* 1954, *18,* 239-252. (b)

Fleishman, E. A. & Hempel, W. E. The relation between abilities and improvement with practice in a visual discrimination reaction task. *J. exp. Psychol.,* 1955, *49,* 301-312.

Fleishman, E. A. & Hempel, W. E. Factorial analysis of complex psychomotor performance and related skills. *J. appl. Psychol.,* 1956, *40,* 96-104.

Fleishman, E. A. & Rich, S. Role of kinesthetic and spatial-visual abilities in perceptual-motor learning. *J. exp. Psychol.,* 1963, *66,* 6-11.

Gagné, R. M. *Conditions of learning.* New York: Holt, Rinehart and Winston, 1964.

Gagné, R. M. & Fleishman, E. A. *Psychology and human performance: An introduction to psychology.* New York: Holt, Rinehart, and Winston, 1959.

Hempel, W. E. & Fleishman, E. A. A factor analysis of physical proficiency and manipulative skill. *J. appl. Psychol.,* 1955, *39,* 12-16.

Melton, A. W. & Briggs, G. Engineering psychology. In *Ann rev. Psychol.,* Stanford U. Press, 1960.

Miller, R. B. Task analysis and task taxonomy: Inventive approach. Contribution to symposium on "Task Taxonomy and its Implication for Military Requirements." APA Convention, 1965.

Parker, J. F. & Fleishman, E. A. Ability factors and component performance measures as predictors of complex tracking behavior. *Psychol. Monogr.,* 1960, *74,* No. 503.

An Information—Theoretic Approach to Task Classification*

WARREN H. TEICHNER

A more theoretical procedure in defining classes of tasks and their nature is provided in the following article. Tasks are categorized as being primarily searching, switching, coding, or tracking by design, and logic is supplied through an information transfer mode. The interpretation of a task may be confusing with regard to its distinction from a process. In

* Speech delivered at the 77th Annual Meeting, American Psychological Association Washington, D.C., September, 1969. Reprinted with permission of the author.

other words, the manner in which the word task is used in this paper would probably be interpreted by many others as a process. Information theory is applied to an evaluation of the input-output "task" of the individual. The material presented is highly speculative and theoretical, but nevertheless is exciting and fresh, demonstrating some of the latest efforts at the American Institutes for Research.

Right now my task can be described as one of transferring information of some sort to you. The goodness of my performance can be described in terms of the amount of information transferred or by a related measure. It seems as simple as that. Problems arise only when we insist that there be more than one kind of task or when we try to use what are really explanatory concepts as task descriptors, e.g., a memory task. In that case the task has no independent definition.

A common approach to task classification provides functional descriptors, e.g., tracking tasks, computational tasks, gating tasks, conservational tasks, etc. There is a certain utility in this providing the task categories are reasonably mutually exclusive, and providing that one does not take them too seriously, but rather gets on to the important business. The important business concerns the relationships and parameters on which performance depends. There is, after all, no point to classifying tasks at all except to be able to denote the relationships involved when a new task is classified.

Back to a task as an information transfer—Diane Olson and I have taken this route by defining all tasks as information transfers and then attempting to identify functional task categories as classes of information transfer. This, like all other suggestions so far, is an approach that starts with the empirical side of things and builds up to abstract concepts. It goes from the specific to the general. I shall describe the rationale that we used, but only briefly, since a report is available. Then I shall outline a more theoretical approach i.e., one that goes from the abstract to the empirical. Both are based upon the same fundamental definition of a task as an information transfer.

Both man and the machine are considered as components of a system. In terms of this conventional diagram, we can think of information or data as being transmitted between components and as being operated upon or processed within components. Any operation on information *within* a component is a *process*. A *task* may be defined as a transfer of information *between* components.

However, what is to be called a process and what is to be called a task depends upon the level of system analysis being employed. When a system (such as mentioned above) is analyzed into its subsystems, what was a process at the more general descriptive level becomes a task. That is, there are now new transfers of information between components which did not exist in the original general system. Clearly, a process is carried out as a subtask and as the level of analysis becomes more detailed, successive processes break down into tasks.

Regardless of the level of analysis, the information transfer is always in the direction of machine-man-machine-machine. It is convenient, but not a requisite, to deal with the transfer of information between each two successive components separately, i.e., in terms of the four major tasks, machine-man, man-man, and machine-machine. Although the psychologist is not concerned with machine-machine tasks, it is important to note that such tasks exist. That is, the concept of a task is not one which necessarily involves people. This is extremely important, and usually ignored. It just will not do to have more than one definition of a concept. Regardless of how we define task, we must be willing to use the concept wherever it fits and to say that the same relationships and parameters are involved in every single instance which falls within a task category. Furthermore, one must be willing to talk about tasks at any level of analysis. For the definition just presented, this means that what are usually vaguely referred to as "underlying processes" must be describable in exactly the same terms as tasks at more detailed levels. Thus, there are tasks between components within the central nervous system as well as between machine components, and between men and machines.

Starting with this as a rationale, Diane Olson and I defined four classes of tasks: searching, switching, coding and tracking. We attempted to provide operational definitions for each and then to consider the parameters and relationships which would justify them as unique. I think that this approach is one which takes maximum advantage of what is already available by way of empirical relationships. It has the disadvantage that the task classification can never be any more reliable than the state of knowledge about these relationships. Right now reliability is probably very low.

The same problem can be approached with a model or a set of abstract concepts for which the relationships within a class are defined. Such an approach is completely reliable, but, of course, the model may not fit, in which case it has no validity. I would like now to outline an information transfer model which we are beginning to develop at the American Institutes for Research as an approach which is complementary to that of Teichner and Olson (1969).

We start with the understanding that a taxonomy is a model. It contains definitions and relationships, i.e., a logic. A classification system, ideally, is what is evolved or derived from the taxonomy when the model is applied to an empirical area of interest. If the model fits for situations involving people, then it is useful for that purpose and people can be said to be involved in tasks as defined. The model may fit situations which do not involve people, however, and these too would be called task situations. For our interests here, we wish a model which is useful in that it fits those situations in which people make responses. But we do not restrict our definitions to just those situations.

We define a task as a transfer of information between an information source and a receiver in any system that can be construed as a communication channel in Shannon's sense. The source information, $H(X)$, is a function of the number of alternative events contained in the source and their probabilities. The receiver information, $H(Y)$, is defined in terms of the number of events the receiver can exhibit and their probabilities. The amount of information transmitted, $H(XY)$, is a function of the joint probabilities of selecting source events and observing receiver events.

In analyzing perception, Garner (1962) has described how sampling constraints introduce redundancies into the sampled events. These constraints may be internal or external. The internal constraints apply to restrictions on the random sampling of events at the source or at the receiver and are stated as sampling rules. Internal constraints, then, are restrictions on how events are sampled. External constraints are restrictions on what events are sampled. Varying either kind of constraint while holding the other constant varies the amount and determines the form of the redundancy. We note that these relationships characterize *all* kinds of information transfers—not just perceptual ones. A characteristic of a task, then, is that it may contain internal and external constraints which limit the amount of information transfer. For our taxonomic model, we define classes of tasks by classes of constraints, with internal and external as the primary task groupings. We define task complexity in terms of amount and form of redundancy. That is, as external constraining increases, redundancy increases and complexity increases. As internal constraining increases, redundancy increases, but complexity *decreases*.

We have presented only the barest outline of a task taxonomy model and that only in terms of some definitions. The model must also have a logic. This is given by a statement of the dependency of information transfer on the constraint classes at different levels of complexity. The model needs to be developed in detail and then tested against human performance situations. We shall try to indicate briefly how the model can be developed and evaluated.

Task Classes. Internal constraints may be stated as sampling rules. Examples of classes of such rules may be found in sequential sampling restrictions, e.g., purposive sampling, stratified sampling, and sampling without replacement. External constraints restrict the size of the ensemble. Examples of possible classes of external constraints are:

1. Combination constraint—sample only one at a time.
2. Rate constraint—sample no faster than a given rate.
3. Range constraint—sample only within a specified range of values.
4. Similarity-dissimilarity constraint—e.g., sample only combinations having no common elements.
5. Probability constraint—e.g., sample only events having probabilities greater than a specified probability.
6. Sequence constraint—sample only sequences having some specified sequential restriction, e.g., no unique event can occur twice in succession.

If these were all of the possible classes of constraints which can operate on sampling from the source and the receiver, and if only zero or one constraint operates on either, there would be $2 \times 5 \times 7 = 70$ task classes. The actual number of classes is much greater than this, of course, since more than one constraint can be present in either sampling operation. However, in applying the model it does not follow that all classes of task must be found in each area of application. For example, some, but not all of these classifications might characterize man-machine tasks; others might characterize machine-machine tasks; still others might describe information transfers within the central nervous system, the planets, etc. Of course, there might be communalities among these as well. Furthermore, although it is unlikely that we will find a stratified sampling of human responses in normal behavior, we can still ask to what degree behavior samples can be approximated this way. It is likely that we will find sequential constraints as in the contraction-relaxation cycle of antagonistic muscles.

A theoretical requirement is the specification of all of the possible sampling constraints. An experimental requirement is that of determining which of these possible contraints are represented in the human receiver.

Most human performance situations are likely to be those in which the man provides external constraints. Sources of human external constraints are indicated by the spectral sensitivity of the eye and ear, size of the visual field, empirical attention span, memory span, coordinative ability, etc. All of these act to limit the reception of transmitted events. Application of the model requires finding out what classes of constraint man can represent. The next step is to identify the sources of the human-imposed constraints. Doing this requires research which is directed toward evaluating how well people can represent the constraints in the presence of sources which themselves are varied in kind of constraint imposed.

Taxonomic Logic. So far we have been considering only the initial input and the final output of a communication system. In the human situation this is, of course, a traditional S-R relationship. We are now calling it a task. The S-R relationship depends upon underlying processes. When we say this, however, all we are saying is that there is a series of intervening tasks. We call them processes only when the level of analysis is so gross as to leave them unspecified, as in the case with S-R relationships. Analysis at the S-R level, however, offers some interesting possibilities for raising questions about underlying processes in a rational way. That is, looked at only in terms of S-R or initial input and final output, there are three possible kinds of effect which can be produced by constraining:

1. There can be less information in the output than in the input; that is, the amount of information transmitted is less than the maximum possible. This implies constraints present in the receiver not present at the source. For illustration, suppose that it could be determined that a range type of constraint were present and that it could not be accounted for by known range type constraints such as those in the eye, the empirical attention span, etc. Under these conditions it might be inviting to postulate the presence of an underlying mechanism with properties such as to impose a range type of constraint. We might call this mechanism *attention* and then we might either develop a model of it which provides the needed constraint or we might try to apply available models, for example, a particular kind of band-pass filter.

2. In an S-R analysis there can be more information at the receiver than at the source. This can happen only if the communication system has more sources than are accounted for. If there is only one external source, other sources must be internal to the receiver. Examples of how this could happen might be the following. (1) The input from a second source might be contingent upon the occurrence of events from the first source and the receiver reports both. In this case, if the second source were internal, it might be called *memory*. (2) Successive inputs from a single source might be operated upon internally to produce a third event and the receiver reports them all. In a human performance situation, the source might present the numerical events 2 and 3; the receiver might report, "2 and 3 are 5." A process that could be postulated to provide this third event might be called *computation*. Then again, it might also be called *memory*. . . .

3. Finally, the output information might equal the input information. In this case, there may be no need to assume any receiver constraints to be operating.

We are interested primarily in the question of what classes of constraint operate in human performance situations and what relationships hold between them and information transfer as the complexity of the task is varied. Our approach is twofold. On the one hand we shall attempt to identify classes of human constraints which might appear to be operable. Then, for each such class, we shall attempt to determine its effects on information transmission at different levels of redundancy as a strictly theoretical function. At the same time we shall test the model experimentally. This can be done in laboratory situations in which the human subject provides the constraint while other constraints are manipulated at the source or stimulus ensemble. If the theoretical result and the laboratory result agree, we shall say that the model fits at that point, i.e., there are tasks of that sort in human affairs and they are describable by the logic of the model. In this way we shall avoid the development of the model in its entirety and shall concentrate on those aspects of it which can be expected to have relevance to human performance.

In summary, I am proposing a two-pronged approach to task classification using information transfer as the definition of task in each case. One approach classifies tasks by groupings of common empirical relationships; the other uses a model to state what these groupings should be. In our laboratory we are pursuing both simultaneously.

References

Garner, W. R. *Uncertainty and structure in psychological research.* Wiley, N. Y.: 1962.
Teichner, W. H. and Olson, Diane. Predicting human performance in space environments. *NASA CR-1370,* June, 1969.

The Development of a Response Taxonomy*

ELMO E. MILLER

WHEREAS in some of the articles presented in this chapter experimentation and statistical analysis served as the bases for the conclusions drawn, Miller extracts material from accepted concepts and experimental findings in the literature to develop his own performance taxonomy. The ideas are stated clearly and simply. The major purpose of these efforts are, in the words of the writer, "to provide a classification system for relating training methods to the types of job requirements with which they are most effective." Educational and training techniques are instructional and can equally benefit from an analysis of Miller's training strategies. Any vocational or recreational skill fits into response taxonomy. This reading contrasts with the preceding one in that it is far more applied in context.

During the last few years, there has been increasing activity and interest in taxonomies of human performance. I want to share some of my experiences in developing one such taxonomy with the hope that this may prove helpful to others involved in developing such systems.

My taxonomy is restricted to perceptual-motor skills—a term I have not attempted to define precisely. I have tried, rather, to set the limits broadly in order to include most of the tasks that are generally listed under this topic.

There is another restriction on my taxonomy: It was specifically designed to help in the design of training programs. Thus, if the taxonomy achieves its purpose, each category of tasks would call for a different set of training strategies.

As to the performance being classified, I am concerned with the functions, or operations, which a person must perform in a system, such as a man-machine system, rather than with internal processes. I will stress the approach

* Miller, Elmo E. *The Development of a Response Taxonomy.* Presentation at the 77th Annual American Psychological Association Convention, Washington, D.C.: issued as HumRRO Professional Paper 32-69, October 1969. Reproduced with permission of the Human Resources Research Organization (HumRRO). Also reprinted from HumRRO Professional Paper 32-69 by permission of the American Psychological Association and the author.

I followed, so as to help those who are trying to decide whether to follow a similar approach.

First, my approach was *not* experimental, at least not directly. I did not begin by designing and performing experiments. It seemed that a comprehensive taxonomy would require far more resources than I could muster. Instead, I collected a large body of task distinctions and other considerations, from both the experimental literature and common observation, and tried to form these into a system by a process of *explication*—that is, by systematically developing the interrelationships among the terms.

The fruitfulness of this approach increases sharply with the number (in this case, several hundred) and variety of items considered.

In order to extract relationships, I used a technique that I call "connotative clustering." This is simply listing the terms, then copying them, one by one, on a large sheet of paper, placing each new term near other terms that are most similar in their connotations. As more terms are added, clusters of related terms seem to emerge, and it becomes relatively easy to define the clusters and their interrelations. I suppose that there are many similar devices for listing, then juggling and shuffling terms. The important thing, when dealing with such complex and abstract relationships, is to have some effective means of structuring one's activities so as to evolve an increasingly coherent logical structure.

A second major feature of the approach is the development of a second taxonomy—a taxonomy of training strategies. Since our purpose in classifying tasks is to facilitate the use of training strategies, it seems only reasonable to try to formulate these strategies explicitly. Actually, the two taxonomies were developed concurrently and were frequently compared, so that the distinctions among tasks would tend to reflect differences in training strategies.

The training strategies are listed in figure 1. The first section, A, "Operational Conditions of Practice," seems fairly traditional—such concerns as the practice environment, dividing the task for allocation into practice sessions, telling the person what he must do in the situation, and so forth.

However, the second section, B, "Diagnosis of the Behavioral Process," seems somewhat unusual for a psychologist. These seem to be the sorts of things commonly done by coaches. For example, look at 4, c, "Inducing set to avoid common mistakes." Specifically, in water skiing, a coach will say "When the boat first pulls you up out of the water, you'll tend to fall forward on your face, so lean way back." In this second group of training strategies, it may be dubious what the coach or instructor actually does, in behavioral terms. Most often, he only talks to the student, stating his diagnosis and leaving it to the student to adjust his responses accordingly.

In the taxonomy of response processes section (Figure 2), only the four major divisions are listed (the subdivisions were omitted in the interest of simplicity). In the "reactive" tasks, the performance stays fairly homogeneous over time. For example, if you observe a typist for five seconds, her performance will be essentially the same in character as it would be in another sample taken a few minutes later.

In the first category, Adjustive, the person must try to bring about an alignment in the stimulus dimension. A feedback loop is thus established so that what is not corrected at one moment will remain in the system for later correction. In the second category, however, in tasks like typing, if a mistake is made, it's like water over the dam—there is no way to modify the next response to make up for it. It's a difference in the nature of the feedback loop—and I believe this is the basic difference between what are usually called "continuous" tasks and "discrete" tasks.

DEVELOPMENT OF A RESPONSE TAXONOMY
Training Strategies

A. Operational Conditions of Practice

1. Representation of the task environment
   a. Unmodified task environment
   b. Purposeful modification
      (1) Stimulus predifferentiation
         (a) Terminology practice
         (b) Progressive narrowing of discrimination
         (c) Demonstrating tolerance limits
         (d) Recalling differences
      (2) Response differentiation
         (a) Practicing at slower rate
            Task-paced Tasks
            Self-paced Tasks
         (b) Reducing force or amplitude required
         (c) Relaxing qualitative standards for responses

2. Analysis into subtasks
   a. Successive phases
   b. Concurrent subtasks
      (1) Independent subtasks
      (2) Interdependent subtasks

3. Performance requirements information (telling S what to do)
   a. Size of behavioral unit described
   b. Contingencies for prompting
      (1) Time in training
      (2) S's past performance
      (3) Properties of responses required
      (4) Speed of response
      (5) S's request for prompt
   c. Completeness of prompts
      (1) Cue (partial)
      (2) Prompt (complete)

4. Supplementary knowledge of results (KR)
   a. Size of response unit
      (1) KR after each step
      (2) KR after end result
         (a) General KR
         (b) KR specific to a particular step
   b. Form of KR
      (1) Providing comparison
      (2) Giving assessment

5. Manipulating incentives
   a. Adding incentives
   b. Emphasizing existing incentives

B. Diagnosis of the Behavioral Process

1. Promoting intrinsic KR
   a. Clarifying goal state
   b. Calling attention to subgoal images
   c. Providing supplementary KR

2. Fostering conception of underlying process

3. Establishing a more effective response set
   a. Promoting movement consistency for better feedback
   b. Establishing response set which permits sensing of feedback

4. Inducing set for appropriate response pattern
   a. Physically guiding responses
   b. Describing desired modifications of responses
   c. Inducing set to avoid common mistakes
   d. Instructing on grip or stance

5. Inducing cue sensitivity
   a. Signaling, during task performance, the moment for a response
   b. Describing situation which is to trigger the action

6. Encouraging anticipation of the response (reading ahead)

Figure 1

TASK TAXONOMY (Response Processes)

Major Task Category	*Common Reference Terms: Examples*
Reactive Tasks	
I. Adjustive	Tracking or adjusting: adjusting a knob, steering a car, stick control in flying a plane, steering a bicycle.
II. Selection from a set of responses	(No common reference term): Typing, sight reading in playing a piano.
Developmental Tasks	
III. Procedural	Procedures: aircraft flight procedures, procedure for assembling an M1 rifle, starting a tank.
IV. Skilled performance	Skilled act: batting a ball, throwing a ball, laying a single brick, a hand stand, vaulting over an obstacle.

Figure 2

The definition of Category II tasks requires that there be a series of conventional signs in the environment such as letters or numbers which specify the series of actions to be performed. If these signs are not apparent, as when a person composes as he types, then it is assumed that generating the symbols—that is, composing—is a separate task.

In performing tasks of the last two categories, the task functions *do* change in character during any particular performance of the task. Each performance goes through several phases—beginning, middle, and end. The third category, Procedural, includes the categorical or qualitative aspects of performance, and the last category covers the quantitative, fine-skill aspects of performance. Learning procedures involve the chaining together of simple, already learned acts.

One can make reasonably sharp distinctions among tasks because of two very pervasive features of our culture: the use of machines, and the use of language. (The most primitive category is "Skilled performance," in which we find complex, subtle behavior developing toward an objective. Most athletic performance is of this sort.)

The combination of machines, which have identifiable parts, and language, which deals with the world in terms of categories, causes the emergence of procedural tasks. Also, with the complexity of our technology, we find it increasingly *useful* to form long chains of essentially simple acts, that is, procedures. These factors also affect the training strategy; the classic method for teaching procedures is to put the student into a reasonably realistic work situation (Training Strategy A,1,a) and then tell him what he is to do (some variation under A,3, such as prompting him before each step).

The use of machines also creates Category I, Adjustive tasks, such as tracking, for it is the machine that creates the requirement for maintaining a roughly optimal condition, and also provides the structure necessary for consistent dynamic properties. Category II, covering such tasks as typing and sending Morse code—is peculiarly dependent upon a series of conventional signs in the environment. Such tasks, in reality, are probably an information-processing kind of function which happens to keep the person busy on the effector side.

The two taxonomies, for tasks and for training strategies, were interrelated in detail, both during development and later in trying to assess how well they had accomplished their purposes.

For example, consider the training strategies B,1, a and b, which refer specifically to goal images and goal states. These would *not* refer to the "reactive" categories, I and II, because the reactive task functions are homogeneous over time, and hence do not involve development toward a goal. These strategies are often implied to tasks of type IV, Skilled performance. In such tasks, the image of the goal situation sets up a feedback loop with the current situation, to guide development toward the goal. These training strategies may also apply to procedural tasks, but in the somewhat more trivial sense of a mnemonic device rather than forming a feedback loop.

As another example, consider B,6 (reading ahead), the last training strategy listed. In the very literal definition of this strategy, there would have to be some signs in the environment that tell what future responses must be, thus allowing a person to organize his responses into larger units. Category II tasks are of this sort by definition, and in these tasks coaches or teachers do in fact encourage students to "read ahead," as in sight reading on the piano. In tracking tasks, Category I, however, one would have to be able to see the track ahead, as when driving along a road. Incidentally, this establishes sub-categories of tracking tasks on the basis of whether the person can see the track ahead. Of course, one could apply the training strategy in a somewhat different version—that is, "imagine the track ahead." However, the effectiveness of this modified strategy would be limited by the degree of coherence, or autocorrelation, in the task. Similarly, the "read ahead" strategy would *not* apply to "procedural" tasks or "skilled performance" tasks, except in situations where extensive job aids were used.

In summary, the taxonomy of perceptual-motor tasks was developed by *explication* from existing concepts, rather than through experiments. The project also involved developing another taxonomy, that of training strategies, so that development could reflect its purpose—more effective use of the training strategies. The major task categories depend upon the prevalence in our society of machines and language. The effort seems to offer some encouragement for further development of taxonomies of human performance.

Task Taxonomy: Science or Technology?[*]

R. B. MILLER

IN the final article in this chapter Miller explains the foundations and rationale for taxonomies. It might have been better to place this paper first for the understanding it brings to the development of classification systems; hence, greater insight into the efforts of the other reporting authors. On the other hand, Miller presents some assessment of existing

[*] From *Ergonomics*, 1967, *10*, 167-176. Reprinted with permission of the author and publisher.

attempts at classifying tasks and then goes on to make suggestions for new direction in this area. In this respect, his material can be used in part to evaluate the worth of the other papers. For instance, he is highly critical of factor analysis and intercorrelation techniques as a means to meaningful information related to a task taxonomy. Also, the worth of nonsense tasks, e.g., the pursuit rotor, as a useful reference base in the development of a meaningful task taxonomy is questioned. The student should ask himself whether he agrees with Miller or whether he considers the positions of such researchers as Fleishman and Guilford defensible.

May I begin by showing a proper respect to the whole business of constructing a taxonomy. This respect may seem pedantic. It will be useful, however, if it lights up some of the alternatives and general issues in approaching taxonomic design. Perhaps I should at this point ask the reader's indulgence for a rather large proportion of personal references later in the text.

What is a Taxonomy?

Let us agree that a taxonomy is a means of classifying objects or phenomena in such a way that useful relationships among them are established. A taxonomy is therefore not a mere list of labels with semantic definitions: it also has an inner syntactic structure. Thus, the *Dewey* and *Library of Congress* schemes of classifying books enable the person with a topical interest to find references physically close to each other on the shelves; and also assist the librarian to maintain balance in library purchasing policies. The classification schemes in natural history attempt to establish etiological parallels, as well as to cluster physiological and structural identities. Geological classifications have as their principles of division both etiological and morphological characteristics.

A taxonomy is therefore a way of simplifying a complicated universe of individual events and objects according to some useful way of identifying and labelling the way in which groups of individuals (or observations) have things in common and differ from other groups of individuals.

Explanatory versus Descriptive Taxonomies

The periodic table in physics and the identifying of different particles in nuclear physics are examples of explanatory taxonomies. I would say that Hull's "principles of behavior" aimed at being an explanatory taxonomy. An explanatory taxonomy is the near-equivalent of a theory: the syntactic structure whereby terms in an explanatory taxonomy are related to each other is the structure of an equation.

In a descriptive taxonomy we ordinarily find some salient structural characteristics of similarity within a genus which we can use in predicting other structural and functional characteristics we have learned to expect to be associated with the genus. Thus, the ungulates or hooved animals share many characteristics in addition to their being hooved, but a hoof is an easy way to identify the class. Sheldon and Stevens' attempts to relate types of physique to temperament is an example of a descriptive taxonomy which sought to identify clusters of correlated characteristics, although perhaps their attempt to formulate equations between types of body measurements and types of temperament suggests an explanatory aspiration.

Certainly the *Dewey* system of classifying subject matter is descriptive rather than explanatory. You may object, however, that the difference between description and explanation is one of degree and a philosophical matter anyway. Having mentioned the point, I will not further belabour it.

Rigorous versus Non-rigorous Taxonomies

In a rigorous taxonomy the terms are mutually exclusive. Membership in one class is absolutely exclusive of membership in another class. One may be black or white. If there is a gray category, it is defined so as to be exclusive of either white or black. With considerable historical labour, the periodic table in physics provides such an example. Note that in this example, membership in a given class is based on a *count* of some kind. If the count of discrete entities is of a given magnitude, the count itself is equivalent to a discrete category.

It is my belief that the only kind of rigorous taxonomy which is logically possible is one which is based on some kind of count of discrete entities. All other kinds of taxonomy are non-rigorous, if not in concept then in application, which is where the taxonomy is tested.

A special case may be pleaded for a taxonomy derived from factor analysis. Here, mutual exclusivity is an outgrowth of an analytic process applied to data. But we have neglected the assumptions generated by the operations of measurement which provide the data. These assumptions are not inconsequential. Perhaps we can differentiate one purpose of a taxonomy: to analyse objects or phenomena efficiently by a limited number of measurements from another purpose of perhaps a different taxonomy: to control, synthesize and predict behaviour given some minimum base of information about it in terms of the taxonomy. We are driven back to the pragmatic criteria of purpose and utility.

Later, I hope to show that a taxonomy which does not claim mutual exclusivity of its terms can be, and is, useful, and possibly convince you that the quest for mutual exclusivity in behavioural classification is a *will-o-the-wisp*.

Classifying Objects and Classifying Phenomena

Different concepts, techniques and objectives may apply to a classification system for *objects* as contrasted with *phenomena*. It can be argued that no set of attributes can provide unambiguous characterizations of objects, much less of class characteristics of objects. This has been the argument of semanticists. On the other hand, as physics has more or less demonstrated, it is possible to frame and name a set of *variables* which are sufficient and necessary to account for certain restricted kinds of phenomena. These variables, and the control or measurement techniques derived by them, are mutually exclusive both conceptually and operationally: although there may be room for debating this latter issue.

I hope these sketchy comments have at least made one point. Formal taxonomy development has many approaches and possible aspirations. Some aspirations with some kinds of subject matter may be logically absurd and operationally doomed, and these may be predictable from the outset. The philosophic and semantic literature plus some hard-boiled thinking can avoid some expensive blind alleys. Let us now pick up pace by becoming more concrete.

Objectives for a Task Taxonomy

One school of thought about behavioural taxonomy seeks to discover some underlying or "fundamental" set of elements and building block units, like the periodic table, whereby behaviour can be rigorously categorized, quantified, designed, predicted, controlled. My own aspiration has been more modest, and, I think, realistic. My intention was to invent a useful tool. In order to be useful (that is, to yield a payoff with reasonable effort) it should, I believe, have the following objectives.

It should have a starting set of less than 15 to 20 kinds of behaviour that in some degree were a part of any segment of repeatable, purposeful activity. This seemed a reasonable number of terms for any analyst to work with.

Since the behaviours would be functional (and for other reasons), the categories should permit discriminations among the activities observed, but not necessarily mutually exclusive ones.

The categories as a set could be learned and applied by an experimental psychologist (or perhaps anybody else) in a few hours.

The categories should tend to parallel the segmenting of training into part-task training.

The characterizations would at least foster the anticipation of types of error.

The level of detail in analysis should suggest a point beyond which predictions from available observation or knowledge are no better than random.

In summary, the objective of the taxonomy was to assist in making design decisions and predictions rather than being an end in itself. I was (and still am) ready to settle for a non-quantitative tool which would help me structure and search my own knowledge of the literature plus observational experience, interpret them and apply them with professional judgment. It was intended as a heuristic instrument, modifiable in the course of its use.

Here are my assumptions about behaviour, stated in oversimplifications:

The description or specification of any behavioural phenomenon or class of phenomena is necessarily an abstract: selective and incomplete. There may be a limitless number of equally truthful ways of describing any denotable sets of events, although some descriptions will better serve some purposes than others.

At different degrees of practice, behaviour becomes organized in different ways. By "organized" I refer to what stimuli become sufficient and necessary to elicit (or lower the threshold for) various patterns of response. The dropping out of various kinds of mediating activities with much task practice is an example.

The conditions of what is practiced with what, and in what order, determine what clustering of associations will be formed and, therefore, what the psychological boundary of the "task" will be.

This last point justifies a digression. I believe that I (and others) can structure different training regimens of externally identical tasks so that entirely different and inconsistent patterns of intercorrelations would emerge. And I believe these differences would interact with the kind of differences we call "individual differences." The more complex the task—and especially in intellectual involvement—the greater the range of inconsistency in correlations of analytic components between one training strategy and another.

Let us look at this issue in another light. I believe that a task taxonomy produced through factor analysis and intercorrelations is predominantly a measure of similarities and differences in what behaviours are grouped with what other behaviours in a given training procedure. I doubt that we will have any more success in finding task traits than we have had in finding personality traits or executive traits, and for the same reason. Individual experience is the glue that makes behaviours stick together in habit associations, and not natural structures. (I might make some exceptions in perceptual-conceptual behaviour, but this would confuse the point).

We can put it still another way with the analogy of computers. Task taxonomy is more like the study of computer programming and programmes than it is comparable to the study of computer hardware. An identical set of functions can be (and unfortunately often is) put together into a programme in many different ways. Several commonplace examples might help. Some years ago, children were taught to read solely by learning the names and sounds of letters of the alphabet, then by putting these sounds together into words. Some students never seemed to get past phonetic reading. So, instead, pupils were taught to read by recognizing words all at once. The reading skill now grew out of a different 'task' and task family. The same kind of thing happens when we learn a new language by conversation rather than by constructions of vocabulary and grammar.

A different organization of typing skill arises when we learn touch typing from the very start, rather than "hunt and peck," and the typing of patterns of characters rather than one at a time: both perceptual and motor organizations differ from those of "hunt and peck." Similarly in swimming.

Therapy for the personality consists largely of learning new (shall I say?) task organizations for symbolic and conceptual behaviour associated with attitudes. A properly trained musician learns to translate musical notation into a concept of the sound and what he plays (in sight reading) is a translation of this tone concept (or image) into more or less automatic muscular actions. I myself was poorly trained, and read poorly; only my muscles remember what to do—at least I cannot translate what I hear conceptually into appropriate finger movements.

In all these cases the facade of performance may appear identical, but behind it are different behaviour organizations, and factor analysis which showed up these differences as inconsistencies could lead to perplexing conclusions. And if a task analysis cannot generalize across any task domain, any task subject matter, then it is of doubtful utility.

The reason for my selecting factor analysis as an opponent is that it has been, and is, offered as a rational, quantitative and quasi-experimental, data-oriented approach, in contrast to what I must blushingly accept as the arm-chair, intuitive approach which under duress of respectability I prefer to call "inventive."

Example of Task Classification

Thus far I have avoided defining one of the two central concepts of this paper. You ask "What is a task?" The answer I give will beg the question. A task is any set of activities, occurring at about the same time, sharing some common purpose that is recognized by the task performer.

In 1951 I was faced with a contract obligation to develop a procedure for anticipating from prototype equipment task requirements for human engineering and training purposes. The simple-minded premise (which turned out to be a revolutionary one, and still is today) was that training should be based on what the operator or maintenance man had to do, rather than on theory of operation of the machine or the physics of the phenomena. I quickly became aware that I needed some rubrics to clump and bundle task information. So I asked myself, if I were to build a robot that could simulate human capabilities, what kind of boxes would I have to design into him: what kinds of general function would he need that could be independent of the mechanism which implemented the function? Like the human, he is an associative mechanism. I was also guided by the objectives and assumptions mentioned in earlier paragraphs. The following emerged as a set of classifying terms.

Concept of Purpose. A function which could be programmed so that sooner or later he could discriminate relevant from irrelevant cues, responses and feedback, and to enable him to be turned "on" by inciting cues and turned "off" by criterion-matching cues. Concepts of purpose may be single-values (such as reeling off a programmed procedure to a predictable series of cues) or multiple-valued (such as in inductive decision making). This "concept of purpose" function, by the way, is the most difficult to design into a box.

Scanning function. Active or passive search for exposing his perceptive apparatus to task-inciting cues in the environment, or to cues generated by himself.

Identification of Relevant Cues Function. A function whereby he identifies or differentiates a pattern of cues as a pattern either from a background of noise or from other patterns of cues. A label or some other discriminatory action would be attached to the identifying operation.

Interpretation of Cues. Interpretation according to the "meaning" or implication apart from the physical nature of the cue itself.

Short-term Memory. For holding together, during a task cycle, the fragments of information that will be acted upon later or combined into a clump. This function is much broader than apperception span, by the way. It operates as extensively and as elaborately as the continuation of my concept of purpose and my recall of what I have said during presentation.

Long-term Memory. The case of recallable associations between and among stimuli and responses. The associations may be automatic perceptual-motor, or they may be symbolic in cognitive awareness. In relatively simple form, long-term memory is seen in strict procedural performance. But memory may also consist of trains of symbolic associations such as images of a map or a terrain.

Decision Making and Problem Solving. Techniques which may be divergent and convergent, computational or strategic, and so on; a tradeoff against long-term memory (or "table lookup"): response selection or formulation in the absence of a sufficiently dominant association between the cue pattern, the response pattern and the concept of purpose. Problem solving requires information provided by the functions already mentioned plus processing by strategy rules or concepts with symbolic response repertoires. Decision making and problem solving can be useful if divided into further categories.

Effector Response. The outputs that do work on the environment, including symbolic work.

Most of you have heard of this list before, with expanded descriptions. These rubrics would guide my examination of the robot's environment. They should help me match his mechanisms with their programming so that he could cope with this environment according to the purposes we had specified.

As evaluated according to many criteria of scientific elegance, this list is a mess. One definition overlaps others. The definitions, even in their more extended and refined form, are ambiguous for observing activities. They lack handles for quantification. But I have emphasized that this list is an invention, not a discovery in nature. Its test is in utility, not validity in the sense of physical experiments.

Like any tool, its effectiveness depends as much on the knowledge and skill of the user as in any of its intrinsic properties. That is why even its utility cannot be measured as an entity in itself. (But it shares this same difficulty with most scientific theory: if I may distinguish a "theory" from a "hypothesis.")

Some of my associates and I have used this analytic structure with modest professional success in examining work situations, actual and planned, in reasonable amounts of time, sometimes in a few minutes. With its help we have made substantial proposals about procedure design, human engineering, concentrations of training and part-task training (note that the list itself offers a psychologically reasonable structure for training segments, not necessarily in sequence as given) and, in a gross way, for selection. On the latter I am tentative for reasons I have already suggested: a task can be performed in many different ways, hence with different combinations of "ability."

I have found this structure useful in predicting the kinds of errors likely to be made under performance, and the conditions (such as external stress) under which relative increases in errors will occur. At present I am finding this scheme highly useful in adapting complex human activities (teaching-learning, engineering design, diagnosis, concept retrieval as examples) to inventing new applications for computers. I am hampered very little during the important stages of conceiving system functions by lack of quantitative behaviour predictors or by overlapping categories of classification.

A Taxonomic Grid

If I were to assume responsibility for further formalizing a task classification, I would proceed in the following way.

First, I would subdivide several of the present categories into one further level. Problem solving and decision making would be redefined and sub-categories found. The basis would be "intuitive."

More significantly, as a second step I would attempt to design a classification matrix. The row headings would consist of the present functional categories. The column headings, or cell entries, would be names of classes of task content. At present I have no organizing principle clearly in mind, but I suspect it would develop from some concepts of differences among (a) strategy, (b) the handling of noise and uncertainty implied by the task conditions and objective, plus (c) the form of information stored in long- and short-term memory. For example, the convergent strategy of diagnosis, or trouble-shooting, affects how and what following activities take place: search and scan, identification, interpretation, short-term memory (of other symptoms and progressively eliminated hypotheses, as well as of relationships between diagnostic diagrams and physical objects). In fact, I strongly suspect that what happens (or should happen) in short-term memory will be a key differentiator of types of task content.

The fact that a classification grid existed would point out that scanning a radar scope for targets *might* require different human engineering principles, error predictions, training operations than, say, scanning traffic during the guidance of a vehicle, or scanning a page in a telephone directory.

A third dimension would be needed for this grid. The term "dimension" as used here refers only to the layout of the grid; not to some continuum of task phenomena. This dimension would consist of degree of learning. A succession of writers since Bryan and Harter (1899) have pointed out the role of qualitative changes in task performance with progressively higher degree of learning. Fleishman in 1962 obtained some evidence of these changes in perceptual-motor tasks. Some of these changes are attributable to the dropping out of mediating behaviours, others to perceptual reorganization (reading through noise, set and so on) and still others to changes in the operation of motor patterns. Perhaps the most far-reaching ones may be changes in the mnemonic structures active in short-term memory.

This "degree of learning" dimension in the grid should help us to see that what early in the learning series may have been a decision-making activity, making heavy demands on short-term memory, has become formatted and proceduralized to such an extent that the activity is almost automatic: that is, the activity now uses up relatively little of the range of attention, or awareness, or whatever you choose to characterize short-term memory.

3

In summary, the taxonomic grid is proposed as having three dimensions. One dimension consists of categories which may be thought of as psychologically functional. A second dimension would consist of categories of task content.

The third dimension would be made up of characterizations of successive stages of learning. The structural relations of the grid should be sufficiently flexible that boundaries can be changed, added or eliminated in order to adapt to new data or new theory. (Notice, for example, that I have omitted reference to "social" task behaviour.)

Nonsense Tasks and Correlations

Parenthetically, I believe it will be a waste of time to try to build a useful task taxonomy from a reference base of nonsense tasks. The rotary pursuit and the syllable list are nonsense tasks and are designed to be so. The puzzle-solving tasks typical of laboratory studies in "problem solving" are a close relative to artificial nonsense situations. There will be attempts to make meaningfulness a scalar dimension of tasks. I predict these attempts will be abortive. If meaningfulness is defined in the objective stimulus-response sense, then the "meaning" of a stimulus is the response(s) made to it, overt or covert, actual or incipient. This definition offers no hope for a scale or dimension. If meaningfulness is defined as some subjective cognitive content (such as number of associations the stimulus evokes), we are again among qualitative differences.

Rather than attempting to reify "meaning," I would ask, "What are the forms of 'meaning'—that is, of mnemonics—that can be introduced as technique in learning and purposive performance?" Thus, I might try to make trouble-shooting easier to learn, to remember and to apply by making the graphic aids compatible with the strategy I gave the troubleshooter for sequencing a series of tests and inferences leading to further tests. The task and the meanings would change together. Only the most artificial of scales could relate one to the other in some linear fashion.

By the same argument, I doubt that a task taxonomy can be developed from nonsense tasks and be extrapolated to real tasks, that is, purposive tasks which, by that description alone, are meaningful. In addition, real life tasks have contingencies, options and choices that are fundamentally absent in rote learning.

There have been, and I am sure there will continue to be, attempts to discover task categories through clusterings derived by correlational operations on work performances. But this means we are limited to whatever the investigator hypothesizes it is important to measure, and here he must borrow and invent variables. He is also restricted to what is feasible to measure. Whatever he discovers will be limited to the variables sampled because his extrapolative skill is hidden within numerical equations rather than exposed in conceptual stipulations and definitions. But even if the correlational approach were theoretically valid, the sampling problem would be prodigious: people, task variables, task contexts, training contexts, degrees of training. We would still have to depend on the skill and imagination of the person who selects from the universe of these variables.

But even after we had parsed out task "factors" in this way, what could we do with them? Add the findings to the literature shelf?

As a person trained as a scientist, I would like to see tools developed out of theory. But even in engineering this is not altogether the case. It is possible that useful tools may get generalized into useful theories.

Acceptance by psychologists at large as a criterion of the validity of any taxonomy is a forlorn hope, but probably the only one if my analysis is even reasonably right. Acceptance is a matter of acculturation: perhaps literally the number of times that a group of sentences appears in textbooks, and especially when the sentences have become anonymous. And of course the attitude towards acceptance differs, depending on whether the outcome is a professional paper or a pilot who can fly an airplane.

Comments for Progress

At best I can suggest what I would do if I assumed responsibility for a substantial motion forward, aimed at use by a large professional community.

I would try to assemble as diverse a collection of job-task samples as I could, perhaps several hundred of them. They would be drawn from real-life: industry, military, sports. Special care would be taken to sample as widely as possible from intellectual tasks. These would be analysed, perhaps in several passes, by the information processing model I described above. The model would be changed as dictated by convenience. I would be sure to try to get such information as I could about the strategies used consciously or unconsciously in optimizing task performance. I would also obtain qualitative (and, if possible, quantitative) error data, especially at different levels of learning and practice on the task.

Then I would take one or two introductory psychology texts and, topic by topic, cross reference findings and phenomena to my list of task analyses. Where I could not make sensible matches, I would add a category. (Of course, my work would be checked by friendly consultants if I could afford them.) The same phenomenon might go under several categories. My criterion for a matched reference would be hunch as to whether a system designer could match a concrete task situation (and conditions of performance) with a finding, and from it make some substantive choice or evaluation of a design either for operation by human or learning by human. Then, after finishing with the textbook, I would tackle the 1965 psychological literature in the same way. And so forth.

I would end, I hope, with a functional information retrieval system that was keyed to human action descriptions. It is possible that a large percentage of the literature would remain unreferenced in this system. The reason would be either that the investigator didn't know what task behaviour he was working with, or couldn't describe it in a way that I (or my consultants) could interpret. Hopefully, we could do better on a later pass. I would test the utility of what I had both by my ability, and that of others, to apply this structure to design problems in tasks ranging from ditch digging to piano-playing; proof-reading to computer design.

If all went well, I would try to construct a set of training modules and matrices. I would hope that perhaps less than 50 such modules could specify effective conditions for part-task training, assimilation into larger behaviour contexts, error anticipation, strategy and technique, practice sequencing and any other know-how that psychology might lend to learning and performance. These constructions would be unabashed inventions based, we might hope, on technical underpinning. I would be happy to be right, by practical measures, at least 85 per cent of the time.

To a scientist, what I have described must seem a miserable state of affairs. It would have been intolerable to me when I was a graduate student running subjects on a *Hull* memory drum. No numbers: or very few of them. Uncertain validity measurements aside from practical usage. No objective, invariant definitions. The requirement of interpretive judgment. With effective promotion, of course, the enterprise might create a new psychology which later on would "validate" the enterprise.

PART 3

LEARNING CURVES

The Nature of Learning Curves

Data can be examined and analyzed in many ways. In a great number of learning studies, the major concern of the investigator is behavioral change over time. He is interested in measures of performance on a motor skill as a function of practice (usually trials or time). The plotted learning curve is a visual and graphic representation of how learning progresses in one practice period or over a number of sessions.

There are those who inspect the learning curve in a "typical" situation, attempting to determine the orderliness and predictability of skill acquisition. Negative and positive acceleration aspects of the curve are viewed in a wide assortment of tasks. Phenomena such as the warm-up decrement and the plateau are of concern to some researchers. Treatment of the curve may range from describing general observable features, to analyzing statistically for linear, cubic, and quadratic components, to developing sophisticated mathematical predictive formulae.

Not only is the typical learning curve for a given task or group of tasks the source of inquiry. The manipulation of environmental conditions such as practice variables also has come under the scrutiny of researchers. The resultant learning curve has been analyzed in similar ways as mentioned previously. Regardless of the experimental conditions leading to the learning curve in question, group data rather than individual data are usually plotted and become the source of inference. Group data are more orderly; they are not so irregular and haphazard as individual data. Unfortunately, at the same time, they may conceal certain phenomena that would be revealed by individual curves.

The techniques employed in formulating learning curves, from the more simple to the intricate, are discussed in a few of the following papers. Also suggested are those measures which might yield better indicators of learning and improvement. Dangers in the misuse and misinterpretation of curves are described in some of the sources. The plateau, a commonly accepted condition in the process of mastering skills, is also discussed from an experimental point of view, raising some penetrating questions as to its very existence.

Chapter 3

THEORIES AND MEASUREMENT OF
LEARNING CURVES AND PLATEAUS

A Method of Constructing Learning Curves
for a Motor Skill Involving Total Body
Speed and Accuracy*

GERALD EHRLICH

Most motor skills demand both speed and accuracy on the part of the
learner for successful performance, and any measurement of learning must
be carefully constructed to take them into consideration as well as such
variables as initial status, final achievement, and rate of gain. Ehrlich
explains the formulation of learning curves and possible analysis of data
for a real-life skill, the fencing lunge. Techniques and results are compared, with suggestions made for curve-fitting.

The purpose underlying this investigation was the determination of a
method of constructing learning curves for a motor skill involving speed and
accuracy of a total body movement.

Procedure in Organizing and Collecting the Data

The subjects used in this investigation consisted of a group of eighty-seven
male subjects selected at random from the student population of the City
College of New York. Where medical records indicated physical disability of
any type, the individual in question was excluded from participating in the
experiment.

The group was heterogeneous from the point of view of socio-economic
status, nationality, and attitudes and interests in motor skills, but was relatively
homogeneous with respect to the number of years of school experience and
intelligence.

Selection of the Motor Skill. The fencing lunge was selected as the motor

* Reprinted from the *Journal of Applied Psychology*, 1943, 27, 494-503 by permission of the author and the American Psychological Association.

skill to be subjected to investigation for the following reasons: (1) it represents a bodily movement in which comparatively few people have had any previous experience; (2) improvement in the skill may be measured objectively by the use of precision instruments; and (3) the skill offers an excellent opportunity to observe the development of new muscular patterns and coordinations. Furthermore the complete action of the skill contains the "four properties of action systems which stand at the root of our habits, skills and posture,"[1] namely, strength, quickness or speed, coordination and accuracy.[2]

Speed-Accuracy Apparatus.   A device originally designed by E. R. Elbel,[3] but modified for the present investigation, was employed in measuring the accuracy and speed of the fencing lunge. Elbel's original design consisted of two main parts, a target by means of which accuracy was measured and a chronoscope which was used for recording time intervals. A preliminary tryout of this apparatus revealed certain functional and structural inadequacies. For example, the accuracy score values, while adequate for one administration of the test, did not permit a large enough variation among accuracy scores of individuals. This point was important because as individuals learned, the development of a skewed curve would bring all high scores into a coarse collection interval and obscure differentiation of abilities. A second inadequacy was found in the use of 110 volts for wiring the foil. A current of this voltage is dangerous and is definitely a source of shock despite all precautionary measures. Accordingly the apparatus was modified but the basic design maintained throughout.

The apparatus as utilized in this experiment consists of three major parts: the target, the clock, and the control cabinet. The target was constructed by using nine galvanized tin circles, ranging in size from ¼ inch in diameter to 13½ inches in diameter. Each respective larger circle was ¾ of an inch greater in radius than the preceding smaller circle. A wire was soldered to each circle and passed through ³⁄₁₆ inch holes that had been drilled previously through the entire set of circles. Furthermore, each circle was insulated by placing cardboard circles between them. The materials were next fastened to a wooden backing board by a bolt that passed not only through the metal target but also the backing board. This was attached to the apparatus framework by means of two strap iron hinges. The electrical wires were then numbered to correspond to the score values of the circles, the smallest circle representing a score of 9, and proceeding outward to scores of 8, 7, 6, 5, 4, 3, 2, and 1. Nine long extension wires were attached to these and wired to bulbs in the control cabinet. Thus when the electrically wired foil struck any one of the circles, the score value immediately flashed.

Electrical Design of the Apparatus.   The device was so wired that the moment the operator pulled the starting switch, a signal light flashed and the electric clock began to operate.[4] When the subject saw the stimulus he lunged toward the target. The impact of the foil not only flashed the accuracy of the lunge but broke the electrical circuit operating the clock, thus indicating the speed with which the lunge was performed

Two electrical circuits were housed within the control cabinet, one circuit controlling the accuracy scores, the other controlling the clock. A transformer

---

[1] C. R. Griffiths, *Psychology applied to teaching and learning,* Farrar & Rinehart, 1939, p. 250.

[2] *Ibid.,* p. 250.

[3] E. R. Elbel, A study of response time before and after strenuous exercise. *Res. Quart. Amer. phys. Educ. Ass.,* 1940, *11,* 86-95.

[4] The electric clock is manufactured by the Standard Electric Time Company of Massachusetts. The face of the clock is calibrated to indicate 1/1000 of a second.

was used to reduce the 110 volt circuit to 6 to 8 volts and the foil was wired to this circuit by placing a small tip-jack in the rear of the control cabinet. By using an extension cord the foil could be moved to any distance. When the foil touched any area of the target, the circuit was completed and one of the bulbs flashed the score.

The speed circuit drew current from two sources, A.C. and D.C., since the motor of the clock operated upon 110 volt A.C. current while the clutch which operated the second hand worked on 110 D.C. current. Since the room in which the experiment was conducted had only D.C. current a converter was used in order to have available both types of voltages. The control cabinet drew only 110 volt D.C. current so that breaking the circuit would leave the motor running while the second hand stopped.

Reliability of the Apparatus. The reliability of the instrument was determined by means of the re-test method. A group of 116 subjects was selected from the summer session student body during the summer session of 1941. For purposes of expediency and accuracy the group was divided into four groups of twenty-nine in each group. The purpose of this preliminary test was explained in detail with emphasis placed upon the need for conscientious cooperation. Two days were used in determining the length of the lunge of each individual, two days were required for the first set of data while an additional two days were used for the collection of data for the second trial. A period of one week elapsed between the administration of the first and second tests. Using the average of ten trials, a reliability coefficient of 0.937 was obtained for speed with a reliability of 0.921 for accuracy.

Administration of the Speed-Accuracy Test. The experimental group met twice a week for twelve weeks with each weekly period of forty-five minutes' duration. These sessions were used for purposes of training and instruction. Individual appointments were arranged so that each subject was examined once a week for the total period of twelve weeks. The length of the lunge was determined for each individual by demonstrating the correct position for the lunge and noting the distance along a ruler placed on the side of the fencing strip. A movable foot cleat was used to mark off the correct distance each time the subject appeared for the weekly test.

Collection of Data. Five or six preliminary lunges were utilized as a warming up period and the subject was then asked to start the trials. The subject was told not to look at the stimulus unit, but at the target, since the light was strong enough to be seen without staring directly at it. As soon as this flashed the subject lunged toward the target as accurately and as quickly as he could. The interval between the stimulus was varied in order to avoid mechanization of the lunge. Each trial was recorded upon forms specifically prepared for recording these data. Using the average of the ten trials in speed and accuracy, these data were transferred to a large posting sheet where it could be seen by all individuals participating in the experiment.

Treatment and Analysis of Data

It is important to emphasize that the present investigation was directed toward a description of the differences involved in a learning process rather than attempting to account for factors and reasons underlying learning *per se.* Therefore the basic problem consisted of analyzing the data obtained over a period of twelve weeks in order to supply an answer to the theoretical question, "What does the shape of the learning curve look like?" Two approaches were used; the first approach assumed that there was some generalized law in operation tending to influence the data in such a way as to produce a curve typical of the learning function. In this case it was a question of selecting a second degree parabola, a log curve, or any one of a number of curves commonly encountered in learning experiments. The second approach was based upon a preliminary examination of the data with the express purpose of proceeding upon the information obtained from such statistical analysis.

Since the concept of individual differences was of paramount importance, three elements were selected by means of which these differences might be distinguished, namely, initial status, rate of learning, and maximum learning at the end of the experimental period. Several mathematical techniques were capable of producing such information but it appeared important to select a technique that was related logically to the data at hand. Hence, two methods were selected, the Courtis Isochronic technique[5] and the freehand method. The Courtis technique was selected because it uses the Gompertz equation and curve as the function underlying growth. If learning was accepted as a type of growth then there was a very logical basis for the choice of this particular technique. This reasoning is corroborated by Ezekial who indicates that "When there is some logical basis for the selection of a particular equation, the equation and the corresponding curve may provide a definite logical measurement of the nature of the relationship."[6] As an alternative the freehand method was also investigated in the event that the Courtis method was found to be inadequate. This particular point is again confirmed by Ezekial: ". . . a curve fitted freehand by graphic methods, and, conforming to logical limitations on its shape, may be even more valuable as a description of the facts of the relationship than a definite equation and corresponding curve selected empirically."[7]

Of the two methods discussed above, the freehand method was chosen for reasons presented in the following section.

Technique Employed in This Study. Originally the intention was to combine the speed and accuracy scores into one index number that would represent an individual's performance at any one testing period. This was to be accomplished by dividing accuracy by speed. However, after some deliberation this method was not employed. It was felt that an arbitrary combination of this nature might be open to sound criticism. Therefore the speed and accuracy scores were treated independently.

Means and sigmas were computed for both speed and accuracy scores for each of the twelve-week testing periods and Pearson product-moment coefficients were computed between successive weekly periods; that is, the correlation between the first and second week was determined, then the correlation between the second and third week, etc.

The means were used to determine the progress of learning for the entire group; the measures of variability yielded an analysis of the relative weight ascribed for portions of the learning curves and the successive weekly correlations were computed in order to ascertain the degree to which the group tended to level off. It was reasoned that as individuals reached a peak of learning and development, the degree of association existing among the scores made during the final weeks would tend to become high.

The values of sigma and r obtained for the tenth, eleventh, and twelfth weeks were considered extremely significant. During this specific time interval, the sigmas are approximately equal as are the correlation coefficients. This apparently confirmed the use of the above mentioned computations and indicated that some type of maximum development had occurred. Because of the slight numerical differences existing among the sigmas and coefficients the

[5] S. A. Courtis. *The measurement of growth.*
[6] M. Ezekial. *Methods of correlation analysis,* p. 127.
[7] *Ibid.,* p. 127.

question then arose as to whether these differences were statistically significant or had occurred because of chance fluctuations. While the use of Critical Ratio could answer the question of significant differences, it did not consider changes in individual status. Hence some expression of the relationship between sigmas and correlation coefficients was needed. The following principle appeared to offer just such solution. *Individual differences in learning cannot be measured when the correlation coefficients of successive time intervals are equal and when the sigmas of the same successive time intervals are also equal.* While such statement presumably suggested a reason for the similarity of numerical values among the sigmas and *r*'s for the accuracy scores, rigorous statistical proof was lacking. Such proof was developed by assuming that the correlation between the differences of successive correlations would be equal to zero only if chance errors were involved. Since chance errors are uncorrelated a numerical value of zero would indicate the absence of any other experimental factor tending to make for such slight differences.[8] On the basis of this evidence it was then possible to combine the scores of the last three weeks into one score that represented maximum learning. Thus, one of the factors essential in describing individual differences was obtained.

The sigmas of the first two weeks were large relative to succeeding ones. This constituted evidence that they failed to represent reliable initial points for learning rates, though they *may* be used as indices of initial ability. It is pointed out that no individual in the experimental group had had any previous experience in the fencing lunge. Therefore, theoretically the sigmas should have been somewhat the same for the first two weeks and thereafter should have become larger as individual differences manifested themselves. However the obtained large variance at the initial stage includes factors of pre-training and previous experience in skills involving similar bodily movements, and hence unduly affects the rate of learning of those who have lower starting points on the learning curve. It was for this reason that the Courtis technique was not found to be completely adequate. In many cases when this method was used, the percentages of development at the very beginning of the experiment were found to be fairly high; in some cases as high as forty-five per cent. This fact tended to obliterate the bottom portion of the Gompertz curve and resulted in a segment of the curve. Furthermore, curves of individuals starting fairly low, continuing with a large gain the subsequent week, and proceeding thereafter at a slow rate of learning, were overweighted because of the necessity of fitting a line to the data. Apparently then, information regarding the rate of learning based on such overweighting would tend to obscure much of the actual evidence. Hence the scores of the first two weeks were combined to represent the initial status, but were not included in the rate of learning calculations. In this way, the second independent factor, initial status, was obtained. The scores within the period extending from the third to the ninth week were then used to compute the third factor necessary for distinguishing individual differences, namely, rate of learning.

The speed scores were examined in the same fashion and in this instance the independent treatment of speed and accuracy was more than justified. The speed scores show some startling facts that would not have been brought to light had speed been combined with accuracy. The means increase by week and also demonstrate a total group improvement. There is a rapid acceleration for the first four weeks followed by a decrease in acceleration up to the sixth week, with scores leveling off thereafter. The characteristic end-spurt appears

---

[8] A complete mathematical development of this proof is contained in a paper written by Dr. Raymond Franzen and the author.

in this instance as well as in the accuracy data. One bit of interesting information that is not clearly evident is the very small time interval within which improvement manifested itself. The mean score for the sixth week was 0.613 of a second, while the mean score for the twelfth week was 0.561 of a second, a difference of only 0.052. Therefore the group appeared to be functioning closely to its maximum speed efficiency after the sixth week of the experiment. Because of similarities in the sigmas, they could not be used as reliable indices for learning rates. Two factors might have accounted for such similarities; the refined unit in which speed was measured, or the fact that subjects who were slow at the beginning of the experiment remained slow for the duration of the experiment and similarly, subjects who were initially fast remained fast. As in the case of the accuracy data, there is a decided shifting around in positions during the first three weeks after which the high correlations signify a status quo. This is shown by the size of the correlation coefficients, which range in size from .834 at the end of the fourth week to .961 at the end of the twelfth week. Such numerically high coefficients could not have been obtained had the reverse been true. Therefore the measurement of individual differences on the basis of speed scores could be accomplished only by three broad time intervals with the scores achieved during the first three weeks serving as initial scores, the scores for the fourth, fifth, sixth, and seventh weeks serving as rates of learning and the remainder being used for maximum end points.

Application of the Method of Least Squares.   On the basis of the above statistical analysis the method of least squares was used to construct learning curves. The principle underlying the use of this technique is one wherein "the curve of a given type which best fits a given set of points is one in which the constants of the equation are so chosen as to make the sum of the squares of the errors a minimum."[9] Since the initial starting points and the terminal end points were already available this method of least squares yielded rates of learning and thus produced the third item essential for describing individual differences in learning.

Conclusion

1. In experiments involving speed and accuracy of total body movements the construction of learning curves may be best accomplished by analyzing the data from three points of view, initial status, rate of learning, and maximum end points.

2. Curve fitting techniques should be examined and analyzed to see whether the function underlying any one curve adequately fits the data at hand.

3. Skills involving speed and accuracy of total body movement do not necessarily follow the normal curve, the ogive, the autocatalytic curve, or the Gompertz equation, since factors of pre-training and conditioning negate the possibility of a zero origin and thus exclude the lower portion of these curves.

Bibliography

1. Beise, D., and Peaseley, V. The relation of reaction time, speed and agility of big muscle groups to certain sport skills. *Res. Quart. Amer. phys. Educ. Ass.,* 1937, *13,* 133-42.
2. Bunch, M. E. Transfer of training in the mastery of an antagonistic habit after varying intervals of time. *J. comp. Psychol.,* 1939, *28,* 189-200.

[9] C. C. Peters and W. R. Van Voorhis. *Statistical procedures and their mathematical bases,* p. 426.

3. Buxton, C. E., and Henry, C. E. Retroaction and gains in motor learning. *J. exper. Psychol.*, 1936, *19,* 616-620.
4. Courtis, S. A. *The measurement of growth.* Ann Arbor, Michigan: Brumfield and Brumfield, 1932, pp. ii+155.
5. Ezekial, M. *Methods of correlation analysis.* New York: John Wiley and Sons, 1941, pp. xix+531.
6. Kao, D. Plateaus and the curve of learning in a motor skill. *Psychol. Monogr.,* 1937, *49,* 1-94.
7. Philip, B. R. The relationship between speed and accuracy in a motor task. *J. exper. Psychol.,* 1936, *19,* 24-50.

Comparative Analysis of Methods of Scoring Tests of Motor Learning*

L. W. McCRAW

ALTHOUGH the illustrated learning curve provides a general trend of the data, in reality most researchers statistically analyze scores to determine if significant improvements in learning have occurred. The particular trials to use as a comparison base or formulae that take into consideration gain scores and/or initial status have usually varied with the investigator. The following paper includes a comparison of techniques commonly used in scoring improvement in motor learning. They by no means exhaust the list of possible methods, for there are far more sophisticated techniques that might be employed. Nevertheless, the different results obtained from the different methods serve to warn us that oftentimes research conclusions and implications will be dependent on the learning score selected as the criterion.

A method used quite frequently to evaluate the ability of an individual to learn a specific motor skill is the so-called practice test. In using such tests, the objective is to determine the amount of improvement occurring during the performance of a definite number of trials on an activity involving the motor skill. The assumption is that if a fast learner and a slow learner having the same initial ability perform an act the same number of times, the fast learner will show more improvement during the performance than will the slow one.

It is generally agreed that an interpretation of the learning occurring under such circumstances is contingent on several factors. For example, Greene[11] stresses that, in order to compare the improvement of two individuals on the same learning test, every effort should be made to provide equal practice for all, equal motivation, constant behavior patterns, similar types of scores, equal units of measurements, and expression of improvement in terms of the difficulty of improvement. One of the hardest of these conditions to achieve is that of expressing the improvement in terms of difficulty.

* From *The Research Quarterly,* 1955, *26,* 440-453. Reprinted with permission of the author and the American Association for Health, Physical Education, and Recreation.

Although many methods have been proposed to evaluate improvement, there is no indication that a satisfactory solution has been achieved. Rather it would appear that many of the methods yield entirely different results. It is the purpose of this study to examine certain of these methods, particularly with regard to the selection of scores to indicate initial and final status and to the interpretation of improvement made during repeated trials.

Discussion of the Problem

Various studies have indicated that there is little relationship or perhaps a low negative correlation between the initial status and improvement on repeated performances of a test.[1,8,10] It is argued that it is harder for a person with the higher initial score to improve because he is much nearer the physiological limit of performance than is the person with the lower score. The same difficulty arises even when two individuals start with identical scores, for as the individual improves over the initial score, it becomes increasingly more difficult for him to show additional gain. The measurement of improvement during a practice test then should be made in terms of where the individual is at the beginning of the practice period and of the relative difficulty of improvement.

The problem of interpreting the improvement made from an initial to a final status is not confined to learning tests but would be encountered in many experimental and practical situations in the use of pre-tests and post-tests to measure learning. Of those methods that have been used to express the improvement made under such circumstances, perhaps the simplest and most easily understood is that of computing the actual difference in raw scores by subtracting the initial score from the final score. Some advocate that raw scores should be converted to standard scores before obtaining such differences.[6,7] A most popular method[14] consists of dividing the difference in either raw scores or standard scores by the corresponding initial scores to obtain a per cent of improvement. It has been advocated by many investigators that this procedure penalizes unduly the individuals with high initial scores, and it has been suggested that the improvement should be divided by the possible gain rather than the initial score.[3,4,14] The possible gain in this instance is computed by subtracting the initial score from the highest possible score that can be made on the test. Other methods of expressing improvement include an increased increment method[2,5,13] wherein more credit is given for performance as one progresses up the scale, and the absolute zero scale,[11,12] which is constructed by arbitrarily assigning zero to the highest negative standard representing the lowest raw score and then placing all other standard scores on the scale according to their distances from this lowest score. Although there are many similarities among these methods, there is evidence that several of them yield quite different results.[14]

Another problem presented in the use of successive trials as a measure of learning is that of determining an initial score and a final score, particularly the latter. In most instances, the initial score consists of the first N number of trials at the beginning of the learning period. However, quite often, as a result of warming-up or familiarization, individuals exhibit a marked increase in scores immediately after the first two or three trials. It is usually recommended that these "warm-up" trials be discarded and not used as part of the initial score.[9] Although there is no general agreement regarding the number of trials to be used, the initial score should include enough trials to insure its being a valid measure of the individual's initial status yet not so many as to involve improvement within itself.

It would seem logical that the final score should consist of a corresponding number of trials at the end of the practice period. Such procedure would be based on the assumption that there is improvement on each of the successive trials in the test so that the score on the final trials will be greater than that on the initial trials. In actual practice, however, the scores are not always distributed in this manner. In many instances the learning curves reveal that many individuals achieve their maximum efficiency before the final trials, perhaps near the middle of the test, and then drop off because of fatigue, disinterest, or some unknown reason. It would appear therefore that in selecting the final score, consideration should be given to the maximum performance no matter where it occurs after the initial score.

Subjects, Tests, and Procedures

The subjects used in this study consisted of 134 seventh grade boys in the University High School, Austin, Texas. The ages of these boys ranged from 11 to 14, with 90 per cent of them between 12 and 13 years of age.

The tests used were a Rope Skip test and a Mirror Target Toss test. The Rope Skip test was taken by 128 boys and the Mirror Target Toss by 134. Both tests were administered in the regular physical education class period by the physical education instructor assisted by students from the Department of Physical and Health Education of the University of Texas.

The Rope Skip test consisted of having the subject skip a rope as rapidly as possible for 10 seconds while turning it himself. The subject stood with the rope behind his heels and started it on the command "Go." When a skip was missed, he stepped over the rope and continued until the 10-sec. trial was completed. Any type of skip was permitted as long as the subject jumped clearly over the rope as it passed beneath his feet. The score for a trial was the number of legal skips completed during the 10-sec. period. The highest score made on any one trial was 20. For the administration of the Rope Skip test, the class was divided into ten squads of four persons each. The 10-sec. trials on the test were given simultaneously to one person from each of the squads. Individuals within each squad alternated on the trials so that no one took two trials in succession. Each subject was given 21 trials with approximately 2 minutes' rest between trials. The entire test of 21 trials was administered during one class period.

The Mirror Target Toss test involved the subject's bouncing a volleyball off a smooth, hard-surfaced wall at a concentric target lying on the floor while he watched the image of the target in a mirror. The target consisted of three concentric circles, with diameters of 1, 3, and 5 feet respectively. The target was painted on a mat with its center 11 feet from the wall. The subject stood 5 feet from the wall and 11 feet to the left and slightly in front of the target. The mirror was placed to the right of the target and against the wall with its surface at a 45° angle from the wall. Such position caused the image in the mirror to be rotated 90° from the true position of the target. The subject was thus able to observe the target in the mirror as he faced the wall, but a screen placed between him and the target prevented him from looking directly at it at any time during the test. The test was scored by awarding three, two and one points for hitting the inner, middle, and outer circles respectively. Each trial consisted of three throws, making a possible score of nine for one trial. Fifty such trials were taken by each of four subjects during one class period. Each subject was allowed 5 trials in succession, and the four subjects alternated so that there was approximately 4 minutes of rest for each person between performances.

Methods of Scoring Tests

The two learning tests were scored by eight methods. With the exception of the Total Learning Score Method, the computation of scores required the selection of initial and final scores. Some of the methods differ only in the procedure for computing the final score, whereas the initial score was the same for all methods.

The initial score for the Rope Skip test was the sum of the fourth and fifth trials after discarding the first three. In comparing the scores on the various trials, a significant difference was found between the means of the third and fourth trials. Since, as previously discussed, this increase in performance was probably due to familiarization or warming-up, the first three trials were discarded. Inasmuch as performance thereafter was consistent, it was felt that two trials were adequate to indicate initial status. No significant increase was found among the initial trials for the Mirror Target Toss test; therefore, no trials were discarded. The first four trials were used as the initial score for this test since it was about twice as long as the Rope Skip test.

The final score was determined by three different procedures. The first, the one most commonly used, was the sum of the last two trials for the Rope Skip test and the sum of the last four trials for the Mirror Target Toss, the number of trials in each instance being comparable to that used for the initial score. The second procedure consisted of selecting the highest two successive trials for the Rope Skip and the highest four successive trials for the Mirror Target Toss occurring at any point after the initial score. A third procedure was simply using a total of all trials after the initial score. Each of the methods used in this study is described below:

I. Total Learning Score Method: This method consists of adding the scores on all trials in the learning test, including the initial and final scores.

II. Difference in Raw Score Method No. 1: The difference in raw score was obtained by subtracting the initial score from the final score, consisting of the sum of the last "N" trials as follows:

(Sum of last "N" trials) minus (Sum of first "N" trials)

III. Difference in Raw Score Method No. 2: This method differs from No. 1 above only in the computation of the final score.

(Sum of highest "N" successive trials) minus (Sum of first "N" trials)

IV. Per Cent Gain of Possible Gain Method No. 1: In the 3-per cent gain of possible gain methods, the learning scores were computed by dividing the actual gain from the initial score to the final score by the possible gain from the initial to the highest possible score. The three methods differed in the selection of the final scores as indicated in the formulas.

$$\frac{\text{(Sum of last ``N'' trials) minus (Sum of first ``N'' trials)}}{\text{(Highest possible score on ``N'' trials) minus (Sum of first ``N'' trials)}}$$

V. Per Cent Gain of Possible Gain Method No. 2:

$$\frac{\text{(Sum of highest ``N'' successive trials) minus (Sum of first ``N'' trials)}}{\text{(Highest possible score on ``N'' trials) minus (Sum of first ``N'' trials)}}$$

VI. Per Cent Gain of Possible Gain Method No. 3:

$$\frac{\text{(Sum of all trials) minus (Sum of first ``N'' trials)}}{\text{(Highest possible score on all trials) minus (Sum of first ``N'' trials)}}$$

VII. Per Cent Gain of Initial Score Method No. 1: In the 2-per cent gain of initial score methods, the scores were computed by dividing the gain from the initial to the final score by the initial score. Two different procedures of selecting the final score were used as indicated in the formulas.

$$\frac{(\text{Sum of last "N" trials}) \text{ minus } (\text{Sum of first "N" trials})}{(\text{Sum of first "N" trials})}$$

VIII. Per Cent Gain of Initial Score Method No. 2:

$$\frac{(\text{Sum of highest "N" successive trials}) \text{ minus } (\text{Sum of first "N" trials})}{(\text{Sum of first "N" trials})}$$

Findings

The analysis of the eight methods of scoring the two tests of motor learning used in this study is made by examining (1) the variability of scores yielded by the various methods, (2) the relationship among the methods, and (3) the validity of the different methods. For this analysis, the subjects were divided into three approximately equal groups on the basis of low, moderate, or high initial scores and into three groups on the basis of small, moderate, or large gain. The gain used for this subdivision is the gain in raw scores from the initial to the final score (II. Difference in Raw Score Method No. 1).

Comparison of Variability. There were marked differences in variability among most of the methods for both the total group and each of the subgroups. Likewise, substantial differences were noted within each method for the various subgroups.

With few exceptions the lowest coefficients are found for the Total Learning Score Method and the Per Cent Gain of Possible Gain Method No. 3, which involves the total score in the computation (Methods I and VI). The highest coefficients are found for the Per Cent Gain of Initial Score Methods (Methods VII and VIII). Very little difference is noted between the coefficients for the Difference in Raw Score Methods and the Per Cent Gain of Possible Gain Methods (Methods II, III, IV, and V). These conclusions are based on a comparison of methods with similar procedure of selecting the final score. When the different methods of selecting the final score are compared, it is found that in general the larger coefficients were obtained in those methods using the sum of the last N trials as the final score (Methods II, IV, and VII) rather than the sum of the highest N successive trials (Methods III, V, and VIII). No consistent pattern is noted among the various subgroups; however, by far the largest coefficients are found for the groups with small gain and the lowest for the ones with large gain.

Relationship among Methods. In order to determine the relationship among methods, intercorrelations were computed for the total group and the subgroups. An examination of the correlations reveals that there is practically no difference between the Total Learning Score Method and the Per Cent Gain of Possible Gain Method No. 3 (Methods I vs. VI). All correlations are .93 or above, with most .99. Such relationship is not surprising since the total score is used as the final score in the computation of this Per Cent Gain of Possible Gain Method. In view of this close relationship, further comparison will be made only on the basis of the Total Learning Score Method. Very high correlations are also found between the Difference in Raw Score Methods and the Per Cent Gain of Possible Gain Methods (Methods II vs. IV and III vs. V). With the exception of those for the subgroups with moderate and large gains, the correlations are all above .80 with most above .90. The most pronounced disagreement among the methods of scoring exists between the Total Learning Score Method and each of the two Per Cent Gain of Initial Score Methods (Methods I vs. VII and I vs. VIII). Very low positive or moderately high negative correlations are found for these combinations.

The relationship among the different procedures of selecting the final score may be ascertained by examining the correlations between the two methods for the respective systems of computing gain (Methods II vs. III, IV vs. V, and VII vs. VIII). Although there is no consistent pattern with the correlations ranging from .90 to —.18, it is apparent that there is only moderate or slight relationship among the scores yielded by these two procedures.

There seems to be no indication that higher or lower correlations exist for any of the three subgroups. Where differences among methods do exist, they are more pronounced for the subgroups with small, moderate, or large gains. Such marked deviations are probably due to the fact that individuals within each group start from varying initial scores rather than that they have different gains.

Validity of Methods of Scoring

An indication of the validity of the scoring methods may be obtained by comparing the scores yielded by the different methods for the various subgroups. This comparison is made on the basis of mean T-scores computed for each subgroup for each method. The T-score scales used for these computations were based on the total distribution for each method of scoring.

In Table I are presented the mean T-scores for the subgroups arranged on the basis of initial score. For example, the first three subgroups all start with a low initial score but the three have small, moderate, and large gains respectively; the second three subgroups all start with a moderate initial score and have small, moderate, and large gains; while the last three start with a high initial score. To be valid a scoring method should yield increasingly larger scores within each of the three subgroups starting from the same initial score, i.e., the score for the subgroup with Low Initial Score and Moderate Gain should be larger than that for the one with Low Initial Score and Small Gain and so on. While there are differences among the methods with regard to the amount of increase among subgroups, all methods meet this criterion.

In Table II the same mean T-scores have been arranged on the basis of improvement rather than initial score. The first three, for example, all have small gain but start with low, moderate, and high initial scores; the second three have moderate gain from varying initial scores; and the third three have large gain. Again, to be valid a scoring method should yield increasingly larger scores within each set of subgroups. This is based on the contention that it becomes more difficult to exhibit the same improvement as one approaches his physiological limit. Thus the subgroup with a Small Gain over a High Initial Score should have a larger learning score than those with Small Gain over a Low or Moderate Initial Score. When evaluated on the basis of this criterion, only three methods are valid; namely, I. Total Learning Score Method; V. Per Cent Gain of Possible Gain Method No. 2; and VI. Per Cent Gain of Possible Gain Method No. 3. It will be recalled that Method V uses for the final score the highest N successive trials no matter where they occur after the initial score and Method VI uses the total score as the final score. The two Per Cent Gain of Initial Score Methods (Methods VII and VIII) are the least desirable of all methods; in fact, they appear to be wholly invalid when comparing individuals starting from different initial scores.

Summary and Conclusions

The purpose of this study has been to compare eight methods of scoring improvement on learning tests in which individuals were given a definite number of repeated trials on a specific motor skill. Some of the methods

TABLE 1

Mean T-Scores on the Different Methods of Scoring Learning for the Various Subgroups Arranged on the Basis of Initial Score

Subgroup	I TLS		II DRS 1		III DRS 2		IV PPG 1		V PPG 2		VI PPG 3		VII PIS 1		VIII PIS 2	
	RS	MTT	RS	MTT	RS	MTT	RS	MTT	RS	MTT	RS	MTT	RS	MTT	RS	MTT
Low Initial Score Small Gain	37	30	45	44	40	38	44	43	44	35	38	30	48	51	46	49
Low Initial Score Moderate Gain	39	39	54	50	51	51	50	48	51	47	39	39	61	57	62	57
Low Initial Score Large Gain	45	51	59	61	60	63	55	59	58	59	45	52	61	66	64	68
Moderate Initial Score Small Gain	44	38	43	40	39	39	44	39	45	37	44	37	43	44	40	44
Moderate Initial Score Moderate Gain	48	49	48	51	50	52	47	52	54	52	48	49	47	46	49	46
Moderate Initial Score Large Gain	54	58	60	59	63	60	59	59	65	60	55	57	55	49	57	49
High Initial Score Small Gain	56	54	39	42	40	39	41	44	49	42	56	54	40	44	39	43
High Initial Score Moderate Gain	62	56	48	45	50	49	51	47	61	54	62	56	44	45	43	44
High Initial Score Large Gain	66	58	55	53	60	47	61	56	74	61	66	59	48	46	48	46

TLS—Total Learning Score; DRS—Difference in Raw Score; PPG—Per Cent of Possible Gain; PIS—Per Cent of Initial Score; RS—Rope Skip Test; MTT—Mirror Target Toss Test.

TABLE 2

Mean T-Scores on the Different Methods of Scoring Learning for the Various Subgroups Arranged on the Basis of Improvement

Subgroup	I TLS		II DRS 1		III DRS 2		IV PPG 1		V PPG 2		VI PPG 3		VII PIS 1		VIII PIS 2	
	RS	MTT	RS	MTT	RS	MTT	RS	MTT	RS	MTT	RS	MTT	RS	MTT	RS	MTT
Small Gain Low Initial Score	37	30	45	44	40	38	44	43	44	35	38	30	48	51	46	49
Small Gain Moderate Initial Score	44	38	43	40	39	39	44	39	45	37	44	37	43	44	40	44
Small Gain High Initial Score	56	54	39	42	40	39	41	44	42	42	56	54	40	44	39	43
Moderate Gain Low Initial Score	39	39	54	50	51	51	50	48	51	47	39	39	61	57	62	57
Moderate Gain Moderate Initial Score	48	49	48	51	50	52	47	52	54	52	48	49	47	46	49	46
Moderate Gain High Initial Score	62	56	48	45	50	49	51	47	61	54	62	56	44	45	43	44
Large Gain Low Initial Score	45	51	59	61	60	63	55	59	58	59	45	52	61	66	64	68
Large Gain Moderate Initial Score	54	58	60	59	63	60	59	59	65	60	55	57	55	49	57	49
Large Gain High Initial Score	66	58	55	53	60	47	61	56	74	61	66	59	48	46	48	46

TLS—Total Learning Score; DRS—Difference in Raw Score; PPG—Per Cent of Possible Gain; PIS—Per Cent of Initial Score; RS—Rope Skip Test; MTT—Mirror Target Toss Test.

differ only in the selection of the final score—the sum of the *last* two to four trials in one instance and in the other the sum of the *highest* two to four successive trials occurring after the initial score. The initial score was the sum of a comparable number of trials at the beginning of the practice period. Four different procedures were used in the computation of improvement as follows: the summation of scores of all trials on the test, subtracting the initial score from the final score, dividing the gain from the initial to the final score by the initial score, and dividing this gain by the possible gain after the initial score.

The learning tests were two activities in which the subjects had little or no experience. A Rope Skip test consisted of determining the number of times an individual could skip a rope while turning it himself during each of 21 10-sec. trials. A Mirror Target Toss test involved bouncing a volleyball off a wall at a concentric target lying on the floor while watching the image of the target in a mirror. Fifty trials of three throws each were allowed.

Comparison of the eight methods was made on the basis of coefficients of variation, product-moment correlations, and mean T-scores computed for the total group and for subgroups with varying initial scores and gain. The following conclusions seem warranted:

1. There are marked differences in variability of scores yielded by the different methods, suggesting that some of the methods allow unusually high or low scores for certain individuals.

2. In general, there is rather low or negative relationship among most of the methods of scoring, particularly when comparing improvements of individuals starting with widely different initial scores.

3. Of those methods used in this study, the Total Learning and the three Per Cent Gain of Possible Gain Methods seem to be the most valid methods when comparing individuals with different initial scores.

4. The two Per Cent Gain of Initial Score Methods seem to be the least desirable and should not be used to measure improvement on learning tests.

References

1. Anastasi, Anne. Practice and variability. *Psychological Monographs, 45*: 155, 1934.
2. Bovard, John F., Frederick W. Cozens, and E. Patricia Hagman. *Tests and Measurements in Physical Education.* Philadelphia: W. B. Saunders Co., 1949.
3. Brace, David K. Studies in motor learning of gross bodily motor skills. *Research Quarterly, 17*: 242-253, 1946.
4. ————. Studies in the rate of learning gross bodily motor skills. *Research Quarterly, 12*: 181-185, 1941.
5. Cozens, Frederick W. A curve for devising scoring tables in physical education. *Research Quarterly, 2*: 67-75, 1931.
6. Cureton, Thomas K. The physiology of fitness. *Scholastic Coach, 13*: 14-20, 1944.
7. ————, Warren J. Huffman, Lyle Welser, Ramon W. Kireilis, and Darrell L. Latham. *Endurance of Young Men.* Monograph of the Society for Research in Child Development, 1945, 1.
8. Gates, Georgina Strickland. Individual differences as affected by practice. *Archives of Psychology, 8*: 1-74, 1922.
9. Gire, Eugenia, and Anna Espenschade. The relationship between measures of motor educability and the learning of specific motor skills. *Research Quarterly, 13*: 43-56, 1942.
10. Goodenough, Florence L., and Clara R. Brian. Certain factors underlying the acquisition of motor skill by pre-school children. *Experimental Psychology, 12*: 127-155, Apr., 1929.

11. Greene, Edward B. *Measurement of Human Behavior.* New York: The Odyssey Press, 1941.
12. ———. Practice effects on various types of standard tests. *American J. of Psychology, 49*: 67-75, 1937.
13. McCloy, Charles H. *The Measurement of Athletic Power.* New York: A. S. Barnes and Co., 1932.
14. McGraw, L. W. A comparison of methods of measuring improvement. *Research Quarterly, 22*: 191-200, 1951.

Learning Curves—Facts or Artifacts*

HARRY P. BAHRICK, PAUL M. FITTS, and GEORGE E. BRIGGS

The shape of the learning curve is greatly dependent on the response measures utilized in the plotting of data. Tracking tasks are very often used by experimental psychologists as the basis of understanding how an individual learns skills, and the results can be scored in various ways. Therefore, tracking is a good skill to illustrate the effects of errors in measurement on the learning curve. Indeed, the curve may be misinterpreted at various stages of practice, and effects deemed important are in reality confounded by the artifacts produced. Theory and research are discussed, and warnings are made against possible artifact-inducing measurements, some of which are identified.

From an operational viewpoint, theory and method are intimately related. A theory has little value if no method is available for testing its predictions, and a method has no validity if it is not representative of the operations specified by some theory. Yet there are many instances in learning research in which behavior measures are chosen as a matter of convenience, rather than on theoretical grounds. This is done despite the fact that most theories of learning emphasize the distinction between the basic process of learning and indicants of this process[12,16,17] and despite the fact that the importance of this distinction is demonstrated in studies reporting low correlations among various indicants of presumably the same learning process.[5; 10, p.138]

One of the most common instances of the arbitrary choice of response measures in learning studies is the use of a dichotomous score as an indicant of an underlying process which is known or assumed to be continuously distributed. We have reference to the use of arbitrary criteria of success and failure, or arbitrary criteria of the occurrence of a response, such as the extent of entry into a cul-de-sac necessary for recording an error in maze learning, the magnitude and latency of a reaction necessary for recording the occurrence of a conditioned response, or the size of the target used in determining the number of hits in a skilled task. A continuity viewpoint holds that the processes underlying these phenomena will produce a continuous and often normal distribution of response measures.

* From the *Psychological Bulletin*, 1957, *54*, 256-268. Abridged and reprinted with permission of the authors and the American Psychological Association.

It is our purpose in this paper to show that the arbitrary choice of a cutoff point in the dichotomizing of continuous response distributions can impose significant constraints upon the shape of resulting learning curves, and that this can form the basis of misleading theoretical interpretations. We have chosen for illustration of this point the use of time-on-target scores as indicants of the level of skill attained in tracking tasks. However, we believe that the principles developed are quite general and apply to many learning situations.

Time-on-target scores reflect the amount of time during a trial that S is able to remain within an arbitrarily specified region around a target. A great many reports have been published during the last few years in which E has made use of such scores. In a few studies the effects of target size upon transfer of training have been examined.[3,8] Two studies[7,14] have dealt with the validity of time-on-target scores, and one of these[7] concluded that their usefulness is limited because the correlations between such scores and average error scores vary as a function of target size and problem difficulty. However, emphasis has not been placed on the importance of the constraints which the choice of a scoring zone exercises upon the shape of learning curves plotted from the recorded data and upon the conclusions which can be drawn from these functions.

It is our purpose here to show that the same tracking behavior, when scored with different target-tolerance standards, will result in learning curves which differ greatly in shape, and that the differing shape of learning curves obtained with various-sized scoring zones can be predicted theoretically from assumptions regarding the error-amplitude distributions. In further support of this view we present empirical data which indicate, in the case of tracking behavior, that the underlying error distribution to which all conventional scores can be related is continuous and normal. Finally, we point out that a lack of understanding of these differential characteristics of response measures can easily lead to incorrect conclusions regarding the effects of other variables.

Empirical Data

The data reported here are taken from two studies[1,5] in which Ss practiced one-dimensional tracking tasks on an electronic tracking apparatus described elsewhere.[18] The tracking problems in the two studies varied in difficulty. We shall present first the learning curves obtained for the more difficult problem.[5] In this study the target motion consisted of a 10 cpm sinusoidal motion of a line on a cathode-ray-tube (CRT) display. A filter with a time constant of .4 sec. introduced an exponential lag between the output of S's arm control and its effect on tracking error. A compensatory display was used which provided a target line that remained stationary in the center of the display, and a cursor that moved to the right or left depending on the direction of the error from moment to moment. Two types of performance measures were taken on even-numbered 90-sec. trials: RMS error scores and time-on-target scores.

An electronic circuit provided a means of continuously obtaining the magnitude of the error (in the form of an electrical voltage), squaring this voltage, and integrating it over the period of a trial. The output of this circuit appeared on a voltmeter and the square root of this meter reading provided an index of the root mean squared error (RMS). The error voltage is computed with respect to an absolute reference of zero volts, whereas S's error amplitude distribution may show some constant bias toward plus or minus voltages (i.e., error to the right or left of the target). As a result, the error RMS reflects both the variability of S's distribution of amplitudes and any small constant error in average cursor position.

Time-on-target measures give the total time that the absolute magnitude of the error voltage was smaller than a given magnitude. Three such scores were taken for target zones of 5%, 15%, and 30% of ±5 v., which was the maximum problem voltage. These zones correspond to errors of .1, .3, and .6 in. of displacement of the cursor to either side of the target line, respectively. The three zones (from smallest to largest) will be referred to hereafter as zones A, B, and C in order to avoid confusion when it is desired later to refer to the percentage of time S was "on target." Similarly, the time-on-target scores will be referred to as scores A, B, and C.

Fifty male and 50 female Ss were used, and since the male Ss were superior trackers on the average, separate learning curves were formed for the two groups.

The various learning curves suggest different accounts of the relative and absolute improvement during practice. The curves for time-on-target scores all suggest that absolute as well as relative improvements during tracking were greater for the male than for the female Ss. This effect is particularly apparent for the smallest target zone (zone A) and becomes progressively less pronounced for the larger target zones. Between trials 2 and 14 the males improved by 33.2%, 31.9%, and 18.7% for scores in zones A, B, and C, respectively, while the corresponding improvements for the females are only 2.5%, 17.6%, and 11.8%. The RMS curves, however, indicate a greater improvement for the females, with a 22.3% reduction of error as contrasted with a 20.4% error reduction for the males. And all of these scores, it should be remembered, are derived from a single error voltage!

The widely divergent picture of the amount of improvement resulting from practice, given by the four scores described above, can be accounted for on theoretical grounds, which will be developed in the next section. Briefly, it will be shown that time-on-target scores are nonlinear, being relatively insensitive to changes in level of performance both above and below a critical region. Most of the female Ss who served in the study referred to above, for example, were relatively poor trackers at the beginning of practice, and the zone A time-on-target score was almost completely insensitive to any improvement at this level of skill. Improvements at this level, however, were reflected in fairly large reductions in the error RMS score.

We shall now present data from the second study[1] which illustrate the same kind of scoring artifact with a less difficult tracking task. As in the first study, the problem was that of compensating for a 10 cpm target oscillation. However, no lag was introduced between the control output and the cursor movement. Several control loading conditions were used in this study as independent variables. We have selected four learning curves from the condition in which both a spring and a mass were used to load the control, since this condition of the study generally resulted in the best performance. Twenty-five males served as Ss. Mean learning curves were obtained for the RMS score and for three time-on-target scores employing the same relative target zones as were used in the previous study.

The empirical curves again give different accounts of the improvement in performance at different stages of practice. The zone C curve is negatively accelerated and shows most of the improvement during the early trials, with smaller improvement during the last few trials. The curve for zone A, on the other hand, shows the largest gain during the last two trials, and relatively less gain during the early trials. . . .

It can be shown that the differential sensitivity of the scores in these two studies is determined by the variation in task difficulty. The change of sensitivity of individual scoring zones as a function of task difficulty has been mentioned earlier, but will now be dealt with more systematically.

Prediction of Learning Curves for Various Time-on-Target Zones

If we assume that the amplitudes of tracking errors form a normal distribution during a trial, it is apparent that the percentage of this distribution which would fall within a given target zone can be determined, provided the standard deviation of the distribution of tracking errors is known. To illustrate the differential sensitivity of various scoring zones, time-on-target scores for five target zones of differing size were predicted as a function of the magnitude of the RMS value of the error distribution.

Successive values for these curves are found by determining the ratio of the scoring zone, in volts, to the RMS values of the error distribution, also in volts. The ratios are z scores and the percentage of a normal distribution between zero and each z score is found from a table of the normal curve. These values are multiplied by two to include errors on both sides of the target, and are plotted on the ordinate opposite the assumed RMS value.

Each of the curves shows a maximal slope at a different range of variation of the RMS value, and becomes insensitive to variations outside that range. The ranges of maximal sensitivity shift toward smaller RMS values as we move from larger to smaller target zones. The sensitivity of a time-on-target score is maximal when the zone is of a size that includes ± 1 SD of the error distribution, so that S is on target about 68% of the time. For smaller or larger target zones the score becomes progressively less sensitive to changes in the RMS value of the error distribution.

Functions similar to those described above can be plotted for target zones of any desired size, and it is apparent that curves for very small target zones would show their maximal sensitivity in an RMS range in which the curves of larger target zones have already approached an asymptote.

It is obvious that a score cannot reveal improvements once performance is approaching an asymptote of 100% time-on-target. However, the relative lack of sensitivity of each score at low performance levels is not generally recognized.

Empirical learning curves can be expected to depart from the curves just described for at least two reasons: (*a*) the theoretical curves are plotted for linear decreases in error RMS, while the observed decreases of error RMS during practice are usually a negatively accelerating function; and (*b*) the theoretical curves are also based upon the assumption that the amplitude distribution of error is normally distributed on all trials. . . . The divergence of the predicted curves from the corresponding empirical ones can be attributed in large measure to departures of the error distributions from normality. Unreliability of the electronic scoring equipment would, of course, also contribute to such divergence, but is believed to be quite small in the present case.

The empirical curves in the simple tracking task correspond moderately well to those predicted from the assumption of a normal distribution of error amplitudes. In the difficult tracking task the correspondence of empirical and predicted curves is close in the case of the zone C curves. For the zones A and B curves, male Ss performed better than would be predicted on the assumption of normality, and for the zone A curves this divergence is quite pronounced, particularly during the last few trials of practice. On the basis of our analysis we would expect these relations only if the amplitude distribution of tracking error were more peaked than a normal distribution, i.e., if the area near the center of the distribution were greater than predicted from the z scores. In order to check this prediction we shall need to examine in detail the empirical error-amplitude distributions of Ss during tracking. This we proceed to do in the next section.

Empirical Error-Amplitude Distributions

Empirical distributions were formulated of the error amplitude on trials 2, 6, and 14 for the data reported on the difficult tracking task. These distributions were obtained by means of an error-amplitude analyzer, an apparatus that has been described in more detail elsewhere. . . .[5] It can be seen that the error distributions of female Ss do not depart greatly from normality, and neither do the predicted values of their learning curves vary greatly from the observed ones. For male Ss, however, the obtained distributions are more peaked than the corresponding normal ones, particularly on later trials. This confirms our interpretation of the departure of the empirical learning curve from the predicted curve for zone A scores.

Because the data dealing with error amplitudes are pooled for 50 Ss, the peaking of the combined error-amplitude distribution may be the result of at least two different conditions. It is possible that this type of departure from normality characterizes the individual error distributions of the majority of Ss, or it may be that all or most individuals show normal error distributions, but that we have an abnormal distribution of individual differences among our 50 male Ss. In other words, the combining of 50 normal distributions with different SDs can yield a curve such as we obtained, provided sizable proportions of these curves (i.e., individuals) represent unusually good and unusually poor performance.

To determine which of these two situations prevailed we analyzed in more detail the data for the 50 males on trial 14, since this distribution shows the most pronounced departure from normality. The error amplitude distributions of each of the individual Ss on the trial were converted into z scores after the SD of each S's own amplitude distribution was determined. The ordinates for successive z-score values of .1 were averaged for the 50 Ss. . . . The peaking effect is not due to departures from normality in the error-amplitude distributions of individual Ss, but rather, to the combining of normal distributions which among themselves are not normally distributed. We are apparently dealing with a situation in which individual differences are normally distributed early, but not later in learning.

The problems involved in interpreting learning curves based on group data have been the concern of several recent papers.[2,4,15] In the present instance, however, we are chiefly interested in accounting for the departures of the obtained curves from the predicted curves in the difficult tracking task. The progressive peakings of the group amplitude distributions for male Ss appear to be a sufficient explanation for this phenomenon. During the later stages of practice the change in the shape of the pooled amplitude distribution has made the zone A curve more sensitive and the zone C curve less sensitive than would be the case if the group error-amplitude distribution had remained normal.

Confounding of Effects Produced by the Manipulation of Independent Variables and Artifacts Produced by Scoring

We have shown in the preceding section that learning curves based upon a particular-sized time-on-target zone will be maximally sensitive over a relatively narrow range of RMS values, and be relatively insensitive to variations of RMS outside that range. This means that large differences in the RMS value of the error-amplitude distribution may exist and may result in small or large differences of performance on a time-on-target score, depending upon the sensitivity of the score over the RMS range in question. If we now use a time-on-target score as a means of determining the functional relation between two variables, functions at various stages of learning, or functions for several versions of a task which differ in difficulty, the change in sensitivity of our measure must be taken into account. Particularly must we guard against scoring artifacts when we look for interaction effects. Otherwise we may conclude that the independent variable produces important effects at one stage of training and not at other stages, or important effects on a simple-task version and not on a difficult-task version, when in fact we are dealing with artifacts produced by the nonlinearity of our measures.

There are many instances in the literature where authors have failed to consider the above effects in their interpretation of results based on time-on-target scores. In order to call attention to this problem we have chosen two reports of work done in our own laboratory.

In a recent paper[9] which evaluates the effect of stimulus and response amplitudes upon tracking performance, a 5% time-on-target score covering an error voltage range of $\pm.325$ v. was used. In discussing the interactions of stimulus and response amplitude upon performance, the authors conclude from statistical tests of their scores that as the stimulus amplitude was magnified, Ss found it increasingly advantageous to use a large response motion. This conclusion appears quite reasonable if we examine the progressive separation among response-amplitude curves for increasing values of stimulus amplitude. However, the small stimulus amplitudes resulted in scores of only 20% to 30% time on target, while time-on-target scores as high as 50% to 60% were achieved under conditions of large stimulus amplitude. In the present article the acquisition curve for a time-on-target zone that provides scores near 50% on target is found to be very sensitive to variations of RMS, whereas a time-on-target zone giving scores in the range near 20% is relatively insensitive to identical variations in RMS error. Thus, assuming a normal distribution of error amplitudes, slight variations in the RMS value of the error would produce large effects on the time-on-target score if the stimulus amplitude is large, but only small effects when the stimulus amplitude is small. The range of RMS values occurring in this study varied from about .4 to 1 v. If a larger target zone had been used, for example one covering $\pm.75$ v., it is possible that the statistical analyses would again have shown a significant interaction, but the obtained curves would have shown more separation for small than for large stimulus amplitudes and the authors would have been forced to make an opposite conclusion regarding the direction of the interaction effect among stimulus and response amplitudes.

In this same study the absence of significant stimulus- and response-amplitude effects upon performance in the compensatory version of the task may have arisen because of a similar artifact of scoring. Time-on-target scores under the compensatory 30-plus-20-plus-10-cpm-frequency condition did not greatly exceed 10%. In the present article the curve for a target zone giving 10% time-on-target scores has extremely poor sensitivity in terms of the RMS criterion. Using their particular target zone for this version of their task, it would be difficult to demonstrate the effect of any independent variable upon performance. We do not believe, therefore, that a comparison of the relative effect of amplitude factors on compensatory vs. pursuit versions of the tracking task is possible on this basis. Thus, whereas the authors were careful to use the same criterion measure (a particular time-on-target zone) for all of their task variations, the very use of a standard measure, which was differentially sensitive to tasks of varying difficulty, limits the validity of some of their conclusions. This should, however, not be interpreted as a criticism of the major findings of the study, which do not depend upon assumptions of linearity.

In another study[12] evaluating the effects of control loading upon tracking performance, a similar effect can be observed. In summarizing their results the authors conclude that the differential effects of control loading upon performance seem to increase during the first 20 practice sessions. The various curves show increasing separation as practice progresses, and this fact forms the basis for the conclusion of the authors. However, the initial performance level is only about 12% time on target, a range in which time-on-target scores are insensitive, while the terminal performance level is one which brings the scores into a much more sensitive range of the performance measure. This increasing separation among learning curves is an artifact of the gradually increasing sensitivity of the scoring zone. . . .

Implications for Performance Measurement

It should be pointed out that the nonlinear relation between RMS and time-on-target scores does not invalidate all use of the latter scores. For certain gross comparisons, intended only to determine the presence or absence of a significant effect, either type of score may be adequate. Indeed, the two types of scores would be expected, and have been found[5,6,7] to correlate rather highly. Artifacts in the interpretation of results occur primarily when attempts are made to test for interaction effects or to interpret functional relations over an extended range of task difficulty or over an extended period of learning.

Thus it would appear that a single target zone can provide a score of only limited value as an indicant of tracking performance. This is particularly true if performance on different tasks or at different stages of learning varies over a wide range, so that the percentage of time on target is either very low, or very high for some of the conditions to be evaluated.

Simultaneous recording of scores for several target widths is one method of obtaining performance records which are less likely to lead to confounding of the effects produced by independent variables and the scoring mechanics (although perhaps this presents E with a difficult choice of functions). Another possible approach would involve transformation of time-on-target scores to yield an estimate of the RMS score or by direct reference to a table of the normal curve. This procedure may be of limited value, however, because of excessive demands upon the reliability of the scoring apparatus near the extremes of the scale.

The use of the RMS measure itself appears to us as the best method of avoiding the problems discussed in this paper. The best single statistic (in addition to the mean) for describing a normal or near-normal distribution is generally accepted to be the SD. Furthermore, this score does not impose an artificial ceiling upon improvement as do the time-on-target scores. Other advantages lie in the fact that the RMS value provides a score equally useful for problems of all difficulty levels, and that the measure reflects the entire distribution of error amplitudes rather than just a dichotomized version of the distribution. The selection of this measure is, of course, also arbitrary in one sense, since RMS does not change linearly as a function of practice. The lack of true scales for the measurement of learning, and the consequent difficulty of comparing variability at different stages of practice has been pointed out before,[11, p.635] and the use of the RMS measure does not solve these problems. The advantage of the RMS measure simply lies in the substitution of a single function for an unlimited number of functions determined by all possible target dimensions. As a consequence, there result advantages of comparability of data and ease of interpretation. If the RMS score is computed with respect to zero error equals perfect performance, rather than with respect to zero equals S's own mean, then the score will reflect constant error as well as variable error (i.e., $MS_{\text{total error}} = MS_{\text{variable error}} + MS_{\text{constant error}}$). It would appear from the amplitude distributions presented here that such constant errors are relatively minor and can usually be disregarded. This is likely to be true in most studies of continuous tracking, where lead or lag of the cursor relative to the target will each result in positive and negative voltage errors depending upon the momentary direction of motion. However, the mean plus or minus error can usually be determined by the use of slightly more complex scoring equipment and the RMS score can then be reduced to the variable error in pure form. Thus, we can conclude that the best single measure of tracking performance is error RMS (or perhaps simply mean error). A more complete picture of performance can be gained by recording the complete amplitude distribution of error.

Although the present analysis has dealt only with the measurement of tracking performance, the conclusions have much wider implications for psychology. Similar problems exist wherever response characteristics follow a continuous and normal distribution and where learning results in diminished variance of this distribution, but performance is scored according to an all-or-none criterion of frequency of occurrence. Not only are performance scores in tracking tasks such as that provided by the rotary pursuit apparatus subject to artifacts arising from the arbitrary choice of the size of the target zone, but so are scores in many other tasks such as steadiness tests, dotting tests, tweezer dexterity tests, pegboard tests, etc., where success is scored against an all-or-none criterion. It even appears likely that the records of many other types of behavior, including such diverse responses as conditioned eyelid responses, leg flexion, and maze turning, which are recorded in terms of frequency of occurrence, may show similar artifacts provided the underlying habit strength varies as a continuous function of practice.

References

1. Anderson, Nancy. Factors of motor skill learning related to control loading. Doctor's Dissertation, The Ohio State University, 1956.
2. Bakan, D. A generalization of Sidman's results on group and individual functions and a criterion. *Psychol. Bull.*, 1954, *51*, 63-64.
3. Bilodeau, E. A. Accuracy of response as a function of target width. *J. exp. Psychol.*, 1954, *47*, 201-208.
4. Estes, W. K. The problem of inferences from curves based on group data. *Psychol. Bull.*, 1956, *53*, 134-141.
5. Fitts, P. M., Bennett, W. F., & Bahrick, H. P. Application of autocorrelation and crosscorrelation analysis to the study of tracking behavior. In G. Finch & F. Cameron (Eds.). *Symposium on Air Force human engineering, personnel, and training research*. Baltimore: Air Research and Development Command, 1956. Tech. Tep. 56-8.
6. Fitts, P. M., Marlowe, E., & Noble, M. E. The interrelations of task variables in continuous pursuit tasks: I. Visual-display scale, arm-control scale, and target frequency in pursuit tracking. *USAF, Hum. Resour. Res. Cent., Res. Bull.* Sept., 1953, No. 53-34.
7. Gray, Florence E., & Ellson, D. G. The validity of time-on-target (clock) scores as an estimate of tracking error magnitude. USAF, Air Material Command, Wright-Patterson AFB, *Memo. Rep.* TSEAA-694-2F, June, 1947.
8. Green, R. F. Transfer of skill on a following tracking task as a function of task difficulty (target size). *J. Psychol.*, 1955, *39*, 355-370.

9. Hartman, B. O., & Fitts, P. M. Relations of stimulus and response amplitude to tracking performance. *J. exp. Psychol.,* 1955, *49,* 82-92.
10. Hilgard, E. R., & Marquis, D. G. *Conditioning and learning.* New York: Appleton-Century, 1940.
11. Hovland, C. I. Human learning and retention. In S. S. Stevens (Ed.), *Handbook of experimental psychology.* New York: Wiley, 1951. Ch. 17.
12. Howland, D., & Noble, M. E. The effect of physical constants of a control on tracking performance. *J. exp. Psychol.,* 1953, *46,* 353-360.
13. Hull, C. L. *Principles of behavior.* New York: Appleton-Century, 1943.
14. Humphrey, C. E., Thompson, J. E., Ensor, H. L., & Versace, J., The measurement of tracking error: time-on-target. Johns Hopkins Univer., *Applied Physics Lab. Rep.* APL/JHU TG-196, April, 1953.
15. Sidman, M. A note on functional relations obtained from group data. *Psychol. Bull.,* 1952, *49,* 263-269.
16. Stevens, S. S. Mathematics, measurement, and psychophysics. In S. S. Stevens (Ed.), *Handbook of experimental psychology.* New York, Wiley, 1951. Ch. 1.
17. Tolman, E. C. The determiners of behavior at a choice point. *Psychol. Rev.,* 1938, *45,* 1-41.
18. Warren, C. E., Fontaine, A. B., & Clark, J. R. A two-dimensional electronic pursuit apparatus. *USAF, Hum. Resour. Res. Cent. Res. Bull.* August, 1952, No. 52-26.

*The Phantom Plateau**

F. S. KELLER

THE possible existence of a plateau in the learning curve created a real stir among psychologists in the early portion of the nineteenth century. Difficult to obtain in experimentally contrived situations but accepted as occurring in the learning of real-life skills, the plateau is debated as a real or a phantom phenomenon. Furthermore, assuming its existence, is it a natural phenomenon involved in complex skill acquisition or a product of bad learning habits? Keller reviews some of the more significant early research on the topic, discussing findings and theoretical explanations. Although the basis of the paper is the learning of the Morse code, which is a unique task, the problems raised are universal to learning.

Not so long ago, I overheard a laboratory assistant in general psychology telling one of the boys in his section about a file of old examinations that we keep in the college library for students to consult. He ended brightly with the comment that it wouldn't do much good to study these exams. "You see," he said, "we use the same questions from year to year, but we change the answers."

This disturbed me at the time. It seemed like a dangerous quip to make. What if word got around that we actually did change our answers? Might we

* From the *Journal of the Experimental Analysis of Behavior,* 1958, *1,* 1-13. Abridged and reprinted with permission of the author and the Society for the Experimental Analysis of Behavior, Inc. Copyright 1958 by the Society of the Experimental Analysis of Behavior, Inc.

not be investigated for Unacademic Activities? A little reflection, however, suggested that changing answers was, in truth, a sign of good health in any course of study. It suggested, too, that such changes are really quite uncommon—especially in the beginning course. And, finally, it suggested a few answers that ought to be changed. One of these makes up the burden of the present discussion.

The answer to which I refer is commonly given in textbook chapters on learning, or habit-formation. Under such headings, it may fall within a treatment of skill, practice, or, occasionally, learning-curve plateaus.

In conformity with a well-known teaching procedure, the question itself comes after the answer, usually by several weeks. In an old-fashioned essay-type examination, it might read like this:

> What is the normal course of progress in the mastery of a skill? How might a curve for ball-tossing or pursuit-meter learning differ from that for Morse code receiving? Explain this difference. (10 points)

An A-student's answer to this question might go as follows:

> The progress curve for most skills is negatively accelerated. The amount of improvement from one trial to the next decreases as the number of trials increases. This is true of ball-tossing and of keeping contact with the target of a pursuit-meter. However, progress in Morse code receiving typically shows a long period of no advance—a *plateau*—midway in training. This plateau occurs only in the case of receiving plain-language material. It is said to be due to the fact that code proficiency depends on learning to respond to phrases and sentences as units, rather than to letters or words. The plateau represents the period in which word habits have not yet become sufficiently automatic for progress with phrases and sentences to take place.

This is the answer that I would like to change. It is wrong in two respects. First, the receiving curve for plain-language Morse code does *not* typically show a plateau. Secondly, our student has offered a faulty analysis of the receiving process. Since both errors are widespread, and since the second reaches well beyond a purely Morse code problem, it will be my aim, in what follows, to suggest some corrections.

All of you have seen the receiving curve to which our student refers. It has been a standard fixture of our textbooks for more than half a century. It is sometimes found in company with a sending curve, and sometimes with two other receiving curves. . . .

The two studies from which these curves were taken are classics in the psychology of skill.[1,2] Both were published in the *Psychological Review,* one in 1897 and the other in 1899; and both resulted from the joint endeavor of two men: *William Lowe Bryan* and *Noble Harter.* Bryan, the senior author, was then professor of psychology at Indiana University; Harter, an ex-telegrapher, was a graduate student working under Bryan's direction.

The 1897 Bryan and Harter paper contained the first known records of advancement in sending and receiving Morse code. These records were obtained in several ways. First, Harter cross-examined 37 railway and commerical telegraphers, asking them about their experience in mastering the code. From their answers he was led to construct the pair of curves. Four more pairs of "typical" curves were drawn from data supplied by schools of telegraphy with which he made contact.

Then Harter got some first-hand information. He tested for himself the weekly progress of two young students in the Brookville, Indiana, Western

Union office. Except for their greater irregularity, the curves are like all the others, especially in showing the same receiving-curve plateau at a point just below the main-line level of acceptability.

In their first paper, Bryan and Harter point out the existence of this plateau in all of their receiving curves for connected discourse. They note that many students become discouraged at this level of their code-receiving proficiency. They suggest that foreign-language learning goes through a similar phase of no improvement. But they do not tell us why the plateau occurs.

In 1899, they went further. They began with a report of some new findings. Harter had followed the progress of John Shaw, a student in the Brookville office, from the sixth through the thirty-fifth week of code practice. Shaw had been tested every Saturday in sending and receiving. The receiving tests made use of three kinds of material: disconnected letters, disconnected words, and connected words—i.e., plain English.

Three receiving curves were generated from these tests. The plain-language curve resembles all the earlier curves that had been plotted. The same plateau is there, with a main-line breakthrough at about the same place as before, in the twenty-fourth week of practice. The word and letter curves, however, appear to have reached their limit of advance. This limit, even for the curve of disconnected words, is well below the main-line requirement of 72 letters per minute.

The second aim of the 1899 paper was to explain the plateau. Bryan and Harter had by this time questioned more telegraphers; they had considered the way in which blind children read Braille; they had heard of a "period of depression" in learning college chemistry; and, especially, they had John Shaw's word and letter curves to think about.

The result of all this is now an old story, but still appealing. It runs as follows. In learning Morse code, one acquires a *hierarchy of habits*. Letters must first be mastered; then syllables and words; and, finally, phrases and sentences. Mastery of the higher-order habits depends on mastery of the lower-order ones. To receive sentences, that is, one must first have acquired the component word-habits; to receive words, one must have acquired the letter-habits.

As for the plateau, let us go straight to Bryan and Harter:

> A plateau in the curve means that the lower-order habits are approaching their maximum development, but are not yet sufficiently automatic to leave the attention free to attack the higher-order habits.[2]

As the receiving curve ascends from the base line, "no plateau appears between the learning of letters and of words, because very soon these are learned simultaneously." It takes a large vocabulary of words, however, before one can form the phrase and sentence habits needed for high-speed receiving; hence the plateau. When the vocabulary has become automatic, the curve ascends for the second time, to a level that marks the peak of achievement for most telegraphers.

Bryan and Harter have little to say about those who go still higher, beyond noting that "complete freedom in the telegraphic language" is reached only after years of apprenticeship, and comes as suddenly as did the ascent from the first plateau. Presumably, this depends upon one's mastery of language units that are highest in the habit hierarchy.

There were some puzzling features of these two papers. More puzzling today, perhaps, than they were in 1890. For example, there is the remarkable resemblance of all the receiving curves in the first report. We know, from more recent studies, that progress in receiving the *International* form of

Morse code is affected by many factors. It depends on the number of hours of practice per day; on the content of the practice materials employed; on the criteria of perfection used in passing a student from one speed to another; on the size of the steps in practice speed; and so on, and on. We know, too, that progress curves from different schools today are often quite unlike. Was there more uniformity of procedure in the code schools of the '90's than in those of our time? Is American Morse less affected by these variables than International Morse? Or, was Thorndike[6, p.285] right when he suggested that the similarity of the Bryan and Harter curves was due to the inadequacy of the questionnaire used in collecting the data?

Then, in the second paper, there is the matter of John Shaw's curves for receiving disconnected words and letters. Why did these curves never reach the main-line level? Even in those days there must have been telegraphers who copied stock-market reports and ciphered messages at speeds higher than 72 letters per minute. In Signal Corps schools today, even low-speed operators receive mixed letters and digits at rates well above this; and high-speed operators using typewriters reach nearly twice that rate. Had this student really reached his limit? Or did he fail to go further because he had so little chance to copy disconnected words and letters in his daily practice sessions?

We shall never know the answers to such questions. Except for a brief mention of the manner in which Harter conducted the speed test in the Brookville office, Bryan and Harter tell us nothing about training methods, practice material, steps in speed, criteria of passing, or any other influence that might be at play. For more light upon such matters, we are compelled to await the studies of later men.

The investigation of code learning requires an intimate acquaintance with a rather unusual training situation. It depends on more than a casual interest in practical goals. Also, it requires special experimental subjects—young men or women on whom one can rely for long-term class attendance and high motivation. It is for these reasons that war time has been the best time for research in this field. There is then a shortage of men with code skill. Investigators are then willing to work long and hard in the interest of the purely useful; and the government is usually ready to help them with funds and facilities. Experimental subjects, often in uniform, are plentiful and tractable.

The first major attack upon the Bryan and Harter position came in World War I. It was made by Rees Edgar Tulloss,[7] at Harvard University, as part of a doctoral dissertation entitled, "The Learning Curve—with Special Reference to the Progress of Students in Telegraphy and Typewriting." In the code-learning field, this was a very important study; yet, for some reason, it was never published. In fact, its existence was barely noted until early in World War II. At that time, Donald W. Taylor,[5] another Harvard code researcher, dug it out of Widener Library for a *Bulletin* review.

In the section of his dissertation that deals with telegraphy, Tulloss offers us, first, an improved method of testing speed in code receiving—a method in which each test was based on two or three short runs of signals, sent at each of several different speeds, and including as many as four distinct types of test material. There were runs of English text in which all the letters of the alphabet were represented; there were runs of disconnected letters, covering the alphabet, but with a frequency of appearance like that in plain English. Finally, there was a special test, called "alphabetical code," in which the 26 letters were represented randomly in each of two or three alphabet runs.

Using one or more of these tests, Tulloss measured the weekly progress of 23 students in International Morse code, including 19 from a Navy school that had been set up at Harvard. The latter were tested, during most of their training, with all four kinds of test material, along with a plain-language test that was given by the school itself.

Three members of this class had no prior experience with any form of Morse code when they started training. The record for one of these men was clearly atypical, for known reasons. The other two records were remarkably alike, and typified the progress of the entire group throughout most of the training period. Letters per minute were plotted against weeks of practice, with about 20 hours of practice to the week. Progress was most rapid at the start, followed by a slower, fairly straight-line advance, or a slight deceleration up to the end of training. All of the curves reach a level well above the Bryan and Harter main-line speed—even in the case of disconnected letters, as in Tulloss' alphabetical code. Finally, except for one or two obviously abnormal records, there is *no sign of a plateau* in any of the Tulloss curves—plain-language or otherwise.

These curves are, of course, for progress in *International* Morse, a code that differs from American Morse in two important ways. Its signals are composed of long and short tones, rather than patterns of clicks; and six of its letter signals are different from those of the older code in their dot-dash construction. Hence, one might fairly argue that Tulloss had no right to expect a confirmation of the Bryan and Harter findings.

To meet this objection, Tulloss measured the progress of four students of *American* Morse in a special class at Simmons College. As test material, he used only the alphabetical code, although the Western Union instructor of the class added his own weekly tests with plain-language material.

These students received approximately 10 hours of practice every week, and all four of them went ahead at about the same pace. The curves from the subjects are like the ones obtained with the International code. Even the slowest student showed a fairly steady climb in speed with disconnected letters to a point beyond that reached by John Shaw; and it appears that plain-language receiving may pass the main-line test without the appearance of a plateau.

The Tulloss studies did much to advance our knowledge of Morse code learning. They were not, however, without flaws, one of which Tulloss himself had found in Bryan and Harter. In trying to account for their plateau, he concluded that it was due to lack of practice with the more difficult signals of the code. Yet, in his own work, except in the case of one student whose only training came while taking tests, there was no control of the practice materials employed. His results, it might be argued, were equally a function of an unknown state of an unknown state of affairs.

The code researches of World War II were free from this defect. In service schools especially, both practice and test materials were commonly specified from start to finish of a student's training. As a rule, however, they lacked variety, being restricted mainly to military cipher, with little or no plain-language code. It was not until 1953, 35 years after Tulloss' work, that the problem of practice materials was faced in an adequate manner.

The study to which I refer was conducted at Columbia University, under Air Force contract, by Donald A. Cook.[3] Its aim was to measure progress in receiving International Morse code when students were not only tested, but trained, with five different kinds of material. . . .

Progress went on quite steadily for each kind of material throughout the practice hours in which it was employed. There are ups and downs, as in the Tulloss curves, but nowhere do we find the classical plateau. Moreover, the old main-line speed is again, in every case, exceeded. This would be true even if we were to handicap the International code severely in making our comparisons. . . .

From the findings of these two investigations, you will probably be led to agree that the answer should be changed to our original question about "the normal course of progress in the mastery of a skill," at least when this answer states that Morse code progress *typically* shows a plateau. There is, however, one more study to be noted here, as a sequel to the John Shaw story, and as one last look for the classical curve.

This study deals with the progress, in American Morse, of one experimental subject, who was given daily code practice during 10 weeks of the summer of 1955. This subject, Anne Simmons, was an 18-year-old high-school graduate who was working to earn money for college expenses. Her instructor, who shall be nameless, was an elderly ex-telegrapher trained in American Morse and with a lively interest in the proper conduct of the experiment.

Practice sessions for Anne Simmons were held on 7 days of the week, usually in the early afternoon. The practice material included four of the five kinds of material used by Cook in the study just described, with supplements from *Treasure Island* and *Tom Sawyer*. The material omitted was Cook's second-order approximation to English. Digits were included with the letters, as before, but punctuation was limited to the comma and the period.

Initial mastery of the 36 basic signals was brought about with the code-voice method.[4] This is a procedure in which the instructor names each signal a few seconds after sending it, and the student tries to respond with the correct letter or digit during the pause. All 36 of the signals were used from the start. They were sent in runs of 100 each, in random order, and with rest-pauses and error-tallies between runs.

For the first 12 days of training, this method was in effect, with 1 hour practice daily. There were two 100-signal runs on the first day, and three on each day thereafter. The number of correct responses per run was plotted against the number of runs. The over-all picture was crudely linear, up to the point of near-perfection, but there was a cyclical effect that is clearly due, in the first half of training, to overnight losses of skill.

Then the speed runs were begun, for 2 hours a day and with all four types of material. The speed at the start was one of four words (20 letters) per minute. It was increased, in 1-word-per-minute steps, as the subject met each passing criterion of 95-per cent correct copy in three runs for a given material. The runs were generally 1 minute long (never shorter) and, in all but a few cases, they were checked for errors by the "call-back" method immediately after being copied. Each run, in a sense, was treated as a test, and the subject was informed of each test score. . . .

The curves of her results, unlike Cook's, are based on American Morse, the code that Bryan and Harter studied. Unlike the Tulloss curves, they deal with the entire code and they result from a known and equal amount of practice on all the types of material with which the student was tested. Yet, in their appearance, they are little more than smoothed-out and speeded-up versions of the Cook and Tulloss curves. There is no plateau, at any place, for any kind of material. In addition, the curves for disconnected discourse and disconnected letters (plain-English frequency) reach heights that John Shaw never dreamt of. . . .

This little experiment was brought to an end, at a prearranged date, to provide the subject with a well-deserved vacation. It could have gone no further, anyhow, without drastic changes in procedure. Anne Simmons was close to her limit in speed of *handwriting,* and her instructor, using a standard telegraph key, was barely able to reach the topmost speeds employed with each material. By using a typewriter, and a higher-speed transmission of signals, the curves would surely have continued to climb. Perhaps they would have paused for a while in their ascent, on that *second* plateau of which Bryan and Harter made mention. Or perhaps they would have marched on, at a slowing pace, but steadily, into the realm of the expert. I would guess the latter, but I might be wrong. This is country into which no Morse code researcher has ever yet entered.

In 1918, having looked in vain for plateaus in all his progress curves, Rees Tulloss began to re-examine the code-receiving process. The result was a multistage analysis of this skill which has not yet been improved upon, and which I venture to outline here as an alternative to the Bryan and Harter view.

At the very start of training, according to Tulloss, the code beginner has usually memorized a list of visual dot-dash symbols, one for each letter and digit. Hence, his first response to an *auditory* signal is one of visualizing or covertly verbalizing its dot-dash elements. This reaction sets off, in turn, a subvocal articulation of the appropriate character; and this articulation is itself followed immediately by the copying response—the writing (or speaking) of the letter or digit. In every case of reaction to a signal, there is this little chain of events. In responding to a simple combination of a short and long tone, for example, a student might visualize a dot and a dash, utter subvocally the letter "a," then write the letter down—all within a second or two of time.

As practice continues, however, several more things happen. First, the initial visualizing or verbalizing within each chain is replaced by a "duplicative" or "imitative" response. Instead of reacting to the tonal compound by saying "dot-dash" or seeing the dot and dash, the student says to himself something like "di-dah"—a muscular approximation to the tonal pattern. The complete sequence will then be as follows: (1) the auditory dot-dash; (2) the imitative "di-dah"; (3) the silent articulation of "a"; and (4) the copying response— the writing of "a."

With further practice, the duplicative response drops out of the chain. The signal pattern now leads directly to covert articulation of the letter, after which the copying response occurs. The reaction time of the copying response to each signal is thus appreciably shortened, first to the "easy" signals, and then to the "hard" ones, and the student's code speed is correspondingly increased.

The next main feature of the process, with still further practice, is one in which each response chain begins to *overlap* in time with its neighbors. The student is gradually enabled to begin a second, or even a third, linkage before the first one has come to its end. This permits, of course, another increase in his speed of receiving, and lets him "copy behind," at least by one or two letters.

You might imagine that the next advance would be another shortening of reaction time—that the middle link of each chain, the covert articulation of letters and digits, would then drop out, and that each signal would come to evoke, directly, the copying response. Tulloss would possibly have agreed that for students who deal mainly with meaningless transmissions of disconnected letters and numbers, something like this might really occur. But he would certainly have denied that the link drops out for those who go on to the next stage of the code-receiving process.

This stage is one of *word-articulation*. It is a kind of "spelling-out" stage, in which the articulation of letters is still a basic feature. Consider the case in which plain language is being sent. The signals come along as usual, one by one. Each signal continues to evoke the articulation of a letter—however fragmentary, however covert, this letter response may be. The letters, of course, spell out words, and if they come in close enough succession, they lead the student to say the words to himself. Thus, having subvocalized "t," "h," and "e," as the signals call these letters up, he finds himself, like any other speller, articulating "the." To each sequence of his own letter responses, he makes a single, unitary word response, even before he puts his pencil to the paper.

To appreciate this argument fully, and to get the feel of code-receiving at high speed, you have only to listen to someone's dictation of the letters in a series of words, at a rate of two or three letters per second. The effect will be even better if you try to write the letters as the message is sent. For example, see if you can "copy" the following:

THISISASIMPLIFIEDVERSION

("This is a simplified version")

You can understand, after listening to this message, how unlikely it is that ten successive letters, as in the word "simplified," or seven, as in "version," could ever function as an auditory whole. There may be word *responses*, just as there are letter responses, but code signals are never word *stimuli*, except in the case of very short words or uncommonly high speeds.

You can also see how word articulations arise from the articulations of letters and must always depend upon them in the receiving process. These word responses are not compounds of letter responses, but are merely evoked by them, just as any response evokes another. Often the word response comes up before the letter chain has been completed. Some of you may have uttered "simple," subvocally, before the sixth letter of "simplified" had been spoken; or you may have articulated "version" before that word was half spelled. In the first case, a mistake was made, which may or may not have disrupted the receiving process. In the second case, no harm was done, since the letters that followed your precocious word response served simply to confirm it.

This "guessing" behavior occurs primarily in the case of plain-language or disconnected-word receiving. It is obviously related to one's spelling experience, and it probaly accounts for the fact that progress with text and mixed words may actually be *slower* than with almost any other kind of material. As I have already noted, both Cook and Tulloss had students who gave them such results. In the case of Anne Simmons, there was no clear effect of this sort; but even at the end of her training she was still copying "close behind"— responding letter by letter to most of each transmission. Ultimately, in her case, as in others, we would expect words to be articulated in advance of being written. We would also expect that with increased knowledge of common pitfalls—the different ways in which letter sequences may get off the track— there would be fewer and fewer mistakes. Plain English would, in the end, be easiest to copy.

Tulloss goes two steps further in dealing with high-speed code reception. First, he argues for a second stage of overlapping, in which each of several word articulations may, at the same time, be in process of arousing its own copying response. He likens the process to that of ordinary writing, in which the word being written may be several words behind the one from which it stemmed. Secondly, he has something to say about the expert's ability to copy behind by 10 or 12 words or more:

> What we can and do have (here) is a present articulation of the word, without immediate writing response, and then later a *repeated* articulation of the word which does result in its writing. . . . The words are articulated as they are spelled out. They are remembered and repeated.[7]

These analyses, however, carry less conviction than the earlier ones. In particular, Tulloss' appeal to "memory" in the final stage is not very helpful;

and the need for repeating a word sequence before writing it is not very helpful; and the need for repeating a word sequence before writing it is not very clear. One might just as plausibly argue that successive words, like successive letters, *directly* induce the writing of those familiar patterns to which they belong.

This is the Tulloss story, told briefly and, perhaps, with distortion. It is probably incorrect in detail, and it is certainly incomplete. It also assumes the existence of events that you may think of as undesirably subjective, as, for example, the subvocal articulation of letters, words, and "duplicative" responses. But nothing metaphysical is involved here; the private events differ from the public only in their magnitude, not in kind.

Tulloss did not explain the plateau because he had no plateau to explain; for him, the plateau was a phantom, or the outcome of bad training methods. But he did throw light on the Bryan and Harter doctrine. He helps us see how they could talk of receiving words and sentences, without asking us to believe that a series of 20 to 100 or more dots and dashes of code, requiring many seconds for transmission, may function as an auditory unit.

His analysis fits readily within the framework of modern reinforcement theory, and it suggests a much closer tie between code learning and other verbal activities than we have been wont to consider in the past. I am thinking of its relation not only to such skills as those of shorthand, typing, and reading Braille, but also to those involved in reporting, listening, and understanding. The theoretical gain that accrues from relating code to such transactions should be more than enough to compensate us for the loss of that mysterious power bequeathed by Bryan and Harter to the telegraphic art.

The further study of this problem need not involve Morse code at all. High-speed receiving is simply a form of taking dictation, and can be investigated with signals that are no more elaborate or unfamiliar than the spoken letters or words of our mother tongue. Indeed, the patterns of Morse code are but awkward, slow-moving, and hard-to-master counterparts of letters, digits, and marks of punctuation. For some rather special purposes, they may still be preferred. For others, we ought to employ their less-demanding mates. From the study of dictation, by letters and words, we might then move on, in orderly fashion, to verbal report and note-taking, testimony and rumor, and the "comprehension of ideas."

References

1. Bryan, W. L., and Harter, N. Studies in the physiology and psychology of the telegraphic language. *Psychol. Rev.,* 1897, *4,* 27-53.
2. Bryan, W. L., and Harter, N. Studies on the telegraphic language. The acquisition of a hierarchy of habits. *Psychol. Rev.* 1899., *6,* 345-375.
3. Cook, D. A. Message type as a parameter of learning to receive International Morse code. Paper read at Eastern Psychological Association Meetings, New York, April, 1957.
4. Keller, F. S. Studies in International Morse code: I. A new method of teaching code reception. *J. appl. Psychol.,* 1943, *27,* 407-415.
5. Taylor, D. W. Learning telegraphic code, *Psychol. Bull.,* 1943, *40,* 461-487.
6. Thorndike, E. L. Educational psychology. Vol. 2. The psychology of learning. New York: Teachers College, 1913.
7. Tulloss, R. E. The learning curve—With special reference to the progress of students in telegraphy and typewriting. Unpublished doctoral dissertation, Harvard Univer., 1918.

PART 4

ABILITIES RELATED TO MOTOR SKILL PERFORMANCE

The Generality of Abilities

The nature and development of abilities have been of interest to differential psychologists and growth and development psychologists for a long time. The measurement of cognitive abilities and their relation to academic achievement have occupied the efforts of researchers and educators. Of concern, too, has been the relationship between intellectual variables, motor abilities, and physical characteristics. Before examining such associations, let us address a major problem. What is an ability and how is it to be measured?

Presumably, abilities are inborn and developed through experience. They underlie potential for success in a number of given tasks in that they set limits in which skills can be acquired. A task or skill usually refers to a specific set of responses in a situation whereas an ability is a more general trait. In many skills, abilities interact to influence performance at various stages of practice. They help to explain how and why individuals differ from each other. Although in theory an ability can be adequately defined, in practice it is typically measured with a task designed by the investigator. Therefore, in fact, an ability is denoted by performance in a task arranged by an individual and labeled either as a result of common sense, intuition, or correlational or factor analysis.

Tests may attempt to measure performance in specific skills, general mental ability, or general motor ability. There more than likely exist abilities that are more general and those that are more specific to certain situations. Fleishman in his article in Part 1 identifies a number of psychomotor abilities and physical proficiency items. Books dealing with measurement and evaluation in such areas as education, psychology, and physical education contain tests used to tap certain abilities. The use of a test to measure mechanical ability in order to predict success in an industrial task is also reported. In other literature, the relationship of abilities to each other is indicated. One of the questions asked is whether individuals who possess certain highly developed abilities have a tendency to perform well in tests of other abilities?

With regard to the nature of abilities and their interaction with motor performance, three considerations have been selected for emphasis in Part 4. First of all, papers are included that deal with the generality of abilities in the broad sense; that is, the relationship of so-called cognitive, or academic, abilities to motor abilities is examined. The second group of readings is concerned with the predictive worth of ability tests in the acquisition of motor skill. In the third grouping of papers, abilities apparently related to proficiency at different stages of practice and learning are discussed.

Chapter 4

THE GENERALITY OF ABILITIES

Correlation Between Motor and Verbal Skills*

CLARENCE E. RAGSDALE

THE tendency to achieve well in assorted motor and verbal tasks, a "going-togetherness" if you will, has been speculated upon and researched throughout this century. The purpose of this material by Ragsdale is to demonstrate that the problem is by no means new, as indicated by the 1930 publication date. He addresses the possibility of the existence of a so-called general motor ability, and the degree to which motor and verbal abilities correlate. In general, the conclusions reached by Ragsdale appear to be reasonable today. Research since the publication of this work has usually verified his contentions.

Psychologists have commonly assumed that there is a parallel between the mental and the physical. Theoretically we should be able to find a fairly high correlation between physical and mental traits. Many studies have been made to determine the amount of such correlation. These correlations have ordinarily been disappointingly low. Baldwin finds that mental age has a correlation of —.15 with weight and .095 with height. Other measures of physical development and physical maturity have been used, some of which show higher correlation, but in no case are the correlations great enough to be of practical value. A zero or slightly positive correlation has been found between ossification of wrist bones and mental age. A low positive correlation has been found between anatomical age and physiological age. A composite of several physical measurements gives a more significant correlation with mental age than any one index. Gates found that mental age has a correlation of .212 with the combined measures of nutrition, ossification, chest girth, height, and grip. Naccarati found that mental age has a correlation of .356 with a composite of several physical measurements. Intercorrelation of different physical mea-

* From *The Psychology of Motor Learning*, Ann Arbor, Michigan: Edwards Brothers, Inc., 1930, pp. 71-76.

sures with each other range from .11 to .69, indicating that no two measures are indices of exactly the same physical development. In general, we can conclude that there is a low positive correlation between intelligence and various measures of physical development, and that there is a low positive intercorrelation between different measures of physical development. In no case are the correlations sufficiently high to have much practical significance.

Terman made a study of approximately 1000 gifted children from grades one to eight in the larger cities of California. These gifted children were given extensive examinations in mental and physical traits. They were given complete medical and physical examinations as well as character and personality tests. The minimum degree of intelligence of those under 11 years was an intelligent quotient of 140. These gifted California children, as a group, are above the standards for American-born children in standard height and weight. The gifted children are, on the average, one pound heavier at birth than normal children. Their health is better than that of normal children. They walked slightly earlier than normal children, and learned to talk four or five months earlier than normal children. The gifted children are less often rated as nervous. The proportion of stuttering, morbid fears, etc. is about the same in gifted and normal children. The gifted children sleep thirty to sixty minutes more daily than normal children. Gifted children reach puberty earlier than normal children. With some exceptions, gifted children are more interested than normal children in the abstract subjects in school. Their interest in manual training and sewing is weaker than in literature and dramatics. However, gifted children rank shop work as much easier than unselected boys. In their play interests, gifted children are less social and more mature than normal children. Gifted boys are more "masculine" in their play interests than normal boys, and gifted girls lose their interest in "masculine" play earlier than normal girls. This study by Terman indicates that there is a tendency for superior ability in manual and motor activities to be present in children who also have superior ability in the academic school subjects.

Lehman and Witty found that there was no appreciable difference in the number or diversity of play activities engaged in by children of widely varying progress quotients. Pedagogically retarded children engaged in more social play activities than children who had progressed normally. Pedagogically accelerated children did not differ much from normal children in the social character of their play: they were, however, slightly more social in their play interests. With increasing mental age there was a tendency for children to engage in fewer play activities and in smaller numbers of plays and games of a social nature. In general, retarded children avoid individual activities and show an unusual interest in games in which others take part. Children with high intelligence quotients were more solitary in their play than normal children. Gifted children engaged more often than normal children in gymnastic stunts, but less often in running, jumping, boxing, and baseball.

Musico investigated the intercorrelation between a number of tests of motor capacity. He used such tests as aiming, tapping, tracing auditory reaction time, and muscular strength. The tests were made as simple as possible in order that the mental element might be excluded. In most cases the right hand was used. He found, in general, that the intercorrelations between this type of motor tests were positive. From a somewhat similar investigation, Perrin concludes that motor ability is not general; that it is somewhat generally specialized. As a statement of fact, this means merely that there is an absence of correlation between the scores of various tests, both complex and simple. From the results of Musico and Perrin, we may conclude that an individual's performance in one motor activity does not, in general, furnish much indication of what his performance in another motor activity will be. There is no "motor type." Motor capacities are relatively independent of intelligence.

Abel carried on a study to determine to what extent differences in mentality would determine differences in ability to learn skilled trades. He used two groups of girls, with about one hundred in each group. The more intelligent group were graduates of the eighth grade. The less intelligent group were those who had not finished the eighth grade or had failed to pass the entrance tests in the Manhattan Trade School in New York. Both groups of girls were taking training in millinery and dressmaking. Abel gave a series of intelligence tests and motor tests to both groups of girls. He found that the more intelligent group were superior in mechanical and motor tests. After leaving the Manhattan Trade School, the girls of the more intelligent group, in general, secured work at better wages than those in the less intelligent group. From his investigations, we can conclude that a higher degree of intelligence in a worker is accompanied by greater mechanical ability, more motor speed, quicker speed of decision, and greater persistency of effort than are found in a worker of subnormal intelligence.

Rudisill gave a series of intelligence and motor tests to a group of junior and senior students in the school of economics at the University of Pittsburgh. He used the Army Alpha Tests and academic grades to estimate their intelligence. For motor tests, he used tracing, tapping, strength of grip, vital capacity, and endurance of grip. In every case the correlations were quite low. Miss Glenn carried on a series of tests of grade children in grades six, seven, and eight to determine the relationship between ability in academic and manual subjects. She used intelligence tests and standardized subject matter tests on the one hand and motor tests such as tapping, paper folding, and peg-board on the other. The correlations between the school subjects and the motor tests were quite low; many were negative. The correlations between academic subjects and handwork ranged from .12 to .42, as compared with an intercorrelation between the academic subjects of .60 and .80. Wooley found a correlation between mental and manual ability of .21, probable error .064 at fourteen years and .33 with a probable error of .060 at fifteen years. She found that the individuals could be divided into five groups. (a) Those low in both abilities; this group is probably destined to enter the unskilled trades and occupations. (b) Individuals low in mental ability but high in manual ability; this group of individuals could probably be trained in the skilled trades. (c) Individuals medium in both abilities; these individuals are probably destined for secondary positions in business and industry. (d) Individuals with high mental ability and low manual ability; these people could probably be successful in law, literature, finance, etc. (e) Individuals high in both mental and manual abilities; these individuals should be directed into occupations such as engineering and experimental science.

Johnson studied the learning ability of three groups of women inmates of the State Reformatory for Women at Bedford Hills, New York. They were grouped as high, medium, and low in intelligence. The skill to be learned consisted of throwing darts at a circular target ten feet distant. The average scores of the group corresponded to their degrees of intelligence. The lowest group, however, made great improvement. These results indicate that individuals of a low degree of intelligence may start at a low point in motor ability but can improve greatly, although their final score will not be so high as that of individuals of a higher degree of intelligence.

Brace, in devising his motor ability tests, has assumed the existence of a general motor ability. The investigation which we have just quoted does not justify this assumption. Attempts to make use of Brace's motor ability tests for predicting success in various specialized types of physical activity have been uniformly unsuccessful.

These investigations show that there is no unitary capacity which we can name "general motor ability." There seem to be many specific abilities concerned with motor ability. There seem to be many specific abilities concerned with motor activity. These abilities have low correlations with one another and low correlations with verbal ability or intelligence. In order to discover an individual's ability to perform a task of a motor nature, it is necessary to devise a test dealing specifically with the task in question. An individual who has good motor ability may have either high or low ability in academic school subjects. There is just a slight tendency for those who have good motor abilities to also have a good ability in academic school work. It seems that human beings have many special abilities. One of these special abilities is that which we have ordinarily called "general intelligence," which seems to be specifically the ability to use words or symbols in abstract thinking. This specific ability is of such great importance in determining life success that it has been extensively investigated. On the same level with literary ability there are many other specific abilities, which we ordinarily call manual or motor. No one of these manual or motor abilities has, for human beings as a whole, as much importance as ability to deal with words and symbols.

For some years, in many school systems, the assignment of children to various departments has been based more or less on the theory that all those who have low intelligence quotients should be given the bulk of their work in the motor activities as found in the manual arts and physical education. These departments have been made the general dumping ground for those who cannot or will not keep up with the average child in strictly academic lines. It has been commonly assumed that the children who cannot do well with the academic subjects will be able to do well with the manual and motor activities. It is assumed that the child who is backward in general intelligence is likely to be good in motor intelligence. This assumption, as shown from the investigations which we have quoted, is not founded on fact. The problem reduces itself to the question of whether there is less competition in occupations which demand manual and motor activity than in occupations in which the manual and motor element is relatively small. If this is true, children of a low degree of intelligence may well be directed into these occupations, not because they are especially well fitted for them, but because they can in this way avoid the competition of their more gifted fellows. On the other hand, there are many occupations such as engineering, surgery, agriculture, and physical education which give opportunity for the exercise of the highest type of intelligence. In these occupations there may be room for some relatively unskilled workmen, but there is also room for many workmen of the highest degree of intelligence.

In our schools participation in athletics is ordinarily restricted to students who have attained a certain minimum scholastic standing. This fixing of eligibility requirements is based, in part, upon the assumption that athletics represent a waste of time and should be participated in only by those students who can prove that they have time to waste. This assumption, that athletics and physical abilities represent a waste of time, has been effectively challenged during recent years. The conclusion has been rather widely reached that athletics and physical activities have a definite educational and cultural value which should give them an important place in the school program. If we approach the problem of participation in athletics from the standpoint of the welfare of the individual students, the decision of whether he should participate in athletic and physical activities should be based upon an understanding of his ability in this and other kinds of work. He should be directed into the kinds of work in which he has the most ability, and in which he has most possibility of gaining a satisfactory and useful position in the community when his school life is finished. Advice concerning participation in the manual and motor activities of the school program should be based upon ability in this kind of work in connection with opportunity in this type of occupation, and should not be based merely upon the lack of ability in academic subjects.

When we eliminate individuals with low verbal ability from participation in sports and other so-called extra-curricular activities by reason of eligibility requirements, we are in danger of preventing these students from following out the lines of their special ability. Participation in any activity, whether of a physical or purely academic nature, should be determined by ability in that activity rather than by *ability in something else*. The problem of eligibility for interscholastic athletics and other extra-curricular activities is complicated by other practical considerations, but these should not be permitted to outweigh the needs of the individual student. The principle that he should be permitted to develop along the lines of his own special interests and abilities should outweigh other considerations.

Occupations which yield the greatest individual and social returns ordinarily demand good verbal ability, while many occupations which yield less social and economic returns require good ability of the motor and manual type. In these latter occupations there are many *low-grade* jobs in which there is less competition than in the former. The *highest* degree of success in this latter class of occupation also demands, in addition to the specific motor or manual ability, good verbal ability, that is, good intelligence. When we direct students with low ability in academic school work into a motor occupation, we are justified in doing so only because of the less intensive competition they will meet, and not because we can expect them to have outstanding ability in manual and motor activities except in specific cases where this outstanding ability can be demonstrated. Those who are to become teachers of motor activities such as physical education need to possess both high ability in one or more motor activities and high verbal ability—that is, high intelligence. Neither good motor abilities nor good intelligence alone is sufficient to insure the highest type of success; the two kinds of ability must occur together.

Bibliography

Abel, T. M.: Tested Mentality as Related to Success in Skilled Trade Training. Ph.D. Thesis at Columbia University, 1925. *Arch. Psych.,* Columbia University Press, #77.

Bolton, T. L.: The Relation of Motor Power to Intelligence. *Amer. J of Psych.* 1903, pp. 615-631.

Brace, D. K.: *Measuring Motor Ability.* A. S. Barnes Co., New York, 1927.

Johnson, B.: Practice Effects in a Target Test. *Psych. Rev.* 1919.

Lehman, A. C. and Witty, Paul A.: *The Psychology of Play Activities.* A. S. Barnes and Co., New York, 1927.

Musico, B.: Motor Capacity with Special Reference to Vocational Education. *Brit. J. of Psych.* Vol. 13, pp. 157-184.

Perrin, F. A. C.: An Experimental Study in Motor Ability. *J. of Exp. Psych.* 1921, pp. 24-56.

Reaney, M. J.: The Correlation between General Intelligence and Play Ability as Shown by Organized Group Games. *Brit. J. of Psych.* 1914, pp. 226-253.

Rudisill, E. S.: Correlation between Physical and Motor Capacity and Intelligence. School and Society, 1923, pp. 178-179.

Terman, L. M.: Genetic Studies of Genius, Part 1. Stanford University Press, 1925.

Wooley, Helen T.: Relation between Manual and Mental Ability as Shown by Tests. *J. of Ed. Psych.* 1915, p. 532.

Relationships Among Intellectual and Nonintellectual Variables[*]

A. H. ISMAIL, JOHN KANE, and D. R. KIRKENDALL

CERTAINLY not all research efforts have yielded data indicating that motor and verbal measures are independent among and within each other. It has been suggested that perhaps there is "a positive association between some motor items, especially in terms of coordination and balance, and well-established measures of intelligence and scholastic ability." Examined here is this hypothesis. The reader is requested to note and compare the statistical analyses utilized to reach conclusions in the study reported below as well as in other investigations. In the latter case, intercorrelations among the variables of direct concern are usually positive and low to moderate. However, in the investigation of Ismail and his associates, factor analysis was the basis for optimistic confirmation of the hypothesis, while intercorrelations alone were employed by others to reject it.

The concept of integrated development drawing attention to the interrelationship between the nonintellectual (especially motor, emotional, and social) and intellectual aspects is at the foundation of a number of theories of child development. Olson[20] has proposed an "organismic age" theory; Kephart[15,16] in his work has stressed the importance of considering the complete perceptual-motor development while Doman[5] and Delacato[4] emphasize "neurological organization" as an essential feature in child development.

These and other theories have stimulated much speculative research into the nature of the association between various aspects of development. The present report is part of a research program designed to clarify the relationship between measures of motor aptitude and intellectual ability. In this area of research difficulty has been found in making valid interpretations due to both conflicting results and to the variety of measures used to assess motor aptitude—Sloan,[21] Klausmeier,[17,18,19] Brown and Henderson,[3] Weber,[23] Barry,[2] Jenny,[12] and Asmussen and Heiball.[1]

Two earlier stages of the present research program have already been reported. The initial step was taken to identify by factor analytic procedures the factors underlying tests which authorities claim to measure motor aptitude—Ismail and Cowell[7]; Ismail, Kephart, and Cowell.[11] Six factors were described as follows: (a) speed and strength; (b) growth and maturity; (c) kinesthetic memory of the arms; (d) body balance on objects; (e) body balance on the floor; and (f) coordination.

After defining motor aptitude, Ismail and others[8,9,10,11] studied the relationship between this dimension and intellectual achievement. In each of four studies reported a factor was identified which had high loadings on intellectual, coordination, and some balance items. In addition, these studies demonstrated

[*] From *The Research Quarterly*, 1969, *40*, 83-92. Reprinted with permission of the authors and the American Association for Health, Physical Education, and Recreation.

the possibility of adequately predicting intellectual performance utilizing motor aptitude measures. Moreover, it was found that the factor structure was similar among boys and girls.

The study reported here was conceived as a further step in the research project attempting to clarify the relationship between motor aptitude and intellectual achievement. In particular, this study aimed to identify the factors explaining the relationship between these two domains among British children. The procedures and measures employed by Ismail and his coworkers in the studies with American preadolescent children were included, together with assessments of personality and appropriate British measures of scholastic achievement. The study, therefore, might offer some evidence relative to the cross-cultural validation of the earlier findings.

Procedures

Selection of Subjects. The children involved in the study were from four mixed (coeducational) primary schools in the Richmond-Upon-Thames Borough of Greater London. The population from which the subjects were chosen was made up of students in their final year at primary school (N = 130). Utilizing a six-point criterion measure previously established by Ismail and others,* 94 children were selected for this study (48 boys and 46 girls). The 94 children represented a balance of high, middle, and low achievement levels. The groups were representative of a wide socioeconomic stratum.

Variables Included in the Study. The variables were intellectual and nonintellectual measures. The nonintellectual items comprised, in addition to age, height and weight, 18 motor aptitude items identified and described by Ismail,[7,11] and two personality dimensions. More particularly these were:

1. Three general motor items—shuttle run, wall pass, and standing broad jump.
2. Two kinesthetic items.
3. Seven coordination items based on hopping activities.
4. Six balance items.
5. Two personality items—neuroticism and extroversion scores as measured by the Junior Maudsley Personality Inventory.

The nine intellectual variables measured were:

1. Otis IQ Test (Beta form).
2. Standard Academic Achievement subtest scores in paragraph meaning, word meaning, arithmetic reasoning, arithmetic computation, and total achievement.
3. General Scholastic Ability Test (NFER Test 2) which measures verbal reasoning.
4. The NFER TEST C_2 which measures English achievement (including vocabulary and comprehension) and the NFER Test C_3, which measures knowledge of mathematical concepts.

Statistical Procedures. In order to identify the factors which are present in the selected 32 nonintellectual and intellectual variables, factor analysis using the principle axis form of solution was utilized. The varimax rotation of the factor matrixes in accordance with the Kaiser[13] criterion was undertaken as a further step in the clarification and interpretation of the factors

* A. H. Ismail and J. J. Gruber, *Motor Aptitude and Intellectual Performance* (Columbus, Ohio: Charles E. Merrill Books, 1967), p. 52.

extracted. Three factor analyses were run, one for boys, one for girls, and one for the total group.

The operations were carried out on the I.B.M. 7094 at Purdue University and on the Atlas Computer, London University.

Results and Discussion

The correlation matrix for the total group shows that the correlations between the intellectual items and the coordination items (except one) were positive and ranged between .05 and .43. Balance items (especially those performed on the floor) also show some correlation with the intellectual items. On the other hand, the general motor items show negligible correlations with the intellectual items. The personality items show relatively highest correlations with general motor, kinesthetic, and size items.

The pattern of the correlation matrixes for boys and girls was similar to that for the total group.

Interpretation of the Factors

Eight factors were extracted for each of the three factor analyses. The amount of extracted variance accounted for 68.7% of the total variance in the boys' matrix, 72.1% in the girls' matrix, and 61.1% in the combined (total) matrix. For the purposes of interpretation, the order of the factors described is given regardless of the amount of variance involved. To a very large extent the pattern and identity of the factors for each of the three groups are similar.

Factor I. Intellectual Development. Observing the factor loadings associated with the total, boys and girls groups, it is found that high loadings are related to academic achievement and IQ, with relatively lower loadings on coordination items. The factor pattern for the three groups was found to be similar; hence for each group it is reasonable to name this factor Intellectual Development. The same factor structure was obtained previously by Ismail, Kephart, and Cowell and Ismail and Gruber.

An important observation is that all intellectual items have positive loadings with all of the coordination items except one. The reason behind the negative loading on this item is that children performed it incorrectly by treating it as a power item instead of a coordination item. . . .

Due to the presence of positive significant relationships between four of the motor coordination items and intellectual items, as shown in the correlation matrix, it could be postulated that the motor coordination items involved are either confounded with intelligence or that there is a common neurophysiological process which takes place in performing intellectual as well as motor coordination items. Such a neurophysiological process may be such that it enhances facilitation in performing both intellectual and motor coordination items in high achievers, while it inhibits such facilitation in low achievers. Or the presence of such positive relationships may be due to the similarity of the perceptual process in both the intellectual and motor coordination tasks. Hypotheses should be formulated and tested along this line to investigate the validity of the suggested propositions.

Although this factor structure in the three analyses is very similar, an interesting difference is seen concerning the loading of neuroticism. For boys the loading is —.31, indicating that stability, as opposed to neuroticism, is associated with intellectual ability and motor coordination, while the loading for girls (.08) indicates this is not the case with girls.

Factor II. Coordination of the Lower Limbs. High factor loadings are found on the coordination items . . . and moderate loadings on academic performance items. This second factor is similar in each of the three groups and is a reflection of Factor I reported above, since the pattern involving the intellectual and coordination items is reversed. Since all the coordination items are primarily performed by the legs and feet, this factor is defined as Coordination of Lower Limbs and appears to be the same factor as that previously identified by Ismail and coworkers.

As with the first factor, the neuroticism loading differs for boys and girls. While neuroticism loads —.22 (indicating stability) with this coordination factor among girls, a moderate loading of .14 (indicating neuroticism) is associated with the factor among boys. It could be that the normal, stable pre-adolescent girl in our culture tends to be more coordinated at hopping and skipping skills than the average stable boy because of the difference in the play and games expectations of the sexes.

Factor III. The Effect of Size on Dynamic Balances. Observing the factor loadings in the total group, high factor loadings are associated with weight, height, and beam walking in that order. These findings are supported by the intercorrelations among the three variables. Height correlated .70 with weight, and beam walking correlated —.39 with height and —.42 with weight. At the pre-adolescent stage children increase in both height and weight as a part of their normal growth. The scores on beam walking are adversely affected by both height and weight of children. This is reflected by the negative factor loading associated with beam walking on this factor and by the negative correlation coefficients of the item with either height or weight variables. Similar results are obtained on both boys and girls. Consequently, for each group it is reasonable to name this factor The Effect of Size on Dynamic Balance. These findings are supported by Travis[22] and Ismail and coworkers.

The personality loadings for the three groups indicate that extroversion and stability go with physical size. Among the girls the emphasis is apparently on the stability loading (.39) and among boys on the extroversion (.23). At this age boys who are physically big might seem to be well equipped to develop extrovert tendencies, while for girls between 10 and 12 years stature might well be regarded as an index of satisfactory development towards maturity and hence, associated with stability.

Factor IV. Speed and Power Involving the Lower Limbs. The highest loadings on this factor are for the 40-yard shuttle run, standing broad jump and wall pass. These items measure speed and power though the wall pass additionally is a good measure of hand-eye coordination. The factor structure in the three groups is again seen to be very similar with the exception of the approximately zero loading for the boys' group on the wall pass item. It seems reasonable therefore to name this factor Speed and Power Involving the Lower Limbs. A similar factor has been identified and described in the earlier research by Ismail and Gruber.

The moderately high loading of extroversion (.31) on this factor for the boys' group supports the finding of Kane,[14] who showed that extroversion was consistently associated with general motor ability among boys. The explanation may be found either in types of games and out-going athletic activities which are regarded as suitable for boys, or it may be that "in-group acceptance" among boys at this age favors the athletic extrovert.

Factor V. Kinesthetic Memory of the Arms. The two important items in this factor are the kinesthetic variables and the pattern is much the same in the three groups, with loadings ranging from —.66 to —.87. The factor is, therefore, described as Kinesthetic Memory of the Arms. Less important but of interest are the personality loadings, where for the girls there is a moderately high association with neurotic extroversion (.44 and .26) which is not reflected for boys. Indeed for them it is introversion (opposite of extroversion) which has a moderate loading (.22) on this factor. It would seem that refined kinesthetic ability tends to be present only in those boys who vouchsafe the gross physical activities which seem particularly suited to the extroverted individuals. The substantial loading on neuroticism for girls is difficult to explain unless kinesthetic sensitivity is increased in association with mild tendencies towards anxiety among girls. Further experimentation to test this hypothesis would be interesting and rewarding.

Factor VI. Static Balance on Objects. Static balance items on sticks have substantial loadings on this factor on each of the three groups and hence the name Static Balance on Objects is given. Apart from this pattern there emerge some intergroup differences. For boys, but not for girls, there are additional moderate loadings for two coordination items. . . . Moreover, whereas this factor is associated with the personality dimension of stability (.43) and to a lesser degree with extroversion among boys, the girls' matrix shows the personality loadings to be in exactly the opposite direction; i.e. towards neurotic introversion. This finding represents a clear-cut sex difference with respect to the personality traits going with static balance and deserves further investigation.

Factor VII. Static Balance on the Floor. For the three groups, loadings ranging from .46 to .77 are shown on the two floor balance items with loadings on floor balance eyes closed being consistently high. The factor is consequently named Static Balance on the Floor. The girls' group shows a loading of .51 on standing on stick eyes closed which may indicate the general facility of girls compared with boys in balance tests, especially when the eyes are closed. There is some previous research support for this suggestion.[6,10,11,22]

The personality loadings indicate a general understandable tendency for emotional stability to go with physical stability. There is also a clear indication among boys for extroversion to be associated with this factor of motor control, as it was seen to be associated with Factors III and IV.

Factor VIII. Age (For the Girls and Total Group) and General Motor Performance (For Boys). In this factor, the structure for girls and the total group are similar but the boys' factor loadings are somewhat different. Coordination loadings of a low to moderate type are common to all three groups but while the other significant loadings for boys are spread over a wide range of physical aptitude, the other two groups highlight age. In these circumstances, it seems important to distinguish between what may well be two different factor structures. Consequently, the factor is named General Motor Performance for the boys' group and Age for the other two groups.

Conclusion

The findings of this study allow reasonable conclusions to be drawn concerning the relationship between measures of intellectual ability and chosen measures of nonintellectual aptitude. In particular, the evidence points to a positive relationship between some motor aptitude items, especially coordination and balance, and well established measures of intelligence and scholastic ability. This conclusion, based on the testing of British children, is similar in pattern to the one arrived at by Ismail and others with American children in an earlier study in the same research program. It serves, therefore, as a cross-cultural validation of the earlier American results. The present study, however, in including personality measures to the variables, has added a dimension which will need further study in order to understand more clearly the way in which personality is associated with the interaction of motor and intellectual performance. Neuroticism and extroversion were found to load substantially on four of the extracted factors but the extent and direction of the associations varied with the factor and the sex of the children.

References

1. Asmussen, E., and Heiball, N. K. Physical performance and growth in children—influence of sex, age, intelligence. *J. appl. physiol. 88*:371-80, January 1956.
2. Barry, Alan J. *A factorial study of motivation, physical fitness, and academic achievement in college freshmen.* Unpublished material, University of Illinois, 1961.
3. Brown, R., and Henderson, E. *The use of a developmental index to predict pupil achievement.* Unpublished paper, New York University, 1963.
4. Delacato, Carl H. *The Diagnosis and Treatment of Speech and Reading Problems.* Springfield, Ill.: Charles C Thomas, 1963.
5. Doman, Glenn. Lecture given at the Institute for the Achievement of Human Potential on January 10, 1966.
6. Furneaux, W. D., and Gibson, H. B. A children's personality inventory designed to measure neuroticism and extroversion. *Brit. j. educ. psychol. 31*: 204-07, June 1961.
7. Ismail, A. H., and Cowell, C. C. Factor analysis of motor aptitude of preadolescent boys. *Res. quart. 32*:507-13, December 1961.
8. Ismail, A. H., and Gruber, J. J. Predictive power of coordination and balance items in estimating intellectual achievement. *Proceedings of First International Congress of Psychology of Sports.* Rome, April 1965.
9. Ismail, A. H., and Gruber, J. J. Utilization of motor aptitude tests in predicting academic achievement. *Proceedings of First International Congress on Psychology of Sports.* Rome, April 1965.
10. Ismail, A. H. and Gruber, J. J. *Motor Aptitude and Intellectual Performance.* Columbus, Ohio: Charles E. Merrill Books, 1967.
11. Ismail, A. H., Kephart, N., and Cowell, C. C. *Utilization of motor aptitude test batteries in predicting academic achievement.* Technical Report No. 11, Purdue University, Research Foundation, August 1963.
12. Jenny, John H. The m. q. is as important as i. q. *J. hlth. phys. educ. recreat.* 30:23, April 1959.
13. Kaiser, H. F. The varimax criterion for analytic rotation in factor analyses. *Psychometrika. 23*:187-200, September 1958.
14. Kane, J. E. *Physique and physical abilities of 14-year-old boys, in relation to their personality and social adjustment.* Master's thesis, University of Manchester, England, 1962.
15. Kephart, Newell C. *The Slow Learner in the Classroom.* Columbus, Ohio: Charles E. Merrill Books, 1960.
16. ————, The needs of teachers for specialized information on perception. In William M. Cronickshank (Ed.), *The Teacher of Brain-injured Children.* Syracuse, N. Y.: Syracuse University Press, 1966.
17. Klausmeier, H. J. Physical, behavioral, and other characteristics of high and low achieving children in favored environments. *J. educ. res. 51*:573-82, 1958.
18. ————, Breeman, A., and Lehmann, I. J. Comparison of organismic age and regression equations in predicting achievement in elementary school. *J. educ. psychol. 49*:182-86, 1958.
19. Klausmeier, H. J., and Check, J. Relationships among physical, mental achievement, and personality measures in low, average, and high intelligence at 113 months of age. *Amer. j. ment. defic. 63*:1059-68, 1959.
20. Olson, W. C. *Child Development.* Boston: D. C. Health, 1959.
21. Sloan, W. Motor proficiency and intelligence. *Amer. j. ment. defic. 55*:394-406, 1951.
22. Travis, R. C. An experimental analysis of dynamic and static equilibrium. *J. exp. psychol. 35*:216-34, 1945.
23. Weber, R. J. Relationships of physical fitness to success in college and personality. *Res. quart. 24*:471-74, 1953.

*Athletes Are Not Inferior Students**

WALTER E. SCHAFER and J. MICHAEL ARMER

MUCH research has dispelled the myth of athlete and non-athlete differences in I.Q. and academic achievement; notably the inferiority of the athlete. It is usually found that they score similarly within a given school population. The next article strongly suggests that, in fact, athletes do better scholastically than non-athletes. Exactly why this is the case is difficult to determine, although Schafer and Armer present a list of possible explanations. The study, of course, does not directly indicate that academic and athletic abilities go hand-in-hand. It is highly probable that the athletes had greater motivation, encouragement, and assistance to reach loftier academic goals than the non-athletes. Certainly though, there is no reason to believe that excellence as displayed by the development of skills and abilities in one field of endeavor, e.g., athletics, is related to deficiency in another area, e.g., scholastics.

Does the heavy emphasis on sports evident in most of our high schools interfere with what is supposed to be the central purpose of all high schools—education? Does sports downgrade the value that students put on intellectual effort? Does it reduce the learning of the athletes themselves?

Fewer than one out of four high-school boys play in interscholastic sports. But if we consider the immense amount of time and money spent on stadiums and gymnasiums, on teams and on their equipment and training, and on pep rallies, marching bands, and cheerleading, it is easy to believe that athletics must seriously interfere with schooling. As James S. Coleman has observed, a stranger in an American high school could easily conclude that "more attention is paid to athletics by teenagers, both as athletes and as spectators, than to scholastic matters." To many observers, it has become a self-evident article of faith that athletics is overemphasized in our high schools, and that the effect of athletics is, overall, bad.

One of the difficulties with this belief, however, is that it is based on very little research. And studies that my colleagues and I have conducted strongly indicate that this belief is, in most respects, probably untrue. Not only does participation in sports generally seem to have little or no effect on a student's scholarship, but it seems to actually *help* certain students academically—especially those students from the poor and disadvantaged groups that usually have the most trouble in school.

The arguments of the critics run something like this:

Whatever athletics may contribute to a player's character development, sportsmanship, physical fitness, or to the pride and fame of the town, there are at least five different ways in which it interferes with the central academic objectives of a school:

* From *Trans-Action*, 1968, *6*, 21-26, 61-62. Abridged and reprinted with permission of the authors and publisher. Copyright © June, 1968 by *TRANS-action*, Inc., New Brunswick, New Jersey.

An excessive amount of resources, personnel, and facilities of the high school is diverted from more fruitful activities.

Although sports may get many parents and other adults apparently interested in school affairs, this interest is not in education itself but in a marginal activity—and therefore it may actually distract from any real educational involvement on their part.

Pep rallies, trips, attending games, floats, displays, and all the other paraphernalia combine to draw students away from their studies.

Many potentially good students become discouraged about trying for academic excellence because the big rewards of popularity and status go to athletes and cheerleaders. Rather than being rewarded, the serious student may actually be ridiculed as a "square" and a "grind."

Sports demands so much time, energy, and concentration from the athletes—and gives them so much prestige compared to their studies—that their school work must inevitably suffer. . . .

If these assumptions are stated as hypotheses, they can be put to an experimental test. For if these assumptions are true,

1. Athletes should not perform as well scholastically as nonathletes.

2. The greater the student's participation in sports, the greater the detriment to his studies.

3. A student's participation in those sports that are given the greatest recognition and attention—generally, football and basketball—should harm his academic performance more than the minor sports that do not require so much time, or give as great social rewards.

Data have now been gathered from one medium-sized and one large senior high school to test each of these hypotheses. During the summer of 1964, we examined the complete high-school records of 585 boys. These boys had been tenth-graders in 1961, attending two Midwestern senior high schools. By 1964, most had already graduated from high school.

One of the three-year high schools had an enrollment of 2565 in the fall of 1963, and was situated in a predominantly middle-class university community of about 70,000 people. The other school had an enrollment of 1272, and was situated in a nearby, predominantly working-class industrial community of about 20,000 people. For this study, the boys from both schools were treated as a single sample.

Of the 585 boys, we classified 164 (28 percent) as athletes. During the three years of high school, these boys had completed at least one full season in some interscholastic sport (varsity or junior varsity). Thirty percent of these athletes had completed one sports season during the three years; 34 percent had completed two or three seasons; 21 percent, four or five seasons; and 15 percent six to nine seasons. (Any boy could complete three seasons a year—for example, football, basketball, and track.)

What we did was to compare the grade-point averages and dropout rates of athletes with those of nonathletes. At first, no account was taken of possible differences between athletes and nonathletes in motivation, or ability, to get good grades or to stay in school. These factors were then taken into account by matching each athlete with a nonathlete on intelligence-test scores, occupations of fathers, curriculums, and G.P.A.s for the final semester of junior high school. Several studies of the grades and dropout rates of athletes had been made before, but this is the first one to reduce the effects of other influences, or to measure the relationships by the students' social background and amount and form of their participation in athletics.

In Table 1 we have compared the grade-point averages (A=4=excellent, B=3=good, C=2=fair, D=1=passing, F=0=failure) of 585 boys in the two high schools, contrasting the athletes and nonathletes. Clearly, *the athletes obtained better grades*. The athletes, on the average, got over C, the nonathletes got less than C. There may, of course, be many reasons for this finding apart from the students' participation in sports. Athletes could start high school with a greater potential or motivation, and get higher grades not because of but *despite* athletics, and so on. But even when we control for these initial differences, by matching athletes with nonathletes, we still find the athletes getting slightly higher grades (See Table 2).

Variation by Amount of Participation. What about the effects of *amount* of participation in sports? Dividing the athletes into those who completed one or two seasons on the one hand, and those who completed three or more on the other, again we found that the results did not support the hypothesis. *The more the athletes participated in sports, the greater the positive gap between their grades and those of their matched nonathletes* (See Table 3). The difference between the grades of the less-active athletes and their matches was .03. Between more-active athletes and their matches, the difference was .18—six times as much.

Viewed another way, 51.5 percent of the less-active athletes exceeded their matches, compared with 60.4 percent of the more-active athletes. Again, rather than eroding academic performance, extensive participation in interscholastic sports seems to slightly increase a student's scholastic success.

Variation by Type of Sport. According to the prediction, playing football or basketball would hurt a student's grades more than playing in minor sports such as track, swimming, wrestling, and gymnastics, in which the rewards, effort, and competition might be less. Table 4 clearly shows that, while par-

TABLE 1

Mean Grade-Point Average for Athletes and All Boys in Their Class

	Mean G.P.A.*	Number
Athletes**	2.35	164
All Other Boys	1.83	421

* Grade-point averages are based on the following scale: A=4, B=3, C=2, D=1, F=0. Each student's G.P.A. is based on his final marks in all major courses during the six semesters of his three-year high school. (Physical education is not included as a major course.) G.P.A.s may be based on anywhere from one to six semesters, depending on how long the student remained in school.

** Boys who completed at least one full season as a member of an interscholastic athletic team are classified as athletes.

TABLE 2

Mean G.P.A. of Athletes and Matched Nonathletes & Percentage of Athletes Who Exceed Their Matches in G.P.A.

	Mean G.P.A.	Percent of Athletes Higher Than Match	Number
Athletes	2.35		152
		56.6	
Matched Nonathletes	2.24		152

TABLE 3

Percentages of Athletes with Higher, Same, & Lower G.P.A.s Than Their Matches, & Mean G.P.A.s of Both Groups by Amount of Participation

Amount of Participation	With Higher G.P.A.		Percentage of Athletes With Same G.P.A.	With Lower G.P.A.		Total	Number of Pairs	Mean G.P.A.	
	.25 or more difference	.01 to .24 difference		−.01 to −.24 difference	−.25 or more difference			Athletes	Matched Nonathletes
Three or More Seasons	48.8%	11.6%	1.2%	10.5%	27.9%	100%	86	2.45	2.24
(Total)	(60.4%)		(1.2%)	(38.4%)		(100%)			
One or Two Seasons	37.9%	13.6%	3.0%	9.1%	36.4%	100%	66	2.26	2.23
(Total)	(51.5%)		(3.0%)	(35.5%)		(100%)			

TABLE 4

Mean G.P.A. for Athletes & Matched Nonathletes, & Percentage of Athletes Who Exceed Their Match in G.P.A., by Type of Sport

Type of Sport	Mean G.P.A.	Percent of Athletes Higher Than Match	Number
Major Sport*			
Athlete	2.20		83
		60.2	
Matched Nonathlete	2.02		83
Minor Sport**			
Athlete	2.53		69
		52.1	
Matched Nonathlete	2.50		69

* Major sports include football and basketball, according to our coding criteria. Participants in major sports sometimes participated in one or more minor sports also, but the reverse is never true, according to these criteria.

** Minor sports in both schools include baseball, track, cross-country, swimming, wrestling, tennis, and golf; the larger school also fields teams in gymnastics and hockey.

ticipants in the two major sports have somewhat lower average G.P.A.s than participants in minor sports, those in major sports exceed their *matches* to a greater extent than those in minor sports do. Therefore, the prediction does not hold up.

Variations Among Types of Boys. Having found no support so far for the various "interference" hypotheses, we can now legitimately ask whether the major prediction holds true among *any* of the boys. For instance, does participation in athletics have a greater positive effect on academic achievement among white-collar boys than among blue-collar boys? Among high-I.Q. boys than low-I.Q. boys? Among college-bound boys than work-bound boys? Or among high achievers than low achievers in junior high school?

The data in Table 5 reveal two clear patterns. First, the slight positive association between athletics and scholarship persists in *all* subgroups. In no case is the relationship negative. More than half the athletes in each category exceed their matches, and the average G.P.A.s of athletes is always higher than that of their matched nonathletes. Moreover, on father's occupation and curriculum, the gap is greater between athletes and their matches in the *lower* categories than in the higher. For example, greater percentages of blue-collar athletes than white-collar athletes exceed their matches in G.P.A.s (63.0 percent versus 53.7 percent). An even greater spread separates non-college-preparatory athletes from college-preparatory athletes (69.0 percent versus 53.7 percent).

In short, the boys who would usually have the most trouble in school are precisely the ones who seem to benefit most from taking part in sports.

Interpretation. These findings, of course, do not tell us whether athletics diverts a high school's resources, staff manhours, and facilities at the expense of the scholastic program; whether the support of parents is channeled away from education; whether the academic achievement of student fans suffers from their support of school teams; or whether potentially top students are discouraged from trying because social rewards go to athletes instead.

But these findings do bring into serious question the notion prevalent among

TABLE 5

Mean G.P.A. for Athletes & Matched Nonathletes, & Percentage of Athletes Who Exceed Their Match in G.P.A., by Father's Occupation, Intelligence-Test Score, Curriculum, & G.P.A. for Last Semester of Junior High School.

Characteristic	Mean G.P.A.	Percent of Athletes Higher Than Match	Number
Father's Occupation			
White Collar			
Athlete	2.53		95
		53.7	
Matched Nonathlete	2.48		95
Blue Collar			
Athlete	2.05		54
		63.0	
Matched Nonathlete	1.84		54
Intelligence-Test Scores			
Upper Half of Class			
Athlete	2.64		94
		56.4	
Matched Nonathlete	2.55		94
Lower Half of Class			
Athlete	1.88		58
		56.9	
Matched Nonathlete	1.74		58
Curriculum			
College Preparatory			
Athlete	2.47		123
		53.7	
Matched Nonathlete	2.40		123
Non-college Preparatory			
Athlete	1.85		29
		69.0	
Matched Nonathlete	1.56		29
G.P.A. for Last Semester of Junior High School			
Upper Half of Class			
Athlete	2.82		78
		57.7	
Matched Nonathlete	2.70		78
Lower Half of Class			
Athlete	1.85		74
	1.75	55.4	
Matched Nonathlete			74

many teachers, parents, and social scientists that the supposed overemphasis on athletics in the American high school results in the lowering of academic achievement among athletes. At the very least, the data cast doubt on the validity of Jules Henry's irate judgment that "athletics, popularity, and mediocre grades go together with inarticulateness and poor grammar."

If there is in fact a positive effect of participation in athletics on grades, as the data suggest, why does it occur? Here we are forced to speculate.

1. Perhaps athletes are graded more leniently because teachers see them as special or more deserving.

2. Perhaps exposure, in the sports subculture, to effort, hard work, persistence, and winning spills over into nonathletic activities such as schoolwork.

3. Perhaps the superior physical condition of athletes improves their mental performance.

4. Perhaps some athletes strive to get good grades to be eligible for certain sports.

5. Perhaps athletes make more efficient and effective use of their limited study time.

6. Perhaps the lure of a college career in sports motivates some athletes to strive for good grades.

7. Perhaps the high prestige that students obtain from sports gives them a better self-concept and higher aspirations in other activities such as schoolwork.

8. Perhaps athletes benefit from more help in schoolwork from friends, teachers, and parents.

Why does participation in athletics appear to have its greatest positive effect on the academic performance of those boys with blue-collar backgrounds and a non-college-prepartory label? A plausible interpretation of this finding is that, compared to nonathletes with the same characteristics, blue-collar and non-college-bound athletes are more likely to associate and identify with white-collar and college-bound members of the school's leading crowd. Illustrative cases are abundant of blue-collar boys who were not at all academically-oriented or college-oriented until they began to "make it" in sports, and to be increasingly influenced by white-collar boys (and girls) with whom they would not otherwise have associated or identified.

Another important type of educational achievement is graduation from high school. Does participation in interscholastic sports keep boys in school? The data presented in Table 6 strongly suggest a Yes answer. Whereas 9.2 percent of the matched nonathletes dropped out of school before graduating, less than one-fourth as many (2.0 percent) of the athletes failed to finish. (These figures do not include boys who transferred to another school.)

This finding suggests that athletics exerts a holding influence on students which might operate in four different ways. First, the high prestige that athletes are likely to receive probably makes them want to remain in school. Second, athletes who are potential dropouts are likely to associate and identify with college-oriented (or at least graduation-oriented) boys more often than are nonathletes who are potential dropouts. Third, some athletes might stay in school simply to be able to participate in high school sports—or, later, college or professional sports. Fourth, potential dropouts who are athletes are likely to get encouragement and counseling from coaches and others, while nonathletic potential dropouts are likely to get much less encouragement from anybody.

Whatever the reasons, it is clear that participation in athletics exerts a holding influence over some boys who might have otherwise dropped out. Of the nine matched nonathletes who dropped out with G.P.A.s of below 2.0, eight could be paired with athletes who ended up with equal or lower G.P.A.s

TABLE 6

Percentage of Athletes & Matched Nonathletes Who Dropped Out of School Before Graduation

	Percent	Number
Athletes	2.0	152
Matched Nonathlete	9.2	152

but did *not* drop out. This finding provides limited support for Coleman's suggestion that "if it were not for interscholastic athletics . . . the rate of dropout might be far worse. . . ."

An assertion often heard, but little studied, is that competitive sports serve as an important vehicle for upward mobility. Numerous examples can be cited, of course, of college or professional athletes' having risen above their fathers in income and status solely or primarily because of athletic achievements.

We know of no prior systematic studies in the United States, however, to determine how often this is true. Yet information about the relationship between a student's participation in interscholastic athletics and his expectations of attending college is of interest for two reasons: It provides a basis for understanding the role of athletics in upward mobility, insofar as mobility is dependent on someone's attending and graduating from college; and it provides additional data about the extent to which athletics impedes or facilitates the attainment of one of high school's educational goals: to send a maximum number of youths to college.

Pertinent data on this point have been gathered from questionnaires filled out by 785 twelfth-grade boys in three public and three Catholic high schools in three middle-sized (50,000 to 100,000) Pennsylvania cities during the spring of 1965. (See "Participation in Interscholastic Athletics and College Expectations," Richard A. Rehberg and Walter E. Schafer, *The American Journal of Sociology*, LXXIII, 1968.) Among other things, the boys were asked to name the extracurricular activities they participated in during their senior years, how far they expected to go in college, their fathers' education and occupation, and how often their parents encouraged them to go to college. The students' rank in their graduating classes was obtained from school records.

Table 7 shows that, in comparison with nonathletes, athletes are slightly more likely to expect to complete at least two years of college (82 percent versus 75 percent), and considerably more likely to expect to complete at least four years of college (62 percent versus 45 percent). And if we hold the factors of background and early ability and aspirations about equal, we still get the same results (See Table 8).

To what extent participation in athletics directly *causes* higher educational expectations is, of course, still open to question; but there is little doubt that more athletes intend to go to college than matched nonathletes. Earlier, we noted that higher scholastic achievement was especially marked among athletes who were from working-class backgrounds and who were not college bound. Are expectations of attending college, therefore, relatively more common among athletes who are less "earmarked" for college? Our findings indicate that the answer is Yes. (See Table 9.) That is, a greater percentage of athletes than nonathletes expect to complete four years of college among working-class

TABLE 7

College Expectations of Athletes & All Other Boys in Their Class

| | Percent who expect to complete. . . | | |
	at least two years of college	at least four years of college	Number
Athletes	82%	62%	284
All Other Boys	75	45	490

TABLE 8

College Expectations of Athletes & All Other Boys in Their Class—With Controls

| | Percent who expect to complete. . . | | |
	at least two years of college	at least four years of college	Number
Athletes	80%	61%	284
All Other Boys	76	45	490

Note: Social status, the amount of encouragement from parents, and the students' rank in their graduating classes have been controlled for.

TABLE 9

College Expectations of Athletes & All Other Boys in Their Class, by Social Status, Parental Education Encouragement, & Rank in Graduating Class

| | Percent who expect to complete. . . | | |
Characteristic	at least two years of college	at least four years of college	Number
Social Status			
Middle			
Athletes	91%	78%	90
All Other Boys	89	67	144
Working			
Athletes	78	55	194
All Other Boys	69	36	346
Parental Educational Encouragement			
High			
Athletes	90	68	208
All Other Boys	88	56	298
Low			
Athletes	58	45	66
All Other Boys	55	26	164
Rank in Graduating Class			
High			
Athletes	94	85	116
All Other Boys	89	78	205
Low			
Athletes	74	46	164
All Other Boys	66	21	280

rather than middle-class boys; among boys with less, rather than more, parental encouragement; and among boys in the lower rather than the upper half of their graduating classes.

It would seem, then, that interscholastic athletics serves a democratizing or equalizing function. It represents a vehicle for upward mobility, especially of those otherwise not likely to complete college. And the data suggest that, at least as far as participants are concerned, athletics fosters rather than interferes with the educational goal of sending a maximum number of youth to college.

The question arises whether all of these findings apply to Negro boys. We know that sports is an important channel to success for many Negroes, but we do not know *how* important, or to what extent it varies in time and place. Nor do we know how often Negro boys put all their hopes into becoming a Willie Mays, Wilt Chamberlain, or Bob Hayes in college or professional sports, but fail, and end up disillusioned and unprepared for more conventional routes of mobility.

In this article, we could not deal with the results of a student's relative *success* in sports. Obviously, athletics will effect the star and the substitute differently. Success means greater prestige; and this *might* mean higher self-regard, higher aspirations, and higher academic performance. On the other hand, it might mean more praise and distraction than most teenage boys can handle and still do good school work.

It is a frequent claim of coaches, playground directors, and Little League promoters that athletics deters students from deviance within the school and delinquency in the community. Over 30 years ago, Willard Waller noted that many teachers deliberately supported interscholastic sports because they felt that it

> makes students more teachable because it drains off their surplus energies and leaves them less inclined to get into mischief. . . . Part of the technique, indeed, of those who handle difficult cases consists in getting those persons interested in . . . athletics.

But we don't really know. Again, it seems that nobody has systematically investigated the problem.

A striking feature of varsity sports—college and high school—is the great authority of the coach in controlling the athletes' off-the-field behavior. The coach usually has the unquestioned authority to suspend or drop a boy from the team if he is caught smoking, drinking, staying out too late, or violating a law. Some coaches even decide the hair styles, dress, friendship patterns, and the language of their boys. A few "training rules," of course, are laid down for the sake of the athletes' physical conditioning and efficiency, but others can be understood only as part of the "moralism" associated with sports. The high-school athlete is supposed to be a "good American boy." A fascinating question for research, therefore, is: What are the long-term effects on the athlete from this rigid and often puritanical control by coaches? A related question: Does high-school sports really contribute to the "character development" that coaches so often claim?

Finally, what of the lifetime and career effects of a student's participation in athletics, after he has left high school and even college? Of course, many examples can be cited of individuals who have been successful through sports—either by staying in as players or coaches, or through the education or contacts that sports has made possible. But what of the others? And what are the direct and indirect factors and mechanisms involved?

These are all matters that call for careful and rigorous research. Clearly, interscholastic athletics is far more important in the American educational process—for good or ill—than most social scientists seem to want to recognize. And the extent of that importance cannot be determined by the unsupported rhetoric of those who have personal reasons to applaud, or denounce, high-school athletics.

Chapter 5

PREDICTIVE ABILITIES IN MOTOR LEARNING

The Relationship Between Measures of Motor Educability and the Learning of Specific Motor Skills*

EUGENIA GIRE and ANNA ESPENSCHADE

IN the 1930's and 1940's, a fairly concentrated effort was displayed by physical educators to develop tests that might predict the ease with which a person might learn a new skill, and, in a sense, his motor aptitude. What appeared then to be a fertile area for research has since been recognized as a relatively fruitless venture. There is simply no acceptable means of measuring a person's general motor ability, motor capacity, or motor educability. Verbal IQ tests have been more successful in predicting achievement in a number of academic areas than motor "IQ" tests have been with regard to a variety of athletic skills. The following article is one of the earlier ones to point out the limitations of motor tests designed to measure this ability.

The term *motor educability* was introduced into the literature of physical education by McCloy in 1934 and was defined as "the ability to develop high skill quickly."[23] Since that time there have been published a number of studies in the measurement of motor educability and the relationship of this quality or factor to other motor factors and to performance. The progress of this research has been viewed with interest by many in our profession; the concept of motor educability is a valuable one. A test of motor educability which would analyze accurately the ability to learn, or the aptitude of the individual for learning, would contribute to a better understanding of physical perfor-

* From *The Research Quarterly*, 1942, *13*, 43-56.   Reprinted with permission of the authors and the American Association for Health, Physical Education, and Recreation.

mance and would provide an effective tool for the administration of the physical education program.

It seems certain that the term *motor educability* has been interpreted somewhat differently in the various studies which have been published. Although all definitions imply a close relationship between motor educability and learning, only one study has utilized a learning criterion in an effort to validate an "educability" test. The relative value of the various tests as measures of "motor educability" has not been experimentally determined. Studies have been confined in general to the isolation and definition of the factor of motor educability through empirical or statistical means, to comparisons between two types of tests of motor educability, and to the relation of these tests to achievement, not to the ability to learn.

It was with the belief that a better understanding of the concept of motor educability could be obtained that the present study was undertaken. The purpose of this study was to determine the relationship between the Brace, the Iowa Revision of the Brace, and the Johnson tests, which have been designated as measures of "motor educability,"[25, p.20] and the achievement and learning by high school girls of specific motor skills in the three activities of basketball, volleyball, and baseball.

One hundred ninety-five girls in a four-year senior high school in California served as subjects for this study. These girls were the students of the junior author. All girls who were physically able to participate in the regular physical education program of the school were included in the study. The girls ranged in age from thirteen through eighteen years and in experience from no participation in some of the physical activities to twelve years (seasons) of experience in one or more activities. All girls reported some previous experience in at least one of the sports tested.

An intensive program of measurement was included as a part of the regular girls' physical education program during the spring semester of 1939. The tests selected for the experiment were representative of the activities taught in class, sampled all possible techniques, and were given as an integral part of the regular program. The physical education course for the semester of testing was of the "block" or seasonal type in which one activity was scheduled daily for a number of weeks. During the weeks of teaching basketball, volleyball, and baseball, the program was organized so that each girl participated in the game for two-thirds of the class period and took tests during the remaining one-third of the time.

"Motor educability" was measured by the three designated tests of this factor: the Brace Scale of Motor Ability Tests,[4] the Iowa Revision of the Brace Test (for Senior High School Girls),[22] and the Johnson Physical Skill Tests for Sectioning Classes into Homogeneous Groups.[19] The Brace and Iowa-Brace tests were administered outside of school hours; the Johnson test was given in the regular class period. In all tests, each subject performed individually and was scored by the administrator. Scoring of the test items in this study was strict; good form in performance was demanded for success in the events of the Brace and Iowa-Brace tests, and precise performance of the exercises of the Johnson test was required.

The reliability of the Brace test was .7421 $\pm$ .0230, the reliability of the Iowa-Brace .611 $\pm$ .0320, and the Johnson .6111 $\pm$ .0320. Since these tests do not have parallel forms and could not well be repeated, these reliability coefficients were obtained by correlating the comparable halves of the Brace and Iowa-Brace tests (as equated by Brace and McCloy) and estimating the reliability of the whole test by means of the Spearman-Brown formula. The "split-half technique" was used in the Johnson half-test reliability.

TABLE 1

Interrelationships of "Motor Educability" Tests*
(Number = 162)

	Brace	Iowa-Brace	Johnson
Brace		.7664 ± .0217	.2018 ± .0512
Iowa-Brace	1.0000 ± .0000		.4817 ± .0410
Johnson	.3019 ± .0485	.7897 ± .0196	

* Lower half of table presents coefficients corrected for attenuation.

Scores in the three "educability" tests were complete for 162 cases. To determine their interrelationships, each test was correlated with each of the other two tests. The results are shown in Table 1.

It may be seen that there is a fairly high relationship between the Brace and Iowa-Brace tests, substantial relationship between the Iowa-Brace and Johnson tests, but only a very slight relationship between the Brace and Johnson tests. Evidently these three tests of "motor educability" are not measures of the same ability to the same degree.

When the coefficients of correlation were correlated for attenuation, it became apparent that the Brace and Iowa-Brace tests are measures of the same ability and might be expected to correlate perfectly with each other if errors of measurement could be eliminated. The Johnson test, on the other hand, seems to sample somewhat different functions.

Achievement and learning of basketball, volleyball, and baseball skills were measured by frequently repeated achievement tests. The techniques which should be sampled by the achievement tests were determined by analyses of the games. Eight basketball tests were administered from three to seven times each over an eight-week period. Two volleyball tests were administered five times each over a three-week period. Five baseball tests were administered from three to six times each over a five-week period. The first series of tests in each sport was completed before any of the subjects received instruction or practice in the game.

Since specific instructions and practice in all activities were given between repetitions of tests, the correlations between first and second trials are not, strictly speaking, reliability coefficients. . . . In order to increase the reliability of the measurement and so obtain as stable criteria as possible, all achievement test scores for one sport were combined. Raw scores were converted into T-scores and these scores were added. The total scores which were obtained before the subjects were given instruction and practice in the game were named "Total Basketball I," "Total Volleyball I," and "Total Baseball I." The scores from the final testing in each sport were labeled "Total Basketball IV," "Total Volleyball V," and "Total Baseball V." The intervening series of tests were similarly distinguished. These scores represent the achievement of the subjects at specific intervals.

In analyzing the problem, there appeared to be three different measures of learning which might be used to study the "educability" of the subjects. The initial learning or change which takes place at the beginning of the season may be attributed in part to neuromuscular adjustment to the activity and in part to a more thorough understanding of the procedure and mechanics of the test situation. In any case the difference between the first and second total test scores may be taken as a measure of quick adjustment. After the subject has become familiar with the nature of the activity, the learning brought about as a result of continued practice may be considered primarily motor. The difference between the second and last test scores has been used, then, as the criterion of motor learning. A combination of these two measures or the change from the first to the last test series includes the total learning for the season. Thus three learning scores were computed for each subject in each of the three sports.

To find the relationships of the measures of "motor educability" to the learning of the subjects in this study, the Brace, Iowa-Brace, and Johnson tests were correlated with these difference scores. In addition, correlations between the three tests of "motor educability" and the first and last test series of each sport were computed to determine the relationships between "motor educability" and the skill status or achievement of the subjects at the beginning and end of each sport season. These results are presented in Tables 2, 3, and 4.

TABLE 2

Relationships Between Measures of "Motor Educability" and Achievement and Learning in Basketball.

	Brace	Iowa-Brace	Johnson
Total I	.3617 ± .1072	.3117 ± .1113	.2709 ± .1142
Total IV	.6565 ± .0695	.5371 ± .0872	.3061 ± .1113
Diff: II-I	.5045 ± .0924	.2456 ± .1155	.0724 ± .1226
Diff: IV-II	−.1990 ± .1187	−.2913 ± .1128	−.2015 ± .1182
Diff: IV-I	.2934 ± .1128	.1219 ± .1214	.0456 ± .1228

TABLE 3

Relationships Between Measures of "Motor Educability" and Achievement and Learning in Volleyball.

	Brace	Iowa-Brace	Johnson
Total I	.2209 ± .0677	.3004 ± .0647	.1916 ± .0686
Total V	.2395 ± .0670	.2949 ± .0647	.2260 ± .0674
Diff: II-I	.1218 ± .0701	−.0323 ± 0711	.0441 ± .0710
Diff: V-II	−.0475 ± .0709	−.0355 ± 0710	−.0236 ± .0711
Diff: V-I	.0039 ± .0711	−.0305 ± .0711	.0426 ± .1710

TABLE 4

Relationships Between Measures of "Motor Educability" and Achievement and Learning in Baseball.

	Brace	Iowa-Brace	Johnson
Total I	.3923 ± .0738	.3392 ± .0770	.4046 ± .0724
Total V	.3809 ± .0745	.2834 ± .0802	.2689 ± .0807
Diff: II-I	.1120 ± .0860	.1311 ± .0856	−.1913 ± .0840
Diff: V-II	.0451 ± .0869	−.0269 ± .0870	.1724 ± .0846
Diff: V-I	.1463 ± .0851	.1054 ± .0860	−.0274 ± .0870

Of the correlations computed for the basketball study (Table 2) only three were wholly significant, i.e., four times their probable errors. The Brace test shows a fair relationship to the criterion of initial learning (Total Basketball II-I) and so may be said to indicate to some degree the ability of the subjects to develop skill quickly. Both the Brace and Iowa-Brace tests are correlated somewhat with final achievement (Total Basketball IV). The Johnson test shows no significant relationship with any measure studied.

All correlations of the "motor educability" tests with the volleyball data are low (Table 3). Only two are four times their probable errors; these are the correlations between the Iowa-Brace test and Total Volleyball I and the Iowa-Brace test and Total Volleyball V. Thus, the Iowa-Brace shows a slight tendency to correlate with the skill level of the subjects both at the beginning and end of the teaching period. Although the correlation between the Brace test and initial learning (difference, II-I) is very low and of doubtful significance, it should be noted that this relationship is the largest of any between a learning criterion and an "educability" test.

In general, the baseball correlations (Table 4) are higher than the volleyball correlations but are more similar to the latter than to those of basketball. The three tests of "motor educability" correlate low but significantly with Total Baseball I, and the relationship of the Brace test to Total Baseball V is similarly significant. All three tests tend to correlate slightly with the skill level of the subjects at the beginning and end of the baseball season, but no one test shows a significant relationship to any criterion of learning. The Brace test is more stable in its relationships to all items studied, both to the learning and to achievement, than are the Iowa-Brace and Johnson tests.

The degree of relationship of the three tests of "motor educability" to the learning and achievement criteria seems to be proportionate in a rough way to the number of weeks of participation, and, in addition, to the number of achievement tests used. In basketball, with eight weeks of participation and eight different achievement tests, the highest correlations were found. In baseball, with five weeks of participation and five achievement tests, the order of correlation was somewhat lower, and in volleyball, which covered a period of three weeks and in which two different achievement tests were used, the lowest order of correlation was noted. This finding suggests that the degree of relationship is a function of both length of the practice period and reliability of the criteria.

In summary, the Iowa-Brace test was found to be most consistent throughout in relationship to the skill level of the subjects at the beginning of each season. The Brace test tends to be most closely related to final achievement. In the relationships to initial learning differences (between the first and second series of tests), the Brace test is highest in basketball and volleyball but is equaled by the Iowa-Brace in baseball. All correlations are very low and in most instances not significant. Negative relationships are the rule in the correlations of all "educability" tests with the criterion of "motor" learning (IV-II or V-II). These negative relationships indicate that those individuals who are the best early in the season make the least progress, i.e., achieve less. This may be attributed to the fact that these individuals have more nearly reached their limit of development and so have less possibility for improvement. The Brace test shows the highest relationships with total learning (IV-I or V-I) in basketball and baseball. The order of the correlations is small and especially in volleyball is too low to be of significance.

From this analysis of the results of the correlations of the three tests of "motor educability" with the criteria of achievement and of learning, the conclusion may be drawn that the highest relationships are shown by the Brace test, the second highest by the Iowa-Brace test, and the lowest by the Johnson test. However, the degree of relationship in all cases is too low to obtain reliable prediction of any one criterion.

Motor educability has been defined frequently as the ability to learn *new* skills easily. Since many of the subjects in this study reported previous experience in the game skills tested, the number of inexperienced subjects was not sufficient for reliable statistical study. The mean scores of these latter subjects were compared with the means of the whole group and with those of the most experienced subjects in order to examine the effect of experience on achievement and learning.

In the basketball comparison, the inexperienced group was slightly below the group average and markedly below the experienced group in scores on the Brace, Iowa-Brace, and Johnson tests and in the mean scores of Total Basketball I and IV. However, the inexperienced group showed the greatest improvement in learning as measured by the differences between I and II, II and IV, and I and IV. The mean score of the inexperienced group, after this one season of participation, was above the mean score of the experienced group at the beginning of the season and was almost equal to the mean of the whole group at the end of the season.

In volleyball, the "educability" test scores of the inexperienced group were inferior to those of the experienced group but approximately equal to those of the total group. The experienced group here, as in basketball, was superior in achievement but showed less gain than the inexperienced group.

In baseball, the inexperienced group was inferior to both experienced and total groups in all "educability" measures and in achievement scores. The inexperienced group was slightly superior to the total group in all measures of learning, but only in the percentage of improvement between II and V did the former exceed the experienced group.

In order to study further the relationships between the tests of "motor educability" and achievement and learning in new skills, rank order coefficients of correlation between "educability" scores of the inexperienced groups and learning and final achievement in the three sports were computed. The samples were so small that the findings must be interpreted with caution.

The order of relationships with all measures was similar for both the Brace and Iowa-Brace tests. Apparently these tests measure to a small degree the "ability to learn new skills quickly" but are inversely related to "motor" learning. The most consistent relationship shown was that of the Brace and Iowa-Brace with final scores in all sports. Both measures may be said to indicate roughly the level of ability attained over a period of time.

The correlations of the Johnson test with all measures of achievement and learning were negative in basketball, low and in general positive in baseball, and positive and somewhat higher in volleyball. This trend suggested a negative relationship between the Johnson score and length of season, number of achievement tests, and time interval between test series. However, this negative relationship was not sufficiently marked to be of practical value.

Comparisons were made between groups scoring more than one standard deviation above and below the mean in the Brace, Iowa-Brace, and Johnson tests to show the differences in learning and achievement of the two extreme groups. It was found that in the extremes of the range, all three measures of "educability" were adequate to differentiate groups according to initial and final ability. The mean difference between the high and low scoring groups was most substantial in the Brace comparisons, somewhat less so in the Iowa-Brace, and smallest in the Johnson. According to the Iowa-Brace and Johnson test selections, the low scoring groups in the last test series reached or exceeded the skill level which the high scoring group had attained at the beginning of the seasons; the Brace high scoring group, on the other hand, displayed a level of skill at the beginning of each season which was not reached or approximated by the low scoring group in the last test series, and the difference between the two groups increased substantially during the entire period.

The high scoring group selected by the Brace test was superior in all sports to the low scoring group in initial learning (II-I). For this same period of learning the Iowa-Brace high group exceeded the low group in increase in mean scores in all activities. The relation between high and low Johnson groups was not consistent throughout.

The results were less clear cut for the period of "motor" learning (II to end) and for the total learning. The low group, according to all three tests, tended to exceed the high group in the amount of change from the second to the last test series, but this was not invariably true.

It would appear, then, that even in the extremes of the range only the Brace test can distinguish accurately the ability to make quick adjustments (II-I), and that no measure studied will invariably distinguish those who learn most from those who learn least over a period of time.

Thus, it may be concluded that no test of "motor educability" studied measured accurately the ease with which the subjects in this study learned new skills or relearned old ones in basketball, volleyball, and baseball in regular physical education classes. In general, the Brace test showed the highest relationships to the criteria of learning utilized to study the "educability" of the subjects. Of the three "educability" tests, the Brace measured most accurately, and the Iowa-Brace to some degree, the ability of the subjects to attain a relatively high level of skill over the period of participation in the activities studied.

Bibliography

1. Basset, Gladys, Ruth Glassow, and Mabel Locke. "Studies in Testing Volleyball Skills," *Res. Quart.* 8: (Dec. 1937) 60-73.
2. Bovard, John F., and Frederick W. Cozens, *Tests and Measurements in Physical Education* (New York: A. S. Barnes and Company, Revised 1938).
3. Brace, David K., "The Development of Measures of Pupil Achievement in Physical Education," *Res. Quart.*, 2:3 (Oct. 1931) 32-37.
4. Brace, David K., *Measuring Ability* (New York: A. S. Barnes and Company, 1927).
5. Carpemer, Aileen, "The Measurement of Motor Ability and Motor Educability for First-, Second-, and Third-Grade Children," report presented before Convention of American Association for Health, Physical Education, and Recreation, April, 1939.
6. Cozens, Frederick W., and Hazel J. Cubberley, "Achievement Scales in Physical Education for College Women," *Res. Quart.*, 6:1 (March 1935) 14-24.
7. Cozens, Frederick W., Hazel J. Cubberley, and N. P. Neilson, *Achievement Scales in Physical Education Activities for Secondary School Girls and College Women* (New York: A. S. Barnes and Company, 1937).
8. Cubberley, Hazel J., and Frederick W. Cozens, "The Measurement of Achievement in Basketball," *Spalding's 17R* (New York: American Sports Publishing Company, 1935-36).

9. Cubberley, Hazel J., "Achievement Scales in Athletics for Secondary School Girls and College Women," *Res. Quart.,* 6:3 (Oct. 1935) 113-19.
10. Dimock, Hedley, "A Research in Adolescence: I, Pubescence and Physical Growth," *Child Development,* 6 (Sept. 1935) 176-95.
11. Edgren, H. D., "An Experiment in the Testing of the Ability and Progress in Basketball," *Res. Quart.,* 3:1 (Mar. 1932) 159-71.
12. Espenschade, Anna, *Motor Performance in Adolescence* (Washington, D.C.: Society for Research in Child Development, National Research Council, 1940).
13. French, Esther L., and Bernice I. Cooper, "Achievement Tests in Volleyball for High School Girls," *Res. Quart.,* 8:2 (May 1937) 150-7.
14. Garrett, Henry E., *Statistics in Psychology and Education* (New York: Longmans, Green and Company, Revised 1937).
15. Glassow, Ruth B., and Marion R. Broer, *Measuring Achievement in Physical Education* (Philadelphia: W. B. Saunders Company, 1938).
16. Glassow, Ruth B., Valarie Colvin, and Marguerite M. Schwarz, "Studies in Measuring Basketball Playing Ability of College Women," *Res. Quart.,* 9:4 (Dec. 1938) 60-8.
17. Holzinger, Karl J., *Statistical Tables for Students of Education and Psychology* (Chicago: The University of Chicago Press, 1925).
18. Hoskins, Robert N., "The Relationship of Measurements of General Motor Capacity to the Learning of Specific Psycho-Motor Skills," *Res. Quart.,* 5:1 (March 1934) 63-72.
19. Johnson, Granville, B. "Physical Skill Test for Sectioning Classes into Homogeneous Units," *Res. Quart.,* 3:1 (March 1932) 128-36.
20. Keeler, Lindsey D., "The Effect of Maturation on Physical Skill as Measured by the Johnson Physical Skill Test," *Res. Quart.,* 9:3 (Oct. 1938) 54-8.
21. Kistler, J. W., "The Establishment of Bases for Classification of Junior and Senior High School Boys into Homogeneous Groups for Physical Education," *Res. Quart.,* 8:4 (Dec. 1937) 11-18.
22. McCloy, C. H., "An Analytical Study of the Stunt Type Test as a Measure of Motor Educability," *Res. Quart.,* 8:3 (Oct. 1937) 46-56.
23. ———— "The Measurement of General Motor Capacity and General Motor Ability," *Res. Quart. Supp.,* 5:1 (March 1934) 46-61.
24. ———— "A Preliminary Study of Factors in Motor Educability," *Res. Quart.,* 11:2 (May 1940) 28-39.
25. ———— "A Program of Tests and Measurements for the Public Schools," *Journal of Health and Physical Education,* 6:8 (Oct. 1935) 18.
26. McCloy, C. H., *Tests and Measurements in Physical Education* (New York: F. S. Crofts and Company, 1939).
27. Metheny, Eleanor, "Studies of the Johnson Test as a Test of Motor Educability," *Res. Quart.,* 9:4 (Dec. 1938) 105-14.
28. Moser, Helen A., "The Use of Basketball Skill Tests for Girls and Women," *Journal of Health and Physical Education,* 6:3 (Mar. 1935) 53.
29. Neilson, N. P., and Frederick W. Cozens, *Achievement Scales in Physical Education Activities for Boys and Girls in Elementary and Junior High Schools* (Sacramento: California State Department of Education, 1934).
30. Rodgers, E. G., and M. L. Heath, "An Experiment in the Use of Knowledge and Skill Tests in Playground Baseball," *Res. Quart.,* 2:4 (Dec. 1931) 113-31.
31. Schwartz, Helen, "Knowledge and Achievement Tests in Girls' Basketball on the Senior High School Level," *Res. Quart.,* 8:1 (March 1937) 143-56.
32. Wellman, Elizabeth, "The Validity of Various Tests as Measures of Motor Ability," *Res. Quart. Supp.,* 6:1 (March 1935) 18-25.
33. Wendler, Arthur J.. "A Critical Analysis of Test Elements Used in Physical Education." *Res. Quart.,* 9:1 (March 1938) 64-76.
34. Wettstone, Eugene, "Tests for Predicting Potential Ability in Gymnastics and Tumbling," *Res. Quart.,* 9:4 (Dec. 1938) 115-25.
35. Young, Genevieve, and Helen Moser, "A Short Battery of Tests to Measure Playing Ability in Women's Basketball," *Res. Quart.,* 5:2 (May 1934) 3-23.

The Relationship Between Certain Measures of Ability and the Acquisition of a Psychomotor Criterion Response*

JACK A. ADAMS

THERE is concern about the ability to predict end performance from various measures, ranging from intra-task scores, e.g., pre-test, to performance in other initial tests. The relationship of the beginning to the final performance in a simple skill is reported by Adams. Although relative performance status remains the same for many of the subjects, it is important to realize that the task is a relatively simple one, involving very few abilities. It might be expected that with complex tasks, which require the interaction of more abilities, final performance and initial performance measures need not be highly related, especially if ample practice time is allowed. In the second experiment described by Adams, other possible predictive tests, which presumably tap assorted abilities, are related to final proficiency as well as to various practice stages. This work and those by Fleishman reveal the nature of the changing patterns of abilities which have primary importance at different stages of practice.

Introduction

When individual differences in the acquisition of a psychomotor response are studied, two pertinent questions arise: (a) what is the nature of acquisition curves for Ss having different levels of initial ability in the task, and (b) how well can performance at various stages of training be predicted from intra-task measures, measures from other psychomotor tests, and printed test scores. The first question bears on such problems as the interaction between ability measures and learning variables, and what might be expected in the training of Ss differing in initial ability in a task. The second question involves such problems as ability patterns at various stages of training and what measures give the best prediction of performance at these different stages.

Two experiments are to be reported on individual differences in the acquisition of a psychomotor skill in which speed of an arm-hand response to a visual discrimination is measured. The first experiment analyzes acquisition curves as a function of initial level of ability in the task. The second experiment evaluates ability patterns present at initial and final stages of practice by examining the zero and higher order correlations between scores on a printed test battery of known factorial composition, a simple reaction time test, and the criterion task.

Experiment I

Method: **a. Apparatus.** The apparatus used was a four-unit Discrimination Reaction Time Test (CP611D2) described in detail elsewhere.[8] In this

* From *The Journal of General Psychology*, 1957, *56*, 121-134. Reprinted with permission of the author and the Journal Press.

test, S is confronted with a panel having four colored cue lights arranged in a square pattern. The upper light on the left is red and the lower light is green. The upper light on the right is green and the lower is red. S's control panel has four snap-return toggle switches arranged in a diamond pattern with eight inches between the points of the diamond. A pair of lights, one red and one green, is presented and S is required to snap the toggle switch whose position relative to the other switches corresponds to the relationship of the red to the green light. If the red light is to the right of the green light, S snaps the switch on the right corner of the diamond pattern of switches; if the red light is below the green light he snaps the switch nearest to him in the diamond pattern; if the red light is to the left of the green light he snaps the left switch; if the red light is above the green light he snaps the switch which is directly in front and furthest from him on the control panel. There is a white light placed above the four cue lights on the panel and this is illuminated simultaneously with the presentation of each pair of colored cue lights and is turned off by the correct response. S is instructed to respond as rapidly as possible and to continue responding until the white light is turned out. The colored cue lights remain on for three sec. There is a foreperiod of either .50 sec., 1.0 sec., or 1.5 sec., in duration before each paired-light presentation. These three foreperiods and the four different pairs of cue lights are randomly distributed throughout a sequence of 40 paired light presentations and are presented automatically. S is seated during the test and rests his first two fingers on a small cross whose center is 2⅛ in. from the lower toggle switch. The response requires movement of the whole arm. A trial was defined as the presentation of 10 settings and the score recorded for the trial was cumulative reaction time in min. for the 10 settings.

b. Subjects Ss were 860 basic airmen trainees selected from the population available at Lackland AFB, Texas. They were tested in subgroups of four.

c. Experimental Procedure. All Ss were given 160 continuously presented settings. When collection of the data had been completed, Ss were stratified into deciles on the basis of Trial 1 score.

The range of performance and the mean for each decile on Trial 1 were as given in Table 1.

Results: The groups exhibit considerable difference in the form of their curves. Decile 1, which is comprised of the lowest 10 per cent of the Ss, has a performance curve with a rather extended initial curvilinear segment. As the level of initial ability increases, the initial curvilinear segment becomes less prominent, until, by Decile 10, the performance curve is approximately linear throughout. All groups show relatively little gain in performance over

TABLE 1

Decile	Interval	Mean
1	.331-.439 min.	.370 min.
2	.293-.330	.311
3	.267-.292	.279
4	.251-.266	.258
5	.232-.250	.241
6	.217-.231	.223
7	.203-.216	.209
8	.186-.202	.195
9	.169-.185	.177
10	.108-.168	.156

the later trials. The 10 curves are essentially parallel in the final trials and there is little indication that they will eventually converge to a common level. Each group appears to be approaching its own asymptote. Between-groups differences decrease with training as shown by the mean difference between Decile 1 and Decile 10, decreasing from .215 min. on Trial 1 to .062 min. on Trial 16. All groups show improvement with practice and this improvement is more pronounced with low than with high ability Ss. Decile 1 has a gain in mean performance of .182 min. from Trial 1 to Trial 16 whereas Decile 10 displays a gain of only .029 min. over this period.

Although the mean performance curves of the deciles maintain about the same rank order and remain fairly well differentiated throughout training, some individual Ss show a tendency to shift status with practice. Decile 1, for example, was initially separated from Decile 10 by 80 per cent of the Ss. But by Trial 16, a substantial number of Decile 1 Ss are equal or superior to the performance of Decile 10 Ss. One possible hypothesis is that Ss with low initial ability lacked the opportunity to acquire responses in extra-experimental situations that would transfer to the experimental task. Some of these Ss, however, when given an opportunity to practice these responses, acquire them readily and attain the level of initially proficient Ss over a fairly short span of trials. This hypothesis will be discussed in greater detail in Experiment II.

Experiment II

Method: **a. Apparatus.** Four-unit Discrimination Reaction Time Test described in Experiment I. Also, a test of simple reaction time to the onset of a light stimulus was given in which S had to move his hand a distance of 2¼ in.

b. Subjects. Ss were 197 basic airmen trainees drawn from the population available at Lackland AFB, Texas.

c. Experimental Procedure. The data to be reported in this experiment are abstracted from an extensive study soon to be reported in detail which was directed at the general problem of predictability of psychomotor performance at advanced stages of training. A large battery of simple psychomotor tests, complex psychomotor tests, and printed tests were administered during a three-day testing period and a correlational analysis was made of the scores. Since one of the complex psychomotor tests administered was a *DRT,* and since the present paper is concerned with individual differences in *DRT* performance, it would seem that pertinent features of the correlation matrix could most profitably be presented here.

Three blocks of eight trials each were administered on *DRT* with a two-min. rest between blocks. A trial on *DRT* has the same definition as in Experiment I. Score recorded on simple reaction time was cumulative time to 10 stimuli. Scores on the printed tests comprising the Airman Classification Battery were also obtained. This battery has been described elsewhere.[4,9]

Results: Since the abilities measured by the Airman Classification Battery are well known,[1,2,3,5,6,12,13] and since the importance of reaction time ability can be reasonably assumed for *DRT* performance, correlation of these measures with *DRT* measures should yield information on abilities required for performance on *DRT*. Two *DRT* measures were correlated with these tests: (*a*) total score for the first five trials, and (*b*) total score for the last five trials.* These are referred to as initial *DRT* and final *DRT,* respectively. A

*In computing the r's, raw scores were coded for convenient machine computation. In the case of *DRT* and Reaction Time, the highest coded scores were assigned to the lowest raw scores since low raw scores represent superior performance. The r's between each of these two tests and printed tests were therefore positive

TABLE 2

CONTRIBUTIONS OF TESTS TO PREDICTION OF INITIAL AND FINAL STAGE OF
CRITERION TASK

Test	Principal factors measured	Initial DRT r	Initial DRT β	Final DRT r	Final DRT β
Word Knowledge	Verbal	32	−11	25	−10
Arithmetic Reasoning	Numerical	48	13	34	06
Dial & Table Reading	Numerical, Perceptual Speed	54	14	39	07
Numerical Operations II	Numerical	39	09	34	13
Aviation Information	Verbal	38	04	29	03
Background Current Affairs	Verbal	35	−02	24	−09
Electrical Information	Mechanical Experience	42	10	32	22
Mechanical Principles	Mechanical Experience	37	−05	25	01
General Mechanics	Mechanical Experience	30	−06	15	−12
Tool Functions	Mechanical Experience	29	09	14	−03
Speed of Identification	Perceptual Speed	52	13	44	22
Memory for Landmarks	Visualization, Rote Memory	43	14	34	13
Pattern Comprehension	Visualization	54	22	34	02
Reaction Time		23	17	41	35
R^2			47		39
R			69		62

Decimal points omitted.

multiple correlation coefficient (R) was then computed between the tests and each *DRT* measure. For each test at each stage of *DRT* training, Table 2 presents the zero-order correlation coefficient (r) and β weight. R and R^2 for each stage of *DRT* and the generally accepted name for the most prominent factor or factors measured by each printed test are also given in Table 2.

Table 2 shows that the test battery is not as effective in predicting final *DRT* as initial *DRT* although the differences between R's is not large. An examination of the r's between tests and initial *DRT* indicates that all printed tests have a higher value than Reaction Time. But, for final *DRT*, just the opposite is true. All printed tests show some reduction in the magnitude of r from initial to final whereas Reaction Time shows a substantial increase. With the exception of Speed of Identification, Reaction Time has the highest r with final *DRT*. It is noteworthy that the decrease in r from initial to final *DRT* observed for most variables is not a function of decreasing reliability of measurement with practice. The use of total score for five trials for the initial and for the final *DRT* measure permitted reliability in each instance to be estimated by an analysis of variance of a Trials X Ss table.[11] Both reliability coefficients were high and with little difference between them—being .87 for initial and .93 for final.

The β weights show that several printed tests have considerable weight in predicting initial *DRT*. These tests are Arithmetic Reasoning, Dial and Table Reading, Speed of Identification, Memory for Landmarks, and Pattern Comprehension. It is interesting to note that Pattern Comprehension has greater weight in predicting initial *DRT* than Reaction Time. These printed tests measure numerical, perceptual speed, visualization, and rote memory abilities. Numerical ability has been defined as the ability to perform arithmetic computations speedily and accurately, perceptual speed as the ability to observe and compare visual details rapidly and accurately, visualization as the ability to manipulate visual images mentally, and rote memory as the ability to recall learned associations immediately.[5] Reynolds[9] has suggested that numerical ability and rote memory ability involve facility in the use of learned responses and as such are analogous to speed of response measures employed in learning studies.

By the final stage of *DRT* training, Reaction Time has the largest β weight. The printed tests most potent in predicting initial *DRT* tend to decrease in weight with the exception of Speed of Identification, which increases. Electrical Information and Numerical Operations, which are measures of the mechanical experience factor and the numerical factor respectively, both had moderate weight in predicting initial *DRT* and show an increase in β for final *DRT*. Since the other tests measuring the mechanical experience factor are tests of mechanics and do not contribute appreciably to the prediction of final *DRT*, it would seem that Electrical Information, which is a test of electronics experience, involves somewhat different abilities. Another possibility is that test items involving circuit diagrams measure some perceptual ability present in final *DRT* performance.

It is interesting to note that the two largest contributors to prediction of final *DRT* (Speed of Identification and Reaction Time) are both measures of speed. An r of only .15 between these two tests indicates the relative independence of these two speed measures.

Discussion

It would seem profitable to discuss the term "ability," its meaning for complex psychomotor tests, and how it relates to learning. Ability studies typically involve the statistical evaluation of a set of test scores. Since these test scores are responses obtained in defined situations, an ability can be interpreted as some aspect of one or more of the measured responses. Let an *ability,* therefore, be defined as a certain response class associated with a specified set of stimuli and *ability level* as the strength of this response class. Anything that affects response level, such as learning variables, will thus also affect ability level. A printed test, for example, provides one simple means of evaluating relative response strength in a specified stimulus situation. If the test is heterogeneous, several classes of stimuli are present such as numbers, words, forms, etc., and each class serves to evoke its associated response class. The score on a heterogeneous test is complex and represents a weighted average response strength for all response classes present. If the test is homogeneous, only a single stimulus class and its associated response class is present.* A correlation between two tests indicates the presence of common response classes (abilities). Assuming perfect reliability, two parallel homogeneous tests will have a perfect correlation since a score on each test is an index of the strength of the same response class and the rank order of *S*s on both tests will be the same. Correlation between two parallel heterogeneous tests will also be perfect except that more than one response class is present in each test although they are the same for both tests. Tests having a correlation greater than zero but less than one have only part identity of response classes. If the correlation is zero, the response classes in each are completely different. It should be noted that identity of response class is sufficient for two tests to be correlated and that it is probably not necessary to have identity of stimulus class also. There are at least three possibilities of response evocation when the stimuli have been changed: (*a*) stimulus generalization when the stimuli

---

*A more precise definition of test homogeneity and heterogeneity would be in terms of inter-item and item-test correlation.

vary along some specified dimension, (b) mediated generalization, and (c) learning sets when repeated experience in problem situations with the stimuli changed for each problem yields positive transfer. A summary of these findings on positive transfer in human learning is presented elsewhere.[10] Any one of these three possibilities could yield evocation of a response under different stimulus conditions and could account for a correlation between two quite different printed tests or a printed test and a psychomotor test.

In an analysis of abilities required in complex psychomotor performance, an important consideration is that a task is not as simple as the single performance score typically recorded on a trial might suggest. What a complex task seems to require is the learning of a number of component response classes as well as their integration into the appropriate pattern and sequence necessary for proficiency. The score recorded, therefore, represents a weighted average performance level in these activities at any stage of training. As an example, consider a task where a number is flashed on a screen and the measured response is the speed with which S moves his hand from a given point to a knob and adjusts the knob to a setting that is the square root of the number. In this hypothetical task, at least five component responses (abilities) can be tentatively specified: (a) speed in recognition of the number on the screen (perceptual speed), (b) speed of arm movement (reaction time), (c) facility in manipulating the knob (dexterity), (d) facility in extracting square roots (numerical), and (e) organization of the four basic responses into the sequence and pattern required for successful performance (patterning). A single performance measure at any stage of training in this task would represent the composite strength of all five response classes. To the extent that a previously administered test, either printed or psychomotor, evokes one or more of the component responses, it should correlate with an initial performance measure on the criterion task since it would be a strength index of a component response or responses present in the total response. A test's β weight is an index of the extent to which a test measures a component response class or classes in the criterion not measured by other tests in the battery.

One interpretation of changes in r and β for a test from the initial to final stage of practice on a complex criterion task would be in terms of a changing organization of factors or abilities. The present paper, however, considers the counter hypothesis that ability or component response requirements for a complex task are the same at any stage of training but that training changes the strength of certain component responses. Individual differences in acquisition curve characteristics for each of the component responses result in a change of rank order of Ss in the single overall measured response with a consequent change in r and β. It would seem that this change in rank order of Ss from early to late in training can be attributed to two characteristics of individual acquisition curves for the component responses of the criterion task: (a) rate or *aptitude*, and (b) asymptote or *capacity* under the conditions holding. Initial proficiency in the criterion task is a function of the strength of various component responses developed in extra-experimental situations and some Ss will have low initial status because of lack of prior experience in one or more of them. But when given opportunity to practice, a number of these initially poor Ss transition to a performance level equal or superior to that of initially proficient Ss because of rapid acquisition rates and/or high asymptote levels on one or more of the component responses. If a previously administered test measures the strength of a response class present as a component response in the criterion task, the test will correlate with an initial performance measure on the criterion task. Since the component response is a source of variance in the overall response measured, differential improvement of Ss on the component response should affect the rank order of Ss in the measured overall criterion response such that the r between test and criterion should shrink from initial to final stage of practice on the criterion task. Most tests are heterogeneous to some degree and learning on any one of the response classes measured by it should result in a shrinkage of r. If criterion response classes measured by the test are highly learned and at near asymptote levels, further practice of them will have little effect on the rank order of Ss and consequently will not appreciably change r. The same explanation would apply to changes in β except that β is in reference to a response class (or classes) measured by a test when response classes in common with other tests in the battery have been partialled out.[7]

In some instances the r and β between test and criterion will increase with training on the criterion task. One possibility is that a certain sequence is imposed on the practice of component responses by the nature of the task or special instructions. In the initial stages of training, a component response appearing late in the sequence will tend to be subordinate to those component responses that are earlier in the sequence and do not have a level commensurate with its strength as indicated by test scores. A consequence will be that the test and an initial criterion measure will have a low r and β. As training progresses and this component response is eventually practiced, the level of response strength indicated by the test will be more accurately represented and r and β will increase. If this component response is a highly learned one, the r and β will remain high with further practice. Tests showing a decrease in r with training but an increase in β weight are probably heterogeneous ones measuring several component responses in the criterion task—one of which is probably not practiced until late in training. Thus, the r will decrease with training because of learning on some component responses but β will increase because an important component response is receiving practice.

In terms of the foregoing analysis of complex tasks, total response on DRT can be grossly reduced to three principal component responses: (a) the perceptual response which entails speed of stimulus pattern recognition, (b) the visualization response which involves learning the relevance of any given stimulus pair for the arm-hand response, and (c) the reaction time response involving speed of arm-hand movement. The importance of printed tests measuring speed and visualization in predicting initial DRT suggests that stimulus pattern recognition and acquisition of the S-R connections required for task proficiency are prominent at this stage. The tendency for Reaction Time r and β to be less prominent initially than finally suggests that Ss are relatively indifferent to arm-hand speed in the initial stages where preoccupation is with perceptual and visualization responses. By final DRT, speed responses are important and Pattern Comprehension, which is a measure of the visualization response, ceases to contribute to prediction. On the basis of the learning interpretation presented, it would not be assumed that the evaluational response has ceased to be important but only that considerable change in strength for it has taken place and the ordering of Ss in this ability has changed. The outcome is that the scores on Pattern Comprehension, which gave an index of status in this response prior to DRT practice, is no longer an important source of DRT variability.

The data shed some light on the problem of what class or classes of tests tend to give better prediction of performance at advanced stages of training. It would seem that tests measuring highly learned responses should yield best prediction at advanced levels on tasks where these responses are present as component responses. Since strength of these responses is high, the ordering of Ss on tests evaluating their strength will change little with further practice on the criterion task and will not tend to lose their ability to predict. Conversely, tests evaluating component responses that change strength considerably with training will tend to lose their ability to predict. Speed of Identification and Reaction Time tests, which measure perceptual and motor speed respectively, give the best prediction of final DRT and are probably tests evaluating highly learned responses. This is consistent with Reynold's finding that measures of speed are important in the prediction of performance in advanced stages of training.[9] It might seem on *a priori* grounds that an initial measure from the criterion task would yield better prediction of a measure at an advanced stage of training on the criterion task than external tests, either singly or in composite. Yet, this is not true. The r between initial and final DRT was found to be .55 whereas the R between other tests and final DRT was .62. It is interesting to note that a battery of tests can be assembled capable of a better job of predicting final criterion performance than a measure from the initial stage of the criterion task itself.

One additional comment on the present analysis seems pertinent. The equating of ability level with strength for a particular response class does not necessarily lead to the conclusion that there are as many abilities as there are types of responses. The component responses required by complex tasks are probably limited in number, as the factor analysts have hypothesized. Although an infinite number of variations can be devised for tasks with a consequent infinite variation in the required overall response, a certain limited number of component responses in various combinations probably comprise the overall response in all of them. What may be unique to a complex task is the particular patterning response required for proficiency. However, it is equally tenable that the patterning response is general and that an S's facility in organizing the component responses of a complex task into the pattern required for proficiency is some positive function of experience with complex devices. If the patterning response is a general response, it probably is present in advanced stages of training on complex tasks where the component responses have been fairly well learned and the emphasis is now on their patterning. This leads to the interesting hypothesis that measures at advanced levels of training on complex tasks should have a certain communality due to the presence of the patterning response, and that such measures should contribute to the prediction of performance at advanced levels of training on complex criterion tasks. The present study provides no information on this topic. Additional research seems required to elucidate this important problem.

Summary

Two experiments were reported on individual differences in response acquisition on the Discrimination Reaction Time Test.

Experiment I evaluated the form and level of acquisition curves as a function of initial proficiency in the task. The 860 Ss were stratified into deciles on the basis of Trial 1 score. Mean performance curves for the deciles generally maintained their initial rank order throughout training. A number of initially poor Ss made transition to the level of initially proficient Ss as training progressed.

Experiment II was concerned with the predictability of DRT performance where printed tests of the Airman Classification Battery and a simple reaction time test were employed as independent variables. The ability of the battery to predict DRT decreased from initial to final stage of training on DRT. Differences in the zero-order r's and β weights from initial to final stage of DRT were interpreted in terms of characteristics of individual acquisition curves for component responses comprising the total response measured.

References

1. Abt, J. C., & Friedman, G. M. A factor analysis of the Airman Classification Battery AC-1B with Control Tower Operator (27251) technical school final grade. USAF Training Command Human Resources Research Center *Research Note 52-46*, Dec., 1952.
2. Christal, R. E. A factor analysis of Airman Classification Battery AC-1A and radar operator final school grade. USAF Training Command Human Resources Research Center *Research Note 52-37*, Dec., 1952.
3. Cox, J. A., Jr. A factor analysis of Airman Classification Battery test scores for airplane sheet metal worker technical school graduates. USAF Training Command Human Resources Research Center *Research Note 51-23*, Sept., 1951.
4. Dailey, J. T., Brokaw, L. D., & Lecznar, W. B. The development of the Airman Classification Test Battery. *Research Bulletin 48-4*, Barksdale AFB: Hq., Air Training Command, Nov., 1948.
5. Fruchter, B. The factorial content of the Airman Classification Battery: I. Factor analysis of 1948 Normative Survey Battery. USAF Training Command Human Resources Research Center *Research Bulletin 49-1*, Nov. 1949.
6. Gordon, M. A. Orthogonal and oblique rotations of axes, Airman Classification Battery and selected tests from the 1949 Normative Survey. USAF Training Command Human Resources Research Center *Research Note 52-28*, July, 1952.
7. Kendall, M. G. *The Advanced Theory of Statistics.* Vol. I. London: Griffin, 1948.
8. Melton, A. W. (*Ed.*). Apparatus Tests. Report No. 4, Army Air Forces Aviation Psychology Programs Research Reports. Washington: U.S. Govt. Print. Office, 1947.
9. Reynolds, B. The effect of learning on the predictability of psychomotor performance. *J Exp. Psychol.,* 1952, *44,* 189-198.
10. Stevens, S. S. (*Ed.*). *Handbook of Experimental Psychology.* New York: Wiley, 1951.
11. Thorndike, R. L. *Personnel Selection.* New York: Wiley, 1949.
12. Zachert, V., & Ivens, F. C. Factor analysis of the Airman Classification Battery AC-1B and the Texas Battery. USAF Training Command Human Resources Research Center *Research Note 52-45,* Dec., 1952.
13. Zachert, V., & Shibe, E. H. Factor analysis of the Airman Classification Battery with clerk-typist final school grade. USAF Training Command Human Resources Research Center *Research Note 52-39*, Dec., 1952.

Chapter 6

ABILITIES RELATED TO DIFFERENT STAGES OF SKILL ACQUISITION

Ability Correlates in Learning a Psychomotor Task*

J. R. HINRICHS

VERY recent evidence supports the earlier findings of Fleishman and others. Although Hinrichs also used laboratory artificially-contrived tasks, the implications for predicting achievement at any stage of training are clear. The complex situation one confronts when attempting to predict skill acquisition can be realized from the results of this study. The changing relative importance of abilities as a task is being learned indicates the qualifications one must place on a motor aptitude test in terms of its potential value. Also indirectly suggested is an instructional methodology that would emphasize those abilities apparently of most importance as skill is acquired. Hopefully, we will soon be at the point where real-life skills, e.g., athletic, industrial, dance, and aviational, will be analyzed for ability relationships in a similar and appropriate manner. As one might or should expect, reference tests more similar to the task at hand are more highly related to performance than are more general tests. The usage of designated general ability tests to predict well in a number of skills is rightfully questioned.

A number of studies have shown that the abilities required for performance on certain psychomotor tasks may change during the course of learning of the task (e.g., Fleishman, 1957; Fleishman & Hempel, 1954, 1955). Similar results have been found in an analysis of abilities involved in learning to receive Morse code (Fleishman & Fruchter, 1960). These studies suggest that the

* From the *Journal of Applied Psychology,* 1970, *54,* 56-64. Reprinted with permission of the author and the American Psychological Association.

pattern of abilities related to performance changes in a relatively systematic fashion from one stage of practice to the next, until some point at which learning is mastered and the pattern of abilities required for performance at the final level of proficiency on the task has been stabilized.

Clearly, the possibility of different ability requirements for initial stages of learning in comparison with ability requirements at final stages of proficiency can have important implications for the prediction of ultimate performance on any task. Such shifts also have important implications regarding the nature of skill training and the emphasis which should be placed at various stages of practice. If the abilities required by a task change during the course of the learning period, a clear distinction between final proficiency and proficiency during training must be maintained in developing predictive instruments. Also, it may be possible to increase the efficiency of skill training by concentrating throughout the training period on those abilities required for final proficiency, rather than on those abilities required only in the early stages of skill acquisition. At least this would seem to be a fruitful area for research.

An additional result emerges from these studies of skill acquisition, however, which tends to complicate the issue of predictability of attained proficiency. Frequently, in factor analytic studies of learning data for psychomotor tasks, an increasingly important "specific habits" or "within-task" factor has been found. The variance accounted for by such a factor consistently increases with successive stages of practice and is usually not shared with reference tests external to the specific task under study (e.g., Fleishman & Hempel, 1954).

In one study utilizing a rotary pursuit task, in addition to finding an increasingly important task-specific factor, a decreasing within-task factor was identified (Fleishman, 1960). This decreasing task-specific factor, like the increasing task-specific, was not explainable by any of the external reference tests included in the analysis. In this study, while the within-task factors were most strongly related to performance at all stages of practice, a factor of "control precision" (the ability to make highly controlled precise muscular adjustments) contributed to rotary pursuit performance throughout learning and "rate control" (the ability to make continual anticipations and adjustments relative to changes in speed and direction of a continuously moving object) contributed slightly early in training but decreased in importance over time. Fleishman's analysis was based on data collected from 224 basic trainee airmen at Lackland Air Force Base covering eight stages of rotary pursuit performance and 17 apparatus and printed reference tests.

With regard to the two task-specific factors, Fleishman (1960) stated that

the increase in importance of a factor common only to the task itself agrees with our findings with other kinds of psychomotor tasks (Fleishman, 1957; Fleishman & Hempel, 1954, 1955). This is consistent with the view that skill in later performance is more a function of specific habits acquired during practice on the task itself, relative to transfer from previous abilities, skills, and habits. While factors of *decreasing* importance have been found in other tasks, this is the first study in which such a factor was not defined by external ability measures. The nature of this decreasing factor is not immediately apparent. It is possible to speculate that this factor represents a "learning" set of some kind which facilitates learning early but which drops out as a contributor as all Ss gained experience with the task. Whatever explanation is adopted would have to account for the fact that we have not found this decreasing "within-task" factor in our studies with other motor tasks (pp. 168-169).

Fleishman's speculation regarding a "learning set" suggests that perhaps individual differences in method of approaching the task may be related to performance during initial stages of learning, but that this method-based source of individual differences washes out as the task becomes learned. In effect, method of approaching the task may serve as a moderator variable in predicting performance early in the learning process but not at final stages of proficiency. If Ss approach the rotary pursuit task with different basic methods, a declining task-specific in the factor analysis of proficiency data from various stages of practice might result.

The present study was designed to shed further light on these issues. The intent was to (a) replicate the major aspects of Fleishman's (1960) analysis, though some important changes in the task and reference tests were included. The replication was designed at least to look for the presence of increasing and decreasing task-specific factors in rotary pursuit skill acquisition, (b) identify further different abilities related to early and late stages of practice in rotary pursuit through a series of reference tests, and (c) attempt to explain the decreasing task-specific factor by forcing, through the experimental design, the use of two different "methods" of approaching the rotary pursuit task.

Method

Apparatus. A rotary pursuit tracking device with variable speed was utilized as the practice task. The apparatus is contained in a rectangular box 12.5 in. square $\times$ 5.75 in. high. Beneath the top of the apparatus, which consists of a glass pane, a cylindrical 25 w. light bulb, 5 in. long, rotates just below the glass around an axis through the center of the apparatus face. Various tracking patterns cut from black paper can be placed on the glass face and covered with another glass sheet so that as the light bulb rotates, the tracking target appears as a spot of light moving around the tracking pattern. Although the light rotates at a constant rate, the target speed and path may be varied through the course of a single revolution by using various irregular patterns.

The D-shaped pattern was utilized for the learning trials in this study. Due to the shape of this particular pattern, the spot of light which is the tracking target for the task appears to move at a relatively steady rate over the curved portion of the pattern and then speed up suddenly as it enters the straight portion. Thus, this practice pattern emphasizes both speed and accuracy in rotary pursuit tracking.

The tracking stylus consists of a photo electric cell, 0.5 in. square, mounted at an angle of 20° on the tip of a 10 in. long wand. Time on target is recorded by the photo electric cell, which operates a timer calibrated to .01 sec. The entire apparatus rests on a table 35.75 in. high. The Ss stand during practice on the task.

Subjects. The Ss were 50 students enrolled in an undergraduate course in industrial psychology representative of the much researched "college sophomore" S population. No distinction was maintained between male and female Ss. Individuals were randomly assigned to experimental conditions as they arrived to participate in the study.

Reference Tests. Both printed and apparatus tests were used as reference tests in an effort to identify abilities required at different stages of practice. While the battery of reference tests does not match those utilized by Fleishman, an effort was made to include tests which it was felt would be predictive of performance in rotary pursuit and which would tap the major ability factors of control precision and rate control found in Fleishman's research. The reference tests were

1. *Jump Visual Reaction Time.*—This is a measure comparable to the one utilized by Fleishman in which *S*'s task is to respond to a light stimulus and extinguish it by pressing a button as rapidly as possible. The score was recorded as the total time required for 10 trials.

2. *Purdue Pegboard, Preferred Hand.*—The *S*'s task is to place as many pegs as possible in a series of holes in a 30-sec. trial utilizing his preferred hand. Two trials were administered and the mean score was recorded.

3. *Purdue Pegboard, Assembly.*—This task requires as many assemblies of peg, washer, and collar as possible within a specified time interval. This test was also used by Fleishman.

4. *Flanagan Aptitude Classification Test, 7A (FACT), Coordination.*—This is a paper-and-pencil test designed to measure the ability to coordinate hand and arm movements. "It involves the ability to control movements in a smooth and accurate manner when these movements must be continually guided and readjusted in accordance with observations of their results (Science Research Associates, 1953)." The test consists of a series of spirals between which *S* must trace with a pencil, and his score reflects both accuracy and speed. Two practice trials are given and four test trials; the score is the total of the four test trials.

5. *"Kinesthetic Tests."*—These are two paper-and-pencil tasks developed for this study which were intended to measure individual differences in the ability to utilize kinesthetic cues in a tracing task. Blindfolded, *S* is required to trace a pattern which had been presented to him, starting with the tip of his pencil at a specified position on the figure. One task involved tracing a square, 5 in. on each side, attempting to remain within a ¼ in. wide path. The other task involved tracing a circle with a 5-in. diameter, again within a ¼ in. wide path. Two trials for both the square and the circle were completed by each *S*. Several scoring procedures for these tests were evaluated, including a measurement of the linear separation between the beginning and end of the tracing, a ratio of the vertical measurement of the trace to the horizontal measurement (as an index of symmetry of the trace), and a rating of "goodness of fit" of *S*'s trace to the stimulus pattern in terms of a scale running from (1) Much too small to (5) Much too large. This goodness-of-fit evaluation was done separately for both vertical and horizontal directions by two independent judges. Following an evaluation of all of these measurements, the final score decided on for these tests was a pooled goodness-of-fit rating, pooling judgments for both vertical and horizontal directions, for both judges, for the two trials on the squares test, and a separately pooled overall rating for the circles test. The decision to pool these ratings was based on the determination of adequate interrater reliability of judgments (average of four interrater coefficients: $r = .82$ for squares and $r = .72$ for circles).

6. *Apparatus Test, Speed.*—This is a reference test utilizing the rotary pursuit apparatus described above and a circular pattern 8 in. in diameter. Target speed was 65 rpm—an extremely rapid tracking task which clearly emphasized the speed component in rotary pursuit performance. The score was recorded as total time on target for five 20-sec. test periods, each period separated from the next by a 15-sec. rest pause.

7. *Apparatus Test, Accuracy.*—A pattern was employed as an apparatus test emphasizing accuracy of tracking. This irregular pattern was presented at target speed of 25 rpm, but due to the irregular shape of the pattern the target speed of the blip varied widely over the course of the pattern. Again,

TABLE 1
Three Factor Analyses of Test and Performance Data

Data	Varimax factor loadings*								
	Factor 1			Factor 2			Factor 3		
	M1	M2	Tot	M1	M2	Tot	M1	M2	Tot
Reaction time	-11	-25	-11	13	39	18	-09	-13	-24
PB—Preferred Hand	15	-15	-07	-17	-14	-12	81	65	70
PB—Assembly	05	-13	-08	-09	-09	-06	75	82	73
FACT—Coordination	-20	24	02	14	07	11	74	81	67
Apparatus—Speed	74	78	70	21	22	25	-22	10	01
Apparatus—Accuracy	-05	41	18	68	76	73	-19	-02	-12
Trial 1	17	65	42	91	67	82	-03	-06	-03
Trial 3	27	72	49	89	61	76	03	-09	-02
Trial 5	48	97	76	83	14	55	-05	-04	-07
Trial 7	45	97	74	86	08	51	04	01	-06
Trial 9	56	96	79	77	16	49	12	-05	-05
Trial 11	91	96	93	20	14	16	14	-13	-03
Trial 13	92	98	94	19	11	14	05	-02	05
Trial 15	94	98	96	24	02	12	02	-04	02

Note.—Method 1—Accuracy (M1), $N = 23$; Method 2—Speed (M2), $N = 27$;
Total group (Tot), $N = 50$.
* Decimals omitted.

the score was recorded as total time on target for five 20-sec. periods separated by 15-sec. rest pauses.

These reference tests were given prior to learning in the order indicated. In addition, all tests were administered again following the learning trials, in counterbalanced order from the pretest administration.

Practice Task. The experimental trials consisted of 15 practice sessions utilizing the D-shaped tracking pattern. Each trial consisted of five 20-sec. test periods, each of these separated by 15-sec. pauses. Score for a trial was recorded as time on target or the total 100-sec. trial period. The 15 trials were in turn each separated by 30-sec. rest pauses. A 5-min. rest pause was introduced between Trials 8 and 9.

The learning task was designed as one of attaining proficiency in rotary pursuit under conditions of increasing task difficulty. This was achieved by systematically increasing the speed of the target during the learning process from an initial speed of 25 rpm to a criterion speed in finals trials of 45 rpm.

To test the hypothesis of a method variable playing a role in a decreasing task-specific factor, two different methods of practice were utilized, and *S*s were assigned to the two method groups at random.

Method 1 was intended to emphasize accuracy in the task, and for the first 8 trials the target moved at a relatively slow speed (25 rpm). On Trials 9-13 the speed was increased linearly to 45 rpm, and the final 3 criterion trials were at 45 rpm.

Method 2 emphasized speed. The first 3 trials were at the slow speed of 25 rpm, and the speed was increased linearly through Trials 4-8 to 45 rpm. Trials 8-15 were at 45 rpm. Thus, the two method groups ended up at the same speeds, but got there by different "routes."

Factor Analyses. To evaluate whether task-specific factors emerged in this study as in Fleishman's research, selected variables were factor analyzed. Because essentially two different tasks were involved for the two different methods, separate factor analyses were conducted of the data for each method, as well as a factor analysis of data for combined samples. Since the samples were relatively small, it was necessary to limit the number of variables in the analysis to scores on six of the reference tests given prior to the practice task and performance results for every other practice trial. R^2 was used as the estimate of communality, and factoring was continued until the characteristic roots dropped below 1.0.

Utilizing these criteria, three factors were extracted for Method 1, three for Method 2, and three for the analysis of the combined sample. The principal axis factor matrix was rotated to simple structure utilizing the varimax procedure. Table 1 presents the results of these three separate factor analyses.

Factor 1 is clearly an increasing task-specific factor. For the combined sample, loadings increased from .42 on Trial 1 to .96 on Trial 15, and corresponding increases are evident in the separate factor analyses for both Method 1 and Method 2. Since successive stages of the task entailed a greater speed component, the large loadings for the pretest for speed are reasonable. As was characteristic of the increasing task-specific factor from Fleishman's analysis, none of the other reference tests seem particularly related to this factor (with the possible exception of some hint of a loading for the accuracy apparatus test in the analysis for Method 2).

Factor 2 seems to be a decreasing task-specific one and occurs consistently in all three of the analyses. It appears most related to the accuracy pretest and seems to reflect the emphasis placed on accuracy early in the learning period which tends to be supplanted by an emphasis on speed in later trials.

Factor 3 appears to reflect a composite of three of the reference tests—the two pegboard scores and the coordination test. These tests do not appear to be related to performance in the various stages of learning.

While the increasing task-specific (Factor 1) and the decreasing task-specific (Factor 2) appear to develop in a relatively orderly fashion over the various trials for the combined sample (i.e., factor loadings consistently increase or decrease with successive trials), it is clear that the different methods injected into the task do have an impact on the emergence of these factors. Under Method 1, which stressed "accuracy" and entailed a relatively late increase in speed in the learning task, the major changes in the patterns of loadings occur relatively late in the series of learning trials. For Method 2, which emphasized speed, the break in the level of loadings occurs relatively early between Trials 3 and 5. Thus, it would appear that the task-specific factors are susceptible to influence by the design of the task which "forced" different methods of approaching the job.

But it is also evident that these patterns of increasing and decreasing factor loadings were beginning to occur without any changes in the speed requirements of the task, as is evident by the trends over the first series of trials under Method 1 which were conducted at a constant speed. The trends suggest that, at least to some extent, it may be that increasing and decreasing task-specifics are a function of different methods of approaching the job.

Comparison of Learning Curves for the Two Methods. The performance curves are very different, but this is to be expected as the speed increase for Method 1 occurred late in the series of trials (between Trials 8 and 13), while for Method 2 it occurred early (between Trials 3 and 8). During the period of speed increase, performance under each method very sharply declined.

However, the final degree of learning achieved appears quite comparable for the two groups. An analysis of covariance comparing the two method groups for the total scores for Trials 13-15 with covariance controls for total scores for Trials 1-3 yielded $F = 0.25$. Thus, there are no significant differences between the two groups in final level of proficiency attained. It is also interesting that final level of proficiency does not differ significantly from total scores for the first three trial periods; except for the fact that the task during final periods was considerably more difficult than it was during the initial periods, one might assume that no learning had taken place!

However, when we transform the learning curves by a factor taking into account differences in speed of the target, the two learning curves are relatively comparable. The mean performance score for each method in each trial period was multiplied by a fraction equivalent to target speed for that trial over 45 rpm (the maximum target speed in the final trials of the learning series). The adjusted curve for Method 1 exhibits a plateau following Trial 4, probably reflecting considerable boredom with the task through the series of early trials which were all performed at a constant relatively slow speed. (Questionnaire responses by Ss frequently indicated that the task rapidly became boring at slower speeds.) The curve assumes a positively accelerating form as speed was increased, suggesting that the method change injected additional requirements for attention into the task.

For Method 2, a negatively accelerating curve occurs relatively early in the data during the period of speed increase, and performance reaches an asymptote at about Trial 9. One may suppose that under Method 2, high initial attention and learning is forced through the experimental manipulations associated with the method.

Based on these curves and the analysis of covariance of final proficiency, it certainly does appear that the experiment entailed two different tasks in the middle stages of learning, but that the starting and ending points for the two groups are comparable. That is, it would appear that the experiment was successful in forcing two different methods of achieving the same level of rotary pursuit learning. Parenthetically, it would also appear that Method 2, which entails an early increase in speed, is probably the most efficient approach for attaining learning in this task and that "acceptable" levels of performance in rotary pursuit could be obtained in roughly half the number of trials utilized in this study.

Abilities Contributing to Performance at Different Stages of Practice. To evaluate any possible differences in the patterns of abilities contributing to performance in early, middle, and late stages of practice for the two different methods, multiple regression analyses between reference tests and scores for early (total of Trials 1, 2, and 3), middle (Trials 7, 8, and 9) and late (Trials 13, 14, and 15) performance in learning were computed for each method group. The results of these analyses utilizing pretest data are presented in Table 2, and comparable results were obtained for the posttest battery except as noted below.

Based on the multiple R's obtained, it is evident that performance on this task at all stages of practice can be predicted with considerable accuracy from the battery of reference tests employed. It is also clear that most of the common variance between task performance and reference tests occurs with the apparatus tests. However, there are some interesting trends in these relationships.

Apparatus Test, Accuracy. This test appears most related to early stages of practice for both method groups and washes out completely as a predictor of late performance in Method 1. It does, however, correlate significantly with late performance under Method 2, but not as strongly as it does with early performance. One may speculate that tracking accuracy skills measured by this pretest are important early under slow speeds. However, under Method 1 which emphasizes learning at slow speeds, accuracy skills more clearly specific to the learning tracking pattern have an opportunity to become organized. On

TABLE 2

Correlations Between Pretest Scores and Performance on Early, Middle, and Late Practice Trials for Both Methods

Test	Method 1—Accuracy (N = 23)			Method 2—Speed (N = 27)		
	Early	Middle	Late	Early	Middle	Late
Reaction Time	29	18	−20	−17	38*	−43*
PB—Preferred Hand	−06	04	06	−23	−17	−18
PB—Assembly	−10	00	−01	−14	−14	−14
FACT—Coordination	03	08	−12	10	20	20
"Squares"	28	28	32	−27	−49**	−50**
"Circles"	41*	31	18	−31	−33	−37
Apparatus—Speed	41*	49*	71**	62**	74**	74**
Apparatus—Accuracy	60**	43*	05**	73**	49**	41*
R	78	68	81	82	80	82

* $p < .05$.
** $p < .01$.

the other hand, under Method 2 (speed) in which there was less opportunity for pattern-specific accuracy skills associated with the learning task itself to become organized, possibly, the Accuracy pretest still retains significant common variance with the accuracy component of variance required for final performance on the task. The fact that Accuracy apparatus test scores administered *after* training are as strongly correlated with late trials (Method 1, $r=.51$; Method 2, $r=.78$) as they are for early trials (Method 1, $r=.59$; Method 2, $r=.75$) for both methods, may result at least in part from the building up of pattern-specific accuracy skills which transfer in turn to the Accuracy posttest. Pre/Post Accuracy tests themselves correlate $r=.53$, a level of test reliability indicating considerable potential for influence by practice effects from the experimental task.

Apparatus Test, Speed.   For both methods, this test becomes more predictive of performance in later stages of practice than in early stages. This is no doubt a reflection of the increasing speed of the learning task for both methods, and it is interesting that the jump in predictability from this test occurs precisely at the points at which speed was increased—between middle and late learning periods for Method 1 and between early and middle periods for Method 2. This test exhibited higher pre/post reliability ($r=.74$) than the Accuracy apparatus test, perhaps reflecting less susceptibility to influence from specific skills acquired during practice.

Squares and Circles.   The nature of these tests is not completely clear; possibly because of low retest reliability (pre/post squares $r=.37$, circles $r=.05$) even if scores do exhibit adequate interrater agreement. These tests appear most related to criterion performance in middle and late trials for Method 2 (speed), and the relationship suggests that the ability to "hold in" while drawing these blindfolded figures is related to performance where speed is emphasized. Perhaps these tests are tapping some sort of kinesthetic cues which people utilize in counteracting centrifugal force in a speeded tracking task. But this is largely speculation.

Pegboard.   Neither the Preferred Hand nor the Assembly Pegboard task appear related in a meaningful way to rotary pursuit performance. It is interesting that there has clearly been a shift in the relationship between the two different Pegboard tests as a result of the intervening 15 practice trials on rotary pursuit; before training, Assembly and Preferred Hand correlated $+.56$. After training, they correlated $-.48$. This reversal in the direction of correlation between the two Pegboard tasks is consistent for both the Method 1 and Method 2 groups, and it is not surprising that pre/post reliabilities are low: (Preferred Hand, $r=.18$; Assembly, $r=.34$). Skills on the Pegboard appear unduly susceptible to influence by rotary pursuit practice and not sufficiently reliable as a reference test for this type of task.

Reaction Time.   This does not contribute significantly to performance at any stage of learning under Method 1, but does appear more important under Method 2, suggesting that a quick reaction time is positively related to performance on the task under learning conditions emphasizing speed. Retest reliability is high ($r=.85$).

The *FACT* test of Coordination does not appear to be related to any stage of practice on this task for either method. *FACT* exhibits moderate retest reliability ($r=.65$).

Conclusions

This study, like the Fleishman study (1960), identified both increasing and decreasing task-specific factors in the acquisition of skills on a rotary pursuit task. Fleishman selected the rotary pursuit task for his analysis because it seemed to be less complex than some of the other psychomotor tasks which he employed and because

> the initial factor structure indicated it to be a more "pure" task (than other tasks available). With regard to this latter point, it was of interest to note whether a relatively "pure" task would most resist changes in factor structure as a function of practice (p. 168).

However, from Fleishman's results it would appear that rotary pursuit, even utilizing an invariant circular target as he did, is not a completely "pure" task but requires different patterns of ability for proficiency and that these ability patterns change over the course of learning of the task. And as additional variables of complexity are interjected into the task, as in the present study, which utilized an irregular pattern and varying speed during learning, the identification of ability patterns required for proficiency becomes even more complex. In all probability, task-specific factors account increasingly for most of the variance in task proficiency as task complexity increases.

However, at the same time, it does appear that different approaches to the task or different methods utilized in the learning process can be associated with these increasing and declining task-specific factors. In this study, an emphasis on the skill requirements which seem to be associated with proficiency late in learning (tracking under conditions of speed) is associated with the increasing task-specific factor, and an initial emphasis on factors as associated with tracking accuracy (the component which seems most related to performance early in training) is associated with the declining task-specific factor. Thus, these increasing and decreasing task-specifics are associated with different patterns of proficiency on apparatus tests which are very closely similar to the task, as well as with a shifting emphasis on these differing components during the course of learning resulting from different methods of approaching the learning situation.

It is also clear that the most precise prediction of proficiency at any stage of training on the task comes from either reference tests which closely resemble the task itself, or as a prediction of later stages of practice from performance in early stages, rather than from reference tests which are intended to measure more generalizable abilities. If the best prediction of motor skills comes from highly task-specific tests on as relatively "pure" a task as rotary pursuit, we would expect this to be even more the case in actual job situations requiring considerably more complex patterns of abilities.

This suggests for the applied situation that job sample tests or training progress data will probably provide a better prediction of ultimate performance in industrial training settings than will ability tests and other instruments used for initial selection of trainees. As a result, management should possibly orient its thinking with regard to the selection of personnel for skills training toward a prediction and "reselection" partway through training, with initial entry into any training program relatively open to self-selection by the trainees.

These results also point to the need for careful job analysis of the types of skills required for final proficiency in a task and, if initial selection tests are utilized, designing the tests to measure these final proficiency skills to the greatest extent possible. Also, there may be some very marked savings in training time by focusing primarily on skills required for final proficiency early in training, rather than employing a more gradual progression in training emphasis from early to final skill requirements. These are certainly variables which should be investigated carefully in any specific applied situation.

References

Fleishman, E. A. A comparative study of aptitude patterns in unskilled and skilled psychomotor performances. *Journal of Applied Psychology,* 1957, *41,* 263-272.

Fleishman, E. A. Abilities at different stages of practice in rotary pursuit performance. *Journal of Experimental Psychology,* 1960, *60,* 162-171.

Fleishman, E. A., & Fruchter, B. Factor structure and predictability of successive stages of learning Morse code. *Journal of Applied Psychology,* 1960, *44,* 97-101.

Fleishman, E. A., & Hempel, W. E., Jr. Changes in factor structure of a complex psychomotor test. *Psychometrika,* 1954, *19,* 239-252.

Fleishman, E. A., & Hempel, W. E., Jr. The relation between abilities and improvement with practice in a visual discrimination reaction task. *Journal of Experimental Psychology,* 1955, *49,* 301-312.

Science Research Associates, Inc., 1953, *FACT* (Examiner Manual).

Role of Kinesthetic and Spatial-Visual Ability in Perceptual-Motor Learning*

EDWIN A. FLEISHMAN and SIMON RICH

THAT spatial-visual and kinesthetic abilities underlie success in motor learning is a statement few individuals would attempt to refute. Exactly how they relate to achievement has been analyzed for us by Fleishman and Rich. In beginning learning the spatial-orientation factor is of greater impact; later on, kinesthetic sensitivity explains much more of the achievement variance. The extent to which appropriate abilities are developed within individuals will reflect their potential for accomplishment at various points in practice. Special emphasis or training may be necessary for those who are deficient in abilities important for sucess during the course of motor learning.

It is generally recognized that responses to kinesthetic stimuli play a role in perceptual-motor skill performance. But relatively little is known about the manner in which these cues operate or about their relative importance during the course of motor skill learning. The main difficulty, of course, is that the relevant proprioceptive stimuli are inaccessible to direct experimental manipulation.

Attempts to investigate such cues, at least remotely, generally manipulate physical features of a control in terms of such variables as mass, spring loading, friction, viscous damping, and amplitude of control displacement (e.g., Bahrick, 1957). Especially illuminating are the recent studies by Adams and associates (e.g., Adams & Creamer, 1962) which attempt to specify, more precisely, the role of proprioception in skilled motor behavior. Their work indicates that proprioception serves not only a regulatory function (feedback for overt responses) but also as a time-perception mechanism which assists *S*

* From the *Journal of Experimental Psychology,* 1963, *56,* 6-11. Reprinted with permission of the authors and the American Psychological Association.

in anticipating temporal regularities in stimulus events. Still unanswered are questions of the relative contribution of kinesthetic and nonkinesthetic factors to the learning of a complex perceptual-motor skill, the learning of which may be dependent on responses to *many* classes of stimuli.

The fact that kinesthetic factors play a role in motor performance raises questions of individual differences in ability to make use of proprioceptive cues, and the interaction of such differences with motor skill learning. Are there stable individual differences in sensitivity to kinesthetic cues? Jenkins (1951) stresses that "kinesthesis—the sense of position and movement, is probably the most important sensitivity that man possesses." Yet, we know almost nothing about the existence of possible "kinesthetic ability" traits which may distinguish one individual from another.

A line of research by the author and associates (summarized most recently in Fleishman, 1962) has shown that the particular combinations of abilities contributing to performance on complex tasks may change as practice on these tasks continues. The approach used in these studies is to exploit the fact of individual differences to gain insights into the mechanisms of skill learning.[1] The Ss' pretask abilities become major "treatment" variables with significant interactions with learning trials. The magnitude of the differences produced by these "organismic" trait variables are often quite large (e.g., Fleishman & Hempel, 1955) when compared with the small effects often achieved by the manipulation of procedural or environmental variables.

Lately, this program has turned toward the search for external reference measures which might better describe the variance at advanced levels of learning. One of our hypotheses was that at least part of this variance is "kinesthetic" in nature (Fleishman, 1956, 1957a, 1959, 1962) and represents individual differences in sensitivity to kinesthetic cues.

Fitts (1951) stressed the need to investigate the relative importance of exteroceptive vs. interoceptive feedback, and the optimum combination of both in motor performance. He goes on to say that "visual control is important while an individual is learning a new perceptual-motor task. As performance becomes habitual, however, it is likely that proprioceptive feedback or 'feel' becomes the more important." Fitts' hypothesis is directly in line with our own speculation growing out of our extended practice correlational studies. But as far as we know this hypothesis has never been subjected to experimental test.

The present study represents a preliminary attempt to investigate this hypothesis within the framework of our ability-skill paradigm. According to our reasoning, if kinesthetic cues predominate, mainly, later in motor learning, then Ss who have superior sensitivity to these cues should be superior to other Ss at advanced stages of learning a complex motor task; but these Ss would not necessarily excel during initial stages of learning. Also tested was the related hypothesis that early in learning, spatial-visual abilities would play a dominant role in perceptual-motor learning, but that these abilities would decrease in importance as practice continued.

Reliable measures of spatial abilities exist but first, we needed to develop a reliable measure of individual differences in "kinesthetic sensitivity."

[1] The ability-skill paradigm used here has been elaborated elsewhere (Fleishman, 1956, 1959, 1962; Gagné & Fleishman, 1959). Briefly, the term *ability,* as used here, refers to a more general, stable trait of the individual which may facilitate (transfer to) performance in a wide variety of different tasks. The term *skill* is more specific, referring to level of proficiency on a specific task. Thus, flying an airplane is a skill, while spatial orientation is a more general ability related to performance on many diverse tasks (e.g., dentistry, navigation). Of course, abilities themselves are often products of earlier learning.

Method

The Ss were 40 males, all Yale University undergraduates enrolled in a second semester psychology course. Each S received extended practice on the Two-Hand Coordination apparatus and in addition was administered two ability measures: a standardized test of spatial orientation and a newly developed test of "kinesthetic sensitivity."

Ability Measures. **Kinesthetic sensitivity measure.**—The measure used was based on the classical psychophysical procedure of determining difference limens for judgments of lifted weights. Such a measure is relatively easy to administer and brings into play some of the same hand and arm muscles to be used with the Two-Hand Coordination (THC) apparatus. Despite the widespread use of these materials in classical studies of difference thresholds, little is known about the reliability of such measures as indicators of individual differences. Variability among individuals in threshold determinations is error variance in psychophysical study, but it is precisely those differences that we are interested in here. We were not even sure that kinesthetic sensitivity, as measured in this way, represents a dependable ability trait. Considerable pretesting was carried out to arrive at the desirable number of trials, the range of weights to be used, the specific instructions to give, and the type of score to derive.

The weights used were identical (in size) brass cylinders of 100, 102, 104, 106, 108, 110, and 112 gm. The standard was the 106-gm. weight. The method of limits was used, in which blindfolded Ss compared each variable weight in a pair with the standard, making the judgment of whether the second weight was lighter, heavier, or the same, as the first in each pair. Each S was blindfolded and received 24 such pairs, where each weight was lifted one at a time. The S's arm was on the table with lifting done from the wrist. The difference limen (DL) calculated for each S was the measure of kinesthetic sensitivity used. The procedure for deriving this is outlined in Woodworth and Schlosberg (1954, pp. 197-198).

Test-retest reliability of the DLs derived by this test procedure, with at least 24 hr. between the two administrations, was .85. As far as we know, this is the first demonstration that individuals vary consistently in their DLs.

Spatial ability measure.—The measure used was the United States Air Force Aerial Orientation Test found to load consistently on a spatial orientation factor in many previous factor analyses (Fleishman, 1957b; Guilford & Lacey, 1947; Michael, Guilford, Fruchter, & Zimmerman, 1957; Parker & Fleishman, 1960; Roff, 1951). The test presents a printed booklet containing a series of aircraft cockpit views of land-sea-sky horizons. For each item S is required to match the cockpit view of the horizon that corresponds to the position of one of five airplanes from which this view would be seen. Score is the number right. The reliability of this test, in these previous studies, averages approximately .84.

Perceptual-Motor Practice Task. The Two-Hand Coordination apparatus has been described in detail by Melton (1947), and is pictured in reports by Fleishman (1956, 1958, 1960), Parker and Fleishman (1960), and in Gagné and Fleishman (1959). Briefly, S attempts to keep a target-follower on a small target disc as the target moves irregularly and at various rates around a circular plate. Movement of the target-follower to the right and left is controlled by one lathe-type handle; to-and-from movement of the target-follower is controlled by the other handle. Consequently, simultaneous rotation of both handles moves the follower in any *resultant* direction. Score is the total time-on-target during a trial.

In the present study Ss received 40 1-min. trials. These were separated by 15-sec. rests, except after Trials 8, 16, and 32 when there was a 1-min. rest.

Results

Prediction of Two-Hand Coordination Performance from the Ability Measures.—The correlations between the Aerial Orientation Test (number correct) and kinesthetic sensitivity (DL) measures, with total time-on-target during the 40 trials of Two-Hand Coordination performance were found to be .49 and .58, respectively. Both of these coefficients are significant at the .01 level. The correlation between Aerial Orientation and the DL was .12, not statistically significant. These results indicate that our two ability measures tap independent ability traits, each of which accounts for substantial variance in the perceptual-motor practice task. The combination of these two tests yields a multiple R of .73 with overall Two-Hand Coordination performance. Thus, over half the variance ($R^2 = .53$) in total time-on-target on the perceptual-motor task is "accounted for" in terms of two ability traits developed by S prior to practice with this task.

Relation of Ability Measures to Different Stages of THC Learning.—The 40 THC trial scores were grouped into 10 blocks of four trials each. Correlations of each of these 10 time-on-target scores with the ability tests were obtained. These are presented in Table 1.

It is clear from Table 1 that as practice continues the correlations of Two-Hand Coordination (THC) performance decrease with the spatial ability measure and increase with the kinesthetic sensitivity measure. These changes are quite systematic, with the spatial measure showing significant relations only early in THC learning, and the kinesthetic measure showing significant relations only late in learning.

Ss were also ranked on the basis of their scores on the spatial test measure. The group was then stratified at the median into "high spatial ability" and "low spatial ability" Ss. The THC acquisition curves were then plotted for each group. The groups are separated at the beginning of learning, with those Ss who have a higher spatial ability superior in two-hand coordination ability. As practice continues the curves *converge* until there is no superiority of the high spatial ability group. (A t test between the groups during the first trial is significant at the .01 level; differences at the last trial are not significant.)

The total Ss were stratified (at the median) on the basis of their "weight lifting" DLs. Here we have the Two-Hand Coordination acquisition curves

TABLE 1

Correlations of Spatial and Kinesthetic Tests with Successive Trials of Two-Hand Coordination Task Performance

THC Trial	Aerial Orientation	Kinesthetic Sensitivity
1	.36**	.03
2	.28*	.19
3	.22*	.15
4	.19	.15
5	.08	.10
6	.07	.09
7	.09	.23*
8	−.05	.28*
9	−.02	.38**
10	.01	.40**

* $p < .05$, one-tailed.
** $p < .01$, one-tailed.

for Ss with above average kinesthetic sensitivity (low DLs) and for Ss with below average kinesthetic sensitivity (high DLs). These curves *diverge* with continued practice. There is absolutely no difference between these groups during early THC performance, but this variable produces a significant difference later in learning. (A *t* test between the groups at the last trial is significant at the .01 level.)

Discussion

The limitation is that we have stratified a relatively small group at the median. Consequently, the groups overlap considerably and individuals in the middle of the range dominate both groups, making it difficult to demonstrate the predicted differences. In spite of this, the effects are clearly shown to be in the hypothesized directions. What is shown is an interaction effect between different abilities and the effects of practice on still another perceptual-motor skill. More importantly, we have identified an ability variable which is predictive of more advanced proficiency levels in psycho-motor performance.

These findings are consistent with the ability-skill paradigm, previously described, as well as with an information processing model of human learning. In fact, abilities can be thought of as "capacities for utilizing different kinds of information." It would seem that initially, exteroceptive cues (spatial-visual) provide information which guides Ss' movements into the appropriate patterns indicated by the target course. These cues assist S in learning the spatial relationships between the proper control handle and proper direction of handle movement required for S to move the target-follower toward the moving target. The Ss who are especially good at using this type of spatial information make more rapid progress at this stage in the sense that they are in the target area more frequently. At this stage, kinesthetic cues are of relatively little use. Furthermore, S has had little opportunity to experience the appropriate proprioceptive feedback as his errors continue to be large ones. As all Ss learn to utilize these spatial cues, so also do they learn the accompanying proprioceptive cues which accompany the movements originally controlled by the exteroceptive feedback. Once a given level of proficiency is reached and errors tend to be smaller, spatial cues are not as effective in facilitating more precise control over the target-follower. The Ss high in spatial ability have an advantage only in the earlier stages of learning. To achieve a higher score, finer motor adjustments are required. Those Ss who are especially sensitive to proprioceptive cues are able to make use of this information earlier in the practice period. In a sense, they may be able to switch from a dependence on exteroceptive (visual-spatial) feedback to the more direct proprioceptive channels. The Ss who are limited in this sensitivity are more limited in the level of proficiency they can achieve at advanced levels of practice.

The study also illustrates how the use of external reference tests of Ss' abilities provides a way of describing the components of skill learning. Elsewhere (Parker & Fleishman, 1961) we have shown that knowledge of how these components interact with practice at different stages of skill learning can facilitate skill training.

References

Adams, J. A. & Creamer, L. R. Proprioception variables as determiners of anticipatory timing behavior. *Hum. Factors,* 1962, *3,* 217-222.

Bahrick, H. P. An analysis of stimulus variables influencing the proprioceptive control of movements. *Psychol. Rev.,* 1957, *64,* 324-328.

Fitts, P. M. Engineering psychology and equipment design. In S. S. Stevens (Ed.), *Handbook of Experimental Psychology.* New York: Wiley, 1951.

Fleishman, E. A. Predicting advanced levels of proficiency in psycho-motor skills. In G. Finch & F. Cameron (Eds.), *Air Force Human Engineering, Personnel, and Training Research*. (NAS-NRC Publ. No. 455) Washington, D.C.: National Academy of Science-National Research Council, 1956. Pp. 142-151.

Fleishman, E. A. A comparative study of aptitude patterns in unskilled and skilled psychomotor performances. *J. appl. Psychol.*, 1957, 41, 263-272. (a)

Fleishman, E. A. Factor structure in relation to task difficulty in psychomotor performance. *Educ. psychol. Measmt.*, 1957, 17, 522-532. (b)

Fleishman, E. A. Dimensional analysis of movement reactions. *J. exp. Psychol.*, 1958, 55, 453-483.

Fleishman, E. A. Abilities and the learning of psychomotor skills. In P. H. Dubois, W. H. Manning, & C. J. Spies (Eds.), *Factor Analysis and Related Techniques in the Study of Learning*. Technical Report No. 7, 1959, Washington University, Contract Nonr-816(02), Office of Naval Research.

Fleishman, E. A. Psychomotor tests drug research. In J. G. Miller & L. Uhr (Eds.), *Drugs and Behavior*. New York: Wiley, 1960.

Fleishman, E. A. The description and prediction of perceptual-motor skill learning. In R. Glaser (Ed.), *Training Research and Education*. Pittsburgh: Univer. Pittsburgh Press, 1962.

Fleishman, E. A., & Hempel, W. E., Jr. The relation between abilities and improvement with practice in a visual discrimination reaction task. *J. exp. Psychol.*, 1955, 49, 301-310.

Gagné, R. M., & Fleishman, E. A. *Psychology and Human Performance*. New York: Holt, 1959.

Guilford, J. P., & Lacey, J. T. (Eds.) *Printed Classification Tests*. Washington: United States Government Printing Office, 1947.

Jenkins, W. O. Somesthesis. In S. S. Stevens (Ed.), *Handbook of Experimental Psychology*. New York: Wiley, 1951.

Melton, A. W. (Ed.) *Apparatus Tests*. Washington: United States Government Printing Office, 1947.

Michael, W. B., Guilford, J. P., Fruchter, B., & Zimmerman, W. S. The description of spatial-visualization abilities. *Educ. psychol. Measmt.*, 1957, 17, 185-199.

Parker, J. F., & Fleishman, E. A. Ability factors and component performance measures as predictors of complex tracking behavior. *Psychol. Monogr.*, 1960, 74(16, Whole No. 503).

Parker, J. F., & Fleishman, E. A. Use of analytical information concerning task requirements to increase the effectiveness of skill training. *J. appl. Psychol.*, 1961, 45, 295-302.

Roff, M. F. Personnel and classification procedures: Spatial tests. *USAF Sch. Aviat. Med. Rep.*, 1951, No. 21-29-002.

Woodworth, R. L., & Schlosberg, H. *Experimental Psychology*. New York: Holt, 1954.

Effects of Practice Upon Individual Differences and Intra-variability in a Motor Skill*

A. V. CARRON and J. L. LEAVITT

ANY concern one might have for human abilities must also be framed within the context of individual differences. Traditionally norms are

* From *The Research Quarterly*, 1968, 39, 470-475. Reprinted with permission of authors and American Association for Health, Physical Education, and Recreation.

established for personality traits, intellectual aptitude, or motor abilities, and individual variations around the median examined. However, practice itself may cause individuals to differ more or less from each other and to become more or less consistent within their own performances. Thus far we have seen how specific ability tests relate to motor learning. In the present article, a description is offered of intra-individual (within subject) and inter-individual (between subject) changes coinciding wth practice. Franklin Henry and his many graduate students at the University of California at Berkeley have researched this topic at a fair amount of depth in recent years as well as a theoretical exponential mathematical model for a learning curve.

Differences observed in the performance scores of a group of individuals do not necessarily demonstrate that there are individual differences. These score differences may reflect nothing more than a fluctuation in individual performance from moment to moment or trial to trial. It is only to the extent that this variation *within* individuals is small as compared to the variation *between* individuals that individual differences assume importance.

While there has been interest for some time in the question of how practice affects variability,[12] this interest has until recently centered around total variance. During the past few years however, Henry and his students have examined the effect of practice on individual differences (true-score variance, S^2_t) and intra-variability (S^2_i). While usually combined as well as confused with error variance, it should be noted that the biological variability of performance within an individual (or intra-variability) seems to be large as compared with experimental error.[5]

Review of Literature

The first of the theses and dissertations from the University of California laboratory which reported results bearing on this problem is a study by Grose.[2] He tested 51 college male students in a coincidence timing task involving a finger press, a horizontal arm movement, and a whole body progression movement. For all three tasks the intra-variance decreased over the 25 practice trials, while mean performance scores and the individual difference variance were not affected.

Using Henry's constant tension kinesthetic task,[6] Morford[9] found that the intra-variance of a group of 30 subjects practicing without visual feedback decreased over the practice period of 10 one-minute trials. The performance level and individual difference variance remained unchanged during this period. When two additional groups of 30 subjects were tested, with each group receiving a different amount of visual feedback to supplement their kinesthetic information, mean performance level improved, individual difference variance decreased, and intra-variance was unaffected.

Lersten[7] noted an eightfold increase in the individual difference variance during the first 60 practice trials (with a practice-rest ratio of 25-sec. practice and 15-sec. rest) on the pursuit rotor. During this same period, the intra-variance doubled. For the 60 college males tested in this experiment, additional practice over a period of five additional days had little effect on these variances even though the mean performance level continued to improve.

Meyers[8] tested 100 high school girls for two practice sessions which consisted of 10 one-min. trials on the Bachman ladder climb. A varied layoff for five subgroups (10 min., one day, one week, four weeks, and 13 weeks) separated the two practice sessions. Although the mean performance level showed a large improvement with practice, no appreciable change was evidenced for either the individual difference or intra-variances.

In a comprehensive study by Welch and Henry,[11] 70 freshman college women were tested on the stabilometer over a six-day practice period (twelve 300-sec. trials per day). Performance level improved throughout the practice period while both types of individual variance decreased exponentially. Relative variability increased 200 percent over the practice period.

In view of the relatively small amount of information in this area, and the different results obtained by Meyers with the Bachman ladder[8] versus Welch and Henry[11] with the stabilometer,[11] it would seem desirable to pursue the influence of practice on individual difference (true-score) variance and intra-variance in a learning situation. An experimental design such as that used by Welch and Henry[11] (i.e., a six-day interrupted practice period) ensures that the practice period will be sufficiently long to observe any changes which might occur in these parameters well into the learning. Also, by using the same experimental design and the same motor learning task used by Welch and Henry,[11] it will be possible to determine if the mathematical model used to describe the learning curve for freshman college women can also be applied to the learning curve for children.

Procedures

Thirty boys from the University of California Children's Recreation School (mean age = 10.9 yr., S.D. = 1.0) participated in the experiment. All were volunteers who had had no previous experience on the stabilometer or similar apparatus. The subjects were tested for six days, with an interval of one-to-two days between each practice day. Within a test day, the performance schedule consisted of 12 trials of 30-sec. duration with a 30-sec. rest period between each trial.

The subjects stood erect on a horizontally pivoted platform (stabilometer), straddling the middle supporting axle with knees slightly flexed and hands either on the hips or hooked into the belt. The task required balancing the board with a minimum of movement. The less motion that is displayed in the maintenance of position, the greater the level of skill. A work-adder recorded the movement of the board (12° of movement represented one movement unit). Scores were recorded to the nearest 1/10 division.

Results

Intra-variance and Individual Difference (True-score) Variance. The error variance (S^2_e, the instrumental and observational error) was calculated to be .02 movement units by Welch and Henry.[11] They found that the average intra-variance (S^2_i) per trial was 25.0 scale units, while S^2_e was only .02 scale units. For this reason, the observed within-individual variance could be accepted as representing S^2_i. Their stabilometer was used in the present study.

The standard deviations of the true-score variance and intra-variance were plotted as a function of practice. These results agree with those of Welch and Henry with college women,[11] since both true score and the intra-variances in the present study show parallel decreases with practice. They differ from the findings of Meyers,[8] who used a different task (ladder climb) and found no influence of practice on either type of variability in high school girls.

The decrease in true-score variance meant that the effect of practice is to cause individuals to become more nearly like each other in this particular skill. This may or may not be true for other skills. True-score variance *is* the quantitative measure of individual differences.

The decrease in intra-variance with practice means that the subjects are becoming more consistent in their own individual performances. This does not necessarily mean that reliability is increasing. In fact, in the present study it tends to *decrease* with practice. The reliability coefficient can be computed as S^2_t/S^2_x, where $S^2_x = S^2_t + S^2_i$.[3,4] At trials 6, 24, 36, and 72, for example, the reliabilities estimated from the variance trend curves are $r = .82, .76, .73$, and .67.

Reynolds[10] has suggested that with practice there is a discarding of extraneous responses which hinder correct performance and/or a cessation by the subject of any experimentation with different approaches to perform the task, and the settling on one or two convenient and appropriate techniques. This may offer an explanation for the mechanism responsible for the current findings.

The changes in these two kinds of variation are not proportional to the changes in mean performance. When the learning effect is partialed out by examining the relative variation (S_t/M and S_i/M) at various stages of practice, both kinds of variation are approximately doubled with practice. This agrees with the findings of Welch and Henry on their study of college women.

Theoretical Learning Curve.   The theoretical significance of the exponential mathematical model for the stabilometer learning curve has been adequately discussed by Welch and Henry[11] and will not be elaborated here. The present data fit this model quite well. The points represent actual obtained values while the smooth curve is drawn according to the exponential equation $y = a_1 e^{-k_1 n} + a'_3 e^{-k/n'} + C$, where $a_1 e^{-k_1 n}$ represents the main (slow) component, $a'_3 e^{-k/n'}$ represents rapid learning on day 1 and the relearning component on days 2 through 6. The symbol C represents the asymptote or a plateau on the sixth (last) practice day. The symbol n in the first exponential term represents the number of any particular trial minus one, a_1 is the magnitude of the component at the first trial, k is the rate constant of that exponential term, and e is the Naperian log base 2.718. The symbol n' is the number of a trial minus one within a particular day (i.e., it is two for the third trial on day 1, or the third trial on day 2, or the third trial on day 3, etc.); a'_3 and k'_3 are the curve constants for this relearning component.

The initial performance level of the boys in our study is 50.4 movement units, and the estimated C at the end of day 6 is 5.0 movement units. The parameters for the first component are $a_1 = 23.8$, and $k_1 = .0357$. They are comparable to those found by Welch and Henry[11] which were $a_1 = 19.7$, and $k_1 = .0469$; the C is slightly higher than their value of 1.75.

The above formula for the curve does not contain the $a_2 e^{-k_2 n}$ component included in the Welch and Henry formula. The reason it was not found possible to resolve this component is probably because of irregularities occasioned by our much smaller number of subjects. Consequently our $a_3' e^{-k/3 n'}$ probably represents an average of their second and third components for day 1; our k'_3 for day 1 (.661) is almost identical with the average of their k_2 and k_3 (.674); but our a'_3 (22.7) for day 1 is noticeably higher than their average of a_2 and a_3 (16.3). A value of $k'_3 = .340$ for days 2 through 6 was used, since with fewer subjects and greater irregularity daily differences could not be distinguished. The a'_3 values are 8.2 for day 2; 5.1, 4.1, 2.3, and 2.1 for the remainder of the practice days.

Similarity is noted between Bachman's results[1] using a single day of practice and the results in this experiment. Averaging his figures for boys aged 10 to 11 and 11 to 12 yr. (N=32), the initial scores were 57.5, the final scores (trial 10) were 24.7, and the learning score 32.8 movement units. Our corresponding day 1 scores are 50.4, 22.7, and 27.7 for 30 boys. Assuming that his standard deviations for initial and tenth trials were the same as ours (14.3 and 9.7), the differences could be accounted for by sampling error since the t ratios are only 1.93 and 1.87. His instrument was not identical with ours, and there must have been some differences in technique. It seems that the results with the stabilometer are fairly reproducible.

The amount of learning, estimated as the change in performance from the initial score to the position of the trend line at the end of the 12 trials of each day's practice, progressively decreases day by day. The improvement is 30.4 score units for the first day, 5.0 for the second, 3.4 for the third, 2.2 for the fourth, 1.4 for the fifth, and 1.0 for the sixth.

The first three or four trials on each day were always poorer than the end of practice on the preceding day. In other words, there is a considerable loss of performance during the 24-hr. layoff between practice days. It requires three or four trials just to catch up from the effect of the layoff, and three or four additional trials to reach the level of performance that presumably would have been reached on the six or eight practice trials if there had been no layoff (assuming no fatigue or inhibition from these additional six or eight trials). Using the trend line at the end of each day's practice as a reference point, the drops in performance between these points and the first trials after the layoff, for the first to fifth layoffs, are 10.0, 5.2, 4.1, 3.9, and 3.1. Using a'_3 from the mathematical curves, these values are somewhat smaller in some instances. As stated earlier, a'_3 is 8.2 for the first layoff and 2.1 for the last; the only other discrepancy is 2.3 (instead of 3.9) for the next to last layoff.

Thus, as learning becomes more complete, the amount of performance loss from the layoff becomes progressively less. This finding is similar to the trend reported by Welch and Henry; but the performance-drops after layoff in our young boys are approximately twice as large as in their college women.

Conclusions

During this large muscle motor coordination task, both individual differences (true-score variance) and within-subject variance decreased with practice, although they increased when calculated as relative variations. Reliability decreased with practice.

An exponential mathematical model was found to describe the six-day practice curve for these boys, including the relearning after the interposed rest days. The parameter values were similar to those reported by Welch and Henry for college women for a six-day practice curve, and the initial and tenth trial scores were similar to those reported by Bachman for boys aged 10 to 13.

Large amounts of performance loss occurred with each one-day layoff, with consequently large amounts of relearning. This effect diminished in the later stages of learning.

References

1. Bachman, J. C. Motor learning and performance as related to age and sex in two measures of balance coordination. *Res. quart.* *32*:123-31, 1961.
2. Grose, J. E. *Training ability in finger, arm and whole body movements.* Unpublished doctoral dissertation, University of California, Berkeley, 1963.
3. Henry, F. M. Reliability, measurement error and intra-individual difference. *Res. quart. 30*:21-24, 1959.
4. ————. Influence of measurement error and intra-individual variation on the reliability of muscle strength and vertical jump tests. *Res. quart. 30*:155-59, 1959.
5. ————. Stimulus complexity, movement complexity, age and sex in relation to reaction latency and speed of limb movements. *Res. quart. 32*:353-66, 1961.

6. ————. Dynamic kinesthetic perception and adjustment. *Res. quart.* *24*:176-87, 1953.
7. Lersten, K. C. *Inter- and intra-individual variations during the progress of motor learning.* Unpublished doctoral dissertation, University of California, Berkeley, 1966.
8. Meyers, Judith L. *Relearning and retention of a balance coordination.* Unpublished master's thesis, University of California, Berkeley, 1965.
9. Morford, W. R. *The value of supplementary visual information during practice in dynamic kinesthetic learning.* Unpublished doctoral dissertation, University of California, Berkeley, 1964.
10. Reynolds, B. The effect of learning on the predictability of performance. *J. exp. psychol.* *44*:189-98, 1958.
11. Welch, Marya, and Henry, F. M. *Individual differences in various parameters of motor learning.* Unpublished manuscript, University of California, Berkeley.
12. Woodrow, H. The effect of practice on groups of different initial ability. *J. educ. psychol.* *29*:268-78, 1938.

PART 5

DEVELOPMENT AND AGING

The Influence of Developmental Variables on Performance

Genetic endowment and developmental factors predispose individuals to emit behaviors and excel at certain activities. Instruction, training, and experiences help to fulfill potentialities. Researchers delving into the learning process of motor skills have generally either overlooked or paid lip-service to the developmental aspects of learning. Yet, in order to understand the behaviors of mature organisms, some insight as to what went on before is in order. Furthermore, learning and performance expectations according to maturational status or chronological age provide other important data.

Psychologists who study development from birth to maturity or aging inform us that the individual undergoes a series of fairly predictable and orderly events and changes. There are some characteristics that are relatively stable and others that are not. It has been written elsewhere that development and aging involve irreversible changes that are continuous and cumulative. To be aware, then, of behaviorial norms is of benefit in anticipating proficiency in skill.

With regard to the influence of early and timely experiences on later behaviors, research is accumulating on lower forms of organisms but is still woefully lacking on man. Enriched cultural environments in which movement and exploration are not only possible but also encouraged are recognized in the development of general gross motor skills. The difficulty in isolating optimal, or critical, learning periods in which the organism is maturationally ready to learn any motor skill is much more apparent with man than with subhuman organisms. In this portion of the book, Part 5, critical learning research with lower forms of life is described. The classic Johnny and Jimmy study, with its apparent limitations, is included to indicate an attempt to designate periods of critical development with children.

Other articles range from performance expectations in children and adolescents to aged individuals. Comparisons between varying age groups in motor performance lead to inferences about the aging process. Various motor skills demand different requirements of the performer, many of which are age and maturation reflected in output. Although many learning "principles" can hold fairly true regardless of the learner's developmental stage, unique considerations according to age and maturational status deserve recognition.

151

Chapter 7

EARLY LEARNING

Critical Periods in Behavioral Development*

J. P. SCOTT

THEORETICALLY, there is a point in the developmental process of every organism at which it is best able to respond most effectively to a certain stimulation, to a given experience. Research concerned with man presents great hazards in attempting to uncover this optimal period. Research with lower organisms has been far more rewarding. Scott has contributed much of our knowledge on the development of behavior in many forms of life, and it is logical that one of his writing efforts be included here. The article is all-encompassing in summarizing research and suggesting theories. The recurring theme throughout the article is that the potential critical period for any organism is not so much dependent on chronological age as on the timeliness of introduction.

A number of years ago I was given a female lamb taken from its mother at birth. My wife and I raised it on the bottle for the first 10 days of life and then placed it out in the pasture with a small flock of domestic sheep. As might have been expected from folklore, the lamb became attached to people and followed the persons who fed it. More surprisingly, the lamb remained independent of the rest of the flock when we restored it to the pasture. Three years later it was still following an independent grazing pattern. In addition, when it was mated and had lambs of its own it became a very indifferent mother, allowing its offspring to nurse but showing no concern when the lamb moved away with the other members of the flock.[1]

Since following the flock is such a universal characteristic of normal sheep, I was impressed by the extensive and permanent modification of this behavior that resulted from a brief early experience. The results suggested that Freud was right concerning the importance of early experience, and pointed toward the existence of critical periods in behavioral development. As I soon discovered, there is considerable evidence that a critical period for determining early social relationships is a widespread phenomenon in vertebrates; such a critical period had long been known in ants.[2]

The theory of critical periods is not a new one in either biology or psychology. It was strongly stated by Stockard in 1921, in connection with his experiments on the induction of monstrosities in fish embryos, although he gave credit to Dareste for originating the basic idea 30 years earlier.[3] In experimenting with the effects of various inorganic chemicals upon the development of *Fundulus* eggs, Stockard at first thought one-eyed monsters were specifically caused by the magnesium ion. Further experiments showed him that almost any chemical would produce the same effect, provided it was applied at the proper time during development. These experiments and those of Child[4] and his students established the fact that the most rapidly growing tissues in an embryo are the most sensitive to any change in conditions, thus accounting for the specificity of effects at particular times.

Meanwhile Freud had attempted to explain the origin of neuroses in human patients as the result of early experience and had implied that certain periods in the life of an infant are times of particular sensitivity. In 1935, Lorenz[5] emphasized the importance of critical periods for the formation of primary social bonds (imprinting) in birds, remarking on their similarity to critical periods in the development of the embryo, and McGraw soon afterward[6] pointed out the existence of criticial periods for optimal learning of motor skills in the human infant.

Since then, the phenomenon of critical periods has excited the imagination of a large group of experimenters interested in human and animal development. In describing this fast-moving scientific field, I shall point out some of the most significant current developments. More detailed information is available in some excellent recent reviews.[7,8]

To begin with, three major kinds of critical-period phenomena have been discovered. These involve optimal periods for learning, for infantile stimulation, and for the formation of basic social relationships. The last of these has been established as a widespread phenomenon in the animal kingdom and consequently receives major attention in this article.

Periods Are Based on Processes

In the dog, the development of behavior may be divided into several natural periods marked off by important changes in social relationships (Table 1). Only a few other species have been studied in sufficient detail for making adequate comparisons, but enough data have been accumulated to show that similar periods can be identified in other mammals and in birds.[9,10] I originally expected to find that the course of postnatal development, like that of embryonic development, would be essentially similar in all vertebrates, and that while the periods might be extended or shortened, the same pattern of development would be evident in all.[11] However, comparison of only two species, man and the dog, shows that the periods can actually occur in reverse order, and that there is an astonishing degree of flexibility in behavioral development.[12]

This leads to the conclusion that the important aspect of each developmental period is not time sequence but the fact that each represents a major developmental process. Thus, the neonatal period is chiefly characterized by the process of neonatal nutrition—nursing in mammals and parental feeding in many birds. The transition period is characterized by the process of transition to adult methods of nutrition and locomotion and the appearance of adult patterns of social behavior, at least in immature form. The period of socialization is the period in which primary social bonds are formed. If we consider processes alone, it is apparent that they are not completely dependent on each other and that they can therefore be arranged in different orders. It is also apparent that certain of these processes persist beyond the periods characterized by them. For example, a mammal usually retains throughout life the ability to suck which characterizes the neonatal period, although in most cases this ability is little used.

Process of Primary Socialization

Since one of the first acts of a young mammal is to nurse, and since food rewards are known to modify the behavior of adult animals, it once seemed logical to suppose that the process of forming a social attachment begins with food rewards and develops as an acquired drive. However, the experimental evidence does not support this extreme viewpoint. Brodbeck reared a group of puppies during the critical period of socialization, feeding half of them by hand and the other half by machine, but giving all of them the same degree of human contact.[13] He found that the two sets of puppies became equally attached to people. This result was later confirmed by Stanley and his co-workers,[14] who found that the only difference in response between the machine-fed and the hand-fed puppies was that the latter yelped more when they saw the experimenter. Elliot and King[15] fed all their puppies by hand but overfed one group and underfed another. The hungry puppies became more rapidly attached to the handlers. We can conclude that, in the dog, food rewards per se are not necessary for the process of socialization, but that hunger will speed it up.

Fisher[16] reared fox terrier puppies in isolation boxes through the entire socialization period. The puppies were fed mechanically (thus, food was entirely eliminated as a factor in the experiment), but they were removed from the boxes for regular contacts with the experimenter. One group of puppies was always rewarded by kind social treatment. A second group was sometimes rewarded and sometimes punished, but in a purely random way. Still a third group was always punished for any positive approach to the experimenter. The puppies that were both rewarded and punished showed most attraction and dependency behavior with respect to the experimenter, and the puppies that were always punished showed the least. After the treatment was discontinued, all the puppies began coming toward the experimenter, and the differences rapidly disappeared. This leads to the surprising conclusion that the process of socialization is not inhibited by punishment and may even be speeded up by it.

At approximately 3 weeks of age—that is, at the beginning of the period of socialization—young puppies begin to bark or whine when isolated or placed in strange places. Elliot and Scott[17] showed that the reaction to isolation in a strange place reaches a peak at 6 to 7 weeks of age, approximately the midpoint of the critical period and begins to decline thereafter. Scott, Deshaies, and Morris[18] found that separating young puppies overnight from their mother and litter mates in a strange pen for 20 hours per day produced a strong emotional reaction and speeded up the process of socialization to human handlers. All this evidence indicates that any sort of strong emotion, whether hunger, fear, pain or loneliness, will speed up the process of socialization. No experiments have been carried out to determine the effects of pleasant types of emotion, such as might be aroused by play and handling, but these were probably a factor in Brodbeck's experiment with machine-fed puppies.

The results of these experiments on dogs agree with evidence from other species. While they were going on, Harlow[19] was performing his famous experiments with rhesus monkeys isolated at birth and supplied with dummy "mothers." When given the choice between a comfortable cloth-covered mother without a nipple and an uncomfortable mother made of wire screening but equipped with a functional nursing bottle, the young rhesus monkeys definitely preferred the cloth-covered models from which they had received no food rewards. Harlow concluded that the acquired-drive theory of the origin of social attachment could be discarded.

Later, Igel and Calvin[20] performed a similar but more elaborate experiment with puppies. These animals had more opportunity to choose, being provided with four kinds of mother models: comfortable and uncomfortable, each type with and without nipples. Like rhesus monkeys, the puppies preferred the comfortable "mother" but usually chose one with a nipple. Thus, it appears that food rewards do contribute something to the social relationship, although they do not form its prime basis.

Since then Harlow[21] has raised to maturity the monkeys raised on dummy mothers, has mated them, and has observed their behavior toward their own young. They become uniformly poor mothers, neglecting their offspring and often punishing them when they cry. In spite of such rejection, the young rhesus infants desperately crawl toward their mothers and give every evidence of becoming attached to them, although perhaps not as strongly as in the normal relationship. Here again punishment does not inhibit the formation of a social bond.

The hypothesis that the primary social bond originates through food rewards had already been shown to be invalid in the precocial birds, many of which form attachments prior to the time when they begin to feed. Lorenz[5] was the first to point out the significance of this phenomenon, which he called "imprinting." He also stated that it differed from conditioning primarily in that it was very rapid and apparently irreversible. However, rapid formation and great persistence are also characteristic of many conditioned responses and other learned behavior. Fabricius[22] pointed out that no sharp line can be drawn between imprinting and conditioning, and Collias[23] concluded that imprinting is a form of learned behavior that is self-reinforcing.

The process of imprinting in young ducklings and chicks has since been experimentally analyzed in much detail, with results that invariably confirm the conclusion that it takes place without any obvious external rewards or reinforcement. Hess[24] found that if he caused young ducklings to follow a model over varying distances or over hurdles, the ducklings which had to make the greater effort became more strongly imprinted. He also found that the drug meprobamate and its congener carisoprodol, which are muscle relaxants as well as tranquilizers, greatly reduce imprinting if given during the critical period. James[25] found that chicks would become attached to an object illuminated by a flickering light, even though they were not allowed to follow, and Gray[62] later showed that they will become attached to a motionless object illuminated by a steady light and viewed from an isolation box. It is therefore apparent that chicks can become imprinted without following, although muscular tension may still be important.

Guiton[27] found that chicks allowed to follow a model in a group become less strongly imprinted than chicks exposed singly, and he attributed the results to the greater fear shown by the isolated chicks. Recently, Pitz and Ross[28] subjected young chicks following a model to a loud sound and found that this increased the speed with which they formed a social bond. Hess[29] has given a mild electric shock to chicks following a model and finds that this also increases the strength of imprinting. Instead of avoiding the model, the distressed chick runs after it more closely.

We may conclude that these young birds become attached to any object to which they are long exposed during the critical period, even when their contact is only visual. We may also conclude that the speed of formation of a social bond is dependent upon the degree of emotional arousal, irrespective of the nature of that arousal. Whether attachment is the result of the emotion itself or of the reduction of emotion as the chick or duckling approaches the model is still a matter of conjecture.[30]

Timing Mechanisms

The basic timing mechanisms for developmental periods are obviously the biological processes of growth and differentiation, usually called maturation. For various reasons, these are not precisely correlated with age from birth or hatching. For example, birds often retain newly formed eggs in their bodies overnight, thus incubating them for several hours before laying. By chilling duck eggs just before placing them in an incubator (thus killing all embryos except those in the earliest stages of development) Gottlieb[31] was able to time the age of ducklings from the onset of incubation rather than from hatching and found that variation in the timing for the critical period was much reduced. No such exact timing studies have been made in mammals, but I have estimated that there is at least a week's variation in development among puppies at 3 weeks of age, and the variation among human infants must be considerably greater.[32]

TABLE 1

Periods of Development in the Puppy and Song Sparrow*

Puppy			Song sparrow		
Name of period	Length of period (weeks)	Initial event	Name of period	Length of period (days)	Initial event
I. Neonatal	0–2	Birth, nursing	Stage 1 (nestling)	0–4	Hatching, gaping
II. Transition	2–3	Eyes open	Stage 2	5–6	Eyes open
III. Socialization	3–10	Startle to sound	Stage 3	7–9	Cowering—first fear reactions
			Stage 4 (fledgling)	10–16	Leaving nest— first flight
			Stage 5	17–28	Full flight
IV. Juvenile	10–	Final weaning	Stage 6 (juvenile)	29–	Independent feeding

* The six periods of development described by Nice[10] for the song sparrow correspond to the first four periods in the puppy, as indicated in the table. The young of the two species are born or hatched in an immature state, require intensive parental care and feeding, and go through much the same stages before becoming independent. Development is much more rapid in the bird than in the puppy, although small mammals such as mice mature at about the same rate as birds.

Another approach to the problem is to try to identify the actual mechanisms which open and close a period. Since an important part of forming a primary social relationship appears to be emotional arousal while the young animal is in contact with another, it is obvious that the critical period for socialization could be timed by the appearance of behavioral mechanisms which maintain or prevent contact, and this indeed is the case. There are demonstrable positive mechanisms, varying from species to species, which bring young animals close to other members of their kind: the clinging response of young rhesus monkeys; the following response of chicks, ducklings, and lambs and other herd animals; the social investigation, tail wagging, and playful fighting of puppies; and the visual investigation and smiling of the human infant.[33] These are, of course, accompanied by interacting responses from adult and immature members of the species: holding and clasping by primate mothers, brooding of mother hens and other birds, calling by mother sheep, investigation and play on the part of other young puppies, and the various supporting and nurturing activities of human mothers.

If contact and emotional arousal result in social attachment, there must be negative mechanisms which prevent such attachment once the critical period is past. Perhaps the most widespread of these is the development of a fear response which causes the young animal to immediately leave the vicinity of a stranger and hence avoid contact. This developing fear response is found in young chicks,[7] ducklings,[22,34] dogs,[35] rhesus monkeys,[36] and in many other birds and mammals. Even in children there is a period between the ages of 5 and 12 months in which there is a mounting fear of strangers,[37] sometimes called "8-months anxiety."[38] As already pointed out, there is a time in development when certain fear responses actually facilitate imprinting, but, as they grow stronger, the escape reaction follows so quickly that it prevents contact altogether.

Another sort of negative mechanism is the rejection of strange young by adult sheep, goats, and many other herd animals.[39] In these species the mothers become strongly attached to the young within a few hours after birth and refuse to accept strangers thereafter. This indicates that the rapid formation of emotional bonds is not limited to young animals.

These timing mechanisms all depend primarily on the development of social behavior patterns, but both sensory and motor development can also influence timing. For example, a very immature animal cannot maintain contact by following, and in slowly developing altricial birds such as jackdaws and doves,[5,40] the period of imprinting comes much later than it does in the precocial species. In the human infant the process of socialization begins before the adult motor patterns develop, but contact is maintained by visual exploration and by the smiling response to human faces.[33] Thus, understanding the process of socialization and its timing mechanisms in any particular species requires a systematic study of the development of the various capacities which affect the time of onset and the duration of the critical period. These include sensory, motor, and learning capacities as well as the ability to perform essential patterns of social behavior.

The fact that emotional arousal is so strongly connected with the process of primary socialization suggests that the capacity to produce emotional reactions may also govern the time of onset of a critical period. If puppies are kept in large fields totally isolated from people, fear and escape responses toward human beings very nearly reach a maximum by the time the puppies are 14 weeks old—a finding that fixes the upper limit of the period of socialization.[35] On the other hand, the peak of the emotional response to isolation in a strange place occurs when puppies are approximately 6 to 7 weeks old, as does the peak of the heart-rate response to handling. At this age, such emotional arousal actually contributes to the strength of the social bond. Fuller[41] was unable to condition the heart-rate response consistently until puppies were 5 weeks old. This indicates that one of the factors that brings the critical period to a close may be the developing ability of the young puppy to associate fear responses with particular stimuli.

All this suggests that if the development of the escape response to strangers could be held in check, the critical period might be extended indefinitely. Raising puppies in small isolation boxes during the critical period inhibits the development of the escape response, but they still show obvious signs of fear when they are first removed from their cages. Fuller[42] reports some success in socializing these older pups by overcoming their fear responses, either by careful handling or through the use of tranquilizing drugs.

Fear responses thus have the dual effect of facilitating the formation of the social bond during the critical period (along with other emotions) and of bringing the period to a close. This is understandable because the type of fear which terminates the critical period is a developing fear of strange animals. In the early part of the critical period the escape reaction is either lacking or is momentary and weak. At the close of the period it is strong enough to prevent contact altogether.

Formation of Affectional Bonds in Adult Life

Until recently, most investigators have concentrated their attention on the critical period for primary socialization or imprinting and few have gone on to study similar phenomena in later development. This field of investigation is just beginning to open up, though many related facts have long been known. For example, many birds form strong pair bonds which are maintained as long as both members survive. In studying the development of various types of social bonds in different species of ducks, Schutz[43] finds that, while attachments to particular individuals may be formed in the early critical period from 12 to 17 hours after hatching, the critical period for the attachment to the species may not come until some time later, in some cases as late as 30 days after hatching, and the attachment to a particular member of the opposite sex, or the pair bond, does not come until the age of 5 months or so. Schutz also finds that female mallards cannot be sexually imprinted with respect to other species but always mate with other mallards no matter what their earliest experience has been. A similar phenomenon is reported by Warriner,[44] who finds that male pigeons prefer to mate with birds whose color is similar to that of the parents who reared them, whether of the same or another color from themselves, but females show no preference.

Certain species of mammals, such as foxes,[45] form long-lasting mating bonds. It is possible that the violence of the sexual emotions contributes to the formation of the adult bond, just as other sorts of emotional arousal are important to the primary socialization of the infant. Klopfer[46] has suggested that the rapid formation of the social bond in a mother goat toward her kid is the result of the high degree of emotional arousal which accompanies the birth of the offspring.

In short, it seems likely that the formation of a social attachment through contact and emotional arousal is a process that may take place throughout life, and that although it may take place more slowly outside of certain critical periods, the capacity for such an attachment is never completely lost.

At this point it may be remarked that, in attempting to analyze the development of affection and social bonds objectively, scientists have often tried to simplify the problem by postulating various unitary, unromantic, and sometimes unesthetic explanations. One of these was the "acquired drive" hypothesis—that children love you because you feed them. Taking a more moderate view Harlow[19] has emphasized "contact comfort" as a major variable—that the young monkey begins to love its mother because she feels warm and comfortable—but that a number of other factors are involved. As this article indicates, evidence is accumulating that there is a much less specific, although equally unromantic, general mechanism involved—that given any kind of emotional arousal a young animal will become attached to any individual or object with which it is in contact for a sufficiently long time. The necessary arousal would, of course, include various specific kinds of emotions associated with food rewards and contact comfort.

It should not be surprising that many kinds of emotional reactions contribute to a social relationship. The surprising thing is that emotions which we normally consider aversive should produce the same effect as those which appear to be rewarding. This apparent paradox is partially resolved by evidence that the positive effect of unpleasant emotions is normally limited to early infancy by the development of escape reactions.

Nevertheless, this concept leads to the somewhat alarming conclusion that an animal (and perhaps a person) of any age, exposed to certain individuals or physical surroundings for any length of time, will inevitably become attached to them, the rapidity of the process being governed by the degree of emotional arousal associated with them. I need not dwell on the consequences for human behavior, if this conclusion should apply to our species as well as to other animals, except to point out that it provides an explanation of certain well-known clinical observations such as the development by neglected children of strong affection for cruel and abusive parents, and the various peculiar affectional relationships that develop between prisoners and jailors, slaves and masters, and so on. Perhaps the general adaptive nature of this mechanism is that since the survival of any member of a highly social species depends upon rapid development of social relationships, a mechanism has evolved which makes it almost impossible to inhibit the formation of social bonds.

Critical Periods of Learning

Unlike the process of socialization, the phenomenon of critical periods of learning was first noticed in children rather than in lower animals. McGraw's[47] famous experiment with the twins Johnny and Jimmy was a deliberate attempt to modify behavioral development by giving one of a pair of identical twins special early training. The result varied according to the activity involved. The onset of walking, for example, was not affected by previous practice or help. Other activities, however, could be greatly speeded up—notably roller skating, in which the favored twin became adept almost as soon as he could walk. In other activities performance was actually made worse by early practice, simply because of the formation of unskillful habits. McGraw[6] concluded that there are critical periods for learning which vary from activity to activity; for each kind of coordinated muscular activity there is an optimum for rapid and skillful learning.

In an experiment with rats, Hebb[48] used the technique of providing young animals with many opportunities for spontaneous learning rather than formal training. Pet rats raised in the rich environment of a home performed much better on learning tasks than rats reared in barren laboratory cages. Since then, other experimenters[49] have standardized the "rich" environment as a large cage including many objects and playthings and have gotten similar effects.

Forgays[50] finds that the age at which the maximum effect is produced is limited to the period from approximately 20 to 30 days of age, immediately after weaning. A similar experience in adult life produces no effect. In rats, at any rate, the critical period of learning seems to coincide with the critical period of primary socialization, and it may be that the two are in some way related. Candland and Campbell[51] find that fearful behavior in response to a strange situation begins to increase in rats between 20 and 30 days after birth, and Bernstein[52] showed earlier that discrimination learning could be improved by gentle handling beginning at 20 days. It may well be that the development of fear limits the capacity for future learning as well as the formation of social relationships.

In addition to these studies on motor learning and problem solving, there are many experiments demonstrating the existence of critical periods for the learning of social behavior patterns. It has long been known that many kinds of birds do not develop the characteristic songs of their species if they are reared apart from their own kind.[53] More recently, Thorpe[54] discovered a critical period for this effect in the chaffinch. If isolated at 3 or 4 days of age, a young male chaffinch produces an incomplete song, but if he hears adults singing, as a fledgling 2 or 3 weeks old or in early juvenile life before he sings himself, he will the next year produce the song characteristic of the species, even if he has been kept in isolation. In nature, the fine details of the song are added at the time of competition over territory, within a period of 2 or 3 weeks, when the bird is about a year old. At this time it learns the songs of two or three of its neighbors, and never learns any others in subsequent years. The critical period for song learning is thus a relatively long one, but it is definitely over by the time the bird is a year old. There is no obvious explanation for its ending at this particular time, but it is possible that learning a complete song pattern in some way interferes with further learning.

King and Gurney[55] found that adult mice reared in groups during youth fought more readily than animals isolated at 20 days of age. Later experiments showed that most of the effect was produced in a 10-day period just after weaning, and that similar experience as adults produced little or no effect.[56] Thus, there appears to be a critical period for learning to fight through social experience, and this experience need be no more than contact through a wire. In this case the effect is probably produced by association with other mice before the fear response has been completely developed. Similarly, Fisher[16] and Fuller[57] inhibited the development of attacking behavior in fox terriers by raising them in isolation through the critical period for socialization. The animals would fight back somewhat ineffectually if attacked, but did not initiate conflicts. Tinbergen[58] found a critical period in dogs for learning territorial boundaries coinciding with sexual maturity.

The results of corresponding experiments on sexual behavior vary from species to species. In mice, rearing in isolation produced no effects.[59] Beach[60] found that male rats reared with either females or males were actually slower to respond to sexual behavior than isolated males, and he suggested that habits of playful fighting established by the group-reared animals interfered with sexual behavior later on. In guinea pigs, contact with other young animals improves sexual performance.[61]

On the other hand, young chimpanzees[62] reared apart from their kind can only be mated with experienced animals. Harlow[21] discovered that his rhesus infants reared on dummy mothers did not develop normal patterns of sexual behavior, and he was able to obtain matings only by exposing females to experienced males. Normal behavior can be developed by allowing 20-minute daily play periods with other young monkeys, but if rhesus infants are reared apart from other monkeys beyond the period when they spontaneously play with their fellows, patterns of both sexual and maternal behavior fail to develop normally. These results suggest that play has an important role in developing adult patterns of social behavior in these primates, and that the decline of play behavior sets the upper limit of the critical period during which normal adult behavior may be developed.

Such great changes in the social environment rarely occur in human beings even by accident, but Money, Hampson, and Hampson[63] have studied the development of hermaphroditic children who have been reared as one sex and then changed to the other. They find that if this occurs before 2½ years of age, very little emotional disturbance results. Thus, there is a critical period for learning the sex role, this capacity persisting unchanged up to a point in development which roughly corresponds to the age when children begin to use and understand language. Perhaps more important, this is the age when children first begin to take an interest in, and play with, members of their own age group.

It is difficult to find a common factor in these critical periods for learning. In some species, such as rats, mice, dogs, and sheep, certain critical periods for learning coincide with the period for primary socialization and seem to be similarly brought to a close by the development of fear reactions. Other critical periods, in chaffinches and dogs, coincide with the formation of adult mating bonds. However, the critical period for sexual learning in the rhesus monkey comes later than that for primary socialization,[64] as do critical periods for various kinds of learning in human beings.

Part of this apparent inconsistency arises from our ignorance regarding timing mechanisms. One such mechanism must be the development of learning capacities, and we have evidence in dogs,[65] rhesus monkeys,[66] and human infants[12] that learning capacities change during development, sometimes in a stepwise fashion. One element in these capacities is the ability to learn things which facilitate subsequent learning.

It is equally possible, however, to "learn not to learn," and such a negative learning set may act to bring the critical period to a close. At this point, we can only state a provisional general hypothesis: that the critical period for any specific sort of learning is that time when maximum capacities—sensory, motor, and motivational, as well as psychological ones—are first present.

Critical Periods for Early Stimulation

Experiments to determine the effects of early stimulation have been mainly performed on infant mice and rats, which are usually weaned at about 21 days at the earliest, and have been concerned with the effect of stimulation during this pre-weaning period. All investigators beginning with Levine[67] and Schaefer,[68] agree that rats handled during the first week or 10 days of life have a lessened tendency to urinate and defecate in a strange "open field" situation, learn avoidance behavior more readily, and survive longer when deprived of food and water. In short, early stimulation produces an animal that is less timorous, learns more quickly, and is more vigorous. Levine found that the effect could be obtained by a variety of stimuli, including electric shock and mechanical shaking as well as handling. This ruled out learned behavior as an explanation of the effect, and Levine, Alpert, and Lewis[69] discovered that animals handled in the early period showed a much earlier maturation of the adrenocortical response to stress. Levine interpreted these results as indicating that the laboratory environment did not provide sufficient stimulation for the proper development of the hormonal systems of the animals. This interpretation is in agreement with Richter's finding[70] that laboratory rats are quite deficient in adrenocortical response as compared with the wild variety. Schaefer, Weingarten, and Towne[71] have duplicated Levine's results by the use of cold alone, and have suggested temperature as a possible unitary mechanism. However, their findings are not necessarily in disagreement with those of Levine, as the hormonal stress response can be elicited by a variety of stimuli, and temperature may simply be another of the many kinds of stimuli which produce the effect.

According to Thompson and Schaefer[72] the earlier the stimulation the greater the effect. If the hormonal mechanism is the chief phenomenon involved, we can say that there is a critical period during the first week or 10 days of life, since the adrenal response in any case matures and becomes fixed by 16 days of age.

Denenberg[73] takes a somewhat different approach, pointing out that there should be optimal levels of stimulation, so that either very weak or very strong stimulation would produce poor results. He suggests that there are different critical periods for the effect of early stimulation, depending on the intensity of stimulation and the kind of later behavior measured. Working within the critical first 10 days, Denenberg found that the best avoidance learning was produced by stimulation in the second half of the period, whereas the best survival rates were produced by stimulation in the first half. Weight was approximately equally affected, except that there was little effect in the first 3 days.[74]

Analyzing the effect on avoidance learning, Denenberg[75] and his associates found that both unhandled controls and rats handled for the first 20 days performed poorly, the former because they were too emotional and the latter because they were too calm to react quickly. An intermediate amount of emotional response produces the best learning, and this can be produced by handling only in the first 10 days of life; handling during the second 10 days has a lesser effect. No handling produces too much emotionality, and handling for 20 days results in too little. Irrespective of the effect on learning, the data lead to the important conclusion that emotional stimulation during a critical period early in life can lead to the reduction of emotional responses in later life.

More precisely, there appear to be two critical periods revealed by research on early stimulation of rats, one based on a physiological process (the development of the adrenal cortical stress mechanism) and extending to 16 days of age at the latest, the other based on a psychological process (the reduction of fear through familiarity),[51] beginning about 17 days when the eyes first open and extending to 30 days. The effects of handling during these two periods are additive, and many experiments based on arbitrary time rather than developmental periods undoubtedly include both.

The deleterious effects of excessive stimulation in the life of the infant may also be interpreted as a traumatic emotional experience. Bowlby,[76] in studying a group of juvenile thieves, found that a large proportion of them had been separated from their mothers in early infancy, and he postulated that this traumatic emotional experience had affected their later behavior. Since this conclusion was based on retrospective information, he and his co-workers have since studied the primary symptoms of separation and have described in detail the emotional reactions of infants sent to hospitals, and thus separated from their mothers.[77] Schaffer[78] found a difference in reaction to separation before 7 months and separation afterward. Both sets of infants were disturbed, but they were disturbed in different ways. Infants show increasingly severe emotional reactions to adoption from 3 through 12 months of age.[33] It seems logical to place the beginning of the critical period for maximum emotional disturbance at approximately 7 months—at the end of the critical period for primary socialization, which Gray[79] places at approximately 6 weeks to 6 months. Infants whose social relationships have been thoroughly established and whose fear responses toward strangers have been fully developed are much more likely to be upset by changes than infants in which these relationships and responses have not yet been developed.

However, not all apparently "traumatic" early experiences have such a lasting effect. Experimental work shows that young animals have a considerable capacity to recover from unpleasant emotions experienced in a limited period in early life,[80] and that what is traumatic in one species may not be in another. While young rats become calmer after infantile stimulation, young mice subjected to excessive auditory stimulation later become more emotional.[81] At this point it is appropriate to point out that critical periods are not necessarily involved in every kind of early experience. Raising young chimpanzees in the dark produces degeneration of the retina, but this is a long and gradual process.[82]

Another approach to the problem is to stimulate emotional responses in mothers and observe the effect on the offspring. Thompson[83] and other authors[84] have shown that the offspring of rats made fearful while pregnant are more likely to be overemotional in the open-field situation than the offspring of animals not so stimulated. Since any direct influence of maternal behavior was ruled out by cross-fostering experiments, it seems likely that the result is produced by modification of the adrenocortical stress mechanism—in this case, by secretion of maternal hormones acting on the embryo rather than by stimulation after birth of the young animal itself. No precise critical period for the effect has been established, but it is probably confined to the latter part of pregnancy. Similar effects have been obtained in mice,[85] and if such effects can be demonstrated in other mammals, the implications for prenatal care in human beings are obvious.

It is interesting to note that, whereas shocking the mother both before and after parturition has the effect of increasing emotional responses in the young, the emotional responses of young rats are *decreased* when the treatment is applied directly to them. The explanation of this contradiction must await direct experiments on the endocrine system.

General Theory of Critical Periods

There are at least two ways in which experience during critical periods may act on behavioral development. The critical period for primary socialization constitutes a turning point. Experience during a short period early in life determines which shall be the close relatives of the young animal, and this, in turn, leads the animal to develop in one of two directions—the normal one in which it becomes attached to and mates with a member of its own species, or an abnormal one, in which it becomes attached to a different species, with consequent disrupting effects upon sexual and other social relationships with members of its own kind.

The concept of a turning point applies equally well to most examples of critical periods for learning. Up to a certain point in development a chaffinch can learn several varieties of song, but once it has learned one of them it no longer has a choice. Similarly, the human infant can learn either sex role up to a certain age, but once it has learned one or the other, changing over becomes increasingly difficult. What is learned at particular points limits and interferes with subsequent learning, and Schneirla and Rosenblatt[86] have suggested that there are critical stages of learning—that what has been learned at a particular time in development may be critical for whatever follows.

A second sort of action during a critical period consists of a nonspecific stimulus producing an irrevocable result, not modifiable in subsequent development. Thus, almost any sort of stimulus has the effect of modifying the development of the endocrine stress mechanism of young rats in early infancy.

Is there any underlying common principle? Each of these effects has its counterpart in embryonic development. Up to a certain point a cell taken from an amphibian embryo and transplanted to a new location will develop in accordance with its new environment. Beyond this turning point it develops in accordance with its previous location. Some cells retain a degree of lability, but none retain the breadth of choice they had before. Similarly, specific injuries produced by nonspecific causes are also found in embryonic development: damage to an embryonic optic vesicle results in a defective eye, no matter what sort of chemical produces the injury. It is obvious that the similarity between this case and the critical period for early stimulation can be accounted for by the single common process of growth, occurring relatively late in development in the case of the endocrine stress mechanism and much earlier in the development of the eye. The effects are nonspecific because of the fact that growth can be modified in only very limited ways, by being either slowed down or speeded up.

Both growth and behavioral differentiation are based on organizing processes. This suggests a general principle of organization: that once a system becomes organized, whether it is the cells of the embryo that are multiplying and differentiating or the behavior patterns of a young animal that are becoming organized through learning, it becomes progressively more difficult to reorganize the system. That is, organization inhibits reorganization. Further, organization can be strongly modified only when active processes of organization are going on, and this accounts for critical periods of development.

Conclusion

The concept of critical periods is a highly important one for human and animal welfare. Once the dangers and potential benefits for each period of life are known, it should be possible to avoid the former and take advantage of the latter.

The discovery of critical periods immediately focuses attention on the developmental processes which cause them. As these processes become understood, it is increasingly possible to deliberately modify critical periods and their results. For example, since the development of fear responses limits the period of primary socialization, we can deliberately extend the period by reducing fear reactions, either by psychological methods or by the use of tranquilizing drugs. Or, if it seems desirable, we can increase the degree of dependency of a child or pet animal by purposely increasing his emotional reactions during the critical period. Again, if infantile stimulation is desirable, parents can be taught to provide it in appropriate amounts at the proper time.

Some data suggest that for each behavioral and physiological phenomenon there is a different critical period in development. If this were literally true, the process of development, complicated by individual variability, would be so complex that the concept of critical periods would serve little useful purpose. Some sort of order can be obtained by dealing with different classes of behavioral phenomena. For example, it can be stated that the period in life in which each new social relationship is initiated is a critical one for the determination of that relationship. Furthermore, there is evidence that critical-period effects are more common early in life than they are later on, and that the critical period for primary socialization is also critical for other effects, such as the attachment to particular places,[87] and may overlap with a critical period for the formation of basic food habits.[88]

We may expect to find that the periods in which actual physiological damage through environmental stimulation is possible will turn out to be similarly specific and concentrated in early life.

A great deal of needed information regarding the optimum periods for acquiring motor and intellectual skills is still lacking. These skills are based not merely on age but on the relative rate of maturation of various organs. Any attempt to teach a child or animal at too early a period of development may result in his learning bad habits, or simply in his learning "not to learn," either of which results may greatly handicap him in later life. In the long run, this line of experimental work should lead to greater realization of the capacities possessed by human beings, both through avoidance of damaging experiences and through correction of damage from unavoidable accidents.[89]

References and Notes

1. J. P. Scott, *Comp. Psychol. Monogr.* 18, 1 (1945).
2. A. M. Fielde, *Biol. Bull.* 7, 227 (1904).
3. C. R. Stockard, *Am. J. Anat.* 28, 115 (1921).
4. C. M. Child, *Patterns and Problems of Development* (Univ. of Chicago Press, Chicago, 1941).
5. K. Lorenz, *J. Ornithol.* 83, 137, 289 (1935).
6. M. B. McGraw, in *Manual of Child Psychology,* L. C. Carmichael, Ed. (Wiley, New York, 1946), pp. 332-369.
7. E. H. Hess, in *Nebraska Symposium on Motivation* (Univ. of Nebraska Press, Lincoln, 1959), pp. 44-77.
8. H. Moltz, *Psychol. Bull.* 57, 291 (1960); J. L. Gewirtz, in *Determinants of Infant Behaviour,* B. M. Foss, Ed. (Methuen, London, 1961), pp. 213-299.
9. J. P. Scott, in *Social Behavior and Organization among Vertebrates,* W. Etkin, Ed. (Univ. of Chicago Press, Chicago, 1964), pp. 231-255.
10. M. M. Nice, *Trans. Linnaean Soc. N.Y.* 6, 1 (1943).
11. J. P. Scott and M. V. Marston, *J. Genet. Psychol.* 77, 25 (1950).
12. J. P. Scott, *Child Develop. Monogr.* 28, 1 (1963).
13. A. J. Brodbeck, *Bull. Ecol. Soc. Am.* 35, 73 (1954).
14. W. C. Stanley, private communication (1962).
15. O. Elliott and J. A. King, *Psychol. Repts.* 6, 391 (1960).
16. A. E. Fisher, thesis, Pennsylvania State Univ. (1955).
17. O. Elliot and J. P. Scott, *J. Genet. Psychol.* 99, 3 (1961).
18. J. P. Scott, D. Deshaies, D. D. Morris, "Effect of emotional arousal on primary socialization in the dog," address to the New York State branch of the American Psychiatric Association, 11 Nov. 1961.
19. H. Harlow, *Am. Psychologist* 13, 673 (1958).
20. G. J. Igel and A. D. Calvin, *J. Comp. Physiol. Psychol.* 53, 302 (1960).
21. H. F. Harlow and M. K. Harlow, personal communication (1962).
22. E. Fabricius, *Acta Zool. Fennica* 68, 1 (1951).
23. N. Collias, in *Roots of Behavior,* E. L. Bliss, Ed. (Harper, New York, 1962), pp. 264-273.
24. E. H. Hess, *Ann. N.Y. Acad. Sci.* 67, 724 (1957); in *Drugs and Behavior,* L. Uhr and J. G. Miller, Eds. (Wiley, New York, 1960), pp. 268-271.
25. H. James, *Can. J. Psychol.* 13, 59 (1959).
26. P. H. Gray, *Science* 132, 1834 (1960).
27. P. Guiton, *Animal Behavior* 9, 167 (1961).
28. G. F. Pitz and R. B. Ross, *J. Comp. Physiol. Psychol.* 54, 602 (1961).
29. E. H. Hess, "Influence of early experience on behavior," paper presented before the American Psychiatric Association, New York State Divisional Meeting, 1961.
30. H. Moltz, L. Rosenblum, N. Halikas, *J. Comp. Physiol. Psychol.* 52, 240 (1959).
31. G. Gottlieb, *Ibid.* 54, 422 (1961).

32. J. P. Scott, *Psychosomat. Med.* 20, 42 (1958).
33. B. M. Caldwell, *Am. Psychol.* 16, 377 (1961).
34. R. A. Hinde, W. H. Thorpe, M. A. Vince, *Behaviour* 9, 214 (1956).
35. D. G. Freedman, J. A. King, O. Elliot, *Science* 133, 1016 (1961).
36. H. F. Harlow and R. R. Zimmermann, *ibid.* 130, 421 (1959).
37. D. G. Freedman, *J. Child Psychol. Psychiat.* 1961, 242 (1961).
38. R. A. Spitz, *Intern. J. Psychoanalysis* 31, 138 (1950).
39. N. E. Collias, *Ecology* 37, 228 (1956).
40. W. Craig, *J. Animal Behavior* 4, 121 (1914).
41. J. L. Fuller and A. Christake, *Federation Proc.* 18, 49 (1959).
42. J. L. Fuller, private communication.
43. F. Schutz, private communication.
44. C. C. Warriner, thesis, Univ. of Oklahoma (1960).
45. R. K. Enders, *Sociometry* 8, 53-55 (1945).
46. P. H. Klopfer, *Behavioral Aspects of Ecology* (Prentice-Hall, Englewood Cliffs, 1962).
47. M. B. McGraw, *Growth: a Study of Johnny and Jimmy* (Appleton-Century, New York, 1935).
48. D. O. Hebb, *Am. Psychologist* 2, 306 (1947).
49. D. G. Forgays and J. W. Forgays, *J. Comp. Physiol. Psychol.* 45, 322 (1952).
50. D. G. Forgays, "The importance of experience at specific times in the development of an organism," address before the Eastern Psychological Association (1962).
51. D. K. Candland and B. A. Campbell, private communication (1962).
52. L. Bernstein, *J. Comp. Physiol. Psychol.* 50, 162 (1957).
53. W. E. D. Scott, *Science* 14, 522 (1901).
54. W. H. Thorpe, in *Current Problems in Animal Behaviour*. W. H. Thorpe and O. L. Zangwill, Eds. (Cambridge Univ. Press, Cambridge, 1961).
55. J. A. King and N. L. Gurney, *J. Comp. Physiol. Psychol.* 47, 326 (1954).
56. J. A. King, *J. Genet. Psychol.* 90, 151 (1957).
57. J. L. Fuller, "Proceedings, International Psychiatric Congress, Montreal," (1961).
58. Tinbergen, *The Study of Instinct* (Oxford Univ. Press, Oxford, 1951).
59. J. A. King, *J. Genet. Psychol.* 88, 223 (1956).
60. F. A. Beach, *ibid.* 60, 121 (1942).
61. E. S. Valenstein, W. Riss, W. C. Young, *J. Comp. Physiol. Psychol.* 47, 162 (1954).
62. H. Nissen, *Symposium on Sexual Behavior in Mammals, Amherst, Mass.* (1954), pp. 204-227.
63. J. Money, J. G. Hampson, J. D. Hampson, *Arch. Neurol. Psychiat.* 77, 333 (1957).
64. H. Harlow, in *Determinants of Infant Behaviour*. B. M. Foss, Ed. (Wiley, New York, 1961), pp. 75-97.
65. J. L. Fuller, C. A. Easler, E. M. Banks, *Am. J. Physiol.* 160, 462 (1950); A. C. Cornwell and J. L. Fuller, *J. Comp. Physiol. Psychol.* 54, 13 (1961).
66. H. F. Harlow, M. K. Harlow, R. R. Rueping, W. A. Mason, *J. Comp. Physiol. Psychol.* 53, 113 (1960).
67. S. Levine, J. A. Chevalier, S. J. Korchin, *J. Personality* 24, 475 (1956).
68. T. Schaefer, thesis, Univ. of Chicago (1957).
69. S. Levine, M. Alpert, G. W. Lewis, *Science* 126, 1347 (1957).
70. C. P. Richter, *Am. J. Human Genet.* 4, 273 (1952).
71. T. Schaefer, Jr., F. S. Weingarten, J. C. Towne, *Science* 135, 41 (1962).
72. W. R. Thompson and T. Schaefer, in *Functions of Varied Experience*, D. W. Fiske and S. R. Maddi, Eds. (Dorsey, Homewood, Ill., 1961), pp. 81-105.
73. V. H. Denenberg, in *The Behaviour of Domestic Animals*, E. S. E. Hafez, Ed. (Bailliere, Tindall and Cox, London, 1962), pp. 109-138.
74. ———, *J. Comp. Physiol. Psychol.* 55, 8 (1962).
75. ——— and G. G. Karas, *Psychol. Repts.* 7, 313 (1960).
76. J. Bowlby, *Intern. J. Psychoanalysis* 25, 19, 107 (1944).
77. C. M. Heinicke, *Human Relations* 9, 105 (1956).

78. H. R. Schaffer, *Brit. J. Med. Psychol.* 31, 174 (1950).
79. P. H. Gray, *J. Psychol.* 46, 155 (1958).
80. M. W. Kahn, *J. Genet. Psychol.* 79, 117 (1951). A Baron, K. H. Brookshire, R. A. Littman, *J. Comp. Physiol. Psychol.* 50, 530 (1957).
81. G. Lindzey, D. T. Lykken, H. D. Winston, *J. Abnormal Soc. Psychol.* 61, 7 (1960).
82. A. H. Riesen, in *Functions of Varied Experience*, D. W. Fiske and S. R. Maddi, Eds. (Dorsey, Homewood, Ill., 1961), pp. 57-80.
83. W. R. Thompson, *Science* 125, 698 (1957).
84. C. H. Hockman, *J. Comp. Physiol. Psychol.* 54, 679 (1961); R. Ader and M. L. Belfer, *Psychol. Repts.* 10, 711 (1962).
85. K. Keeley, *Science* 135, 44 (1962).
86. T. C. Schneirla and J. S. Rosenblatt, *Am. J. Orthopsychiat.* 31, 223 (1960).
87. W. H. Thorpe, *Learning and Instinct in Animals* (Methuen, London, 1956).
88. E. H. Hess, in *Roots of Behavior*, E. L. Bliss, Ed. (Harper, New York, 1962), pp. 254-263.
89. Part of the research described in this article was supported by a Public Health Service research grant (No. M-4481) from the National Institute of Mental Health.

The Effect of Prolonged Motor Restriction Upon Later Behavior of the Rat*

RICHARD J. RAVIZZA AND
AUSTIN C. HERSCHBERGER

ENVIRONMENTAL restrictions or enrichments early in life may have quite noticeable effects in later years. Although there are apparent dangers in making comparisons from animal behaviors to those displayed by man, insights and implications can certainly be drawn. The difficulty in controlling human variables for experimentation purposes, especially in longitudinal studies, suggests the application to man of research with other organisms, with whom greater manipulation is possible. Such is the case with the next article, in which rats are subjects. Early movement experiences are shown to be related to later activity levels, intelligence, and emotional behavior.

Several studies have investigated the effects of early, enriched motor experience (Baron, Antonitis, & Schell, 1962; Forgays, & Forgays, 1952; Forgus, 1954; Forgus, 1955 a, 1955 b; Meier, & McGee, 1959; Montgomery, & Zimbardo, 1957; Walk, 1958). However, little has been done to determine the effects of extreme motor deprivation and isolation.

Forgus (1955a) reported that rats raised in enriched visual conditions learned an 11 unit elevated maze with significantly fewer errors than rats having both enriched visual and motor experiences. When visual cues were reduced, however, the performance of the early visual-motor enrichment group

* From *The Psychological Record*, 1966, *16*, 73-80. Reprinted with permission of the authors and publisher.

was superior. This finding was further substantiated by another study (Forgus, 1955b). Walk (1958) closely replicated Forgus (1955) and found that rats having only enriched visual experience were superior when visual cues were present, but when these cues were reduced, no differences were found to exist between visual and visual-motor enriched groups. Walk attributed his failure to confirm Forgus' reversal in performance to the width of the alleys used, Forgus having used 4 in. alleys while Walk used 1¼ in. alleys.

Whereas the above investigators manipulated several variables simultaneously, Baron, Antonitis and Schell (1962) studied the effects of one variable, early differential climbing experience, upon later behavior, and found that mice raised in groups under severely restricted climbing conditions climbed significantly less when tested at maturity than Ss not so restricted. The present study was designed to determine the effects of restricting a particular motor activity, climbing, upon later exploratory, emotional activity and learning behavior of the white rat.

Method

Subjects.   Twenty-nine female rats, 12 experimental (F-E) and 17 controls (F-C), and 30 male rats, 16 experimental (M-E) and 14 control (M-C), offspring of 6 pregnant albino rats obtained from the Charles River Breeding Farms, were used as Ss.

Differential Rearing Procedures.   Five days prior to giving birth, three of the pregnant females were placed in separate living cages 7 in. wide, 7 in. high and 9 in. deep. The front and bottom of each cage were constructed of ¼ in. hardware cloth; the two sides and back were of solid sheet metal. The remaining three pregnant females were placed in identical cages which had clear plexiglass surfaces fitted to the front and to the top inside the hardware cloth of each cage. The cages were placed on a bed of wood shavings on a plastic tray with ad lib food and water. All six cages were located in a secluded part of the vivarium and were disturbed only to replenish food and water.

After the Ss were born the cages were disturbed only when it was necessary to replace food and water, and for periodic cleaning. On the nineteenth day after birth Ss were weaned, each S being placed in its own cage, identical to the one in which it was born. These cages, containing no wood shavings, were hung in a Wahman cage rack. From weaning until the twenty-third day Ss were fed wet mash with water available. From the twenty-fourth day until termination of the experiment they were fed Purina Lab Chow with water continuously available except for specific periods to be noted.

From the thirteenth day until the eightieth day each S was handled for a period of about 30 sec. every day. Each S was picked up by placing the palm of the hand on its back with E's fingers wrapped around its abdomen. The S was then held upright. In this manner Ss were unable to use their limbs to support themselves. Each S was then stroked on the top of the head and across the abdomen. Each S remained in its assigned living cage for the duration of the experiments.

Experiment I: Table Top Exploration, Satiated

Subjects.   The 59 Ss described above (ad lib food and water) were 81 days old at the start of the experiment.

Apparatus.   The apparatus consisted of a white 6 ft. $\times$ 6 ft. table top surface marked with a 6 in. grid of black lines. A black cloth was suspended 1 ft. beyond the perimeter of the table. The top of the cloth was 6 ft. above the floor of the room and 30 in. above the table, while the lower edge of the cloth extended 6 in. below the level of the table. This arrangement provided a uniform visual field. A single 15 watt light source was suspended 3 ft. above the center of the table. A standard timer in circuit with a telegraph key enabled E to record the total amount of time S was in motion. A stop watch was used for additional time measures. Gridded data sheets were used to record squares traversed.

Procedures. Each S, fully satiated, was removed from its cage and placed in the center of the table top, and after a 5 min. period was replaced in its cage. There was a 48 hour rest period between each of five exposures. All animals were run between 7:00 and 10:00 p.m., the order of any particular animal being changed randomly. After completion of this phase, all animals were given a five day rest period during which food and water were continuously available.

Two Es were involved, E_1 recording the time required for each S to traverse a distance of 6 in. after being placed upon the table top, "starting latency," and sketching the path of each S on a gridded data sheet. The E_2 recorded total time that all four legs of S were in locomotion and noted the number of defecations and times an animal fell from the table.

Results. The mean number of defecations for the first trial was 0.59 for F-C; 0.72 for M-C; 1.67 for F-E; and 3.81 for M-E. Using the Kruskal-Wallis test, the differences among the groups were found to be significant ($p<.001$). The mean number of 6 in. squares traversed by each group for all five trials was 120.61 for M-E; 177.60 for F-E; 170.42 for M-C; and 231.22 for F-C. Analysis of variance for a 2 $\times$ 2 factorial design with unequal cell frequencies indicated significant differences between experimental and control conditions ($F=8.74$, $df=1/54$, $p<.01$) as well as between sexes ($F=11.33$, $df=1/54$, $p<.01$). The mean running time for all five table top trials was 55.2 sec. for M-E; 68.96 sec. for F-E; 91.38 sec. for F-C; and 91.76 sec. for M-C. The same analysis of variance technique indicated a significant difference between experimental and control conditions ($F=14.02$, $df=1/54$, $p<.01$), but no difference between sexes. Interaction for both squares traversed and mean running time was not significant, neither were significant differences found for starting latencies. Nine of the 16 M-E fell from the table on the first trial, whereas only one of each of the other groups fell. Over all trials the total of falls was 14 for M-E, 3 for M-C, 3 for F-E, and 1 for F-C.

Experiment II: The Hebb-Williams Closed Field Intelligence Test for Rats 23½ Hour Deprivation Schedule.

Apparatus. The apparatus was similar to the maze described by Rabinovitch and Rosvold (1951) with the following alterations. The floor of the maze was painted white and lined with a 5 in. black grid; the walls and the movable partitions were painted black. In addition, a wooden framework was constructed to support a curtain of black cloth which extended from the top of the maze to a distance of 30 in. above the sides of the maze. The entire maze was placed on a turntable which allowed E to rotate the maze 180°. A 5 ft. $\times$ 5 ft. piece of translucent plexiglass was suspended 3½ ft. above the floor of the maze. Eleven in. above this sheet of plexiglass were 30 small, clear white Christmas tree lights spaced evenly over the area such that the resultant illumination was a diffuse glow. The light source was sufficiently homogeneous so that no shadows were evident in the maze regardless of the position of the partitions, and the light source was sufficiently large that it was all that was visible from the floor of the maze. The same standard timer circuit used in Experiment I was used to measure latencies during habituation trials.

Habituation. The Ss used in Experiment I, now 100 days old, were used. At this time all animals were placed on a 23½ hour water deprivation schedule. On the first three exposures each animal was placed in the maze without partitions present and allowed to explore for 5 min., goal and starting box doors being closed. On the fourth exposure each S was placed in the goal box and given access to water for 5 sec. The S was then placed in the center of the maze and allowed to run to the goal, where it had access to water for 5 sec. This procedure was repeated five times. On the fifth exposure each S was given access to the goal box with water for a 5 sec. period and then given three runs from the center of the maze to the goal box. The S was then placed in the starting box and given two runs to the goal box. After each run from the starting box to the goal box, the maze was rotated 180°. The sixth through the ninth exposures consisted of five starting box to goal box runs. On the tenth exposure each S was given a total of ten runs. Latency leaving the starting box was recorded from the fourth through the thirty-second exposure. In addition, one E rated the quality of these runs on a scale of three: 1 being hugging the walls, 2 being a significant departure from the walls, and 3 being a direct diagonal route from starting box to goal box. After each exposure and prior to being placed in its individual living cage, each S was allowed to drink freely in special watering boxes for 30 min.

Habituation Results. Quality rating of runs yielded no significant differences. All latencies were subjected to a log transformation. Using analysis of variance for unequal cell entries (Winer, 1962), the log latencies for the first trial were found to be significant between experimental and control animals ($F=12.92$, $df=1/54$, $p<.005$), and differences between sexes were also found to be significant ($F=6.71$, $df=1/54$, $p<.05$). The means for each group were 27.7 sec. for M-E; 13.4 sec. for F-E; 12.7 sec. for M-C; and 7.8 sec. for F-C. On the last five trials the differences between control and experimental remained ($F=15.57$, $df=1/54$, $p<.005$) while sex differences disappeared. In no instance was interaction significant.

Pattern Learning on Test Items

Procedure. The patterns used, a series of maze pathways of graded difficulty, were those standardized by Rabinovitch and Rosvold (1951). The procedure used on each of the 18 items was as follows: Each S was placed in the starting box of the apparatus; the guillotine door of the starting box was raised and after S had entered the maze proper this door was closed; once S had entered the goal box, its guillotine door was closed. After a five sec. reward period S was removed from the goal box, the maze rotated 180°, and S replaced in the starting box for a subsequent trial. Upon completion of the ten trials, S was moved to a drinking box and allowed to drink freely for 30 min., and then placed in its home cage where it remained until the next evening. A single test pattern was given every night between 5:00 and 11:00 for 18 consecutive nights.

During the course of this phase of the experiment one S died and another had to be discarded because it refused to enter the goal box, leaving 13 Ss in the M-C group, and 16 Ss in the F-C group. The two experimental groups remained the same.

Results. The mean number of errors for all 18 patterns on the last three trials was 197.6 for M-E; 223.3 for F-E; 156.2 for M-C; and 189.4 for F-C. Analysis of variance indicated significant differences between experimental and control conditions only ($F=5.89$, $df=1/53$, $p<.05$). Sex differences and interaction were not significant.

Experiment III:[1] *Table Top Activity under 23½ Hours Water Deprivation*

Subjects. The same Ss, now 130 days old, were continued in this experiment.

Apparatus. The apparatus employed was the same as that used in Experiment I.

Procedure. For three days after the completion of the Hebb-Williams task, Ss were maintained on a 23½ hour deprivation schedule. All Ss were then given two additional table top trials following the exact procedure described under Experiment I with the same data being recorded. After completion of the second trial Ss were taken off the water deprivation schedule and given both food and water ad lib. A six day interval was interposed between this Experiment and Experiment IV.

Results. There were no significant differences either for experimental conditions or sex differences in the mean distances traversed. Analysis of variance revealed significant differences between experimental and control conditions for mean running time ($F=10.29$; $df=1/54$, $p<.01$) but not for sexes. The means were 101.84 sec. for M-C; 74.67 sec. for M-E; 102 sec. for F-C; and 84.65 sec. for F-E. Differences among the groups in falls from the table top and number of defecations were not significant.

Experiment IV: Table Top Activity, Satiated

Subjects. The same Ss used in Experiment III, 139 days old, were used.

Apparatus. The apparatus employed was the same as that used in Experiments I and III.

Procedure. Six days after Experiment III, during which time all Ss had food and water ad lib, Ss were given two additional table top trials. The procedure and measures taken were the same as for Experiments I and III.

Results. Analysis of variance indicated no significant differences between experimental and control conditions for mean distances traversed, but significant sex differences were found ($F=8.19$, $df=1/54$, $p<.01$). The differences between experimental and control conditions for mean running time were found to be significant ($F=12.42$, $df=1/54$, $p<.01$) but not for sex. The means were 84.62 sec. for M-C; 54.46 sec. for M-E; 88.78 sec. for F-C; and 69.78 sec. for F-E.

Experiment V: Activity Wheel Behavior

Subjects. The Ss used were those of the preceding experiment, now 145 days old.

Apparatus. The apparatus consisted of six Wahman activity wheels with adjacent living cages. Those cages used by the experimental Ss had plexiglass surfaces fitted to the inside walls and ceilings of the living cages. The cages of control Ss were not so altered.

Procedure. Three days after conclusion of Experiment IV, the first group of six Ss was placed in the activity wheels at 9 a.m. The number of revolutions by each S was recorded at 9:05, 9:10, 9:15, 9:30, 10:00, 12:00, 3:00 p.m., 9:00 p.m. and 8:00 a.m. the following morning. One hour later, that same day at 9:00 a.m., the next group of six Ss was placed in the activity wheels. The assignment of Ss to the various groups and wheels was on a random basis.

[1] The authors wish to thank William D. Dukes for assistance in gathering data in this particular experiment.

Results. The mean number of revolutions for the first 15 min. period was 25.00 for M-E; 42.69 for M-C; 43.00 for F-E; and 45.12 for F-C. Using analysis of variance, these differences were found to be significant for experimental and control ($F=5.76$, $df=1/54$, $p<.05$) and for sex ($F=6.13$, $df=1.54$, $p<.05$). For the remaining 23 hours the differences between experimental and control conditions disappeared, while sex differences remained significant ($F=32.20$, $df=1/54$, $p<.001$). The mean revolutions for this period were 222.56 for M-E; 448.69 for M-C; 958.08 for F-E; and 910.71 for F-C.

Discussion

This study demonstrated that animals raised in an environment which prohibited climbing activity were inferior by several measures to animals not so restricted. The controls exhibited more activity in table top exploration, superior performance in the Hebb-Williams intelligence test, more activity in activity wheels after a fifteen minute period, and less emotional behavior in novel situations than did experimentally restricted animals. Significant sex differences were found on many of the measures, yet in testing for interaction effects, not one was found to be significant, indicating that the treatment, when effective, affected both sexes in the same direction and extent.

There is evidence that the effects of prolonged restriction disappeared on some of the experimental measures (differences in table top distances, falls off the table, and improvement in the experimental animals' general motor coordination). On the other hand, differences in the amount of time spent running on the table top and latencies leaving the starting box in the Hebb-Williams intelligence test during the ten day habituation trials remained constant.

It is impossible to ascertain whether the observed differences were due to motor restriction during the animal's early experience or to the prolonged restriction into adult life. However, several observations support the hypothesis that the early period of this motor restriction had the greater effect upon the performance of the adult subjects. The first is that long before the start of the first experiment, climbing activity was no longer observed in the control groups, although they were not restricted from doing so. With continued exposure to similar experimental situations certain forms of the experimental Ss' behavior changed, although the climbing restriction remained.

In Experiment I the distances traversed by each group were highly significant, but by Experiment IV these differences had disappeared. It was also observed that the experimental animals exhibited difficulty in motor coordination, particularly in the rear legs, but as Experiment I progressed, these difficulties disappeared. In addition, the male experimental group fell off the table top considerably more than any other group on the first trial, and this tendency persisted, although with less frequency, on subsequent table top exposures in Experiments I, III, and IV. Thompson and Heron (1954) found considerable motor incoordination in dogs as a result of early restricted experience.

The alterations made on the Hebb-Williams apparatus were concerned with limiting visual cues. These precautions were taken because of a study by Forgays and Forgays (1951) in which it was reported that Ss reared in an enriched visual and motor environment used distant visual cues to a much greater extent in the Hebb-Williams apparatus than did Ss reared in a restricted visual and motor environment. It was hoped that by limiting such visual cues the Ss would have to rely heavily upon motor cues. If motor cues are important in learning in a visually restricted test situation, and if motor restriction is effective, then animals so restricted should exhibit inferior performance to non-restricted animals. This was the finding with regard to the Hebb-Williams test.

The findings of this experiment pertaining to exploratory behavior are not in agreement with earlier work reported by Ehrlich (1959), who found that no differences in exploratory behavior resulted from early motor and visual-motor deprivation. In addition, Zimbardo and Montgomery (1957) found that rats reared in normal cages explored a simple Y maze significantly more than did rats reared in an environment offering complex visual and motor stimulation. These experimenters tested for exploratory behavior using either a Y or Dashiell maze, whereas this experiment employed a table top situation.

It may well be that the table top is more sensitive to "shyness and timidity" as well as exploratory behavior than the closed maze. Hebb and Williams (1946) imply that on initial exposure to the open field animals would tend to hug the perimeter and explore less than upon subsequent exposures; i.e., a measure of both exploration and timidity. In the large open field, the table top, significant differences were found while in the more confined field, the Hebb-Williams test during adaptation procedures, no qualitative exploration differences were obtained. The differential activity during the first 15 min. in the activity wheel and its disappearance during the ensuing 23 hours might also be due to initial timidity. An alternative explanation of the differences in table top activity is that the restricted group simply had more difficulty moving around. This interpretation is supported by the many observations of motor difficulty among the experimental animals during the early phases of testing.

References

BARON, A., ANTONITIS, J. J. & SCHELL, S. F., 1962. Effects of early restriction and facilitation of climbing on later climbing behavior of mice. *J. comp. physiol. Psychol.*, 55, 808-812.

EHRLICH, A., 1959. Effects of past experience on exploratory behavior in rats. *Canad. J. Psychol.*, 13, 248-254.

FORGAYS, D. G., & FORGAYS, J. W., 1952. The nature and effects of free environmental experience in the rat. *J. comp physiol. Psychol.*, 45, 322-328.

FORGUS, H. H., 1954. The effect of early perceptual learning on behavioral organization of adult rats. *J. comp physiol. Psychol.*, 47, 331-336.

FORGUS, R. H., 1955. Early visual and motor experience as determiners of complex maze learning ability under rich and reduced stimulation. *J. comp. physiol. Psychol.*, 48, 215-220. (a)

FORGUS, R. H., 1955. Influence of early experience on maze learning with and without visual cues. *Canad. J. Psychol.*, 9, 207-214. (b)

HEBB, D. O., 1949. *Organization of behavior: A neuropsychological theory.* New York: Wiley.

MEIER, G. W., & McGEE, R. K., 1959. A re-evaluation of the effects of early perceptual experience on discrimination performance during adulthood. *J. comp. physiol. Psychol.*, 52, 390-395.

MONTGOMERY, K. C., & ZIMBARDO, P. G., 1957. The effects of sensory and behavioral deprivation upon exploratory behavior in the rat. *Percept. mot. Skills*, 7, 223-229.

THOMPSON, W. R., & HERON, W., 1954. The effects of early restriction on activity in dogs. *J. comp. physiol. Psychol.*, 47, 77-82.

WALK, R. D., 1958. "Visual" and "Visual-motor" experience: A replication. *J. comp. physiol. Psychol.*, 51, 785-787.

ZIMBARDO, P. G., & MONTGOMERY, J. C., 1957. Effects of "Free environment" rearing upon exploratory behavior. *Psychol. Rep.*, 3, 589-594.

Later Development of Children Specially Trained During Infancy: Johnny and Jimmy at School Age*

MYRTLE B. McGRAW

ONE of the more famous and intensive projects at examining critical periods in children was undertaken by McGraw. Her data suggest the values and disadvantages in initiating various motor skills at an early point in life. Also, childhood behaviors are related to early experience in varied motor activities. The effectiveness of the case study approach is limited by possible observer bias, but the contribution of McGraw's work to the literature and to our understanding of behavioral development should not be taken for granted. The use of twins as subjects helps to minimize complaints that might be voiced if the children had been raised in separate households or if they had been born with significantly different characteristics and aptitudes. Unfortunately, because of great variability between children, we still do not know the optimal period or stage in which to introduce any kind of athletic skill. One thing is certain though. Many skills can and should be experienced, in modified form, much sooner in childhood than is typically believed or practiced.

Introduction

In 1932 Johnny and Jimmy, twins, became the subjects of an intensive study of behavior development at the Normal Child Development Study of the Babies Hospital, Columbia-Presbyterian Medical Center. Before the study had been under way for two years, it attracted wide interest because of the reports of a baby less than a year old swimming with his face under water, ascending steep inclines and by the time he was sixteen months old moving around with considerable skill on roller skates. These were the achievements which gave the study a popular interest, but such performances were incidental to the primary objectives which were 1) to analyze the sequential phases or changes through which a growing infant passes in the achievement of a given performance, and 2) to determine whether these phases are altered by certain prescribed conditions, viz., the daily stimulation of activity on the one hand and the restriction of activity on the other.

Such an investigation was timely because of the current pediatric and psychiatric notion that infants should not be over-stimulated and because of a general assumption following a co-twin study by Dr. Gesell[1] that the immature nervous system of the infant is unresponsive to practice effects and that development during infancy is essentially a matter of neural maturation. It is proverbial that among older children and adults practice leads to improvement in performance. If the infant is unresponsive to practice-effects, and if,

---

* From *Child Development*, 1939, *10*, 1-19. Abridged and reprinted with permission of the author and The Society for Research in Child Development, Inc.

on the other hand, the adult is responsive, it is a reasonable assumption that there must come a time in the course of the child's development when improvement by virtue of experience begins. It therefore seemed to the writer that if one began soon after birth to stimulate one member of a set of twins in certain activities and within certain limits to restrict the activities of the other, it might be possible to ascertain that period in life when the individual begins to profit by experience or repetition of performance. Johnny and Jimmy were selected as the subjects for this investigation and a group of 57 infants, examined at weekly or bi-weekly intervals, served as controls. The general procedure during the first twenty-two months of life was to observe both babies in the laboratory five days a week from nine until five. During this time Johnny was stimulated daily to engage in activities to the extent of his capabilities, whereas Jimmy was left with a few toys unhindered in his crib except for disturbances accompanying routine care. When they were twenty-two months old, Jimmy was given a period of two and one-half months of intensive practice in those same activities in which Johnny had been given earlier and more prolonged exercise. A detailed report of this investigation was made in 1935 in "Growth: A Study of Johnny and Jimmy."[2]

In this report it was pointed out that there is no one age period or developmental stage which clearly demarcates an earlier state of immaturity during which the child is incapable of improving through practice from the subsequent state in which improvement through practice becomes feasible. The impossibility of identifying such a critical period in the development of the individual results, it would seem, from the fact that the nervous system does not mature uniformly. There are critical periods dependent upon the maturational status of the nervous system, but these periods vary with respect to the particular activity under consideration. Before training or practice can be economically provided, it is essential to determine, by the observation of behavior symptoms, the periods of greatest susceptibility for each type of activity. It will be recalled that while Johnny was induced to roller-skate with considerable skill by the time he was sixteen months old, repeated daily practice in a seemingly simple activity like tricycling evoked no improvement either in technique or performance until he approached nineteen months of age. The discrepancy in these two activities affords a striking example because under ordinary conditions a child learns to tricycle much younger than he does to roller-skate.

It has been four years now since this special study of Johnny and Jimmy was discontinued. Although they have at specified intervals during these four years been given follow-up examinations at the laboratory, their life at home has otherwise been comparable to that of other New York children of their socioeconomic status. However, an immediate question arises as to the sequelae of their contrasting experiences during the first twenty-two months of life. Now that they are just attaining school age, when a new chapter of a child's life is opened, it is desirable that we consider their relative development to date in the light of their earlier experiences.

At the time of the original report, before there had been an opportunity of observing the subsequent influence of special exercise, the writer commented, "The permanency of the expansion which an action-pattern gains through additional exercise is contingent upon the degree of fixity the behavior pattern had achieved at the time the modifying agent, i.e., the factor of special exercise, was withdrawn. It does not necessarily follow that a performance which has been developed under special conditions will be retained after those conditions are removed. Unless the behavior-pattern has become fixed, it is only reasonable to expect that there will be a loss in performance when the conditions which brought it about are discontinued. Correspondingly, if the growth of a behavior-pattern has been hindered through restriction, it is to be expected that recovery will be evident when the restrictions are removed."[3] The early investigation brought out the fact that certain activities of infants can, through exercise, be brought to a much higher level of achievement than is normally assumed, but it will require new and longer studies to determine the extent to which practice should be enforced in order to render its results comparatively permanent. It is well known that many adults who learn a performance such as bicycling in childhood can, after a lapse of years without practice, pick it up in fairly short order. On the other hand, an adult resuming his attack on a language which he has not spoken since early childhood will show more than an initial awkwardness in re-learning the language although he may acquire it with greater facility than someone who had never been exposed to it before. In other activities an adult often appears to be a virtual tyro despite his childhood accomplishments in a given field. An adult's loss of childhood skills in marble-shooting, ball throwing, etc., is such a common occurrence that it is a familiar subject for the cartoonist and other humorists. General conclusions concerning the permanent effects of practice are therefore impossible since different types of skills exhibit wide variation in their tendency to be retained or lost.

In evaluating the permanency of practice effects with Johnny and Jimmy, we shall consider first those laboratory activities in which Johnny had been given long and intensive training during infancy but in which Jimmy had received only two and one-half months of intensive training beginning when he was twenty-two months old. During the past four years, they have been examined in these same performances at intervals from two weeks to six months.

Laboratory Studies

Tricycling. One of the most interesting attainments of Johnny and Jimmy during their period of intensive study was that of manipulating a simple tricycle. The initial practice period was begun with Johnny when he was eleven months old. It was pointed out in "Growth"[4] that this activity was initiated before his neuro-muscular mechanisms were ready for such a performance, as it was eight months before he began to show distinct comprehension of the situation. After he showed some degree of mastery he acquired an easy, skillful performance in about two months. It was also pointed out that Johnny had apparently suffered by his long and futile practice periods. Jimmy, whose training began when he was twenty-two months old—presumably when his neuro-muscular mechanisms were in a state of readiness—accomplished an easy performance in a shorter time than did Johnny. After the period of intensive training was discontinued, both boys were observed at the laboratory in their tricycling behavior, and at no time did either of them show any distinct loss in this particular skill. The twins were living at home during this time. Although they did not possess a tricycle in their own home it was impossible to ascertain whether they had had access to one in the nursery school or on the playground. On the other hand, it may be that tricycling, like bicycling, automobile driving, etc., is a type of skill which does not deteriorate appreciably through lack of practice once it has been definitely acquired.

Skating. In some of the other gross motor skills we find a different story. It was pointed out in the earlier report that Johnny, who began his roller-skating experience when slightly less than a year old, enjoyed an advantage over his twin, whose practice in this activity was begun at the age of twenty-two months. This advantage appeared to be attributable to several factors. In the first place, from purely mechanical considerations, a child who is just learning to walk possesses because of his relatively wide base and short legs greater static equilibrium than does the child who is older and therefore taller.[5] In the second place a child who is just beginning to walk has ample experience in falling, less distance to fall, and is therefore less disturbed when he falls on skates than is the older child. Furthermore, a child's achievement in a particular skill like skating is determined to some extent by the number of distracting or interfering interests which play upon a performance at a given time. The toddler of a year is less responsive to the world about him than is the child of two years or older. Johnny was at the threshold of independent walking when the skating practice was initiated and apparently experienced an advantage in static equilibrium. Also, having had less general experience at the age of twelve months, he was less hindered by distractions and emotional factors and therefore could exert himself to the limit of his neuromuscular abilities, whereas Jimmy's performances at the age of two years were modified considerably by interference from broader interests, so that his activities at the time were not the result of optimum neuro-muscular coordinations. Even after a practice period of two and one-half months, Jimmy had still not acquired a well-integrated skating movement.

The children were given skates as a present shortly after their daily laboratory visits were terminated, but these skates were demolished within a few weeks and their parents report that they have had no other skating experience except for the follow-up laboratory tests. Their performances on these occasions corroborate the parents' report. In brief summary of the notes which have accrued on their skating behavior during these four years, it may be said that soon after their practice period both children began to show a loss in skill and disorganization of the skating pattern. When the children were about three years old, it was noted that the chief source of their difficulty was in maintaining the erect posture on skates. The aspect of balance had undergone greater disorganization than the actual progressive movements. Disorganization of the skating behavior was more pronounced in Johnny's performances than in Jimmy's. This difference, however, appeared to be due to Johnny's attitude of abandon and a tendency to lunge forward even though he had lost in equilibrium, whereas Jimmy adhered more to the short, stiff strokes characteristic of his early practice period. Despite this difference both children began to show an increased tendency to lose their balance and tumble compared with their earlier performances. Neither of them skates well today. The fact that the children showed no loss of skill in tricycling but complete disorganization of roller-skating raises the question as to why certain skills deteriorate through lack of exercise and others do not. The answer to this question is, of course, problematical since the factors which control a growing behavior are multiple and were not in this study controlled by laboratory measurement. However, from observations of other children in our study as well these particular boys it seems clear that at least three factors play an important role in determining the permanency or deterioration of a motor skill when no special exercise of the function has occurred during a period of years. The first factor is the lack of practice *per se;* the second is the influence of the child's attitude toward the performance, and the third is the changing configuration of the bodily structures as a result of physical growth. It is impossible to evaluate the effect of disuse of function without taking into account the factors of attitude and organic structures. From direct observation of the twins' skating behavior the writer is of the opinion that changes in bodily proportions were of considerable significance in the disorganization of skating behavior. Actually the child of five or six years, because of his relatively long legs and narrow base, has a set of structures with which to perform the task of skating different from those of the toddler. With the set of structures characteristic of the toddler, Johnny developed a well coordinated skating movement. Johnny's attitude toward skating continued to be cooperative and favorable during the entire four years. There are other motor activities in which he showed no appreciable loss of skill despite the lack of exercise. It seems reasonable to infer, and certainly the character of his behavior indicated, that the disorganization was brought about not solely because of disuse of function but also because during the non-practice period important growth changes occurred in the bodily mechanisms which function in the act of skating. It is reasonable to assume that if the practice had continued he would have altered his behavior gradually to meet the new and slowly developing structural demands. Jimmy, who was less skillful in skating than Johnny at the end of their practice periods, has also shown deterioration. The fact that both began to show marked difficulty in balancing at about the same age lends support to the contention that physiological growth was an important influence in the disorganization of their skating behavior.

Slides. Another activity which seems to have undergone alteration in the course of years, though it was not so completely disorganized as roller-skating, was that of ascending steep slopes. It may be recalled that[6] at the end of the experimental period, Johnny was able to ascend easily a slope of 70 degrees and Jimmy could with somewhat less ease scale the incline of 61 degrees. For some months immediately following their practice period Johnny showed, on follow-up examinations, no loss in motor skill in mounting even the steepest slopes. Jimmy, on the other hand, showed some initial loss, then began to improve both in motor skill and in persistence. Alterations in their methods of ascending the slides became most obvious when the children were about three years old. At this time it was noted that they had great difficulty in managing their longer legs. They would attempt to ascend on their knees while grasping the ridges and pulling vigorously with their upper extremities. The most outstanding individual difference was Jimmy's persistence in trying to ascend in this manner while Johnny, after a few trials, would shift to the more efficient method of using his toes. He also climbs the steep slopes with greater ease and muscular coordination. He gives the impression of having better gripping power in his toes than Jimmy or most six year old children whom we have had occasion to observe in this activity.

At the present time the writer is less impressed as to the extent to which daily practice might have functioned in Johnny's achievements on the slopes than she was at the time of the original report. Practice undoubtedly operated in his ascending slopes of 61 and 70 degrees respectively. Other infants in our laboratory, however, have ascended slopes as steep as 40 or 48 degrees without great difficulty even when they had not been given systematic practice in such performances. To the experienced observer, it is obvious that infants can more easily ascend slopes of this order than can older children. The advantages enjoyed by the infant appear to be due somewhat to differences in body configurations. The center of gravity in the infant's body is relatively higher and his legs are relatively shorter. It is therefore possible for him to get his chest, and thereby his center of gravity, nearer to the slide without raising his pelvic girdle too high. It is also possible that the texture of infant skin is such as to create a higher friction coefficient between his hands and feet and the underlying surface. Whatever the reasons may be, the fact remains that the babies can stick to and ascend these slopes with greater facility than the older children. The difficulties of older children are manifested by slipping or a deficient gripping power in the toes and in managing their long legs. Alterations in the slide climbing behavior of Johnny and Jimmy during the past four years were of a similar nature. It is a reasonable inference, therefore, that growth changes in body proportions played a large role in altering their method of ascending slopes. Any permanent effects of the early practice which Johnny enjoyed are general, as indicated by superior motor coordinations, except for the comparative readiness with which he shifted from an inferior to a more effective method of managing his long legs and using his toes.

In descending these slopes neither Johnny nor Jimmy at any time showed any distinct loss of motor skill or alteration of method. During the first few months following the practice period Jimmy was more timid and required greater urging to descend but after the first three or four months he overcame this hesitancy and manifested no lack of motor skill.

Getting Off Pedestals. Post-practice behavior of the children in getting off pedestals is similar to that of descending the slides, since no definite deterioration of motor skill was manifested by either of the boys. The pedestals ranged in height from 14½ to 63¼ inches. At no time during the four-year interim has Johnny shown any loss of skill or hesitancy in getting off these pedestals. At the time the practice period was terminated Jimmy was easily and deliberately climbing off the 63¼ inch pedestal. During the months immediately following his two and one-half month practice period, there appeared a regression in his general attitude or emotional adjustment to the situation which interfered with his motor performance. He would complain even on the lower pedestals and would refuse to get off the higher ones. Behavior of this character continued more or less until he was about four and one-half years old when his attitude seemed to change to cooperation and some enjoyment of the situation. The failure of Jimmy to get off the higher pedestals was not so much a deterioration of the motor coordinations formed during his practice period, but rather a recurrence of attitudes established prior to his practice period. Once he could be induced to climb down he could do so with considerable ease. He has never, however, attained the agility which Johnny manifests in this performance. At the present time the individual differences are indicated not so much in terms of their achievements as in the degree of coordination which they show when performing the same act. This superior motor coordination on Johnny's part is reasonably attributable, in a measure, to the difference in amount of exercise the children received in the activity during their first two years of life. Climbing off pedestals is another type of performance the motor aspects of which do not suffer appreciable loss through lack of exercise once the motor habits are well established.

Jumping. In the report of early behavior of the children in the jumping activity,[7] it will be noted that in this type of performance the attitude of the child played a major role in determining the somatic response. At the end of the experimental periods the investigator felt not only that Johnny had established a cooperative attitude, but that the integration of the essential movements in jumping had been accelerated. Jimmy, on the other hand, even after two and one-half months of daily exercise could not be induced to jump off a tall pedestal into the outstretched arms of an adult. It seemed unquestionable that Johnny experienced an advantage in this performance by having had practice in the activity before his increased perceptive and emotional capacities added complexities to the somatic or motor aspect of the behavior. During Jimmy's two and one-half months of practice (at two years of age) his attitude became definitely more acquiescent, but the alteration of attitude was not sufficient to effect an integrated jumping performance. At the end of the exercise periods, when they were 26 months old, Johnny was gleefully leaping from tall pedestals with even a slight "spring" as he threw himself forward. Jimmy, happy enough, would stand on the pedestal, shifting his weight from

7

one foot to the other, squatting, and in other ways indicating his urge to go forward, but was not quite able to consummate the performance. During the first few months after their practice periods were terminated, Johnny began to show a less cooperative attitude and for a while there was even less motor skill in his action, that is, when he did jump there was noticeably less grace in his movements. This loss or deterioration was, however, temporary and intermittent, appearing at intervals over a period of six or eight months. After that relatively brief period jumping was again one of his most enjoyable activities and he subsequently showed no distinct loss in motor coordinations. It appeared to the experimenter that this early change in attitude was due in part to imitation of his brother's behavior rather than to real hesitancy in carrying out the act.

For some months after their practice periods terminated Jimmy showed a definite regression in his behavior. He would cling tenaciously to the adult, refuse to stand up on the pedestal and cry lustily. When he was about three years old, however, his attitude became more acquiescent, and his behavior comparable to that manifested during his exercise period. He would stoop or squat on the pedestal, reach toward the adult, and if the adult was only about eight or ten inches away he would throw his shoulders forward. He has steadily shown improvement and is now willing to jump, but he has not manifested the abandonment nor been willing to jump as far as Johnny. In this activity there has been a definite residual of the early training period in Johnny's favor.

Purposive Manipulation of Graded Stools. "Growth"[8] offers an analysis of the children's development in manipulating stools of various heights in order to obtain lures which had been placed out of reach. At the time the experimental or practice period terminated, neither of the children had attained the maximum degree of proficiency in this activity. At that time Johnny would juggle eight different pedestals, ranging from 7½ to 63¼ inches in height, in order to climb up and obtain an object hung some nine feet above the floor. However, he still had a tendency to push all the stools in a cluster, not seriatim, usually with the tallest one beneath the lure. On a few occasions he had shown some tendency to eliminate unnecessary pedestals, but this aspect had not become a fixed part of his behavior activity when the practice period ended. Jimmy, on the other hand, was, at the same time, able to manipulate two or three stools successfully in order to obtain the lure placed upon the 63¼ inch pedestal, but he had at no time successfully obtained the object hung from the ceiling, which arrangement demanded his making use of the taller pedestals for climbing. Johnny's practice period began in this activity when he was eighteen months old, and Jimmy's when he was twenty-two and one-half months old. It was pointed out in the original report that the time span between the inception of the practice periods for the two children was not great and therefore came nearer to striking the critical period for both children, i.e., that period when development in this type of activity would be most susceptible to advancement.

It would require too much detail in order to delineate the various changes in their performances in this situation during the four years they have been returning to the laboratory for follow-up examinations. It is sufficient to state that at the present time, as a rule, Johnny and Jimmy both arrange the pedestals purposively to obtain the lure when it is hung at least nine feet above the floor. Both children carefully discriminate in placing the tallest pedestal under the object. Johnny, however, carelessly and dexterously pushes all the other seven pedestals in a cluster about the tallest one with no definite order or arrangement. He then goes clambering up two or three of the stools, as may be necessary, for him to gain the top of the tallest one. He shows no hesitancy or difficulty in bridging wide gaps in order to pass from one stool to another when they are not in juxtaposition, and he shows no hesitancy in standing erect on the tallest stool in order to reach the lure. It never seems to trouble him that he has pushed all the pedestals in a cluster although he makes use of only two or three for the purpose of climbing.

Jimmy, in contrast, works diligently arranging the stools in a graded sequence with the tallest one carefully placed under the object. Once he has them arranged in a stairway he will climb up and stand on the one next to the tallest pedestal, but it is only rarely that he can be induced to climb up on the tallest one so as to obtain the lure. He has definitely less courage and less motor coordination in handling his body. It is the writer's impression that Johnny's failure to arrange the pedestals in order according to their relative height is a residual of his habits established earlier when his discrimination was inadequate to allow him to do so. The fact that it is not lack of discrimination at the present time was brought out one day when he was shown some movies of his performances taken before he was two years old. This particular reel included an occasion when he had arranged most of the pedestals in stair formation. Johnny's remark was, "That isn't me. I didn't put them straight like that." With his greater agility he doesn't feel the need of an orderly arrangement, whereas Jimmy, who is more cautious in climbing, tries to make that aspect of the situation as easy as possible. The impression that the tendency of Johnny and Jimmy to employ all eight stools even though three properly selected ones would have sufficed is a residual of their early practice in this situation was substantiated by the behavior of a small group of children from six to eight years of age who had never been exposed to this particular situation before. At this stage of maturity these children would make use of only a few of the pedestals, even if they were not properly chosen. In other words, they had developed beyond the stage of thinking an additional one would help solve the problem.

Purposive Manipulation of Graded Boxes. This situation[9] called for the stacking of two or more boxes of different size on top of each other in order to obtain a lure suspended from the ceiling. When the practice periods were discontinued Johnny was skillful in stacking three boxes in order and had occasionally successfully stacked four boxes, but he was actually lacking in physical height to stack the fourth box easily. Jimmy, by contrast, at the same chronological age and after a period of two and one-half months' practice, had not arrived at the stage of placing one box on top of another for the purpose of climbing up to reach the lure. Therefore, in this situation neither child had attained his maximum development in performances of this order, though Johnny was considerably advanced beyond Jimmy.

In the four year interim during which they have been given follow-up examinations in this situation Johnny has shown many fluctuations, the details of which would be too laborious for the reader if reported here. Jimmy was three years old before he began placing one box on top of another, and it may be that this is about the age when children would normally begin to engage in activities of this order if they were not given specific stimulation to do so. At the present time both children usually pile all four boxes on top of one another in order to obtain a suspended lure. Jimmy is more careful in arranging the boxes in order according to size, that is, with the largest one on the bottom and the smallest one on the top. He often shows a reluctance to climb up after he has neatly arranged the boxes. Johnny, who is careless and less discriminative in the order of arrangement, shows greater skill in climbing and maintaining his balance on even a quite unstable structure. It would seem that in this particular situation Johnny's advanced motor skill and courage operate to make him either careless or less discriminative of the relative sizes and placement of the boxes. Again, Jimmy, who has less courage in motor performances, is more meticulous in making arrangements, so that the motor aspect will be as easily accomplished as possible.

When a long range view is taken covering the twin's behavior in these several laboratory situations during the past four years, it is clear that there are at least three different situations in which Johnny showed no loss of proficiency and in which any loss which Jimmy might have shown could be attributed more to his emotional or attitudinal status than to motor inadequacy. These activities are (a) tricycling, (b) getting off pedestals, and (c) descending slides. When we examine their mode of performance in these activities we are struck with the fact that it has suffered no major alteration. In other words, so far as the motor aspect of these performances goes, the twins had achieved a high degree of integration or maturity at the time the practice periods were terminated. Given relatively the same heights and slopes and a tricycle of relatively the same size, the two year old and the six year old child tend to get off pedestals or go down slides in essentially the same manner, and also to propel a tricycle in the same fashion.

In at least two different activities, and in certain aspects of a third, the mode of performance seems to have changed primarily because of alterations in the boys themselves in terms of physical growth, specifically because of their relatively longer legs and the shift in their centers of gravity. These alterations are especially noted in skating and in ascending steep slopes. The influence of changes in bodily growth upon behavior was also observed in the way in which the boys manipulated graded pedestals to obtain suspended lures. Actually, because of his short stature, the two year old child who strikes the tall pedestals nearer their base is less liable to tip them over and can, therefore, move them with greater ease than can the six year old whose contact point in pushing strikes the pedestal nearer its center of gravity.

Purposive arrangement of pedestals and manipulation of boxes were activities which were probably in the most fluid state at the time the special practice periods were terminated. For that reason the performances of both children have shown greater fluctuations in these situations than in activities which were more stabilized. While the achievement difference of the two boys was great when special practice was abandoned their relative efficiencies have, during the past three years, approached each other though the two children adopt somewhat different methods in demonstrating their merits. As might be expected there is comparatively less diversity in their present achievements in those activities which were not so stabilized when practice was abandoned.

Jumping from a tall pedestal seems to stand in a class by itself. It appeared that through practice the motor aspects of this performance had been greatly accelerated in Johnny. However, his performance had reached a high degree of fixity and suffered only a temporary loss immediately following the practice period, whereas, the attitude which prevailed with Jimmy during his period of isolation had become so fixed that the two and one-half months of practice he experienced when he was about two years old were inadequate to counteract it. With increasing maturity Jimmy's emotional disturbance was somewhat abated, but it has never become sufficient to eliminate obvious muscular tension in his performance even though he will complete the jump.

Swimming. No follow-up study has been made of the swimming behavior. It will be recalled that the original investigation of this activity[10] terminated when the children were seventeen months old. During the ensuing four years there have been three or four occasions when their aquatic behavior was observed. Until the age of six years Johnny showed noticeably greater fortitude in jumping into the water and playing about, though he was not able and was not urged to engage in independent swimming. However, on the last occasion they were taken to a lake, when they were a little more than six years old, Jimmy was quite brave about jumping into the water with a ring around him for support, whereas Johnny showed some inhibition about doing so. Just why this change in attitude should have taken place is a matter for conjecture. An interesting difference was noted in their swimming strokes. When supported by a ring, both would venture out beyond their depth, but Jimmy maintained a vertical position as he made rapid treading movements with his legs. Johnny, on the other hand, assumed the horizontal position and engaged in graceful crawl strokes of the more advanced swimmer. Just why he should have taken up a method of movement which by experts is considered to be more efficient than the natural dog paddle of beginners, is beyond present explanation as no attempt was ever made to teach Johnny strokes during his period of infantile swimming and at that time he used the typical dog paddle. It is unfortunate that this behavior could not have been studied further, especially since it appears that this is another activity in which the body proportions constitute a large influence in determining the manner of behavior. An infant, whose head is relatively heavier with respect to his total body, cannot maintain his face above the water level. Beginning swimmers between the ages of four and six years have a tendency to maintain a vertical position if they are allowed artificial support, and their first movements without support are of the struggling order.

Interpretation.   In the light of their subsequent behavior, both in and out of the laboratory, it is safe to state that at the present time Johnny usually manifests greater motor coordination and daring in physical performances. Jimmy, who is more awkward and timid, exercises devious methods of rendering more easy the motor aspect of a given activity, so that both children may end up with the same result in terms of final accomplishment.

It has been pointed out that the degree to which an accelerated activity may retain its advanced status after the modifying factor of intensive exercise has been withdrawn is proportional to the degree of fixity the behavior pattern had attained when practice was discontinued. Fixity in this connection means whether the manner of performance had stabilized into a well integrated movement. Examples of well stabilized activities which manifested no major alteration through lack of practice are tricycling, getting off pedestals and descending slopes. Manipulating pedestals and boxes was in a fluid state, and their subsequent performances have shown many fluctuations.

Fixity in mode of behavior, however, is not the only factor determining the permanency of acceleration. Another important factor, viz: organic change within the individual, has been recognized only by the analysis of later performances in skating and ascending slides. Johnny's mode of performance in these activities when he was two years old was highly skillful and of an order comparable to that of the efficient adult engaging in a similar activity. If one considered the activity in the abstract, one would say that his skating and slope-climbing behavior had attained a high degree of fixity. Yet these activities suffered alteration, or loss in skill. This loss of skill appears to have been due primarily to change in bodily proportions. Thus it seems that a child may, in a given activity, attain a high degree of skill and his manner of operation may be the most approved or efficient with the organic structure he has to work with at the time. If, however, at a later age he has a different set of organic structures for performing the same activity, then his behavior may show disorganization characteristic of the novice. Retention of general muscular coordination may persist but the actual patterning of the particular skill or behavior will be interrupted until the child has learned to operate the new set of body mechanisms. The comparative behavior of Johnny and Jimmy in roller-skating illustrates this point. Even though the activity became disorganized in both children as they grew taller, superior general motor coordinations could be detected in Johnny's movements.

Johnny's superior motor coordination is evinced not only in adaptive skills as mentioned above but also in the common, more organic motor movements such as the assumption of an erect posture, walking and falling. Quantitative determinations of their efficiency in walking were ascertained periodically at six month intervals from the time they were about two years old. While these measurements are too scattered to justify elaborate treatment, they do show that Johnny was consistently a little ahead of Jimmy, and to that extent these objective measurements corroborate the observational data.

In summary it might be said that the alteration or deterioration of performance, particularly motor performance, through lack of exercise or practice over a long period of time is determined 1) by the state of maturity the activity had attained at the time the practice was withdrawn, 2) by alteration in body mechanics or other physical changes which necessitate an alteration in the form of the behavior pattern, 3) by change in emotional or attitudinal adjustment which operate as an inhibiting or facilitating factor in a particular performance. . . .

Personality Development. In view of the importance to the early experiences of life in determining later personality makeup, and in consideration of the rather popular notion that over-stimulation during infancy forecasts a neurotic child, two attempts were made to evaluate the personality and social adjustments of the children as of six years of age. Dr. William S. Langford, through psychiatric interviews with the mother and children, arrived at the following evaluation of the children's emotional and social adjustments as of today:

"It is difficult to discuss these two children without stressing the differences between them and without speculating as to possible causes of these differences. Johnny and Jimmy both are regarded by the mother as happy children who benefited by their experiences in the Normal Child Development Clinic. There are no particular difficulties in home management with either of the boys. The mother believes that both, as a result of the clinic experience, are able to meet with people and adjust better in social contacts outside of the home than do her other children. When playing with the older siblings, they both are able to adapt their play to the situation; when playing with the girls it is dolls, and when playing with the boys it is guns and cowboys; they are equally happy at each type of play.

"There has been a difference in the attitude toward the two children at home, in part coming out of the fact that Johnny was the 'subject' in the clinic. This difference in attitude would seem important in the genesis of some of the differences between the two boys. Although the family tried to realize that the selection of Johnny for the conditioning experience in the clinic was not because of any favoritism, it was difficult for them not to favor Jimmy and not to try to make up for some of the things he did not get. During the latter part of the second year, after newspaper reports of the experimental studies had been published, they would, among other things, take Jimmy and encourage him to jump off the icebox. However, the experiences in the home, which would seem to have given Jimmy the greater security there, were more a result of circumstance. In their infancy when, at the end of the clinic day, they were returned home, Johnny would be tired and go to sleep; Jimmy on the other hand would be wide awake and ready for play and socialization with his parents and siblings. For a time Jimmy would strike Johnny and take away his toys; Johnny would not seem to dare to hit back. One wonders strongly if this, too, was not a result of attitudes in the home.

"Jimmy seems to be more at ease in the home situation where he is the leader of the two boys. He usually bosses Johnny about. Jimmy is quite apt to come home with tales about Johnny and tell what he had done outside. The parents, one feels, do not particularly encourage him in this activity. Jimmy wakes up quickly and is on the go all day as a rule chattering a blue streak about whatever comes into his mind. He seems closer to his mother; talks more with her and likes to sleep with her. When he is put to bed with another sibling, he will frequently come into his mother's bed. He definitely prefers his mother to his father and feels that she likes him best. He is helpful about the house and likes to assist his mother in tidying up and washing dishes. Jimmy cries easily when things do not go his own way or if he is scolded. He indulges in mild temper tantrums consisting of stamping his feet when he cannot get what he wants. Earlier, at about two years of age, he went through a period of severe temper outbursts with breathholding.

"Johnny gives evidence of some tension; he has always been a nailbiter, and the mother states that he is a 'wiggler,' cannot sit still in a chair and from time to time displays quite restless sleep. In addition, Johnny has always been enuretic nightly. This is difficult to interpret as enuresis seems to be a family failing. There was difficulty in establishment of the day habit with all of the older siblings and one brother did not stop his bedwetting until nearly eleven years of age. Jimmy still wets his bed occasionally although the mother did not tell of this until some time after the initial interview. In addition, an adult member of the family will occasionally wet his bed. The mother feels that this tendency comes from the father's family where all the members have a tendency toward urinary frequency and urgency. Johnny, among all of the Woods children, is a thumb sucker; this began in early infancy and continues at bedtime even today although it used to be more marked and occur in the daytime also. He sucks the left thumb, and as an accessory movement pulls his own or bed partner's hair with the other hand; usually the latter. The sucking is rather vigorous and the accessory movement is so pronounced that most of the siblings prefer not to sleep with him. Johnny is somewhat ashamed of this habit and was disinclined to discuss it at first. Johnny is the quieter of the two children and rarely holds conversations with the other members of the family. Mother believes he is 'deeper' and 'when you least expect it Johnny will say something.' He is dependent on his mother in being washed and dressed and tends to play in his bath. One feels that this slowness is more a result of preoccupation than of a desire to have the mother do these things for him as the mother becomes irritated at his slowness and finally does it herself rather than wait for him to complete it. Johnny is not thoughtful or helpful about the house, but tends to be 'destructive and throw things around.' The mother feels that Johnny has no fears and thinks that he would be better off if he were a little more cautious, especially in his attitude towards dangerous occupations, such as crossing streets. In the home, Johnny has a philosophical attitude and takes things as they come; he is not upset when he cannot get his own way. There are no temper outbursts and he rarely cries. During the past year he has shown a tendency to play with fire, but otherwise has shown no overt behavior difficulties. Both children when observed in the interview were friendly and cooperative and talked freely. Both boys, in common with two older siblings, speak indistinctly with a lisping difficulty in articulation suggestive of 'baby-talk.'

"Jimmy showed a good deal of spontaneous chatter, but was quite apt to grow almost incoherent in the rapidity with which he spouted out detail after detail and leaped from topic to topic. He showed no marked preoccupations, but reacted to the questions immediately without taking thought as to how he answered. He talked a good deal of Johnny and showed a warm affection towards him. At the same time, he tended to bring out Johnny's bad points, telling of his enuresis and hair pulling and stating that Johnny is 'the bad one at home; bad at home and bad in school.' He said that Johnny wanted to be a drunken man when he grew up. He likes to play with Johnny best, and brags about how funny he is. Many of Jimmy's statements seemed to be made for effect and with a desire to produce a laugh as he would immediately contradict himself. His general attitudes and behavior seem quite typical of an outgoing, exuberant and quite usual six year old boy. He reacted without thinking and was responsive to environmental changes. In one interview when the examiner was weary, Jimmy reflected the subdued and more quiet atmosphere. Jimmy in his drawing drew a watch which he then cut out and pinned to himself, strutting around with evident pleasure at his self adornment.

"Johnny in the interview presented a quite different picture from that of his brother. He was friendly and cheerful but not so spontaneous. Attention was difficult to hold; he would be distracted by extraneous noises, but more often by passing thoughts of his own which would result in a seemingly irrelevant answer. He was thoughtful in answering questions and seemed to weigh his answers. His interviews came after Jimmy's and he seemed to feel that he should have everything that his brother had had; making sure that he sat in the same chair, had his words written down, drew pictures, and took home a pencil as a gift. His attitude towards the members of the family was somewhat different from Jimmy's. He definitely prefers his mother and sister whereas Jimmy prefers the 'toughest' brother to the sister whom he soundly denounces as being dumb. Johnny is quite fond of his twin brother, but does belittle Jimmy's ideas of wanting to grow up twice; he himself would prefer to keep on growing until he became a giant. He did tell of a dream which he was careful to point out was 'make believe' in which an old witch hits Jimmy. Johnny talks of most of his difficulties quite freely, but is hesitant about mentioning the hair pulling. He shows a definite tendency towards self evaluation and self criticism which is not present in his brother's output. He also shows good imaginative ability and reveals in his stories evidence of a rich phantasy life although he will not express these when questioned directly. His drawings are rather well done and are not, as were Jimmy's, copies of something he sees, but rather a product of his own imagination.

"Attitudes of both children toward the clinic were those of its being a pleasurable experience with the exception of having to take their clothes off. Jimmy, however, tended to protest that he liked Dr. McGraw better than Johnny, although both felt sure she had no preferences. In the clinic situation it would seem that Johnny has the greater security and tends to be the leader and to boss Jimmy about. His reactions at the birth of Dr. McGraw's child would tend to bear out his need to be wanted there.

"In conclusion one might say that the boys present quite different pictures. Johnny exhibits in the home certain evidences of tensions; nail biting, motor restlessness, persistent thumb sucking as well as enuresis. The last symptom, however, is difficult to evaluate because of its prevalence in the family, and it is also present to a lesser degree in Jimmy. These symptoms could well come out of Johnny's lessened security in the home situation where his brother has been preferred and given more attention, and earlier, a greater amount of affectional demonstration. It would not seem that the 'conditioning' in the clinic had much to do with these. The restlessness, nail biting, and sucking do not occur in the clinic setting, and the boy has great security in his relationship with the clinic personnel, especially Dr. McGraw. I should not feel that undue pressure for success in various accomplishments was a factor in this as the boy enjoyed his work. This latter, however, would seem of importance in giving Johnny his attitude of evaluating and looking over a situation.

"Jimmy is the outgoing, helter skelter type of child who lives for the moment. Johnny is the more serious, thoughtful and contemplative youngster who looks to the consequences before he acts. Jimmy reacts mostly to external stimuli, Johnny as a result of his more active inner life reacts in a less direct manner to external stimuli and frequently gives the impression of preoccupation. Johnny gives the impression of being capable of weathering more serious environmental difficulties without blowing up because of his greater capacity for working things through; but once upset, he would respond more slowly to efforts for readjustment. Neither child seems to have suffered from the experimental study. Both make adequate social adjustments although in different fashions. The differences in their personalities may well be largely constitutionally determined and not entirely the result of their diverse earlier experience. However, one feels that these experiences are of importance. I should feel that the home attitudes were of great importance as well as Johnny's 'conditioning' and they do seem a little easier to evaluate."

Dr. Langford is in a peculiarly favorable position to make these interpretations since he knew the children during their experimental period and has had occasion to see them from time to time around the laboratory in addition to the specified psychiatric interviews. It is especially interesting that the opinion concerning the personality make-up of the two children as expressed by Dr. Langford is corroborated by an interpretation of their reactions to the Rorschach test. These tests were administered by Miss Jane Sills and a blind analysis was made by Dr. Z. Piotrowski. Excerpts from Dr. Piotrowski's reports referring to Jimmy's record state "this boy probably makes the impression of a rather typical average child of his age, emotionally immature. Toward the environment he appears to react in a rather self-centered and labile emotional manner, and he seems to have a rather poorly developed inner life. His reasoning power is not above the average, and he does not seem especially observant. He appears to lack the capacity to preoccupy himself with imaginative and instructive games. Compared to his brother's record, he is childish, as one would expect a child of his years to be. His brother appears more independent in his actions, more individual, while this boy seems to be more dependent, more appealing to adults who like to play the role of protectors to young children." Concerning Johnny's record Dr. Piotrowski writes, "The complete lack of color responses in the presence of a good human response suggests that the child's reactions to the environment are determined by promptings from within himself rather than by changes in the outward situation. Probably, the child tends to be rather impersonal in his relations with people, and one might find a certain lack of emotional warmth in his attitude toward people. Although his reactions seem to be rapid, he is fairly well aware of his psychic experiences. Occasionally he is given to feelings of insecurity and uneasiness, and it is my impression that at such times the boy tends to be brave against his liking. Intellectually he seems to be above the average since only the intelligent among the small children tend to have a human movement response. Since the boy seems to lack the capacity for an immediate and effortless emotional adjustment to the environment, it is the intellect which carries the burden of adjusting. It is probably best to make a contact with him on a rather intellectual and impersonal basis. His thinking would appear to have a common sense quality with occasional excursions into imaginative fantasies. His mental independence does not, however, seem to be characterized by negativism or aggression. On the whole, this child is rather self-confident and probably would impress one as capable of taking his future into his own hands. He probably gets along well with only a few children while his brother fits in better with any children's group." On the basis of the child's reactions Dr. Piotrowski correctly surmised Johnny's record to represent that of the "trained" twin since from the nature of Johnny's earlier experiences "he would have had a better chance to develop his inner abilities and the habit of self-observation for the purpose of avoiding future mistakes in well standardized situations."

In the main, these two interpretations of the personality differences of the children are in agreement. They are also in accord with the general opinion of the writer, whose observations of the children during their entire life have been both intensive and extensive. According to the writer's observations, outstanding personality differences are Johnny's stoical and rather philosophical attitude in disagreeable situations, and his escape by indulging in his own phantasies. Jimmy is more loquacious, is more conscious of, and bids for the approval of his audience. Consequently, he is more appealing to the casual observer. Since infancy he has looked and played the part of a clown. He is rather happy-go-lucky, and reflects his home environment more directly. Johnny employs a more subtle method of revealing his feelings. It appears that the less frequent contacts with the laboratory after the age of two years have been a handicap to Johnny. Apparently having heard that younger twins came here, he spontaneously inquired "Dr. McGraw, did you need another baby when you sent me home?" When they left here, Jimmy went to a home admittedly more favorable to him; he also had less of an adjustment to make. In some ways Johnny's experience here was poor preparation to meet the rough and tumble of a large family life. He had learned in many ways "to take it" and the reports indicate that he has had more than his share of taking. At home and at school Jimmy is rather the bully, often casting aspersions on Johnny and threatening his confidence. For all that, the affection between the two boys is warm. Despite the amount of public notice they have received, they are remarkably free from self-consciousness.

To evaluate the extent to which these personality differences are constitutional, or determined by their early experimental experiences or their later home environment, is beyond achievement at the present time and will probably remain beyond the scope of actual determination for all time. However, their experiences and behavior have been studied and chronicled as to detail in a way which is not obtainable for the average school child. If these reports and opinions serve a useful purpose in guiding the educational careers of these two children, they may at the same time be of even greater significance in showing the extent to which knowledge of early childhood experiences is of educational and psychiatric value in the adjustments of the adolescent or adult.

Intellectual and Physical Development. Both Johnny and Jimmy have consistently rated within the normal range on standardized intelligence tests. The Rorschach test indicates that Johnny is somewhat accelerated in intelligence. This paper is not the occasion to discuss the correlation of the Rorschach with the Stanford-Binet, the Minnesota, or other well-known intelligence scales. It may be that the Rorschach taps a quality of intellectual processes which is not measured by the items included in these various tests.

There is one fairly common opinion among the laity at least which might at this occasion be corrected. Some have labored under the belief that special training during the first few years of a child's life will in some way raise his general intellectual endowment. It has been previously pointed out that the effect of training or exercise as applied in these studies was highly specific to those activities in which the child received daily practice. Certainly, whatever are the factors measured by standardized intelligence tests, they have not been appreciably altered by the different experimental experiences to which the twins were subjected.

There is one aspect of mental development which deserves mention, although it has no direct bearing upon the training program. In parlor discourse the earliest individual memory is a common topic. Psychologists are usually skeptical of reports of direct memories of experiences which have occurred during infancy. The usual explanation is that the person had heard the experience referred to and therefore could not distinguish between direct and verbal memories of it. Because of the peculiar circumstances of the twins' first two years, it is possible to know precisely whether reference had been made to certain incidents in their early experiences. There are several instances in Johnny's behavior indicating remote memory. When Johnny was sixteen and seventeen months old, he would skate through the tunnel joining Babies Hospital and Neurological Institute as he journeyed to the swimming pool in Bard Hall. These journeys through the tunnel were terminated when he was seventeen months old, and he never entered the tunnel again until he was 43 months old, i.e., twenty-six months later. On this occasion he was walking with three other children. As he entered the tunnel his eyes widened and he suddenly remarked, with a sweeping gesture, "This is where we go skating." This recall is interesting beyond the mere indication of memory for early experiences. At the time the tunnel journeys were ended Johnny had no verbal means of expressing the act of skating. He recognized skates by name, but he had no word in his own vocabulary to indicate them. Here his remote memory is entirely integrated with verbal expression which was acquired at a later date. A year later, when he was four and one-half years old, Johnny was again escorted to the tunnel. On this occasion he asked, "Where's the bathroom?" When told he would have to wait until he returned to the laboratory, he replied, "Oh, there's one way, way down there," pointing in the direction of Neurological Institute. It was then recalled that when Johnny was seventeen months old he was being trained in toilet habits, and as soon as he arrived at Neurological Institute during those days, he was rushed to the toilet. Another instance illustrates his incorporating into his vocabulary recollection of an experience which occurred before he had language facilities for expressing such experiences. Johnny and Jimmy were just two years old when they entered the elevator of an apartment house alone and Johnny pulled the lever, sending the elevator to the basement. The occasion was subsequently never referred to, and other persons who have been associated with the children did not even know about it. More than three and one-half years later, as Johnny sat somewhat meditatively watching the dial indicate the floors of the elevator in Babies Hospital, he quietly remarked, "Dr. McGraw, remember when Jimmy and me went in your house in the elevator and it went down boom!" These incidents are cited because they are comparable to citations of many parents in reporting the early memory of their children; and because of the peculiarity of experiences to which the twins were exposed during their first two years, it is possible to know definitely whether or not subsequent reference had been made to the situations. If the direct memory of experiences during the first two years of life is as indelible as these incidents indicate, then the weight attributed to influences imposed upon the infant and young child gains significance.

There is nothing of experimental significance in the physical history of the two children. Although Johnny was smaller during the first seven months of his life, he began at about eight months to maintain a superior weight gain as compared to that of Jimmy. This advantage in body weight he has sustained during the four years they have been at home. While Johnny began to show this superiority in weight gain about the same time as he showed improvement in motor performances, there is no claim of a direct relationship between the two. Their health records compare favorably with those of other children of their socioeconomic level, and their value to this study is only in so far as they indicate no serious sequelae of their experimental experiences during their first two years of life.

Summary

Studies of the performances of Johnny and Jimmy in particular laboratory situations indicate that the amount of retention of a motor performance, once the factor of repetition has been reduced or abandoned, is contingent upon the state of fixity the activity had attained at the time the practice-factor was withdrawn. Activities which have attained a high degree of integration may be appreciably altered if the body mechanisms are so modified through growth as to introduce new structures or elements into the situation. The natural and gradual maturing of emotional or attitudinal factors seems to influence appreciably the somatic or motor performance in particular activities.

In general endowment the two children have consistently fallen within the normal range as measured by the standardized intelligence tests. There is no reason to believe that exercise in special activities will accelerate mental functions as measured on standardized scales. There seems to be a superiority of general muscular coordinations on the part of Johnny, who received the longer and more intensive practice in motor activities. In general personality make-up, Johnny also appears to be more complex as indicated both by psychiatric interviews and by analysis of responses to the Rorschach ink blots. There is no way to evaluate the extent to which their early experimental experiences operated in determining their respective personality components.

The two boys today present the picture of lively, normal six year old children who show no deleterious sequelae of the different regimes to which they were subjected during the first two years of their lives.

References

(1) Gesell, Arnold and Thompson, Helen. Learning and growth in identical twin infants. *Genet. Psychol. Monographs*, July, 1929, 6, No. 1, 1-124.
(2) McGraw, Myrtle B. *Growth: A study of Johnny and Jimmy.* New York, Appleton-Century Company, 1935.
(3) Ibid. Pp. 310-311.
(4) Ibid. P. 255.
(5) McGraw, Myrtle B. and Weinbach, A. P. Quantitative measures in studying development of behavior patterns. *Bull. Neurol. Inst.*, April, 1936, IV, No. 4.
(6) McGraw, Myrtle B. *Growth: A study of Johnny and Jimmy.* Pp. 136-143.
(7) Ibid. Pp. 167-174.
(8) Ibid. Pp. 174-183.
(9) Ibid. Pp. 183-190.
(10) Ibid. Pp. 122-136.

Age Differences and Inter-relationships Between Skill and Learning in Gross Motor Performance of Ten- and Fifteen-Year-Old Boys*

FRANKLIN M. HENRY AND GAYLORD A. NELSON

VARIOUS parameters of task performance between two age groups are compared, with unique differences and similarities pointed out. The num-

* From *The Research Quarterly*, 1956, 27, 162-175. Reprinted with permission of the authors and the American Association for Health, Physical Education, and Recreation.

ber of differences found between ten- and fifteen-year-old boys in motor skill learning emphasizes age considerations and expectations when skills are introduced to these age groups. Most particularly, greater task generality exists among the younger children, and with age there is more specificity in the kind of skill demonstrated for a particular task. Achievement differences that are attributed to age are consistent with other research findings. Amount of learning and rate of learning factors are contrasted in this study (at the same time suggesting techniques for measuring learning).

McGeoch and Irion, after reviewing the published research on changes in learning as a function of age, conclude that the rate increases during the first two decades of life.[7,(p.535)] Munn, on the other hand, interprets the evidence as showing that the amount of improvement that can be attained from practice is not systematically related to age.[8,(p.395)] These investigators have concerned themselves almost entirely with *verbal* rather than *motor* learning because of the paucity of experimental studies in the latter area.

It is well known that motor skills are highly specific—appreciable intercorrelations between tasks occur only when there are obvious common elements. This topic has been reviewed by Lindeburg.[6] There has been less attention to the question of whether *learning* as such is also characterized by a high degree of task specificity. Woodrow[10] found evidence that this is so, although the data available to him were obtained mostly with verbal material and his conclusions do not necessarily apply to motor problems. Heese[4] studied some of the so-called fine motor skills. Very low intercorrelations were found between individual differences in learning. There was one exception: Improvement scores in tracing a figure in the mirror-drawing test correlated $r = 0.57$ with improvement scores in tracing the same figure with a two-handed apparatus that controlled the movement of the pencil. Even though the common task element was substantial, the observed relationship was not large since it accounted for only 33 per cent of the individual difference variance.

If gross motor skills are not completely specific, there is a possibility that the degree of specificity may be less in the younger individuals. Another question of interest is whether the ability to learn motor tasks is related to age within a range that is of particular interest with respect to physical education instruction in the schools. In addition there are several related problems, such as examination of the extent that it is possible to estimate motor educability from performance ability rather than directly from the learning scores. Stated in more fundamental terms, this is the problem of assaying the relative contribution of initial skill and amount of learning to individual differences in final skill attainment. It is too complex to be solved by simple examination of the correlation between performance and learning.

Methodology

One group of subjects (n = 73) included all boys in the tenth year of age from a small-town grammar school, with the exception of a few who did not complete the test because of illness or some other complication. Another group (n = 72) was a random sample of high school boys in their fifteenth year of age, from the high school of the same town.

The three motor tasks were chosen partly for their suitability with respect to the range of ages being investigated, and partly because they involved important basic elements of game skills. They were intentionally quite similar.

One of them was very easy to perform. The subject held a celluloid ball in his hand next to his belt buckle, and responded to the stimulus by throwing this ball downward into a wastebasket and then reaching forward to grasp a tennis ball which was suspended in front of him at one-arm's-length distance. In this task the stimulus was a sound, and the response was simple, i.e., no stimulus discrimination or choice of movement was required. An electric chronograph measured the time required to respond to the stimulus by completing the forward arm movement.

The other tasks were inter-related, involving the performance of one or the other of two movements in a visuo-motor discrimination problem. This problem was unusual in that the perceptual discrimination was made as simple and unequivocal as possible through the use of multiple discrimination cues. Having discriminated and identified which stimulus had occurred, the subject performed the movement specified by that stimulus. The complete testing schedule required about one hour.

Apparatus. In front of the subject, and within his normal visual field, there were two corona glow lamps, an unmarked orange one and vertically below it a striped blue one. Also within the visual field, placed one arm's length away, were two colored balls hanging on strings. The upper one was orange; it was the larger. Below it was a blue striped ball. The task of the subject was to respond to the orange light by grasping the orange ball with a forehand movement, first dropping a table tennis paddle held in his hand. If the lower (blue) light came on, the subject retained the paddle and used it to hit the lower (blue) ball with a backhand stroke. These movements were made from the standing position, with the hands and paddle touching the knees. One trial followed another at intervals of about one minute.

The strings supporting the balls were suspended by small metal strips held between spring contacts; if either ball was touched, the metal strip fell out immediately, opening the chronoscope circuit. This circuit was placed in action automatically by the same switch that turned on the stimulus light. In order to prevent undesirable swinging of the balls, their supporting strings passed downward to terminate at screw eyes attached to the floor of the device. The apparatus was very similar to one illustrated in certain other studies done at this laboratory,[5] although the physical dimensions were about twice as large. An electric chronoscope measured the elapsed time from the first flash of the stimulus light to the completion of the motor response, with an accuracy of somewhat more than 0.01 sec.

A prepared randomized order was used to decide which stimulus (orange or blue) would be used in a particular trial, and whether the interval between the warning signal (a bell) and the stimulus light would be one, two, or three seconds. The same order sheet was used for all subjects. Timing of the fore-period was controlled automatically by an electronic time-delay circuit. All subjects had at least 30 trials (15 forehand and 15 backhand) on this problem, and somewhat more than half of each group practiced 40 trials.

It will be seen that these two tasks had an identical element in common, namely, the discrimination reaction time which has been found in subsequent (unpublished) studies to be about 0.35 sec. Approximately half of the measured performance time was therefore used for the reaction phase of the response and the other half was net movement time. Since only a single chronoscope was available, the motor performance scores included both reaction and movement times. The simple (non-discrimination) task described earlier was similar to the backhand task in that an object had to be released before proceeding with the principal movement, and was similar to the forehand task in that a forward arm movement was performed in order to grasp the ball. Only 40 per cent of the subjects in each age group were tested with the simple task, as the need for it was not recognized until the experiment had been in progress for some time.

In all three of these tasks there was no particular requirement for accuracy of response; speed was the factor emphasized to the subjects and measured by the apparatus. Motivation seemed to be high in both age groups. All the boys seemed interested in the tests and appeared to try to improve throughout the experiment. Naturally, the experimenter made every possible effort to keep the psychological factors constant. An additional degree of control was secured by testing an equal number of boys from each age group at any one experimental period, so that any changes in effectiveness of instruction or seasonal influences would affect both groups.

Experimental Results

Age Differences in Mean Performance. Learning curves were plotted for three tasks. In view of the irregularities of single trials (a typical characteristic of learning curves in general) it has seemed desirable to average the first three trials as a measure of the initial performance level, and the last three trials as a measure of the final performance achieved. One is faced with a dilemma in this sort of situation—the reliability of the individual differences is increased as a large number of trials is used to define the measures, but at the same time the amount of learning (i.e., the differences between the initial and final measures) becomes less. One factor in the choice of three trials rather than some other number was the observation that, as will be explained later, a statistically significant improvement in performance can just be demonstrated beginning with the fourth trial (for all three problems) if the initial performance is taken as the average of at least three trials.

Using these measures of initial and final performance, it may be seen in Table 1 that the younger subjects are definitely slower than the older boys at the beginning of each task. They are also slower at the end of the training period. The percent improvement due to the practice is not greatly different for

TABLE 1

Descriptive Statistics for Two Age Groups in Three Motor-Learning Tasks

Statistic	Simple Forehand			Discrim. Forehand			Discrim. Backhand		
	Initial	Learn.	Final	Initial	Learn.	Final	Initial	Learn.	Final
M_{10}	0.672	0.135	0.537	0.842	0.145	0.697	0.794	0.192	0.602
M_{15}	0.552	0.088	0.464	0.671	0.102	0.569	0.594	0.109	0.485
Diff.	0.120	0.047	0.073	0.171	0.043	0.128	0.200	0.083	0.117
t	4.97	1.97	4.52	6.38	1.91	6.44	9.86	4.45	7.25
10 yr	*(n = 28)*			*(n = 73)*			*(n = 73)*		
σ	0.091	0.102	0.067	0.186	0.152	0.131	0.131	0.130	0.096
σ/M	0.135	—	0.125	0.221	—	0.188	0.165	—	0.159
r_{11}	0.530	0.396	0.744	0.814	0.678	0.684	0.566	0.394	0.572
15 yr	*(n = 29)*			*(n = 72)*			*(n = 72)*		
σ	0.095	0.072	0.085	0.130	0.110	0.104	0.111	0.089	0.097
σ/M	0.172	—	0.183	0.194	—	0.183	0.187	—	0.200
r_{11}	0.818	0.258	0.927	0.831	0.267	0.669	0.712	0.624	0.719

NOTE: The σ's for learning scores have been computed directly from the distributions. When computed indirectly from initial and final scores and the intercorrelation, there may be as much as 10 per cent discrepancy, presumably caused by cumulated grouping errors. Means are in seconds; individual instrumental error is negligible ($\sigma = 0.0035$ sec), influencing the average only 0.0005 sec.

the three tasks. Averaging all age groups and tasks, the percent gain is 18.4, ranging from 15.2 per cent for the older boys in the discrimination forehand problem to 24.2 per cent for the younger group for the backhand movement. The younger boys improve relatively more in all tasks—on the average, they gain 20.3 per cent in speed compared with only 16.5 per cent gain by the older boys.

The absolute amount of gain in speed by practice is greater in the younger age group for all three motor tasks. However, the advantage is statistically significant for only one, namely the backhand movement (t = 4.45). The absolute differences due to age are only about half as large as this in the other two tasks, and the t ratios are not quite significant—1.91 for the discrimination forehand task compared with 1.98 required for the 5-per-cent level of confidence, and 1.97 compared with 2.00 required for the simple forehand (the number of cases was smaller for the latter task).

Inter-task Differences. In order to compare inter-task differences in learning, it seems reasonable to require that practice be continued until a stable plateau is reached. In the 38 older subjects who had 20 trials in these tasks, the average of trials 18, 19, and 20 is 0.5 per cent slower than the average of trials 13, 14, and 15 for the discrimination forehand movement; the corresponding figure for the backhand is 2.4 per cent slower, so it may be said that learning did not progress after trial 15. In the 41 younger subjects who practiced 20 trials, there was a slight improvement in the forehand (1.0 per cent, t = 1.53) and also in the backhand (1.4 per cent, t = 1.84); it would seem that the learning was so nearly completed for these boys that the use of trials 13, 14, 15 as the final score is justified for most purposes. The slight additional gain would, however, be sufficient to cause the age difference in the discrimination forehand speed to be significant, since the estimated t ratio would be 2.00 compared with the previously non-significant value 1.91. In the case of the simple forehand movement, it is necessary to use the 20-trial learning period, because the gain between trials 13, 14, 15 and 18, 19, 20 is about 3 per cent, and is statistically significant in both age groups. However, the amount of gain from the last 5 trials is small, and it is doubtful if additional practice would have caused any important change.

It is rather curious that the amount of learning actually differs so little among the three tasks. As explained earlier, the inter-task differences in per cent improvement are not very large. Using the absolute gains, it is found that none of the mean differences in the older group are significant, since the inter-task t ratios are 0.44, 0.77, and 1.39. In the younger subjects, there is no important difference in the amount of learning as between the simple and discrimination forehand movements (t = 0.52), but the backhand learning is definitely greater than the simple forehand learning (t = 2.76) and also greater than the discrimination forehand learning (t = 2.33). All of the task averages differ significantly from each other in initial performance levels within the older subjects and within the younger subjects. The final performance means are in exactly the same rank order as the initial performances, and all inter-task differences are highly significant with a single exception—in the older group, the t ratio between backhand and simple forehand is only 1.42. The major differences between tasks, therefore, are in *performance level difficulty* rather than ease of learning.

Individual Differences

Inter-task Relationships. Even though the striking differences in average response are seen as characterizing initial and final response levels rather than amounts of learning, individual differences in ability persisting through

TABLE 2

Inter-Task Correlations

Task	Type of Data	Age 10			Age 15		
		Initial	Learn.	Final	Initial	Learn.	Final
Simple forehand vs.	Raw	0.456	0.438	0.284	0.478	0.085	0.707
Discrim. forehand	Corrected	*0.694*	*0.838*	*0.438*	*0.580*	*0.322*	*0.869*
Simple forehand vs.	Raw	0.387	0.317	0.260	0.264	0.254	0.470
Discrim. backhand	Corrected	*0.643*	*0.801*	*0.298*	*0.357*	*0.622*	*0.576*
Discrim. forehand vs.	Raw	0.551	0.276	0.434	0.503	0.122	0.583
Discrim. backhand	Corrected	*0.740*	*0.528*	*0.760*	*0.674*	*0.301*	*0.814*

NOTE: True-score intercorrelations (italics) have been corrected for attenuation in both variables.

the three tasks are more prevalent in the initial and final performances than in the learning phase. None of the inter-task correlations of amount of learning are significantly different from zero at the 1-per-cent level of confidence. In contrast, two-thirds of the possible inter-task correlations between performance levels have this degree of significance (Table 2).

For more direct statistical evidence of this tendency, it is necessary to inspect the correlations between the discrimination forehand and the backhand movements, because this is the only inter-task comparison that involves a sizable sample of individuals (73 in the younger group and 72 in the older). The learning score intercorrelation is significantly lower than either initial or final performance correlations in the older group (t = 2.61 and 3.29). In the younger group, it is also lower than the initial score intercorrelation (t = 2.03), but not significantly lower than the final score intercorrelation (t = 0.96). The lower inter-task correlation for learning is intrinsic rather than just a reflection of lower reliability of learning scores, because when the inter-task correlations are corrected for attenuation in both variables (Table 2), the coefficient for learning remains significantly smaller than the coefficients for either initial or final scores, in both age groups.

Inter-task correlations are higher for the younger subjects in all cases insofar as learning is concerned, and are also higher in the case of initial scores. The age differences are not statistically significant. However, they are in consistent directions in all the inter-task comparisons using corrected coefficients and all but one using uncorrected coefficients, so there is a suggestion that there may be a genuine tendency for the younger subjects to have less task-specificity in learning these skills. Any such tendency has disappeared in the case of final skill level.

Regardless of any age tendencies, one cannot fail to be impressed with the high degree of task specificity. In examining this question, it must be remembered that the corrected correlation coefficients give the relation present after the removal of error variance, so that the square of a coefficient (multiplied by 100) gives directly the percentage of individual difference variance that is common to the performance (initial or final) or the learning of any two of the tasks. It will be recalled that a considerable amount of similar elements was incorporated in these tasks; even so, the correlations are far from high. Evidently the learning of motor tasks, at least those of the type used in this experiment, is not a matter of motor-learning ability—rather, it is a matter of specific aptitudes for learning specific tasks.

Individual Differences at Final Skill Level. As practice progresses, improvement follows a law of diminishing return until the learning curve approaches either an asymptote or at least a line of very little slope. It is important to know whether individual differences tend to disappear in this region, or whether they persist at full effect. One way of estimation is to use the size of the standard deviation as an index of the degree of individual differences, although it must be recognized that it is made up of two components—true individual difference variance and error variance. Also, the individual difference variance (in contrast to error variance) is not necessarily independent of the mean. For this reason, the coefficient of relative variation ($V = 100$ σ/M) is sometimes used. The size of the reliability coefficient is probably a better index than either.

It can be seen by inspection of Table 1 that the standard deviation is somewhat smaller in the final performance as compared with the initial performance. The coefficient V changes very little. When the tasks are averaged, there is a 9.4 per cent drop in V in the younger group, and a 2.4 per cent rise in the older boys. The average reliability coefficient rises 4.7 per cent in the younger group and declines 1.9 per cent in the older group. Since these changes are small and inconsistent, it seems likely that the extent of individual differences does not change from the initial performance level to the final level.

Within-task Correlations. If one defines motor educability as ability to learn, it may be inferred from the pattern of intra-task correlations (Table 3) that performance scores cannot be substituted for improvement scores in the assaying of individual differences in *educability*. The pattern is somewhat different in the two age groups, but there are certain features common to both. Individual differences in amount of learning are negatively related to degree of initial skill—slow performers have greater possibilities for improvement, and they do indeed tend to improve more than those with a higher degree of initial skill. In other words, a *good* initial score indicates *poor* educability.[1] The coefficient of determination,[3, (p.223)] however, averages only 40 per cent for the older boys and 52 per cent for the younger group, so the predictability is certainly not high.

In the older subjects, the tendency is just about equally great for boys who start in a certain relative position to end in the same relative position as it is for boys who start with a poor initial score to improve more than those who start with a high score. In other words, the correlation of individual differences in initial score is as large with final score as it is with amount of learning. In the younger boys, the situation is somewhat different; the coefficients involving initial score give only about half as large a correlation with final score as with learning, and the differences in correlation are statistically significant for each of the three motor tasks ($t = 2.32$, 2.67 and 2.48).

A point of view of more practical interest is the final performance attainment. One may ask how important *is* learning as a determiner of individual

---

[1] The term "motor educability" is commonly used to mean *ability to learn motor skills easily;* sometimes the definition is *ability to develop a high degree of skill quickly,*[2] thus implying the involvement of motor skill capacity (i.e., the ability to reach a high final score as learning approaches completion). Presence of a substantial negative correlation would seem to require the acceptance of the latter, more complex, definition. In another article a "W" score is developed in order to meet this definition of educability and to provide a means of escaping the dilemma imposed by the negative relationship. See Henry, F. M., Evaluation of motor learning when performance levels are heterogeneous, *Research Quarterly* 27:176-181, 1956.

TABLE 3

Within-task Correlations

		Age 10		Age 15	
Task	Score	Learning	Final	Learning	Final
Simple forehand	Initial	−0.747	0.266	−0.618	0.758
	Learning		0.437		0.008
Discrim. forehand	Initial	−0.714	0.460	−0.722	0.656
	Learning		0.280		0.009
Discrim. backhand	Initial	−0.712	0.406	−0.551	0.583
	Learning		0.326		0.315

NOTE: In this table the measures have been treated as speed scores rather than time scores, so that the negative relation between performance and learning will be seen clearly.

differences in the completely learned performance. For the backhand movement, the coefficients relating learning to final score, while low, are significant at the 1-per-cent level of confidence for both age groups. (Incidentally, the reliabilities of scores in this task tend to run somewhat *lower* than in the other two.) As the correlations are negative in sign, the relationship is in the direction of large improvement being associated with fast performance in the final tests. In the other two tasks the same pattern is evident for the younger subjects, but the coefficients are smaller and only pass the significance test at the 5-per-cent level of confidence. In the older subjects the corresponding correlations are zero; amount of learning is unrelated to final performance level in either the simple or the discrimination backhand movements. It seems that individual differences in learning are subject to both age and task influences in their extent of determination of final attainment.

It may be noted that the systems of intra-task correlations are internally consistent within each task and for each age group. As a test of this, all of the partial correlations have been computed, and are found to fall within the range $r = 0.93$ to 0.99. Therefore, one may with some confidence compute the beta coefficients and by utilizing their products with the associated correlation coefficients[3, (p.261)] estimate the per cent contribution of individual differences in initial score and learning as factors determining individual differences in the final performance level in each task. This has been done in Table 4. The multiple R's are also shown in the table. Since they are all close to unity, it is evident that the intra-task correlations require no correction for attenuation (this would be expected, since the learning scores are fully determined by initial and final score magnitudes).

Age Differences in Effects of Learning. It is evident from this analysis that initial scores are in general more important than the amounts of learning in determining individual differences in the final level of skill. There is one exception; in the simple forehand response, learning is more important than initial score in determining the final score. Learning exerts a much larger influence in the younger subjects than in the older boys—in fact, the learning plays a negligible role in two of the three tasks for the 15-years-olds and is less important in the remaining movement than it is for any of the three in the 10-year-olds. This does not mean in any sense that the older subjects do not learn—rather, it means that *individual differences* in learning are small as compared with the individual differences in initial performance in the older

TABLE 4

Relative Contribution (in Per Cent) of Individual Differences in Initial Score and Learning to Final Score

	Age 10			Age 15		
Task	Initial	Learning	R	Initial	Learning	R
Simple forehand	35.6	62.7	0.992	93.6	0.6	0.971
Discrim. forehand	62.0	34.8	0.984	90.8	1.1	0.958
Discrim. backhand	52.4	40.6	0.965	63.3	28.7	0.960

NOTE: The relative contributions have been computed as the products of the beta coefficients with the corresponding r's.

subjects. It will be recalled that the evidence in Table 1 showed that the amount of learning was highly significant in both age groups, and the mean differences in amount of learning in the two age groups was only of borderline statistical significance in the very tasks in which the most striking differences are now found with respect to the relative contribution of individual differences. This is an example of the necessity of supplementing analysis of mean differences by correlational analysis in order to understand the role of individual differences.

Age Differences in Learning Rate

With respect to age differences in rate of learning, it was shown in Table 1 that there is a definite tendency for the younger subjects to improve somewhat more than the older boys when both age groups receive the same amount of practice. This does not necessarily mean that the *rate* of learning is faster in the younger group. For example, if one asks how many trials are required to secure a single trial mean performance that differs by a statistically significant amount (at the 5-per cent level of confidence) from cumulated average score up to that point, it turns out that three trials are required for the simple forehand response in each age group. In the discrimination problem, two forehand trials are required, with no age difference. The backhand response yields somewhat equivocal results because of irregularities in the curve of the older subjects, but a smooth curve through the graph would indicate three trials are required for them, which is the same as the requirement for the young group in this task.

Attempts to fit a mathematical curve system to these graphs in order to quantify the learning rates with greater accuracy has not been fully satisfactory due to the irregularity of the points. The impression gained through these attempts is that there is little if any age difference in rate of learning. Cozens[1] found that a parabolic equation of the form $Y = X^2$ described the improvement due to a semester of practice in such events as the dash, half-mile run, broad jump, discus, etc. Of course, this improvement was due to athletic training as well as learning, and the equation may not be theoretically correct for true learning curves. It is found that a general form of the parabola does describe the learning in the present experiment quite as well as certain other formulae that were tried (as for example, an exponential equation). The equation used is $y = at^{-k}$ where y is the time required to perform the motor act, a is the initial performance, t is the number of practice trials, and k is the rate coefficient.

It is rather interesting that the same rate coefficient ($k = 0.076$) seems correct for both the simple and the discrimination forehand movement data, whereas the backhand movement requires a considerably larger coefficient ($k = 0.117$). Identical rate coefficients have been used in both age groups. It seems that the learning progresses slightly faster in the younger age group, since the points tend to fall below the line for them in the later part of the learning period, but the difference is small.

Discussion

It would seem that the position of Munn,[8] rather than McGeoch and Irion,[7] is substantiated by these data. If the rate of motor learning changes with age, it tends to become *slower* rather than faster in the older subjects. Any possible difference in rate is, however, not impressive in the present experiment. There is more consistent evidence that the *amount* of learning is greater in the younger group. While small in comparison with the large age differences in initial and final performance levels, it seems to be definitely present and contradictory to the general expectations of McGeoch and Irion.

The finding of moderately high correlations, negative in sense, between amount of learning and initial amount of skill, is quite different from the intra-task relationships observed by Woodrow[9] for problems in which the motor-learning component was small or absent. He reported low correlations ranging between $r = 0.24$ and -0.05 between initial scores and learning in digit substitution performed by 82 subjects, whereas his correlations between learning and final score for these tasks ranged from $r = 0.75$ to 0.82. In the present experiment, the comparable correlations are quite small, and several are zero, although they are positive in sense (*i.e.,* the large learning scores are associated with fast performance in the final test). The other problem for which he made this type of analysis was horizontal adding (essentially a mental task); in this case the relation between learning and final score was very high, $r = 0.93$. It seems very likely that the inter-relationships may be quite different in motor and non-motor learning.

In the Heese study of fine motor skills,[4] the only intra-task correlations reported are those between initial and final scores. The coefficients found for his 50 subjects range from $r = 0.25$ for maze tracing to 0.55 for mirror tracing and 0.65 for the typing test. These results are similar to those obtained in the present study.

With respect to task specificity of motor learning, the results obtained by Heese on the precision type of fine motor skills are confirmed for an entirely different type of response using gross motor movements of a non-precise type. There is, however, suggestive evidence that the degree of specificity of the latter type of response may be somewhat less in the younger subjects.

The evidence presented to illustrate the danger of confusing motor *educability* with *ability* (the former being necessarily identified with ability to learn and the latter with performance level) agrees with certain conclusions of Gire and Espenschade.[2] While these investigators did not compare individual differences in learning with differences in performance level in the same task, as was done in the present experiment, they did fail to find any consistent or substantial correlation between non-learning tests purporting to measure motor educability and the actual amounts of motor learning in several activities. It should also be mentioned that Woodrow[10] has been fully cognizant of the hazards of confounding performance level with learning. He has shown that certain types of widely used learning scores such as total errors or total successes in the practice period are uninterpretable because, even though correlated with learning, they may be correlated even more highly with performance level. The latter *may* in some cases be strongly influenced by prior learning, but on the other hand it may not be, and there are certainly other factors that are always operative in determining its magnitude. . . .

Summary and Conclusions

Seventy-three boys age 10 years and 72 boys age 15 learned a sensory-motor problem involving stimulus discrimination and choice of a forehand or backhand movement depending on the stimulus. Forty per cent of the boys also learned a non-discrimination problem utilizing similar movements but a different stimulus.

The younger boys averaged 22 per cent slower than the older ones in initial performance for the simple motor task; in the discrimination tasks they were 25 and 33 per cent slower. Their amount of learning was greater than that observed in the older group, although this age difference was considerably less significant, statistically, than was the case for initial and final performance scores. Age differences in *rate* of learning, estimated from a parabolic learning curve, were negligible. Inter-task differences in amount of learning were small, even though initial and final performance scores were considerably different in the three tasks.

The correlations between individual differences in the performance of the three tasks were not high, even when corrected for attenuation in both variables. Inter-task correlations of amount of learning and also of individual differences in initial skill were larger in the younger boys, suggesting that the relative specificity of motor learning increases between ages 10 and 15 years.

Individual differences in final performance of the two forehand movements were almost entirely determined, and backhand speed was 63 per cent determined, by *initial amount of skill* rather than by *learning* in the older age group. In contrast, *learning* was an important determiner (35 to 41 per cent) of final performance of the younger boys in the discrimination tasks and accounted for 63 per cent of individual differences in final skill in the simple forehand response. Approximately 50 per cent of individual differences in learning in the younger boys and 40 per cent in the older group were predicted by the initial performance scores, but the sense of the relationship was negative rather than positive, indicating the futility of measuring motor educability by using performance scores without including direct estimates of learning aptitude. The intra-task relationships were quite different from those reported by others for non-motor tasks such as addition.

Evidently, the 10-year-old differs from the 15-year-old in being slower in motor performance of the type measured. On the average, he learns more than the older boy before the plateau is reached, but probably approaches the plateau at the same rate. His final skill is more determined by his ability to learn than is characteristic of the 15-year-old. Individual differences in the final skill of the latter are chiefly determined by initial skill. Even among gross motor tasks that are similar, task-specificity is great; it tends, however, to be less in the younger boy. Individual differences in final score are relatively as great as in initial performance, although this conclusion must be qualified by consideration of the possibility that learning was not yet completed for some individuals in this experiment, even though it was substantially completed for the average.

References

1. Cozens, F. W. A curve for devising scoring tables in physical education. *Research Quarterly*, 2(4):67-74, 1931.

2. GIRE, EUGENIA and ANNA ESPENSCHADE. The relationship between measures of motor educability and the learning of specific motor skills. *Research Quarterly,* 13:43-56, 1942.

3. GUILFORD, J. P. *Fundamental Statistics in Psychology and Education.* New York: McGraw-Hill, 1942.

4. HEESE, K. W. A general factor in improvement with practice. *Psychometrika,* 7: 213-223, 1942.

5. HOWELL, M. L. Influence of emotional tension on speed of reaction and movement. *Research Quarterly,* 24:22-32, 1953.

6. LINDEBURG, F. A. A study of the degree of transfer between quickening exercises and other co-ordinated movements. *Research Quarterly,* 20:180-194, 1949.

7. MCGEOCH, J. A. and A. L. IRION. *The Psychology of Human Learning.* New York: Longmans, Green and Co., 1952.

8. MUNN, N. L. Learning in children. In: Carmichael, L. (Ed.), *Manual of Child Psychology,* New York: Wiley, 1954.

9. WOODROW, H. Factors in improvement with practice. *Jour. Psychol.,* 7:55-70, 1939.

10. WOODROW, H. The ability to learn. *Psychol. Rev.* 53:147-158, 1946.

Chapter 8

MATURATION AND AGING

Age and Sex Parameters in Psychomotor Learning*

CLYDE E. NOBLE, BLAINE L. BAKER, AND THOMAS A. JONES

ALTHOUGH longitudinal data would be most desirable, cross-sectional data of subjects ranging from childhood to old age performing the same task reveal important performance output comparisons as a function of age. In the present study, with the most favorable response times produced at age sixteen for females and age twenty for males, one is led to believe that those skills requiring fast discriminatory responses would be best performed about these ages. A gradual decline in performance with age verifies other research findings and common logic. Although sex differences exist, the shapes of the performance curves as related to age are reasonably similar. For those interested in learning theory and learning curves, an exponential operation is suggested to describe the data.

Psychologists interested in the theory of human learning and performance have devoted increasing attention during the past two decades to the role of individual-difference parameters. One specific hypothesis (Hull, 1945) maintains that human-factor differences affect the numerical constants rather than the mathematical forms of behavioral equations (cf. Reynolds & Adams, 1954; Spence, 1956; Adams, 1957; Noble, 1961). This implies that empirical laws of learning obtained inductively as group averages from statistically representative samples are *general* (nomothetic) laws in the sense that, when stratified parametrically into families of curves, no new formal characteristics should emerge in the full range of *particular* (idiographic) traits or abilities.

* Reprinted with permission of authors and publisher: Noble, C. E., Baker, B. L., and Jones, T. A. Age and sex parameters in psychomotor learning. PERCEPTUAL AND MOTOR SKILLS, 1964, 19, 935-945.

Two of the major individual-difference variables affecting human learning and performance are *age* and *sex*. In studies of age researchers generally report a rapid increase in average proficiency from a chronological age of about 8 yr. up to the end of the second decade, then a brief period of relative stability followed by a slow, almost linear decrease in proficiency as the ninth decade is approached (Thorndike, 1928; Hovland, 1951; McGeoch & Irion, 1952; Welford, 1958; Morgan, Cook, Chapanis, & Lund, 1963; Birren, 1964). Cross-sectional sampling techniques applied to a number of learning-performance situations with different populations of Ss have repeatedly produced this non-monotonic type of age-performance function, although the exact shapes of the curves are contingent upon task characteristics and the dependent variables measured (Koga & Morant, 1923; Jones, 1928; Willoughby, 1929; Miles, 1931; Miles, 1933; Miles, 1935; Ammons, R. B., Alprin, Ammons, C. H., 1955; Birren & Botwinick, 1955; Braun & Geiselhart, 1959; Botwinick, Robbin, & Brinley, 1960; Shephard, Abbey, & Humphries, 1962).

There is rarely any consistent superiority of one sex over the other except when the task evokes specific motivational or associative processes that are culturally different between the sexes (McGeoch & Irion, 1952). This difference is marked in the area of perceptual-motor skills where males usually excel in tasks which capitalize upon speed or amplitude of response (Jones, 1944; Hunsicker, 1958; Noble, Fuchs, Robel, & Chambers, 1958; Francis & Rarick, 1959). Little of a systematic nature is known about possible interactions among age, sex, and amount of training in determining scores in psychomotor skills.

Our principal objectives in this research were to discover the quantitative relationships between *response speed* (R) as a function of 320 *practice trials* (T) on a discrimination reaction time apparatus, *chronological age* (A) in 15 categories over an 80-yr. range, and *biological sex* (S). The dependent variable, R, is theoretically related to the major independent variable, T, by the familiar exponential equation $R = m(1 - e^{-iT}) + c$, whose form has been rationalized by Hull (1943) and Spence (1956). Constants m, i, and c are empirical, representing the asymptote, rate, and R-intercept parameters, respectively, for each experimental group. Goodness-of-fit tests will be used to evaluate the extent to which the exponential hypothesis remains invariant over differences in the A and S factors as they affect m, i, and c.

Method

Apparatus. Four units of the USAF Discrimination Reaction Time apparatus, Model D2, described in detail elsewhere (Melton, 1947) were used. S's task was to snap one of four toggle switches in response to the simultaneous lighting of a pair of red and green signal lamps. The relative position of the red lamp with respect to the green determined which of the four switches was correct. Reinforcing knowledge of results was provided by the offset of the white light.

A trial was defined as a single 3-sec. stimulus presentation. There was a variable fore-period between stimulus patterns which ranged from .5 sec. to 1.5 sec. and averaged 1 sec. Reaction time was cumulated on .001-min. synchronous clocks and recorded in blocks of 20 trials. The inter-block interval was 40 sec. except between Blocks 4 and 5, Blocks 8 and 9, and Blocks 12 and 13, when it was increased to 80 sec. to allow E time to reset the apparatus to the first pattern.

Subjects. Six hundred persons, ranging in chronological age from 8 to 87 yr. and divided equally between the two sexes, were recruited for the investigation. Ss were assigned to 30 experimental groups, each group including 20 males (Groups 1 to 15) or 20 females (Groups 16 to 30). The age of each S

TABLE 1
CHRONOLOGICAL AGE RANGES AND MEDIAN AGES (A) IN YEARS FOR 30 GROUPS

Males			Females		
Group	Range	*Mdn*	Group	Range	*Mdn*
1	8-9	8.73	16	8-9	8.41
2	10-13	10.50	17	10-13	11.07
3	14-17	16.06	18	15-17	16.14
4	18	18.00	19	18	18.00
5	19	19.00	20	19	19.00
6	20	20.00	21	20	20.00
7	21	21.00	22	21	21.00
8	22-23	22.25	23	22-23	22.73
9	24-25	24.50	24	24-25	24.21
10	26-29	27.50	25	26-30	28.17
11	31-40	35.00	26	31-40	35.50
12	41-50	46.50	27	41-50	46.50
13	51-60	55.00	28	51-60	54.17
14	62-70	67.50	29	61-70	65.25
15	71-84	75.50	30	72-87	76.50

was recorded in whole years rounded to the nearest birthday. Table 1 shows the chronological age ranges and medians for each group. An effort was made during original selection to have the median ages for the two sexes coincide. Examination of Table 1 reveals close spacing at those age levels where proficiency changes were expected to be greatest, i.e., from 18 to 21 yr.

In addition to psychology students enlisted routinely in classes at Montana State University, Ss included young adult volunteers from a local high school, a school for nurses, and a business college. Older adults were recruited through the auspices of fraternal orders, civic organizations, women's clubs, associations for retired employees, agencies of the Federal government, and rest homes for the aged. Some children and adolescents were provided by an education class conducted during the University Summer Session; others were obtained through interested friends in the community. No Ss had had prior experience with the apparatus and all served without remuneration.

Once Ss had been selected, the only criteria of rejection were: (1) apparatus malfunctions, (2) inability of S to understand and comply with instructions, or (3) S's physical impairment in sensory or motor capacities which are directly relevant to discrimination-reaction performance. Although the conventional procedures of recruiting Ss for developmental studies of this type do not lend themselves to statistical evaluations of the amount of sampling error incurred with respect to variables other than age and sex, it is known that performance differences in psychomotor skills are not highly correlated with educational or occupational levels (Welford, 1958).

Procedure. In the interest of efficiency and because of the importance of social influences on discrimination-reaction scores (Noble, Fuchs, Robel, & Chambers, 1958; Noble, Chambers, Fuchs, & Robel, 1959; Noble, Fuchs, Walters, & Chambers, 1959), the data were collected from groups of 2 to 4 Ss at a time. When only 2 Ss participated, they were positioned next to rather than opposite one another.

All 30 groups received standard USAF instructions, reported verbatim elsewhere (Melton, 1947; Noble, Alcock, & Frye, 1959). The instructions, accompanied by 4 demonstration trials, placed equal emphasis upon speed and accuracy. E corrected any S who deviated from the standard operating procedure and encouraged to greater effort those who appeared to be poorly motivated. Following the instructions, Ss received 6 familiarization trials, then 320 training trials grouped into 16 blocks of 20 trials each. Except for the convenience of 8-yr.- and 9-yr.-old children in Groups 1 and 16, who were allowed to stand while performing, Ss were seated in front of the apparatus. They used the preferred (dominant) hand in manipulating the switches throughout the experiment.

Results and Discussion

After transforming the 16 cumulated reaction time (latency) scores for each S to reciprocals, the resulting measures of response speed (R) were combined for each group of 20 Ss. Graphs of the arithmetic means of these R-scores plotted as a function of the 16 successive 20-trial blocks were constructed, with male and female curves of corresponding age groups plotted together. Best-fitting exponential curves were calculated from the equation, $R = m (1 - e^{-iT}) + c$, by allowing the parameters m, i, and c to vary simultaneously in order to satisfy the criterion of minimizing the variance of the residuals, defined as the discrepancies between the empirical (R_e) and theoretical (R_t) scores.[1] As a measure of goodness of fit, an index of determination $d (= 100\sigma_t^2 \sigma_e^2)$ was computed for each of the curves by a method given in Noble (1957) for response probability curves. The statistic d is analogous to the coefficient of determination in linear regression; it specifies the percentage of variance in the dependent variable (R) which is predicted by the exponential equation. These goodness-of-fit indexes, rate, and intercept parameters ranged from a low d of 95.93% for Group 7 to a high d of 99.30% for Group 4. Mean predictability for males was 97.91%, for females 98.05%. The grand mean predictability for the 30 curves in the experiment was 97.98%, indicating excellent support for Hull's equation and for the invariance hypothesis.

An alternative analysis of the curves was performed to test the simpler hypothesis (Noble, S. E., Noble, J. L., & Alcock, 1958) that merely differences in rate of acquisition (i) might account for the major portions of the response variance associated with the age levels within each sex. Accordingly, for all Ss of a particular sex we selected the group which had the highest m parameter, then used this value in fitting the curves of the remaining 14 groups. A similar procedure was followed for the lowest c parameter. Thus a maximum m and a minimum c value were taken as constants, with only i allowed to vary in determining the theoretical curves and the resulting values of d. For males the two pairs of fixed values were $m = 2.4472$, $c = 1.1836$; for females $m = 2.0607$, $c = 1.2308$. When these arbitrary parameters were inserted in the above curve-fitting procedure as "floor" and "ceiling" restrictions, the outcome was a very unsatisfactory set of curves. The mean predictability in terms of d value for males dropped to 60.24%, for females to 69.29%; the grand mean was only 64.76%. Thus our attempt to reject the initial hypothesis [that, given constant amounts of practice, $\Delta R = f(m, i, c)$] in favor of the alternative hypothesis [$\Delta R = f(i)$] was unsuccessful.

[1] This method of successive approximations was programmed by the IBM 1620 Computer in collaboration with Prof. John A. Peterson, Director of the Montana State University Computer Center. The constant e has its conventional mathematical value of 2.718 (natural logarithmic system) rather than the special value of 10 (common logarithmic system) which Hull (1943) favored.

The second major set of results concerns relationships between over-all proficiency and age for the two sexes. The mean total response speed scores (R) earned by each group over the 16 blocks of 20 trials was plotted as a function of median chronological age (A). As we were led to expect from the literature, the classical non-monotonic age-learning function was found, together with a general superiority of males over females in psychomotor speed. In only two age segments (10 to 13 yr. and 71 to 87 yr.) were females faster. The mean speed score of males (Groups 1 to 15) was 3.391 while that of females (Groups 16 to 30) was 3.018, a mean difference in R-units of .373. For both sexes the slope of the pre-maximum or "growth" segment was greater than the post-maximum or "decay" segment.

To determine the significance of the main effects of Trials (T), Age (A), Sex (S), and their interactions, a $16 \times 15 \times 2$ mixed-factorial Type III analysis of variance (Lindquist, 1953) was performed upon the R-scores. According to the summary, all sources of variance except the three-factor $T \times A \times S$ interaction were significant ($P < .001$). In addition, the $T \times A$ and $T \times S$ interactions establish the non-parallelism of the age and sex acquisition curves; the $A \times S$ interaction is consistent with the response speed data; and the marginal $T \times A \times S$ interaction ($P < .10$) implies that amount of training may itself interact with the two-factor age-sex interaction.

The two sexes appear to be quite similar in performance level and rate of growth up to the age of about 16, after which the females begin a fairly linear decline into the 70s. The males continue to improve to the age of 20, after which they, too, undergo a progressive impairment with advancing longevity. A slight curvilinearity in the post-maximum portion of the male curve causes a gradual narrowing of the gap in proficiency between the sexes until, in the seventh decade, the males ($R = 1.68$) finally fall below the level of the females ($R = 1.82$). It is interesting to note that, while there are many pre- and post-maximum correspondences in the two curves where the psychomotor performances of the young and old are statistically equivalent, men and women must attain septuagenarian status before their discrimination-reaction proficiency descends again to the level of childhood.

Two final analyses were made, one in terms of gain scores, the other in terms of variability. Gain scores were measured for each S as the difference between his performance on Blocks 1 and 16. Variability was computed as the standard deviation of the R-distributions. There was little support in our data for Welford's (1958) belief in a universal positive relationship between inter-individual variability and chronological age. The product-moment correlation coefficients (r) between σ and A were only .23 for males and .24 for females. Neither r is significantly greater than zero ($P > .05$, $df = 13$).

Our data indicate that the exponential invariance hypothesis relating R to T is tenable over a wide age span and holds for both sexes, with coefficients of determination exceeding 95% in all cases. This provides additional verification of Hull's (1945) original theorem that individual differences affect the numerical constants rather than the mathematical forms of behavior equations. The goodness-of-fit tests make it clear, moreover, that rate of acquisition alone cannot be employed to describe differences in discrimination-reaction performance attributable to variations in age and sex. Asymptote and R-intercept parameters must also be considered. For compound trial-and-error learning, where response probability measures are employed to measure the growth of Ss' capabilities to select pre-established responses on cue (Noble, 1957), individual differences seem to influence the rate parameter alone (Noble, C. E., Noble, J. L., & Alcock, 1958). In the development of discrimination-reaction skill, where response-learning is a critical element alongside S-R association formation, not only rate but also initial proficiency, and probably asymptotic level as well, are affected (Adams, 1957); the same is true of rotary-pursuit performance (Reynolds & Adams, 1954). Although an adequate solution is still lacking, we recognize the problem of experimentally isolating the variance components attributable to "ability" and to "capacity" as one of fundamental importance, as Adams (1957) has suggested. To this distinction we now add an emphasis on the need for appropriate analyses to task factors in theorizing about human learning.

With respect to relationships between the acquisition of proficiency and age for the two sexes, the present results confirm the classical findings and extend our knowledge to include a broader principle of age-sex interaction, with amount of training. The abstract form of this multiplicative law is: $R = f$ ($T \times A \times S$). But why is $A \times S$ significant? The initial rise in the age-performance curve from 8 to 20 yr. for males and from 8 to 16 yr. for females is doubtless a combination of sensorimotor maturation and transfer of (non-specific) training; one might, by experimental manipulation of Ss' generalized experience in discriminating spatial cues and reacting promptly in selected directions, account for the differential maxima. As for the post-maximal decline, older Ss are expected to perform less well than are teen-agers on tasks requiring speed in discrimination reaction for a number of reasons which have been reviewed by Welford (1958) and Birren (1964).

References

ADAMS, J. A. The relationship between certain measures of ability and the acquisition of a psychomotor criterion response. *J. gen. Psychol.,* 1957, 56, 121-134.

AMMONS, R. B., ALPRIN, S. I. & AMMONS, C. H. Rotary pursuit performance as related to sex and age of pre-adult subjects. *J. exp. Psychol.,* 1955, 49, 127-133.

BIRREN, J. E. *The psychology of aging.* Englewood Cliffs, N. J.: Prentice-Hall, 1964.

BIRREN, J. E., & BOTWINICK, J. Age differences in finger, jaw, and foot reaction time to auditory stimuli. *J. Geront.,* 1955, 10, 429-432.

BOTWINICK, J., ROBBIN, J. S., & BRINLEY, J. F. Age differences in card-sorting performance in relation to task difficulty, task set, and practice. *J. exp. Psychol.,* 1960, 59, 10-18.

BRAUN, H. W., & GEISELHART, R. Age differences in the acquisition and extinction of the conditioned eyelid response. *J. exp. Psychol.,* 1959, 51, 386-388.

FRANCIS, R. J., & RARICK, G. L. Motor characteristics of the mentally retarded. *Amer. J. ment. Defic.,* 1959, 63, 792-811.

HOVLAND, C. I. Human learning and retention. In S. S. Stevens (Ed.), *Handbook of experimental psychology.* New York: Wiley, 1951. Pp. 613-689.

HULL, C. L. *Principles of behavior.* New York: Appleton-Century, 1943.

HULL, C. L. The place of innate individual and species differences in a natural-science theory of behavior. *Psychol. Rev.,* 1945, 52, 55-60.

HUNSICKER, P. A. *Youth fitness test manual.* Washington, D. C.: Nat. Educ. Assn., 1958.

JONES, H. E. Psychological studies of motion pictures: II. Observations and recall as a function of age. *Univer. Calif. Publ. Psychol.,* 1928, 3, 225-243.

JONES, H. E. The development of physical abilities. In *Adolescence, Forty-third Yearbook.* Chicago: Univer. of Chicago Press, 1944. Pp. 100-122.

KOGA, Y., & MORANT, G. M. On the degree of association between reaction times in the case of different senses. *Biometrika,* 1923, 15, 346-372.

LINDQUIST, E. F. *Design and analysis of experiments in psychology and education.* Boston: Houghton Mifflin, 1953.

McGEOCH, J. A., & IRION, A. L. *The psychology of human learning.* (2nd ed.) New York: Longmans, Green, 1952.

MELTON, A. W. (Ed.) *Apparatus tests.* Washington, D.C.: U. S. Gov't Printing Office, 1947. (AAF Aviat. Psychol. Program Res. Rep. No. 4.)

MILES, W. R. Measures of certain human abilities throughout the life span. *Proc. Nat. Acad. Sci.*, 1931, 17, 627-633.

MILES, W. R. Abilities of older men. *Person. J.*, 1933, 11, 352-357.

MILES, W. R. Training, practice, and mental longevity. *Science*, 1935, 81, 79-87.

MORGAN, C. T., COOK, J. S., CHAPANIS, A., & LUND, M. W. (Eds.) *Human engineering guide to equipment design.* New York: McGraw-Hill, 1963.

NOBLE, C. E. The length-difficulty relationship in compound trial-and-error learning. *J. exp. Psychol.*, 1957, 54, 246-252.

NOBLE, C. E. Verbal learning and individual differences. In C. N. Cofer (Ed.), *Verbal learning and verbal behavior.* New York: McGraw-Hill, 1961. Pp. 132-146.

NOBLE, C. E., ALCOCK, W. T., & FRYE, R. L. The point influence of practice and instructions on discrimination reaction time. *J. Psychol.*, 1959, 48, 125-130.

NOBLE, C. E., CHAMBERS, R. W., FUCHS, J. E. & ROBEL, D. P. A further study of individual vs. social performance in discrimination reaction. *Proc. Mont. Acad. Sci.*, 1959, 19, 150 (Abstract)

NOBLE, C. E., FUCHS, J. E., ROBEL, D. P. & CHAMBERS, R. W. Individual vs. social performance on two perceptual-motor tasks. *Percept. mot. Skills*, 1958, 8, 131-134.

NOBLE, C. E., FUCHS, J. E., WALTERS, H. A., & CHAMBERS, R. W. One-man vs. two-man performance on the discrimination reaction time test. *Proc. Mont. Acad. Sci.*, 1959, 19, 151. (Abstract)

NOBLE, C. E., NOBLE, J. L., & ALCOCK, W. T. Prediction of individual differences in human trial-and-error learning. *Percept. mot. Skills*, 1958, 8, 151-172. (Monogr. Suppl. 2)

REYNOLDS, B., & ADAMS, J. A. Psychomotor performance as a function of initial level of ability. *Amer. J. Psychol.*, 1954, 67, 268-277.

SHEPHARD, A. H., ABBEY, D. S., & HUMPHRIES, M. Age and sex in relation to perceptual-motor performance on several control-display relations on the TCC. *Percept. mot. Skills*, 1962, 14, 103-118.

SPENCE, K. W. *Behavior theory and conditioning.* New Haven: Yale Univer. Press, 1956.

THORNDIKE, E. L. *Adult learning.* New York: Macmillan, 1928.

WELFORD, A. T. *Ageing and human skill.* London: Oxford Univer. Press, 1958.

WILLOUGHBY, R. R. Incidental learning. *J. educ. Psychol.*, 1929, 20, 671-682.

Toward an Experimental Psychology of Aging[*]

JAMES E. BIRREN

SINCE he has contributed so much research and writings to the topic of aging, a summary article by Birren is very much in place here. He makes a plea for an experimental psychology of aging, but more important for us are the conclusions reached on the basis of research concerned with the accuracy and speed of responses as affected by the aging process. Neurological theories suggest explanations of the research findings. The current state of research on aging and its future directions are clearly expressed in

[*] From *American Psychologist*, 1970, 25, 124-135. Abridged and reprinted with permission of the author and the American Psychological Association.

this paper. Although the practical applications of the research are not reported in depth, the reader can certainly draw his own inferences regarding the aged and their unique problems in mastering assorted skills.

With the passage of time the human organism is changed as a result of biological, psychological, and social influences. Some of these influences are amenable to experimentation, but most are not as yet. The psychologist often must resort to descriptive studies to gain clues about the basis of some of the most profound changes we undergo as individuals and as members of a species. While studies of identical twins as children have become part of the literature of psychology, more recently studies of one-egg twins over the age of 65 have been reported. Similarities are observed in the psychological and biological changes in one-egg twins late in life. Photographs of such twins taken throughout their life span indicate remarkable persistence of resemblance while also showing the transformations of aging (Kallmann & Jarvik, 1959). In a similar way, one can see in the pictures evidence of differences in dress which represents cultural change. One also has the impression that within the range of cultural change, the individuals have selected age-appropriate dress. Were one able to hear samples of the speech of these individuals corresponding to the various phases of the life span pictured, their word choices would very likely reflect contemporary culture and age-appropriate word choice since our word choices reflect the idioms and colloquialisms of the periods through which we live and suggest to our listeners how old we are. The studies of identical twins by Kallmann and Jarvik, and their subsequent follow-up, indicate that there are inherited characteristics of likely length of life, cause of death, and persistence of twin resemblances in measured intellect. Beyond the involvement of our academic egos in the question of whether there is late life change in intellectual function, there is clearly a broad range of problems of considerable scientific importance. . . .

While practical reasons slow dramatic progress, the science seems to be moving toward an experimental psychology of aging or, more properly, toward a comprehensive developmental psychology that embraces the entire life span.

Some Longitudinal Data on Intellectual Functions

Many observers have noted that investigators tend to study readily available captive populations, often in institutions. This is often true of school children and indeed of older adults as well. In 1963, my colleagues and I studied a small number of community residents—men all over the age of 65—in an effort to get an estimate of the capacities of older independently living individuals. In the study there were 47 men all over the age of 65, average age 72 years. The survivors were measured again five years later, and again six years later (Birren, 1968). Of considerable interest to me is the strange distribution of change in these men with time. Differences in scores on such standardized tests as the Raven Progressive Matrices and the Wechsler Adult Intelligence Scale show some aged individuals as having slight or no decrements while still others show dramatic declines in scores. While the sample is not large, the nonnormality in the distribution of change beginning to be reported on older adults is provocative of a tentative hypothesis, that is, that change in intelligence in late life, as measured by conventional techniques, is not normally distributed. It may show little or no change in some healthy men in the seventh, eighth, and ninth decades of life, while concurrently individuals, possibly comprising a subpopulation suffering erosion of health, may show dramatic decline related to their likelihood of survival.

If changes in measured intelligence are part of a process of primary biological aging, every individual would be expected to show some change during the second half of life. The fact that some individuals beyond the age of 70 show large changes and others show none at all suggests that the terminal or near terminal phases of the life span can be accompanied by unique and relatively rapid or precipitous changes in individuals when their health fails. The importance of this is one of establishing our concept of ourselves in old age. There is the possibility that the psychological norm for the species is one of little change in intellectual functions in the years after 65, given good health. Chronic diseases of later life, particularly those involving cardiovascular disease and cerebral insufficiency, can, of course, result in an appreciable number of the population showing marked decline in intellectual function with age, but such need not be accepted as the norm for the species. Thus one of the implications of the study on the elderly men was that some of the higher cognitive processes measured by standard intelligence tests were more related to the health status of the individual than to chronological age. In contrast to intellectual measurements, however, the slowness observed in perceptual and motor tasks seems more intimately associated with chronological age than with health status. The role of speed and timing in cognitive processes of the older adult is far from explained (Birren, 1964, chap. 5). One may, in fact, reverse the usual equation and regard slowness of behavior as the independent variable that sets limits for the older adult in such processes as memory, perception, and problem solving (Birren, Riegel, & Morrison, 1962).

Age Differences in Response Time to Visual Tasks

One of my long-standing interests in research has been that of explaining the slowness of behavior seen in adults after middle age. In this regard, I will point out some implications of the relations of response time and task difficulty in young and elderly subjects. In one of the earliest experiments that Botwinick and I (1965) conducted on this topic, we varied the difference between two lines, requiring a judgment as to which was the shortest. In 1906, Henmon reported an elegant experiment in which he found that the time required to make a judgment as to which of two lines was the shorter varied with the amount of the difference between the two lines. Our study was an attempt to test the hypothesis that the increased response time shown by older adults lies in the difficulty of perceiving the stimulus to which they are to respond. If this were so, older adults should show a relatively greater increase in speed of judgment as stimuli are made easier to judge. In the experiment, subjects were required to simply say right or left, indicating the side of the smaller of two lines presented tachistoscopically. The variable line differed from the standard by 1–50%. The work confirmed the report of Henmon for young subjects but found a displaced curve for older adults.

The judgments of older subjects slow down more when the difference between the two line lengths is less than 15%. Beyond 15% the difference in response time is roughly a constant. These data can be related to the question of whether the older subjects *want* more time or *need* more time to make perceptual judgments. The data would seem to answer yes to both parts of the question in the sense that when the perceptual judgments become difficult, in this case less than 15% difference in line length, elderly adult subjects would appear to require more time to respond. On the other hand, above a 15% difference there is no systematic variation. In this range, the data may suggest that older individuals want more time to respond.

The basic condition of the experiment was such as to present the lines to be judged for two seconds. This is longer than the subjects required to respond, thus the subjects had ample time to view the stimulus before responding. A subsequent experiment (Botwinick, Brinley, & Robbin, 1958) not only used a two-second exposure but also a shorter exposure time of .15 seconds, which is less time than it takes even the fastest subject to respond.

Under the shortened exposure time, both young and elderly subjects speeded up their responses. However, the largest reductions in time were for the older group for the most difficult discriminations. It is worthwhile to note that under the two-second exposure time, both elderly and young subjects maintained the same percentage of accuracy. The median accuracy for both groups was 100% correct judgment for 2% or greater difference in line length, and at 1% difference the accuracy diminished to 88%. However, when the exposure time was reduced to .15 seconds, the median accuracy for the elderly subjects dropped to 62% for the 1% line length difference and 88% for the young subjects (elderly subjects, 65-79 years; young subjects, 18-35 years; N was 24 and 36, respectively).

These data clearly indicate that both elderly and young subjects are not at their limit of response time at a two-second exposure time, even maintaining a very high criterion of accuracy. When the duration of the stimulus is reduced to .15 seconds, both young and elderly subjects reduced their accuracy of response. The experiment did indicate that even for difficult discriminations, a considerable decrease in time to make the judgments could be brought about by reducing the exposure duration, and that this decrease does not seem to take place at a greater relative expense of accuracy. This suggests that the evidence lies on the side of the older person taking more time but not requiring more time to make difficult judgments. The effect of a brief stimulus may be to somehow drive or induce a state of need to respond more quickly than the usual self-pacing of the subject. It should be noted, however, that the elderly "driven" subject at short exposures does not respond as quickly as young subjects at long exposures. The age difference in response time was about two-tenths of a second for a two-second exposure. Under the conditions of short exposures the age difference in time to respond was reduced to .15 seconds. Considering the major results of this study the data would seem to lie outside the range of explanations offered by the perceptual difficulty hypothesis or the cautiousness hypothesis as to why older subjects are slow in their judgments.

The conditions of the two previous experiments led Rabbitt and Birren to conduct another experiment on the same topic, but using a broader range of conditions. Also, the decision was made to use circles of varying diameter as stimuli, believing that they would provide a more uniformly judged stimulus than line lengths. A broader range of exposure intervals (from .05 to 2.0 seconds) was used than in the previous experiments, and the exposure interval was randomized together with the percentage difference in stimuli. The experiment of Botwinick and his associates (1958) first exposed all stimulus cards at two seconds and then followed it with the second study in which the same subjects judged the stimuli at exposure of .15 seconds. Furthermore, in the analysis of the data, we analyzed separately the times to respond for correct and incorrect judgments. As in the previous experiments, both young and old subjects are slow in their judgments when the percentage difference in the two stimuli was small. Response time rises as a function of percentage difference in circle diameters. These data have also been analyzed with respect to the means of the minimum and maximum response times for old and young subjects. If one examines the data with respect to response times of correct or incorrect judgments, the aged appear to be slower in their response times when they are making errors.

One of the important conditions varied systematically was the exposure time. Exposure time was varied randomly from the two seconds in the earliest experiments down to one-twentieth of a second. There was not a very dramatic following of response time in relation to the exposure duration. This lack of relationship held for both the correct and incorrect responses for both young and elderly subjects. The results of the experiment differ from those obtained by Botwinick and his associates (1958), in which they found a relationship between two exposure intervals of two seconds and .15 seconds, when the subjects were run through a long series at each level. To me this implies that the subjects could develop a set to respond quickly, given brief exposures, and maintain it over a long series of judgments (see Brinley, 1965). That is, there is a "driving effect" of a short stimulus on both young and elderly subjects, but only if one has a sufficient number of short stimuli so as to develop an expectation. In explaining why older subjects tend to be slow in response, one may invoke a set explanation, or a forcing of response by short duration stimuli, but only if there is a sufficiently large number of stimuli so the subject can develop an expectation. In general one must return either to the explanation of the slowness in terms of perceptual difficulty of input, or a generalized slowing yet beyond our concepts or explanation.

In young subjects there is clearly no evidence that the exposure time is influencing their correctness of response or modifying in any important way their speed of judgment. With old subjects one sees a slight tendency for errors to occur for somewhat slow responses to short exposure times. Their correct responses are not faster to short exposure times. Considering the total phenomena of the slowness of judgments in older subjects, I would submit that only a small portion of the variance has been explained by the concept of a cautious reaction to perceptual difficulty or to the driving effects of stimulus duration. In brief, then, the major variance to be accounted for in the slowness of responses of older subjects remains to be explained.

It is quite possible to conceive of experiments that would attempt to partition the large and important age variance neurophysiologically, that is, to attempt to find out where in the nervous system the additional time is required in the older subjects (see Hicks & Birren, 1970). However, there are still some useful experiments to be done at the phenomenal level, using psychological variables. Craik (1969) has suggested that older subjects demand a high degree of sensory information before committing themselves to a response. This would appear to be a variation of the cautiousness hypothesis. Using a signal detection theory approach, Craik thought that the judgment criterion would become relatively higher for the older subjects as they were allowed additional time. In the present experiment, additional time in a sense was allowed them by the wide range of stimulus durations. They did not exercise the option, however, of taking more time to make judgments when given long duration stimuli. While the cautiousness of older persons may be slowing their responses, it is not an adequate explanation to account for the majority of the time required in the responses of older subjects in these experiments. . . .

Activation and Neural Noise

The general tendency for older adults to be slow in their responses can be attacked through a test of two alternative hypotheses. One is that it takes longer for signals to be discriminated because the older nervous system is noisy (Crossman & Szafran, 1956). Alternatively the older nervous system may be in a less activated state so that any stimulus yields a slower response. Essentially the neural noise hypothesis holds that with age the nervous system becomes increasingly noisy, such that the signal to be discriminated must be discriminated against a higher background noise. The reduction of the signal-to-noise ratio thus means that longer time is taken, for example, for perception of input information. The picture is one of a constantly active nervous system into which signals arrive to be discriminated against a level of background neural activity. Random firing of neurons would constitute a limiting factor in all signal recognition. Contributing to an increase in noise with age might be a hyperirritability of cells, and also prolonged aftereffects on brain cells following stimulation. Aftereffects of previous stimulation would constitute noise for subsequent stimulation or signals. Another hypothesis which attempts to explain the slowness of discrimination and response, which I favor, does not emphasize that the signal is competing with a higher background noise level, but rather that the signal itself is weak due to a less excitable nervous system. An attempt was made recently in our laboratory at the University of Southern California to test the two hypotheses. The doctoral dissertation of Dwight Jeffrey (1969) involved the performance of old and young adult subjects on a visual discrimination task. The response was a rapid movement of a finger. Control conditions were the ambient light and noise level of the building. The experimental conditions were those of increased muscular tension or auditory white noise. Under one experimental condition, the subject held a constant 20% of his maximum weight in his left hand while making responses with his right hand. Under the other condition, a 75-decibel white noise was presented to the earphones of the subject while he performed the task. The experimental conditions were thought to result in slower performance of elderly subjects if the neural noise hypothesis was true. That is, tension and auditory white noise should result in greater slowness on the part of the older adult. In contrast, the activation hypothesis would predict that the performance of the older subject would improve under conditions of muscular tension and white noise. Neither of the hypotheses was supported by the results. Instead, the almost classical results were obtained that older subjects are significantly slower in discrimination tasks than young subjects, and that the time difference between the two age groups grows with increasingly complex discrimination tasks (Jeffrey, 1969).

New Research Areas

The hypotheses tested by Dwight Jeffrey may also be examined by lowering ambient stimulation. That is, old and young subjects can be placed in environments where the visual and auditory stimulation is reduced. The neural noise hypothesis suggests that older adults will improve their performance relatively more when ambient stimulation is reduced. The activation hypothesis, on the other hand, would hold that older subjects will slow down relatively more under conditions of reduced ambient stimulation. There is, of course, the possibility that the kind of relative sensory deprivation or activation one is attempting to study in older adults is not readily reversible in hours but may require days to shift.

Other approaches to research on the slowness of behavior with age can also be undertaken using recordings of the latencies of evoked potentials in response to visual or auditory signals. Such latencies could help to indicate something of the cortical timing involved in the older nervous system. Where one finds significant differences with age in the latencies of such potentials, one could explore more directly the effects of chronic or short-term stimulation.

The laboratory rat is still a useful experimental animal with which to study some problems of aging. Some time ago it was established that the old rat also showed a slowness in responses with advancing age. Such slowness was not reversible with practice although susceptibility to fatigue was (Kay & Birren, 1958). For the more physiologically minded, it is possible with such animals to implant electrodes in a further effort to partition the slowness or the additional time required by the older nervous system.

At the human level, considerable important experimental work remains to be done. Following the lead of Rabbitt, for example, there is more to be learned about the conditions of slowness of older adults when irrelevant information is introduced into the stimulus and when errors are made (Rabbitt & Birren, 1967). A question to be answered is whether the older subject is more distractible to irrelevant information because he cannot maintain vigilance to an assigned task, or whether some other factor accounts for the fact that older subjects may find difficulty in responding to increasing amounts of information in a stimulus display.

The scientific importance of this line of experimentation lies in its contribution to our understanding of the nature of the altered functioning of the nervous system with age. A practical outcome of the experimentation lies in its potential for indicating the conditions of optimum learning for the older adult and for the optimum utilization of stored experience. I have not commented here about some of the subjective aspects of performance and the reasons why older adults change in their life contentment and goals that may bear on their performance. Such have been, and can be, the topics for objective study eventually leading to experimental testing of alternative hypotheses.

The widespread evidence of slowness of behavior with advancing age will no doubt continue to be studied as a dependent variable in relation to other things we can manipulate. On the other hand, slowness of behavior with age, since it appears somewhat independently of disease and a wide range of environmental circumstances, may be used as an independent variable in studying other processes. If, with age, there is a change in the speed with which the central nervous system can mediate responses, it would, in fact, limit not only the speed with which information could be acquired from the environment, but also the speed of retrieval of relevant stored memories, and the likelihood of combining these effectively in new perceptions, novel hypotheses, and complex motor responses. Several studies of adult intelligence have shown that vocabulary scores tend to rise with adult age. Concurrently, however, speed of performance on a decoding task declines with age. This suggests the rather common sense hypothesis that with age one's experience grows, but the speed of manipulation of this experience declines. An important hypothesis should be tested that with advancing age over the adult years, one enlarges one's unit of information by concept formation. Thus, by grouping past experience under new abstractions, one's previous "bits" can become "chunks," if you like—so that while one grows older, one may process fewer units of information per unit time, but the "chunks" become larger, and thereby effectiveness in an environment may stay the same if not improve. Some exploratory data obtained from interviews with middle-aged men and women would seem to fit this tentative hypothesis and may lead to more designed experimental investigations (Birren, 1969). Subjects between the ages of 30 and 60 years were interviewed around the significant areas of their current life, family, career, health, participation in organizations and clubs, and relations to time. The number of interviews varied from subject to subject from one to six interviews, with the interviews varying in length from one and a half to two hours. Commonplace were reports of reduced energy for carrying out all tasks associated with being middle aged. One of the important qualities of the interviews was the evidence that the subjects had evolved goals that extended over much of their life span and had evolved various strategies in relation to achieving these goals. Preliminary analysis of the interviews led to the isolation of statements that had the properties of strategies. Subjects appeared to be aware of the fact that when they were younger, they reacted differently to situations and people. The changes imply to me a greater level of abstraction with age. Apparently competent individuals project ahead a tentative plan for action over a several year period, and in relation to these plans use various broad strategies and individual tactics to advance toward their goals. Interestingly enough, despite the opinions of contemporary young adults, middle-aged adults view themselves as increasingly allowing others to behave autonomously, delegating responsibility, and having a direct approach. It is most interesting, although tangential to the present line of thought, that the middle-aged adult is acutely aware of the extent to which he needs others, including the young, and how much of his time is given to planning to raise individuals to positions of authority, responsibility, and autonomy.

While middle-aged and older adults seem to be increasingly aware of the limitations of their performance, and frequently in their energy and health, they do seem to be increasingly effective in their careers by virtue of the abstractions and strategies they form. While in one sense they are processing less information in the same situations than they did when they were younger, they also appear to deal with more significant information, since they are looking for crucial issues according to the abstractions they have formed. By grouping their experiences, the information load placed on the aging adult may be therefore less than on the young adult.

Study of the cognitive strategies used by older persons may be a very promising line of research, particularly if one can isolate the strategies used by productive, competent adults. It is possible that such strategies and related tactics could be transmitted verbally. It is, however, questionable whether abstract strategies derived through experience can be transmitted effectively to younger adults without their having at least some of the intervening experience that led to the formation of the strategies. The concept of evolving cognitive strategies and tactics over the adult life span is, at minimum, a useful addendum to qualifying the results of our measuring instruments that purport to measure intelligence in the adult. The level of component capacities may be less critical in the adult than are the strategies that the individual uses in the deployment of these capacities. For example, interviews with physicians and lawyers reveal a strategy of protecting themselves from cognitive overload or affective overload by not becoming as involved with clients as they did in the earlier years of their practice. This again suggests that the older professional is reducing the total information while concentrating on more crucial information.

A question many of us would like to answer at this stage is whether man's effectiveness for decision changes over the life span. We do not know very much about the conditions that give rise to optimum development and maintenance of man's capacity for making the decisions in a complex and changing society. Guilford (1969) reviewed the relations of decision making to age and discussed the various types of decision that face individuals. Altered perception and capacity of the aging nervous system for dealing with the wide range of input of information and complexities may influence the type of decisions reached. Any particular hypothesis should be tempered by recognition of the point of departure of the investigator, that is, whether he is analyzing perception, intellectual processes, learning and memory, psychomotor skills, or the evaluation of brain deficits. One can place side by side contemporary hypotheses regarding behavioral changes associated with aging as being due to changes in set, disuse, interference of previous learning, retrieval mechanisms, increased neural noise, brain damage, reduced activation, psychosocial disengagement; to some extent these and other hypotheses may be all partially correct, since they tend to apply only to the function of a subsystem of the organism (Birren & Hess, 1968; Heron & Chown, 1967; McFarland, 1969; Welford, 1969). . . .

References

BIRREN, J. E. *The psychology of aging.* Englewood Cliffs, N.J.: Prentice-Hall, 1964.

BIRREN, J. E. Increments and decrements in the intellectual status of the aged. *Psychiatric Research Reports,* 1968, 23, 207-214.

BIRREN, J. E. Age and decision strategies. In A. T. Welford & J. E. Birren (Eds.), *Decision making and age.* Basel: S. Karger, 1969.

BIRREN, J. E., & BOTWINICK, J: Speed of response as a function of perceptual difficulty and age. *Journal of Gerontology,* 1955, 10, 433-436.

BIRREN, J. E., & HESS, R. D. (Eds.) Influences of biological, psychological and social deprivations upon learning and performance. Chap. 2. In, *Perspectives on human deprivation.* United States Department of Health, Education and Welfare. Washington, D. C.: Government Printing Office, 1968.

BIRREN, J. E., RIEGEL, K. D., & MORRISON, D. F. Age differences in response speed as a function of controlled variations of stimulus conditions: Evidence of a general speed factor. *Gerontologia,* 1962, 6 1-18.

BOTWINICK, J., & BIRREN, J. E. A follow-up study of card-sorting performance in elderly men. *Journal of Gerontology,* 1965, 20, 208-210.

BOTWINICK, J., BRINLEY, J. F., & ROBBIN, J. S. The interaction effects of perceptual difficulty and stimulus exposure time on age differences in speed and accuracy of response. *Gerontologia,* 1958, 2, 1-10.

BRINLEY, J. F. Cognitive sets, speed, and accuracy of performance in the elderly. In A. T. Welford & J. E. Birren (Eds.), *Behavior, aging, and the nervous system.* Springfield, Ill.: Charles C Thomas, 1965.

CRAIK, F. I. M. Applications of signal detection to studies of aging. In A. T. Welford & J. E. Birren (Eds.), *Decision making and age.* Basel: S. Karger, 1969.

CROSSMAN, E. R. F. W., & SZAFRAN, J. Changes with age in the speed of information intake and discrimination. *Experientia Supplementum,* 1956, 4, 128-135.

GUILFORD, J. P. Intellectual aspects of decision making. In A. T. Welford & J. E. Birren (Eds.), *Decision making and age.* Basel: S. Karger, 1969.

HENMON, V. A. C. The time of perception as a measure of differences in sensation. *Arch. Psychol.,* 1906, 14.

HERON, A., & CHOWN, S. M. *Age and function.* London: J. & A. Churchill, 1967.

HICKS, L. H., & BIRREN, J. E. Aging, brain damage, and psychomotor slowing. *Psychological Bulletin,* 1970, 74, 377-396.

JEFFREY, D. W. Age differences in serial reaction time as a function of stimulus complexity under conditions of noise and muscular tension. Unpublished doctoral dissertation, University of Southern California, 1969.

KALLMANN, F. J. & JARVIK, L. F. Individual differences in constitution and genetic background. In J. E. Birren (Ed.), *Handbook of aging and the individual.* Chicago: University of Chicago Press, 1959.

KAY, H., & BIRREN, J. E. Swimming speed of the albino rat. *Journal of Gerontology,* 1958, 13, 378-385.

MCFARLAND, R. A. The sensory and perceptual processes in aging. In K. W. Schaie (Ed.), *Theory and methods of research on aging.* Morgantown: West Virginia University, 1969.

RABBITT, P. M. A., & BIRREN, J. E. Age and responses to sequences of repetitive and interruptive signals. *Journal of Gerontology,* 1967, 22, 143-150.

RIEGEL, K. F., & BIRREN, J. E. Age differences in associative behavior. *Journal of Gerontology,* 1965, 20, 125-130.

WELFORD, A. T. Age and skill: Motor, intellectual and social. In A. T. Welford & J. E. Birren (Eds.), *Decision making and age.* Basel: S. Karger, 1969.

PART 6

EMOTIONS

Stress, Anxiety, and Performance

As a result of the perception of a situation, psychological and physiological responses and reactions are emitted. The circumstances surrounding the learning task may be interpreted as stressful. The very nature of the learner may cause him to respond with a greater or lesser degree of emotion. At any rate, emotions may have organizing or disorganizing effects on behavior. In this way they operate much like motivation for the successful completion of any task.

Research has indicated that the nature of the task, the proficiency level of the performer, and his personality are important variables of consideration when predicting output under stress-induced conditions. These factors are investigated by the researchers whose reports are included in Part 6. Of course apparent stressful conditions do not affect everyone in the same manner or to the same extent. Nevertheless, current research indicates certain important trends with regard to explaining the relationship of emotions to skill acquisition.

The degree of "activation" within an individual is thus very much associated with emotions. A person operating under a great amount of stress and/or anxiety is extremely activated and is highly responsive. Situations bear upon the level of activation and, in conjunction with the particular activity to be learned and the anxiety state of the organism, reflect performance outcomes. Behavior under emotional states usually differs from that expressed under relatively unemotional states. It will be our concern to determine how and why. Although the three readings included here cannot possibly provide nearly all the answers, they indicate important findings concerning the interrelationship of stress, anxiety, and performance.

Chapter 9

EMOTIONAL INFLUENCES ON PERFORMANCE

Relation of Stress and Differential Position Habits to Performance in Motor Learning*

ALFRED CASTANEDA AND LEWIS P. LIPSITT

It is apparent that induced stress may facilitate or impair performance. The article by Castaneda and Lipsitt demonstrates the validity of a proposed theory concerned with the emitting of dominant and nondominant responses. Apparently stress encourages dominant responses to occur, and during the early stages of learning, where incorrect responses are usually dominant, stress can be predicted to be harmful. When higher levels of skill exist and correct responses are more dominant, reasonable stress should be beneficial. Other theoretical issues are also discussed in this reading. In a motor learning situation, the relative strength of the response (appropriate or inappropriate) can be effectively tempered with the application of a stressor. It should be emphasized that the stressor in this study, although conceivably interpreted differently by the subjects, is of a generally moderate nature. Different kinds of stressors will not necessarily lead to similar findings.

In several previous studies (Castaneda, 1956; Castaneda & Palermo, 1955; Palermo, 1957) stress (time pressures) has been introduced during a transfer task involving re-pairing of several S-R associations acquired during original learning while the remaining S-R associations are left unchanged. Under these conditions, the effects of stress have been found to depend on whether re-pairing is involved, i.e., stress has been found to impair performance where re-pairing is involved but to facilitate where it is not. On the assumption that this form of stress affects the level of drive in young human Ss, these results have

* From the *Journal of Experimental Psychology*, 1959, *57*, 25-30. Reprinted with permission of the authors and publisher.

been interpreted to be consistent with those theoretical implications (Spence, 1956; Taylor, 1956) derived from Hull's (1943) assumption that all existing habits aroused by the stimulus situation are indiscriminately strengthened by the total drive level that is momentarily operative. Thus, if the stimulus situation gives rise to more than one response, the effects of increased drive, according to this assumption, are expected to depend on the strength of the to-be-learned (correct) response relative to other competing (incorrect) responses.

The present study is concerned with the relation of this form of stress to performance in a motor-learning task in which initially dominant (pre-experimentally acquired) position habits are arbitrarily designated either correct or incorrect. The task consisted of two horizontally parallel rows of eight lights and eight switches. The present version is a modification of one described by Morin and Grant (1955) which, in turn, is based on suggestions by Fitts and Seegar (1953). Morin and Grant have reported findings in line with the assumption that under conditions in which the various lights are successively activated the initially dominant response is to the response element which is in direct spatial correspondence, i.e., directly underneath. Half of the to-be-learned S-R combinations in the present situation (No. 1, 4, 5, and 8) involve the initially dominant response while the remaining half (No. 2, 3, 6, and 7) do not. According to the previously outlined assumptions, the effects of stress would also be expected to interact with the particular S-R combination involved. For those combinations in which the initially dominant response is compatible with the correct one, performance under stress should be facilitated in comparison to nonstress, but impaired where it is incompatible with the correct response.

Method

Subjects. The Ss were 108 fifth-grade boys and girls randomly assigned in equal numbers, 54 per group, to the stress and nonstress conditions. The last 38 Ss, 19 per group, were added at a later time in order to obtain information as to the specific types of errors occurring to those S-R combinations (No. 2, 3, 6, and 7) in which the dominant position tendency was incompatible with the correct response. Records of these errors had not been obtained for the first 70 Ss.

Apparatus and Procedure. The apparatus consisted of a sloping panel 20 × 12 in., painted flat black. Eight green, jeweled reflectors, illuminated by 6.3-v. pilot lamps, were arranged horizontally on the panel spaced 2 in. apart. A small push button was situated 2 in. directly below each light. A 6.3-v. red, jeweled reflector was centered at the top of the panel. By means of appropriate switching devices on the back of the panel not visible to S, any single light could be activated and any single button could be set to turn it off. Selection of the correct button by S simultaneously terminated the green light and activated the red light which indicated that the response was correct. For the stress condition, duration of the stimulus light was electronically controlled and responses occurring after the automatic offset of the light did not activate the red signal lamp.

The Ss in the nonstress condition were informed that the task required them to learn which of the buttons turned off a given light and that for "some" of the lights the button directly underneath was correct but that for "some" of the lights an immediately *adjacent* button was correct. The intent in this portion of the instructions was to limit the number of response elements from which S was to make his selection. No time limits were placed on responding for the nonstress group. In addition to these instructions, Ss in the stress condition were given a demonstration in which a stimulus light was activated for 1 sec. and were informed that failure to respond within this interval would be scored an error. As in the previous studies, in order to reduce the incidence of nonresponding, the timer was set for a 2-sec. exposure during the test trials. If a response failed to occur during this interval, the light was re-presented until a response could be recorded for that trial. The data reported, however, do not include failures to respond. Two Ss each failed three times to respond on the first presentation of a light while seven Ss failed once. Three of these failures occurred on lights which were associated with the button directly underneath and 10 on lights involving an adjacent button.

Each light was presented 10 times. Defining each presentation for which a response was recorded as a trial, training consisted of a total of 80 trials. The lights were successively activated in the same prearranged order for all Ss. This consisted of one presentation of each light in every block of eight trials and no light was activated twice in succession (a qualification to this aspect of the procedure may be noted in the preceding paragraph). No attempt was made to hold the interval between presentations constant and Ss were *not* permitted to correct for errors.

Since principal interest is in the differential effects of stress in relation to the two types of S-R combinations, those combinations for which the correct response involves the button directly underneath will be hereafter designated DTC (dominant tendency correct), and those involving adjacent buttons designated DTI (dominant tendency incorrect).

Results

Table 1 presents the percentage of correct responses made by the stress and nonstress groups on all trials to the DTC and DTI combinations separately. Both groups made fewer correct responses on the DTI than the DTC combinations with performance starting out well below 50% on the DTI at the first block of trials. More importantly, however, these data indicate that the effects of stress are contingent on the type of S-R combination. Thus, it is apparent that the stress group, in comparison to the nonstress group, made more correct responses on the DTC combinations at all stages of training and, with the exception of the last block, fewer correct responses on the DTI. It is of interest to note that the point at which the DTI performance curves converge approximates the 50% level of performance. The mean percentage of correct responses on the last block of trials was 48.70 for the nonstress and 48.14 for the stress group.

Analysis of variance of the data indicated that the differential effects of stress (facilitation, impairment) were statistically reliable as reflected in the interaction of stress with the type of S-R combination. Comparisons of the

TABLE 1

PERCENTAGE OF CORRECT RESPONSES

| | S-R Combination | | | |
| | DTC | | DTI | |
Group	Mean	SD	Mean	SD
Stress	70.60	13.42	33.29	15.13
Nonstress	62.92	11.00	42.18	14.07

difference between the stress and nonstress groups on the two types of combinations separately, based on the means shown in Table 1, indicated that the difference on the DTC combinations was reliable at beyond the .005 level ($F = 10.64$, $df = 1$ and 106), and on the DTI at beyond the .005 level ($F = 9.77$). The apparent tendency for the effects of stress to depend on the stage of training on the DTI combinations would be reflected in the triple interaction. It can be noted, however, that the reliability of this effect falls just short of the .05 level. However, because of its theoretical implications and the possibility that this effect may have been partially obscured in the over-all analysis, an additional analysis based on the two curves alone was performed with the main interest being in the interaction of the effects of stress with that of stage of training. This effect was found to be reliable at beyond the .05 level ($F = 3.20$, $df = 3$ and 318), providing evidence for rejection of the hypothesis of parallel curves.

While the finding indicating that the stress group made more correct responses than the nonstress group on the DTC combinations provides evidence that stress enhanced the strength of the dominant tendency, the opposite results on the DTI stimuli do not necessarily permit this same inference. That is to say, it is possible that this latter effect may have been the result of an increased frequency in responses to incorrect buttons other than the one in direct spatial correspondence. The data of the last 38 Ss, for whom records were kept of the type of error occurring to the DTI combinations, provide the relevant information. Responses occurring to the button in direct spatial correspondence are designated DTE (dominant tendency errors), and responses made to any other incorrect button designated RE (random errors).

The percentage occurrence of the two types of errors made by each group was recorded separately in blocks of 10 trials. On the basis of these data it is apparent that both groups made more errors of the DTE than the RE type, with this difference being more pronounced during the early stages of training. It is also apparent that the stress group made consistently more errors of the DTE type than the nonstress group. On the other hand, the stress group also tended, but not consistently, to give slightly more errors of the RE type than the nonstress group. An analysis of variance of these data yielded three statistically reliable effects. These were Stress ($P < .025$), Blocks of Trials ($P < .001$) and the Type of Error ($P < .001$). Although the magnitude of the

TABLE 2

ANALYSIS OF VARIANCE OF CORRECT RESPONSES

Source	df	MS	F
Stress (C)	1	.78	
Error (b)	106	804.66	
Blocks (A)	3	167.13	84.40**
S-R Type (B)	1	1820.04	255.26**
A × B	3	7.38	2.64*
A × C	3	4.01	2.02
B × C	1	148.34	20.80**
A × B × C	3	6.48	2.32
Error₁ (w)	318	1.98	
Error₂ (w)	106	7.13	
Error₃ (w)	318	2.79	

* $P = .05$.
** $P = .001$.

difference between the two groups appeared to depend on the type of error, the interaction of stress and type of error did not reach reliability at the .05 level. However, when the difference between the two groups was compared on the total number of each type of error separately, the difference was reliable at beyond the .05 level for errors of the DTE type but considerably short of the .05 level on errors of the RE type.

Discussion

From a theoretical standpoint the results of the present experiment indicating differential effects of stress (facilitation, impairment) are of special interest and are in line with the previous studies. The effects of stress were found to be contingent on the relative strength of the to-be-learned response. For those S-R combinations in which the initially dominant response was arbitrarily designated correct, performance was found to be significantly facilitated under the stress as compared to the nonstress condition. On the other hand, deleterious consequences of stress were found for those combinations in which the initially dominant response was incompatible with that required for correct performance. In the latter case the results indicated that this effect could be partly attributed to the relatively greater enhancement in the strength of the initially dominant response.

Of additional interest for its possible theoretical implications was the finding that the magnitude of the deleterious effects of stress was dependent on the stage of training for those S-R combinations in which the initially dominant response was incompatible with that required for correct performance. As training progressed, the initial relative superiority of the nonstress condition tended to diminish so that at the end of training the performance of both groups was nearly identical. The fact that this equality in performance occurred when the frequency of correct responding approximated 50% is of theoretical interest. That is, assuming that such a level of performance indicates equality in the strengths of the correct and the initially dominant, incorrect tendency, i.e., $H+ = H-$, an increase in drive, according to theory, would not be expected to affect performance under these conditions, and neglecting other factors. Since drive is assumed to combine indiscriminately with *all* existing habit tendencies, the resultant effect would be one of augmenting the absolute strengths of the correct as well as the incorrect response by equal amounts. Providing that the equality in the habit strengths of the correct and incorrect responses occurs at approximately the same stage in training for both a high- and a low-drive condition, performance under the higher drive would not be expected to differ from that of low-drive condition. However, once the strength of the correct habit, though initially the weaker, supersedes the strength of the incorrect one through the process of differential reinforcement, performance under the higher drive condition would be expected to be facilitated thereafter. Thus, on the basis of these implications, had training been continued in the present experiment, eventual facilitation under stress would be expected on those S-R combinations in which the initially dominant tendency was incompatible with the correct response even though its initial effect is that of impairment. As implied by the theory, the change from relative inferiority to superiority in performance would be expected to occur beyond that point in training when the strengths of the correct and incorrect responses have become equal.

Summary

The present experiment was concerned with the relation of time pressures (stress) and pre-experimentally acquired differential position habits to performance of children in a motor-learning task. The main interest was in the effects of stress as a function of the compatibility of the dominant position habits with the correct response in the task. An interaction between stress and compatibility was found based on statistically reliable effects for stress to facilitate performance, in comparison to a nonstress condition, where the dominant position habit was compatible with the correct response but to interfere where it was incompatible. The experiment was designed to test implications relating to the role of drive in situations involving competing responses based on Hull's basic assumption concerning the manner in which drive and habit combine to determine response strength.

References

CASTANEDA, A. Effects of stress on complex learning and performance. *J. exp. Psychol.*, 1956, 52, 9-12.

CASTANEDA, A., & PALERMO, D. S. Psychomotor performance as a function of amount of training and stress. *J. exp. Psychol.*, 1955, 50, 175-179.

FITTS, P. M., & SEEGAR, C. M. S-R compatibility: Spatial characteristics of stimulus and response codes. *J. exp. Psychol.*, 1953, 46, 199-210.

HULL, C. L. *Principles of behavior.* New York: D. Appleton-Century, 1943.

LINDQUIST, E. F. *Design and analysis of experiments in psychology and education.* New York: Houghton Mifflin, 1953.

MORIN, R. E., & GRANT, D. A. Learning and performance on a key-pressing task as a function of the degree of spatial stimulus-response correspondence. *J. exp. Psychol.*, 1955, 49, 39-47.

PALERMO, D. S. Proactive interference and facilitation as a function of amount of training and stress. *J. exp. Psychol.*, 1957, 53, 293-296.

SPENCE, K. W. *Behavior theory and conditioning.* New Haven: Yale Univer. Press, 1956.

TAYLOR, J. A. Drive theory and manifest anxiety. *Psychol. Bull.*, 1956, 53, 303-320.

Effects of Stress on Motor Performance and Learning*

E. DEAN RYAN

IN this particular study, the nature of the task—simple and complex— is investigated as to the performance effects of induced stress. Since stress can be expected to have a different influence on the performance of easy tasks as compared to difficult tasks, the implications for instruction are reasonably clear. With increasing task complexity, a greater possibility of the emission of many alternate and incorrect responses is present. Hence, the previous investigation and the present one reinforce each other's findings. Although shock was the stress-inducer in Ryan's study, other stimuli serve in this capacity in real-life learning situations. The importance placed on successful performance and the presence of spectators, possible consequences in the form of criticism, punishment, or a bad grade and the like

* From *The Research Quarterly*, 1962, *33*, 111-119. Reprinted with permission of the author and the American Association for Health, Physical Education, and Recreation.

⌐are typical stressors. They might be expected to act in one way on complex task performance and in another way on easy task performance.

The purpose of the present study was to test the hypothesis that externally induced tension will facilitate performance on a relatively easy motor skill but impair performance on a more difficult motor skill and to test the further hypothesis, based on Hullian theory, that the learning per se will not be influenced by tension.⌐

Review of the Literature

It has long been the common belief that tension and stress are detrimental to performance. Lazarus, Deese, and Osler[7] in a review of the literature up to 1951, indicate that these factors usually impair both verbal and perceptual motor performances. More recently, however, learning theorists have contended that tension will improve performance in some situations. This has been related to Hullian theory in the 1956 review by Taylor.[10]

Farber and Spence,[4] using the Taylor Anxiety Scale, tested a high anxiety group and a low anxiety group in an eyelid conditioning experiment. The anxious subjects gave a larger number of conditioned responses than the non-anxious subjects. They subsequently learned a conventional stylus maze. The performance of the anxious subjects was significantly poorer than that of the non-anxious, with the more difficult choice points providing the greatest difference between the two groups.

Castaneda and Lipsitt[3] investigated the effects of speed stress on a paired associate type motor learning task (lever positioning) in which pre-experimentally acquired position habits were arbitrarily designated as either correct or incorrect. When the pre-experimentally acquired positions were correct, the stress group made significantly more correct responses than the non-stress group, but when the pre-experimentally acquired positions were incorrect the stress group made fewer correct responses.

Using a real life stress situation to study the effects of stress on serial learning and conditioning, Beam found that stress facilitated conditioning but hampered serial learning.[2] The stress group (those taking a doctoral examination) made significantly more conditioned responses than did the non-stress group, but made significantly more errors and took longer to reach a criterion in serial learning.

Howell[6] employed a relatively simple motor performance. This consisted of hitting a ball with an arm movement, reversing direction to touch a key, and then hitting a second ball. There was no particular demand for accuracy, but speed was emphasized. He used electric shock to produce motivation and tension. The most tense half of his subjects exhibited a significantly greater increase in speed of motor performance under motivation than was observed in the less tense subjects.

From these studies it seems that tension, or stress, may improve or impair performance, depending upon the difficulty of the task and the anxiety state of the subject. In a simple task, tension can facilitate performance, while in a more difficult task, tension can impair performance. It should be noted that the previous investigations have mostly been concerned with conditioning or with verbal tasks. While some have involved perceptual-motor skills, only the Howell study used a large muscle task, and it did not include motor learning.

Methodology

Learning Task. The task selected to be learned was balancing on a horizontally pivoted platform (stabilometer) described in a recent study.[1] It involved movements made by large muscles in contrast to the typical small muscle perceptual motor tasks frequently used by psychologists. In addition, it permitted measurement of learning in a short period of time using only 12 trials of 30 seconds each.[5]

Difficulty was altered by varying the vertical position of the balance platform in relation to its center of rotation. For the easy skill, the platform was 25 cm. (10 in.) below the center of rotation. For the difficult task, the platform was 25 cm. (10 in.) above the center of rotation. The nature of the task reduced the involvement of previous experience as a complicating factor.

Tension. Electric shock was used to produce experimental stress or tension. The objective stimulus value (strength of shock) was controlled and equal for all subjects. The apparatus to produce the shock has been described in a previous publication.[9]

To ensure that a high degree of tension was maintained, the shock was administered on 7 of the 12 trials. The trials that received shock were randomly determined, as was the point of time that the shock was administered within each trial. This prevented the subject from anticipating the shock or relaxing after once receiving it.

Subjects. One hundred and twenty male university students, all volunteers, were used as subjects. None had ever practiced on a bongo board or any device similar to the stabilometer. Because it was impossible to match subjects or groups in advance as to ability to learn the stabilometer task, and because no known motor task correlates high enough with stabilometer performance to justify grouping by a matching variable,[8] the subjects were assigned to the subgroups randomly.

Experimental Design. There were 6 groups of 20 subjects each. Groups #1, #3, and #5 were experimental, #2, #4, and #6 were control. The task was easy for #1 and its control #2, and difficult for #3 and its control #4, as well as for #5 and its control #6. The differentiation between #1 and #3 (both experimental) was that one had the easy task and the other had the difficult task; prior to the testing both had knowledge that they would be shocked, and both were shocked randomly throughout the test. The differentiation between #3 and #5 (both difficult) was that the latter group had no knowledge that shock would be given until trial 2 had been completed. They were then shocked on trial 3 and randomly thereafter. Thus, the first two trials for #5 were made under control conditions, and the third and subsequent trials were made under experimental conditions. Group #6 was the control for #5.

Procedure. The subject was told that the purpose of the experiment was to investigate differences in learning to balance on a pivoted platform and was asked if he had discussed the experiment with anyone or if he had heard it discussed. (This was a particularly important point for group #5.) Questions relating to height, weight, age, and medical defects were asked. The purpose, while disguised, was to discover any defects that might make the admission of shock inadvisable. (One subject was rejected because he had cardiac trouble.)

At this point, Groups #1 (experimental-easy) and #3 (experimental-difficult) were informed that they would receive a series of very severe electric shocks that they could do nothing to avoid. They were told that they might receive 1, 2, or even 3 shocks per trial and that on some trials they might receive no shock. It was explained and emphasized that their performance had nothing to do with the shock. Whether they did well or poorly, they would receive the same number of shocks. All subjects were given a chance to quit at this point if they so desired. (Only two did not continue.) After trial two, group #5 (experimental-delay) was told about the shocks and given the same instructions as the other experimental groups. Stabilometer performance scores were recorded after each trial.

At the end of the testing period, the true nature of the experiment was explained. The subjects were then requested not to discuss the experiment with anyone, so that other potential subjects could be called upon to complete the experiment.

Results

Easy Task. For purposes of statistical analysis, the data for each group were assembled into three sections, averaging trials 1-4, 5-8, and 9-12. Differences in performance between experimental and control groups were negligible. The largest difference (trials 9-12) yielded at ratio of only 0.70, which is nonsignificant.

Difficult Task. On trials 1 and 2 of Group #3 (experimental-difficult) the subjects were under tension, while the other three groups on Stabilometer-D were not aware that shock was part of the experiment. On trial three, Group #5 (experimental-delay) was introduced to shock. Because the two control groups did not differ significantly at any point, as will be demonstrated later, a single average control curve was plotted. Further, since the effect of the trials for trials 4-12 was nonsignificant, these trials have been averaged in order to simplify the graph. Because the experimental treatment was changed during the progress of learning, and because it was desirable to analyze results before and after the change in treatment, the data were divided into two parts, consisting of the first 2 trials and the last 9 trials.

There was little difference between the two control groups and Group #5 (experimental-delay), which performed under control conditions at this stage of the experiment. Group #3 (experimental-difficult) was poorer in performance than any of the controls. Analysis of variance showed that there was a significant difference between trials 1 and 2. However, the interaction of trials by groups was not significant, signifying that while all groups make progress from trial 1 to trial 2, there was no significant difference in the rate at which the groups progressed.

Since there was a significant difference between groups in their performance level, the t test can be used to determine the significance of the difference between any 2 of the group means.[8] The t ratios indicate that there was no significant difference between the two control groups (t = 0.38), and no significant difference between Group #5 (experimental-delay) and the average of the two control groups (t = 0.34). Group #3 (experimental-difficult) was significantly poorer in performance than Group #5 (experimental-delay) (t = 2.29) and significantly poorer than the average of the control group (t = 2.25). These findings are in agreement with the hypothesis that tension will impair performance on a difficult skill.

In the variance analysis for trials 3 through 12, subjects in Group #5 (experimental-delay) were treated the same as those in Group #3 (experimental-difficult), that is, shock was given randomly in both. The analysis shows that the effect of the trials was not significant (F = 1.42); there was only random variation among the trials from 4 through 12. This interpretation is confirmed by the nonsignificance of the trials-by-groups interaction (F = 0.82). The F ratio for the groups' effect was significant (F = 3.52 with 2.76 required for significance at the 5 percent level); therefore, the postlearning performance levels of at least some of the groups were different. Since the effect of the trials was nonsignificant, it is possible to average the nine postlearning trials of each group to compute t for the difference between groups.

There was no significant difference between the 2 experimental groups (t = 0.32) and no significant difference between the 2 controls (t = 0.87). The average of the experimental group was significantly poorer in performance than the average of the 2 control groups (t = 2.19 with 2.09 required for significance at the 5 percent level). This further confirms the hypothesis that tension impairs performance on a difficult skill.

Discussion

Some studies show that tension impairs performance, others show facilitation by tension, and a few show no effect at all. When these studies are examined as a group, however, a pattern seems to emerge. Most of the investigations on tension in difficult learning tasks (usually verbal or conditioning) have shown that performance tends to be impaired. Some of these have considered the rate of learning, which seems to be unaltered by tension. Other studies have investigated relatively simple tasks, reporting improved performance with no effect on learning in those few cases where it was considered. The present writer contends that in gross motor learning tasks (which had not previously been investigated in this connection), tension will impair performance in a difficult task and facilitate it in an easy task but will not influence rate of learning.

For the most part, the results have confirmed the hypothesis; tension does impair performance in a difficult task. This occurs both during learning and after learning (when the latter is defined as the attainment of a plateau). It does not influence the rate of learning.

In the case of the easy task, the results are somewhat equivocal. Performance is not impaired, and to this extent the hypothesis is not contradicted. However, the expectation was that tension would improve performance in the easy task. It did not. In fairness, it must be admitted that this failure to find improvement could be ascribed to inadequate variation of the experimental variable. The specification of task difficulty as easy or difficult is relative rather than absolute, and the so-called easy task may in fact have been too difficult to have permitted tension to cause improvement. It is doubtful if the failure to secure improvement could justly be ascribed to statistical inadequacy. Two other groups of the same size (n = 20) showed positive results in the difficult task.

Summary

The purpose of the study was to test the hypothesis that externally induced tension would facilitate performance on a relatively easy motor skill, but impair performance on a more difficult skill and would not influence learning.

Tension was produced in the experimental groups by an irregular series of unavoidable electric shocks, a current density of 4.4 ma. per square cm. Two groups of 20 subjects each performed the easy stabilometer task. The experimental group received the unavoidable electric shock and the control group received no shock. There was no significant difference between groups in learning or performance. Four groups of 20 subjects each performed the difficult stabilometer task. Two groups served as controls, while 2 experimental groups received the unavoidable shock. One of the 2 experimental groups received shock from the beginning of the experiment while the other performed under control conditions until the third trial, when the shock procedure was started. Under the influence of tension during the first 2 trials, the experimental group exhibited significantly poorer performance than the others, which did not differ among themselves. After the third trial, when both experimental groups were under tension, both exhibited poorer performance than the controls. The amount of improvement during practice, in contrast to performance level, did not differ among the groups.

The results of the study support the hypothesis that increased tension impairs performance of a difficult motor task, and that rate of learning is independent of the state of tension for either difficult or easy skills. They fail to support the hypothesis that tension improves performance of an easy motor task.

It is to be understood that these conclusions imply the usual reservations with respect to the conditions of the experiment and the type of subjects used. Moreover, it is possible that the easy task was actually not sufficiently easy to offer a fair test on the expectation of improvement.

References

1. BACHMAN, J. C. "Specificity vs. Generality in Learning and Performing Two Large Muscle Motor Tasks." *Research Quarterly* 32:3-11, March 1961.
2. BEAM, J. C. "Serial Learning and Conditioning Under Real Life Stress." *Journal of Abnormal and Social Psychology* 51:543-51; November 1955.
3. CASTANEDA, A., and LIPSITT, L. P. "Relation of Stress and Differential Position Habits to Performance in Motor Learning." *Journal of Experimental Psychology* 57:25:30; January 1950.
4. FARBER, I. E., and SPENCE, K. W. "Complex Learning and Conditioning as a Function of Anxiety." *Journal of Experimental Psychology* 45:120-125; February 1953.
5. HENRY, F. M. "Evaluation of Motor Learning When Performance Levels are Heterogeneous." *Research Quarterly* 27:176-81; May 1956.
6. HOWELL, M. L. "Influence of Emotional Tension on Speed of Reaction and Movement." *Research Quarterly* 24:22-32; March 1953.
7. LAZARUS, R. S.; DEESE, J.; and OSLER, S. F. "Anxiety and Stress in Learning; The Roll of Intraserial Duplication." *Journal of Experimental Psychology* 47:111-14; February 1954.
8. McNEMAR, Q. *Psychological Statistics.* New York: John Wiley and Sons, 1955.
9. RYAN, E. D. "The Effect of Differential Motive-Incentive Conditions on Physical Performance." *Research Quarterly* 32:83-87; March 1961.
10. TAYLOR, J. A. "Drive Theory and Manifest Anxiety." *Psychological Bulletin* 53:303-20; July 1956.

Motor Performance Under Stress*

ALBERT V. CARRON

IN this final reading, high and low anxiety subjects are compared on the basis of introduction of stress early and late in practice. The ability to cope with stress in learning is shown to be a function of one's anxiety state. Although high and low anxious subjects perform similarly in the latter stages of practice when stress is present or absent, performance dissimilarities in early practice suggest consideration for the nature of the learner as he undertakes the learning of a motor skill. Instructors sensitive to the

* From *The Research Quarterly*, 1968, *39*, 463-469. Reprinted with permission of the author and the American Association for Health, Physical Education, and Recreation.

personalities of learners will be better able to create learning environments more compatible with their temperaments. It can be observed from the readings in this section that the type of stress, anxiety level, task complexity, and practice stage are interacting variables in motor performance./

In recent years anxiety (or level of emotionality) as measured by the Taylor manifest anxiety scale[17,18] has frequently been considered to be one of the factors contributing to the total effective drive level of the organism. In the Hullian-Spence[5,14] framework, habit strength (sHr) and drive (D) jointly determine response strength (sEr). Thus, whether performance will be facilitated or deterred by high drive will depend upon the relative strengths of the competing response tendencies. In regard to simple tasks, i.e., those tasks with only a small number of habits or competing response tendencies, the implication is clear—the performance level of the high-anxious subjects should be superior to that of the low-anxious subjects by virtue of their higher drive, which theoretically will combine with the simple correct habit. This has been confirmed by Montague,[10] Spence, Farber, and McFann,[15] Spence, Taylor, and Ketchel,[16] Taylor,[19] and Taylor and Chapman.[20]

On the other hand, in complex tasks, i.e., those tasks containing a large number of habits or competing response tendencies, it may be expected that the performance of high-anxious subjects will be inferior to that of low-anxious subjects.

While the results of Axelrod, Cowen, and Heilizer[1] and Spence, Taylor, and Ketchel[16] failed to verify this latter prediction, it was confirmed by the findings of Farber and Spence,[4] Korchin and Levine,[6] Lucas,[9] Montague,[10] Ramond,[11] Spence, Farber, and McFann,[15] and Taylor and Spence.[21] Unfortunately, only two of the above studies were concerned with tasks of a "motor nature" and consequently, the implications of drive theory for large muscle motor tasks are not clear. In what appear to be the only studies concerned with this problem, Ryan[12,13] observed that although a shock stressor impaired performance in a difficult task when it was introduced early in the learning process,[13] it had no effect on performance when it was introduced late.[12]

Purpose

/ The present study is concerned with the effect of an electric shock stressor upon the performance of high-anxious and low-anxious subjects practicing on a difficult motor task. The shock stressor was introduced early in practice when the strength of the correct habit would be expected to be approximately the same as that of the incorrect competing response tendencies, and late in practice when the strength of the correct habit should be stronger than that of the competing incorrect tendencies. Thus it was hypothesized that the early stress would have a detrimental effect upon the performance of the high-anxious subjects and would either not affect or would improve the performance of the low-anxious subjects. It was further hypothesized that the late stress would have a facilitative effect upon both groups, but this improvement would be most marked in the high-anxious subjects.

Method

Subjects. The 120 subjects (60 high-anxious and 60 low-anxious) were selected from the University of Alberta freshman male population (1,272 students) on the basis of their extreme scores on the Taylor manifest anxiety scale. (A score of 7 or below was designated low-anxious and a score of 21 or above was designated high-anxious.) When they arrived to be tested, the subjects were assigned in a fixed order to one of the following three conditions:

Control. The 20 high-anxious and 20 low-anxious subjects practiced for 2 days (35 trials per day) on the stabilometer. They were never exposed to the experimental stress.

Stress-early. On trials 4, 5, and 6, the 20 high-anxious and 20 low-anxious subjects were given the electric shock stressor.

Stress-late. On trials 65, 66, and 67, the 20 high-anxious and 20 low-anxious subjects were given the electric shock stressor.

Apparatus. The task consisted of balancing on a stabilometer. The range of motion of the platform was $\pm 20°$ from the horizontal. Motion of the board over this arc was measured in electrical "movement units" with $1°$ of movement scored as one movement unit. All subjects were given 20-sec. trials over a two-day period (35 trials per day). The rest interval between trials was 20 to 30 sec.

A model 250 constant current electronic stimulator was used to administer the shock stressor. The stimulus was applied through finger electrodes fastened to the right index finger.

Experimental Design. On day 1, the control and stress-late subjects were given 35 20-sec. trials. The stress-early subjects were given 3 practice trials and then, before trial 4, it was explained that they would receive either 0, 1, 2, or 3 electric shocks per trial for 3 trials. It was emphasized that these shocks were unavoidable and were in no way related to performance. Although the subjects were given the option of dropping out of the experiment at this point only 3 chose to do so. After trial 6, the electrodes were removed and the stress-early subjects then practiced under control conditions.

On day 2, the stress-early and control subjects were given 35 20-sec. trials under normal (control) conditions. The stress-late subjects were given 29 trials and then, prior to trial 65, the shock stressor was introduced. After the stress period of 3 trials, the stress-late subjects were given the remaining 3 trials under control conditions.

Results

Stress-Early. When a variance analysis was used for the data from the prestress, stress, and poststress periods an average of 3 trials was used to represent each period. There were no differences in the performance levels of the 6 groups in the prestress period. In the stress period there were differences between the high-anxious and low-anxious subjects ($F = 6.55$, $p < .05$) as well as between the 2 stress-early experimental groups and the other 4 groups ($F = 4.26$, $p < .05$). However, when the ordered means from this latter variance analysis were subjected to the Duncan multiple range test, only the high-anxious stress-early group was inferior in performance level to the other groups.

In the immediate poststress period (trials 7 to 9) there were no differences in the performance levels of the 6 groups. That is, once the shock stressor was removed, the differences between the 2 stress-early groups and the other 4 groups seem to have been erased.

Another way of analyzing the effect of the shock stress upon performance involves studying the amount of change from period to period, i.e., from the prestress to the stress, and from the stress to the poststress. This resulting score is designated the delta, or difference score.

The results from an analysis of variance of the delta scores for the changes from the prestress to the stress period indicated a significant experimental conditions effect ($F = 5.004$, $p < .05$). The improvement of the stress-early groups during the stress period was less than that shown by the other 4 groups. When these results were subjected to a Duncan multiple range test, the amount of improvement of the high-anxious stress-early group was found to be significantly inferior to that of all other groups (except low-anxious stress-early, with this difference just failing to reach significance) while the low-anxious stress-early group did not differ from any other group in amount of improvement during the stress-early period.

The high-anxious stress-early and low-anxious stress-early groups did not differ from the other four groups in amount of improvement from the stress period to the poststress period. It would seem, therefore, that while the shock stressor had a depressant effect upon the amount of improvement shown by the high-anxious group during the stress period, this effect did not persist once the electric shock threat was removed.

Stress-Late. There were significant differences between the performance levels of the high-anxious and low-anxious subjects in the prestress, stress, and poststress periods but there was no "experimental condition" effect during these periods. However, studying the performance level alone is not adequate since both the high-anxious stress-late and the low-anxious stress-late did show a marked decrement in performance level during the stress period. This is not reflected by the variance analysis of performance levels because the low-anxious stress-late group was superior to all other groups prior to the introduction of the shock stressor. Thus, the performance decrement during the stress period resulted in their achieving approximately the same performance level as the other groups.

The more meaningful analysis of the changes in performance resulting from the electric shock stressor was provided by the delta-score technique. The 2 stress-late groups exhibited a change in performance from the prestress to the stress period that was significantly ($F = 9.45$, $p < .01$) inferior to that of the other 4 groups while the low-anxious stress-late group differed from the 2 stress-early groups only.

In the poststress period, the 2 stress-late groups showed a significant improvement in performance ($F = 17.01$, $p < .01$). A Duncan analysis indicated that both the high-anxious stress-late and the low-anxious stress-late groups improved significantly more ($p < .05$) than any of the other groups for this period.

Discussion

According to Ryan,[12] two important factors which help to determine the effect that stress will have upon performance are the difficulty of the task and the proficiency of the individual when the stress is introduced. In the Hullian framework where the difficulty of the task is related to the number and strengths of the competing response tendencies present, it may be expected that when stress is introduced early in a difficult task, it will have a detrimental effect upon performance, while stress introduced late may be expected to be beneficial to performance. However, the anxiety level factor (with the underlying assumption that manifest anxiety scale scores reflect emotional responsiveness, which in turn reflects drive level) complicates this picture. The available literature in which stress was used on manifest anxiety scale subjects[2,7,8,19] indicated that both levels of anxiety were affected in the same direction and to the same degree by stress. In the single exception, Deese, Lazarus, and Keenan[3] found that while the differences between high-anxious and low-anxious subjects increased under shock stress, this was due primarily to the disruptive effect of the shock on the low-anxious subjects.

In the present study, the results for the stress-late period were in the opposite direction expected—the stress was detrimental to performance.

In the stress-early period, the results closely approach theoretical expectations: namely, the stress was detrimental to the performance of the high-anxious subjects while the low-anxious subjects were essentially unaffected.

Some possible explanations for this failure to meet theoretical expectations for the stress-late period are as follows: First, sufficient practice might not have been given before the stressor was introduced. Thus, although the habit strength of the correct response tendency was probably stronger relative to the strengths of the incorrect response tendencies, the latter might not have been sufficiently reduced in the response hierarchy with regard to their excitatory potential (E) to ensure that they would not appear. The increase in drive level (by virtue of the shock stressor) would then have been sufficient to bring the incorrect tendencies over the minimum threshold level (L) necessary to make their probability of occurrence possible.

The second possibility which arises relates to the nature of the stressor. Since the shock was unavoidably introduced, the subject could do nothing to prevent its administration. It was nondirective and unrelated to performance, and consequently, rather than contribute to drive level, the shock may have been distractive and a detriment to the effective drive level. Thus, it is possible that had the subject been informed that he could avoid the electric shock by showing an improvement in performance, a facilitative effect might have resulted. The weakness of this explanation is its inability to explain the differences between the high-anxious and low-anxious subjects in magnitude of reaction to the early stress.

Conclusions

Within the limitations of the present study, the following conclusions appear justified:

Stress introduced early had a differential effect upon the improvements in performance of the high-anxious and low-anxious subjects. The low-anxious stress-early group was not affected by stress, but the performance improvement of the high-anxious stress-early group was significantly inferior to that of all other groups during the stress period.

During the stress-early period, the level of performance of the low-anxious stress-early group did not differ from any other group, while the level of performance of the high-anxious stress-early group was significantly inferior to that of the low-anxious control and stress-late groups.

Stress introduced late resulted in a significant decrement in amount of performance improvement for both high-anxious and low-anxious subjects. Upon removal of the shock stressor, both the high-anxious and low-anxious subjects significantly improved in performance, thereby achieving their prestress levels of performance.

References

1. AXELROD, H. S.; COWEN, E. L.; and HEILIZER, F. The correlates of manifest anxiety in stylus maze learning. *J. exp. psych.* 51:131-38, 1965.
2. DAVIDSON, W. Z.; ANDREWS, T. G.; and ROSS, S. Effects of stress and anxiety on continuous high speed color naming. *J. exp. psych.* 52:13-17, 1956.
3. DEESE, J.; LAZARUS, R. S.; and KEENAN, J. Anxiety, anxiety reduction, and stress in learning. *J. exp. psych.* 46:55-60, 1953.
4. FARBER, I. E., and SPENCE, D. W. Complex learning and conditioning as a function of anxiety. *J. exp. psych.* 45:120-25, 1953.
5. HULL, C. L. *Principles of behavior.* New York: D. Appleton-Century, 1943.

6. KORCHIN, S. J., and LEVINE, S. Anxiety and verbal learning. *J. abnorm. soc. psych.* 54-55:234-40, 1957.
7. LAZARUS, R.; DEESE, J.; and HAMILTON, R. Anxiety and stress in learning: The role of intraserial duplication. *J. exp. psych.* 47:101-14, 1954.
8. LEE, L. C. The effects of anxiety level and shock on a paired-associates verbal task. *J. exp. psych.* 61:213-17, 1961.
9. LUCAS, J. D. The interactive effects of anxiety, failure and intraserial duplication. *Amer. j. psych.* 65:59-66, 1952.
10. MONTAGUE, E. K. The role of anxiety in serial rote learning. *J. exp. psych.* 45:91-96, 1953.
11. RAMOND, C. K. Anxiety and task as determiners of verbal performance. *J. exp. psych.* 46:120-24, 1953.
12. RYAN, D. E. Motor performance under stress as a function of the amount of practice. *Percept. mot. skills* 13:103-106, 1961.
13. RYAN, D. E. Effects of stress on motor performance and learning. *Res. quart.* 33:111-19, 1962.
14. SPENCE, K. W. Theoretical interpretations of learning. In S. S. Stevens (Ed.), *Handbook of experimental psychology.* New York: Wiley, 1951.
15. SPENCE, K. W.; FARBER, I. E.; and McFANN, H. H. The relation of anxiety (drive) level to performance in competitional and noncompetitional paired-associates learning. *J. exp. psych.* 52:296-305, 1956.
16. SPENCE, K. W.; TAYLOR, J.; and KETCHEL, R. Anxiety (drive) level and degree of competition in paired-associates learning. *J. exp. psych.* 52:306-10, 1956.
17. TAYLOR, J. A. A personality scale of manifest anxiety. *J. abnorm. soc. psych.* 48:285-90, 1953.
18. TAYLOR, J. A. Drive theory and manifest anxiety. *Psych. bull.* 53:303-20, 1956.
19. TAYLOR, J. A. The effects of anxiety level and psychological stress on verbal learning. *J. abnorm. soc. psych.* 55-56:55-60, 1953.
20. TAYLOR, J. A., and CHAPMAN, J. P. Paired-associates learning as related to anxiety. *Amer. j psych.* 68:671, 1955.
21. TAYLOR, J. A., and SPENCE, K. W. The relation of anxiety level to performance in serial learning. *J. exp. psych.* 45:61-64, 1952.

PART 7

PERFORMANCE VARIABLES

Fatigue, Sleep and Sense Deprivation, and Warm-Up

Performance, or behavioral output, has traditionally been used as an index of learning status. Learning is an inference based on a relatively permanent increase in appropriate behavior or on some type of motor performance over successive trials or practice sessions. Those experimental or environmental factors producing permanent increments in performance are considered learning factors. Those producing temporary increases or decreases are considered performance factors. Although performance represents the best indicator of level of skill, many times it leads to an incorrect assessment of achievement.

A number of factors temporarily facilitate or inhibit performance. For example, certain variables may appear to depress rate of improvement, but after they are removed no residual effect is noted. It thus becomes apparent that the activities of the learner prior to and during practice on a particular skill need to be recognized and evaluated. This section of the book will contain readings dealing with learner status prior to the actual practice and performance on the task of concern. Such influences on performance as fatigue, sleep loss, sense deprivation, and warm-up are represented with selected readings.

Each reading contains a particular technique for inducing and measuring a performance factor. When one, therefore, examines the effect of fatigue on learning versus performance, the fact that fatigue can be brought about in many ways should be considered. And that which is relatively fatiguing for one subject may not be for another. Confounded with subject characteristics, e.g., age, sex, state of training, practice conditions and the nature of the task, conclusions beyond any immediate study are dangerous to make. Of course, this problem is generally true of most investigations reported in the area of behavioral science. Considering these limitations, the readings that follow depict reasonable trends. They have not been chosen for unusual or unreasonable findings (when weighed against other similar research).

With the exception of reports on the topic of warm-up (as traditionally employed by coaches and physical educators and uniquely interpreted by experimental psychologists), most performance variables have not been well-researched. We have long conjectured on the effect of performance factors on performance and learning. Current research, some of it represented here, is verifying popular notions in some cases and refuting them in other cases.

Chapter 10

LEARNER STATUS PRIOR
TO PRACTICE

Performance and Learning a Gross Motor Skill Under Conditions of Artificially-Induced Fatigue*

RICHARD A. SCHMIDT

It has been assumed for some time that fatigue detrimentally affects learning and performance. In recent years, the possibility that fatigue might influence performance rather than learning is becoming more substantiated by experimental data. Literature on massed practice has usually supported the concept of a temporary fatigue factor, and an actual separate fatiguing task is incorporated in the design of the present reading. The conclusions of Schmidt's study suggest that the practice of real-life skills can conceivably be learned even under reasonably fatigue-like conditions. Those tasks that are dangerous and therefore involve a concern for safety deserve special considerations. Furthermore, it is doubtful whether extremely tiring conditions will produce effective learning situations, especially early in the acquisition of a skill.

Introduction

Recently there has been some interest in distinguishing between performance and learning variables in various learning situations. Performance variables temporarily affect the level of proficiency during practice, whereas learning variables will cause more permanent changes in behavior and thus influence learning. A given variable can be both a learning and a performance

* From *The Research Quarterly,* 1969, *40,* 185-190. Reprinted with permission of the author and the American Association for Health, Physical Education, and Recreation.

variable, but the fact that a variable has been found to affect the performance on some task (relative to subjects practicing without that variable) is not sufficient evidence that the learning has also been affected. A proper design to test for learning differences would be to compare the subsequent performance of the two groups under equivalent levels of the variable in question. If differences exist at this point, the variable has had a more permanent effect on performance, which is evidence that it is a learning variable.

Reynolds and Adams,[13] Adams and Reynolds,[2] and Bilodeau[5] all conclude that the degree of massing has a potent degrading effect on performance during the massed trials, but that when massed groups were later shifted to distributed practice the effect disappeared. They concluded that massing was a performance variable, but not a learning variable. Other studies have indicated that visual display "noise",[6] the percentage of pursuit component in tracking tasks,[7] and distraction[8] and pacing[1] in pursuit rotor practice resulted in serious performance effects during the time the variables were in effect, but had no effects upon performance when they were withdrawn, indicating that they were not learning variables.

Some recent research has been concerned with the performance versus learning characteristics of physical fatigue. Since fatigue is evidenced by a decrement in performance, fatigue must be a performance variable, but it was not known whether fatigue also affected learning. Phillips,[12] using the rho task and the stabilometer, and later Alderman[3] using the rho task and the pursuit rotor, inserted a single fatiguing exercise bout approximately halfway through the learning of the tasks on Day 1, and measured the effects on learning by comparing the fatigued groups during subsequent Day 1 trials and during practice on a second day (Day 2). No differences existed later on Day 1 or on Day 2 and the author concluded that fatigue was not a learning variable. However, the designs used did not permit this conclusion. Since the fatiguing activity was inserted approximately halfway through the learning on Day 1, there was a sizable number of Day 1 trials subsequent to the exercise). (Alderman used 60 rho trials and 40 pursuit rotor trials after the exercise). Thus there may have been ample time on Day 1 for subjects to recover from the exercise, and therefore to be practicing the final Day 1 trials in a relatively unfatigued condition. Alderman's curves showed that the fatigue effects lasted for only 10 trials, and that his subjects had 50 rho task and 30 pursuit rotor trials of relatively unfatigued practice on Day 1. Thus fatigue could have been exerting a substantial effect while it was operating, but the large number of relatively unfatigued trials on Day 1 may have allowed the subjects to recover and to "catch up" with the control group. An adequate test of the performance versus learning characteristics of physical fatigue should not permit recovery from fatigue and subsequent practice on Day 1.

Gutin used the pursuit rotor and determined the effect of treadmill running[9] and a locally-fatiguing exercise[10] on performance and learning. He found no differences in learning (measured on Day 2), but his experiments failed to provide an adequate test because fatigue did not depress performance on Day 1. Nunney,[11] using treadmill running and bicycle ergometer work, investigated the effects on learning a mirror tracing task. He concluded that fatigue reduced the amount of learning but he did not use a design in which all groups were transferred to a common nonfatigue condition, so that the estimate of learning for the fatigue groups was depressed by fatigue. This failed to provide an adequate test of the effect of fatigue on learning.

The present study used a fatigue exercise between each pair of trials to keep the subjects fatigued, and used a transfer design in which all subjects were transferred to a nonfatigue condition two days after original learning.

Method

Learning Task. The learning task in the present study was the Bachman Ladder Climb, the apparatus for which has been described in detail elsewhere.[4] It involved climbing and balancing a free-standing ladder with a special, unfamiliar rung spacing. The subject was instructed to begin with the feet on the bottom rung, start climbing with the right foot, and climb as high as possible without skipping steps. As soon as he toppled over, he began climbing from the bottom again, and continued this process until the completion of a 30-sec. trial. Each time the subject began from the bottom (defined as an "attempt"), the highest rung reached before falling (subtracting any skipped rungs) was recorded by the experimenter, and the subject's score was the total number of rungs climbed during the 30-sec. trial. An alternative score (rungs-per-attempt) was the total number of rungs climbed in a trial divided by the number of attempts. The last attempt in a trial was always disregarded since the end of the trial occurred during the last attempt. Instructions emphasized that the score was the total number of rungs climbed in 30 sec., and stressed the need to move quickly and to climb as high as possible on each attempt.

Design. On Day 1, all subjects practiced ten 30-sec. ladder trials, with an intertrial interval of 90 seconds. Three groups, each with a different intensity of intertrial exercise, are described below:

Group I—750 (mild exercise). Before Trial 1, the subject rode a bicycle ergometer (750 kg m/min.) for 2 min., after which he immediately began the first ladder trial. During each of the intertrial intervals which followed, the subject rode the bicycle for 75 sec. at the same work load.

Group II—1200 (moderate exercise). This group used the same procedures as Group I, except that the work load was 1200 kg m/min.

Group III—M (mental task). The subjects used the same procedures as Groups I and II, except that a vowel-cancelling task was substituted for ergometer work. Intertrial vowel-cancelling was used in place of rest to control for possible differences in the opportunity for rehearsal.

The sample sizes for the various groups were 13, 14, and 20, respectively for Groups I, II, and III. The subjects were male graduate and undergraduate volunteers.

The subjects began ladder trials and either ergometer or vowel-cancelling work on the experimenter's command. When the time for that activity had elapsed, the experimenter said "stop," and the subject took about 7 sec. to disengage himself from the present apparatus, cover the few feet to the other apparatus and get ready to begin. As the subject was moving from the intertrial task to the ladder for the next trial, his score on the previous trial (total rungs climbed in 30 sec.) was reported to him.

On Day 2 (48 hrs. ± 1 hr. later), all groups were treated identically, having four 30-sec. trials with 30-sec. intertrial intervals. During the intertrial interval, the subjects sat quietly and rested. Knowledge of results (total rungs) was given during the last 7 sec. of the interval as on Day 1. The mean of the four Day 2 trials was the criterion measure of amount learned. The subjects always wore tennis shoes to prevent the feet from slipping on the rungs.

Results

Day 1 Performance. The mean differences between groups on Trial 1 were small, with Group I falling between Groups III and II, indicating that the effect of the 2 min. exercise before the first trial had little effect on Trial 1 performance. A between-groups F ratio using Trial 1 scores was clearly nonsignificant ($F = 1.14$), indicating that the pre-Trial 1 activity exerted neither a fatiguing nor a warming-up effect on Trial 1 performance.

The curves indicated that the effect of intertrial work on performance increased as practice continued, with the curves diverging noticeably near Trial 4 or 5: Past Trial 5 the performance appeared to be negatively related to the level of intertrial work. Using the mean of Trials 5 through 10 as the criterion of Day 1 performance, differences between groups were significant at the .05 level ($F = 3.32$). A Scheffé test indicated that only Groups III and II differed on Day 1. Using rungs-per-attempt as the score, the between-groups differences (Trials 5-10) failed significance ($F = .75$), indicating that the exercise did not significantly reduce the height climbed on each attempt. Since Day 1 differences must obtain in order to show that fatigue was operating, the rungs-per-attempt score was not further analyzed.

Day 2 Performance. The differences present at the end of Day 1 appeared to diminish. The ordering of the groups changed, with Group I having the poorest performance, and Groups III and II having nearly identical performances. However, using the mean of Day 2, Trials 1 through 4 as the criterion of amount learned, the between-groups variance was clearly not significant ($F < 1.00$). Thus, even though the groups practiced with differential intertrial fatiguing activity which interfered with performance on Day 1, the performance two days later (under nonfatigued conditions) was not statistically different, offering no evidence that the fatigue affected learning. It appears that fatigue may be a performance variable only, and may not affect learning in gross motor skill.

Discussion

The finding that fatigue is a performance rather than a learning variable seems in agreement with the literature, which shows that degree of massing is a performance, not a learning, variable. It seems reasonable that at least part of the decrement in performance due to heavy massing of practice might be due to muscular fatigue. However it seems that muscular fatigue was not active in reducing learning.

How subjects can practice under seemingly unfavorable conditions of fatigue and learn as well as subjects practicing under the most favorable conditions is difficult to explain. One possible explanation might be that the subjects had acquired the majority of the skill before they became highly fatigued. Fatigue effects did not appear large until after Trial 4 on Day 1, and over one-half of the control group's learning had occurred by Trial 4. Thus it could be that the fatigued subjects gained nearly half of the learning while the differences in fatigue between the groups were minimal; the procedure of having 2 min. ergometer work before Trial 1 was designed to minimize this possibility. It is quite possible that longer and harder work before Trial 1 would have increased the between-group differences in fatigue level during early Day 1 practice, and that the greater differences in performance when learning rate was highest would have produced differences in learning. Progressively increasing the pre-Trial 1 work load should eventually lead to a situation in which fatigue finally produces differences in learning. Indeed, the upper limit of pre-Trial 1 fatigue would be complete exhaustion, rendering the subject helpless to attempt Trial 1. It seems clear that learning differences would occur in this case. However, a more important consideration seems to be that physical fatigue exerts much less influence on learning than has been formerly assumed. The effects of fatigue on the subjective quality of practice (e.g., stumbling, skipping rungs, and lower height per attempt) make it difficult to understand how the fatigued subjects could learn as well as the nonfatigued subjects. Yet the fact that learning was not affected gives some encouragement for trying to teach motor skills when the students have been engaged in earlier fatiguing activity.

References

1. ADAMS, JACK A. The effect of pacing on the learning of a psychomotor response. *J. exp. psychol.* 47:101-09, 1954.
2. ———, and REYNOLDS, B. Effect of shift of distribution of practice conditions following interpolated rest. *J. exp. psychol.* 47:32-36, 1954.
3. ALDERMAN, R. B. Influence of local fatigue on speed and accuracy in motor learning. *Res. quart.* 36:131-40, 1965.
4. BACHMAN, JOHN C. Specificity vs. generality in learning and performing two large muscle motor tasks. *Res. quart.* 32:3-11, 1961.
5. BILODEAU, E. A. Massing and spacing phenomena as a function of prolonged and extended practice. *J. exp. psychol.* 44:96-100, 1952.
6. BRIGGS, G. E.; FITTS, P. M.; and BAHRICK, H. P. Learning and performance in a complex tracking task as a function of visual noise. *J. exp. psychol.* 54:379-87, 1957.
7. BRIGGS, G. E., and ROCKWAY, M. R. Learning and performance as a function of the percentage of pursuit component in a tracking display. *J. exp. psychol.* 71:165-69, 1966.
8. EYESENCK, H. J., and THOMPSON, W. The effects of distraction on pursuit rotor learning, performance, and reminiscence. *Brit. j. psychol.* 57:99-106, 1966.
9. GUTIN, B. *Effect of a treadmill run to exhaustion on rotary pursuit performance, learning, and retention.* Unpublished paper, Hunter College of the City University of New York, 1967.
10. ———. *Effect of local fatigue on rotary pursuit performance and learning.* Paper read at the American College of Sports Medicine conference, State College, Pa., May 1968.
11. NUNNEY, D. N. Fatigue, impairment and psychomotor learning. *Percept. mot. skills,* 16:369-75, 1963.
12. PHILLIPS, W. *The effect of physical fatigue on two motor learning tasks.* Doctoral dissertation, University of California, 1962.
13. REYNOLDS, B., and ADAMS, J. A. Effect of distribution and shift of distribution of practice within a single training session. *J. exp. psychol.* 46:137-45, 1953.

An Investigation of Accumulative Acute Fatigue in Participants at the 1966 World Modern Pentathlon Championships, Melbourne (Victoria, Australia)*

FREDERICK C. HAGERMAN

FATIGUE as a performance variable in motor learning has invariably been investigated in and related to the confines of a research laboratory. Although Hagerman measures fatigue with an apparatus task, his direct

* From *The Journal of Sports Medicine and Physical Fitness,* 1968, *8,* 158-170. Reprinted with permission of the author and publisher.

applications to athletic accomplishments should hearten practitioners and applied researchers. Also, his excellent overview of related research provides the reader with a broad understanding of fatigue and performance relationships as well as common problems in measuring fatigue. Athletic coaches will obviously be most interested in and intrigued by the findings of this experimenter.

Introduction

Fatigue tolerance is vital to the achievement of high performance in any form of vigorous sport. It is particularly magnified in sporting activities which extend over long duration and demand the utmost of an individual's physical and mental resources. The decathlon, automobile racing, repetitive qualifying heats and subsequent final events in rowing, running, and swimming that take place at the Olympic Games and other international sporting competitions and the modern pentathlon are outstanding examples of these activities.

At present there is no precise or agreeable definition of fatigue among physiologists and experimental psychologists who, with few exceptions, have studied this problem in its greatest depth and scope. Those who hold to the belief that fatigue is exclusively a physical phenomenon suggest that tiredness arises from the depletion in fuels for muscular work and accumulation of metabolites resulting from gross energy output.[1,17,19] In contrast, supporters of the theory which strictly associates all forms of fatigue with the deterioration in the central nervous system suggest that fatigue is a subjective feeling of tiredness and is not related to amount of work done or biochemical changes taking place within the tissues.[12,23,26,30] Merton[25] proposed that muscular fatigue was a protective mechanism caused by a complex nerve-muscle inhibitory association designed to inhibit further voluntary contraction when there is danger of damage to the neuromuscular system.

Most attempts at defining fatigue purport that tiredness associated with exercise cannot be separated into purely physical and mental components. Instead, the disturbance in function seems to involve a psychosomatic relationship resulting in general fatigue.[18] Brouha[10] suggested that the inclusion of specific variables in a definition of fatigue is further complicated by the involvement of many situations produced by many factors and characterized by numerous symptoms. McGrath and his associates[24] classified fatigue into two categories: a transient or normal fatigue which can be alleviated by sleep and adequate rest, and cumulative fatigue represented by a negative response to sleeping. The latter type is often accompanied by minor pathological changes. Schwab[30] also contended that chronic or pathological fatigue would not disappear with rest, but acute fatigue, that fatigue which is a direct result of a specific physical or mental stress, can be relieved with normal sleep. Bartlett[5,6,7] distinguished between fatigue resulting from hard physical effort and fatigue from work requiring no gross muscular movements, but involving mental concentration and a high degree of skill, and along with Broadbent,[9] defined fatigue as the deterioration in an activity as a direct result of being engaged in it. There appear, therefore, to be two types of acute fatigue associated with sport; one resulting from vigorous muscular activity (i.e., long distance running) and the other, the after-effect of work demanding concentrated mental effort and a high degree of neuromuscular coordination (i.e., automobile racing). Both types seem to be exaggerated by prolonged engagement in such activities.

Since fatigue cannot be adequately defined, it is reasonable to assume there are no existing means to measure this variable accurately. The study of fatigue has been related to such parameters as strength decrement, lowered physiological responses, inadequate nutrition and rest, disturbance of psychomotor function, dulled intellect, low morale, abnormal endocrine activity, increased environmental stresses, reduction in sensory activity and the inability to resist disease. Welford[34] regarded the study of fatigue as one of close contact between physiology and environmental psychology, being careful to note that the problems of these two sciences are not identical and that changes of function in peripheral organs which typify what may be called fatigue at a physiological level are not explanations of so-called mental fatigue. However, differentiation as to sites of deterioration correlating to either specific mental or physical fatigue are still unknown. According to Crawford[11] the most satisfactory index of fatigue would be a physiological measurement of some description, but there are none practical at present. Schnore[29] studied a number of selected physiological variables and their association with fatigue and concluded that physiological methods in general are more likely to be useful in indicating the changes in emotional stress during a task rather than the cumulative effect of it in the form of fatigue. Whether a primarily based physiological test or one founded on psychological criteria is administered, the evaluation cannot discern between purely physical and strictly mental fatigue. The measurement appears to be an appraisal of general fatigue, the results of which imply a close association between physical and mental variables.

A review of pertinent literature[2,3,4,8,13,14,15,16,18,20,21,22,23,27,28,29,30,32,33] revealed that specific psychological tests or modifications of these tests have assumed a dominant role as tools of research in the study of fatigue. These tests, administered individually or in combination, purported to measure general fatigue objectively by appraising reaction time, visual and auditory responses, or psychomotor reactions. As previously stated, there is wide disagreement as to the source of deterioration associated with fatigue, but most workers are in accord that fatigue can be represented in the form of disturbances in human function as a direct result of performance in a specific activity.[1,7,9,17,21,31,34] This disturbance in function, in turn, can be reflected in the deterioration of performance in tasks involving neuromuscular responses.[13,20,27,31] Griffith[18] suggested that since success in motor learning often depends considerably on sensory information arising from muscles as their fibers engage in motor activity, it is possible that tasks involving neuromotor responses are highly susceptible to the influence of fatigue.

It must be noted that in many cases tests of fatigue have failed to be validated. This is linked, no doubt, to the complexity of the definition of fatigue and to what variable is really being evaluated. Unpublished data (Cameron C. and Tritt B., Aeronautical Research Laboratories, Fishermans Bend, Melbourne, Australia) have suggested that the failure of some tests, which supposedly measure fatigue, to be valid, is a result of inadequate experimental design. These tests involved the use of only one psychotechnical task and although many were extended over long duration, subjects thought to be severely fatigued demonstrated little or no deterioration in performance. It was thought that uninterrupted concentrated effort, without distraction, on one skill as well as the challenge presented to the subject to achieve a high performance over a long duration contributed to the inaccuracy of measurement of fatigue by a single task test. In most cases the subjects, even after the most stressing fatigue conditions, achieved higher fatigue tolerance scores as the tests were more prolonged. These data were substantiated by similar unpublished data obtained by this worker immediately prior to the conduction of this research. A combination of at least two of the following parameters;

reaction time, flicker fusion test, pursuit rotor test, dotting task or its modifications, or a tapping test seem to best bear out a disturbance in human function as a result of fatigue. Under these conditions one test acts as the primary task while the other assumes the role of a secondary or distracting skill.

Apparatus

The testing equipment was especially designed for this study and consisted of an electrically driven memory drum apparatus (Precision Instrument Co., Sydney, N.S.W., Australia) modified by slipping a cylindrical masonite shell over the metal drum cylinder. The memory drum and its modifications served as the testing device for the primary task (dotting test). Thirty-two contact holes, each seven-eighths inches in diameter, were drilled in the masonite shell before it was attached to the memory drum and these holes were represented in an irregular pattern. The revolving speed of the drum was controlled by the removal of cog-pins and these were adjusted for the experiments to permit time enough, under normal conditions, for the subject to make contact with the minimum, one, or maximum number of responses, three, each time the drum turned. The memory drum's exterior was altered so that each parallel row (twenty rows for one complete drum revolution) containing one, two, or three contact holes appeared before a small window through which the subject made contact with the drum.

A metal stylus electrically connected to a telephone counter served to make contact with the drum. The digital counter cumulatively recorded the number of successful contacts. A flasher lamp was attached to the top of the drum and was electrically connected to a Relion Chronoscope (Relion Pty. Ltd., Melbourne, Victoria, Australia) which measured time to the nearest one-one hundredth of a second. This reaction-time unit represented the secondary task. Microswitches were provided for the investigator and subject to activate and deactivate the lamp and chronoscope.

Procedure

Eighteen competitors, active participants in the World Modern Pentathlon Championships and representing seven different countries, were utilized as subjects. They ranged in age from twenty-two to thirty-two years. The mean height and weight of the subjects were 76.4 kg. and 183.5 cm. respectively. Test demonstration and orientation sessions were conducted with the subjects during the week prior to actual competition. Since there was a language problem in some cases, necessitating the use of interpreters, instructions pertaining to the use of experimental apparatus and information concerning the purpose of the study were given to the teams individually. Three orientation periods on different days were permitted each subject in order to facilitate his familiarization with the test apparatus and experimental procedure. A comparison of the results of these familiarization sessions with experimental results demonstrated the elimination of any learning factor variable.

Prior to the first day of competition, each subject was experimentally tested for a three-minute period and then identical tests were carried out with the subjects following each competitive event. The subject was required to make as many contacts (stylus against metal drum via contact holes) as possible in three minutes, being permitted only one touch per contact hole regardless of the number of possible responses presented for each drum turn (minimum-one, maximum-three). The digital telephone counter measured the accumulative number of successful contacts. In addition, twelve light stimuli were emitted at random during the experiment. The subject was instructed to continue making as many contacts with the drum but to switch off the lamp immediately upon observing its illumination. The investigator controlled the lamp and chronoscope with a concealed microswitch and was in a position to observe continually the chronoscope and digital counter. The subject, seated with the apparatus placed visually and applicably at a comfortable level, was required to hold the stylus with the thumb and forefinger of the dominant hand and in an over-hand fashion, the elbow being maintained lower than the wrist and fingers. The elbow, however, was not permitted to make contact with the test table. The non-dominant hand held the microswitch which served to deactivate the light and chronoscope. The subject operated the microswitch with his forefinger and was required to hold the switch above the table, his elbow, in this case, resting comfortably on the table.

The results of the pre-competition three-minute experimental test, excluding orientation tests, served as the base-line or normal condition scores and were utilized to compare with the results of identical tests which followed each of four competitive events. The rapid departure of most subjects following the fifth and final day of competition necessitated in foregoing the administration of the fatigue test after the final day of competition, the cross-country run. All tests were conducted at the games' village under suitable laboratory conditions. Tests following competition were carried out approximately one hour after the conclusion of the event.

Scoring and Analysis

The subjects' performances on the fatigue tests were scored in terms of the total number of successful contacts on the dotting task and aggregate reaction time in seconds for twelve lamp stimuli for a three minute time period. The subjects were naive as to their achievements on all fatigue tests.

In order to facilitate analysis, task and reaction time data for each test were converted to standard scores utilizing the Hull Scale. These scores were weighted equally and combined to yield a composite test performance score. A high fatigue test score indicated better performance on the test (greater fatigue tolerance). Evaluation of pentathlon event performance was taken as actual points scored for that event and total event performance refers to the total accumulation of points at the end of four competitive events. In order to obtain a correlation between total event score (after four events) and total accumulative fatigue test performance, the results of the final fatigue test following swimming were utilized. Since this test score was obtained after what was the final event in this experiment, it reflected the total possible accumulative fatigue response from each subject. Individual composite test scores, deviation from the base-line score, and event scores and rankings are shown in Table 1.

Results

In order to ascertain whether a significant relationship existed between accumulative acute fatigue and pentathlon performance, comparisons were noted between: 1. pentathlon event performance and deterioration of post-event fatigue test performance from base-line test score ($r_{1.2}$), 2. event performance and base-line test score ($r_{1.3}$), 3. deterioration of post-event test performance from base-line test score and base-line test score ($r_{2.3}$) and 4. event performance and deterioration of post-event test performance from base-line test score and base-line test score ($r_{1.2.3}$). The Pearson-Product Moment Correlation statistic was applied in cases 1, 2, and 3 and a partial correlation, designed to intercorrelate all experimental parameters, was utilized for case

4. Also, individual pentathlon event performances and corresponding post-event fatigue test data were compared $(r_{1.2})$ and $(r_{1.3})$ with hope that inferences might be realized concerning the relationship of the individual event and degree of severity of subsequent fatigue.

The correlation between event performance and the deviation of post-event test score from base-line test score, for the accumulative effect, revealed significant positive relationships between these variables for riding, shooting, and total event performance. In contrast, a high negative relationship of -.61 was obtained for fencing.

The individual event effect for $(r_{1.2})$ (including total performance) disclosed significant positive correlations for riding and shooting, a significant negative correlation for fencing, and a low negative relationship between event performance and test deterioration for swimming.

Significant positive correlations were obtained after comparing accumulative and individual event performances with base-line test scre $(r_{1.3})$ for all five conditions.

Positive correlations ranging from .75 to .83 were noted for all events, with fencing the only exception, when deterioration of post-event test performance from base-line test score was compared with base-line test score $(r_{2.3})$. A coefficient of -.77 was obtained for fencing.

Results of the partial correlation analysis $(r_{1.2.3})$ demonstrated a progressively increased positive relationship among the three variables. A summary of correlation coefficients and their statistical significance for the five conditions are presented in Table 2.

Discussion

The significant positive correlations relating to accumulative acute fatigue which were obtained for riding, shooting, swimming, and total event performance after comparing accumulative pentathlon performance and deterioration of post-event test performance from base-line test score $(r_{1.2})$ indicated that those subjects achieving higher accumulative pentathlon point totals demonstrated greater deterioration from the norm on these post-event tests. Subjects with poorer event performances showed less accumulative fatigue. These findings were also applicable for riding and shooting when individual event performance was compared with fatigue tolerance. The high negative correlations obtained for fencing after analyzing both accumulative and individual event effects disclosed that subjects excelling in the fence were less fatigued at its conclusion, as indicated by a more diminutive deterioration on the post-event fatigue test, than those individuals recording lower fencing points. Similar, but less significant correlation data were obtained for swimming. The negative data obtained for fencing and swimming, particularly fencing, seemed to reflect the strenuosity of these activities and most important, they emphasized the close association between the skill demands of fencing and those required to attain better performance on the fatigue test. The similarity of skills involved in the success of fencing and superior performance on the fatigue test were demonstrated consistently in all analyses of the results of this study. The greater motor efficiency of the superior fencer must certainly be considered to be a vital factor in his ability to withstand fatigue. Of the four events investigated, success in fencing and swimming is probably more dependent upon a greater combined physical and mental response from the competitor. Besides the greater inherent psychosomatic demands of fencing, the manner in which this event was conducted lended itself favorably to the study of acute fatigue. Each competitor, with only brief respites, was required to endure an entire day (10-12 hours) of continuous fencing facing every

TABLE 1.—*Individual and Total Pentathlon Event Scores and Fatigue Test Data.*

Scores*	Riding				Fencing			Shooting			Swimming			Total		
Subject	BLT	FTS	DBL	ESR	FTS	DBL	ESR	FTS	DBL	ESR	FTS	DBL	ESR	FTS	DBL	ESR
P 1	96	69	−27	1060 (4)	115	+19	667 (9)	110	+14	868 (6)	114	+18	961 (8)	114	+18	3555 (11)
P 2	79	70	−9	1100 (1)	91	+12	593 (11)	52	−27	956 (4)	62	−17	931 (12)	62	−17	3580 (8)
P 3	101	90	−11	1020 (7)	109	+8	556 (12)	112	+11	846 (7)	130	+29	793 (18)	130	+29	3215 (15)
P 4	103	140	+37	1070 (3)	100	−3	815 (5)	108	+5	802 (9)	108	+5	844 (17)	108	+5	3531 (12)
P 5	135	120	−15	1100 (1)	127	−8	926 (3)	135	0	846 (7)	146	+11	1051 (2)	146	+11	3923 (4)
P 6	100	120	+20	935 (10)	127	+27	741 (7)	116	+16	1000 (2)	119	+19	901 (15)	119	+19	3577 (9)
P 7	102	102	0	1090 (2)	81	−21	556 (12)	79	−23	978 (3)	109	+7	949 (10)	109	+7	3573 (10)
P 8	107	89	−18	970 (8)	112	+5	926 (3)	111	+4	846 (7)	110	+3	1009 (5)	110	+3	3751 (6)
P 9	45	116	+71	1090 (2)	102	+57	630 (10)	96	+51	936 (5)	100	+55	1036 (4)	100	+55	3715 (7)
P 10	51	92	+41	405 (12)	87	+36	667 (9)	92	+41	824 (8)	96	+45	922 (14)	96	+45	2818 (18)

	BLT	FTS	DBL	ESR	FTS	DBL	ESR	FTS	DBL	ESR	FTS	DBL	ESR	FTS	DBL	ESR
P 11	91	132	+41	955 (9)	132	+40	667 (9)	120	+29	758 (11)	27	−64	1042 (3)	27	−64	3422 (14)
P 12	133	113	−20	1100 (1)	118	−15	1111 (1)	109	−24	868 (6)	102	−31	1054 (1)	102	−31	4133 (1)
P 13	136	114	−22	1100 (1)	100	−36	1037 (2)	107	−29	978 (3)	96	−40	877 (16)	96	−40	3992 (2)
P 14	118	120	+ 2	1070 (3)	104	−14	889 (4)	102	−16	1022 (1)	102	−16	997 (6)	102	−16	3978 (3)
P 15	113	76	−37	1100 (1)	82	−25	926 (3)	88	−25	824 (8)	97	−16	946 (11)	97	−16	3796 (5)
P 16	94	54	−40	1040 (5)	58	−36	704 (8)	71	−23	780 (10)	46	−48	925 (13)	46	−48	3449 (13)
P 17	75	74	− 1	1025 (6)	50	−25	519 (13)	68	− 7	714 (12)	32	−43	955 (9)	32	−43	3213 (16)
P 18	120	113	− 7	440 (11)	117	− 3	778 (6)	113	− 7	714 (12)	110	−10	976 (7)	110	−10	2908 (17)

BLT = Base-Line Test Score. FTS = Fatigue Test Score. DBL = Deviation From Base-Line. ESR = Event Score and Rank in ( ).

*1. Base-Line Test Score refers to performance on fatigue test under normal or pre-competition conditions.

2. Event Score is actual points scored for that event; however, rank (in parentheses) represents comparison of 18 subjects only and does not represent rank when compared with the 31 participants taking part in these championships.

3. Total Event Score represents accumulative pentathlon point total after four events.

TABLE 2.—*Summary of Correlation Coefficients.*

Correlation		Effect	Event				
			Riding	Fencing	Shooting	Swimming	Total
Event Performance ($r_{1.2}$)	• Deterioration of Post-Event Test Performance From Base-Line Test Score	Accumulative	.54	−.61	.65	.72	.72
		Individual Event	.54	−.72	.69	−.20	—
Event Performance ($r_{1.3}$)	• Base Line Test Score	Accumulative	.71	.80	.79	.81	.81
		Individual Event	.71	.74	.60	.61	—
Deterioration of Post-Event Test Performance From Base-Line Test Score ($r_{2.3}$)	• Base Line Test Score	Accumulative	.75	−.77	.83	.82	.82
Event Performance and Post-Event Test Performance From Base-Line Test Score ($r_{1.2.3}$)	• Base Line Test Score	Accumulative	.017	.35	.43	.66	.66

Significance: $P_{.05} = .47$ (16 df); $P_{.01} = .71$ (16 df).

competitor. Another significant consideration in the close association that existed between excellence in fencing performance and less fatigue is the relative importance of specific events and their effect on the competitor's total pentathlon score. The participant could not afford, on the basis of the amount of possible points to be scored, to fail to do well in the fence. The scoring system utilized in the modern pentathlon provides for greater point-weighting in fencing than in any of the other four events. In addition, fencing is the only pentathlon event which permits the competitor to depreciate his opponent's score. It appeared then that the combined effect of potentially obtaining the highest possible individual event point total and the ability to lessen an opponent's score prompted those subjects demonstrating greater fencing proficiency also to condition themselves better to tolerate fatigue even if they were extended to near maximum physical and mental limits.

The positive associations obtained for riding and shooting performances for both the accumulative and individual event effects implied that those subjects scoring high in these events exhibited greater fatigue than their low scoring counterparts. It appeared that in these events the high scoring competitor was extending himself to near maximum psychosomatic limits. The results of the comparison of the accumulative fatigue effect and total pentathlon performance also demonstrated the close relationship between superior over-all performance and the willingness of a competitor to consistently work to fatigue.

High positive coefficients were obtained for all five conditions when individual and accumulative event performance was compared with base-line test score $(r_{1.3})$. These data served to validate the fatigue test and accentuated the fatigue predictive powers of the base-line test. Initial success on the test (base-line score) was dependent on a high degree of neuromuscular coordination. Similarly, a high level of performance in each pentathlon event hinged on the vital contribution of superior neuromuscular skill, particularly in the riding, fencing and shooting events. The significant relationships which existed between the neuromuscular requirements of the pentathlon events and similar demands of the fatigue test further substantiated the selection of a composite psychotechnical skill test to evaluate fatigue.

Correlations obtained after analyzing the relationship between deterioration of post-event performance from base-line test score and base-line test score by itself $(r_{2.3})$ paralleled the findings acquired from the computation of $(r_{1.2})$. Only one coefficient was reported for each of the five conditions since this relationship considered both individual and accumulative effects of post-event fatigue testing. This correlation also demonstrated the significance of the base-line score as a variable for predicting acute fatigue. Those subjects recording a poor base-line test score tended to demonstrate less changes in the five subsequent post-event fatigue tests than high base-line test scorers. In contrast, the significant negative correlation of -.77 for fencing indicated that those subjects achieving better base-line test performances tended to endure the fence with less post-event fatigue. The fencing seemed to extract more, physically and mentally, from the poor base-line scorer. The positive correlation results were difficult to interpret, but seemed to point out that the better base-line scorers, who as previously shown had achieved the highest event scores $(r_{1.3})$, extended themselves more readily to fatigue limits.

The results of the partial correlation gave evidence to support the fact that a progressing interrelationship occurred among the three variables as the program of competitive events moved to its conclusion. The analysis of $(r_{1.2.3})$ considered how event performance and change in post-event fatigue test score from base-line score was related to base-line score by itself. Since base-line score appeared to be a significant indicator of fatigue tolerance [see results of

($r_{1.3}$) and ($r_{2.3}$)], a partial correlation which held to base-line score constant was utilized to determine the gravity of previous correlation results involving base-line score as a variable. In other words, the partial correlation adjusted the three variables in such a manner so that this comparison was carried out as if all subjects had recorded the same base-line fatigue test score. In addition, this partial correlation adjusted the negativeness of the fencing coefficient to a positive variable consistent with the other correlations. The correlation data disclosed that initially the base-line test score could, by itself, be utilized to predict acute fatigue. That is, those subjects recording better base-line scores appeared to exhibit greater fatigue tolerance. However, as the competition neared its conclusion, the interrelationship among the three variables was more pronounced. The significant partial coefficient demonstrated that event performance and deterioration of post-event test score from base-line score were also vital in the evaluation of acute fatigue.

The effect of individual event activity on post-event fatigue test performance was difficult to assess. Correlations obtained for ($r_{1.2}$) and ($r_{1.3}$) are some-what deceiving since fatigue test data for all events, riding the only exception, were most certainly masked by the physical and mental requirements of the previous event or events.

Subjective analysis during and following post-event fatigue tests revealed a combination of physical and emotional disturbances and these occurred in greater number and were more exaggerated following fencing. The subjects complained of tiredness and soreness in muscles directly associated with specific muscular performance during the fatigue tests and found it difficult to maintain suitable posture. Frustration and the lack of concentration were also noted. Bartlett[7] and Drew[13] recorded similar subjective data at the onset of what they defined as skill fatigue. They mentioned in their studies that the subject's timing was affected, he ignored some elements of the task, and began to complain of aches and pains. These abnormalities were also noted in this research and certainly must be considered as reflections on the subjects' poor post-event response to the secondary task. Inattentiveness toward the fringe elements of this test was vital in an accurate appraisal of acute fatigue and further substantiated the selection of a dual-task fatigue test.

Motivation, always a problem to consider in behavioral research, assumes an important role in a valid and reliable appraisal of acute fatigue. The subjects in this study, without exception, looked upon each fatigue test as a challenge and a competitive spirit, particularly among fellow team members, was evident throughout the testing. The competition was welcomed by this worker as a means to enhance the validity of the fatigue test. Since deterioration of skill occurred under conditions where subjects were highly motivated, then one may assume that fatigue can be more accurately assessed under these condi-tions. In situations where motivation is definitely lacking, fatigue would be difficult to evaluate since fatigue and lack of interest would be similarly reflected in test performance.

Conclusions

The variableness of each pentathlon event with its inherent physical and mental demands most certainly has contributed to the complexity of this in-vestigation. The subjects' fatigue reactions to fencing were most interesting. According to pentathlon coaches and competitors represented at these cham-pionships, fencing is the single most important event in the pentathlon program. Insurance of success requires not only the highest level of neuromuscular coordination and endurance among the five events, but excellence is achieved primarily from continuous and arduous practice. In contrast, most of the competitors rarely practice riding, devote only limited attention to shooting skill improvement, and although they spend many hours swimming and running, these practice periods contribute primarily to the development of stamina. It was therefore not surprising, after examining the correlation data and noting the psychosomatic requirements of the specific events, to consider the post-fence fatigue test results to be the most vital in their relationship to acute fatigue.

The correlation data for $(r_{1.2})$, with the exception of the results pertaining to fencing, indicated that those subjects achieving better event performance were more fatigued than the low event scorers. A predominance of skill, conditioning to prevent fatigue, and the ability to pace oneself (conserving energy for later bouts) were suggested as possible explanations of the high negative correlation obtained for fencing. After making specific inquiries it was interesting to note that those competitors exhibiting less fatigue after fencing had trained more specifically for this event than the more fatigued fencers. That is, their training sessions consisted of many individual one-touch bouts over long duration and thus these subjects were better prepared to endure the long day of fencing competition. Post-fencing fatigue test results appeared to be the most decisive indicators of accumulative acute fatigue tolerance. Those competitors exhibiting less fatigue following fencing not only showed less total accumulative fatigue as indicated by post-event fatigue tests following swimming (final event for this research), but were also to become the leaders in the pentathlon competition. The final individual competitive results of the pentathlon competition (after five events) showed that the highest scorers were those who had survived the fence with less fatigue.

The significant relationship between event performance and base-line event score $(r_{1.3})$ served to validate the test. The review of literature and unpublished data by C. Cameron and B. Tritt, Australian Sports Medicine Federation, further substantiated the selection of a composite psychotechnical test to evaluate acute fatigue.

A comparison of acute fatigue and base-line test score $(r_{2.3})$ revealed that those subjects recording high base-line test scores extended themselves to fatigue limits for all events except fencing, an event they were found to better endure than the low base-line scorers.

The partial correlation demonstrated a progressing significant interrelationship among the three variables as the competition drew to its conclusion.

Since correlations are interpreted as only associations, and not causes, no causative factors pertaining to the data may be included as part of this research. Each comparison must be accepted as an autonomous statistical analysis and with the exception of the partial correlation, no interrelationships among the three variables can be inferred.

The complex nature of fatigue renders it an elusive variable to measure. The many possible combinations of psychosomatic responses and their interrelationships, which might influence a competitor's level of performance, particularly under highly competitive conditions, do not permit an evaluation of the proportional contribution of specific physiological and/or psychological factors in this study of fatigue. The post-event fatigue test was designed to appraise any deterioration of performance from the normal or base-line test and then any negative deviation from the norm was defined as accumulative acute fatigue. Since the participant's physical energy and mental concentration were continuously directed towards the realization of maximum neuromuscular efforts for five consecutive days, it may be assumed that any progressive negative deviation noted in post-event fatigue tests occurred as a direct result of engagement in pentathlon events.

References

1. Adamson G. L. Fatigue. *J. Avi. Med.*, 23, 584-588, 1952.
2. Alderman R. B. Influence of local fatigue on speed and accuracy in motor learning. *Res. Quarterly*, 36, 131-140, 1965.
3. Bartlett F. C. Fatigue following highly skilled work. *Proc. roy. Soc. B.*, 131, 247-254, 1943.
4. Bartlett F. C. The bearing of experimental psychology upon skilled performance. *Brit. J. Indust. Med.*, 8, 209-217, 1951.
5. Bartlett F. C. Fatigue. *Lancet*, 262, 268, 1952.
6. Bartlett F. C. The effects of flying upon human performance. L'Annese Psychologique Cinquatienne Anse, Volume Jubilaine. Presses Universitaires de France, in honor of Penri Pieron, 1953.
7. Bartlett F. C. Psychological criteria of fatigue. In Symposium on Fatigue (Edited by W. F. Floyd and A. T. Welford). London: H. K. Lewis, 1953, pp. 1-5.
8. Berger, Curt and Mahnehe Axel. Fatigue in two simple visual tasks. *Amer. J. Psych.*, 67 (3), 509-512, 1954.
9. Broadbent D. E. Neglect of the surroundings in relation to fatigue decrements in output. In Symposium on Fatigue (Edited by W. F. Floyd and A. T. Welford). London: H. K. Lewis, 1953, pp. 173-178.
10. Brouha, Lucien. Fatigue-measurement and reduction. *Indust. Med. and Surgery*, 22, 547-554, 1953.
11. Crawford A. Fatigue and driving. *Ergonomics*, 4, 143-154, 1961.
12. Davis I. H. Symposium on fatigue. *Psychosom. Med.*, 5, 152-154, 1943.
13. Drew G. C. An experimental study of mental fatigue. Air Ministry, F.P.R.C. Report no. 227, 1940.
14. Editor. Fatigue. *Brit. Med. J.*, 1, 4702, 805-807, 1952.
15. Fritze C. and Simonson E. A. A new electronic apparatus for the measurement of the fusion frequency of flicker. *Sci.*, 113, 547, 1951.
16. Grandjean E., Egli R., Diday F., Block W. and Gfeller H. Die Versohmelzungsfrequenz intermittierender Lichtreize als Ermüdungsmass. *Helv. Physiol. et Pharmac. Acta* (Basel), 11, 4355-4360, 1963.
17. Graybill A, Lilienthal J. L. and Horwitz D. Flicker fusion tests as a measure of fatigue in aviators. *J. Avi. Med.*, 14, 356-359, 1943.
18. Griffith C. R. Study of exercise in its relation to learning. *Lit. Digest*, 102, 20, 1929.
19. Henley W. E. Fatigue. *New Zealand Med. J.*, 50, 277, 212-221, 1951.
20. Jones B. F. *et al.*, 1947. Fatigue and hours of service of interstate truck drivers. Quoted in R. A. McFarland.
    Human factors in highway transport safety. *Med.*, 24, 143-145, 1952.
    Boston, Mass., U.S.A.: Harvard School of Public Health, 1954.
21. Mackworth N. H. Researches in the measurement of human performance. Med. Res. Coun. Lond., Spec. Rep. No. 268 (H.M.S.O.).
22. Monjauze R., Plas F., Verdeaux G., Bourdinand J., Verdeaux J., Missenard A. and LeFebre R. Clinical research on the subject of a test on aviators fatigue. *J. Avi. Med.*, 24, 143-145, 1952.
23. McFarland R. A. and Moseley A. L. Human factors in highway transport safety. Harvard School of Public Health, Boston, Mass., U.S.A., 1954.
24. McGrath S. D., Wittkower E. D. and Cleghorn R. A. Some observations on aircrew fatigue in the R.C.A.F. Tokyo Airlift. *J. Avi. Med.*, 25, 23-27, 1954.
25. Merton P. A. Problems of muscular fatigue. *Brit. Med. Bull.*, 12 (3) 1956.
26. Pierson W. R. and Rasch P. J. The determination of a representative score for reaction and movement time. *Percept. Mot. Skills*, 9, 107, 1959.
27. Pierson W. R. Fatigue, work decrement, and endurance in a simple repetitive task. *Brit. J. Med. Psych.*, 36, 279, 1963.
28. Pierson W. R. and Lockhart A. Fatigue, work decrement, and endurance of women in a simple repetitive task. *Aerospace Med.*, 35, 724-725, 1964.
29. Schnore M. M. Individual patterns of physiological activity as a function of task differences and degree of arousal. *J. Exp. Psychol.*, 58, 117-128, 1959.

30. Schwab Robert S. and Delorme Thomas. Psychiatric findings in fatigue. *Amer. J. Psychiat.*, 109, 621-625, 1953.
31. Simonson E. and Enzer N. State of motor centers in circulatory insufficiency. *Arch. Int. Med.*, 68, 498, 1941.
32. Suzuki K. Professional differences of fatigue as revealed by the method of electrical flicker. *The Tohoku J. Exper. Med.*, 52, 1-7, 1950.
33. Teichner W. H. Recent studies of simple reaction time. *Psych. Bull.*, 51, 128, 1954.
34. Welford A. T. Psychological and physiological aspects of fatigue. *Nature*, 169, 4305, 728-729, 1952.

Effects of Limited Sleep Deprivation on Performance of Selected Motor Tasks*

GEORGE J. HOLLAND

IT is conceivable that another type of fatigue associated with learner performance can be attributed to a lack of sleep. Will sleep deprivation hinder or not influence the performance of motor skills? Will different kinds of tasks be affected in dissimilar ways? Questions like these are raised and answered by Holland in an interestingly designed project. Unfortunately, it appears by Holland's discussion (from the data analyzed and the methods by which they were collected) that more questions may be provoked than solved. State of training, for example, would appear to be an important variable in expecting resistance to the possible handicap of sleep loss. Nonetheless, the results are suggestive for the instructor as well as the researcher wishing to do follow-up work in this area.

Teachers, coaches, military trainers, industrial psychologists, and others concerned with human efficiency have traditionally emphasized the relationship between a normal night's sleep and the quality of ensuing human performance. Studies of prolonged sleep deprivation have demonstrated that man can tolerate as much as two weeks' sleep deprivation or longer before profound psychological disturbances occur. Such periods of sleeplessness also result in gross deterioration of several kinds of human performance.[3] There is, however, only limited substantive evidence to support the popular belief that a more limited level of sleep deprivation necessarily results in deteriorated human motor performance. In most experimental studies the point of concern has been the effect of sleep deprivation on cognitive performance.[6,8,9,10,11,12,15] Very few studies relate sleep loss directly to motor performance, and the findings of those studies are quite limited, as well as contradictory. Brožek and others[4] reported a significant decrease in the accuracy of pipe ball catching and pattern tracing, as well as reaction time following 62 hr. of sleep deprivation. They reported that the speed of plate tapping and pattern tracing, as

* From the *Research Quarterly*, 1968, *39*, 285-294. Reprinted with permission of the author and the American Association for Health, Physical Education, and Recreation.

well as grip and back strength, were not significantly affected by the same stress. Wilkinson[13] found that after only 32 hr. of sleep deprivation there was a significant decrease in speed and increase in errors on a 30-min. choice serial reaction test. Apparently no investigations have been concerned with the effects of sleeplessness on the ability of subjects to sustain heavy work loads. In view of the fact that students in physical education classes and athletes competing away from home often have less than a normal night's sleep it seems imperative to develop an experimental basis from which some implications for performance could be drawn.

Purpose

This study was conducted to determine the effects of one night's sleep deprivation on the subsequent performance of two short motor tasks (jumping and manipulation) as well as on work performance of a more extended nature on a bicycle ergometer.

Procedures

Twenty-four male college students from San Fernando Valley State College served as volunteer subjects in the study. The subjects took part in a 4-week training program prior to the sleep deprivation stress. At each tri-weekly test session the subjects were given three trials each on an arm-hand manipulation test and a patterned jump test. These tests were followed by a bout of work on the bicycle ergometer. The bicycle work load was increased progressively in intensity for the first 3 weeks. Only during the last week were the subjects given an "exhausting" bicycle work performance test. On Friday of the last week, the subjects reported to a special laboratory where they were closely supervised during one night's sleep deprivation and retested the next day on the jump and manipulation tasks, as well as on the bicycle work performance test. During the night's sleep deprivation, the subjects participated in a rotating schedule of light recreational activities (reading, television, card playing, checkers, table tennis, etc.) in order to facilitate the maintenance of a wakeful state. Well balanced meals were served at the normal eating times.

Jump Test. The apparatus for the jumping task employed in this study was designed and constructed by personnel of the San Fernando Valley State College Human Performance Laboratory and is described in complete technical detail by Benson.[2] The task involved a series of hopping and stepping movements through a set pattern designated by painted footprints. The stations to be traversed with the left foot were colored blue and the ones for the right foot yellow. The subjects attempted to move through the pattern of 32 footprints, which were laid out on an 8' × 8' plywood square, as quickly and as accurately as possible. Speed and error were measured electronically. Benson[2] reported the following ranges of reliability for this test: speed .94 to .96, accuracy .84 to 88.

Manipulation Test. The apparatus for the manipulation task employed in this study was patterned after and designed to scale (2½" = 12") from the jump test. The task involved moving a configured ink marking stylus in each hand through a set pattern designated by colored arrows. The subject was instructed that the left stylus had to traverse all the stations indicated by the blue arrows and the right stylus followed the yellow arrows. The styluses were configured to the same pattern as the stylus holes, so as the subject moved from one station to the next it was necessary to turn the stylus very precisely to permit entry into the stylus hole and make a mark on the score sheet below. A conventional stop watch was used to increase the time component. The subject was instructed to move through the pattern of 32 stations as quickly and as accurately as possible.

Bicycle Work Performance Test.   This test utilized a Monark bicycle ergo-meter. According to the technique of Åstrand,[1] rate was kept relatively con-stant and resistance was gradually increased. The work time, rate, and resis-tance factors were used to compute work performance in kilopondmeters (kpm). Heart rate was monitored before and during the bicycle work per-formance test by means of a Sanborn Viso Cardiette #100 electrocardiogram (V-III leads) attached to a Cramer electrocardiogram counter.

The bicycle work load was very light during the first week (600 kpm/min.) and was gradually increased in intensity through the third week (1050 kpm/min.). Beginning on Monday of the last week of testing the subjects were given standardized instructions indicating that they should go "all out" and continue to pedal as long as they possibly could while the resistance factor was increased each minute (1 kpm/min. for the first 4 min., and ½ kpm./min. thereafter). When the subject was unable to maintain the rate the test ended and the total kpm were calculated. This measure constituted the bicycle work performance test which was administered during the last week both before and after sleep deprivation.

Results

Reliability.   The range of reliability for the jump test was .77 to .92, and .84 to .94 for the manipulation test. The reliability value for the bicycle test was based upon comparison of Monday and Wednesday's pre-sleep-loss work performance during the last week.

Jump and Manipulation.   With the exception of manipulation accuracy, which tended to be somewhat erratic, there was continuous improvement of performance throughout the 4-week training period. Following the intervention of the sleep loss stress, improvement was virtually unaffected.

A comparison of the mean pre-sleep-deprivation performances (Wednesday of last week) with the mean post-sleep-deprivation performances (Saturday of last week) revealed that none of the mean improvements were statistically significant, with the exception of manipulation time (significant at the .05 level).

Bicycle Work Performance.   Work performance, as measured by the bicycle ergometer in this study, was rather markedly affected by one night's sleep deprivation. Only six subjects improved their performance following the sleep deprivation; for only one of them was the gain a very substantial one. The mean decrement in post-sleep-loss performance was −572.2 kpm, which was statistically significant ($p < .05$).

There was an obvious and consistent drop in working heart rate following sleeplessness. This decrease was statistically significant, however, at only two of the five work loads. It should be noted that post-sleep-loss resting heart rate also decreased significantly. Thus, it is possible that the changes in working heart rate were only phenomenal reflection of a post-sleep-loss bradycardia. When correction is made for the difference in resting rates, the pre- and post-sleep-loss working heart rates were practically parallel. No precedent could be found in the physiology of sleep literature to explain the basis for the observed post-sleep-loss bradycardial adaptation. It seems logical to suggest some sympathetic depression mechanism, but such a response to the stress of sleep deprivation is not substantiated by the limited data of Hasselman and others[7] which showed that the customary rise of urinary adrenaline and noradrenaline caused by very light muscle activity was enormously enhanced by sleeplessness.

Discussion

The results of this study clearly indicate that one night's sleep deprivation had no significant deleterious effect on the performance of the jump and manipulation tasks. In fact, for both tasks there was a slight improvement in post-sleep-deprivation performance. This improvement was observable in both the speed and accuracy dimensions of the two tests. The performance curves showed that the subject's post-sleep-deprivation improvement was comparable to the improvement demonstrated throughout the 4-week training period.

In no previous sleep deprivation studies were tasks similar to the jump and manipulation tasks in this study utilized. Other studies have demonstrated that the performance of pipe ball catching, pattern tracing, choice reaction, and reaction time were significantly altered by comparable levels of sleep loss.[4,13,14]

The failure to find significant changes in jump and manipulation performance in this study may be attributed to several variables. First, in no previous studies was a training program prior to sleep deprivation employed; performance was measured only before and after the sleep stress. Secondly, there is some evidence that decrement in performances following sleep deprivation is a function both of the complexity of the tasks involved and the time required to complete the task.[5] Thus, the tasks required in the present study may have been too discrete and short-term in nature to tax the vigilance of the sleep-deprived subjects. Also the variability of the jump and manipulation learning curves were such that the day-to-day performances of these tasks were not highly reliable. Therefore the results of only one day's testing following sleep deprivation may not have been sufficient to rigorously test the hypothesis. There is also the possibility that the duration of the sleep loss stress in this study was not great enough to affect the kinds of motor performance involved. In most studies in which a significant change in cognitive performance was demonstrated a minimum of 72 hr. sleep deprivation was employed.[6,8,15] It seems appropriate then that some future study in this area should deal with more complex motor tasks as well as a longer sleep deprivation stress.

It appears that this study represents a pioneer attempt to assess the effects of sleep deprivation on work performance. Because of this, all of the interpretations of this finding must denote conjecture. It is possible that the deleterious change in work performance following sleep deprivation was due more to a psychological rather than a physiological efficiency change. If, as Carmichael[5] has suggested, post-sleep-deprivation performance is partially a function of the complexity of the task and the time required to complete it, then both of these could have played a significant role in the work performance phase of the present study. The work test in this investigation required that the subject constantly watch the speedometer needle. If the needle dropped twice below 20 kpm/hr. the test was ended. Thus, it is conceivable that the work performance finding in this study reflected post-sleep-deprivation changes in vigilance or arousal rather than physiological fatigue. This hypothesis is given further support by the demonstration in this study that working heart rate was relatively unaffected by the sleep loss stress (when compensation was made for the differences in resting rates). If one assumes that working heart rate is a valid measure of physiological work efficiency, then it appears that other factors were responsible for the post-sleep-deprivation decrement. Until, however, further exploration is made regarding the correlation between post-sleep-loss work performance and changing cardiorespiratory functions (e.g., oxygen uptake) it is impossible to describe a work decrement as being predominantly physiological or psychological in origin.

Summary of Major Findings

The major findings of this study are summarized as follows:

1. One night's sleep deprivation had no significant effect upon the speed or accuracy with which the jump and manipulation tasks were performed.

2. Work performance, as measured in this study by the bicycle work performance test, showed a significant decrement ($p < .05$) following the sleep deprivation stress. The mean decrement in performance was 572.2 kpm and the range in decrement was from 30 kpm to 4370 kpm.

3. There was a significant decrease in resting heart rate following sleep deprivation. Working heart rate (i.e., the increase over resting rate) was not significantly altered by the experimentally imposed sleeplessness.

Conclusion

The loss of a single night's sleep has no detrimental effect on the performance of motor tasks which are discrete and short-term in nature, but detrimental effects result from performance which is arduous and long-term in nature.

References

1. Åstrand, P.-O. *Work tests with the bicycle ergometer.* Varbarg (Sweden): Monark Offset, 1954.

2. Benson, David. *The effects of fatigue on motor learning.* Unpublished doctoral dissertation, University of Southern California, 1965.

3. Kleitman, Nathaniel. *Sleep and wakefulness.* Chicago: University of Chicago Press, 1963.

4. Brozek, J., and Taylor, H. J. Tests of motor functions in investigations on fitness. *Amer. j. psychol.* 67:590-611, 1954.

5. Carmichael, L.; Kennedy, J. L.; and Mead, L. C. Some recent approaches to the experimental study of human fatigue. *Nat. acad. sci. proceedings,* 35:691-96, 1949.

6. Goodnow, J.; Rubenstein, J.; and Shanks, B. The role of past events in problem solving. *J. exp. psychol.* 58:456-61, 1959.

7. Hasselman, M.; Schaff, G.; and Metz, B. Influences respective en travail, de la temperature ambiante, et la privation du sommeil sur l'excretion urinaire chez l'homme normal. *C. R. soc. biol.* (Paris) 154:197, 1960.

8. Loveland, N. T., and Williams, L. Adding, sleep loss, and body temperature. *Percept. mot. skills* 16:923-29, 1963.

9. Patrick, G., and Gilbert, J. A. On the effects of loss of sleep. *Psychol. rev.* 3:469-83, 1896.

10. Tufts College. *Effects of sleep deprivation upon performance.* N.D.R.C. Contract OE Mar 581, Rep. No. 4, 1942.

11. Weiskotten, T. F., and Ferguson, J. E. A further study of the effects of loss of sleep. *J. exp. psychol.* 13:247-66, 1930.

12. Wilkinson, R. T. The effects of sleep loss on performance. *Med. res. council* (A.P.R.U. Res. Rep. No. 323), 1958.

13. ———. Interaction of noise with knowledge of results and sleep deprivation. *J. exp. psychol.* 66:332-37, 1963.

14. ———. After effect of sleep deprivation. *J. exp. psychol.* 66:439-42, 1963.

15. Williams, H. L., and Goodnow, J. J. Impaired performance with acute sleep loss. *Psychol. monogr.* 73: No. 14 (whole number 484), 1959.

Effect of Sensory Deprivation on Some Perceptual and Motor Skills*

JACK A. VERNON, THOMAS E. McGILL, WALTER L. GULICK, AND DOUGLAS K. CANDLAND

MAN requires sensory stimulation to which to respond. Without it, in time, among other possibilities, his sense organs could tend to demonstrate poorer sensitivity, body control over motor movements could disintegrate, and perceptual distortions could occur. Confined bed rest and its immediate and later effects on skilled performance are real concerns of athletes, performers, and various occupational specialists. In the reading that follows, sense deprivation is induced under extremely controlled experimental conditions. Performance on various tasks as a result of different periods of sense deprivation is examined. The temporary nature of sensory deprivation effects, at least as determined under the limitations of the study, is an indication of why such a condition is referred to as a performance variable.

Interest in the effects of isolation upon human behavior[1,2,3] has prompted at Princeton a series of investigations[4,5,6] one of which the present paper reports. The conditions of isolation employed in our studies so reduced the sensory stimulation available to the individual as to cause us to refer to the confinement as Sensory Deprivation (S.D.). Obviously, S.D. did not produce a total deprivation of sensory stimulation but, as shall be seen, it did effect a drastic reduction in the sensory input.

Method

Subjects. Volunteer Ss were male graduate students between the ages of 20 and 28 yr. Each passed a physical examination administered by the University Medical Staff. For each day of confinement there was a payment of $20.00. There were nine experimental Ss and nine controls. Control Ss were paid $5.00 for each of the three test sessions. Control Ss were not unwilling to enter the S.D. condition but were unable to do so because of the amount of time required for confinement. We requested all confined Ss to make available to us a block of six days of which we would take whatever amount we needed. We adopted this procedure because we considered it desirable that a confined S not know exactly how long he was to be in S.D. Some volunteers could not take six days from their normal school schedule so we used them in one of the control subgroups. It seems important to make this point so that the reader will not misunderstand and believe that the control Ss were merely individuals who were unwilling to enter the S.D. condition due to fear of confinement or the like.

Procedure. Ss were confined in a dark, light-proof, sound-proof (80 db loss) "floating chamber" which measured 15' × 9'. The confinement cell

* From *Perceptual and Motor Skills*, 1959, 9, 91-97. Reprinted with permission of the authors and publisher.

(4' × 9') at one end of the floating chamber contained a bed, a portable ice box, two relief bottles, a panic button, and a large tray of sodium hydroxide placed beneath the bed to absorb S's accumulated CO_2. Ss were allowed access to a chemical toilet located outside the confinement cell but within the floating chamber. The confined individual wore a gauntlet-type glove which was intended to restrict movements and to remind Ss that they were to make as little noise as comfortably possible. The noise of their own breathing and bodily movements was not shut out by ear plugs for the simple reason that the "sea-shell" effect produced by the plugs provided greater auditory stimulation.

Each individual was monitored throughout his confinement by a concealed inter-communication system which revealed almost perfect adherence to the instructions against making noise.

Each of the five tests, to be described later, was administered three times to all 18 Ss. The first testing (A) was prior to confinement, the second testing (B) was upon release from confinement, and the third testing (C) was 24 hr. after release from confinement. Test A provided a "normal" measure, Test B provided an opportunity for the effects of S.D., if any, to be demonstrated, and Test C provided a measure of the relative persistence of any S.D. effects. Since each test was given three times, a change in results at B or C could reflect either the effects of S.D. or a practice effect or both. This dilemma was resolved by comparing the data for the confined group with those of the control group. The comparison was made more meaningful by matching the control Ss and confined Ss. The basis for the matching was the performance at Test A for all five tests. Some 16 individuals were tested before a matching control group of 9 Ss could be selected. The significance of any difference at Test B between confined and control groups was evaluated by a Wilcoxon test,[7] and $p < .05$ was accepted as significant.

The periods of confinement were 24, 48, and 72 hr., hence the nine experimental Ss were assigned to three subgroups of three Ss each. This arrangement made the time between Test A and Test B 24 hr. for one subgroup, 48 hr. for another subgroup, and 72 hr. for the remaining subgroup. The same time lapses between Tests A and B were arranged for the comparable control subgroups.

Tests. The five tests which were administered are fairly well known so only a brief description of them will be given. They were (a) color perception, (b) depth perception, (c) pursuit rotor, (d) mirror drawing, and (e) rail walking.

(a) *Color perception* was tested with the Dvorine Color Test, Plates I through XX. Each plate was presented for 3 sec. under normal illumination. The order of presentation of the plates was randomized.

(b) *Depth perception* was tested with the Howard-Dohlman apparatus. Each test of depth perception was the mean of six binocular trials where half of the trials started with the variable stimulus behind the standard and the other half with it in front. Ss were 20' distant from the apparatus. A head holder prevented the utilization of head movements. Between trials Ss were required to drop the strings to the floor while E, blocking S's view, set the stimuli for the next trial.

(c) *Pursuit rotor* performance was measured by the amount of time a stylus (21 cm. long) was held in contact with a rotating disc (1 cm. in diameter) when the disc rotated at 44 rpm in a circle 13 cm. in diameter. The test lasted 60 sec. and the performance measure was the total time on target which was measured automatically. The stylus and the disc were electrically connected so that, when they contacted, the circuit to an electrical clock was completed and the clock was activated. The clock ran only when contact was maintained, thus cumulating time on target. The scoring procedure was explained to *S*.

(d) *Mirror drawing* performance was tested utilizing the standard concentric six-pointed star where the separation between lines was ¼″ and the total length of path to be traced was 22½″. *S*s were required to trace a path between the pattern lines with a pencil with reference to nothing but the mirror image of the star pattern. The performance measures were the amount of time required to complete the task and the number of errors committed. An error was considered to be any crossing of the lines of the pattern outline. This procedure was carefully explained to each *S* before testing.

(e) *Rail walking* performance was an attempt to get at a more gross motor ability, a type of activity which S.D. *S*s had little opportunity to exercise. The test was of *S*'s ability to walk upon the narrow edge of a 2″ × 4″ U-shaped rail which was 18′ in length. The performance measure was the total time required by *S* to successfully negotiate the railing without falling off. If *S* fell or stepped off the rail he was required to return to the starting point again. The time recorded was the total time spent by *S* on the rail; time required to return to the start after a fall was not counted. The scoring procedure was carefully explained to *S*.

Results

In evaluating the results the reader is urged to be cautious because the *N*s are small and because of the variability of performance measures for some tasks.

Table 1 presents the results of the color perception tests. The data presented are the changes in the number of correct identifications of the Dvorine Color Plates from Test A to Test B expressed as percent. It is obvious that the control subgroups remained unchanged from Test A to Test B in their ability to perceive color regardless of whether the tests were separated by 24, 48, or 72 hr. The S.D. subgroups, on the other hand, showed a loss in color perception from Test A to Test B. When the two tests were separated by 48 or 72 hr. of S.D., the change in color perception was significantly greater than that of the comparable subgroup. A statistically significant comparison between subgroups is indicated by italic numerals for the two subgroups being compared. Thus in Table 1 the performance of the 24-hr. S.D. subgroup is not significantly different from that of the 24-hr. control subgroup. The 48-hr. S.D. subgroup is significantly poorer than the 48-hr. control subgroup as is true also for the two 72-hr. subgroups.

The color perception test was not conducted until *S* had been out of confinement for a half hour so that he was normally light adapted. Examination of the color plates missed at Test B showed that no particular color was con-

TABLE 1

PERCENT CHANGE IN COLOR PERCEPTION FROM TEST A TO TEST B

Group	Hours between Tests A and B		
	24	48	72
Control	0.0	*0.0**	*1.0*
Confined	−3.3	*−13.3*	*−10.0*

* Significant statistical comparisons shown in italics are between control and confined groups within a given period between Tests A and B.

sistently missed and that the failures occurred primarily for the desaturated hues.

The data for Test C are not presented; however, they reveal that the losses shown by the S.D. subgroups no longer obtain 24 hr. after release from confinement. Test C data are not presented in tabular form for any of the tasks for the simple reason that in all cases they can be easily verbalized and because their inclusion would greatly complicate the tables.

The results of the depth perception tests are presented below in Table 2. The data of Table 2 are the changes in mm. from Test A to Test B. They can be explained by considering the case of the 24-hr. control group. The entry, + 7.9 mm., means that at Test B the average error was 7.9 mm. less than that at Test A; therefore, in Table 2 a plus sign indicates improvement at Test B over Test A. Note, in the case of the control subgroups, as the time increased between Test A and Test B, that the practice effect steadily decreased, becoming negative at 72 hr.

Performance of the confined subgroups shows no consistent trend except that the greatest loss occurs for the shortest period of confinement. These data *are not* statistically significant due to the large individual variation. The data for depth perception are presented primarily to suggest one kind of performance upon which S.D. appears to have no significant effect. In fact the data would not have been worth including here were it not for the large loss in performance for the 24-hr. S.D. subgroup.

The results for the rotary pursuit tests presented in Table 3 are increases in the amount of time on target at Test B in comparison with Test A. For example, the 24-hr. control subgroup was on target at Test B on the average 1.5 sec. longer than at Test A. Note the rather unusual practice effect displayed by the control subgroups, that is, as the interval between Tests A and B increased, improvement is observed. The S.D. subgroups confined for either 24 or 72 hr. also show an improvement similar to that shown by the comparable control subgroup. The 48-hr. confinement subgroup, however, not only fails to improve at Test B but actually loses slightly in performance level. The difference between the performance of two 48-hr. subgroups is statistically significant.

TABLE 2

CHANGE IN DEPTH PERCEPTION PERFORMANCE (MM.) FROM TEST A TO TEST B

	Hours between Tests A and B		
Group	24	48	72
Control	+ 7.9	+1.5	−3.1
Confined	−12.9	+1.4	−1.6

TABLE 3

ROTARY PURSUIT IMPROVEMENT (SEC.) FROM TEST A TO TEST B

	Hours between Tests A and B		
Group	24	48	72
Control	1.5	4.3	7.4
Confined	2.4	−0.3	6.0

The data for Test C reveal that the losses suffered by the 48-hr. confinement subgroups were substantially recovered and the other subgroups benefited very little by the additional practice provided by Test C.

With regard to the performance of the 48-hr. confinement subgroup, it is of interest that most S.D. *S*s report that subjectively the "worst" part of a long confinement is somewhere around 48 hr. This duration of confinement also seems critical for mirror tracing performance.

Performance on the mirror tracing task is presented in Tables 4 and 5. Table 4 gives the time data in terms of the percentage of improvement at Test B over Test A. For example, the 24-hr. control subgroup performed at Test B 55 percent faster on the average than at Test A. Note that *all* subgroups improve in time at Test B over Test A; however, the improvement of the 48-hr. confinement subgroup is so slight as to be significantly less than that of the comparable control subgroup, or, for that matter, for any of the other subgroups.

Why the 48-hr. confinement subgroup fails to improve much as indicated by the time scores is partially explained by the error data in Table 5. These data are presented in the same manner as in Table 4 so that, for example, the 24-hr. control subgroup shows 78 percent fewer errors on Test B than on Test A. Once again note that all subgroups show a reduction in errors for Test B over Test A. The interesting point is that the subgroups confined for 24 and 72 hr. significantly fail to improve as much as their comparable control subgroups. The 48-hr. confinement subgroup reduces its errors as much as the control groups. In fact, it seems to improve more than its comparable control subgroup, which for some unexplained reason performs worse, but not statistically significantly worse, than the other two control subgroups. Thus, considering Tables 4 and 5 together, it appears that the 48-hr. confinement subgroup has sacrificed improvement in time in order to improve accuracy and eliminate errors.

Once again the results at Test C reveal the disappearance of previous differences between the various subgroups.

TABLE 4

PERCENT IMPROVEMENT IN TIME (SEC.) REQUIRED FOR MIRROR TRACING FROM TEST A TO TEST B

	Hours between Tests A and B		
Group	24	48	72
Control	55	49	50
Confined	51	17	58

TABLE 5

IMPROVEMENT IN ERRORS (%) IN MIRROR TRACING FROM TEST A TO TEST B

	Hours between Tests A and B		
Group	24	48	72
Control	78	57	88
Confined	43	76	30

TABLE 6
CHANGE IN TIME (%) REQUIRED FOR RAIL WALKING FROM TEST A TO TEST B

| | Hours between Tests A and B | | |
Group	24	48	72
Control	−36	13	*46*
Confined	−21	−56	*−50*

Performance for the rail walking tests was measured in time required to complete the task, and in Table 6 the performance at Test B is compared with that at Test A in terms of percent. For example, the 24-hr. control subgroup required 36 percent more time for Test B than for Test A, or in other words a loss of −36 percent. The 24-hr. confined subgroup shows about the same results, but with that, similarities in Table 6 cease. Note that the 48- and 72-hr. control subgroups show progressive improvement while the 48- and 72-hr. S.D. subgroups show losses. The difference between the two 72-hr. subgroups is statistically significant. The loss, however, was not permanent as indicated by the recoveries made at Test C.

Summary

The effect of Sensory Deprivation (S.D.) lasting 24, 48, 72 hr. was measured for several perceptual and motor skills. It was found that color perception was adversely affected especially when confinement extended to 48 and 72 hr. There was no significant effect of S.D. upon depth perception, probably because of the large individual variations in performance. Rotary pursuit ability was significantly adversely affected by S.D. only when confinement lasted 48 hr. A similar finding resulted for the time required to perform a standard mirror tracing task. However, the errors made on the mirror tracing task were fewer after 48 hr. of confinement and significantly increased after 24 and 72 hr. of confinement. Gross motor behavior as measured by a rail walking task was adversely affected by S.D., especially after 72 hr. of confinement. All S.D. effects were somewhat temporary in nature since tests given 24 hr. after release from confinement revealed a tendency toward elimination of effects produced by S.D. Although results are based upon small Ns and single brief measures at each test period, the effects of S.D. upon performance are fairly consistent.

References

1. BEXTON, W. H., HERON, W., & SCOTT, T. H. Effects of decreased variation in the sensory environment. *Canad. J. Psychol.,* 1954, 8, 70-76.
2. HERON, W. The pathology of boredom. *Sci. Amer.,* 1957, 196(1), 52-56.
3. HERON, W., DOANE, B. K., & SCOTT, T. H. Visual disturbances after prolonged perceptual isolation. *Canad. J. Psychol.,* 1956, 10, 13-18.
4. VERNON, J. A., & HOFFMAN, J. Effect of sensory deprivation on learning rate in humans. *Sci.,* 1956, 123, 1074-1075.
5. VERNON, J. A., & McGILL, T. E. The effect of sensory deprivation upon rote learning. *Amer. J. Psychol.,* 1957, 70, 637-639.
6. VERNON, J. A., McGILL, T. E., & SCHIFFMAN, H. Visual hallucinations during perceptual isolation. *Canad. J. Psychol.,* 1958, 12, 31-34.
7. WILCOXON, F. *Some rapid approximate statistical procedures.* Stamford, Conn.: American Cyanamid Co., 1949.

A Study of "Warming-Up" in the Case of a Task of More Complicated Perceptual-Motor Coordination*

ERNEST B. SKAGGS

WARMING-UP has been interpreted in many ways by researchers, laymen, and practitioners. In the earlier days of experimentation in motor learning, warm-up was designated as a particular activity that improved performance "over and above the improvement due to practice or actual learning" (see Skaggs' article). The warm-up effect was noted by allocating a certain number of trials to practice sessions, with various rest conditions, and by noting with simple computations, distinctions at different sessions. At any rate, direct practice on the particular task served as a warm-up. It is of interest to compare the theories, experimental designs, and research findings of early studies with those in progress today. For instance, designs were relatively simple in the early years of experimentation, statistics unrefined (and perhaps unacceptable by today's standards), and typically, a very small number of subjects was utilized. Nevertheless, the groundwork for later efforts was paved, and many findings in a number of studies have been unified and re-verified through the years.

This paper presents the methods and results of an investigation of the so-called "warming-up" phenomenon in the case of a fairly complicated perceptual-motor task. The Goddard formboard was used, the task consisting in having the subject get all the blocks back into their proper recesses as quickly as possible. As the blocks were placed in a different (random) arrangement before each trial and as the subject could not see the arrangement until a fraction more than a second before he worked the board, the task demanded a very alert state of mind.

We use the term "warming-up" in the sense of the term which is now fairly well established, namely, to signify improvement in any performance or increase in efficiency over and above the improvement due to practice or actual learning. It has been rather generally assumed that warming-up has been a matter of attention adjustment in which the worker developed a more favorable attitude toward the task as he proceeded with the work. In any case where muscular adjustments or coordinations are involved it is probable that one must also take into consideration a warming-up process in the muscle tissue itself. Thus, when muscle tissue is stimulated a staircase or "Treppe" effect is found, the contractions increasing in extent for a considerable period.

Procedure

A Goddard formboard (standard Stoelting Company pattern) was fastened securely to the top of a table which was 30½ inches high. A green blotter,

* From the *Journal of Applied Psychology,* 1931, *15,* 499-511. Abridged and reprinted with permission of the author and publisher.

11½ × 19 inches, was fixed firmly to the table in front of the formboard. At the beginning of each trial the ten blocks were mixed in a random arrangement on the area defined by the blotter. Each block lay flat on the surface, no block was permitted to touch the edge of the board, and the blocks were separated from each other as far as the total area of the blotter permitted.

The experimenter's body formed a screen to hide the board and the arrangement of blocks from the subject before each trial. When all was ready the experimenter called out "Get Ready" and then stepped aside to the right, saying aloud in a slow rhythm, "One, Two, Go." As the experimenter stepped aside the subject stepped up in position before the board. At the signal "Go," he put all the blocks into their proper recesses as quickly as possible. The experimenter started his stopwatch as he said "Go," and stopped it as he observed the last block to be properly placed. This method of procedure was very regular and constant. On the average the subject had about 1.4 seconds in which to view the board before the signal "Go" was given.

In order to have constant illumination the work was done in a dark room with artificial light. The board was illuminated by means of a 200-watt light which was suspended 40″ above the table and somewhat to the front, in order to eliminate shadows. Temperature and air movements were quite constant.

In this investigation our subjects were first given a certain amount of training in the task. Group I received only a small amount of training. Group II received a good deal more training and Group III was relatively highly trained. The meetings or trials devoted to this training will be designated as "practice-meetings" or "trials." In the practice-periods, five trials constituted a meeting. One minute of rest was taken between each trial. Ordinarily each subject met twice a week in the case of Groups I and II. The subjects of Group III met three or four times a week.

In the testing for warming-up, ten trials were taken at a meeting. One-half minute rest was taken between each trial. In all cases, practice- or test-series, the subject was told his time after each trial.

Treatment of the Data

Ideally, one would like to use the subjects in a task in which they had reached their absolute limit of improvement. Actually this is not possible. However highly trained a subject may be in a complicated task of the kind we have used, one can never be certain that he might not improve if he changed his method or technique. Hence we must deal with subjects whose improvement in any experimental series may be due to practice or actual learning. We have applied the principle used by Robinson and Heron for separating true warming-up from practice effects. Unfortunately, this formula may hide actual (especially small) warming-up effects. If, upon application of the formula, warming-up is indicated, one may feel sure that it is a real phenomenon which is independent of the learning factor.

It must be remembered that in our work the smaller the time-figure the greater is the subject's efficiency. With this in mind we may indicate the following application of the Robinson-Heron formula:

Let A represent the average time for the *first five trials* at any given meeting.
Let B represent the average of the *final five trials* at this same meeting.
Let C stand for the average of the *first five trials* of the following meeting.

Now, in order to show a real warming-up, B must not only be *smaller* than A but this difference in favor of B must be *greater* than the difference between C and A, in case C is *smaller* than A. An example will make clear the situation. Let us suppose that A is 8 seconds, B is 6 seconds and C is 7 seconds. We then compute as follows: $(A-B)-(A-C) = +1$. Any positive number which we obtain thus indicates warming-up as distinct from the practice effect.

However, let us suppose that we find the following situation: A is 8 seconds, B is 6 seconds, and C is 6 seconds. Applying the formula we find that there is no warming-up indicated and the fact that B is better than A is due to learning.

In a word, then, $(A-B)-(A-C)$ must equal a positive number in order to indicate warming-up.

Results Obtained

Group I. Subjects with A Small Degree of Training. This investigation was carried out by the writer's assistant, Mr. Samuel Milinsky. About one month preceding the testing, the writer had trained these subjects, students in his beginning psychology course, over a period of six meetings or forty-eight practice-trials. The students were now divided into two groups of equal initial formboard ability, five men and five women to a group. One group, the A Group, was definitely urged to do its best, to make a fine record. The other group, Group B, did not receive this verbal exhortation or urging before the testing.

In order to conserve space the individual tabulations of averages will be omitted in this paper. Only the statements of central tendency will be given in each case, along with statements of relative number of subjects showing or failing to show the phenomenon of "Warming-up." Any reader who is interested in these individual tables may secure them by writing to the author of this paper. A copy of these figures has been placed in the files of the library of the College of the City of Detroit.

The following summary statements may be made on the basis of the data collected with Group I:

Group A: Out of 60 records, 21, or 35 per cent, show warming-up.
　　　　 The average value of warming-up is 0.30 seconds, with a mean variation of 0.209 seconds. Warming-up values range from 0.10 to 0.82 seconds.
Group B: Out of 60 records, 25, or 41.7 per cent, show warming-up.
　　　　 The average value of warming-up is 0.40 seconds, with a mean variation of 0.281 seconds. Warming-up values range from 0.02 to 1.26 seconds.

From the above data we find indications, then, that a definite exhortation or urging to do one's best tends to diminish the warming-up effect. Group B, the non-urged group, shows more warming-up than Group A. On the other hand, it is evident, since the differences between the two groups are not large, that the general experimental situation furnishes a strong incentive to "key-up" the subject to do his best.

The work with these subjects who were only slightly trained in the task indicates a positive warming-up effect in about 38 per cent of the cases, with an average time value of from 0.3 to 0.4 seconds.

Group II. Subjects with A Greater Amount of Training. The writer carried out this investigation with a group of 8 subjects who were students in an advanced course in psychology. Three of these were women. During the training period the subjects practiced twice a week. Twenty-two practice meetings, or 110 practice trials, were obtained before the warming-up tests were given. Due to practical exigencies, only four test-meetings were possible.

Only the first three of the four meetings can be utilized or tested for warming-up as the last meeting serves as a check upon the preceeding meeting. Thus, there are 24 records or cases available for study. Of these the following summary statements may be made:

(1) Out of 24 records, 11, or 45.8 per cent, show a clear warming-up effect.
(2) The average value of the warming-up time is 0.28 seconds with a mean variation of 0.18.
(3) The individual warming-up times range from 0.04 seconds to 0.90 seconds. This gives a considerable range.
(4) In 7 out of 24 cases, the second half of the work was *less efficient* than the first half. In the 6 cases where, after applying the formula, there is no warming-up shown there is still the possibility, of course, that there may be some of this effect which is obscured by the severity of the formula.

Group III. Highly Trained Subjects. Our third group of subjects may be designated as a highly trained group. While we may consider this group as one for most purposes, it is convenient to sub-divide it into two groups. These sub-groups we may speak of as Group III-A and Group III-B.

Group A consisted of three very highly trained subjects, two women and the writer (subjects F, H, and G). These subjects were trained over a period of nine months, having had 93 meetings, or 465 trials.

Group B consisted of five trained subjects, A, B, C, D, and E. Subject D was a woman, the others being men. These subjects had not had quite as much training as Group A. Each had had 59 meetings or a total of 295 practice trials.

We wish to emphasize the data obtained from this group. In the first place these subjects were quite skilled at the time the warming-up tests were introduced. Their curves of progress were either very negatively accelerated or showed a plateau at the time of the testing. In the second place, these subjects were all quite well trained in psychology and can be trusted to have lived up to the conditions of the experiment as far as is humanly possible. In the third place, sufficient records were obtained to give thoroughly dependable results.

Table I presents a summary of results for all subjects after having applied the Robinson-Heron formula. Any positive value signifies warming-up effects. The term NONE signifies that the second half of the performance was actually poorer than the first half. A negative value indicates that there was no warming-up effects according to the formula.

The following are summary statements for the group as a whole:

(1) Out of a total of 113 records or meetings, 46, or 40.7 per cent, show a clear warming-up effect.
(2) The average warming-up time is 0.274 seconds with a mean variation of 0.19 seconds.
(3) The warming-up time values range from 0.02 to 0.76 seconds.

All subjects showed some warming-up effects although not all were equally susceptible to this effect. Some show much more warming-up records than others. If we compare the percentages of warming-up effects in the case of the eight subjects we note that there is a range of from 16.6 to 57.1 per cent, with an average value of 40.3 per cent. Subject E has but little of the warming-up effect whereas subject A has a frequency of 57.1 per cent. Why there should be this individual difference in a group of eight highly trained, determined and interested subjects is a question which must involve a discussion of the analysis of the nature of the warming-up phenomenon as such.

If one considers only the average time-values of the records which showed a warming-up effect, one notes that, with the exception of the average for subject E (0.700 sec.), the individuals are very much alike, at least the differences are small. The mean for the group is 0.246 seconds with a mean variation of 0.056, omitting the average value for subject E. This last value is omitted because it is an average of only two records showing warming-up and is obviously an exceptional circumstance.

Comparison of All Groups

Table I presents a brief summary of the results for the three groups used in this investigation, thus permitting a comparison.

The above data offer little or no support to our original notion that the degree of learning was an important factor. Highly trained subjects, as in Group III, show just as much warming-up as subjects who are far less skilled. At least this is true if we compare the percentages of occurrence of this phenomenon. One might argue that the average time-values (see the figures at the right in Table I) indicate that there is less warming-up in the case of the highly trained group. However, Groups II and III are practically alike in time-values. This fact makes the preceding suggestion very questionable.

The Nature of "Warming-up"

What is responsible for the initial retardation in the attainment of maximum efficiency on the part of any subject in any given task? In many cases it takes the worker some time to attain his best efficiency for any particular assignment of work. In any experimental work it is necessary to rule out the effects of fatigue and practice. The residual effect is true warming-up. That this warming-up phenomenon appears in some cases and not in others is very significant and demands a thorough analysis of the conditioning factors.

Robinson and Heron have contributed a valuable finding. These investigators say, ". . . we secured a warming-up effect separable from the practice effect and dependent for its appearance upon the relative discontinuity of the work." (Page 97.) In other words, one must control the influence of fatigue. In a later work Robinson and Bills have pointed out two factors which may operate to produce work decrement, namely, the factor of relative homogeneity-heterogeneity of the work itself and the factor of competition due to interfering factors within the work elements. Such factors as these would tend to obscure the warming-up effects.

However, we are concerned here, not so much with the conditions which obscure warming-up effects as we are concerned with an analysis of the conditions which are directly responsible for the phenomenon. Most writers

TABLE I

GROUP	PER CENT OF CASES OF W-U	AVERAGE VALUE OF W-U TIMES
I—Little training:		
A, encouraged	35.0%	0.30 (M. V., 0.224)
B, non-encouraged ..	41.7%	0.40 (M. V., 0.293)
II—Greater degree of learning or skill	45.8%	0.28 (M. V., 0.18)
III—Highly trained	40.7%	0.27 (M. V., 0.19)

have explicitly or implicitly held that warming-up is in some way related to attention adjustments. In general, this is the view which we wish to defend. Our general theses are two: first, that the warming-up is due to a process of becoming thoroughly absorbed in the task at hand and, second, that much can be done to eliminate or shorten the warming-up effects.

An examination of most out-put curves which have been obtained from workers in industry indicates a considerable warming-up. On the other hand, our data and that of most laboratory researches indicate far less of this effect. The difference is not difficult to explain in a large part at least. Our subjects stepped up to their task with a keenly competitive spirit, mentally alert and determined to do their very best right at the outset. The result is that in many cases no warming-up at all is shown and, at most, it is small in amount. . . .

Conclusions

1. Using a fairly complicated perceptual-motor task we have found warming-up effects in about 40 per cent of our records. We had expected to find a higher percentage.

2. The degree of skill attained seems not to be of any particular significance in our work. More skilled subjects showed as much of the warming-up effect as did relatively unskilled subjects.

3. Any condition which will make the subject keenly alert and determined to do his very best at the outset will tend to lessen the frequency of occurrence of the warming-up effect.

4. We are inclined to the view that the warming-up phenomenon is largely a matter of attitude, mental alertness and attention. It takes some time for the subject to become absorbed in his task and to disengage his mind from other matters.

5. Stated in purely physiological terms we may say that the warming-up effect represents, for the most part, a phenomenon of the central nervous system. The locus of the phenomenon in the neuro-muscular system is, we believe, in the cortical areas, involving a proper arousal of cortical "sets" or the exercise of nerve-synapse systems.

References

1. ARAI, T. Mental Fatigue. Columbia University Contributions to Education, number 54, 1912.
2. BATTY, A. M. Some Observations upon Practice and Fatigue as They Affect the Rate of Tapping. *American Journal of Psychology,* 1909, 20, 449-455.
3. HERON, W. T. The Warming-Up Effect in Learning Nonsense Syllables. *Journal of Genetic Psychology,* 1928, 35, 219-228.
4. ROBINSON, E. S., and HERON, W. T. The Warming-Up Effect. *Journal of Experimental Psychology,* 1924, 7, 81-97.
5. ROBINSON, E. S., and BILLS, A. G. Two Factors in the Work Decrement. *Journal of Experimental Psychology,* 1926, 9, 415-443.
6. THORNDIKE, E. L. Educational Psychology. Briefer Course. Chapter XIX, pages 283-329.
7. WATSON, J. B. Psychology. 1924. Pages 354-355.
8. WELLS, F. L. Normal Performance in the Tapping Test. *American Journal of Psychology,* 1908, 19, 437-483.
9. WIMMS, J. H. The Relative Effects of Fatigue and Practice Produced by Different Kinds of Mental Work. *British Journal of Psychology,* 1906-1908, 2, 153-195.

PART 8

PRACTICE

Environmental Manipulations

Good practice leads to effective and efficient learning while poor practice (problems that might rest within the learner himself or the surrounding conditions) develops or perpetuates errors, bores the learner, and generally can become meaningless. The obvious question, then, is what can be done to facilitate the learning process? But first, conditions affecting practice must be identified. In order to organize the possible sources of concern, considerations must be provided to that which is initiated immediately prior to practice, that which transpires during practice, and that which occurs following practice.

More particularly, the problems rest with the instructor for the most part. What can he do at these three stages of practice to bring about best results for the learner? Most research in motor learning is found to relate directly to this question. Consequently, prior, during, and post-practice variables, and there are many of them, have been altered drastically or varied slightly in combination or separately in experiments.

Pre-practice considerations include the selection of techniques of guidance, demonstration, and instruction. The learner depends upon modeling and appropriate methods of presentation for direction. The level of aspiration, or goal level, set by the learner prior to beginning practice may reflect performance outcomes. Practice on related tasks will influence skill acquisition; hence task-to-task relativity and difficulty need to be acknowledged. Finally, modification in the display can be effective in instigating effective practice at early or latter stages of practice.

During practice, the sessions themselves may be varied systematically for productive ends. The alternatives are far apart or resolvable on middle grounds, in general theory or specific practice factors. Should learning proceed through trial and error, where the individual is permitted and/or encouraged to learn through his errors? Or is the programed learning technique more desirable, where behavior is "shaped" from the simple to the complex and errors in performance are minimized and indeed hopefully omitted from the repertoire of responses? Is drill (S-R routines) more or less effective than a problem-solving approach in developing skill?

Motivational techniques prior to and during practice are varied and their relative worth needs to be clarified. The use of simulators as compared to "real" practice situations; instructional emphases on one performance component over another, e.g., speed or accuracy; the continual utilization of

271

apparatus, videotape, films, and the like, as contrasted with traditional instruction; and background settings, music, lighting, and ventilation, represent other controversial areas.

The practice attempts, trials, or sessions may be modified to emphasize massed or distributed practice, part or whole practice, mental or physical practice, and actual or overload practice. Length of practice, skill proficiency of the learner, and intervening activities are further confounding variables. The instructor can select from many alternatives when he formulates the nature of the practice sessions.

With regard to post-practice concerns, knowledge of results or feedback first comes to mind. As the learner is executing his task or upon its termination, are the feedback signals sufficient or should auxiliary ones be added to the situation? If they are to be terminal, when should they occur and in what form? There is also real concern over techniques for improving the retention of the learned skill. How well are motor skills retained over time and what factors contribute to this retention?

The design of the practice period as well as a number of sessions entails much effort on the part of the instructor. The readings in Part 8, included in three chapters, are representative of problems typically investigated and results usually found. These readings should assist the trainer or educator in application and the researcher or theorist in direction of further work.

Chapter 11

PRE-PRACTICE CONSIDERATIONS

The Effect of Tuition Upon the Process of Learning a Complex Motor Skill*

DOROTHY R. DAVIES

VERBAL or written instruction typically forms the early direction in motor skill learning. Its effectiveness is usually taken for granted, although some research articles have indicated that there are times when instructions may be of limited value or, in fact, are inhibitory. Too much instruction, especially if the initial task is complex, results in little, if any, worth to the learner. But instructions compatible with the learner's comprehension and skill level certainly do appear to be of value in general. The first article, by Davies, is a simply executed experiment demonstrating the initial and later benefits of instruction in archery shooting.

Introduction

The Problem. The major purpose of this investigation was to study tuition as a condition affecting learning. The investigation was restricted to an analysis of the process of learning the complex motor skill of archery by two groups of women college students under conditions comparable except for the experimental variable of tuition. The members of one group were given regular and systematic instruction in the technique of archery of the type commonly presented by teachers of this sport. The members of the second group practiced archery under the observation of the experimenter, but without instruction. The general purpose was to determine the effects which tuition during practice had on the process of learning the complex motor skill of archery. The investigation was undertaken to discover whether students aided by tuition and other students practicing without this aid learned in a similar manner. . . .

Implications of the Study. In education there has been much interest in

* From the *Journal of Educational Psychology,* 1945, *36,* 352-365. Abridged and reprinted with permission of the author and the American Psychological Association.

the manner in which learning takes place, and in the conditions under which learning is advanced. In the classroom, children actively learn to solve problems. It is the teacher's duty to guide the children in acceptable work methods, and to prevent them from making errors. The teacher also tries to motivate the children to do better work. Tuition is given in order to aid the pupils in learning. It is expected that pupils so assisted will progress more rapidly than those not given instruction. While this matter was given attention in the present study, it was not the main interest of the investigator.

In laboratory studies of the effects of practice on learning a skill, experimenters have almost invariably set up rigid conditions for presentation of the learning problem and for stimulation of the students, and then left the students to their own devices. Teachers of skill do nothing of this sort. Instead, they demonstrate, analyze, and describe the correct process while drilling the students in methods of work which prevent errors.

Investigators have studied the effects of the amount of practice engaged in, the temporal distribution of practice, the loss of achievement without practice, and other similar conditions affecting learning. There have been relatively few investigations which study tuition as a condition of learning, and the effect which this tuition has upon the process of learning. More knowledge on this subject is needed.

Related Studies. The literature which was reviewed before undertaking this investigation included summaries and handbooks on psychology, recent textbooks on psychology, investigations involving motor learning, and investigations involving tuition and learning. The textbooks in archery were reviewed, as well as those investigations which involved this skill. Lashley's investigation was a pioneer use of archery to study the acquisition of skill.[1] His subjects shot outdoors with no control of wind, weight of arrows, tightness of bow string, or of temperature. All of his subjects practiced without being given instruction. The investigator, who took part in the experiment, read books on archery, and in this way received tuition in the skill.

Hyde's study was a survey of achievement in archery, undertaken in order to make standardized rating scales.[2] Included in her study was a report of the correlations she found between achievement in archery and the height, weight, and mental ability of the subjects.

Goodenough conducted an experiment with pre-school children to discover the effects of tuition upon teaching this age group.[3] Her main findings dealt with the amount learned under various types of instruction. The effects of tuition upon animal and human maze learning have been studied by Carr and his associates.[4]

The Method of Procedure

The Subjects. Two classes in archery were formed, with twenty subjects in each. The members of each class were girls studying at Southern Illinois

[1] K. S. Lashley, "The Acquisition of Skill in Archery," *Carnegie Institute Department of Marine Biology Papers.* Vol. vii, pp. 109-10. Washington, D. C.: Carnegie Institute of Washington, 1915.

[2] Edith Hyde, "The Measurement of Achievement in Archery," *Journal of Educational Research,* xxvii (May, 1934), 72-86.

[3] Florence Goodenough and C. R. Brian, "Certain Factors Underlying the Acquisition of Motor Skill by Pre-School Children," *Journal of Experimental Psychology,* xii (April, 1929), 127-55.

[4] Harvey Carr, "Teaching and Learning," *Journal of Genetic Psychology,* xxxvii (June, 1930), 189-219.

Normal University in Carbondale, Illinois. All of the subjects had selected archery from among a group of sports that grant credit toward graduation.

Matching of Groups. No attempt was made to match the individuals in the two groups with each other. The groups were highly similar, however, in terms of certain variables. These were height, weight, mental ability, and previous physical education experience. The two groups were considered at the start of the experiment to be equally able to acquire the skill in archery.

Physical Setting. The experiment was carried on in a gymnasium where the two archery groups were relatively free from the effects of wind and weather. The subjects had no practice away from the gymnasium, and had no opportunity to see other archers shoot.

Experimental Variable. The members of the two groups learned archery under radically different conditions. One class, the tuition group, was taught an accepted technique of shooting a bow and arrow; the other class, the non-tuition group, learned without instruction other than the minimum amount necessary for the manipulation of the equipment with safety. Each group met each Tuesday and Thursday for fifty minutes during March, April, and May, 1943. The experimental period included eighteen practice periods during which arrows were shot and scores recorded. . . .

Effect of Tuition Upon the Aspects of Learning Represented in Curves of Learning

Shapes of the Learning Curves. . . . The learning curves plotted from data obtained in this investigation are similar to those found in the experiments involving typewriting, telegraphy, and ball tossing.

The group curve for the tuition class in archery shows a sharp initial rise in performance from the first through the ninth practice periods. The group curve for the non-tuition class also shows a sharp initial rise in performance. This rise in score extends from the first practice period to the eighth day of practice.

Although the rate of gain is different for each group, the same negative acceleration in performance is common to the curves drawn from the data obtained from each group. The data at hand suggest that learning curves plotted to show the progress of subjects learning a complex motor skill with the aid of an instructor are similar in shape to the curves showing the progress of subjects learning a complex skill by means of practice without tuition. Whether or not this generalization is true, the curves actually plotted for the experimental and control groups are markedly similar in pattern. . . .

Effect of Tuition upon Rate of Learning and Level of Achievement. The tuition group had been given instructions in the technique of archery previous to the time of shooting their first arrows. The instructed subjects started at a higher level of performance than did the uninstructed ones, and maintained superiority throughout the time of this study. The tuition group progressed at a faster rate than did the non-tuition group during both the initial and latter stages of learning.

Since the purpose of any instruction is to aid the learners to acquire skill and progress as fast as possible, it was expected at the outset of the experiment that the tuition group would achieve more than the non-tuition group during the limited time of this study. The data collected corroborate the belief that a skilled teacher can aid students to perform a motor skill during initial trials with much more success than the students could achieve by their own efforts. By instruction, the teacher can assist the student to learn faster than he would without tuition. . . .

10

Implications of the Study

Psychological and Educational Implications. Following is a brief series of statements, based upon this investigation, that suggest possible broad applications for the psychology and teaching of motor skill.

1) Teachers cannot smooth out the irregularities in learning curves. The forward movement of learning is by its very nature tentative and uncertain. Improvement and loss are intermingled in learning, by the very nature of the process, but with improvement outweighing loss.

2) Teaching a skill negates the advantages which some learners derive from their physique, but takes advantage of the superior capacity for intellectual analysis and insight of brighter learners.

3) Teaching, at least through the period of instruction represented in this study, results in increased flexibility of behavior. Apparently, it takes teaching to prevent the learner from early falling into a set pattern, far below his potentialities, yet bringing some measure of success.

4) In at least three ways, the teacher aids the learner to vary his behavior.

(a) He directs the learner's attention to more adequate techniques than those that the learner has been employing. He thus stimulates the learner to break up faulty techniques, even at the temporary loss of achievement. In teaching a complex skill, this process is repeated again and again.

(b) The teacher promotes the growth of intellectual insight on the part of the learner into the factors related to his success. The instructions given by the teacher make a major contribution to the improvement of the learner's conception of the skill that he is attempting to master.

(c) Finally, the teacher's attitudes and encouragement serve to give the learner a feeling of security and confidence in giving up a familiar mode of behavior and seeking one that is better.

Limitations and Applications of the Study. This study is limited in its specific findings to the single motor skill, archery, taught or learned under the conditions of this investigation. The extent to which results apply to other fields of skill and conditions of learning is, of course, unknown. Further research is needed to determine the broader applications of the findings of this study. In addition to archery, such sports as golf, bowling, riflery, swimming, and various field events, industrial psychology, military psychology, and doubtless many other fields might profit by research of the type exemplified in this investigation.

Bibliography

Carr, Harvey. "Teaching and Learning," *Journal of Genetic Psychology,* xxxvii (June, 1930), 189-219.

Cozens, Frederick W. "The Determination of the Efficiency of Group Learning under Different Incentive Conditions and Modes of Activity," *American Physical Education Association Research Quarterly,* iv (May, 1936), 50-62.

Craft, Dave, and Craft, Cia. *The Teaching of Archery.* New York: A. S. Barnes and Co., 1936, pp. v + 82.

Goodenough, F. L. and Brian, C. R. "Certain Factors Underlying the Acquisition of Motor Skill by Pre-School Children," *Journal of Experimental Psychology,* xii (April, 1929), 127-55.

Hicks, James Allen. *The Acquisition of Motor Skill in Young Children: An Experimental Study of the Effects of Practice in Throwing at a Moving Target.* University of Iowa Studies: Studies in Child Welfare, Vol. iv. No. 4. Iowa City, Iowa: The University of Iowa, 1931, pp. 80.

Hyde, Edith. "The Measurement of Achievement in Archery," *Journal of Educational Research,* xxvii (May, 1934), 672-86.

Lashley, K. S. "The Acquisition of Skill in Archery," *Carnegie Institute, Department of Marine Biology Papers.* Vol. vii. Washington, D. C.: Carnegie Institute of Washington, 1915, pp. 105-28.

McGeoch, John A. *Psychology of Human Learning.* New York: Longmans, Green and Co., 1942, pp. v + 633.

Woodworth, Robert S. *Experimental Psychology.* New York: Henry Holt and Co., 1938, pp. iii + 889.

Individual Sports Guide, published by the National Section of Women's Athletics of the American Association for Health, Physical Education, and Recreation. New York: A. S. Barnes Co., 1942-43, pp. vii + 127.

The Psychology of Learning. Forty-First Yearbook of the National Society for the Study of Education, Part II. Bloomington, Illinois: Public School Publishing Co., 1942, pp. ii + 502.

Effect of Knowledge of Mechanical Principles in Learning to Perform Intermediate Swimming Skills*

DOROTHY R. MOHR AND MILDRED E. BARRETT

INSTRUCTIONAL guidance in motor learning may assume many forms. Besides general task descriptions, specific cue and movement analysis, and coding arrangements, principles thought to underly success in certain situations may be introduced. Traditionally, these are usually mechanical principles as far as the motor learner is concerned. Hopefully, the learning of a principle or combination of principles would lead to better and quicker learning of similar tasks. In other words, the learner will presumably transfer and apply the principle to the task and thereby benefit from the experience. Findings of this order were found as early as 1908. Since that time, inconsistent findings from study to study have caused individuals to question the value of teaching principles.

Most teachers of swimming are probably aware of the mechanical principles involved in the performance of aquatic skills, and many of them no doubt apply these principles in their teaching. According to McCloy: "The teacher should teach, in the direction of the learning of motor skills, according to the principles of the mechanical analysis of motor skills."[6] It is not known, however, how many teachers make a definite effort to help their students understand the mechanical principles that are operating in propulsion through the water. It may be important to be able to convey to students not only how the activity is performed correctly, but also why this method is the correct

* From *The Research Quarterly,* 1962, *33,* 574-580. Reprinted with permission of the authors and the American Association for Health, Physical Education, and Recreation.

performance of the activity. Little research has been done to discover whether or not the time spent on this type of teaching would result in better learning of aquatic skills.

Statement of the Problem

The purpose of this study was to expose students to simplified mechanical principles involved in the performance of the front crawl, back crawl, side and elementary back strokes, and to test the hypothesis that this knowledge would enhance the student's learning to perform these swimming strokes. The experiment was conducted at the University of Maryland during the fall semester of 1958-59, using 34 women enrolled in two intermediate swimming classes. The study lasted for a period of 14 weeks, with each class meeting three 35-minute periods a week. Since two regular university classes in physical education were used, there was no selection of students to be included in the study. Therefore, the writers had no control over students' past experience in swimming or knowledge of mechanical principles.

Review of the Literature

Use of Mechanical Principles in Instruction. A study by Scholckow, as reported by Judd,[5] was one of the earliest experiments concerning transfer of knowledge of the principles of refraction. In the first situation, two groups practiced throwing darts at a target placed 12 inches under water. Only one group was given instruction on the principles of refraction. No apparent differences were found between the performances of the two groups. However, when the target was placed four inches under water, the group with the knowledge of the principles of refraction adapted more readily to the new situation.

Ruger[8] conducted an experiment on processes concerned with the solution of puzzles involving mechanical principles. Puzzles in several different forms were given to the students. Those subjects who discovered the underlying principle for the solution of all forms during the solution of the first form were able to use the habits in succeeding forms. Those subjects who merely formed special habits without recognizing the general principles were confused by the changed puzzles.

Colville[2] conducted a study on the learning of motor skills as influenced by knowledge of mechanical principles. Three principles of mechanics pertinent to certain common motor skills and three specific motor skills which utilized these principles were selected. Two equated groups of subjects were established for each skill; one group was taught without direct reference to the principle involved, and the other was taught to understand and apply the principle. In comparing the two groups, Colville found that instruction concerning mechanical principles utilized in the performance of a motor skill did not facilitate initial learning of a skill any more than an equivalent amount of practice, but such knowledge did facilitate subsequent learning of similar or more complicated skills to which the same principles were applicable.

In another study, by Broer,[1] instruction on basic skills which emphasized problem solving and understanding mechanics was given prior to instruction in volleyball, basketball, and softball. The experimental group, in addition to the instruction in mechanics, was given one-third as much specific instruction in volleyball as the control group, two-thirds as much in basketball, and the same amount in softball. An analysis of the data showed that the experimental group surpassed the control group on all skill tests given at the completion of each unit on volleyball, basketball, and softball.

In view of the above findings, the evidence seems to be conflicting as to whether or not a knowledge of mechanical principles is necessary during the initial learning of a skill. Some evidence has been presented that an understanding of these principles aids individuals in transferring knowledge from one situation to another and in learning more complicated skills. The present investigation has been designed to test the hypothesis at an intermediate level of skill.

Mechanical Analysis of Specific Swimming Strokes. Available mechanical analyses of specific swimming strokes were reviewed in order to provide a guide for the analysis of each stroke included in this study. Due to lack of space, these studies are not cited here. The majority of the research was conducted on the front crawl. Apparently more attention needs to be given to the mechanics of other basic strokes, such as the back crawl, side, elementary back, and breast strokes.

Procedures

The 34 freshman and sophomore women used as subjects were enrolled in two required physical education classes. After eliminating those who had to withdraw from the classes during the semester, there were 16 in the control group, which met at 10:00 a.m., and 15 in the experimental group, meeting at 11:00 a.m. These assignments were made by random selection. Both classes were held on Monday, Wednesday and Friday, and were taught by the same instructor. The two groups were found to be equated through a statistical analysis of the data obtained from the initial testing.

The Tests. Form ratings and objective tests measuring speed and power were administered at the beginning and end of the experiment. A rating scale, devised by Mohr and Neyendorf,[7] was used for form to facilitate uniformity and obtain numerical scores for each subject. Using this scale, three DGWS Nationally Rated Swimming Officials rated each swimmer on the elementary back, front crawl, back crawl, and side strokes, and the scores of the three judges were added together to obtain a total score for each stroke. The objective tests consisted of 25-yard sprints with the front and back crawl strokes, and Hewitt's[4] glide test was used to measure the power of the elementary back and side strokes. The latter involved counting the number of strokes it took the student to swim 25 yards, counting the push-off as one stroke.

The objective tests were administered twice at the beginning of the experiment in order that the reliability of the measuring techniques might be established. The American Council on Education test scores for vocabulary, speed of reading, and level of reading comprehension were available for all of the subjects. These scores were used to discover if the two groups were essentially equal in reading ability and comprehension. It seemed logical to consider reading comprehension, since a great deal of reading material was given to all subjects to study and apply to their swimming practice.

Experimental Teaching. Eight weeks of teaching followed the initial three-week testing program. The lesson plans for the two groups were identical except for the use of mechanical principles in explaining the correct performance of each to the experimental group. The stress on the application of these principles was made during class explanations and demonstrations, as in correcting individual performance as the students practiced the strokes.

Each stroke was thoroughly analyzed. Mimeographed copies of the analysis were given to the students during the class session preceding the one in which the stroke was first introduced. The analyses were the same for both groups; however, the papers given to the experimental group had numbers inserted throughout the analyses which referred to the list of mechanical principles given out previously to the experimental group only. Written quizzes were administered to both groups periodically, covering all mimeographed material. Four makeup sessions in the water were scheduled each week for students who were absent, or were present but unable to participate in the water. In this way all subjects were able to have the same amount of practice in the water throughout the experiment.

Statistical Analysis of the Data. The reliabilities of the objective tests were computed by correlating the subjects' scores on the first tests with the scores on the retests. The judges' scores were correlated with each other to assess the objectivity of the form ratings. Small sample formulas were used in the treatment of all other data. The t test was applied to initial mean scores of the experimental and control groups for the purpose of discovering if the groups were equated in form, speed, power, and reading ability. A significance level of .05 was selected for this t test and for all subsequent ones.

In order to compare the progress of the experimental group with that of the control group during the experiment, the differences between the scores on the initial test and the final test for each subject and each stroke were obtained. The means and standard deviations for these improvements were calculated, and the means of the two groups were compared, using the t test to assess the significance of the differences.

Results and Discussion

Reliabilities and Objectivities of the Measures. As a result of the test-retest procedure, the correlations for the 25-yard sprints and power tests were .93 for the front crawl, .94 for the back crawl, .82 for the side stroke, and .80 for the elementary back stroke. Even though these retests were given during the class period immediately following the completion of the initial tests, some variations in performance of the students would be expected. Therefore, these correlation coefficients appeared to indicate satisfactory reliability of measuring techniques.

In the initial form ratings, the intercorrelations of judges' ratings ranged from .70 to .96, indicating satisfactory degrees of objectivity. Because of the subjectivity of these measures, the final form ratings were also studied for objectivity. This time the coefficients ranged from .56 to .87.

Equating of Groups. The means of the experimental and control groups for the initial form ratings, objective swimming tests, and the ACE reading comprehension scores were compared. The mean scores of the form ratings were slightly lower for the experimental group on the front and back crawl strokes and slightly higher on the side and elementary back strokes. The t values ranged from 0.04 to 1.37, thus failing to show a significance at the 5 percent level of confidence. The two groups were, therefore, considered equated in terms of form at the start of the experiment.

The mean scores on the objective tests were lower for the control group on all of the tests with the exception of the back crawl. This meant that the control group swam the front crawl faster than the experimental group and required fewer strokes to swim 25 yards using the side and elementary back strokes. The t values, however, ranged from 0.76 to 1.32, again failing to show significance at the 5 percent level. Similarly, although the control ACE mean score was higher than that of the experimental group, the t value was only 0.09. Thus the groups were judged to be equated with respect to reading comprehension and initial power ability in the four strokes.

Comparisons of Improvement. For all tests of form and power, the experimental group improvement means were higher than the control group means. The differences in improvement for the front crawl sprint, side stroke power, front crawl, back crawl, and side stroke form were significant at the 5 percent level of confidence.

In the cases where significant t values were obtained, a further analysis was made to discover whether a significant difference in the variances existed. All F ratios failed to show significance except that of the distributions for front crawl form, which was significant at the 5 percent level of confidence. Consequently a further test[3] was made to see if the difference in means existed because of a difference in the variances; this test indicated that, regardless of the difference in the variances, the difference in the means was significant at the 5 percent level.

Summary and Recommendations

The two intermediate swimming classes used in this study were shown to be equated initially with respect to form and power in the front crawl, back crawl, side, and elementary back strokes. The experimental group made significantly greater improvement than did the control group, during eight weeks of instruction, in all strokes but the elementary back stroke. Specifically, these improvements were in the front crawl sprint, the side stroke power test, and the form ratings for the front crawl, back crawl, and side strokes.

These findings support the hypothesis that exposing students to an understanding and application of mechanical principles will effect greater improvement than instruction without reference to these principles. They support the findings of Broer[1] in the learning of volleyball, basketball, and softball skills. However, a great deal more evidence is needed regarding the general hypothesis that a knowledge of mechanical principles will facilitate learning of motor skills. It is recommended that further research be conducted along the following lines.

1. Use larger samples and extend the study over a longer period of time; a study should also be conducted with respect to other swimming skills and to diving.

2. Investigate the rate of learning specific swimming strokes when mechanical principles are taught.

3. Investigate the extent of transfer of knowledge of mechanical principles from one stroke to another and the effects of this knowledge on the learning of other sport skills.

4. Refine the methods of testing; those used in this study were extremely time-consuming.

References

1. BROER, MARION. Effectiveness of a general basic skills curriculum for junior high school girls. *Res. Quart.* 29:379-88, 1958.
2. COLVILLE, FRANCES. *The learning of motor skills as influenced by a knowledge of general principles of mechanics.* Unpublished doctoral dissertation, University of Southern California, 1956.
3. EDWARDS, ALLEN L. *Statistical analysis.* (Rev. Ed.) New York: Rinehart & Company, 1958.
4. HEWITT, JACK. Achievement scale scores for high school swimming. *Res. Quart.* 20:282-89, 1949.
5. JUDD, C. H. Special training and general intelligence. *Educ. Rev.* 36:38-42, 1908.
6. McCLOY, C. H. Towards a greater degree of physical literacy (part II). *The Phys. Educ.* 14:126, 1957.
7. NEYENDORF, DORIS M. *The effects of music as a teaching aid in intermediate swimming classes for college women.* Unpublished master's thesis, University of Maryland, 1953.
8. RUGER, HENRY A. The psychology of efficiency. *Arch. Psychol.* 2:85, 1910.

Effects of Pre-Practice Activities on Rotary Pursuit Performance*

ROBERT B. AMMONS

THE importance of "set" in preparing the learner for the task that follows has been realized for some time. It is thought that he should be "psychologically-geared," in a state of preparation or attention, for the learning task. There are many kinds of pre-learning activities that can be experienced, and Ammons compares the effects of a few realistic possibilities on motor performance. The transfer effects of ocular practice, manual practice, and mental rehearsal are noted. Each is a plausible activating technique that might be used to enhance learning. Although Ammon's results are disappointing to advocates of such procedures, the generality of the implications to all kinds of motor skills has not been confirmed.

In analyzing the rotary pursuit performance curve quantitatively, Ammons[1] defined certain variables including temporary work decrement and warm-up decrement. "Warm-up decrement" was defined as the amount that the mean performance level on the first post-rest trial was depressed below a point determined by backward extrapolation of a line fitted to the mean performance levels on several subsequent trials, those in the relatively decremental segment of the curve. It was shown that this need to warm up became less as the S had more experience starting practice, and it was predicted that there might well be almost no warm-up decrement in instances where practice had been initiated many times. This prediction has been found to hold in one study[2] of distribution of practice. Several groups which had started practice on 36 different occasions separated by rests of 2 or more min. showed no appreciable warm-up decrement after a rest 12 to 30 min. in length. These findings justify the backward extrapolation of the subsequent portion of the post-rest performance curve to correct for warm-up decrement in the first minute or two of post-rest practice.

Amount of temporary work decrement was defined as the difference between performance on the first trial after a 10-min. or longer rest, corrected for warm-up decrement, and estimated performance on that trial if no rest had been introduced. Actually, this difference represents *recovery* from temporary work decrement.

In the original theoretical treatment of warm-up decrement, it was tentatively explained as due to loss over rest of "set," or postural and sense organ adjustments favorable to performance. Irion in a recent article[4] reports that if the first 24-hr. recall trial of a paired-associate series is preceded by a period of naming color strips presented on a memory drum in a manner similar to that used with the paired associates, there is significantly better performance than where no such activity precedes the trial. He proposes that much of what is ordinarily lost over rest is "set," and that the color-naming practice reinstates it, minimizing the effects of its loss on recall.

* From the *Journal of Experimental Psychology*, 1951, *41*, 187-191. Reprinted with permission of the author and the American Psychological Association.

TABLE 1

SUMMARY OF EXPERIMENTAL CONDITIONS

Condition	N	Description
I	28	Control with two 12-min. continuous practice periods separated by a 17-min. rest
II	27	2-min. ocular practice before* initial practice period
III	24	2-min. ocular practice before* both practice periods
IV	24	2-min. ocular practice before* final practice period
V	24	2-min. blindfolded manual practice before* initial practice period
VI	26	2-min. blindfolded manual practice before* both practice periods
VII	24	2-min. blindfolded manual practice before* final practice period
VIII	25	2-min. imaginary practice before* final practice period

* Delay between cessation of pre-practice activity and start of regular session was 20 sec. or less.

Problem

Following this line of reasoning, it can be predicted that: (a) practice of various components of the rotary pursuit task immediately before the initial practice period will increase subsequent performance, since set responses will be learned, giving a basis for higher scores; (b) practice of various major components of the task immediately before practice is resumed after a rest should decrease the warm-up decrement.[1]

Method

Materials. Ss practiced on Koerth-type pursuit rotors[2] with ¾-in. brass targets with centers set 3¼ in. out from the center of 10¾-in. bakelite disks and flush with their surfaces. Target plates rotated in a horizontal plane at 60 rpm. The targets were followed during regular practice with the tips of light hinged styluses, and electrical contacts between targets and styluses were recorded cumulatively on timers during 20-sec. periods. Scores were read from the clocks at the end of each 20-sec. period, although subsequent treatment of the data was in terms of 1-min. periods. Timing of trials was manual.

Subjects. The Ss were experimentally naive undergraduate women college students attending the University of Denver or Colorado Woman's College. Although 28 were assigned randomly in groups of four to each of the eight conditions, difficulties with apparatus, instructions, or interruptions led to the discarding of a total of 22 records. Final N's for the conditions are given in Table 1. It will be seen that they varied from 24 to 28.

Procedure. The Ss practiced in groups of four. Each was assigned a rotor. Instructions were then given as follows: The purpose of the study was to find out how people learn a new task; they would find that they would not do too well to begin with but as they kept at it, they would improve; the best way to practice was with body relaxed, following the target with an easy swinging motion of the arm; each was to use her preferred hand to hold the stylus; her grip was to be light, and no attempt was to be made to put extra

[1] Similar predictions are made by Irion[3] in his review of the relation of "set" to retention in verbal learning.
[2] This apparatus has been described in detail elsewhere.[2]

pressure on the tip of the stylus. The Ss' grip and stance were then checked and corrected where necessary. A ready signal was given, and pursuit began approximately 5 sec. later.

All Ss practiced 12 min. continuously, ceased practice for 17 min., then practiced continuously for 12 min. more. They were encouraged periodically and were corrected verbally when they deviated from instructions in stance or stylus grip. The eight conditions are described briefly in Table 1. It will be seen that provision was made for measuring the effects of manual or ocular practice for 2 min. immediately before each session or both sessions. Imaginary practice could only be given meaningfully after S had already had some experience with the task.

Ocular practice consisted of S's standing for 2 min., following the target with her eyes only. In manual practice, S's eyes were blindfolded, and she was shown how to follow with her index finger a small rivet head set into the rotor plate the same distance from the center as the center of the regular target. When she lost it, she attempted to find it again and to resume following. No S was unable to do this. For imaginary practice, S stood before the rotor with eyes blindfolded. She was told to imagine that she was practicing, without, however, making any overt movements. This instruction was continually reinforced with suggested details. It was judged effective in that two Ss showed trance-like behavior in raising their forearms into practice position and were discarded, and all remaining Ss in this group reported being able to imagine the practice quite clearly.

During the rest period, Ss sat in an anteroom and talked or read popular magazines. At the end of each practice period, the rotors were turned off promptly and Ss laid down their styluses.

Results

It is immediately apparent from inspection that all curves show recovery from temporary work decrement over rest, post-rest warm-up decrement, and a decremental segment in the post-rest curve, presumably because temporary work decrement is building up again. It is also apparent that there are no great differences between the various groups in pre- and post-rest performance.

To evaluate the results statistically, scores at various points in practice were used as indices as follows: (a) first minute of pre-rest practice, to indicate effects of pre-practice on initial level of performance; (b) last minute of pre-rest practice, to indicate effects on final level of performance reached in pre-rest practice; (c) first minute of post-rest practice, to indicate effects on warm-up decrement; (d) difference between first and second minutes of post-rest practice, to obtain a second estimate of effects on warm-up decrement; (e) second minute of post-rest practice, to indicate reminiscence or recovery from temporary work decrement over rest; (f) last minute of post-rest practice, to indicate final level of performance. Use of index (d) assumes that there is little or no relationship between warm-up decrement and the score on post-rest trial 2. Simple analyses of variance were performed on scores at each of the points and F-ratios were computed for between-groups versus within-groups variance estimates. It is realized that the distributions in the first minute are considerably skewed, but the F-ratio still provides a convenient index. Results are summarized in Table 2. No F except that based on the first pre-rest minute scores was significant at even the 5 per cent level of confidence, and this one is here interpreted as occurring by chance. To the extent that these indices provide adequate measures of the variables, it can be concluded that pre-practice, imaginative or on components of the skill, has little or no effect on practice level at the very start of regular pursuit

TABLE 2
RESULTS OF SIMPLE ANALYSIS OF VARIANCE OF SCORES AT
VARIOUS POINTS IN PRACTICE

Source of Variance Estimate: Scores from	Obtained F Ratio*
1. Pre-rest min. 1	2.53
2. Pre-rest min. 12	1.77
3. Post-rest min. 1	1.00
4. Post-rest min. 2	1.39
5. Difference between post-rest min. 1 and 2	1.40
6. Post-rest min. 12	(Error term slightly larger)

* For 7 and 194 degrees of freedom, the F ratio must be approximately 2.73 to be significant at the 1 per cent level of confidence[6]

rotor practice, on recovery from temporary work decrement or warm-up decrement, or on final level of performance.

On the other hand, a careful inspection of the original data suggests that imaginary practice may possibly have had an appreciable effect not detected by the present statistics. In condition VIII (imaginary practice) recovery from temporary work decrement was less by about one-third, and warm-up decrement by one-half.

Discussion

Comments seem in order regarding some implications of this study. In the first place, it can be seen that Irion's prediction of set reinstatement by pre-practice does not hold under the present conditions. This is quite impressive in view of the similarity of the pre-practice. It is possible that positive transfer from component practice is just about matched in amount by negative transfer of temporary work decrement. This guess is given some support by Irion's[5] finding with verbal serial learning that pre-recall warming-up activity beyond an optimum amount may produce work inhibition. If temporary work decrement produced by pre-practice were a major factor in the present experiment, one would expect to find significant differences between the groups at least at post-rest trial 2. Its relative unimportance is indicated by the small F based on scores at this point.

In any case, if component pre-practice is to have any considerable importance, it must perhaps be engaged in for much longer periods than those used in the present study. It may also be that rotary-pursuit and nonsense-syllable learning sets will turn out to have quite different properties.

There has been some discussion about the nature of temporary work decrement. On the basis of the present study it can be concluded that it is not directly dependent upon the rate or amount of energy expenditure, since 2 min. of manual pre-practice produced, at most, only a small amount of the effect the same amount of work would have had if S had had her eyes open and been following the target. It would seem that temporary work decrement is mainly central in nature rather than peripheral.

The results of the present study throw some light on the rehearsal hypothesis of reminiscence. Activities comparable to rehearsal were actually encouraged during the "rest" period. If anything, post-rest performance was poorer as a result. Taken in conjunction with similar results reported by Rohrer[7] for verbal material, this study still further discredits the hypothesis that Ss do better after rest because they have somehow rehearsed when they were supposed to be resting.

Summary and Conclusions

Two 12-min. practice periods of continuous rotary pursuit, separated by a 17-min. rest period, were given 202 undergraduate college women. Groups practiced under eight different conditions of pre-practice warming-up activity, consisting of ocular following of the target, blindfolded following of a rivet head, or imagined practice. Pre-practice was given before one or both of the practice periods. Statistically significant score differences between groups appeared at no point in practice.

It is concluded that the present types and durations of pre-practice activity do not produce significant changes in subsequent performance level, warm-up decrement, or temporary work decrement. These results do not support an energy-expenditure explanation of temporary work decrement, or a rehearsal theory of reminiscence. They do seem to indicate that verbal and motor performances are affected differently by pre-practice warming-up activities.

References

1. AMMONS, R. B. Acquisition of motor skill: I. Quantitative analysis and theoretical formulation. *Psychol. Rev.*, 1947, 54, 263-281.
2. AMMONS, R. B. Acquisition of motor skill: III. Effects of initially distributed practice on rotary pursuit performance. *J. exp. Psychol.*, 1950, 40, 777-787.
3. IRION, A. L. The relation of "set" to retention. *Psychol. Rev.*, 1948, *55*, 336-341.
4. IRION, A. L. Retention and warming-up effects in paired-associate learning. *J. exp. Psychol.*, 1949, 39, 669-675.
5. IRION, A. L. Retention as a function of amount of pre-recall warming-up. *Amer. Psychologist*, 1949, 4, 219. (Abstract.)
6. LINDQUIST, E. F. *Statistical analysis in educational research.* Boston: Houghton Mifflin, 1940.
7. ROHRER, J. H. Factors influencing the occurrence of reminiscence: Attempted formal rehearsal during the interpolated period. *J. exp. Psychol.*, 1949, 39, 484-491.

Cognitive Aspects of Psychomotor Performance: The Effects of Performance Goals on Level of Performance*

EDWIN A. LOCKE AND JUDITH F. BRYAN

PERFORMANCE can be stimulated in a variety of ways, one of which concerns the nature of the goal set for the learner. He may be exhorted to do his best, to try harder, or to reach pre-established goals. The reading by Locke and Bryan concerns this problem; a comparison of general versus specific motivators. It has been known for some time that performance goals, or level of aspiration, have a direct bearing on output. How effective specific goal setting was in motor skill achievement in contrast to general encouragement was not truly realized until this study was published.

* From the *Journal of Applied Psychology*, 1966, *50*, 286-291. Reprinted with permission of the authors and the American Psychological Association.

A previous experiment by Mace (1935) on the effects of performance standards on level of performance found that subjects (Ss) given specific scores or standards of performance to beat on each trial (based on their initial ability) improved much faster on a mathematical computation task than Ss told simply to "do their best." The major purpose of the present experiment was to replicate this finding with a complex *motor* task. The task was the Complex Coordination task described previously by Melton (1947) and Fleishman and Hempel (1954).

However, there were a number of intentional differences in procedure between the Mace experiment and the present one. First, Mace did not report just how hard the standards were for the groups with specific standards. The present investigator (Locke, 1966) has shown that the difficulty of reaching the intended level of performance (i.e., the actual *level* of the standard) has a significant effect on performance: the higher the standard the higher the performance. The standards in these previous experiments ranged in difficulty from 93% (the percentage of trials on which Ss were able to beat them) to 4%; in other words, from "very easy" to "very hard." In the present experiment the standards were set at a moderately hard difficulty level, in this case such that Ss were able to beat them less than 30% of the time. Second, as Mace (1935, p. 20) suggests, Ss told to "do their best" could, if given their scores after each trial, set standards for themselves even though they are not told to do so. In fact, in the present investigator's experience it is very difficult to *stop* experimental Ss from doing this especially where the "demand characteristics" (Orne, 1962) of the situation are high. Usually an S not instructed to set goals (but given knowledge of his score) will set himself a goal of "constant improvement" or a specific score to beat that is considerably above his initial performance (i.e., a "long term" goal). In order to prevent this in the present experiment, Ss who were not given standards were also not given their total scores for each trial, though they were given knowledge of the *correctness* of their response sequences (see task description below). It is true that this group therefore lacked specific "knowledge of total score" which the group with standards had. However, this knowledge was not knowledge about the *correctness* of individual responses or response sequences (this was given in the task itself), but knowledge about the *number* of correct responses made. The latter information could not give the Ss knowledge of how to perform the task better; it could only give them knowledge with which they could regulate their level of effort. Payne and Hauty (1955) made this same distinction between these different kinds of knowledge in a previous study. Mace (1935) has suggested that the motivational effects of knowledge of results are entirely a consequence of giving the Ss information with which to set themselves performance standards. Thus, it is argued in the present case that knowledge of total score and standards affect Ss cognitively in the same way, namely, by giving them information which they can use only to regulate their level of effort. Standards were introduced to insure that all Ss used their knowledge in the same way, thus the "confounding" of the two is not considered relevant to the primary purpose of the study which was to examine the effects of standards.

Of secondary interest in the present study were the effects of a specific learning plan or strategy on Complex Coordination performance. Previous research by Fleishman and Hempel (1954) had found Discrimination Reaction Time to be an important ability at the early stages of practice in this task and Simple Reaction Time to be important at the later stages. However, one pilot S who worked at the task for 5 hours indicated that he had eventually tried to learn to memorize and thus anticipate which pattern was coming. This S attained a very high level of performance. It was not known, however, how soon Ss could begin to memorize the pattern sequence successfully nor if all Ss could do it at all. It was thought that 1 hour's practice was a minimum prerequisite for any attempt to memorize the patterns. The interest here was in whether trying to memorize the patterns would improve performance.

Method

Task. The Complex Coordination apparatus consists of two pairs of adjacent rows of horizontal lights separated by a pair of adjacent vertical rows of lights (so that the display looks like an H on its side). One row of each adjacent pair of rows consists of red lights and one of green lights. One red light in each row is illuminated at any given time to form a pattern (consisting of three red lights). The S's task is to move a set of controls in order to illuminate a pattern of green lights to match the pattern of illuminated red lights. The controls consist of foot pedals that control the illumination of the bottom horizontal row of green lights and a "joy stick" which moves laterally and forward and back to control the illumination of the top horizontal and the vertical rows of green lights, respectively. When the S "matches" the red-light pattern with a green-light pattern, the pattern of red lights automatically changes to a new pattern. There are 13 different patterns given in sequence. Actually the apparatus is programed so that after every 3 repetitions of the 13 patterns (in the same order), Pattern No. 11 comes on before the cycle begins again. Thus, for all intents and purposes, it is a 13-cycle pattern "with complications." Thus, feedback about the *correctness* of his movement sequences is given to S automatically, since the red-light pattern changes when it has been correctly matched. However, information as to the total number of matches made during a given time period could be withheld from the S as necessary. The Ss without standards or knowledge of scores could still get some idea of how well they were doing by the relative frequency with which the red-light patterns changed (with which they made successful matches). One S who was in the No Standard group actually counted the number of matches he made on his last trial. Another counted the number of matches on two different trials.

Subjects. The Ss were 29 University of Maryland, paid, male volunteers who responded to an advertisement in the college newspaper. (One S was dropped from the analysis; see Results section.)

Conditions. The design was a 2×2 fixed model with 7 Ss in each cell. (*a*) "Standard" condition—half the Ss were given specific performance goals or standards to beat on each trial. The standards for each coming trial were determined by adding a fixed increment to the S's best previous score after each trial. The increment was 15 (matches) if the S's 10-minute trial score was below 100, 10 if it was over 100 but under 130, and 5 if the previous best score was over 130 (the reduced increments being due to the fact that improvement was more difficult as S's score became higher). The Ss were told that beating these standards constituted "what we considered to be successful performance on the task on the basis of our experience with the task." The Ss were told that the standards represented "above the average performance for college students." The Ss without standards were told at the beginning of the first experimental trial to "do their best" on every trial, and were not given their total scores or any standards. (*b*) Plan condition—at the end of the halfway point in the experiment (i.e., after 1 hour's practice), half the Ss were told to "try and memorize the number and sequence of the red-light patterns." They were told that this would improve their performance since they would be able to anticipate which patterns were coming, and, therefore, to respond faster. They were reminded on each subsequent trial to continue to try and memorize the patterns.

Procedure. The experiment was introduced as a study of the way in which motor skills develop and relate to each other. After preliminary testing on the Jump and Discrimination Reaction Time tests found by Fleishman and Hempel (1954) to predict performance on this task at the late and early stages, respectively, the functioning of the Complex Coordination task was explained to the *S*s, and then all *S*s were given a 2-minute practice trial during which they were told to "do their best." After this it was decided what condition to put each *S* in. In each case, this was decided only on the basis of the practice score and so as to equalize the practice scores of the 4 experimental groups as much as possible. The *S*s were told they would have 12 trials of 10 minutes each, separated by a 2-minute rest period. At this point, the method of goal setting was explained to the groups with standards (the goal for Trial 1 was 5 $\times$ the practice score plus 15) and the remaining *S*s were told to "do their best." Nothing was said to the Plan groups at this point. After each trial the *S*s with standards were given their score on that trial and their standard for the next trial. (Between trials all *S*s made some ratings and described "what they were thinking about" but these data are not of relevance to the present experiment.)

After Trial 6 all *S*s were told that Trial 7 was to be an experimental trial during which they should "experiment with new ways of doing the task." The Plan *S*s, however, were told explicitly to use this trial to begin to memorize the red-light patterns. The No Plan *S*s were told to do as they pleased. The *S*s with standards were told no scores or standards would be given on this trial.

Before Trial 8 the Standard *S*s were given their new goal based on their best performance before Trial 7. The Plan *S*s were told to continue trying to memorize the patterns.

At the end of the experiment *S*s were given a questionnaire asking them (*a*) whether they tried to reach the goals or not (if applicable) and, if not, what goals they were trying for, and (*b*) how many of the patterns they had been able to memorize. This was checked by an actual recall test in which *S*s had to reproduce as many of the red-light patterns (by marking Xs on a paper design) as they could.

Results

Success of Experimental Manipulations. Since the true independent variables in this study were conceived of as "cognitive" rather than "situational," it was necessary to determine whether or not the *S*s followed instructions about the goals they were asked to pursue. It was found that one *S* in the Standard-Plan condition was not doing so at all, so he was dropped from the condition and replaced with another *S*. The decision to drop this *S* was not based on this answer alone. There were other pieces of evidence, that is, his response to another written question; specific questions put to him by the experimenter (*E*) after the experiment; the *S*'s spontaneous comments during the experiment (e.g., claiming he was falling asleep and asking for stimulants); observations of the *S*'s behavior during the experiment (bowing his head and almost falling asleep); and comments made by the *S* on a dictaphone between trials about his "thoughts during the trial." It was only because all these pieces of evidence completely substantiated his questionnaire response that it was felt justifiable to drop him from the analysis. In the case of other *S*s who indicated that they were not *fully* following instructions, such "convergence of evidence" was lacking, thus they were retained.

All remaining Ss in the Standard-Plan condition claimed to have tried to beat the standards. Three of the seven Standard-No Plan Ss claimed they were not trying to reach the goals set by the E. However, one replaced these goals with his own goals which were of equivalent difficulty; another said he tried not to beat the standards by too much since he did not want them to go too high and tire him out; a third said he followed the goals at first, but did not later. It was felt that these Ss were trying for the goals (or equivalent goals) at least to some degree so that removing them was not justified.

Nine of the 11 No Standard Ss who responded to the question about goals indicated they were trying to "do their best" or something similar. One claimed he was trying for gradual improvement and another's answer was not interpretable. Three Ss did not respond to the question. (This was probably due to ambiguous instructions on the questionnaire.)

All the Plan Ss indicated they had tried to memorize some aspect of the patterns, but 2 indicated they emphasized recognition over anticipation, 4 said they tried mainly to memorize the bottom red-light (matched with the foot pedal) sequence and one the top red-light (matched with lateral stick) sequence. However, 9 of the 14 Plan Ss said that memorizing was too difficult and/or that it did not help them and (in some cases) actually hurt their performance. This suggests that the memorizing plan might have been introduced too soon in the learning process.

In terms of the actual difficulty of the goals, the Ss in the goal condition were able to reach or exceed their standards on only 29% of the trials, suggesting that the standards were quite difficult. In Locke's (1966) experiment Ss who were given standards this hard or harder attained the highest output of any group.

Effects of Standards and Plans.   The four experimental groups were successfully matched on the basis of initial ability, as measured by scores on the practice trial ($F_{bet} = < 1$). The groups were also matched successfully on the Discrimination Reaction Time and Jump Reaction Time tests found previously by Fleishman and Hempel (1954) to predict performance at the early and late stages of practice on this task, respectively.

The linear slope of the performance scores from the practice trial (multiplied by 5) to Trial 12 (omitting Trial 7) was calculated for each S, and the individual slope scores were subjected to an F test. The effect of standards was highly significant $F = 17.75$ ($p < .001$). The effect of the standards was immediate and the difference between the groups increased continually during the 12 trials. The mean total number of matches over all trials (excluding 7) was also significantly greater for the Standard group ($t = 2.78$; $p < .01$).

There was no significant effect of Plans on the linear slopes ($F = 1.44$; $p > .05$) and no interaction effect ($F = 3.28$; $p > .05$). Since the Plan instructions were introduced only after Trial 6, the linear slopes were recalculated on the basis of performance from Trial 6 to 12 only (omitting Trial 7), but again the Plan effect was not significant ($F = 1.20$; $p > .05$). The responses to the postexperimental questionnaire indicated that most Ss were not able to make much headway at memorizing in the 2 hours allowed. Most could reproduce only three patterns or less and these were not exact nor were they recalled in order. (The Ss were considered to have "reproduced" a pattern if they could reproduce its "essential shape"; they did not have to name which pattern they were trying to reproduce.)

However, as it turned out several Ss in the Plan condition were not able to reproduce any patterns. On the other hand, several Ss in the No Plan condition were able to reproduce several of the patterns, indicating that they had memorized some of the patterns even though they were not instructed to do so. When all Ss were reclassified according to the number of patterns they were able to reproduce (dividing the Ss at the median), the "High Memory" group made significantly more matches on Trials 8-12 than the "Low Memory" group ($t = 2.12$; $p < .05$). However, this reclassification put 9 of the 14 Standard Ss into the "High Memory" condition; in addition, those 5 Ss in the "High Memory" condition who were No Standard Ss had a lower mean score than that of the 9 Standard Ss. This suggests that the memorizing that was done may have been as much the *result* of a higher level of performance (which the Standard Ss achieved) as a *cause* of such performance.

How Do Standards Have Their Effect? Mace (1935) found that Ss with specific performance goals dropped below their best previous performance (in terms of their trial scores) only 10% of the time whereas Ss without such goals (those told to "do their best") did so 50% of the time. In this study the corresponding figures are 21% and 41%. But the mean difference in number of reversals is highly significant ($t = 4.07$; $p < .001$). This suggests that one effect of goals is to maintain performance between trials, that is, to prevent "lapses in effort."

However, the question still arises, just how is this level maintained? Mace, for instance, found that the between trial improvement of the Standard group was due *entirely* to greater output during the latter part of each trial. During the first 2 minutes of each 20-minute trial there was no difference at all between the Standard and No Standard groups (for all trials combined). Thus, Mace concluded that the effects of the standards were to *prolong* effort during the work period rather than to *intensify* effort at all stages of the trial. . . .

In the present study the difference between the Standard and No Standard groups is substantial for *all* the 2-minute segments. The t values for the mean differences for each 2-minute segment total are, respectively, 2.44, 2.60, 2.81, 2.71, and 3.01, all of which are significant at $p < .05$ or better. The difference in the mean within trial (linear) slopes of the Standard and No Standard groups, however, is not significant ($t = 1.42$; $p > .05$) though it is in the right direction. However, there is a significant difference between the Standard-Plan group and the No Standard-Plan group ($t = 2.24$; $p < .05$) in mean within trial slopes. Apparently, the major effect of the goals in the present case was to improve performance between trials at every stage of the trial, though there was some difference within trials as well.

One of the reasons for the difference of the two studies might have been that Mace's trials were 20 minutes long while they were only 10 minutes long in the present study. The longer the trials, the more likely the Ss without specific goals should be expected to lag near the end of the period (as fatigue increases). However, it appears that standards can *intensify* effort at all points in the trial as well as to *prolong* effort (as in Mace's study) during the work period.

Discussion

The findings of Mace (1935) using an arithmetic computation task were clearly replicated with a psychomotor task, indicating that the principle that performance goals influence level of performance has some generality over tasks. A recent experiment by Church and Camp (1965) yielded a similar finding using a reaction time task (though the theoretical interpretation of these investigators' results is at variance with our own). Although a previous study by Locke (1966) found a strong relationship between the level of the performance goal (level of intended achievement) and level of actual performance, the present findings (along with those of Mace) may have greater practical implications as in the latter two cases, Ss with specific goals performed better than those told to "do their best." The latter is a typical instruction in most industrial, military, and educational training situations, but the present results indicate that such instructions (or goals) may not result in the highest possible level of performance.

A second finding of interest in the present study was that performance goals were shown to influence the *intensity* of the effort per unit time, whereas previously (Mace, 1935) they had been shown only to *prolong* effort better over the work period. The fact that performance goals can have both effects argues for the general importance of such goals.

Finally the present findings are of theoretical interest in that they emphasize the effects of cognitive (intentional) aspects of motivation. Ryan (1958) and Ryan and Smith (1954), for instance, have argued that the "task" or "intention" be taken as the fundamental unit in motivation and that intentions are the direct cause of most human behavior. The present study, in addition to demonstrating how such notions can be put to a test, supports the validity of this approach.

References

CHURCH, R. M., & CAMP, D. S. Changes in reaction time as a function of knowledge of results. *American Journal of Psychology,* 1965, 78, 102-106.

FLEISHMAN, E. A., & HEMPEL, W. E. Changes in factor structure of a complex psychomotor test as a function of practice. *Psychometrika,* 1954, 19, 239-252.

LOCKE, E. A. The relationship of intentions to level of performance. *Journal of Applied Psychology,* 1966, 50, 60-66.

MACE, C. A. Incentives: Some experimental studies. Industrial Health Research Board (Great Britain), 1935, Report No. 72.

MELTON, A. W. (Ed.) *Apparatus Tests.* AAF Aviation Psychology Program Research Report No. 4, 1947.

ORNE, M. T. On the social psychology of the psychological experiment with particular reference to demand characteristics. *American Psychologist,* 1962, 17, 776-783.

PAYNE, R. B., & HAUTY, G. T. Effect of psychological feedback upon work decrement. *Journal of Experimental Psychology,* 1955, 50, 343-351.

RYAN, T. A. Drives, tasks, and the initiation of behavior. *American Journal of Psychology,* 1958, 71, 74-93.

RYAN, T. A., & SMITH, P. C. *Principles of industrial psychology.* New York: Ronald, 1954.

Relative Task Difficulty and Transfer of Training in Skilled Performance*

R. H. DAY

IN a series of related skills to be mastered, teaching progression could conceivably go from the more simple to the most complex or vice-versa. It has probably been taken for granted by most people that indeed the

* From *Psychological Bulletin,* 1956, *53*, 160-168. Reprinted with permission of the author and the American Psychological Association.

instructional process should proceed from the easy to the difficult. Yet Day's summary of the research shows that the best transfer, with regard to the relative difficulty of initial and last-learned skills, depends on stimulus and response variables. In other words, the nature of the tasks as well as the objectives of the instructor should be taken into consideration when developing the order for teaching a sequence of tasks.

A number of recent investigations have drawn attention to the part played by the relative difficulty of two or more tasks in the degree of transfer from one task to another. Results from these experiments have important implications for practical issues in training as well as for transfer theory. Since, however, there are certain inconsistencies in defining difficulty as well as discrepancies among the experimental results this area of investigation is in need of critical evaluation. The main purpose of this review, therefore, is to bring within the scope of one paper evidence from numerous experiments which have been directly or indirectly concerned with the effect of task difficulty on transfer in skilled performance and to subject this evidence to critical analysis. It should be mentioned in this connection that a number of the experiments dealt with here have not been primarily concerned with task difficulty in relation to transfer, but the evidence has arisen more or less incidentally during the course of the experiment. Also, this paper will be limited to a consideration of recent investigations within the field of human skill, although it is known that some earlier work[6] has drawn attention to the relationship existing between task difficulty and transfer of training.

Essentially, a skilled task in its simplest form possesses three basic features. These are: (a) a stimulus complex sometimes called the display, (b) devices by means of which elements in the display are brought under control by the responses of the operator, and (c) a linkage between these two. This broad analysis applies whether the task is a simple one such as writing with a pen upon paper, or a very much more complex one such as is involved in various kinds of tracking behavior. The difficulty of a task may vary as a function of changes in one or more of these features. The manner in which task difficulty has been varied within each of these task features will be treated first in this paper. This will be followed by a review of results obtained after which certain methodological and theoretical issues will be taken up.

For the most part the general procedure used in experiments of this nature involves either training a number of matched groups under different conditions of task difficulty followed by performance under a different condition, or the use of the AB, BA paradigm or an expansion of it in which each S undergoes each experimental condition. Initial task difficulty is usually assessed from the mean score for a number of trials, the score achieved on the final trial, or the mean number of trials required to reach a certain criterion. The method of estimating the extent of transfer also varies between studies.

Method Used to Vary Task Difficulty

Stimulus Variations. Barch,[3] using a following tracking task (Modified Two-Hand Coordination Test) varied difficulty by changing target size. Using the same task Morin[17] varied difficulty in the same manner. A Rubber Control Test (Model CM120C) was employed by Gagné and Bilodeau.[9] Variations in task difficulty were introduced by changing the width of the on-target scoring area. In an experiment by Szasfran and Welford[23] in which Ss were required to throw loops of chain into a box the display was varied in three ways in order to obtain three levels of difficulty. Under the first conditions Ss

threw directly into the box, under the second they threw over a bar placed between S and target, and under the third condition a mirror was placed behind the box and a screen before it. Under the last condition it was necessary to use the mirror in aiming since the screen blocked direct viewing. In this experiment variations in display led necessarily to changes in method of throwing (responding) according to whether S threw directly or over the bar. Alterations in target speed in a following tracking task led to variations in task difficulty in an experiment by Lincoln and Smith.[14] Changes in target speed necessitated corresponding changes in speed of responding. In an experiment by Andreas and his associates[1] task difficulty was varied by altering the number of moving elements in the display of a tracking task. This was accomplished by employing a following (SAM Two-Hand Pursuit Test) and a compensatory (SAM Two-Hand Coordination Test) task. Under the latter condition changes in display-control linkage were also introduced. A motor-discrimination task in which difficulty was varied by changing the nature of discrimination training during the initial task was used by Gagné and his associates.[7] Position and color discriminations only were used during the initial task and in the final phase both kinds of discrimination were involved.

Response Variations. Gibbs[10] used a hand-wheel controlled compensatory tracking task in which difficulty varied as a function of hand-wheel diameter and in which the smaller hand-wheel resulted in a more difficult task. Another method of varying task difficulty used by Gibbs[10] was that of changing the complexity of the path to be followed in a following tracking task. It is conceivable, of course, that a more complicated path provided greater perceptual difficulties as well as demanding more complex responses. A lever and a pressure control were also used to vary difficulty in another investigation by Gibbs[11] using a compensatory tracking task. The tracking task used by Baker and his associates[2] was of the following variety in which variations in gear ratios between hand-wheel control and follower led to changes in the speed of movement of the follower relative to hand-wheel turning rate.

Variations in Control-Display Linkage. In the experiment by Barch[3] above, task difficulty was varied by means of a complete and a partial reversal of control-display relationship used in the standard form of the task. A change from a "natural" or "expected" to an "unnatural" or "unexpected" relationship resulted in an increase in task difficulty in an experiment by Gibbs.[10] A following tracking task (Iowa Pursuit Apparatus) in which difficulty was varied in four ways using standard, reversed, and two partially reversed display-control linkages was employed by Barch and Lewis.[4] Under the condition of partial display-control linkage reversal either the left or right hand linkage was reversed. It is interesting to note that results from this experiment are contrary to those obtained by Gibbs.[10] Lincoln[13] varied task difficulty by using direct velocity, and aided controls.

Results of Experiments

At this point in the discussion it is as well to summarize briefly the general trend of the experimental results when task difficulty is varied in the numerous ways outlined in the previous section. The effects of relative task difficulty on transfer when difficulty is changed along a stimulus dimension are mainly negative when the *stimulus alone* is varied. In three experiments[9,17] greater initial task difficulty produced by changing the target dimensions did not give rise to a greater amount of transfer than when the initial task was relatively less difficult than the final task.* Target size, however, did exercise an effect in a fourth experiment.[3] In the case of this last experiment it should be pointed out that linkage variables, the difficulty effects of which were not

*See footnote on facing page.

determined, could have affected the amount of transfer from initial to final task. Greater initial task tracking difficulty in terms of target speed[14] also failed to give greater transfer to an easier task than did the opposite order. Increasing task difficulty by changing from a following to a compensatory tracking task[1] did result in greater transfer when the difficult task was practiced initially, but only when the second task had an "unnatural" control-display arrangement. This effect was not observed when the final task control-display relationship was "natural" but still less difficult than the first task. In an aiming experiment[23] increasing the complexity of the display did result in greatest transfer in the difficult to easy direction. In this experiment, however, the variations in the perceptual aspects of the task led to changes in the mode of responding. This makes it difficult to attribute the differential transfer effects to stimulus variation alone. Such an argument applies, of course, to other experiments in which variations in the stimulus situation may have given rise to unmeasurable changes in the mode of response. It does appear, however, to be especially pertinent in the case of the aiming experiment. In a motor-discrimination task[8] transfer of training to a total task of the two forms of discrimination was practiced first. It must be borne in mind, however, that in this experiment transfer of training from the components of a task to a total task comprising a combination of the two initial forms of the task was dealt with, rather than transfer from one task condition to another. The results from this investigation may not be altogether comparable with other experiments in which the stimulus situation was varied.

A greater degree of transfer from a difficult to a less difficult condition than from a less difficult to a difficult condition is met with more consistently when task difficulty is varied with respect to response variables. When the task was made more difficult by altering hand-wheel size and course complexity,[10] method of control,[11] and rate of responding,[2] greatest transfer resulted when this form of the task was practiced initially.

Two experiments[4,10] have dealt with the effects on transfer of task difficulty varied with respect to the spatial relationship between control and display in tracking tasks. Whereas one of these investigations[10] has demonstrated that greater transfer occurred in the difficult to easy direction than in the opposite order, the other experiment[4] failed to note this effect. The fundamental differences in the design, extent of control-display relationship reversal, nature of task, and number of control devices must be considered as possible reasons for the inconsistency between these two sets of results. Variation in difficulty as a result of altering the nature of the control-display linkage in tracking[13] also failed to affect transfer of training differentially with respect to the degree of difficulty of initial and final tasks.

It is necessary to direct attention to the fact that the transfer phenomenon under consideration here has been investigated in connection with only a limited number of factors which are known to affect the difficulty level of a skilled task. Thus, with respect to response variables, such factors as hand-wheel inertia, friction, and aiding time-constants,[12] relationship between display and control,[15] control-crank radius,[22] handedness,[21] and planes of operation[18] have been systematically investigated in relation to the extent to which these factors affect ease of control. In the case of stimulus variables, target dimensions,[15] visual magnification of target,[12] structure of target surround[20] as well

* The results from an experiment by Green published after the completion of this paper in which target size was varied over a wide range are in agreement with these previous findings. The task used was a following tracking task. (Green, R. F., Transfer of skill on a following tracking task as a function of task difficulty (target size) *J. Psychol.*, 1955, 39, 355-370.)

as others have been examined in relation to task difficulty. A systematic examination of such variables from the point of view of differential transfer effects in terms of the order of the difficult and easy conditions would be of considerable practical value as well as a contribution to an understanding of the transfer process in skilled performance.

Task Difficulty

The Isolation and Control of Variables. Ordinarily the relative difficulty of two or more tasks is defined in terms of the magnitude of mean scores achieved during whole or part of the training session or sessions, or, in terms of the magnitude of the score reached on a final trial. These scores are then subjected usually to statistical examination in order to establish the significance of differences between them. Should these differences prove to be significant, then that form of the task revealing greatest mean accuracy, least error, least time of performance, or some such, is said to be the least difficult. In transfer studies of the kind reviewed here, it is of importance not only to define operationally the relative difficulty of the tasks, but to establish as far as possible the source or cause of task difficulty differences. This is an essential step if a theory is to be constructed to deal with the effects on transfer of relative task difficulty.

A problem which has become plain from the preceding review is the difficulty of varying one task variable along a scale of difficulty without producing unmeasurable changes in other closely related variables. Even though the relative difficulty of the two tasks may have become obvious from an examination of performance scores, the exact manner in which task difficulty arose, or to which task-variable task difficulty can be attributed has not always been clear. In short, in many of the experiments discussed the *locus* of task difficulty has not always been clearly specifiable. It should be remembered, however, that stimulus or response conditions probably never remain the same from trial to trial, but, as Osgood[19] has been careful to show, stimulus and response may retain identical functions during learning. Even allowing for this fact many of the experiments on the effects of task difficulty on transfer have failed to control adequately the source of difficulty.

In the experiment by Gibbs[10] in which a following tracking or "steering" task was used not only course complexity, but also the complexity of the responses demanded by the course varied under the two conditions. The more difficult of the two tasks presented the operator with a task which required responses of greater complexity than the easier task, as well as with a stimulus situation which may well have been more difficult perceptually. It is by no means easy in this case to state definitely the separate contributions of each of these factors to the difficulty of the task, or to the extent of transfer. A similar problem is met with in the investigation of Lincoln and Smith[14] where variations in target speed may well have given rise to greater perceptual difficulty, as well as greater difficulty in responding. In the experiment by Szasfran and Welford[23] this same problem arises again. The "bar" condition not only demanded an alteration in the response by requiring the subject to throw over it, but changed as well the stimulus situation. It is not possible, of course, to state whether or not the "bar" and "direct" conditions remained functionally identical while at the same time it is equally impossible to state definitely the locus of task difficulty. A similar argument applies when the greater difficulty of the "screen" condition in this investigation is considered. The two task conditions employed by Andreas and his associates[1] varied not only with respect to the number of display elements, but also in relation to course and response complexity and control-display relationships. In this case it is not possible to state the individual contributions to task difficulty nor their possible interactions, all of which could have affected the level of difficulty.

A further kind of problem in the control of variables has arisen when changes along one stimulus or response dimension have led to unmeasurable variations along a closely related dimension. For example, Baker and his associates[2] altered the level of task difficulty by varying the rate of hand-wheel turning necessary to move the target-follower through a certain distance. These authors have pointed out that changes in turning rate altered also the extent of movement as well as the required force of movement. Variations in task difficulty could be due to any one of these factors or to an interaction between two or all of these.

The principal problem, then, in many of the studies reviewed is to state the locus of variations in task difficulty. Without doing this transfer of training of skill as a function of the relative difficulty of the tasks is not easy to deal with theoretically, since the actual experimental evidence remains obscure. The problem of isolation and control of "difficulty" variables in skilled tasks does not lend itself easily to solution, since stimulus and response factors are so intimately related, and therefore exceptionally difficult to isolate under experimental conditions.

Task Difficulty and Performance Standards. In a number of skilled tasks the level of performance required is frequently *implied* rather than demanded by the task itself. This point can be made clearer by illustration. If in a following tracking task the target is 1 in. in diameter, the target follower ⅛ in. in diameter, and the task of the operator is to superimpose the latter upon the former, a greater margin of error is permitted than if both these display elements are ⅛ in. in diameter. The extent of permissible error is implied by the relative sizes of target and follower. In this example, whereas holding the follower superimposed upon the small (⅛ in.) target may not be necessarily a more difficult task than keeping it on a larger target, the structure of the stimulus situation in the latter case is such that there is a wider margin within which the off-target extent does not count as an error. This means that the two conditions mentioned differ with respect to operationally defined "difficulty" insofar as one condition demands higher performance standards rather than a higher level of skill. The more "difficult" task under these circumstances, then, is the one which requires a higher standard of performance by setting narrower error-tolerance limits. The two task conditions do not necessarily differ, or differ only to a small degree, in the actual level of skill which they demand for adequate performance. The differences, sometimes large, between performance curves for two task conditions differing in this manner may be due primarily to the fact that the operator is directing to the task very little, or a great deal of effort, since the task implies by its target and follower dimensions a certain standard of performance. The difficulty differences between the task conditions are more apparent than real.

Szasfran and Welford[23] have suggested that one possible explanation of the phenomenon of greater transfer from a difficult to an easy task may be found in the higher standards of performance established during the difficult initial task, and carried over to the easier final task. Transfer in this case would be expected to be greater than in shifting from an easy initial task to a more difficult final task. The available experimental evidence does little to support this hypothesis. In the experiments reported[9,17] dealing with the relative dimensions of target and follower in following tracking tasks in which the task difficulty was varied by changing error tolerance limits, transfer was positive and about equal in going from difficult to easy and from easy to difficult conditions. In another experiment[3] greater transfer was found in shifting from difficult to easy, but it has been pointed out that control-display relationship factors were confounded with stimulus factors in this study and the experimental design considered only the easy to difficult direction.

The concept of error-tolerance implicit to the task as a determinant of performance is not a new one. Mace[16] has put forward an hypothesis of "implicit standards" which is summarized in the statement ". . . subjects aiming at targets defined to themselves a 'good,' 'fair' or 'poor' shot not in terms of its *absolute* distance from the bull's-eye, but in a way which was *relative to the form of target employed.*"[16] (p.103) A similar view has been expressed by Helson[12] in his hypothesis of par or tolerance.

The present indications are that when the difficulty of a task varies only in terms of the implied extent of error tolerated, neither condition calling for a higher level of skill, the phenomenon of greater transfer from the difficult to the less difficult condition than from the less to the more difficult condition does not occur. So far this has only been observed in relation to the relative dimensions of target and follower in a tracking task. Much needs to be done with respect to both a variety of skilled tasks, and the various features of skilled tasks, before definite conclusions can be drawn or hypotheses clearly formulated.

The **U** *Hypothesis and Transfer.* Bartlett[5] and Helson[12] have each outlined hypotheses which state in effect that performance will remain essentially the same over a certain range of variation in the physical characteristics of the task. Outside this range performance tends to undergo considerable changes. Thus Bartlett states: "The fundamental features of performance will remain stable over a certain range of its conditions. Outside this range they will change often in a dramatic and radical manner."[5] (p.444) Helson's statement is much the same:

> Human performance tends to be optimal as judged by accuracy, efficiency, and comfort, over a more or less broad band of values for a given stimulus variable outside of which it becomes noticeably poorer. When performance is plotted in terms of error or the reciprocal of accuracy, the resultant curve is roughly **U**- shaped.[12](p.493)

Helson has demonstrated such a curve for aiding time-constants, hand-wheel turning speed, and hand-wheel size and inertia.

Employing this notion of the optimal band of performance Gibbs[10] has suggested that:

> . . . transfer between two tasks, one of which lies within the tolerance limits, and one of which lies outside this optimal zone can be (a) positive, (b) large, (c) unequal and unaffected by the order of task presentation; this implies greater transfer when the first task lies outside the optimal zone, and the second lies within it, than when the first task comes within and the second ouside.

This hypothesis lends itself readily to experiment, and since a considerable amount of data is now available concerning the optimal band of performance for a number of task variables, experiments designed to measure transfer from within to without and from without to within the optimal zone would be of great value.

A single **U** curve deals only with a single variable, thus emphasizing again the need for careful isolation and control of task variables in transfer experiments of this kind. Since much of the evidence indicates that the relative difficulty of initial and final task conditions is a transfer determinant of considerable importance it is essential now to study the many factors varying in difficulty and depicted by the **U** shaped curve. This approach would doubtlessly provide data of fundamental importance to practical and theoretical considerations in the transfer of skill.

In conclusion, one further inadequacy in the experimental design of many of the experiments so far mentioned needs to be pointed out. Many of the experiments have been designed so that only the difficult-to-easy, and easy-to-difficult task conditions have been taken into consideration. It is again important, from both practical and theoretical viewpoints, that the degree of transfer from one condition to the same condition should be observed as well. In the experiment by Baker and his associates[2] it was found that the greatest degree of transfer occurred when there was no difference in difficulty between the initial and final task. This means, of course, that greatest facilitation took place when the initial and final tasks were the same task. This is normal learning rather than transfer of skill. Since a large number of the investigations outlined in this paper failed to include the experimental conditions of easy to easy and difficult to difficult, it is not easy to generalize concerning the difficulty conditions of initial and final task for maximum transfer.

Summary

This article has presented a summary of a number of investigations concerned with the effect on transfer of training of the relative difficulty of initial and final tasks. The results from a number of recent studies are regarded as presenting an important problem for practical consideration and theoretical interpretation. The principal findings of these experiments have been briefly summarized. The concept of task difficulty has been discussed in relation to the isolation and control of task variables, subjective performance standards, and the **U** hypothesis.

References

1. ANDREAS, B. G., GREEN, R. F., & SPRAGG, S. D. S. Transfer effects between performance on a following tracking task (Modified SAM Two-Hand Coordination Test) and a compensatory tracking task (Modified SAM Two-Hand Pursuit Test). *J. Psychol.*, 1954, 37, 173-193.

2. BAKER, KATHERINE E., WYLIE, R. C., & GAGNÉ, R. M. Transfer of training to a motor skill as a function of variation in rate of response. *J. exp. Psychol.*, 1950, 40, 721-732.

3. BARCH, A. M. The effect of difficulty of task on proactive facilitation and interference. *J. exp. Psychol.*, 1953, 46, 37-42.

4. BARCH, A. M., & LEWIS, D. The effect of task difficulty and amount of practice on proactive transfer. *J. exp. Psychol.*, 1954, 48, 134-142.

5. BARTLETT, F. C. Some problems of "display" and "control." In A. Michotte (Ed.), *Miscellanea psychologica*. Louvain: Librairie Philosophique, 1947. Pp. 440-452.

6. COOK, T. W. Amount of material and difficulty of problem solving. *J. exp. Psychol.*, 1937, 20, 288-296.

7. GAGNÉ, R. M., BAKER, KATHERINE E., & FOSTER, H. On the relation between similarity and transfer of training in the learning of discriminative motor tasks. *Psychol. Rev.*, 1950, 57, 67-79.

8. GAGNÉ, R. M., BAKER, KATHERINE E., & FOSTER, H. Transfer of discrimination training to a motor task. *J. exp. Psychol.*, 1950, 40, 314-328.

9. GAGNÉ, R. M., & BILODEAU, E. A. The effects of target size variation on skill acquisition. *USAF, Personnel Train. Res. Cent., Res. Bull.*, 1954, No. 54-55.

10. GIBBS, C. B. Transfer of training and skill assumptions in tracking. *Quart. J. exp. Psychol.*, 1951, 3, 99-110.

11. GIBBS, C. B. The continuous regulation of skilled response by kinaesthetic feed back. *Med. Res. Coun., Appl. Psychol. Unit. Rep.* 1953, No. A.P.U. 190/53.

12. HELSON, H. Design of equipment and optimal human operation. *Amer. J. Psychol.*, 1949, 62, 473-479.

13. Lincoln, R. S. Visual tracking III. The instrumental dimension of motion in relation to tracking accuracy. *J. appl. Psychol.*, 1953, 37, 389-493.

14. Lincoln, R. S., & Smith, K. U. Transfer of training in tracking performance at different target speeds. *J. appl. Psychol.*, 1951, 35, 358-362.

15. Lincoln, R. S., & Smith, K. U. Systematic analysis of factors determining accuracy in visual tracking. *Science*, 1952, 116, 183-187.

16. Mace, C. A. The influence of indirect incentives upon the accuracy of skilled movements. *Brit. J. Psychol.*, 1931, 22, 101-114.

17. Morin, R. E. Transfer of training between motor tasks varying in precision of movement required to score. *Amer. Psychologist*, 1951, 6, 390. (Abstract)

18. Norris, Eugenia B., & Spragg, S. D. S. Performance on a following tracking task (Modified SAM Two-Hand Coordination Test) as a function of the planes of operation of the controls. *J. Psychol.*, 1953, 35, 107-117.

19. Osgood, C. E. The similarity paradox in human learning: A resolution. *Psychol. Rev.*, 1949, 56, 132-143.

20. Senders, J. W. The influence of surround on tracking performance. Pt. 1. Tracking on combined pursuit and compensatory one-dimensional tasks with and without structural surround. *USAF, WADC Tech. Rep.* 1953 No. 52-229.

21. Simon, J. R., De Crow, T. W., Lincoln, R. S., & Smith, K. U. Effects of handedness on tracking accuracy. *Percept. Mot. Skills. Res. Exch.*, 1952, 4, 53-57.

22. Swartz, P., Norris, Eugenia B., & Spragg, S. D. S. Performance on a following tracking task (Modified SAM Two-Hand Coordination Test) as a function of radius of control cranks. *J. Psychol.*, 1954, 37, 163-171.

23. Szasfran, J., & Welford, A. T. On the relation between transfer and difficulty of initial task. *Quart. J. exp. Psychol.*, 1950, 2, 88-94.

Cross Education: Ipsilateral and Contralateral Effects of Unimanual Training*

F. A. HELLEBRANDT

Transfer relationships and effects can be studied under many, many conditions. One of the more interesting phenomena has been termed bilateral transfer, or cross-education. Apparently, the training of one limb positively transfers to the non-trained limb. Research conclusions before and since Hellebrandt's excellent report generally confirm this occurrence under assorted conditions. She goes much further than most investigators in this area by attempting to explain transfer, usually reserved for psychology of learning specialists, in physiological terms.

Work done previously in this laboratory[1] demonstrated that exercise of the progressive resistance type not only increases the functional capacity of the contractile tissues subjected to direct training, but has a significant effect on the power and endurance of homologous muscle groups of the contralateral unpracticed limb. At that time the early literature on the phenomenon of cross

* From the *Journal of Applied Physiology*, 1951, 4, 136-143. Reprinted with permission of the author and the American Physiological Society.

education was reviewed. Since then, Slater-Hammel[2] has added a new study showing that a systematic exercise program involving the repetitive flexion of one forearm against an invariable load produces a positive and statistically significant improvement in the muscular performance of the unexercised arm. The number of contractions executed in the prescribed rhythm (duration of exercise) was the independent variable. In his discussion, Slater-Hammel attempts to differentiate the psychologic from the physiologic factors involved in the interpretation of these data. He places particular emphasis on Davis'[3,4] concept of spreading patterns of action, and suggests that herein may lie an explanation of the phenomenon of cross education. In 1947 we had postulated that the mechanism might be a dual one, involving not only diffusion of motor impulses to the unpracticed side, but also the concurrent development of a reflex postural substrate related to the maintenance of balance and not unlike "muscle setting" in its clinical effect, when elicited repetitively.

It is common experience that whenever unilateral exercise of large muscle groups is performed against heavy resistance, widespread postural readjustments always occur. These call forth the synergistic co-contraction of many muscle groups involving the trunk and remote extremities as well as those of the opposite limb. If spontaneous head turning occurs, the postural configuration is modified in a predictable manner by the tonic neck reflexes of Magnus.[5] The magnitude of the tensions thus developed may be estimated readily by attempting to mobilize the joints of the so-called resting limbs during severe unilateral exercise restricted to a single appendage. The importance of the overflow and postural factors to cross education then becomes obvious. They do not, however, provide a universally applicable hypothesis explaining the mechanism of this phenomenon in less rigorous types of exercise.

Many of the early experiments on cross education were concerned with skills rather than exercises demanding strength. If irradiation occurs to the contralateral side during such activities, it is associated with no visible signs. This suggests that the neurological component in cross education may be as important as the involuntary training of peripheral effector organs. Such a concept has practical implications of importance to the technique of applying physical rehabilitation procedures, many of which are more concerned with the acquisition of motor skills than with the development of strength or power. Many years ago Anderson[6] asked, and attempted to determine, whether or not muscles can be trained to perform ordinary gymnastic feats by merely thinking of the movements involved.

The purpose of the study herein reported was to measure the bilateral influence of the unilateral practice of standardized activities requiring manual dexterity. An incidental objective of some practical importance was to determine whether or not the nonpreferred hand gains more from practice of the dominant side than vice versa.

Methods

The subjects of the investigation were 51 normal young adults, 27 of whom were males. All but one, who was a research fellow, were physical therapy students enrolled in a required course in applied physiology. The activity selected was MacQuarrie's[7] paper and pencil test for mechanical ability. Extensive analysis of this test[8-10] had demonstrated it to be a measure of manual dexterity or agility, controlled manual movement and special perception. It is composed of 7 subtests, 4 of which were used for the major observations of this study.

The total test was first taken by the preferred and then the nonpreferred hand. The initial trials were scored and the dextrality quotient of each subject was computed. The group was then divided into two with matching degrees of handedness. One subject subsequently withdrew, leaving 26 in one group and 24 in the other. The mean performance of the two groups was similar on all subtests performed by both the right and left hands. Statistical analysis of the scores attained on the 400 initial subtests indicated that all differences observed were nonsignificant. The division of the experimental subjects into two groups on the basis of equivalent hand dominance thus proved to be a satisfactory selection procedure.

The *location, blocks* and *pursuit* subtests were eliminated because they are primarily measures of spatial perception. One such test, *copying,* was retained. This requires, in addition, considerable controlled manual movement and appears not to be affected markedly by visual acuity. *Tracing, tapping* and *dotting,* all of which were retained, are predominantly motor tests. Dotting measures, in addition, manual agility.

The MacQuarrie test for mechanical ability was administered once weekly. It was given at the same time of day under standardized conditions; though not ideal, they were constant. The tests were given in an amphitheater, necessitating the use of portable writing boards instead of a table or desk. Standard directions were read each time the test was administered. Adaptation to the experimental situation was good by virtue of previous experience with a battery of paper and pencil tests of various types administered during the opening week of the school term. Attitude and emotional set were controlled by prior indoctrination. Cooperation was excellent.

The experimental period covered 8 weeks. In toto, 2373 subtests were administered. Tracing and copying were scored by one individual and tapping and dotting by another, thus keeping variations related to judgment reasonably constant. All scoring dependent on precise inspection was done with a magnifying glass.

Twenty-six subjects practiced the subtests selected with the left hand (*group L*); the remaining 24 practiced with the right hand (*group R*). The mechanical ability of the right and left hands was retested on the final experimental day. Sex differences in mechanical ability, test-retest reliability and the slope gradient of the training curves of the traits under study will be presented elsewhere. Only cross education will be discussed here.

Results and Their Interpretation

The mean initial performance was significantly better on the right than the left only in tapping and dotting. These differences attained a .01 level of significance in both groups. Dotting, which combines agility and controlled movement, is the only trait which was conspicuously poor on the left. The CR was 15.21 and 10.32 for *group R* and *group L,* respectively. Unexpectedly, performance in tracing was quite good on the nonpreferred side; copying, which is affected by the acuity of spatial perception, was virtually as good on the left as on the right.

The traits studied are obviously not static. All increased with practice. The differences are uniformly significant on the 1 per cent level of confidence. In general, the mechanical ability of the right hand improved more with direct practice than that of the left. Dotting is the only exception. No other trait demonstrated so large a difference between the initial ability on the preferred and the nonpreferred side. Starting at a level roughly 50 per cent that of the dominant extremity, there was ample room for improvement with practice.

The unpracticed hand improved significantly in mechanical ability with one exception, left-handed tapping. This may be due to an environmental artifact.

When 50 persons tap simultaneously, individual rhythm of performance is probably affected by that of the group. The mean percentage gain demonstrated by the left hand as a result of practice by the right exceeded that achieved by direct training. The reverse was never true; i.e. cross education on the right never approached that gained by direct practice. Cross education from left to right was, however, clearly demonstrable. If the percentage gain by direct practice is compared with the improvement attained concurrently by the unpracticed contralateral limb, the relative degree of cross education appears to be somewhat greater from left to right than vice versa. The two hands achieve a more nearly equal mechanical ability than that attained during direct practice of the dominant extremity. Early experiments of Welch[11] may explain the seemingly greater transfer of motor learning when the less skilled of the paired upper extremities is subjected to direct practice. She had observed that the innervations to perform rhythmical contractions given to the left hand while the opposite hand applies static pressure to a dynamometer are communicated to the right hand and influence the form of the curve attained, while innervations to perform rhythmical contractions on the right while the left is squeezing the dynamometer are transmitted to the opposite side much less markedly. This suggests that there may be less irradiation to the contralateral side when ipsilateral responses flow over the more highly trained and discrete neural pathways of the dominant limb.

Discussion

In 1892, Bryan[12] studied the rate of tapping with various joints of the upper extremities: shoulder, elbow, wrist and metacarpo-phalangeal. The observations were made on 789 school children. Between the ages of 6 and 16 the right hand and arm outgrew the left in rate of tapping very little if at all, in spite of vastly more use. Bryan therefore concluded that either growth in rate of tapping was not determined by use, or the effects of use on the right side had been shared to a significant degree by the corresponding muscle groups of the contralateral limb. Functional use obviously has bilateral effects of some biological significance. If this were not true, structural and functional asymmetries would far exceed those demonstrable in the average normal adult.[13]

In 1898, Welch[11] observed that whenever the muscles of one hand were maximally innervated by strong volitional effort, other groups were activated concurrently, as for example, those of the resting hand. She therefore estimated the work done when both hands were simultaneously innervated maximally instead of unilaterally and found that the extent and duration of the effort were greater when the exercise was performed bimanually. More recently we[14] have also demonstrated that when fatigue supervenes during the performance of alternate bouts of repetitive exercise against maximal resistance, the simultaneous contraction of homologous muscle groups is significantly dynamogenic.

It is generally agreed that the bulk of the fibers comprising the corticospinal tract cross into the opposite lateral funiculus at the pyramidal decussation in the medulla oblongata. Thus, the motor cortex of one hemisphere is concerned primarily with the innervation of muscles occupying the contralateral half of the body. No one discussing the phenomenon of cross education has yet attempted to explain where and by what neuronal links motor impulses overflow to ipsilaterally disposed muscle groups, or irradiate to call forth a mass response involving remote as well as the contralateral appendage.

It has long been known that some corticospinal fibers take an ipsilateral course assumed to cross to the opposite side in the anterior commissure before synapsing with lower motor neurons. In 1932 Fulton and Keller[15] pointed out that the belief that no uncrossed corticospinal fibers exist was based on a surmise unsupported by direct histological evidence. They found, furthermore, that following ablation of the leg area on one side, its removal on the opposite side in the baboon and chimpanzee produced a slight impairment of locomotor activity of the homolateral limb. Ablation of the second foot area in the monkey caused an increase in the disability of the ipsilateral extremity and an increase in the sign of Babinski. This suggests that uncrossed corticospinal fibers may influence the ipsilateral extremity directly. In 1933 Bucy[16] reported that cortical stimulation could elicit ipsilateral contraction in the extremities of primates. He located an "ipsilateral area" of high threshold, occupying a position largely in area six but extending slightly into four. Bucy and Fulton[17] concluded that one hemisphere of primates is capable of integrating the movement in all four extremities. Clinical evidence was reviewed suggesting that the pyramidal system of man might also have a bilateral cortical representation. Subsequently Fulton and Sheehan[18] were able to demonstrate an uncrossed contingent in the lateral corticospinal tract.

In 1933 Bucy[16] noted that Foerster had observed ipsilateral movements on stimulation of the human cortex. However, Penfield and Erickson[19] concluded that bilateral representation of movement does not exist in man. Stimulation of the human cortex, in their experience, never produced ipsilateral leg movements. They conceded, however, that the preservation of limited control in the presence of large unilateral lesions in infancy may be due to the influence of the normal ipsilateral cortex, but maintained that this was an unproven assumption. Subsequently Erickson[20] pointed out that though the occurrence of ipsilateral movements in man is rare, specific observation had not been directed to the ipsilateral extremities and such movement may have been overlooked. In their most recent monograph Penfield and Rasmussen[21] report that bilateral leg movements were observed and verified repeatedly in one patient on stimulation of the left motor leg area.

Fulton[22] estimates that from 10 to 15 per cent of the corticospinal fibers terminate on the ipsilateral side of the cord. Whether or not the bilateral representation of descending pathways thus implied presupposes a bilateral representation of voluntary power is open to conjecture. The character of the ipsilateral response elicited by Wyss[23] from cortical stimulation in the monkey led him to believe this to be unlikely. It differed considerably from the contralateral effect of stimulation of the excitable cortex, being primarily tonic. However, the oft-observed return of function after lower extremity cortical lesions in the adult suggests that the ipsilateral representation may indeed be functionally useful.

Viewing the evidence in toto, it is tempting to postulate that some grooving of the neuronal pattern thought to be essential to motor learning must take place on the ipsilateral side, while the main stream of descending impulses flows to the contralateral limb. If the quantum of energy released is large, as for example during maximal volitional effort against maximal resistance, copying movements tend to occur in the so-called resting limb. These always have a conspicuously large tonic component. If the subject has been inured to the discomforts of severe exercise and puts forth a genuine all-out effort, all four extremities may be observed to participate in what commenced as a regional exercise limited to the activators of a single appendicular joint. Cross education appears to occur with equal facility whether the exercise performed demands the development of maximal contractile force by large muscle groups or the execution of highly skilled and agile digital movements. The phenomenon is so readily demonstrated as to suggest that it may be no more than the normal resultant of a simultaneous discharge of identical efferent impulses over bilateral pathways differing only in volume.

Nielsen[24] has postulated that ideational motor planning is dependent upon the integrity of the posterior association area of Flechsig. The learning of motor acts requires cerebration. Visualization of the motor act takes place in the posterior margin of the angular gyrus and a part of area 19 of Broadmann, while the post-central gyrus contributes kinesthesia and recognition of the tactile impulses concerned in the act. The impulses then travel forward to areas 4, 4s and 6, where the pattern required takes form in the descending pathways. Known facts suggest that the engrammes concerned in ideational motor planning are harbored on the major side only since lesions located in the dominant hemisphere destroy consciousness of the body scheme as a whole. The ideokinetic apraxia which results is, however, only temporary. This leads Nielsen to postulate that the ideational motor plan can be formed on either side and that the minor hemisphere assumes control when the dominant side is rendered inactive. Thus the planning which precedes the execution of volitional motor acts requiring cerebration has a unilateral representation capable of bilateral coordination. Whether or not the area concerned with the evolution of a bilateral body scheme is responsible for cross education is open to speculation.

The utility of cross education as a physical rehabilitation device is obvious. It is astonishing that so little advantage has been taken of it in the neuromuscular re-education of the disabled suffering from unilateral lesions. Although the dominant limb appears to improve more by direct practice than cross education, the data presented in this study indicate that more may be gained by the less skilled side through training of the more skilled contralateral limb than by ipsilateral practice. We have shown elsewhere[25] that the execution of simple repetitive movements either reciprocally or in alternation augments work output to levels significantly above maximal unilateral performance. Thus there is little justification for limitation of treatment programs to the injured or diseased side, which is, unfortunately, common practice. Whether the facilitating mechanisms underlying cross education and the dynamogenic influence of bilateral, reciprocal and alternate exercise are related awaits further study.

Summary and Conclusions

The bilateral influence of the unilateral practice of four standardized activities included in the MacQuarrie test of mechanical ability was studied on 50 normal young adult physical therapy trainees, 27 of whom were males. The test was first taken by the preferred and then by the nonpreferred hand. The group was then divided into two on the basis of equivalent hand dominance. Twenty-six subjects practiced once weekly with the left hand and 24 practiced with the right. The experiment extended over a period of 8 weeks at the termination of which right- and left-sided performance was again measured. Statistical analysis of the data supports the following conclusions: 1) Manual dexterity improves significantly with direct practice. 2) In general, the mechanical ability of the dominant limb improves more with direct practice than that of the contralateral extremity. 3) The unpracticed contralateral extremity also improves significantly in mechanical ability. 4) Dextral improvement due to cross education does not approach that achieved by direct practice. 5) The sinistral or nonpreferred side may gain more as a result of practice by the contralateral limb than by ipsilateral direct practice but the differences are not significant. 6) The relative amount of motor learning taking place bilaterally appears to spread more nearly equally to the right and the left sides when training involves the less discrete pathways of the non-preferred limb.

The mechanism of cross education is discussed. Analysis of the response of normal individuals to volitional exercise suggests that efferent patterns of discharge may take a bilateral course with the major flow going to the contralateral side, and a smaller but identical component traveling ipsilaterally. It is unknown whether this behavioral pattern has its origin in bilateral representation of the musculature in the motor cortex or because ideational motor planning involves a bilateral visualization of the body scheme as a whole.

References

1. HELLEBRANDT, F. A., A. M. PARRISH AND S. J. HOUTZ. *Arch. Phys. Med.* 28:76, 1947.
2. SLATER-HAMMEL, A. T. *Research Quart.* 21:203, 1950.
3. DAVIS, R. C. *J. Exper. Psychol.* 30:452, 1942.
4. DAVIS, R. C. *J. Exper. Psychol.* 31: 47, 1942.
5. MAGNUS, R. *Körperstellung.* Berlin: Julius Springer, 1924.
6. ANDERSON, W. G. *Am. Phys. Ed. Rev.* 4:265, 1899.
7. MACQUARRIE, T. W. *J. Personnel Research.* 5:329, 1927.
8. HARRELL, W. *Psychometrika.* 5:17, 1940.
9. GOODMAN, C. H. *J. Applied Psychol.* 32:150, 1947.
10. CHAPMAN, R. L. *Psychometrika.* 13:175, 1948.
11. WELCH, J. C. *Am. J. Physiol.* 1:283, 1898.
12. BRYAN, W. L. *Am. J. Psychol.* 5:125, 1892.
13. HELLEBRANDT, F. A. AND S. J. HOUTZ. *Am. J. Phys. Anthropol.* 8:225, 1950.
14. HELLEBRANDT, F. A. AND S. J. HOUTZ. *J. Applied Physiol.* 2:446, 1950.
15. FULTON, J. F. AND A. D. KELLER. *The Sign of Babinski. A Study of the Evolution of Cortical Dominance in Primates.* Springfield: Thomas, 1932.
16. BUCY, P. C. *Science* 78:418, 1933.
17. BUCY, P. C. AND J. F. FULTON. *Brain* 56:318, 1933.
18. FULTON, J. F. AND D. SHEEHAN. *J. Anat.* 69:181, 1935.
19. PENFIELD, W. AND T. C. ERICKSON. *Epilepsy and Cerebral Localization. A Study of the Mechanism, Treatment and Prevention of Epileptic Seizures.* Springfield: Thomas, 1941.
20. ERICKSON, T. C. *Electrical Excitability in Man.* Chap. XIII, The Precentral Motor Cortex (2nd ed.), edited by P. C. BUCY. Urbana: Univ. Illinois Press, 1949.
21. PENFIELD, W. AND T. RASMUSSEN. *The Cerebral Cortex of Man—A Clinical Study of Localization of Function.* New York: Macmillan, 1950.
22. FULTON, J. F. *Functional Localization in Relation to Frontal Lobotomy.* New York: Oxford, 1949.
23. WYSS, O. A. M. *J. Neurophysiol.* 1:125, 1938.
24. NIELSEN, J. M. *J. Nerv. & Ment. Dis.* 108:361, 1948.
25. HELLEBRANDT, F. A., S. J. HOUTZ AND R. N. EUBANK. *Arch. Phys. Med.* In press.

Chapter 12

DURING-PRACTICE CONSIDERATIONS

A Comparison of Traditional versus Programed Methods of Learning Tennis*

MILTON C. NEUMAN AND ROBERT N. SINGER

ALTHOUGH programed learning techniques are endorsed by many educational psychologists, and tests and teaching machines for learnings in the cognitive domain are available, psychomotor skills are not so readily or easily taught in this manner. Therefore, the effectiveness of a learning experience that attempts to minimize errors, encourage immediate reinforcement, and proceed from simple to complex learnings in the shaping of behavior is difficult to determine as compared to a teaching procedure that encourages less controlled behavior, learning from mistakes made, and that is practical in group-oriented motor learning situations. Neuman and Singer suggest a way of applying the programed learning technique to tennis and, in turn, present data concerning programed and traditional methods.

Many physical educators and those persons involved in related physical education fields have questioned whether the present traditional methods of teaching have achieved teacher objectives to the extent desired.

The traditional approach to learning has been characterized by (a) periods of verbal instruction in which the student receives essential information and demonstration regarding the skills involved in an activity, and (b) periods of activity in which the student creates for himself a movement pattern which meets his preconceived needs and goals as well as conforming to teacher objectives. The instruction period serves to create an image of "ideal" movement, and the activity period serves to develop the movement pattern.

In recent years, many of the academic teaching areas have been revolu-

* From *The Research Quarterly*, 1968, *39*, 1044-1048. Reprinted with permission of the authors and the American Association for Health, Physical Education, and Recreation.

11

tionized by the development and implementation of programed materials and teaching machines. The theory of programed instruction was advanced from the Pavlovian experiments associated with respondent conditioning and later from Skinner's experiments associated with operant conditioning.

Methods of programing, as distinguished from the theory of programed instruction, evolved from the technique used by Pressey in his invention of the teaching machine in the 1920's. The implications of such an approach to the learning of motor skills are yet unknown. It seems logical, then, to investigate the possibilities of providing a learning method representing the programed system in a physical education environment. This study was designed, therefore, to compare the relative effects of a traditional method and a programed method on the acquisition of general tennis skills, playing ability, and form.

Review of Literature

The basis of the traditional teaching methods, which are utilized in physical education classes, lies in Thorndike's[9] trial-and-error learning theory. Active participation of students is necessary, and the student learns correct movement patterns as a result of random behavior. That is, he learns from his mistakes as well as from ideal responses. In a sense, then, the learning from mistakes is encouraged.

On the other hand, Skinner[8] proposed that the most effective learning was that which is "programed." In the operant conditioning of human beings, the learner was led through a sequence of specially designed behaviors arranged to increase the probability that the desired behavior will occur. The concept of programed instruction reflects an ordered sequence of small steps (stimuli), each requiring a response by the learner, which is then reinforced. The stimulus-response-reinforcement pattern continues until the material is learned. The learner is not allowed to learn more difficult material until he has mastered the basics.

In Adams'[1] study each of five groups of subjects learned a maze in a different manner. After a mistake was made, group one returned to the beginning; group two returned to the first step of the maze; group three corrected the error and went straight ahead; group four kept going; and group five repeated the error before continuing. Adams concluded that going back to the beginning in this learning situation helped to develop the best and longest-lasting skill.

Tokemasa[10] wrote that when the task becomes more difficult, the individual must revert to a strictly trial-and-error method because the task is too advanced for his reasoning powers to be of help in solving the problem.

There are advantages and disadvantages in the use of any learning method. Olson,[7] Bender,[2] Williams,[11] and Morello[5] have listed the following advantages of both the traditional and programed methods of learning.

The traditional method of learning:
1. permits more creativity in learning because the learner is not necessarily bound to a predetermined learning pattern;
2. allows the student to more readily explore his errors;
3. is more flexible to individual learning styles; and
4. allows the social environment to interact with the learning environment.

The programed learning method:
1. provides for students' individual learning rates;

2. causes constant participation of the students in the learning process because a response must be made in order to proceed;

3. allows for constant and immediate knowledge of results;

4. can be used more effectively to teach groups of large size and varying ability;

5. corrects errors before they persist; and

6. leaves the teacher free from paper work and allows him to be available for individual instruction.

With regard to the learning of motor skills, the investigation of the effectiveness of the traditional versus programed learning is yet to be explored.

Procedures

The subjects for this study were male beginning tennis players enrolled in each of two service classes at Illinois State University. Qualification for inclusion in this investigation was based on each subject's tennis background as determined by a questionnaire. Those subjects who had had previous high school, college, or professional tennis instruction; those who had belonged to an organized tennis team, or who had played intramural or extramural tennis; and those who played tennis more than 10 times in the past two years, were eliminated from the study.

After the unqualified subjects in the classes were eliminated from consideration as subjects in the study, 20 students in each of the two classes remained. One class was designated as the class to be taught by the programed method, the other by the traditional method.

The traditionally taught group (Group A) and the programed group (Group B) were compared in height, weight, the Hewitt Revised Dyer Backboard Tennis Test, (HRDBTT) and on the American College Test scores to determine the homogeneity of the groups before the study was initiated. The t ratios obtained were not significant. The HRDBTT was administered according to Hewitt's suggested procedures.[4] The American College Test scores for the subjects were obtained from each subject's college entrance records.

Both groups met twice a week for a 7-week period, with each session lasting for one hour. Each group had the same physical education instructor who conducted the group activities. In addition to an instructor, Group B was provided with five supervisors whose responsibilities were to see that no subject violated the program in any way. The volunteer supervisors qualified for their positions by having participated in intercollegiate tennis activities at Illinois State University.

Group A learned beginning tennis skills—the forehand, the backhand, and the serve—by a traditional method. The grip, stance, backswing, forward swing, and follow-through of each stroke were discussed and demonstrated. The subjects were then given general drills and activity periods to perfect the skills.

Group B learned the same tennis skills as Group A but through a programed method.* Each subject was given a programed tennis booklet, through which he worked at his own rate. The booklet was designed by the first author according to suggestions for good programing as stated by Mosston[6] and Foshay.[3]

After the 7-week period of instruction, the HRDBTT was administered again to all subjects in both groups. During the seventh week, Group A and Group B were combined and played a single-elimination tournament. The

*The programed material may be obtained from the authors upon request.

instructor subjectively ranked the first 10 subjects according to their playing ability. The remaining 10 subjects were ranked in groups of five: 11-15, and 16-20. Those subjects ranked 1-10 from both Group A and Group B were seeded in the tournament. Those subjects ranked 11-15 and 16-20 were randomly placed in the tournament.

All first-, second-, and third-round matches were played as 15 point games. Fourth-round matches consisted of 20 points, and the fifth of 25 points. One player served four consecutive points before the opponent served four consecutive points. All games were to be won by two or more points.

During the warm-up and playing of the first round of the tournament all subjects were subjectively rated on tennis form. The rating was done by one female and two male raters, experienced in tennis competition, who had no previous contact with the subjects in either group. They were provided with a set of criteria on which to base their ratings. A total composite score for each subject was tabulated by adding the ratings of the three judges.

Results

The HRDBTT, administered again at the end of the experimental period, indicated no significant difference between the groups. However, the t ratio of 2.13 obtained in the comparison of the groups on subjective ratings (SR) was significant in favor of Group B.

The pre-experimental and postexperimental test scores on the Hewitt test were subjected to a one-tailed t test to determine if a significant difference existed within the groups as a result of their respective learning methods. A one-tailed test was used because of the expected rise in the skill level of the groups. Group B, with a t ratio of 1.30 for the two tests, did not significantly improve. However the t ratio of 2.3 obtained for Group A did indicate a significant rise in test performance.

Progression of the subjects in each group through the single-elimination tournament was analyzed by utilizing the chi-square statistic. It was expected that approximately the same number of subjects from each group would progress through each round of the tournament if the groups were not significantly different in tennis playing ability.

In order to be significant at the .05 level a chi square of 3.84 or above was necessary in each of the tournament rounds. None of the chi squares obtained were significant.

The programed tennis text was validated to ensure that it taught what it purported to teach, that is, beginning tennis skills. Three methods of correlation were used. The number of steps completed through the program was correlated with (a) the final HRDBTT scores, (b) the progression of the subjects in the single-elimination tennis tournament, and (c) the subjective ratings of form made during the tournament.

A correlation of .87 of the programed tennis text with the tournament and a correlation of .84 with the subjective ratings demonstrated rather high validity compared to the correlation of .68 found between the programed tennis text and the HRDBTT.

Discussion and Conclusions

In general, the traditional learning method and the programed learning method differed little in their effect on the general tennis skill ability and playing ability of groups which learned by these methods, although the group taught by a traditional method improved significantly and the other group did not. The programed method did, however, produce significantly better subjective ratings of form. This would seem to indicate that form may be unnecessary for successful tennis skill or playing ability at the beginning level. It is possible, however, that form is necessary for success at the inter-mediate and advanced levels in tennis. The early mastery of form, such as that produced by the programed method, might facilitate the achievement of better skill and playing ability in a 10- to 15-week period of instruction more than the traditional method.

Two observations were made during the 7-week period. First, each subject in the programed group was better challenged to learn at all times since he was allowed to progress individually upon mastery of steps in the program. The traditional group contained some subjects who were, at times, far behind and others who were far ahead.

Second, the instructor of the programed group was freed from formal teaching responsibilities, thus allowing him to individualize his instruction even further. In this study, however, the freedom the instructor had was due primarily to the five assistant instructors who were active in the class. There is no reason to doubt, though, that means could be devised for one instructor to handle a programed group. Associated with the traditional group was a more formal instructional setting with considerably less time for individualiza-tion.

Recommendations

Additional investigation is needed on these learning methods with varying lengths of instructional sessions in order to gain further understanding of the development of tennis skills and to determine the best possible program. Varying the number and length of the instructional periods as well as the instructional situations should be of prime consideration in these studies.

Investigations of this sort in other sports activities may also prove beneficial to the development and implementation of better learning methods and ultimately more highly developed sports skills for each learner.

References

1. ADAMS, L. Five methods of serial role learning: a comparative study. *Arch. psychol.* 31, No. 221, 1938.
2. BENDER, ERIC. The other kind of teaching. *Harper's mag.* 230:48-55, 1965.
3. FOSHAY, ARTHUR W. *Programed instruction.* U.S. Department of Health, Educa-tion and Welfare, Office of Education, Washington, D.C.: Government Printing Office, 1964.
4. HEWITT, JACK E. Revision of the Dyer backboard tennis test. *Res. quart.* 36:153-57, 1965.
5. MORELLO, TED. What is it? New world of teaching machines or brave new teach-ing machines. *UNESCO courier.* 18:10-16, 1965.
6. MOSSTON, MUSKA. *Teaching physical education.* Columbus: Charles E. Merrill Books, 1966.
7. OLSON, JAMES. The trouble with programed teaching. *Lib. j.* 90:935-36, 1965.
8. SKINNER, B. F. *The behavior of organisms.* New York: D. Appleton-Century Co., 1938.
9. THORNDIKE, EDWARD L. *The psychology of learning.* New York: Teacher's Col-lege, Columbia University, 1913.
10. TOKEMASA, T. JOJU. An experiment on learning with special reference to accom-plishment. *Psychol. abstr.* 9:518, 1935.
11. WILLIAMS, EVERARD M. Innovation in undergraduate teaching. *Science* 155:974-79, 1967.

Comparison of the Effects of Visual, Motor, Mental, and Guided Practice upon Speed and Accuracy of Performing a Simple Eye-Hand Coordination Task*

LEON E. SMITH AND JOHN S. HARRISON

VARIOUS sense modalities, situational cues, and practice methods can be emphasized throughout practice or at certain stages in practice, if it is so desired. One of the challenges to researchers concerned with motor learning is to determine how practice should proceed for best ultimate achievement scores. A project designed to compare different types of practice would obviously suggest the better of a few alternatives. And so, Smith and Harrison compare visual, motor, mental, and guided (kinesthetic), practice on task performance requiring speed and accuracy.

The learning of hand-eye coordination tasks, that is, the change in scores of previously unpracticed subjects between initial and final tests, is dependent both on the improvement of perceptual recognition of the stimulus objects and on the increase in proficiency of the motor responses resulting from such stimulation.

It would seem to follow from a recently enunciated theory of neuromotor coordination[5] that the "program" of a response has to be learned in the higher centers of the brain (at the conscious level) before it can become automatically reproduced at a lower level of cortical activity. The interplay between the reception of visual stimuli and their consequent effector responses determines how quickly the program can be learned and adequately reproduced. However, the relative contribution of the various factors involved in the learning of the coordination is largely undetermined. It cannot be said whether visual or nonvisual, mental or kinesthetic practice will cause improvement in terms of greater efficiency to the same extent as physical practice alone. (Efficiency is defined as improved speed and accuracy in performance.)

Psychological and educational textbooks predict most transference of practice when the interpolated activity has a high degree of similarity with the test itself.[15] Thus physical practice of a simple neuromotor coordination should improve performance most. The question posed is whether or not visual practice alone, or mental practice alone, or even kinesthetic practice alone is of sufficient value to improve the learning of such a task. A review of the literature reveals anything but clarity on this issue.

Review of the Literature

A number of investigators[1,7,8] have used some form of visual guidance as a supplementary cue in maze learning experiments. Twitmyer[13] tested 300 undergraduate students in an attempt to determine the effect of one type of

* From *The Research Quarterly*, 1962, *33*, 299-307. Reprinted with permission of the authors and the American Association for Health, Physical Education, and Recreation.

visual guidance upon maze learning. He concluded that visual guidance was highly effective in increasing the efficiency for the early acquisition stages of learning in a blindfold cul-de-sac. However, Spiegel and Ammons[9] found that when passive ocular practice was introduced between two consecutive trials in a pursuit rotor task there was a smaller warm-up decrement, a lower level of performance, and less reminiscence. Gephart[4] studied the effect of blindfold, sighted, and no practice on free throw accuracy. His main conclusions were that blindfold practice proved significantly superior in improving free throw accuracy compared to sighted practice, or no practice, while sighted practice was not significantly superior to the no practice group. It was also found that both blindfold and sighted practice reduced distance and direction errors.

Vandell, Davis, and Clugston[14] attempted to isolate the effects of mental practice in the learning of the motor skill of throwing darts. They concluded from the results obtained from their 36 subjects that mental practice was about as effective as physical practice under the conditions of their experiment. In a similar type of experiment, Twining[12] presented 36 college men with a ring-toss experiment. The group that received no physical practice showed no significant learning whereas physical practice improved 37 percent and mental practice improved 36 percent, both of which were highly significant.

Trussell[11] hypothesized that there would be a significant amount of learning in a test-retest situation due to interpolated mental practice of a complex motor skill such as juggling. Her results showed that there was no significant effect of mental practice or physical practice on the immediate juggling. However, different combinations of physical and mental practice tended to show that significant learning of the task did take place, with neither type of practice, done separately, having any clear advantage over the other. Contrary to these results, Eggleston[2] has shown that physical practice is more efficient than mental in the skill required for card sorting and digit symbol substitution tasks.

The Hypotheses

No definite trends appear as to which special type of practice will most likely improve the learning of eye-hand coordination tasks. It is considered almost axiomatic that physical practice of the task itself should, of necessity, improve final performance since the old adage "practice makes perfect" has been proven time and time again. However, the component parts of actual physical practice obviously need study in order to ascertain just what role the visual and nonvisual factors play in the learning of such tasks. Consequently, it is hypothesized that different visual, as well as nonvisual, factors determine the learning of a simple eye-hand coordination task. These factors will produce different end results (increased correct performance and/or a reduced number of errors) when they are practiced separately in a test-retest situation. The order of greatest benefit due to this interpolated activity is hypothesized as being dependent on (a) how much task similarity there is between the interpolated practice and the tested activity, and (b) how much the visual component is controlled in the interpolated activity.

To test the hypotheses a stylus-type, three-hole punchboard was used to determine how quickly and how accurately subjects could perform the task of placing a metal stylus in the three evenly spaced holes when they were given different types of practice. The types were motor, mental, guided, and two kinds of visual practice. Thus, the above hypotheses would predict that most benefit would be obtained from motor practice. Visual practice should improve performance more than mental and guided practice, but less than motor practice. It was anticipated that learning would occur in all groups (including a control group) due to the nature of the task. However, individual differences in the amount of gain between the initial and final tests should be determined by these different experimental conditions. A distinction was made between the two possible kinds of differences in the data obtained. Scores in terms of both speed and accuracy were recorded in order to help clarify the effect of the factors studied.

The available research on questions of speed vs. accuracy indicates no set pattern of emphasis. Relative specificity to the particular learning task appears to be the most probable conclusion that can be reached. Fulton[3] has suggested, in reviewing the results of relevant studies, that there is no consistent relationship between speed and accuracy in any movements, but that only within certain similar classes of movements are any constant relationships found. Thus if we are to improve speed or accuracy or both, we must emphasize speed or accuracy or both respectively. However, if the learner is permitted to arrive at an optimal level of speed and accuracy in doing a task, then different types of practice should, theoretically, reveal how either speed or accuracy is affected by said practice. In this way, it is hypothesized that the different types of practice will affect these two dimensions of successful performance in differing ways but no exact a priori predictions as to the direction of differences can be made.

Method and Procedure

The total number of subjects was 60. All were male university student volunteers. There were six groups, consisting of 10 subjects; membership in the group was determined by serial order of selection from the original list. The average age of the group was 20 years and ranged from 17 to 27.

A rectangular punchboard inclined at a 45° angle was supported by a wooden base. Inserted in the punchboard were three metal cylinders (3/8 in. diameter) which were spaced triangularly 3 1/4 in. apart. At the bottom of each cylinder was a depressible metal disc which connected to a mechanical counter. To record a correct hit only a slight contact by the metal stylus (1/8 in. diameter and 9 in. length) with the metal disc was required.

Standard instructions were given to each group. The first ten subjects tested were the motor group; then followed the visual practice group, the reversed-visual, the mental, the guided, and finally the control group. Prior to the initial test, each subject in each group was given the necessary instructions so that he could do the task as required. Stress was placed on the fact that optimal speed* and accuracy† were preferable to concentration on one at the expense of the other. Then the subject was given a one-minute test on the punchboard (moving in a clockwise direction) in order to measure his initial level of skill. During this test, his errors (the number of times the stylus failed to enter any of three holes) were tallied by visual count. His total number of correct hits was taken from the counters at the end of the test.

After recording the initial score, the experimenter instructed each subject on the interpolated activity, whichever it happened to be, for that subject. If, for example, he was in the visual practice group, he was given periods of 10 seconds of practice going over the actual eye movements involved in doing

---

*The speed score is synonymous with productivity (the number of responses recorded).

†Accuracy is the proportion of correct responses to the total number of responses. Error score is the complement of accuracy and as such is the only real measure of this ability.

the skill. Each practice period was followed by 10 seconds of rest. The inter-polated activity lasted for 2 minutes; thus each subject received a total of six separate distributed practice periods. The same procedure was followed for the mental, motor, kinesthetic, and reversed-visual practice groups respectively.

Longer test periods were not used because preliminary testing indicated that fatigue factors became increasingly obvious when the tests ran longer than one minute. Furthermore, this same preliminary testing indicated that shorter practice periods did not give sufficient opportunity for individual dif-ferences to become apparent. The differences in the types of practice used as interpolated activity are:

The motor practice subjects received six 10-sec. practice periods doing the task in the same manner as in the initial and final tests. During the 10-sec. rest periods each subject read from a simple standard text which was handed open to him immediately following the practice trial. They were required to give a brief account of the material read at the end of practice and before the final test.

The visual practice subjects during the practice period fixed their eyes on each of the holes long enough to complete the three-hole cycle once per sec-ond, each second being tapped off during this practice period. These subjects moved their eyes in the same direction as if they were performing the task manually. They were instructed to treat this practice as similar to the motor practice except that the motor component was absent. Again, the subjects read during the rest periods and were required to recall briefly what they had read.

The reversed-visual practice subjects did exactly as the above-mentioned group except they moved their eyes in the opposite direction during the practice period.

The mental practice subjects were instructed to close their eyes and think about the performance just completed in the initial test during their 10-sec. practice periods; that is, each subject in this group was to rehearse mentally all the component parts of the skill, but, like the subjects in the other groups, was required to read during the rest periods. To ensure no mental practice during these rest periods, these subjects were warned that they would be required to give a factual and detailed account of the material they had just read.

The guided practice subjects were guided through the task by the experi-menter to get the feel of the movement while their eyes were closed. This often meant increasing the speed of the performance of the task during the practice period at the sacrifice of accuracy, but it was hypothesized that by gaining a kind of kinesthetic awareness of the spatial relationships involved final performance would ultimately be improved. The subjects read during the rest periods.

The control group read for the full 2-min. practice period in between the initial and the final test. It should be noted that the writers considered the skill of reading to be unrelated to the experimental task, thus ruling out, for all subjects, any benefits that may have accrued from such reading.

Results

Each subject was instructed to sacrifice neither speed nor accuracy for the benefit of the other when performing the task. It was thus believed that the different types of practice would produce different results in terms of both these dimensions of performance. In the statistical treatment of the data, dif-ference scores (final test minus initial test scores) were used. Because of the specificity of the question of speed vs. accuracy to the particular kind of task being measured, no attempt was made to create some kind of effective score that would give proportional weighting to each dimension; rather the effects of the different experimental conditions were analyzed in terms of total number of correct hits, total number of errors, and a total productivity score (hits-plus-errors). Since the amount of time on the task was constant for all subjects, the correct number of hits (the speed scores) was considered the best estimate of performance.

Correct Hits. Inspection of the data for the different conditions tends to indicate relatively large differences between tests for the motor, visual, and mental practice groups. However, when the data on all six groups are combined for a variance analysis of these differences, the required F ratio for significance is not reached (1.91 where 2.37 is required at the 5 percent level when n_1 is 5 and n_2 is 54).

Since the over-all differences are not significant, the individual group mean differences cannot be examined for possible significant differences between the various experimental groups and the control group. This does not signify, however, that each group cannot be tested to see if there was or was not a significant learning effect.[6] In order to test the difference between the initial and final tests (the practice effect), the correction factor of the variance analysis is divided by the mean square error. In other words, if there were no differences between the two tests, then a significant t^2 (F) would not show up; however, it was highly significant (F was 76.14). When the individual groups were examined for significant differences from zero, all groups (except the guided practice group) evidenced a significant learning effect.

Errors. It was considered important to determine whether or not the trend of apparent differences in visual and mental practice was significant. Variance analysis of the differences showed that there were significant differences between the different groups in the amount of error reduction due to the different types of practice. Again, the over-all practice effect (the correction factor) was found to differ significantly from zero, indicating that there was an over-all decrease in the number of errors made in the final test for all conditions. However, when each condition was examined for the significance of within-group differences, only two groups differed significantly from zero, the visual practice group and the mental practice group. Therefore, the trends of differences described above have been verified by statistical test.

Total Productivity (Hits-Plus-Errors). The data suggested that if any of the groups showed significant final test increases it would be the motor practice group. However, the amount of improvement in total number of responses did not differ between the different groups due to one type of practice or another. Once again there is an over-all improvement in performance between the initial and final test for all groups. When the individual groups are examined, however, only the motor practice group and the control group improved their total productivity scores significantly.

Discussion

The amount of improvement from initial to final test differed significantly in terms of correct hits only when different subject samples were tested on their ability to benefit from different types of practice on a simple eye-hand coordination task. Such was not the case when the total number of trials, that is, the total increase in speed, was analyzed. Consequently, the original main hypotheses are only partially substantiated. Of major importance is the fact that substantiation did not occur in the type of data considered to be the best estimate of improved performance, namely the number of correct hits made.

It is believed that the original best estimate would have shown the same significant differences in improvement due to the different conditions of practice had the practice periods themselves been of greater length. Of course, there is always the danger of having an insufficiently large subject sample size. Even so, it would appear that this particular learning task permits an increase in accuracy due to certain specific types of practice and also that these same types of practice do not produce increases in speed.

The largest variations due to the effects of practice appeared in the total number of errors made where significant differences have shown up partly because some groups did not reduce their errors. However, with the group sizes as they were, and since significant learning was apparent in more than half of the comparisons, the amount of the differences between the groups would have to have been very large before a significant F ratio would appear.

Learning did occur, however, in all groups in the over-all analysis of the test-retest scores. There were large differences, of course, in the amount of this learning, differences which cannot be interpreted as being any more than significant. When the correct number of hits was examined group for group in terms of the practice (or learning) effect, only the guided practice group showed no learning. The control group showed learning even though they read in between the initial and final test. The order from most to least learning was: motor, mental, visual, reversed-visual, control, and guided practice.

When the same comparisons were made for the errors per group it appears that the effects of reduced errors in the mental and visual practice groups have produced over-all significance between the groups in the amount of reduction. On the other hand, even though the motor and the control groups showed significant learning in the total number of trials, in the complete analysis the differences were not large enough to produce variations in the amount of learning due to the effects of the different conditions. In this analysis, the order from most to least learning was: motor, control, guided, reversed-visual, mental, and visual practice. It should be remembered, however, that there were no significant differences between the group means.

As mentioned earlier, the question of speed vs. accuracy appears to be specific to the type of activity being tested. One can create an experiment which can increase speed but not accuracy (or vice versa as the case may be), for example, Sturt's typewriting experiment[10] where first one and then another variable was stressed; learning depended on the emphasis given either component. The use of any such effective score in this situation would have no doubt clouded the outcome between these two issues and may have resulted in confusion. As the results stand now, it seems safe to conclude that accuracy has been influenced significantly under two of the conditions of this study, namely visual and mental practice. However, one practice was done with the eyes open; in the other, the subjects had their eyes closed. Obviously, there are different mechanisms involved for improving accuracy.

It is important to note that the motor practice group speeded up performance but did not improve accuracy between the two tests. Perhaps this finding is restricted to this type of coordination task or perhaps it can be applied more generally. In this specific motor task it appears possible during motor practice that the speed set has a tendency to predominate or interfere with the accuracy set with consequent neuromotor disorganization resulting in a loss of accuracy. This study has insufficient basis for gross generalizations on hand-eye coordination. The same can be said for the guided practice group. The reversed-visual practice appeared to be of hindrance value only to this group of subjects and had no obviously beneficial effects.

However, visual practice reduced the number of errors through the mere practice of doing the eye movements alone (along with the accompanying, but secondary, mental processes involving conceptualization of the task). It is interesting to note that mental practice alone, that is, the visual imagery of the motions involved in the mind's eye, also reduced the total group errors significantly. Further study of this phenomenon in motor learning activities is obviously warranted.

Conclusion

The control, motor practice, and reversed-visual practice groups significantly improved performance in terms of correct hits and the total number of trials but did not reduce their number of errors. The visual and mental practice groups reduced their total number of errors as well as increased their performance significantly in terms of the correct hits and the total number of trials.

These results warrant the conclusion that visual practice and mental practice improved accuracy on a punchboard learning task, whereas motor practice and guided practice did not.

References

1. CARR, H. A. "The Influence of Visual Guidance in Maze Learning." *Journal of Experimental Psychology* 4:399-417; December 1921.
2. EGGLESTON, D. *"The Relative Value of Actual Vs. Imaginary Practice in a Learning Situation."* Unpublished master's thesis. New York: Columbia University, 1936.
3. FULTON, R. E. "Speed and Accuracy in Learning a Ballistic Movement." *Research Quarterly* 13:30-36; March 1942.
4. GEPHART, G. C. *"The Relative Effect of Blindfold, Sighted and No Practice on Free Throw Accuracy."* Master's thesis. Urbana: University of Illinois, 1954.
5. HENRY, F. M., and ROGERS, D. E. "Increased Response Latency for Complicated Movements and a 'Memory Drum' Theory for Neuromotor Reaction." *Research Quarterly* 31:448-58; October 1960.
6. McNEMAR, QUINN. *Psychological Statistics.* New York: J. Wiley and Sons, 1957.
7. PERKINS, N. L. "Human Reactions in a Maze of Fixed Orientation." *Comparative Psychological Monographs* 4:1-92; 1927.
8. SMITH, F. O. "Differential Reactions of Human Beings in the Maze." *Pedagogical Seminary and Journal of Genetic Psychology* 34:394-405; 1927.
9. SPIEGEL, J., and AMMONS, R. B. "The Effect of Ocular Practice on Subsequent Rotary Performance." *Motor Skills Research Exchange* 2:54-56; 1950.
10. STURT, MARY. "A Comparison of Speed with Accuracy in the Learning Process." *British Journal of Psychology* 12:289-300; December 1921.
11. TRUSSELL, E. M. "Mental Practice as a Factor in the Learning of a Complex Motor Skill." Master's thesis. University of California, 1952.
12. TWINING, W. E. "Mental Practice and Physical Practice in Learning a Motor Skill." *Research Quarterly* 20:432-35; December 1949.
13. TWITMYER, E. M. "Visual Guidance in Motor Learning." *American Journal of Psychology* 63:165-187; April 1931.
14. VANDELL, R. A.; DAVIS, R. A.; and CLUGSTON, H. A. "The Function of Mental Practice in the Acquisition of Motor Skills." *Journal of General Psychology* 29: 243-50; October 1943.
15. WOODWORTH, ROBERT S., and SCHLOSBERG, HAROLD. *Experimental Psychology.* New York: Henry Holt and Company, 1956.

Effect of Verbal, Visual, and Auditory Augmenting Cues on Learning a Complex Motor Skill*

LAWRENCE KARLIN AND RUDOLPH G. MORTIMER

EXPERIMENTAL psychologists refer to an apparatus or pieces of apparatus which contain stimuli and response units comprising a task confronting the subject as a display. Broadly speaking, though, a display can be found in any task situation in which there are specific responses appropriate to particular cues. The task of piloting a plane is represented by the flight conditions and response panel. The external information in a given situation, whether or not it is pertinent to the task, represents the stimuli to which the organism will probably attend. The challenge in facilitating learning is to modify the display in such a way that desired outcomes are reached. Additional verbal, visual, kinesthetic, or auditory cues may be added to the display to aid in practice. Karlin and Mortimer compare the effectiveness of cues especially as they serve as activity guidelines or rewarders of correct behavior.

It was the aim of the present study to compare the effects of adding different types of cue to the primary display in learning compensatory tracking tasks, and to evaluate their effectiveness for training purposes on the basis of the resultant performance during transfer tests when these cues were removed.

While a number of studies (Bilodeau, 1952; Goldstein & Rittenhouse, 1954; Houston, 1947; Morin & Gagné, 1951) have shown that augmenting cues which are coincident or synchronized with the primary cue and more convenient to use than the primary cue materially improve performance on training tests, this improvement is lost in transfer tests.

Noncoincident types of cue in which information concerning performance is provided at the end of a trial or delayed in some other way may be effective in transfer tests. This has been shown by Goldstein and Rittenhouse (1954), Reynolds and Adams (1953), and Smode (1958). However, it should be noted that the results of Reynolds and Adams were not confirmed by Archer, Kent, and Mote (1956) and Archer and Namikas (1958).

It is apparent, then, that the differential effects of coincident and noncoincident augmenting cues on transfer trials are not clear-cut. The present study investigates this problem further by using a verbal delayed feedback cue and visual and auditory coincident type cues.

Method

Subjects and Apparatus. The Ss were 60, paid, volunteer, right-handed male college students.

*From the *Journal of Experimental Psychology,* 1963, 65, 75-79. Reprinted with permission of the authors and the American Psychological Association.

The apparatus consisted of three major parts: (*a*) *S*'s control and display assembly, (*b*) an electronic gating system and recording unit, and (*c*) a tracking course generator and timing control.

The *S*'s control consisted of a potentiometer controlled by a smooth round knob 1¼ in. in diameter set in a small console. The display consisted of a Dumont 304-A cathode ray oscilloscope whose tube face was covered by an orange filter on which were inscribed thin vertical lines $1\frac{3}{64}$ in. apart. The center line which represented the target reticle was somewhat deeper and wider than the other lines so that when the CRT face was illuminated from the rear, the center line was seen as a markedly brighter white line than the other lines. Apart from a central horizontal slit $1\frac{5}{16}$ in. wide, the tube face was blanked off and was surrounded by a large matte gray panel. A Dumont 5-ADP-11 short persistence CRT was used in the oscilloscope.

The cursor consisted of a blip on the tube face $\frac{3}{64}$ in. in diameter. The control-display relationship was such that 32° of control knob movement produced 1 in. of cursor displacement.

The visual augmenting cue was provided by placing two vertical red lines $\frac{3}{64}$ in. thick a distance of ±.25 in. on either side of the target reticle.

The electronic gating system and the recording unit consisted of 15 channels in which high speed counters cumulated the time that tracking performance lay within the range of each channel. From two of these channels time-on-target information was obtained. Two additional gating circuits controlled the auditory cue. The latter consisted of an 800-cps tone fed into a headset and sounded whenever *S*'s error was within ±.25 in. from the target line. For a more detailed description of the gating system, the reader is referred to Karlin (1961).

The tracking course generator was designed to control the duration of a trial (36 sec.), the interval during which scoring took place (the last 30 sec.), the appearance of the cursor at the beginning of a trial and its removal at the end of a trial, and the presentation of the tracking input signal. The latter consisted of a simple sine wave having a frequency of 10 cpm with a second and third harmonic of half the amplitude of the fundamental superimposed upon it; and this forced the cursor in a horizontal path along the CRT face. This section of the apparatus is described in greater detail by Karlin and Mortimer (1961).

Procedure. Fifteen *S*s were randomly assigned to each of the three experimental conditions and to the one control condition of the experiment. The *S* was seated before the display and operated the control with his right hand. His task was one of compensatory tracking such that this response was to counteract the horizontal movements of the cursor and maintain it on the target line.

Each *S* was scheduled for 5 consecutive days. On Days 1-3, *S*s in the experimental groups received 15 learning trials with augmenting cues, and on Day 4 they received 20 transfer trials during which the augmenting cue was not presented. The *S*s in the control group received the same trial sequence but augmenting cues were not provided at any time. Although data were collected for 4 days, *S*s were scheduled for 5 days in order to minimize possible endspurt effects.

A trial began when the cursor appeared on the screen of the oscilloscope and ended when it disappeared from the screen. Each trial lasted a total of 36 sec., the last 30 sec. only being scored. An intertrial interval of 30 sec. was used.

Instructions were read to each *S* prior to data collection. The *S*s in the visual augmenting feedback group were instructed to the effect that the area between the two red lines defined a zone of minimally acceptable performance but that the S's aim should be to keep the cursor on the target reticle. The Ss in the auditory group received similar instructions with respect to the auditory cue. The Ss in the verbal cue condition were given a score at the end of each learning trial which they were told could range from 0-1500 and which was a direct function of the time for which they had maintained the cursor within some minimally acceptable error zone about the target reticle. On Day 4, the experimental groups were told that the augmenting cues would not be present.

At the beginning of each trial the control knob was at its maximum counterclockwise position. All Ss wore headphones throughout the experiment. The experimental room was dimly illuminated. A fan was used to provide masking noise. The oscilloscope was given a minimum warm-up time of 1 hr. and the cursor was checked for alignment prior to data collection of any S.

Results

For each S on each trial, time within scoring tolerance (sec.) was obtained. This is defined as the time within an error of $\pm.25$ in. about the target reticle. Integrated error scores were also obtained but since they yielded quite similar results only the former score is reported.

The groups differed consistently from each other on learning and transfer trials with the verbal being superior to the visual, auditory, and control groups, in that order. The first and second days yielded nonsignificant Fs of 1.79 and 2.72 while the third and fourth days yielded Fs of 3.88 and 2.95 which were significant at the .05 level. The within-groups MSs, each based on 56 df, were used as error estimates for the above and were, respectively, (in squared sec.) 9.58, 8.97, 5.41, 7.88. These values show that individual differences diminished over the 3 training days and tended to rise somewhat on the fourth or test day.

The verbal group was significantly superior to the auditory and control groups in the last day of training and maintained this superiority in the transfer trials.

Discussion

The results show that the noncoincident verbal cue was more effective than the coincident visual and auditory cues in all trials. It is possible that the verbal cue in not specifying a fixed tolerance limit for acceptable performance may have encouraged S to set himself more stringent and in some way more appropriate tolerance widths than were given by the visual and auditory cues. More specifically, the total score given at the end of a trial by the verbal cue may have helped S to define more effective standards of performance which varied with the stage of practice.

The presence of reference marks in the primary cue may have made possible this more effective use of the verbal cue at the same time that it minimized the importance of the visual and auditory cues. That the structure of the primary cue may be important in determining the role of augmenting cues is suggested by the fact that Goldstein and Rittenhouse (1954), using similar verbal and auditory augmenting cues in the Pedestal Sight Manipulation Test (PSMT), found that the verbal cue was inferior to the auditory cue during training. The primary ranging cue in the PSMT which is a pursuit tracking task is notably difficult to discriminate and lacks the reference marks provided in the present compensatory tracking task.

The present results may be compared to those obtained by Smode (1958), who also used a compensatory tracking task. He studied the effects of low- and high-level knowledge of results. His low-level condition corresponded approximately to our verbal condition. In his high-level condition he used discrete visual clicks and lights which counted each .5 sec. of cumulated time on target. Our auditory cue in a sense was more informative (since it was continuous and could be used to monitor performance at every instant) yet measured relative to the performance of the verbal group in each study, his auditory cue produced superior results. Nevertheless, these findings are not in conflict if we recognize that all of Smode's cues are essentially noncoincident cues. In comparison with the present study his results suggest that the efficacy of augmenting cues in the two types of task is mainly a result of their motivating properties as incentives and their help in defining standards of performance. For example, it is hypothesized that the clicks of Smode's study rewarded staying longer on target since they counted cumulative on-target time while the continuous cues of the present study may not have done this as well if at all.

These considerations may help to resolve the apparent conflict of results obtained in two other studies of augmenting feedback. Reynolds and Adams (1953) used auditory clicks at various intervals of delay to augment the primary cues of a pursuit rotor task and obtained positive results both for the effectiveness of delay as a variable and for the augmenting cue in general. Archer and Namikas (1953), interested primarily in the delay of feedback variable, tried to replicate this study except that they used a continuous tone instead of clicks as the augmenting cue. They obtained negative results and concluded that "delay of information feedback is not an effective variable." Bilodeau and Bilodeau (1961) in a recent review seem to agree with this conclusion. On the basis of the present analysis we would suggest that the failure to confirm the results of Reynolds and Adams was due to the change from a discrete to a continuous type of cue. It is felt that this change, contrary to the expectation of Archer and Namikas, may have reduced or eliminated the desirable incentive or reinforcing properties of the original cue and in this way reduced the effectiveness of feedback delay as a variable. Whether their augmenting cue was completely ineffective cannot be definitely determined since being interested only in the influence of varying delay in feedback they did not use a control group as did Reynolds and Adams.

On the basis of this discussion, then, we would conclude that augmenting cues are most effective in transfer when they function as incentives and in defining standards of performance; they are least effective in this respect when their major function is to provide information for guiding immediate action (Miller, 1953).

One other question of interest concerns the consistently poorer performance of the auditory cue compared with the visual cue. There is enough evidence here to warrant further research although these two cues differed in other respects so it is not possible at this point to attribute any difference specifically to a modality factor.

References

ARCHER, E. J., KENT, G. W., & MOTE, F. A. Effect of long-term practice and time on target information feedback on a complex tracking task. *J. exp. Psychol.*, 1956, 51, 103-112.

ARCHER, E. J., & NAMIKAS, G. A. Pursuit-rotor performance as a function of delay of information feedback. *J. exp. Psychol.*, 1958, 56, 325-327.

BILODEAU, E. A. Some effects of various degrees of supplemental information given at two levels of practice upon the acquisition of a complex motor skill. *USAF HRRC res. Bull.*, 1952, No. 52-15.

BILODEAU, E. A., & BILODEAU, I., McD. Motor skills learning. *Annu. Rev. Psychol.*, 1961, 12, 243-280.

EDWARDS, A. L. *Experimental design in psychological research.* (Rev. ed.) New York: Rinehart, 1960.

GOLDSTEIN, M., & RITTENHOUSE, C. H. Knowledge of results in the acquisition and transfer of a gunnery skill. *J. exp. Psychol.*, 1954, 48, 187-196.

HOUSTON, R. C. The function of knowledge of results in learning a complex motor skill. Unpublished master's thesis, Northwestern University, 1947.

KARLIN, L. Psychological study of motor skills: Phase I. *USN Train. Dev. Cent. tech. Rep.*, 1961, No. 558-1.

KARLIN, L., & MORTIMER, R. G. Psychological study of motor skills: Phase II. *USN Train. Dev. Cent. tech. Rep.*, 1961, No. 558-2.

MILLER, R. B. Handbook on training and training equipment design. *USAF WADC tech. Rep.*, 1953, No. 53-136.

MORIN, R. E., & GAGNÉ, R. M. Pedestal Sight Manipulation Test performance as influenced by variation in type and amount of psychological feedback. *USAF HRRC res. Note*, 1951, No. MS 51-7.

REYNOLDS, B., & ADAMS, J. A. Motor performance as a function of click reinforcement. *J. exp. Psychol.*, 1953, 45, 315-320.

SMODE, A. F. Learning and performance in a tracking task under two levels of achievement information feedback. *J. exp. Psychol.*, 1958, 56, 297-303.

Effect of Differential Motive-Incentive Conditions on Physical Performance*

E. DEAN RYAN

MOTIVATION encourages purposive behavior which is energized by needs and drives and directed toward some goal. Performance best represents true learning levels when motivation is present. Furthermore, motivation encourages the individual to practice more, hence, possibly learn more. The very nature of the learning situation may serve to motivate the learner, or else, various incentives or reinforcers may be added to induce motivation. One of the problems in the latter case is that the instructor or experimenter assumes that a particular condition is motivating to all students or subjects. But in fact, each person individually interprets the worth of the incentive or reinforcer, and that which is motivating to one may not be for another. Nevertheless, a usual technique employed in research is to compare various types of possible motive-incentive conditions on performance. Ryan shows what happens when the task situation itself may contain sufficient motivation, thereby making additional attempts to raise the level of motivation useless.

The fact that certain motive-incentive conditions have a marked influence on learning and performance of verbal material has been well established.[2,5] While attempts to manipulate the level of motivation in performers of physical

*From *The Research Quarterly*, 1961, *32*, 83-87. Reprinted with permission of the author and the American Association for Health, Physical Education, and Recreation.

skills through special incentives have been common, research as to the effects of those incentives has been limited. Further, those studies that do exist are contradictory to the extent that some show improvement under motive-incentive conditions and others show no effect.

Review of Literature

Ulrich and Burke[7] tested a group of 18 subjects on a bicycle ergometer under two varieties of motivational stress. All subjects received three trials. On the first trial, subjects were told to pedal for one minute, doing as well as possible. Scores were reported at 30 and 45 seconds. On the second and third trials subjects were again asked to do as well as possible, equaling or improving on the first trial. They were instructed that a bell would ring periodically if their performance improved, but if their performance was below the previous standard a buzzer would ring. Unknown to subjects, it was determined prior to testing whether the buzzer or bell would ring during the trials, regardless of performance. All groups heard the bell on one trial and the buzzer on the other. Results indicated no difference in total work output between the two motivating conditions, although both of these conditions were significantly better than the initial trial.

Fleishman,[1] after giving 400 subjects preliminary training on a rudder control test (maneuvering a type of Link trainer in response to visual signals), divided the subjects into two groups, giving one a variety of motive-incentive instructions and the other no instructions or encouragement after the preliminary test. The performance of the motivated group was significantly better than that of the control group. When the groups were divided into best and poorest performers on the basis of test scores, there was no significant difference between the performance of the poorest half of the control group and the poorest half of the experimental group. The best performers in the motivation group, however, had significantly better test scores than the best performers in the control group.

Noble,[6] using 400 subjects, gave a preliminary practice period on a two-handed coordination test (tracking). At varying periods of practice, experimental groups were informed of their average score and told that they must improve if they were to pass. The author concluded that the incentive-motive conditions did not affect performance.

Johnson[3] had 59 junior high school boys, with instructions to do as well as possible, pedal a bicycle ergometer against a fixed resistance of five pounds. The subjects were given eight 30-second trials, with a 30-second rest between each trial. Each subject had two tests, one with continuous verbal encouragement, the other with no encouragement. There was no significant difference between performance under the two conditions.

Problem Investigated

A review of the literature reveals little as to the effect of various types of incentives on physical performance. Therefore the purpose of this experiment was to determine the relative effect of four different motive-incentive conditions on a simple task that required neither endurance nor skill. In addition the effect of the motive-incentive conditions at varying levels of performance was investigated. The specific task studied was grip strength as measured by a hand dynamometer.

Methodology

Eighty male university students participated in the experiment. All were volunteers obtained from voluntary physical education classes. No particular systematic method of selection was used. All subjects, using only the right hand, were given a preliminary test of grip strength, consisting of three trials with a hand dynamometer. They were told that this was a test to determine their grip strength. Special emphasis was placed on the fact that maximum effort was essential. Results were not shown to the performers.

A second test was administered seven days later and the subjects were told that this test would determine, among other things, the reliability of grip strength. The same general procedures used in the first test were followed with one exception. On the second test each subject received one of four different motive-incentive conditions. Group one, the control group, was given the same instructions as on the first test, being told to squeeze as hard as possible and to make a maximum effort on each trial. Group two, the verbal group, was told to try to improve on their first score (they had no knowledge of initial scores), and as they performed were verbally encouraged to improve with such statements as "harder, harder, much harder." Group three, the knowledge of results group, knew their initial scores, were allowed to watch the dynamometer scoring dial, and were told to make every effort to improve on the initial score. Group four, the shock group, had an electrode attached to the left wrist, were informed of initial scores, and were told that failure to improve on each trial would result in receipt of a severe electric shock.

Apparatus

To provide the electric shock a transformer increased the 120-volt supply to 350 volts and insulated the power line and its ground for safety reasons. Sufficient resistance was placed in the circuit to limit the electrode current to 4.4 milliamps per square centimeter of contact area. The electrodes were 9 by 11 millimeters in size, separated by 7½ millimeters distance from edge to edge, mounted in a small plastic strip and held on the wrist by an elastic strap.*

A Lafayette hand dynamometer was used to measure grip strength. Although the dial of the dynamometer was marked in kilograms, it was necessary to multiply obtained scores by 0.88 and add 15.5 to obtain true kilograms. In this study, however, all scores reported were taken directly from the dial without conversion.

Results and Discussion

In designing the experiment the author reasoned that differences in performance between subjects on the initial test might be attributed to varying levels of motivation, with higher levels of motivation resulting in superior scores. If this hypothesis were true, added incentive would be expected to produce greater gains in the lower scoring subjects.

Therefore, this experiment was designed to provide a test to determine whether or not the four types of incentives had the same relative effect at all levels of strength, and at the same time provide a test of the null hypothesis that there were no differences between the four types of motive-incentive conditions.

Subjects were arranged on the basis of their initial strength test, from strongest to weakest and were divided into four levels of strength, with the strongest 20 assigned to the superior group, the next 20 to the good group, the third 20 to the fair group, and the weakest 20 to the poor group. With-

*See description of apparatus used by F. M. Henry in the article "Increase in Speed of Movement by Motivation and by Transfer of Motivated Improvement" which appeared in the May 1951 RESEARCH QUARTERLY.

in each of the four levels the subjects were randomly assigned to one of the four motive-incentive groups, 20 per group. Thus all groups were matched with reference to the initial strength score.

The results of a simple variance analysis on initial strength measures indicate no differences between the four groups (F = 0.02) prior to the application of the motive-incentive conditions. The reliability of the test-retest on the initial strength measures was .88.

Mean scores for the four motive-incentive conditions are shown in Table 1. While three of the four groups appear to be equal, scores for the shock group are considerably higher. Results of analysis of variance, however, indicate that the differences between groups are not significant (F = 2.34, with F = 2.75 required for significance at the 5% level).

When strength scores are broken into groups by levels (Table 1) the mean scores for the superior group are quite similar. At the lower three levels both the shock group and the verbal group appear to have higher mean scores than the control group. These observed differences are not significant, however, with F = 0.46 for the interaction of groups by levels. (For significance at the 5% level, F had to equal 2.02.)

On the basis of studies done in other areas an assumption could be made that threat of electric shock, verbal encouragement, and knowledge of results would improve performance. The results of this experiment indicate, however, that on a simple task that requires neither endurance nor skill, there appears to be no difference in performance under the various motive-incentive conditions.

The apparent contradiction of Fleishman's study[1] can be explained. His primary objective was to design an experiment to obtain improvement. He selected a task that seemed most susceptible to the experimental treatment and loaded the experimental instructions. In the discussion of results, Fleishman states that while the differences were statistically significant, they were not large and should be interpreted with caution. Further he did not compare different types of motive-incentive conditions but utilized several motive-incentive conditions simultaneously in the experimental group. Ulrich and Burke found no differences in performance between the two types of motivational stress, which is in agreement with the present study.

The explanation for differences between performance on a physical task of this nature and performance on verbal material may be due to the nature of the physical test itself. Subjects in physical performance tests appear to be highly motivated, expressing a keen interest in their performance and the performance of others. It seems probable that the nature of simple tests of physical performance provides sufficient incentive to elicit maximal performance without additional motivation.

TABLE 1.—MEAN SCORES FOR THE FOUR MOTIVE-INCENTIVE GROUPS[a]
(Groups X Levels)

	Knowledge	Verbal	Control	Shock
Superior	184.0	179.4	188.8	191.4
Good	154.8	153.4	145.2	163.8
Fair	130.8	151.6	143.8	157.0
Poor	129.0	134.8	130.4	146.6

[a] Scores are the sum of three trials on the dynamometer.

Summary and Conclusions

It was the purpose of this experiment to determine the effects of four types of motive-incentive conditions on grip strength. Eighty male subjects were divided into four subgroups, all groups being matched on the basis of a preliminary grip test. Group one was simply told to do as well as possible on the retest, group two was verbally exhorted to improve, group three was given the results of the previous test and was allowed to watch the dynamometer dial on the retest, and group four was threatened with electric shock for failure to improve.

There were no differences in performance between the four motive-incentive conditions, and no differences in performance between groups at the various performance levels. These results have practical implications for measurement programs in physical education. In the past, very little attention has been directed to the control of motivation when testing strength. This study suggests that as long as an effort is made to have subjects understand the importance of giving a maximum effort, no additional incentive is necessary. Further, additional incentive, if given, should not bias results.

References

1. FLEISHMAN, E. A. "A Relationship between Incentive Motivation and Ability Level in Psychomotor Performance." *Journal of Experimental Psychology* 56:78-81; July 1958.
2. HOVELAND, C. L. "Human Learning and Retention." *Handbook of Experimental Psychology* (Edited by S. S. Stevens). New York: Wiley and Sons, Inc., 1951.
3. JOHNSON, BIRGER. "Influence of Pubertal Development on Responses to Motivated Exercise." *Research Quarterly* 27:182-93; May 1956.
4. LINDQUIST, E. F. *Design and Analysis of Experiments in Psychology and Education.* San Francisco: Houghton Mifflin Co., 1953.
5. McGEOCH, J. A., and IRION, A. L. *The Psychology of Human Learning.* New York: Longmans, Green and Co., 1952.
6. NOBLE, C. E. "An Attempt to Manipulate Incentive-Motivation In a Continuous Tracking Task." *Perceptual and Motor Skills* 5:65-69; June 1955.
7. ULRICH, CELESTE, and BURKE, ROGER K. "Effect of Motivational Stress upon Physical Performance." *Research Quarterly* 28:403-12; December 1957.

Growth of a Motor Skill as a Function of Distribution of Practice*

JOHN M. DIGMAN

IF there is any area in experimental psychology that has been investigated with a wide assortment of approaches and learning tasks, it is massed versus distributed practice effects on learning and performance. Massed practice refers to continuous practice at a task. Distributed practice indicates rest pauses or alternate skill learning between practice trials. Theories of motor learning have been generated on the basis of perfor-

* From the *Journal of Experimental Psychology*, 1959, *57*, 310-315. Reprinted with permission of the author and the American Psychological Association.

mance data collected from varied practice distributions. Digman attempts to bridge the gap between research and theory, and to resolve some sticky issues. It is unfortunate that he does not include retention data comparisons as affected by original practice distributions, for typically very little difference, if any, is found among group performances.

While the influence of massing of practice on performance of a motor skill can be readily demonstrated, studies concerned with the effects of this variable on the rate of growth and asymptote of habit strength have often seemed inconclusive. Theoretical predictions to the contrary, a number of studies (e.g., Archer, 1954; Bourne & Archer, 1956; Digman, 1956; Reynolds & Bilodeau, 1952) have failed to find clear-cut evidence for any permanent decrement such as Hull's (1951) $_sI_R$, or the inhibition variables postulated by Ammons (1947) and Kimble (1949). Denny, Frisbey, and Weaver (1955) found "several lines of evidence" favoring the concept of conditioned inhibition in motor skill learning. However, the fact that the decremental function observed by them extinguished under distributed practice suggests a concept somewhat different from the traditional $_sI_R$ function. A similar phenomenon was observed by Digman (1956), who favored an explanation in terms of transfer theory, although the extinction interpretation is admittedly more basic.

Bourne and Archer (1956), measuring total time on target and time continuously on target (duration of hits), proposed that only one type of inhibition exists. This is the familiar temporary decrement, I_R, which is presumed to dissipate rapidly with rest. (However, Jahnke and Duncan [1956] have found evidence for traces of I_R after 24 hr. of rest.) Concerning I_R, Bourne and Archer (1956, p. 31) suggested that ". . . in addition to reducing performance . . . it interferes with the acquisition of skill and thereby reduces the actual level of learning of the habit . . . [especially that part associated with] smooth pursuit tracking skill."

A study by Adams (1952), which was indirectly concerned with $_sI_R$, suggested the possibility of a convergence of the performances of two practice groups, one with practice well distributed, the other with practice considerably massed. In this study there were five practice sessions on as many consecutive days. Whether the performance of the massed practice group would have risen to the level of the performance curve for the distributed practice group, had there been another day of practice under distributed practice conditions for both groups, is a question immediately suggested by an inspection of Adams' curves, particularly in view of the conclusions reached by Bourne and Archer. It is this question which prompted the study reported here.

Method

Subjects. The Ss were 41 men and women drawn from two classes in psychology conducted by the investigator. Approximately half of the Ss were volunteers from an introductory course; the rest were students in a course in the psychology of learning who participated in the experiment as an essential part of the course. In general, Ss were assigned to experimental conditions in order of their appearance except for an attempt to equalize sexes in the groups. One S was assigned, out of order, to the distributed practice group, Group D. The N in Group D was 22 (11 men and 11 women), and the N in Group M, the massed practice group, was 19 (10 men and 9 women).

Apparatus. A pursuit rotor manufactured by the Ralph Gerbrands Co. was used. The target button was 12.5 mm. in diameter, imbedded in a disc

25.5 cm. in diameter. The target button revolved at the rate of 30 rpm in a clockwise direction and in an epicyclic fashion. A brass stylus, hinged 12.0 cm. from the target end, with a tip 5.5 mm. in diameter, completed a circuit with the scoring element of a Standard Electric clock, whenever the tip was in contact with the target button during a work period. Target-to-floor distance was 35 in. An electronic interval timer manufactured by the Photoswitch Co., with interval accuracy of approximately 99%, was used to obtain the desired work-rest intervals.

Procedure. Six practice sessions were given to both groups over a two-week period on days Monday, Wednesday, and Friday. To eliminate bias associated with the longer rest from Friday to Monday, the first practice session was staggered, with S_1 beginning on Monday, S_2 on Wednesday, etc. Each practice session consisted of eighteen 30-sec. trials. For Group D there was a rest interval of 1.5 min. between trials throughout the experiment. For Group M this interval was 2 sec., which provided E the opportunity to read and reset the scoring clock. On Day 6 both groups were treated alike, with 1.5-min. intervals between trials. Following Trial 108 there were four "test trials."

Throughout the experiment an attempt was made to motivate Ss to maximum effort by stressing the alleged importance of the research, by asking each S to "do his best," and by reporting S's score to him at the conclusion of each trial.

At the final practice session, Ss were told at the conclusion of Trial 108 that there was to be a test of ability consisting of four trials. The Ss were again told of the importance of the experiment and urged to do their best.

Results

Something of the convergence effect obtained by Adams (1952) was observed, a convergence which seems more evident from a comparison of the terminal performances of both groups on succeeding days, and less so from a comparison of initial performances. At the beginning of Day 6, the difference in performance between the two groups is approximately equal to the initial difference for Days 4 and 5, and not much less than that observed for Days 2 and 3.

Performance for Group M on Day 6, when practice conditions were identical to those of Group D, does lend support to the original hypothesis that, had practice continued indefinitely, the performance curves for the two groups would have converged. However, the data suggest rather than demonstrate a convergence, and a one-sided test of the difference between groups for the sum of Trials 109-112 (the test trials) implies that the groups are still operating at different levels. (The test used was the Mann-Whitney signed ranks test, and the obtained z was 2.56, which is significant at the .01 risk level.)

An interesting resemblance may be noted between the performance curve for Group M on Day 6 and the curve for Group D on Day 4. This may be some indirect evidence of Archer's (1954) contention that under massed practice conditions Ss do not practice as much as they would under conditions of distributed practice. Some of the implications of this resemblance are more fully considered below.

Parameters of Growth in Skill. As an index of skill level (Sk) for Group D, the mean of the last two trials of each practice session was computed. This index was used for two reasons: the presence of warm-up decrement during the earlier stages of practice for each session, lasting for some unspecified amount of time, and the need for a more stable index of skill than a single trial mean.

A number of different types of curves were examined for their applicability to the six points determined. Easily the best fit was accomplished by use of a modified Hull (1951) type exponential curve. The equation for this curve is:

$$Sk_d = 15.2(1-10^{-.275n})+13.2 \text{ [1]}$$

where Sk_d represents the skill level for the distributed practice group attained at the end of a practice session, and n the number of practice sessions.

Because of the extensive amounts of work decrement usually present for Group M (except for Day 6), a different procedure was followed to determine skill level at the conclusion of each practice session under massed practice. It was first assumed that the amount of intersession forgetting was the same for both groups. (Indeed, there is evidence [Jahnke & Duncan, 1956] for little, if any, forgetting of rotary pursuit skill over a 2- or 3-day period.) A second assumption was that differences in performance at the beginning of any session reflected differences in skill level at that point. This difference, present at the beginning of a session, was then subtracted from the value for skill level for Group D at the conclusion of the previous practice session, and used as an index of skill level for Group M. Through the five points thus obtained, a modified Hull-type exponential curve was passed. The equation for the curve is:

$$Sk_m = 17.3(1-10^{-.328n})+8.1 \text{ [2]}$$

A measure of warm-up decrement, present at the beginning of each practice session, was computed by subtracting the obtained score for the first trial from the skill level attained at the end of the previous session.

Shrinking the Practice Scale for Group M. Since the performance of Group M on Day 6 bore such a resemblance to the performance of Group D on Day 4, it was tentatively concluded that at the beginning of Day 6, after 90 trials, Group M had received about as much practice as Group D had received at the beginning of Day 4, after 54 trials. Therefore, it was inferred that, under conditions of massed practice, at least for the first three practice sessions, Group M received .60 as much practice per trial as Group D. The practice scale was accordingly shrunken to .60 of the scale for Group D, and skill values, as determined previously, plotted.

Discussion

Two alternative interpretations of the data are available: the traditional two-factor theories of Hull (1951), Ammons (1947), and Kimble (1949); or the single-factor theory of Bourne and Archer (1956). The present study provides some evidence for the former in the failure of the performance curve for Group M to rise to the level of Group D on the last day of practice. The curve for Group M on the final day does, however, strongly suggest a convergence, and it may be argued that there was insufficient practice on the final day to develop those aspects of skill associated with "smooth pursuit tracking skill."

The results of the study are perhaps better understood according to the views of Bourne and Archer concerning the effects of massing of practice. Massing of practice apparently set an asymptote of skill somewhat lower than did distributed practice. The fact that the values for Equation 2, when plotted on a shrunken practice scale, coincide with the Group D skill curve during the early stages of practice, bears out Archer's (1954) contention that under massed practice Ss learn less in part because they practice less. Beginning with Day 3, however, Group D apparently began to learn not only more per trial but also something which Group M failed to learn (at least until

Day 6). This is very likely the "smooth pursuit tracking skill" for which Bourne and Archer (1956) have some evidence. The failure of the performance curve for Group M to rise to the level of Group D may be attributed to a considerable difference in practice in those parts of skill associated with high-level performance. Since the curves would imply that Ss in Group D began to learn these elements of skill perhaps as early as the beginning of Day 3, Group D may have had in this respect, by the end of the experiment, a fourfold advantage in practice over Group M.

While the computed skill values are unusually well described by the equations derived for them, they obviously fail to coincide at the point of zero practice. Extrapolation of the skill curve for Group M to the point of zero practice gives a value of 8.1. Actual performance for Group M on Trial 1 was 5.71. The difference between this and theoretical skill level, 2.4, is, by reference to the warm-up decrement curve, a reasonable value. However, the skill curve for Group D, when extrapolated to zero, gives a value of 13.2. Actual performance was 4.83, which, even with the addition of 2.5 for warm-up decrement, gives a value considerably short of the skill level for zero practice derived from the equation. A possible interpretation of this state of affairs is that the equation is not applicable during the earliest part of practice, and that a different and more rapid growth of skill occurs under distributed practice at this stage.

The advantage of distributed practice over massed practice is, then, possibly threefold: (a) More learning occurs per trial under distributed practice, because more practice is received. (b) The growth of skill under distributed practice continues to a higher final level, very likely because of the acquisition of a type of response difficult to achieve under massed practice. (c) For some reason, early learning under distributed practice may be especially advantageous.

However, the repeated failure to find conclusive evidence for any permanent decrement, even under the severely contrasting conditions of this study, suggests that in some situations massing of practice, far from causing any permanent damage to skill, may actually be a very economical type of practice. While Ss in the present study who learned under massed practice conditions may have received only 60% as much practice per trial as Ss under distributed practice conditions, they spent only 9 min. in the experimental situation; the distributed practice Ss spent more than 30 min., most of which time was devoted to reading magazines or gazing out a window. An implication of the present study might be that some of this time could have been more profitably given over to practice, at least that portion of training after the beginning and before the acquisition of high-level skill.

Summary

The growth of a motor skill (rotary pursuit) was investigated, using two groups of Ss under contrasting degrees of distribution of practice. Both groups received eighteen 30-sec. trials per day for six days. For one group intertrial rests were 1.5 min. throughout the study. For the other group intertrial rests were 2 sec. for the first five days of practice and 1.5 min. on Day 6. A test of four trials, separated by 1.5 min., was given after Trial 108, under conditions assumed to be fairly optimal in respect to motivation and practice conditions.

Results indicate that the chief effect of massing of practice is to reduce the asymptote of skill, possibly by introducing conditions which make difficult the learning of the type of response necessary for high-level performance. It seems likely, however, that a switch in practice conditions, from massed to distributed practice, is accompanied by a corresponding shift in asymptote to that ordinarily associated with distributed practice. There was evidence that under massed practice Ss received considerably less practice per trial than did Ss under distributed practice. Possible evidence for a difference between "early" and "later" learning under distributed practice was tentatively offered.

References

ADAMS, J. A. Warm-up decrement in performance on the pursuit rotor. *Amer. J. Psychol.*, 1952, *55*, 404-414.

AMMONS, R. B. Acquisition of motor skill: Quantitative analysis and theoretical formulation. *Psychol. Rev.* 1947, 54, 263-281.

ARCHER, E. J. Postrest performance in motor learning as a function of prerest distribution of practice. *J. exp. Psychol.*, 1954, 47, 47-51.

BOURNE, L. E., & ARCHER, E. J. Time continuously on target as a function of distribution of practice. *J. exp. Psychol.*, 1956, 51, 25-33.

DENNY, M. R., FRISBEY, N., & WEAVER, J., JR. Rotary pursuit performance under alternate conditions of distributed and massed practice. *J. exp. Psychol.*, 1955, 49, 48-54.

DIGMAN, J. M. Performance under optimal practice conditions following three degrees of massing of early practice. *J. exp. Psychol.*, 1956, 52, 189-193.

HULL, C. L. *Essentials of behavior.* New Haven: Yale Univer. Press, 1951.

JAHNKE, J. C., & DUNCAN, C. P. Reminiscence and forgetting in motor learning after extended rest intervals. *J. exp. Psychol.*, 1956, 52, 273-282.

KIMBLE, G. A. An experimental test of a two-factor theory of inhibition. *J. exp. Psychol.*, 1949, 39, 15-23.

REYNOLDS, B., & BILODEAU, I. McD. Acquisition and retention of three psychomotor tasks as a function of distribution of practice during acquisition. *J. exp. Psychol.*, 1952, 44, 19-26.

Mental Practice: A Review and Discussion*

ALAN RICHARDSON

MANY highly skilled individuals such as athletes admit to mentally rehearsing, self-verbalizing, or, in other words, imagining the routine in which they are to be engaged or the one just terminated. Presumably positive transfer occurs from this art of task conceptualization to the overt performance. Many investigators have designed reasonably controlled experiments to discover the effects of formalized mental practice on overt performance. Diverse practice schedules, dissimilar tasks, and different mental to physical practice ratios have been of concern. Richardson summarizes a portion of the research dealing with mental practice. In a subsequent issue of *The Research Quarterly,* he has another article on the topic which contains an additional review of the material.

Mental practice refers to the symbolic rehearsal of a physical activity in the absence of any gross muscular movements. When a golfer sits with eyes

* From *The Research Quarterly,* 1967, *38,* 95-107. Reprinted with permission of the author and the American Association for Health, Physical Education, and Recreation.

closed and in imagination goes through the motions of putting a golf ball he is engaged in mental practice.

An examination of the literature over the past 30 years shows that at least 25 studies have been explicitly concerned with the effectiveness of this procedure. Though mental practice has been the term most frequently used, the same topic has been investigated under a variety of other names: e.g., symbolic rehearsal,[25] imaginary practice,[22] implicit practice,[19] mental rehearsal,[42] and conceptualizing practice.[11]

Purpose

It is the purpose of this first article to review the experimental literature on the relation of mental practice to performance and to individual differences in the amount of gain obtained.

Mental Practice and Performance

Primary interest in the process of mental practice has focused on its general value in facilitating the initial acquisition of a perceptual motor skill, in aiding the continued retention of such a skill, or in improving the immediate performance of a skill.

Acquisition

Experiments on the acquisition of a skill have usually employed three basic groups of S's drawn at random from a homogeneous parent population or equated on the basis of initial performance. The number of S's has varied from as few as four per group in the work of Vandell, Davis and Clugston[40] to as many as 72 per group in the study of Clark.[7] In most studies, a comparison has been made between the initial physical performance of each group and its final physical performance. Changes in performance level resulting from the type of intervening activity are typically expressed in terms of percentage gains and losses. In the Physical Practice group (PP) the intervening activity consists in physical practice of the skill to be acquired. In the Mental Practice group (MP) the intervening time is occupied in sitting or standing and rehearsing the skill in imagination for periods ranging from 1 min.[22] to 30 min.[40] Some evidence from Twining's[39] study suggests that a period of 5 min. is probably the longest in which concentration can be maintained without a rest pause. Studies have varied considerably in the number of trials per practice session and in the total number and spacing of these trials. The members of the No Practice group (NP) are usually given clear instructions not to practice the skill in any way or to think about it during the interval. A more adequate control which has sometimes been used, e.g., Perry,[22] is to require the members of the NP group to attend the same number of practice sessions as the PP and MP groups but to occupy their time in some activity irrelevant to the task.

With the exception of the investigations by Kelsey[17] and Steel[36] on muscular endurance, the other nine studies shown in Table 1 constitute all the studies on the acquisition of perceptual motor skills that provide results which can be conveniently compared in tabular form. For this reason they should be taken as a selected group not fully representative of all investigations in the MP field. For example, two other studies on acquisition employ additional comparison groups. In a study by Smith and Harrison[27] using a three-hole punch board, six groups of ten university men were used to investigate the effects of five different practice procedures: motor, visual, reversed visual, mental, guided, and no practice. After an initial 1-min. trial, the S's of the five groups each practiced according to their particular practice procedures

TABLE 1. SELECTED STUDIES ON THE EFFECTS ASSOCIATED WITH MENTAL PRACTICE

Research worker	Subjects	Tasks	Percent gain			Comparison between groups		
			NP	MP	PP	PP>NP	MP>NP	PP>MP
Eggleston (1936)	N = 20 per grp 32 men, 28 women Age rge: 20-53 yrs	Card sorting Digit substitution	4.06 8.79**	12.44** 41.51**	17.30** 49.69**	p<.05 p<.01	n.s. p<.01	n.s. n.s.
Perry (1939)	School children N = 16 per grp N = 16 per grp N = 12 per grp N = 14 per grp N = 15 per grp	Tapping Card sorting Peg board Mirror drawing Digit substitution	0.51 5.15* 0.70 29.60** 21.59**	5.72* 20.28** 42.63** 64.60** 64.92**	11.93** 37.55*** 35.39*** 128.20*** 89.31**	p<.01 p<.003 p<.003 p<.003 p<.003	n.s. <p.003 <p.003 p<.01 p<.003	n.s. p<.003 n.s. p<.01 p<.05
Vandell and others (1943)	Jr. Hi Sch. boys N = 4 per grp Sr. Hi. Sch. boys N = 4 per grp College men N = 4 per grp	Darts Basketball free throw Darts	−2.00 2.00 0.00	4.00 43.00 22.00	7.00 41.00 23.00	n.a. n.a. n.a.	n.a. n.a. n.a.	n.a. n.a. n.a.
Twining (1949)	College men N = 12 per grp <18	Ring tossing	4.30	36.20**	137.30**	n.a.	n.a.	n.a.
Trussell (1952)	College women N = per grp >13	Juggling	36.76	62.48	447.88***	p<.05	n.s.	p<.05
Steel (1952)	School boys N = 15 per grp	Tennis ball	7.56	11.90**	15.32**	p<.05	n.s.	n.s.

Study	Group	N	Task						
Clark (1960)	Varsity Jr. / Varsity Novices	N = 72 per grp	Pacific Coast one hand foul shot (basketball)	n.u. / n.u. / n.u.	15.00** / 23.00** / 26.00**	16.00** / 24.00** / 44.00**	n.a. / n.a. / n.a.	n.a. / n.a. / n.a.	n.a. / n.a. / n.a.
Wilson (1960)	University women	PP = 23 / MP = 30 / NP = 22	Tennis forehand and backhand drives	11.86*	7.07*	10.30*	n.s.	n.s.	n.s.
Kelsey (1961)	University men	N = 12 per grp	Muscular endurance for sit-ups	8.70	29.10*	322.80**	p<.05	n.s.	p<.05
Whiteley (1962)	School boys	N = 50 per grp	Tennis ball throws	3.63	12.98**	19.44**	p<.01	p<.05	n.s.
Steel (1963)	School boys	N = 14 per grp	Muscular endurance for bench press	0.84	6.15*	8.54**	n.a.	n.a.	n.a.

** p < .01.
* p < .05.
n.a.—not available.
n.s.—not significant.
n.u.—not used in final study.
NP = No Practice; MP = Mental Practice; PP = Physical Practice.
Samples were too small to measure confidence levels in Vandell and others (1943).
An analysis of variance design was employed by Clark (1960).

for six periods of 10 sec. After each of the 10-sec. practice periods the S's were required to read for a further 10 sec., thus making a total time of 2 min. The NP group read for the full 2-min. practice period between initial and final test. It was concluded that the most significant over-all improvement occurred under the mental practice and visual practice conditions.

In another study by Halverson[15] three comparison groups were employed in addition to an NP group. The S's were first-year university women (N = 15 per group) and the task was a basketball throw. Of the three groups the first (Demonstration) was given a demonstration followed by PP and then criticism; the second (Kinesiological) had practice in basketball throwing but without a basket to aim at; the third (Mental Practice) had MP while standing facing the basket with preferred foot forward. All three groups improved significantly, though the MP group improved least. No improvement occurred in the NP group.

These two studies and the majority of those shown in Table 1 give support to the basic hypothesis that MP facilitates the acquisition of a skill.

The tasks that have been used vary in the extent to which previous learning might be expected to provide positive transfer. Some tasks, like ballthrowing, are likely to be very familiar while others, like mirror-drawing, are relatively unfamiliar to most subjects. The evidence from Clark's[7] study of basketball throwing suggests that with each increase in task familiarity the advantage of PP tends to decline. Among the novices, PP is almost twice as valuable as MP, but with the more experienced junior and senior varsity groups MP appears to be as valuable as PP.

Of those studies for which MP results in a significant improvement in relation to initial performance, some also show a significant gain in the NP group. However, it should be noted that where this has happened it is usually found that the MP group makes a significantly greater improvement. In a study of the tennis forehand and backhand drives, Wilson[43] found that all three groups improved significantly though the MP group showed least gain and the NP and PP groups were almost equal.

Two other studies were found which had definitely negative results. Trussell,[38] using a three-ball two-hand juggling task, found no significant improvement in the performance of the MP group. Gilmore and Stolurow[13] used a Munn type of ball-and-socket task and six groups of six randomly selected, right-handed, male elementary psychology students. Their experimental design was based on Soloman's use of additional control groups in which there is intervening activity and a post-test, but no pre-test.[28] Improved performance resulted for the PP and NP groups, with the PP groups significantly better than the NP groups ($p < .01$). The MP groups declined in performance and were significantly worse than the PP groups ($p < .01$) and significantly worse than the NP groups ($p < .06$). The experiment was independently replicated twice and the same results were obtained on each occasion. Insufficient information is available in the published abstract to attempt an explanation of these very interesting results, but the possibility that massed MP, as used in this study, may produce more interference than massed PP might be considered. A study by Harby[16] on basketball throwing might also be included among these investigations, though the MP procedure involved viewing repetitions of a loop film of the skill rather than MP as defined here. Five groups had observational practice each day for periods ranging from 7 to 21 days. Only one of these groups showed a significant improvement.

An interesting replication of the Vandell and others[40] study of dart-throwing was carried out by Beattie.[4] Using larger groups she not only obtained confirmation of the earlier study but also found bilateral transfer from the preferred to the nonpreferred hand.

Defining muscular endurance as "the ability to continue repeated muscular activity," Kelsey[17] investigated the effect of MP on the total number of sit-ups. To lessen the effect of sheer strength on this ability, the three groups were selected from all those students at the University of British Columbia who scored between the mean and minus one standard deviation of the total university population. Practice periods for the MP and PP groups consisted of 5 min. per day for 20 days. The results of this experiment showed that a significant improvement occurred in the MP group, though it was relatively slight compared with the improvement in the PP group. In an unpublished study of muscular endurance, Steel[36] used four groups of 14 school-boys selected at random. Each member of the PP group performed bench presses, lifting three-quarters of his initial poundage on each of the 8 days intervening between initial and final performance. Each of these daily trials consisted of four lifts and a 60-sec. rest followed by four more lifts. The MP group practiced for 10 min. each day. A fourth group, in addition to the NP group, had four lifts PP followed by five min. of MP each day. Compared with the PP group which gained 8.54 percent between initial and final performance scores, this PP + MP group gained 12.66 percent. Though both groups showed a significant improvement ($p < .01$) the PP + MP group was not significantly superior to the PP group. The problem of controlling unscheduled practice sessions is present in most of the studies reported but is of particular concern in this type of endurance task.

Four other studies were found which investigated the effect on performance of varying combinations of MP and PP trials. Using a two-hand three-ball juggling task Trussell[38] found that following the initial trial, a 5-min. MP period on each of 6 days followed by 14 days of PP resulted in the greatest improvement, with PP alone the next best. A third group in which the initial trial was followed by a 5-min. MP on each of 14 days followed by 6 days of PP was next, with the all MP group in fourth place and the NP group last. In a study by Riley and Start[23] four equated groups of girls aged 14-15 years practiced quoit throwing (as in deck quoits) on each of the 12 days intervening between initial and final performance. The group which received alternate days of MP and PP improved most. Next came the group which had received 6 days of PP followed by 6 days of MP. In third place was the group which received 6 days of MP followed by 6 days of PP, while last of all came the NP group which improved no more than would have been expected by chance. Whiteley,[42] as a subsidiary part of his main investigation, studied the improvement of four groups of 23 boys on a complex gymnastic skill. Each group practiced for 20 min. on each of the 12 practice days. The group which occupied each 20-min. period by alternating 5 min. PP, 5 min. MP, 5 min. PP, 5 min. MP improved most. Next came the group which alternated 10 min. PP with 10 min. MP on each practice day. The group having PP only was in third place while the MP group improved least of all. Egstrom[11] studied six groups of 20 male university students. Each group was given physical performance tests on the first, seventh, and thirteenth day. The pattern of practice on the remaining days varied from all PP, or all MP, to all NP. A fourth group alternated MP with PP, a fifth group received PP on the first five practice days and MP on the last five and lastly, a sixth group which received MP on the first five and PP on the last five practice days. The group which alternated MP and PP gained most but was not significantly better than the all-PP group which came second in amount gained.

The trend in all five of these studies shows that an alternation of PP and

MP tends to produce the greatest improvement in performance. However, as it is known from many other investigations, e.g., Buxton,[6] Knapp and Dixon,[18] alternating PP periods with periods of rest is in general superior to massed PP, and little can be concluded as to the efficacy of MP periods until experiments include a rest condition in their design. In this regard, the brief report by Cratty and Densmore[8] is of interest. Using three groups of 10 female university students, they studied the effect of unrelated physical and mental activities during rest intervals between trials on a locomotor maze. No significant differences were found between the mean traversal speeds of the three groups (knot-tying, symbol-cancellation, no overt activity). The authors reported their intention to investigate the effect of MP during rest periods in a future study.

Ammons[2] used a rotary pursuit task and found that the incorporation of a 2-min. MP session prior to a 12-min. PP session produced no significant changes in subsequent performance when compared with seven other variations in pre-practice activities.

Retention

Only two studies have been found in which the effect of MP on retention has been the focus of research.

Sackett[25] had three groups of S's learn a finger maze to the criterion of 2 errorless repetitions. He then dismissed the PP group, having instructed them to draw the maze as often as possible from memory and in particular to draw 5 independent reproductions of the maze route each night before retiring. The MP group was told to think through the maze as often as possible and to rehearse it 5 times each night before retiring but not to draw or trace it physically at any time. The NP group was told to avoid thinking about the maze or drawing it. Retention was measured one week later by the savings method, but the difference between the two groups was not statistically reliable. Rubin-Rabson,[24] using three skilled pianists in each of three groups, found that five PP trials followed by a 4-min. MP period, then PP trials to the criterion of one errorless repetition led to significantly better retention one week later than occurred in either of the other two groups. One of these other groups had PP to the criterion followed by a period of 4 min. of MP. The other had PP to the criterion followed by 4 min. of further PP.

Immediate Performance

Studies that qualify for discussion in this section are those in which a skill is rehearsed in imagination immediately prior to its performance.

Waterland[41] compared a PP and an MP group on a ten-pin bowling skill. The PP group was coached under standard conditions of instruction. Members of the MP group were encouraged to recapture the kinesthetic "feel" of the bowling action before delivering each ball down the alley. Mental practice under these conditions was found to produce a smoother action, greater speed of delivery, and a higher score than when bowling was carried out under the standard PP condition.

Many gymnasts, jumpers, and divers are known to employ this type of MP and some attempts to study the effectiveness of this procedure have been reported from the U.S.S.R. In a study by Abelskaya and Surkov[1] for example, it was found that when high jumpers were encouraged to imagine the detailed movements of their jump prior to take off, improvement was superior to that of jumpers who did not employ this procedure. However, it should be noted that two jumpers only were coached in each group and that the superiority of the MP group was delayed rather than immediate.

In these two studies related to immediate performance it might be that MP procedures derive part of their value through establishing an appropriate set to the task. Whether there is any added merit in the MP procedure for establishing a set over other methods deserves to be investigated.

Conclusions

The following tentative conclusions on the relation of MP to performance may be made:

1. Despite a variety of methodological inadequacies the trend of most studies indicates that MP procedures are associated with improved performance on the task. Statistically significant positive findings were obtained in 11 studies—Eggleston,[10] Perry,[22] Rubin-Rabson,[24] Beattie,[4] Waterland,[41] Clark,[7] Kelsey,[17] Smith and Harrison,[27] Whiteley,[42] Egstrom,[11] and Steel.[36]

Seven further studies show a positive trend—Sackett,[25] Vandell and others,[40] Halverson,[15] Twining,[39] Harby,[16] Steel,[35] and Abelskaya and Surkov.[1] Three studies report negative findings—Ammons,[2] Gilmore and Stolurow,[13] and Trussell,[38] while the study by Wilson[43] is equivocal.

2. From the report of Beattie's[4] study there is evidence that MP can lead to bilateral transfer effects.

3. There is some evidence (Clark[7]) that degree of familiarity with the physical performance of a task is related to the efficiency of MP relative to PP.

4. Though the evidence is difficult to evaluate, there is a trend which suggests that when MP and PP trials are alternated during the acquisition of a skill the improvement in performance will be as good or better than PP trials only. (Trussell,[38] Riley and Start,[23] Whiteley,[42] Egstrom,[11] Steel.[36])

5. There is an indication from Twining's[39] study that MP sessions should not exceed 5 min. if concentration is to be maintained. If MP trials are massed, as in the study by Gilmore and Stolurow,[13] interference or loss of motivation may result in lowered performance.

Individual Differences in Gain from Mental Practice

In an attempt to obtain a better understanding of some of the individual factors that may facilitate or inhibit the amount of improvement to be gained from MP the following variables have been studied.

Abstract Reasoning. An insignificant correlation (rho −0.282) was obtained by Wilson[43] between amount gained in skill from MP on the tennis forehand and backhand drives and scores on the test of abstract reasoning from the Differential Aptitude Test (D.A.T.) battery.

Games Ability. In a study by Start[30] it was found that those rated high on games ability made a significant improvement in their performance on a basketball task after 5 min. of MP per day for 9 days ($p < .001$). Those rated as average or poor showed no significant improvement. However, it is possible that the good games players were more ego-involved than the other two groups. If this were true, it might be that motivation per se rather than MP per se could account for the significant improvement in this group. It might also be that those with games ability profited more from the initial trials than did the average and poor groups. These alternative hypotheses might also account for the relationship between percent gain scores on a ball throwing task and motor ability reported by Whiteley.[42]

Imagery. Several investigations, e.g., Vandell and others,[40] Trussell,[38] Clark,[7] have mentioned the possible importance of imagery in achieving any benefit from MP procedures. The first attempt to measure an imagery variable was that of Whiteley,[42] who used a simple test of position memory. After

12

seeing two square trays containing a random arrangement of 12 objects on each and exposed in turn for a period of 2 min., S's were given lists of the objects on each tray and two sheets of paper. On each sheet was a large square divided into four quarters. The task was to note down in which quadrant each object had been placed on its original tray. The number of accurately recorded objects was taken as a measure of imaging ability. The correlation between this test and percent gain scores of a ball-throwing task was found to be 0.63 for the MP group. This finding is of great interest but the question might well be asked as to whether this test is a measure of visual imagery. It might be that success on this test of imagery is greater among those who habitually utilize imageless thought or inner speech. Though some evidence exists for an association between visual imaging ability and spatial manipulation[3,9] it might be better to consider the present test as a measure of position memory until its relation to other imagery tests has been established.

In addition to mention of imagery vividness both visual[40] and kinesthetic[41] there has also been a reference to the potential importance of a capacity to control or manipulate imagery. In the study by Clark[7] "one subject reported mentally attempting to bounce the ball preparatory to shooting only to imagine that it would not bounce and stuck to the floor. This disturbed him to a point where he could not successfully visualize the shooting technique." Start and Richardson[34] investigated the relation between combined vividness and control of imagery and percent gain scores from MP on a simple gymnastic skill. Vividness of visual and kinesthetic imagery was measured with the Sutcliffe[37] revision of the Betts[5] test of voluntary imagery while control was measured on a modified version of the Gordon[14] test. It was predicted that those with vivid controlled imagery would perform best, and in descending order of performance scores, those with weak controlled imagery, those with weak uncontrolled imagery, and last of all, those with vivid uncontrolled imagery. The results supported this ordinal prediction and a significant difference was found between the terminal group ($p < .05$, one-tailed test). This study now needs replication using laboratory tasks.

Intelligence. This variable has been investigated by Perry,[22] Clark,[7] Start,[29,32] and Whiteley.[42] Only Perry, using the Kuhlman-Anderson group test, obtained positive results on one of his tasks. Those S's with high IQ's (above the median, IQ 124) performed better on the mirror-drawing task after MP than those with low IQ's (below the median).

Kinesthesia. Using the Wiebe test of kinesthesis, Start[33] found an insignificant correlation with gain scores from MP on a simple gymnastic skill.

Mechanical Reasoning. Wilson[43] obtained an insignificant correlation (rho 0.067) between improvement associated with MP and the test of mechanical reasoning from the D.A.T. battery.

Motor Ability. This variable was studied by Whiteley,[42] and a significant positive correlation of 0.48 was obtained between percent gain scores on his ball throwing task and motor ability as measured on the Iowa-Brace test. Start[31] found insignificant correlations with gains from MP on a single gymnastic skill using both the Brace test of motor ability and the Iowa-Brace test of motor educability. The same problem of interpretation exists here as was mentioned earlier in discussing the variable of games ability.

Selective Attention. Using the Thurstone forms A and B of the Gottschaldt figures test, Start[31] investigated the correlation between scores on each of these measures and percent gain scores associated with MP on a simple gymnastic skill. While the easier Form A measure showed an insignificant correlation (rho + 0.046) the more difficult Form B measure showed a significant correlation (rho + 0.375) with improvement in the skill.

Sex. Perry[22] used mixed groups of school children, but found no significant differences between the sexes in amount of improvement on any of the five tasks employed in his study.

Spatial Relations. In the light of the earlier discussion on imagery it might have been expected that a measure of spatial relations would correlate significantly with percent gain scores from MP. Wilson[43] obtained an insignificant correlation between improvement in the tennis forehand and backhand drive and the space relations test from the D.A.T. battery (rho 0.142). As no other investigators have examined the relation between gain from PP and individual difference variables, it is of interest that Wilson obtained a significant correlation (rho 0.461) between gain from PP and her spatial relations measure.

Summary

In summarizing these individual difference studies, only games ability and one of the two studies on motor ability, imaging ability, and the capacity for selective attention show a significant relation to amount of gain from MP. Of these, the findings for the first two variables are difficult to interpret. The possible significance of imagery will be discussed in the second article. The likelihood that selective attention, position memory (imagery), and spatial relations may all be interconnected with visual imagery needs further investigation. The connection between imagery and spatial ability has already been suggested (Barratt[3]), and that between selective attention as measured by the Thurstone version of the Gottschaldt figures test and the Guilford-Zimmerman spatial orientation test has been shown by Gardner, Jackson, and Messick.[12]

References

1. ABELSKAYA, R. S. and SURKOV, E. N., quoted by A. Mintz. Further developments in psychology in U.S.S.R. *Ann. Rev. Psychol.* 10:472, 1959.
2. AMMONS, R. B. Effects of prepractice activities on rotary pursuit performance. *J. exp. Psychol.* 41:187-91, 1951.
3. BARRATT, P. E. Imagery and thinking. *Aust. J. Psychol.* 5:154-64, 1953.
4. BEATTIE, D. M. Unpublished study quoted by M. B. Arnold. On the mechanism of suggestion and hypnosis. *J. abnorm. soc. Psychol.* 41:107-28, 1946.
5. BETTS, C. H. *The distribution and functions of mental imagery.* New York: Teachers College, Columbia Univ. Press, 1909.
6. BUXTON, C. E. Reminiscence in the acquisition of skill. *Psychol. Rev.* 49:191-96, 1942.
7. CLARK, L. V. Effect of mental practice on the development of a certain motor skill. *Res. Quart.* 31:560-69, 1960.
8. CRATTY, B. J., and DENSMORE, A. E. Activity during rest and learning a gross movement task. *Percept mot. Skills.* 17:250, 1963.
9. DREWES, H. W. *An experimental study of the relationship between electroencephalographic imagery variables and perceptual-cognitive processes.* Unpublished doctoral dissertation, Cornell University, 1958.
10. EGGLESTON, D. *The relative value of actual versus imagery practice in a learning situation.* Unpublished master's dissertation, Columbia University, 1936.
11. EGSTROM, G. H. Effect of an emphasis on conceptualizing techniques during early learning of a gross motor skill. *Res. Quart.* 35:472-81, 1964.
12. GARDNER, R. W., JACKSON, D. N., and MESSICK, S. J. Personality organization in cognitive controls and intellectual abilities. *Psychol. Issues.* 2, 4, 149, 1960.
13. GILMORE, R. W., and STOLUROW, L. M. Motor and "mental" practice of ball and socket task. *Amer. Psychol.* 6:295, 1951.
14. GORDON, R. An investigation into some of the factors that favour the formation of stereotyped images. *Brit. J. Psychol.* 39:156-67, 1949.
15. HALVERSON, L. E. *A comparison of three methods of teaching motor skills.* Unpublished master's dissertation, University of Wisconsin, 1949.

16. HARBY, S. F. Comparison of mental and physical practice in the learning of a physical skill. *U.S.N. Spec. Dev. Cent. Tech. Rep. S.D.C.* 269-7-25, 1952.
17. KELSEY, I. B. Effects of mental practice and physical practice upon muscular endurance. *Res. Quart.* 32:47-54, 1961.
18. KNAPP, C. G., and DIXON, W. R. Learning to juggle: a study to determine the effect of two different distributions of practice on learning efficiency. *Res. Quart.* 21:331-36, 1950.
19. MORRISETT, L. N., JR. *The role of implicit practice in learning.* Unpublished doctoral dissertation, Yale University, 1956.
20. ORNE, M. T. The nature of hypnosis: Artifact and essence. *J. abnorm. soc. Psychol.* 58:277-99, 1959.
21. ORNE, M. T. On the social psychology of the psychological experiment: with particular reference to demand characteristics and their implications. *Amer. Psychol.* 17:776-83, 1962.
22. PERRY, H. M. The relative efficiency of actual and imaginary practice in five selected tasks. *Archives of Psychol.* 34:5-75, 1939.
23. RILEY, E., and START, K. B. The effect of the spacing of mental and physical practices on the acquisition of a physical skill. *Aust. J. phys. Educ.* 20:13-16, 1960.
24. RUBIN-RABSON, G. A. A comparison of two forms of mental rehearsal and keyboard overlearning. *J. educ. Psychol.* 32:593-602, 1941.
25. SACKETT, R. S. The influences of symbolic rehearsal upon the retention of a maze habit. *J. gen. Psychol.* 10:376-95, 1934.
26. ————. The relationship between amount of symbolic rehearsal and retention of a maze habit. *J. gen Psychol.* 13:113-128, 1935.
27. SMITH, L. E., and HARRISON, J. S. Comparison of the effects of visual, motor, mental and guided practice upon speed and accuracy of performing a simple eye-hand coordination task. *Res. Quart.* 33:299-307, 1962.
28. SOLOMON, R. L. An extension of control group design. *Psychol. Bull.* 46:137-50, 1949.
29. START, K. B. Relationship between intelligence and the effect of mental practice on the performance of a motor skill. *Res. Quart.* 30:644-49, 1960.
30. ————. The influence of subjectively assessed "games ability" on gain in motor performance after mental practice. *J. gen. Psychol.* 67:159-73, 1962.
31. ————. *Mental practice.* Unpublished master's dissertation, University of Western Australia, 1963.
32. ————. Intelligence and the improvement in a gross motor skill after mental practice. *Brit. J. Educ. Psychol.* 34:85-90, 1964.
33. ————. Kinesthesia and mental practice. *Res. Quart.* 35:316-20, 1964.
34. START, K. B., and RICHARDSON, A. Imagery and mental practice. *Brit. J. Educ. Psychol.* 34:280-84, 1964.
35. STEEL, W. I. The effect of mental practice on the acquisition of a motor skill. *J. phys. Educ.* 44:101-08, 1952.
36. ————. *Effect of mental and physical practice on endurance on a bench press task.* Unpublished research report. University of Manchester, 1963.
37. SUTCLIFFE, J. P. *The relation of imagery and fantasy to hypnosis.* Progress report on N.I.M.H. Project M3950, University of Sydney, Australia, 1962.
38. TRUSSELL, E. M. *Mental practice as a factor in the learning of a complex motor skill.* Unpublished master's dissertation, University of California, 1952.
39. TWINING, W. E. Mental practice and physical practice in learning a motor skill. *Res. Quart.* 20:432-35, 1949.
40. VANDELL, R. A., DAVIS, R. A., and CLUGSTON, H. A. The function of mental practice in the acquisition of motor skills. *J. gen. Psychol.* 29:243-50, 1943.
41. WATERLAND, J. C. *The effect of mental practice combined with kinesthetic perception when the practice precedes each overt performance of a motor skill.* Unpublished master's dissertation, University of Wisconsin, 1956.
42. WHITELEY, G. *The effect of mental rehearsal on the acquision of motor skill.* Unpublished diploma in education dissertation, University of Manchester, 1962.
43. WILSON, M. E. *The relative effect of mental practice and physical practice in learning the tennis forehand and backhand drives.* Unpublished doctoral dissertation, University of Iowa, 1960.

Speed-Accuracy Tradeoff in Reaction Time: Effect of Discrete Criterion Times*

ROBERT G. PACHELLA AND RICHARD W. PEW

MOST motor skills require some degree of speed and accuracy in movement. Therefore, it is conceivable an instructional emphasis on one or the other or both equally could determine the nature of the ultimate skill acquired. Many complex athletic skills are initially taught with a de-emphasis on speed and an emphasis on accuracy. It is held that once accuracy is attained, speed will naturally follow without any loss in accuracy. Research has generally not supported this proposition, however. Pachella and Pew discuss speed-accuracy tradeoffs with regard to the designation of criterion performance as well as the values and costs associated with a given response.

The relationships between speed and accuracy of performance can be characterized in three ways, depending on the point of view of E. If one is examining the performance of a group of Ss, it is found that those Ss who tend to be fast also tend to be accurate (Fitts, 1959). If one is looking at performance of an individual S throughout a period of learning, there is a tendency for both speed and accuracy of performance to improve. However, if one looks within an S at a particular point during learning, then an increased emphasis on speed results in a loss in accuracy and vice versa (Garrett, 1922; Hick, 1952; Howell & Kreidler, 1963). It is this speed-accuracy tradeoff that will be examined further in this paper.

Fitts (1966) has demonstrated an effective method for controlling this tradeoff by defining a criterion that determines whether a response is fast or slow and assigning a payoff matrix having differential values and costs for the four cells of the matrix formed from fast vs. slow and correct vs. incorrect responding. He found that the use of a payoff matrix emphasizing speed produced rather consistent differences favoring speed over accuracy of performance as contrasted with use of a payoff matrix emphasizing accuracy. In a control condition Ss who were instructed to respond as rapidly and accurately as possible distributed their speed and accuracy of performance over the entire range of performances produced by the two experimental groups. Fitts interpreted his findings as being consistent with a statistical decision model of reaction time based on an earlier model proposed by Stone (1960) and extended by Edwards (1965). The present experiment examines further the factors which contribute to the production of a speed-accuracy tradeoff within an S.

The use of a discrete speed criterion designating responses as fast vs. slow results in two factors contributing to an S's possible earnings. First, there are the relative values used in the payoff matrix which specifies the value or cost of each outcome of an experimental trial. It was these values that Fitts

* From the *Journal of Experimental Psychology*, 1968, *76*, 19-24. Reprinted with permission of the authors and the American Psychological Association.

manipulated to produce a speed-accuracy tradeoff. Second, E has control of the setting of the criterion time. It is of interest to determine whether this variable also influences S's tradeoff between speed and accuracy. Certainly it would be possible to choose a criterion time sufficiently slow so that virtually all his responses would be considered fast and his accuracy would not suffer. On the other hand, the criterion time could also be set so that virtually none of the Ss' responses can be fast without reducing accuracy to the chance level. Alternatively, this experimental task, in which knowledge of results with respect to speed and accuracy are provided immediately following every trial, may be viewed in the context of a variable-ratio reinforcement rate for being fast.

In the Fitts experiment the criterion time was adjusted throughout the experiment so that an average of approximately 85% of Ss' responses were judged to be fast. This choice, however, was rather arbitrary and, in fact, this variable was not closely controlled. In the present experiment both the payoff matrices describing the relative importance of speed and accuracy and the criterion time were manipulated simultaneously in an effort to determine the relative magnitude of the main effects and their interaction.

Method

Apparatus. The apparatus used in the experiment is described in Fitts (1966). It consisted of a punched-tape system that programmed any number of stimulus lights, up to 10, in any combination and automatically recorded stimulus, response, and reaction time on each trial. The S responded by depressing pianolike, microswitch keys that were arranged in a pattern spatially similar to that of small lights on the stimulus panel. The placement of lights and response keys was designed to fit the curvature of the fingers of the hands. Located below the stimulus lights was a feedback panel consisting of four differentially colored lights. Each light was labeled with one of the possible outcomes of an experimental trial (fast correct, slow correct, fast wrong, and slow wrong).

Subjects. Sixteen male, paid volunteers participated in the experiment. All were undergraduate students at the University of Michigan.

Procedure. In a typical session the first stimulus pattern appeared on the stimulus panel approximately 2 sec. after a warning signal. The stimulus remained on for 50 msec. after S initiated his response. One-hundred milliseconds after S's response, one of the feedback lights was illuminated for 1 sec. Exactly 2 sec. after S had initiated his response, the next stimulus pattern appeared and the sequence was repeated. After 100 such trials S was given a short rest during which he was presented with cumulative results for the block of 100 trials, specifying what proportion of the 100 trials had been in each of the four possible categories (i.e., how many responses were fast and correct, fast and wrong, etc.). Eight blocks of 100 trials, which required approximately 50 min. to complete, constituted an experimental session.

When the response required more than one key to be pressed, 50 msec. were allowed for S to complete depression of all required keys. That is, from the time the first key was pressed, all other keys necessary for the response had to be activated within 50 msec. or the chord response was counted as incorrect. Reaction time, however, was recorded as the time from the onset of the stimulus pattern to the activation of the first key.

Matching Procedure. The Ss were arbitrarily divided into two groups of eight. One of the groups worked in the experiment with a payoff matrix that emphasized speed: the other worked with a matrix emphasizing accuracy. Each group was pretested on a spatially compatible 10-choice reaction-time task for one session of 800 trials. The criterion time for the pretest was set at 590 msec. All Ss worked with the same neutral payoff matrix in the pretest. In each group Ss were then ranked according to the amount of money earned on the pretest. The eight Ss in each group were then divided into four strata, two Ss per strata. One of the Ss in each strata was selected randomly for assignment to a group that would work with a criterion time of 360 msec. in the main experiment and the other was assigned to a group with a criterion time of 460 msec.

Experimental Conditions. The two levels of criterion time, 460 msec. (H) and 360 msec. (L), and the two payoff matrices, one stressing speed (S) and the other stressing accuracy (A), produced a 2 × 2 factorial design in which the four groups can be designated as follows: AH, AL, SH, and SL.

All four of these groups performed the same experimental task. Stimuli consisted of the 15 possible patterns provided by a panel of four lights. The lights could appear in any combination. Responses were made by depressing simultaneously all keys which corresponded spatially to the lights that appeared. The middle and index fingers of both hands were used to make the required chord responses.

Each S was tested on the experimental task for three sessions; all sessions being separated by approximately 48 hr. The Ss were guaranteed a minimum pay of $1.00/session in addition to bonuses earned according to the payoff matrix for their assigned group. The approximate earnings for Ss averaged over all groups was $2.00/session.

Results

The ordering of groups on the basis of the reaction-time data was from fastest to slowest: SL, AL, SH, and AH. The only exception to this ordering occurred on Day 1 when Groups AL and SH had the same average reaction time.

The ordering of the error data was exactly the inverse of that of the reaction-time data. That is, the lower the average reaction time for a group on any given day, the higher the group's error rate.

The analyses of variance of both the reaction-time and error data indicated that the main effects of payoff matrix, criterion time, and practice were significant at the .01 level on both measures of performance with the exception that the effect of payoff matrix on errors was significant only at the .05 level. The only significant first-order interaction was that of payoff matrix and practice and it was significant at the .01 level on both measures.

Finally, the only clear exception to the similarity of the two analyses of variance was that the triple interaction of Payoff Matrix × Criterion Time × Practice was significant at the .05 level for the error data and it was not significant (F < 1.0) for the reaction-time data.

Discussion

If the two criterion-time groups are considered separately, it may be seen that in both cases the basic finding reported by Fitts (1966) was obtained. Those Ss working with a speed matrix were significantly faster and made significantly more errors on all 3 days of the experiment than those Ss working with an accuracy matrix.

The significant interactions between payoff matrix and practice suggest that those *S*s who were working with the speed matrix began working rapidly and gradually improved their accuracy with practice. On the other hand, the group working with an accuracy matrix maintained a low error rate during practice but gradually improved their speed of performance.

Consider now the variable of criterion time. It is clear from the data that the choice of criterion time has large and consistent effects on *S*s' speed and accuracy of performance. There is a consistent difference of at least 60 msec. in average reaction time between the two criterion-time conditions for those *S*s who used the speed matrix and for those *S*s who used the accuracy matrix. This difference appears to be maintained across all three sessions of practice as well. Manipulation of the criterion time also produced large and consistent differences in error rates; the longer criterion time producing fewer errors. Thus it appears that another way to manipulate the speed-accuracy tradeoff is by appropriately adjusting criterion times. In fact, the combination of a significant interaction between payoff matrix and practice and the failure of the interaction between criterion time and practice to reach significance taken together suggest that the speed-accuracy tradeoff produced by manipulating payoff matrices tends to wash out with practice while the tradeoff produced by manipulating criterion times remains intact.

These results have implications for the formulation of an appropriate statistical decision model of reaction time as well as methodological implications. In Fitts' (1966) model, *S* accumulates successive samples of the stimulating environment. The arrival of each sample modifies the relative likelihood as to which of the possible stimulus alternatives is actually present. When *S*'s odds in favor of a particular alternative exceed a criterion value, he then executes the appropriate response. The location of this critical odds boundary is determined by the relative values and costs associated with fast vs. accurate responding. When greater emphasis is placed on accuracy, *S* shifts his critical odds boundary so that more samples must be accumulated before this boundary is reached and this results in a longer reaction time. . . .

From a methodological point of view, if it is desired to control an *S*'s criterion for speed vs. accuracy by means of a payoff matrix, the large effects of criterion time present some problems. Suppose one wants to compare the difficulty of two information-processing tasks. Setting equal criterion times may, in fact, produce a sensitive test of differences in difficulty. But suppose instead one wants to examine the effect of some treatment on two tasks of differing overall difficulty. If *E* chooses to use equal criterion times in the two tasks, then he is introducing a differential time constraint with respect to the easy and difficult tasks. If, on the other hand, he chooses to adjust the criterion time in accordance with the difficulty of the task, he has no assurance whether it is the criterion time or the task that is producing the differential performance. Finally, an a priori basis for adjusting criterion times as a function of learning has not as yet been worked out. Some of these difficulties may be avoided by using a continuous payoff for speed in which *S* is penalized a unit amount for every additional increment in time (Edwards, 1965). However, this introduces the additional difficulty of requiring a tradeoff between a continuous cost for time and the inherently discrete criterion implied by correct vs. incorrect performance.

In summary, then, it has been shown that an *S*'s choice of operating point along the speed-accuracy continuum may be brought under experimental control by manipulating either the criterion time or the values and costs associated with fast vs. accurate responding. Any representation of reaction-time performance, whether it be the statistical decision model suggested here or some other one, must be able to account for the effects of both of these variables.

References

EDWARDS, W. Optimal strategies for seeking information: Models for statistics, choice reaction times, and human information processing. *J. math. Psychol.*, 1965, 2, 312-329.

FITTS, P. M. Human information handling in speeded tasks. IBM Research Report No. RC-109, 1959, Yorktown Heights, New York.

FITTS, P. M. Cognitive aspects of information processing: III. Set for speed versus accuracy. *J. exp. Psychol.*, 1966, 71, 849-857.

GARRETT, H. E. A study of the relation of accuracy to speed. *Arch. Psychol., N. Y.*, 1922, No. 56.

HICK, W. E. On the rate of gain of information. *Quart. J. exp. Psychol.*, 1952, 4, 11-26.

HOWELL, W. C. & KREIDLER, D. L. Information processing under contradictory instructional sets. *J. exp. Psychol.*, 1963, 65, 39-46.

STONE, M. Models for choice-reaction time. *Psychometrika*, 1960, 25, 251-260.

Effects of Task Complexity and Task Organization on the Relative Efficiency of Part and Whole Training Methods*

JAMES C. NAYLOR AND GEORGE E. BRIGGS

A major source of difficulty for the instructor is that of determining whether a particular skill should be learned with a whole method, part method, or some combination plan. The older literature could be summarized quite simply: complex tasks should be broken down into component parts and taught by the part method while relatively easy tasks are favored more with whole practice techniques. This statement is still fairly acceptable today. Naylor and Briggs suggest a more sophisticated approach to task analysis to be used in determining the application of whole and part practice procedures. Task organization and task complexity analyses show much promise in this area, and no doubt in the future other task dimensions will be identified and related to procedural policies in practice.

In an attempt to resolve much of the confusion in previous studies on part vs. whole training methods, Naylor (1962) has suggested a task taxonomy by which to categorize systematically several task parameters as determinants of method effectiveness. The basic structure of the taxonomy states that task difficulty, as defined by the relative performance levels of S, is a function of both task complexity and task organization. Task complexity is defined as the demands placed on S's information-processing and/or memory-storage capacities by each of the task dimensions independently, while task organization refers to the demands imposed on S due to the nature of the interrelationship existing among the several task dimensions.

* From the *Journal of Experimental Psychology*, 1963, 65, 217-224. Reprinted with permission of the authors and the American Psychological Association.

It is interesting to note that whereas an increase in task complexity usually results in an increase in task difficulty, an increase in task organization can either increase or decrease task difficulty, depending upon the nature of the interrelationships used to define task organization. For example, Briggs and Waters (1958) manipulated task organization by varying the degree of interaction present in a two-dimensional tracking task, and they found increased task difficulty as task organization (the amount of interaction) was increased; however, in most verbal learning tasks the presence of relationships between dimensions usually results in a decrease in task difficulty (Lyon, 1914; McGeoch, 1930).

In his article Naylor (1962) suggests that training method effectiveness should be related to both task organization and task complexity, plus he hypothesizes a possible interaction between the two variables. A recent evaluation of the effect of task complexity on method efficiency (Briggs & Naylor, 1962) obtained results which failed either to support directly or deny the relationship. Since Naylor's interaction hypothesis would appear to be the most critical relationship, Briggs and Naylor have suggested that this may have caused the ambiguity found in the study evaluating task complexity alone.

The present study was designed as a test of the Naylor interaction hypothesis: there should be an interaction between task complexity, task organization, and training methods such that (a) for tasks of relatively high organization as task complexity is increased, whole-task training should become relatively more efficient than the part-task methods; however (b) for tasks of relatively low organization (all task dimensions being independent) an increase in task complexity should result in a part-task method becoming superior to the whole-task method. The two training methods compared were a progressive-part-task schedule and a whole-task practice method.

Method

There were two levels of task complexity, two levels of task organization, and two training methods (progressive-part and whole) incorporated in the design. There were 14 Ss per group and none had experienced a similar laboratory task prior to service. There were five daily sessions of approximately 1-hr. duration each. Training occurred over the first 3 days and transfer was effected on the last two sessions in a transfer of training paradigm.

Subjects and Tasks. The Ss were 112 undergraduate female students in introductory psychology classes. They were assigned at random to the eight groups subject only to the restriction that all groups be of equal size. All Ss were paid $7.50 for the entire series of five 1-hr. sessions.

The task was basically a Markov prediction situation which required S to predict three aspects of an event just prior to the occurence of the event. The event was a visual stimulus projected on a screen and a series of such stimulus events occurred at the rate of one event per 18 sec. The several discrete events varied in terms of three stimulus dimensions: (a) type of stimulus —aircraft, carrier, or submarine; (b) location of stimuli—left (L), center (C) or right (R); and (c) number of stimuli—one, two, or three objects of a single type. Thus, a given stimulus event consisted of one of three vehicle types in one of three possible locations or zones on the display and in number ranging from one to three vehicles.

Series of stimulus events were photographed on 16-mm. film. There were 60 stimulus events per series and a complete series represented one trial. There were two trials per day. Instructions to S emphasized that she was to predict *what, where,* and *how many* stimuli would appear and that she was to mark down her predictions on special record sheets prior to the occurrence of each stimulus event. The *S* was instructed also to look for any relationships *within and between* the stimulus dimensions because any relationship discovered would help in the predictions since, although there were four different series representing each experimental condition, the basic relationships between and within stimulus conditions did not change from trial to trial for a given group of *S*s.

Since the criterion task was a Markov prediction situation, it was possible to manipulate both task organization and task complexity by varying the sequential dependencies of the inter- and intradimensional events, respectively, as follows:

Task complexity was defined as the degree of predictability present in each of the task components considered in isolation (intradimensional predictability); thus, this parameter was varied by modifying the predictability *within* each of the separate stimulus dimensions. The digram frequencies of a stimulus series were adjusted while keeping the monogram frequencies constant and equal at all times. Thus, for the zone dimension, all three zones were used an equal number of times in each series (20 stimulus events). However, for the highly complex series all nine digrams (LR, LC, LL, CL, CC, CR, RL, RC, RR) were also equated for frequency of occurrence, while for a low-complexity series the digrams LL, CC, and RR never occurred, i.e., the same zone was never used twice in succession. This reduced the average within-dimension information from 3.160 bits in a high-complexity series to 2.577 bits for a low-complexity series. Maximum possible information for independent stimulus events, considering only monograms and digrams, would be $\log_2 9$ or 3.169 bits. Considering *all* higher-order terms, maximum information possible per event is $\log_2 59$, or 5.88 bits.

As indicated above, the definition of task organization is the degree to which separate task dimensions have meaningful relationships with each other (interdimensional predictability). This parameter was varied by modifying the predictabilities existing between dimensions, e.g., the prediction of zone from information concerning type. For the stimulus series of low organization, the cross-dimensional digrams were all equal in frequency, creating essentially a complete independence of dimensions. There are, with three dimensions, a total of six potential cross-dimensional relationships which might be established. These are predicting (*a*) type from zone, (*b*) type from number, (*c*) zone from number, (*d*) zone from type, (*e*) number from type, and (*f*) number from zone. For lists of high organization, predictability was established across dimensions using two of the possible six relationships: number was made predictable on the basis of zone information and zone was predictable from type information. This was done in each case by eliminating six of the nine possible cross-dimensional digrams for these two relationships. This resulted in series having an average cross-dimensional information metric of 2.449 bits for the highly organized series as compared with 3.119 bits for the low-organization series.

These variations resulted in a total average information (summing across both the within and between dimensions) of 2.74 bits for high-organization, high-complexity; 2.50 bits for high-organization, low-complexity; 3.14 bits for low-organization, high-complexity; and 2.93 bits for low-organization, low-complexity conditions.

Procedure. The groups having whole practice (Groups 1, 3, 5, and 7) made all three predictions (type, zone, and number) for every stimulus event throughout the entire 5-day period. The groups having progressive-part practice (Groups 2, 4, 6, and 8) predicted only type on Session 1, type *and* number on Session 2, number *and* zone on Session 3, and all three dimensions on Sessions 4 and 5. Thus, practice for these *S*s stressed those cross-dimensional relationships that led to maximum predictability, and Groups 2, 4, 6, and 8 can be considered as experimental groups in a transfer of training paradigm while Groups 1, 3, 5, and 7 are control groups.

The total number of correct predictions per 60-stimulus-event trial was used as the dependent variable. In order to make the data comparable during the first 3 days when part training was in progress, *percent* correct predictions were calculated and employed in the data presentation.

Results

It was necessary to ascertain the extent to which manipulation of task complexity in the manner described did indeed affect task difficulty. . . . As task complexity was increased, task difficulty also was increased, as measured by total task performance. Thus, for the highly organized task, the more complex version resulted in a smaller number of correct responses. The same was true of the less highly organized task.

The use of the information metric as a useful means of quantifying both task organization and task complexity (and thus predicting task difficulty) appears to be very meaningful. . . . It appears that intradimension information provided a good index of complexity, average interdimension information provided a good measure of organization, and average intra- and inter-dimension information provided a good index of total task difficulty. . . .

Training. The use of sequential dependencies within a stimulus dimension and between stimulus dimensions (to define task complexity and task organization, respectively) appears to have separated groups as predicted: the worst performance at the end of training occurred under the high-complexity, low-organization condition (Groups 3 and 4) and the best performance was attained under the low-complexity, high-organization arrangement (Groups 5 and 6). Groups 3 and 4 could find no relationships between or within the stimulus dimensions of the event series because none were present; however, there were helpful relationships *both* between and within the stimuli for the series viewed by Groups 5 and 6, and their superior performance at prediction was the result. The remaining four groups could discern relationships either within or between stimuli in the series (but not both) and their performance levels, as expected, were intermediate to those of the extreme conditions.

Transfer. One of the more meaningful ways is to express the transfer performance of an experimental group relative to its control group. Further, it is logical to make the comparison relative to the improvement of the two groups from initial training to initial transfer performance. An index to express this is $(C_i = E_T / C_i - C_T) \times 100$, where C_i is the performance of the appropriate (whole task) control group during initial training, C_T is the performance of the same group during initial transfer, and E_T is the performance of the experimental group during the same transfer trials. To the extent that the index is less than 100% for a given experimental group, the particular training method experienced by that group was less efficient than the whole-task training method.

First the low-organization indices: higher relative transfer occurs for the more complex task (233.3%) than for the less complex task (27.2%). However, there is a striking reversal when one compares the two indices for the highly organized task: here, the higher level of relative transfer occurs for the less complex task (67.7%) and the more complex task resulted in less (even *negative*) transfer (−20%). Thus, whereas a progressive-part training method was much worse than a whole-task method under conditions of high task organization (and high complexity), the same method was considerably better than the whole-task method under conditions of low task organization (and high complexity). Naylor's (1962) prediction is borne out thereby in the data: task complexity and task organization *do* interact to influence performance *and* to determine what training method will be most appropriate for the acquisition of skill.

An analysis of variance was performed on the transfer data. Of interest is the fact that the differences due to training method, task organization, and task complexity were all statistically significant at $p < .05$. On the average, groups trained by the whole method (Groups 1, 3, 5, and 7) were superior to the progressive-part groups (Groups 2, 6, and 8) during transfer, with the most notable exception of the progressive-part group (Group 4) which experienced the high-complexity, low-organization condition; on the average, transfer performance was higher on the less complex (Groups 5-8) than on the more complex (Groups 1-4) task; and, in general, the high-task-organization condition (Groups 1, 2, 5, and 6) resulted in performance superior to that under the low-task-organization condition (Groups 3, 4, 7, and 8).

The significance of the Methods $\times$ Complexity $\times$ Organization interaction was the most notable finding of the analysis. This was indicated previously from the results of the transfer indices where an interaction is clearly apparent. This interaction was the essential test of the hypothesis under investigation, indicating that the choice of a training method is dependent upon *both* task complexity and task organization.

The significant variance due to sessions shows the rapidity of adjustment during transfer to the new task, and the Sessions $\times$ Organization interaction indicates that this rapidity differs as a function of the organizational characteristics of the task. Thus, the highly organized tasks are subject to rapid behavioral adjustment as opposed to only slight changes in performance with the low-organization tasks.

Discussion

Several interesting points emerge in examination of the results. The relative transfer indices showed that the progressive-part training group actually exceeded the whole training group in transfer performance on the high-complexity, low-organization task. It is evident that this version of the task was by far the most difficult of the four task conditions used in the study. Thus, for an unorganized task, part practice surpassed whole practice in efficiency when the task was complex. While it is somewhat refreshing to find a condition under which whole training was not superior to another training method, the result was not unexpected. Prior research (Briggs & Naylor, 1962) has shown that increased complexity (and thereby difficulty) increased the size of the progressive-part transfer index from 75% to 91%, the latter group nearly equaling the whole-task group in transfer efficiency. The task used in the previous study was a three-dimensional tracking problem which involved no interaction between components and could therefore be considered to be of low organization. Therefore, the high-complexity, low-organization version of the task used in the present study must have exceeded sufficiently in difficulty the most complex version of the task used in the previous study so that progressive-part training did indeed result in greater transfer performance than the whole method.

The hypothesis that the relative efficiency of the two training methods would be related to an interaction between task complexity and task organization seems substantiated. Both the absolute differences in performance and the relative differences in transfer show the same interactive pattern. Given a task of high organization, increasing the difficulty (via increasing complexity) tends to favor whole-practice efficiency relative to progressive-part efficiency. However, as was pointed out above, exactly the reverse occurs with tasks of low organization. Here, increasing difficulty results in increased relative effectiveness of the progressive-part method.

These results are logical. By definition, a task of low-level organization consists of essentially independent components or dimensions, and S need not be concerned with the learning of relationships or intercouplings *between* task components. Instead, skill acquisition consists primarily of learning and applying the rules of information processing and/or memory storage for each dimension separately. Therefore, an increase in task complexity results in increased component task difficulty, the individual components still being independent, and it is logical that a progressive-part training method would be efficient since this method emphasizes the acquisition of skill in dealing with the individual components of the task. However, for tasks of higher levels of organization, S cannot treat the several task dimensions as separate and individual subtask requirements since, by definition, they are interrelated, and it is important that he acquire skill not only on the specific information-processing/memory demands of the component tasks, but also that he develop time-sharing and other intercomponent skills as required by the cross-dimension relationships. The whole-task training method should be more efficient under these conditions since this method emphasizes the acquisition of skills in dealing with the total (integrated) task.

For a relatively highly organized task, the whole training method should be superior to a part-task schedule regardless of the level of task (individual component) complexity. This follows since manipulations of individual component complexity can only add to or at least leave unchanged the cross-component relationships, and thus S must deal with total task demands regardless of the level of component complexity.

Seymour (1956) has suggested that a part-task method should become superior to the whole-task training method for tasks requiring complex perceptual skills (the high-complexity conditions as defined in the present report). The present data indicate that this conclusion is valid only for tasks of relatively low organization.

References

BRIGGS, G. E., & NAYLOR, J. C. The relative efficiency of several training methods as a function of transfer task complexity. *J. exp. Psychol.,* 1962, 64, 505-512.

BRIGGS, G. E., & WATERS, L. K. Training and transfer as a function of component interaction. *J. exp. Psychol.,* 1958, 56, 492-500.

LYON, D. O. The relation of length of material to time taken for learning. *J. educ. Psychol.,* 1914, 5, 1-9.

McGEOCH, J. A. The influence of associative value upon the difficulty of nonsense-syllable lists. *J. genet. Psychol.,* 1930, 37, 421-426.

NAYLOR, J. C. Parameters affecting the relative efficiency of part and whole practice methods: A review of the literature. *USN Train. Dev. Cent. tech. Rep.,* 1962, No. 950-1.

SEYMOUR, W. D. Experiments on the acquisition of industrial skills. Part 3. *Occup. Psychol.,* 1956, 30, 94-104.

Chapter 13

POST-PRACTICE CONSIDERATIONS

*Feedback and Skill Learning**

MARGARET ROBB

An individual modifies his performance according to the feedback he received from the prior performance. Feedback is information available to the learner as a result of his own activity. For all practical purposes, some form of it is available to him during and/or following the execution of a task. Additional feedback may be provided to the learner by an outsider or through modification of practice techniques. Various kinds of feedback input are analyzed and compared in effectiveness by Robb, with recommendations made for skill learning. Some theoreticians regard feedback as the central focal point in their models, as exemplified by the study of cybernetics and self-regulating operations, or servomechanisms. Perhaps after reading Robb's article, the value of feedback in developing skilled performance will become more apparent.

The importance of feedback in learning is well recognized. According to Bilodeau and Bilodeau[1] feedback is one of the strongest and most important variables controlling performance and learning. Wiener[3] and psychologists working in the human performance area have stated that feedback provides the information which makes possible the comparison between output and a reference or standard. In other words, feedback can be thought of as error information.

Feedback can be further distinguished by the arrival time of information about a performance. If, for example, a summary score is given to a subject after a defined performance has been completed, it is labeled *terminal feedback*. If the information is ongoing or is provided for moment-to-moment regulation of behavior, it is referred to as *concurrent feedback*. In some studies feedback has been defined by classifying the mode used in obtaining

* From *The Research Quarterly,* 1968, *39,* 175-184. Reprinted with permission of the author and the American Association for Health, Physical Education, and Recreation.

information. That is, sense organs which are stimulated from outside the body and provide knowledge of events happening outside the body are known as *external feedback modes*. *Internal feedback modes* refer to those receptors which register or provide information regarding the action of the body itself. Kinesthetic sense, or the more recently used term, proprioceptive sense, is one type of internal feedback.

Purpose

The major purpose of this study was to investigate the course of learning a specified arm movement pattern under conditions which varied as to the type of frequency of feedback information. A secondary purpose was to determine the subject's ability to perform the same pattern in the absence of explicit visual feedback. A movement was planned which resembled a sport movement. Many sport movements have an address or set position, some type of preparation (e.g., backswing), an acceleration or downswing, a follow through or deceleration, and a return to a starting position. The equipment allowed for a one-dimensional arm movement and the above-mentioned characteristics were incorporated into the design of the pattern. A tracking task[1] was employed to determine if information could be gained about methods of training which might enhance learning. The subjects in this study were specifically trained with some type of feedback followed by testing under conditions in which part of the feedback was absent. It was hypothesized that the different modes of feedback used during training would have significantly different effects on the performance of the subjects as demonstrated in the performance of the task without explicit visual feedback.

Method

Subjects. Forty undergraduate students, 20 men and 20 women, served as subjects. They were secured from a pool of right-handed students who had applied to the Department of Psychology, University of Michigan, to serve as paid subjects. Their ages ranged from 18 to 23 years. Males and females were randomly assigned to five different groups so that each group consisted of four men and four women.

Apparatus. The subject sat in a soundproof compartment in front of a display and a control approximately 50 cm from the oscilloscope. Therefore, 1 cm of target displacement corresponded to 1.41° of visual angle. The arm movement pattern to be learned was displayed to subjects as a target moving in the desired pattern on a 5-in. Fairchild oscilloscope. The subject grasped the handle of the control device and moved the control, which in turn moved a cursor on the display. By moving the control properly the cursor could be superimposed over the target. The subject wore Willson sound barrier earphones which allowed the experimenter to communicate with him.

The experimenter's equipment consisted of an analog computer, associated electronic components, a Veriplotter model X-Y plotter, and an 8-channel brush pen recorder.

Data Collected

Two types of data were collected. The mean error score, termed Integrated Absolute Error (IAE), was recorded for each trial. This score was calculated

[1] A pursuit tracking task was used in this study. A pursuit tracking task is one in which a subject is presented with a display containing a target and a cursor. The target is caused to move by an input signal, and the subject's task is to move the control device which in turn moves the cursor and superimposes the cursor over the target.

automatically by the analog computer and was proportional to the average difference between input and output without regard to sign accumulated during each trial. The lower the error score the more closely the output resembled the input. In order to provide some groups with another type of terminal feedback, selected trials were recorded on the X-Y plotter to give graphic knowledge of results. The X-Y plotter graphed the subject's output as the pattern was performed. After a trial was completed the input pattern was superimposed over the output pattern. These graphs were also analyzed to determine position and timing errors during training and testing.

Procedure

Five groups of eight subjects each were trained to perform the movement pattern. Each group trained under a different condition. The five conditions of training were labeled: *blanked, vision, vision-blanked, passive-active,* and *slow-standard.* The specific feedback conditions emphasized during training for each group were as follows:

Blanked. The subjects in group 1 watched the target and cursor disappear from view after 0.5 sec. During this blanked-out period, the subjects relied on cues provided by the manipulation of the control device and memory of the pattern to perform the movement. This group received two types of terminal feedback. The IAE scores were reported to each subject after each practice trial. Immediately following trials 10, 20, and 30, the subject left the booth and was shown the graphic records generated by the X-Y plotter. After viewing these records the subject returned to the booth and performed 10 more trials. By viewing the graphs the subject could see his point-for-point errors during performance of the previous trial.

During the sixth session, the criterion test for the blanked group was just another session like all their training sessions. The training condition for this group was the same condition used by all other groups of subjects as the criterion test.

Vision. Subjects in the second group watched the target, and moved the control device in an attempt to superimpose the cursor over the target, i.e., they performed a pursuit tracking task. Concurrent feedback was obtained from visual viewing of the position of the target and cursor during each trial and from internal cues through manipulation of the control stick. These subjects also received the same two forms of terminal feedback as did the subjects in the blanked group (IAE and graph readings).

Vision-Blanked. Subjects in this group were trained under a combination of the conditions specified for the subjects in groups 1 and 2 by alternating the two conditions in blocks of 10 trials. Subjects performed the first block of 10 trials, and later the third block of 10 trials, under conditions specified for the vision group. The second and fourth blocks of 10 trials were practiced under the conditions specified for the blanked group.

Passive-Active. Subjects in the fourth group combined passive participation with active performance. At the beginning of the first and third blocks of 10 trials, the subjects were instructed to remove the hand from the control device and merely watch the target traverse the screen in the desired pattern. During the second and fourth blocks of 10 trials the subjects performed a pursuit tracking task with vision. This procedure of alternating blocks of watching the target and performing the movement was carried out during each of the five practice sessions.

Slow-Standard. The condition utilized for the subjects in this group consisted of practicing the pattern under two different speeds in alternating blocks of 10 trials. During the first and third blocks of 10 trials, the subjects practiced the pattern while the target traversed the screen at a speed such that the total movement took 8.6 sec. to complete. During the second and fourth blocks the standard speed of 3.46 sec. was utilized. (All the other groups utilized the standard speed time.) Subjects in the slow-standard group were reminded at the beginning of each practice session that the criterion test to be performed after several days of practice would be at the faster of the two speeds.

The subjects in all the groups were run individually for five practice sessions. Each practice session consisted of 40 trials and lasted approximately 30 min. At the beginning of the first session, the subjects received a brief orientation to the equipment. All the subjects, except those in the group that were never to see the target on the scope (blanked group) were informed that after several days of practice they would be asked to move the control device to perform the movement pattern in the absence of visual information.

Results

The main dependent variable was integrated absolute error. It was used as a measure of each subject's improvement with practice in his ability to minimize the difference between desired input and actual output averaged over the time of a trial. It also provided the primary measure for comparing performance under different feedback conditions.

The subjects in each of five groups showed considerable learning during the five training sessions. During the training session the subjects in the vision group displayed the lowest error scores, and the subjects in the slow-standard group had the lowest error scores during the slow speed practice. None of the other methods (vision-blanked, passive-active, or blanked) resulted in error scores as low as those methods where concurrent visual feedback was always provided.

During the sixth session the criterion test was administered. A test of homogeneity of variance failed to reject the hypothesis that the variance obtained during the criterion test was from the same population. Therefore, a two-way analysis of variance of groups by blocks of 10 trials was performed to determine if the difference among the mean error scores of the five groups was significant.

The Newman-Keuls method[4] was used to test the difference between the means of the five groups. The results of this test showed that the mean error score for the subjects in the slow-standard groups during the criterion test was significantly different from the mean error scores of the other four groups. The other groups (vision, blanked, vision-blanked, and passive-active) did not differ significantly from each other.

Four graphic records from the X-Y plotter were selected for each subject per session to study the specific kinds of errors the subjects made while performing the movement pattern. The three peaks on each of the four graphic records were scored. A peak occurred whenever there was a change of direction from right to left, or left to right in the movement pattern. The method of scoring the graphs was patterned after a technique suggested by Poulton.[2]

A position error occurred when the subject moved the control device to the wrong place at the right time, i.e., the subject may have gone too far or not far enough to the right or left and hence he either overshot or undershot the desired amplitude. During the first five sessions the subjects who used some form of visual information (vision, slow-standard, and passive-active) performed the pattern better than subjects who did not have access to visual error information. During the criterion test, subjects in the slow-standard group performed more poorly with regard to the position errors. This difference was not significant. These findings suggest that the subjects in the slow-standard group, although performing at a higher error score, were able to learn the amplitude pattern about as well as subjects who trained under the other conditions.

An examination of the timing errors during the criterion test indicated that subjects in the slow-standard group had higher timing errors than the subjects in the other four groups.

A one-way analysis of variance was performed to determine if the difference in the timing errors which occurred during the performance of the criterion test was significant. A t test between means revealed that the error scores for the subjects in the slow-standard group differed significantly from the error scores of the other groups. This result indicated that the subjects in the slow-standard group were not able to learn the timing requirements of the task as well as the subjects in the other groups.

Discussion

Subjects in the vision group received the optimum amount of feedback information during training. They received both forms of concurrent feedback (visual and proprioceptive) and both forms of terminal feedback (graphic knowledge of results and IAE). During training their error scores reflected the use of this information. The blanked group received concurrent proprioceptive feedback and terminal feedback supplied by the experimenter (graphs and IAE). Their error scores were higher and more erratic than those of the vision group during training. The task appeared to be more difficult because less feedback information was received. When the vision group transferred to the blanked condition during the criterion test their error scores immediately were higher, and the effect of taking away visual error information was noticeable. However, these subjects adjusted to this condition after 10 trials, and showed a drop in error scores which was equal to that of the blanked group after 10 trials.

The subjects in the slow-standard group received the same type of feedback as did the subjects in the vision group. However, the pattern was slowed down for alternate blocks of 10 trials. Their error scores on the slow speed trials were lower than any of the other four groups during training, which indicated that during slow practice, their output was more nearly like the input pattern than any other group. If it is assumed that one must perform the exact response in order to learn the "feel" of the pattern, then these subjects certainly had more opportunity than the subjects in the other groups. When these subjects transferred to the blanked condition and feedback was reduced to only that which was available from internal cues and memory, they had significantly higher error scores than the subjects in the other groups. Although there was an improvement in error scores during the criterion test, this improvement was not great enough to affect the significant difference. Further analysis of the data revealed that these subjects had learned the amplitude pattern as well as the other subjects, but not the timing requirements.

Emphasizing concurrent visual feedback during a block of trials followed by a block of trials in which only concurrent proprioceptive feedback was available did not aid in faster or better learning of the arm movement pattern. This result was somewhat unexpected. The investigator had assumed that under this condition (vision-blanked) the subjects would have had an early opportunity for the practice of a condition equivalent to the criterion test. It was assumed that this practice would aid subjects during the criterion test. The data showed that these subjects did no better than the blanked group during training and testing. Either subjects were more confused than helped by the alternation of conditions during practice, or the early use of this type of feedback during training was not helpful for later performance.

The passive-active group received knowledge of the input pattern during the "watching" trials. If one agrees with Wiener[3] that feedback is error information, then these subjects were not actually receiving feedback during the watching trials. Instead they were receiving information as to the objective of the task, or learning the exact pattern of the input signal. Subjects during their active trials performed at a higher error rate than the vision group. These data appear to agree with Bilodeau and Bilodeau[1] that feedback is one of the more important variables for learning a task. However, when subjects in this group performed the criterion test, they were able to perform it as well as the other groups. Apparently the limited practice on the active-visual condition was sufficient to prepare these subjects to perform the criterion test.

Conclusions

Although practice was very important in learning the arm-movement pattern, the key to effective learning was practice plus feedback information. Concurrent visual feedback was the most important variable for learning the movement pattern.

One conclusion appears valid concerning both terminal and concurrent feedback. A measure of performance obtained during the continuous execution of the skill may be more valuable to the learner than a measure of terminal performance.

The use of slow practice, especially alternating slow and standard speed practice, was questioned as a method of learning a pattern in which timing is important.

The results of the criterion test showed that there was some indication that after a basic pattern was established through practice with some type of visual information, subjects were able to rely on internal cues sufficiently well enough to judge output and regulate performance.

References

1. BILODEAU, E. A., and BILODEAU, I. McD. Motor skills learning. In Paul Farnsworth (ed.) *Annual review of psychology.* Palo Alto, California: Annual Reviews Inc., 1961.
2. POULTON, E. C. On simple methods of scoring tracking error. *Psychol. bull.* 59: 320-328, 1962.
3. WIENER, N. W. *Cybernetics.* Cambridge, Massachusetts: The M.I.T. Press, 1965.
4. WINER, B. J. *Statistical principles in experimental design.* New York: McGraw-Hill, 1962.

Some Effect of Introducing and Withdrawing Knowledge of Results Early and Late in Practice*

EDWARD A. BILODEAU, INA McD. BILODEAU, AND DONALD A. SCHUMSKY

A performer must know how he is doing in order to become more proficient. When such information is witheld, improvement is impossible.

* From *The Journal of Experimental Psychology*, 1959, 58, 142-144. Reprinted with permission of the authors and the American Psychological Association.

Knowledge of results (KR) can be produced by intrinsic cues or extrinsic cues. They can occur during or following performance, and, if in the latter case, they can be immediate or delayed. Furthermore, knowledge of results can be provided through non-verbal and/or verbal routes. The magnitude of the impact of KR in learning motor skills is demonstrated in the study reported below.

An earlier study by Bilodeau and Bilodeau (1958) reported the effect of providing schedules of knowledge of results (KR) according to fixed ratio. It was shown that learning depended upon the absolute frequency of KR, but not upon the relative frequency. That is, whatever the distribution of KR, non-KR trials neither hindered nor facilitated the learning produced by KR trials. The present study also deals with the relevance of KR for learning, but here KR and non-KR trials were administered in blocks. Such blocks were introduced either early or late in practice.

Because of the results of the previous study, it was expected that performance would improve with KR and deteriorate after the withdrawal of KR. The major expectation, however, was that non-KR trials would have no effect on learning when KR was eventually introduced. Actually, the issues involved here are analogous to those of the latent learning, reward context, and the experimental design was structured accordingly. In the latter part of the experiment all Ss were tested with KR. Prior to this, one group practiced without KR, another with KR, and two others with a different number of KR trials followed by trials without KR.

A secondary purpose of the experiment was to provide observations on the rate and level of response deterioration as KR was withdrawn from Ss of diverse proficiency.

Method

Subjects and Apparatus. One hundred and sixty naive male Ss were assigned in equal number and without known bias to each of four conditions of practice on the Manual Lever apparatus. A complete description of the device was published by Bilodeau and Ferguson (1953).

The S's task was to learn to displace the lever by a certain amount. Unknown to S, a displacement of 33° of arc constituted a perfect pull of the lever. Whenever KR was given, it followed the pull by about 5 sec.; "10 units high" and "8 units low" are examples of KR. The task, then, was to learn to pull the lever by an amount which would minimize the error reported verbally by E.

A 20-lb. pull was required to move the lever. Thus, proprioceptive cues were strong as compared with a line drawing task.

Procedure. For each of four groups, 24 pulls were required. The last five pulls were always followed by KR. For Groups 0, 2, 6, and 19, the first 0, 2, 6, and 19 trials, respectively, were also with KR. The remaining trials were not.

All 24 trials were run with a 20-sec. trial cycle. A "ready" signal preceded the "pull" signal by 3 sec. The response was made within 3 to 4 sec., and KR was given 5 sec. after response completion. About 8 sec. remained until the next warning signal. The S released the lever on completion of the pull, returned his arm to his side and waited for the next ready signal.

Results

The mean absolute errors (actual response less 33°) were plotted. The curve labeled Control Comparison showed the effects of 19 successive KRs.

The Control Comparison represented the errors of three groups (2, 6, and 19) averaged whenever KR was in effect. No particular trend in the error was noted when KR is entirely absent and increasing error trends after KR is withdrawn. The increasing error trends of Groups 2 and 6 were marked, though they did not suggest an imminent regression to the level of the initial error. The performance of Group 6 certainly deteriorated no more slowly than that of Group 2 despite the fact that Group 6 had had four more KRs. Groups 2 and 6 did not appear sufficient for a firm conclusion on deterioration as a function of the number of previous KRs. A group with KR withdrawn after 20 or so trials would have been a useful addition to the experimental design.

The second analysis presented a test of the latent effect of repeated responding in the absence of KR. Here, the last five trials of Group 0 represented the *first* trials with KR, after a series of 19 trials without KR. Group 19 served as a control, since their first five KR trials provided their first experience with the apparatus. The mean squares of neither Groups nor Groups by Trials reached the .05 level of significance. Thus, introducing KR immediately or late in practice had no differential effect upon level of performance and rate of learning, i.e., there was no demonstrable latent effect.

The mean *algebraic* errors were also examined. These errors were near zero for Group 19. For the experimental groups, the errors were near zero during KR trials and markedly positive in sign in the absence of KR. Not only did Ss overshoot when KR was omitted, but they also overshot by amounts that increased steadily the longer KR had been absent.

Discussion

The results were consistent with a previous study where KR was given according to fixed ratios. There was (*a*) no improvement without KR, (*b*) progressive improvement with KR, and (*c*) deterioration of response proficiency after the withdrawal of KR. Furthermore, it was shown that an initial series of trials without KR did not serve to acquaint S with properties of the lever system that could be gainfully employed (positive transfer) with the introduction of KR after the twentieth response. However, and lamentably so, a failure to produce latent learning is not to say that latent learning cannot be produced (though we may not know how).

A few KR trials (2 or 6) introduced at the very beginning of practice were effective in producing relatively long-term response modification, though response deterioration did set in immediately upon the withdrawal of KR. The deterioration, marked in quantity and positive in sign, nonetheless remained substantially below the level of errors produced when KR was entirely absent. The positive effect of a single KR trial is probably much greater (and more lasting) than the negative effect of a non-KR trial.

Dees and Grindley (1951) and others have also observed increasing amplitude of response upon withdrawal of KR. A naive application of Hull's I_R theory (1943) to deterioration phenomena would predict *decreasing* amplitude of response, e.g., progressive undershooting would follow the build-up of I_R. Perhaps, it would be better to state that I_R interacts with or damps proprioceptive feedback. Thus, with the accumulation of I_R, responses must progressively lengthen during non-KR trials in order to produce internal feedback sufficient on Trial n to match feedback on Trial $n - 1$. The assumption here is that S is matching proprioceptive feedbacks during trials without KR. If this were done without the accumulation of I_R, a series of responses would be of uniform amplitude. With increasing I_R the amplitude of the response might well rise in compensation for a decreasing proprioceptive feedback.

Summary

This experiment deals with the late introduction and removal of knowledge of results. Its purpose was, by showing in a single experiment the effects of basic manipulations, to reassert the powerful relationships between response and the presence or absence of KR. The task was lever-displacing; the stimulus (KR) was the amount and direction of the reported error.

The experiment showed (a) no improvement without KR, (b) progressive improvement with KR, and (c) response deterioration after the withdrawal of KR. Further, an early series of trials without KR had no latent effect on the learning shown when KR was eventually introduced.

References

BILODEAU, E. A., & BILODEAU, I. McD. Variable frequency of knowledge of results and the learning of a simple skill. *J. exp. Psychol.* 1958, 55, 379-383.

BILODEAU, E. A., & FERGUSON, T. G. A device for presenting knowledge of results as a variable function of the magnitude of the response. *Amer. J. Psychol.*, 1953, 66, 483-487.

DEES, V., & GRINDLEY, G. C. The effect of knowledge of results on learning and performance; IV. The direction of the error in very simple skills. *Quart. J. exp. Psychol.*, 1951, 3, 36-42.

HULL, C. L. *Principles of behavior.* New York: Appleton-Century, 1943.

Relative Effectiveness of Teaching Beginning Tumbling With and Without an Instant Replay Videotape Recorder*

KENNETH PENMAN

IMMEDIATE feedback, in one form or another, is assumed to be either instructional, reinforcing, motivational, or all of these. It is logical to believe that an indication of the appropriateness of the performer's activity upon its completion should be of value to him. He is reinforced in the correct aspects of his behavior and can quickly begin to adjust the incorrect ones. The videotape recorder serves as an auxiliary feedback channel for the learner. It provides him with an immediate model of his performance from which he can proceed to adjust his next practice act. Unfortunately, several studies dealing with the acquisition of gross motor skills such as athletic ones support Penman's conclusion that there are no benefits observed for the videotape beyond the traditional learning situations. Some plausible explanations might lie in (a) a lack of sensitive

* Reprinted with permission of author and publisher: Penman, K. Relative effectiveness of teaching beginning tumbling with and without an instant replay videotape recorder. PERCEPTUAL AND MOTOR SKILLS, 1969, 29, 45-46.

performance tests, (b) inappropriate usage of videotape, (c) student lack of familiarity in using the operation functionally, (d) too much disparity in individual difference performance or (e) lack of sufficient practice time.

Most research on the effectiveness of instructional television indicates that students can learn at least as well, and sometimes better, from televised instruction of some sort than by conventional classroom instruction. In most of these studies, videotape recordings have simply been used as a means of having a "lesson" which can be played back to different classes.

Possibly the biggest advantage of videotape over film recordings has been overlooked. Videotape recordings can be played back immediately because no development process is necessary. The immediate playback can be performed at regular speed, slow motion, and with stop action. Thus, the videotape can be used as a means of immediate reinforcement, or feedback, in teaching. A student can view his performance immediately after he has completed the activity and can learn from his own mistakes or successes. This type of reinforcement is particularly valuable in learning motor skills.

Almost everyone has seen the instant replay used in network sports shown on television. Research, however, has been mainly limited to taped programs concerned with how to execute a particular skill, student teaching evaluation in physical education, and total programs pertaining to the value of activity to the individual. Penman[2] investigated the use of the VTR in teaching beginning trampoline and found no statistically significant difference in group mean scores for Ss using the VTR and those who did not.

To assess possible differences in performance between the experimental and control groups with practice, a posttest-only control group design was used. The reasons for this choice are two. First, it is difficult, if not impossible, to evaluate students if they have never been exposed to the specific stunts involved in beginning tumbling. Second, it is not necessary to have a pretest if randomization is assured.

Method. From large computer-assigned sections of freshman physical education ($N = 130$), groups of 25 students were selected by consulting a table of random numbers. These sub-groups were then randomly assigned as the control and experimental groups. These groups were taught in the same room, with the same instructor, and at the same hour of the day. The control group met on Monday and Wednesday, and the experimental group met on Tuesday and Thursday. *E*s developed lesson plans which utilized the videotape recorder to best advantage. Both groups were taught the same curriculum; however, the experimental group had use of the instant replay videotape recorder. The study lasted for 12 wk. or 24 instruction periods of approximately 35 min. each.

During the last class, each group was evaluated. As part of the instructional unit, the student learned combinations of stunts. The posttest required that each student make three passes on the tumbling mats executing these learned tumbling stunts. Each specified routine became more difficult. The performances were evaluated by a four-man jury composed of two gymnastics coaches and two analyses of sports performance instructors. Each judge rated each of the three routines of the students in both groups. The sum of the four judges' scores was used as the final student score. The means of the two groups were then compared.

Results. Correlations (rank difference method) between the scores given to the students by the various pairs of judges ranged between .91 and .96. The mean of the control group ($N = 25$) was 87.68 ($SD = 31.1$) and that of the experimental group ($N = 24$) 87.38 ($SD = 23.6$). The small difference obviously was not significant ($p > .05$). That the groups did not differ on the posttest may be due to the fact that the actual practice time was less for the experimental group because they spent time in front of the TV monitor. Conversely, however, the benefit of watching themselves perform apparently "made up" for the time lost in actual practice, since their performance was apparently not impaired by sitting and watching.

There were two situations where the use of the VTR seemed most valuable. These were working with the remedial students, that is, the students who were having trouble "getting" a certain skill or stunt and the appreciably "better" students. Other intangible ego-satisfying benefits were noted. These, however, could disappear after repeated exposures to seeing oneself on television.

On these findings, it appears that there is no benefit in using the instant replay videotape recorder to teach beginning tumbling skills to Washington State University freshman students. Further research should focus on the exceptional student.

References

1. PARSONS, H. L., JR. Relative effectiveness of teaching motor learning through television. Unpublished M. S. thesis, Univer. of California, 1961.
2. PENMAN, K., BARTZ, D., & DAVID, D. Relative effectiveness of teaching beginning trampoline with and without an instant replay videotape recorder. *Research Quarterly, 39,* 1060-1062, 1968.

An Evaluation of the Effects of Various Reinforcers Used as Motivation in Swimming*

BRENT S. RUSHALL AND JOHN PETTINGER

REINFORCEMENT has been well-accepted as a modifier of behavior. From Skinner's work with various organisms, reinforcement schedules are designed for most effective results. Programed learning texts, teaching machines, and other forms of instructional methodology utilize the concept of immediate reinforcement. Anything that increases the probability of a response to occur may be termed a positive reinforcer, and certainly rewards for desirable activity fall into this category. In research and practice, no trends appear with regard to the best reinforcers to use in motor learning situations. A comparison of rewards (reinforcers) is brought to our attention by Rushall and Pettinger, and their data suggest means of shaping performances to ideal outcomes.

* From *The Research Quarterly*, 1969, *40*, 540-545. Reprinted with permission of the authors and the American Association for Health, Physical Education, and Recreation.

This study aimed to assess and compare the significance and strength of some reinforcers that may be useful for administering behavior control procedures in the swimming situation. Rushall has indicated the potential use of behavior modification procedures for behavior control and personality change in swimming.[3,4] The development of adequate tests of Rushall's proposed model requires a certain amount of preliminary investigation.

> . . . the coach should determine the reinforcers and punishments which are significant to everyone and those which are individually significant. Reinforcers may be thought of as rewards. Social recognition is a very strong reinforcer for normal people. Praise, attention, recognition, extrinsic rewards (badges, buttons, candy, tokens, etc.) can be used as positive reinforcement for behavior. When an act is done well, it should be reinforced immediately (i.e., the reinforcement is contingent upon behavior). . . .[3]

Review of Literature

Few papers exist that discuss the appropriateness of behavior control methods for athletics. Apart from the two articles mentioned above, Ogilvie and Tutko[2] approach suggestions of some form of consequential and environmental control of behavior. Behavior control and modification techniques appear to be the most appropriate methods for controlling and changing social behavior.[1,5]

If an operant response is followed by a reinforcer, it is more likely to occur under similar conditions in the future. Patterns of behavior are increased, shaped, and maintained through reinforcement. Reinforcers are often difficult to isolate, but it is possible to evaluate those which are significant.

There is considerable documentation to support the use of reinforcements to develop consistent patterns of response.[1,5] . . . Candy, money, and social attention appear the most successful reinforcers.

Rushall's model for the psychological control of swimmers consists of several stages:

1. Define and list desirable and undesirable behaviors, noting their frequency of occurrence.

2. Structure the stimulus situation for teaching and controlling desirable behaviors.

3. Determine significant reinforcers and punishers.

4. Apply operant paradigms for behavior control.

5. Evaluate the effects of attempted control.

Perhaps the most crucial aspect of this model is the role of reinforcement. In this study, the use of some of the reinforcers suggested by Bijou and Baer may validate their applicability to the swimming situation.

Procedure

Three types of possible positive reinforcers and a control condition were compared to determine their significance for behavior control. The three types of reward were: coach's attention, candy, and money. The dependent variable was work volume, i.e., the number of 25-yd. laps of swimming completed by each individual in a 56-min. period.

Members of an age-group swimming club (N = 32) served as subjects. To obtain cooperation for participation, it was advertised that the special sessions for the experiment were extra activities for technique work and the development of new methods of training. Swimmers ranged in age from 9 to 15 years. Five sessions were scheduled, an orientation for the first day, and four experimental sessions.

A set of laminated fabric boards was constructed to keep the progressive lap total of the individuals in each group. The board contained the workout program, each unit of the program, the cumulative total number of laps for each unit, names, and appropriate boxes for checking the completion of each unit. The subjects checked each unit upon completing it. The first orientation session was designed to acquaint the individuals with using the boards and checking each swim unit regularly.

The experimental design used was eight independent replications of a 4×4 Latin square. The alpha level of .05 was agreed upon by the experimenters, as the severity of consequence of either Type I or Type II errors was considered approximately equal. Appropriate randomization procedures for all assignments of subjects, squares, independent variables, and times were followed.

The independent variables functioned in several different ways.

1. The control group received no predetermined social or extrinsic reinforcement for performance.

2. The coach's attention condition functioned with the coach seated at the end of the lane, next to the program board. As a swimmer finished a program unit, the coach gave encouragement and comments upon each swimmer's performance. To equate these comments between sessions, a list of appropriate comments was devised prior to the experiment. With each session, comments were drawn from the beginning of this list. No control was made as to frequency of comments, as it was decided to have this treatment as close to the normal coaching situation as possible.

3. Under the candy condition, subjects received one piece of M & M candy for each lap completed. These rewards were given at the end of the experimental session. The children were acquainted with the intended consequences of their efforts.

4. Under the money condition, subjects received one cent for each lap completed. These rewards were given at the end of each session and the children were acquainted with the intended consequences of their efforts.

In the four experimental sessions, given on every other day, the swimmers received a 10-min. talk on technique from the coach prior to swimming. At the end of this period, members of the experimental groups were assigned to group controllers. The controllers served as session directors. They read standardized instructions to all groups before the swimming commenced. The consequences for behaviors were disclosed to both the candy and money groups. Apart from this participation, controllers were not interactive with the groups.

Upon a given signal, the workout began. Each session lasted 56 min. and was halted by turning off the lights. Only laps completed were counted in the performance measures. The training program was altered in sequence at each session but remained the same in structure. Any effect of change in the program could be partialed out within the experimental design. Interaction between the groups was minimized in the experimental sessions by having the groups start at alternate ends of the pool, each swimming in one and a half lanes of pool space. Training patterns of swimming in circles were utilized to minimize interference between subjects.

Results

Duncan's Multiple Range Test was performed on the means of the treatment groups to determine significant differences. In the total experiment, seven degrees of freedom were lost because of absences. These scores were replaced with best estimates of the data for each of the individual Latin squares. The treatments revealed a significant F ratio. The candy and money groups were significantly better than the control and coach's attention groups in total distance covered by swimming.

The data were then divided into two groups. From the observations of the experimenters and from inspection of the data, it was suggested that the older participants were relatively unaffected by the reinforcement incentives. The data of 11 subjects, 13 years of age and older, were analyzed. An insignificant F for treatments was revealed.

The remaining group of individuals, 12 years and under, was analyzed. No significant treatment difference was revealed although the range of means for the four conditions was greater than 5.5 laps.

Discussion

The results revealed that the reinforcers used were discriminatory in their effect upon work volume of swimmers. The candy and money conditions were comparable in their effect. Each may be considered to be significantly stronger than the control or coach's attention conditions in producing a greater amount of distance covered. The coach's attention condition was the least effective for producing work output. The coach in giving encouragement and advice actually restricted the swimmer's work capacity for covering distance. The coach's attention group was not significantly different from the control group.

The swimming coach has for a long time assumed the role of trainer. A major portion of his interactional time in the training environment is devoted to controlling the working procedures of both individuals and groups. The possibilities for effective and optimal coaching of techniques and appropriate behaviors are reduced when the coach participates in this fashion. This is contrary to the commonly accepted belief that with the coach "driving" his swimmers in the normal way, the swimmers produce more work than they are capable of doing in a noncoaching environment. This study demonstrated that the "normal" approach to coaching inhibited the work output of swimmers.

The experimenters considered that the program boards themselves had reinforcing properties. Attempts will be made in the near future to compare these boards and the reinforcement properties of marking off accomplishments to the noboard, traditional training situation.

Candy was found to be as effective in its reinforcement value as money. Both forms of reinforcement were significantly better in producing work volume than were the other two conditions. It should be noted that these reinforcements were not contingent upon the response of swimming a program unit. Quite often in the money group, as program units were completed, swimmers verbally evaluated the distance in cents rather than laps. If one accepts that the human is able to symbolically represent potential reinforcement and consequently self-administer his own reinforcement, then these two groups could be said to have had a form of self-reinforcement contingent upon completing each program unit.

Both forms of extrinsic reinforcement produced better working performances than did nonextrinsic conditions. It is proposed that coaches set up work schedules and reinforcement situations that will produce optimal working levels in swimmers. It is possible to relieve oneself of the role of traffic director and to assume the role of coach and work more effectively. With such organization, it could be said that swimmers would work better, cover greater distance, and receive more attention on their stroking. The productivity of the training situation would then be increased.

The use of reinforcements for behavior control in this fashion may not be as simple as we have suggested. The problem of satiation with the reinforcers has not been investigated in this situation. In the laboratory, this has been overcome by changing the reinforcer irregularly but often, and by introducing varied-interval/varied-ratio schedules of reinforcement.

Clearly, two strong reinforcers have been located in the forms of money and candy. It is also considered that program boards themselves may have reinforcing qualities. These have good possibilities for use in developing more efficient behavior control in the swimming situation.

Since the children 13 years and older were not affected by the reinforcement conditions, it is probable that more subtle reinforcers existed in the situation. Although no significant difference between treatments was evidenced, the mean of the coach's attention condition was largest. This result suggests that the coaching procedures for a 13 to 15 years age group should be different from those for a younger group.

No significant F was revealed in the analysis of the 12 years and younger group data. The range of means for the treatments was 5.5 laps. Candy and money were at one extreme of this range and the control and attention conditions at the other. This range appears to have some practical significance. Young swimmers worked better when they received tangible reinforcers. The structuring of suitable contingencies would release the coach to attend to other aspects of his role without detriment to the work volume achieved by this group of swimmers. This is a suggested practical application of the results of this study.

The overall implications of this study indicate that methods of controlling work volume and training efficiency in swimmers are effective and possible when extrinsic reinforcements are received at the end of the training session. The coach can be released from his supervisory role if he wishes to establish contingencies of the nature described here. Several significant reinforcers have been found for swimmers and the possibility of establishing behavior control procedures in coaching is very real.

References

1. HONIG, WERNER K. (Ed). *Operant research: Areas of research and application.* New York: Appleton-Century-Crofts, 1966.
2. OGILVIE, BRUCE C., and TUTKO, THOMAS A. *Problem athletes and how to handle them.* London: Pelham Books, 1966.
3. RUSHALL, BRENT S. A model for the psychological control of swimmers. *Bulletin of British Swimming Coaches Association.* 20-33, July 1967.
4. ———. Personality profiles and a theory of behavior modification for swimmers. *Swimming Technique* 4:66-72, 1967.
5. ULRICH, ROGER; STACHNIK, THOMAS; and MABRY, JOHN (Eds.). *Control of human behavior.* Glenview, Illinois: Scott, Foresman and Co., 1966.

Factors in the Retention and Relearning of Perceptual-Motor Skills*

EDWIN A. FLEISHMAN AND JAMES F. PARKER, JR.

ALTHOUGH many training programs are geared for short-term results, there is a general interest in determining (a) the relative "permanence" of

* From the *Journal of Experimental Psychology*, 1962, *64*, 215-226. Reprinted with permission of the authors and the American Psychological Association.

motor skills, once learned; and (b) those factors that might influence degree of retention. Generally it has been shown that motor skills are typically retained very well compared to other kinds of learning matter. The meaningfulness of the task, few competing responses, extensive practice, and total bodily effort are theories advanced to explain the high retention of skills usually noted in the research. Fleishman and Parker's article on retention is one of the most complete in that they examine numerous variables. Retention intervals, predictive measures from the learning situation to the test of retention, and type of initial training and its effects on retention are the factors varied and controlled.

In several previous reports, Parker and Fleishman have described studies of complex tracking performance. The first of these (Parker & Fleishman, 1959, 1960) attempted to predict performance at different stages of learning a complex tracking skill. Special efforts were made to predict high levels of proficiency after extensive practice (17 sessions distributed over 6 weeks) with this task. A second study (Parker & Fleishman, 1961) made use of information about the components of tracking skill to facilitate the learning of this skill. The present study is an investigation of factors in the retention and relearning of this same skill.

Previous studies of motor skill retention (e.g., Ammons, Farr, Bloch, Neumann, Dey, Marion, & Ammons, 1958; Battig, Nagel, Voss & Brogden, 1957; Bell, 1950; Jahnke, 1958; Jones & Bilodeau, 1953; Leavitt & Schlosberg, 1944; Mengelkoch, Adams, & Gainer, 1958; Reynolds & Bilodeau, 1952) all present evidence that continuous control, perceptual-motor skills are well retained over fairly long periods of no practice. What loss occurs appears to be quickly regained. The present study is a more comprehensive study of factors in retention and relearning, using a highly complex continuous control task requiring considerable practice for initial learning.

While essentially a laboratory study, the task was designed to simulate a complex skill, i.e., that of a pilot flying a radar intercept mission. The problem of retention over extended periods without practice is especially critical here. Furthermore, where the skills are of such complexity, the problem of finding the optimum conditions for retraining becomes even more critical.

Specifically, the following questions were investigated. How well is such a skill retained without practice? What is the relation between the length of the "no practice" interval and level of retention? If there is a loss in proficiency, how much practice is required to regain proficiency? What is the relation between retention and level of proficiency after the original learning? Is the *type* of initial training related to retention? What is the relative effectiveness of a distributed vs. massed retraining schedule? Does the type of retraining schedule affect later performance as well as performance during retraining?

Method

Task. The criterion task consisted of a tracking device constructed so as to simulate roughly the display characteristics and control requirements of an air-borne radar intercept mission. The task of S was to maintain the target dot at the center of the oscillograph display, while at the same time nulling a sideslip indicator. That is, S envisioned himself to be flying the attack phase of an air-borne radar intercept mission. Thus, if the target was to the right, S made appropriate control movements to steer the craft to the right. These movements would bring him on target and the dot would return to the center of the display. All turning movements required coordinated action of stick and rudder controls.

Three identical tracking devices were constructed especially for purposes of this study. Photographs and complete schematics of all components are presented elsewhere (Parker & Fleishman, 1959). These devices and related scoring consoles allowed for the testing of from 1 to 3 Ss simultaneously under the control of a single test administrator.

The S's instrument panel contained two displays. The first consisted of a target dot presented on a cathode ray oscillograph. The target course was generated by setting the equation of a swinging pendulum into an analog computer. This produced a sine wave with a frequency of approximately 6 cycles per min. in the horizontal coordinate as the target course. The rate of decay in amplitude was approximately 5% per cycle. However, the dynamic characteristics of the overall task were such that Ss neither perceived this drop in amplitude nor the fact that the target was programed in one coordinate only. Any control imbalances resulted in dot excursions of considerably larger magnitude than those provided by target programing.

Beneath the oscillograph was an inverted 3-in., zero-center voltmeter termed a "sideslip indicator." This meter reading indicated to S a "lack of coordination" in control actions when centering the target dot. This indicator did not constitute an independent task but rather provided S with additional information related to the primary task.

In performing this task Ss used a standard aircraft control system involving a control stick and rudder pedals. These controls were coupled in a manner similar to those of an actual aircraft. Thus, application of right control stick pressure without proper amount of right rudder produced a sideslip to the left and a consequent left deflection on the sideslip indicator.

Control of the target dot in elevation was accomplished by forward and backward movements of the control stick. This was a pure second-order system resulting from the use of two cascaded integrators in the linkage between the control and display. Thus the acceleration of the target dot was directly proportional to stick displacement.

Control of the target dot in azimuth was accomplished by right and left movements of the control stick. This comprised a system involving acceleration control plus an exponential lag network. This dimension was mechanized, using three cascaded integrators with a negative feedback loop around one. The time constant of this lag network is 1 sec., i.e., it requires 1 sec. to achieve approximately two-thirds $(1-1/e)$ of the final signal resulting from a given stick displacement.

Control of the target dot in azimuth (envisioned as turning the aircraft) and centering the sideslip indicator (coordination display) were both affected by rudder pedal displacement as well as by the control stick. This rudder control of the sideslip indicator involves a simple lag network. Thus, the sideslip indicator displacement was directly proportional to rudder pedal displacement. Movement of the sideslip indicator by stick action represents a velocity control operating through two exponential lag networks.

Movement of the target dot by rudder pedal displacement approximates a pure velocity control.

Scoring. The primary score was the *integrated absolute error score*. This was recorded at the conclusion of every trial and was produced by summing algebraically the three absolute error part scores in accordance with this relationship: $T=1/2X+1/2Y+Z$, where T = integrated absolute error score, X = absolute azimuth error, Y = absolute elevation error, and Z = sideslip (lack of coordination) error.

Initial Training. The initial learning data upon which this study is based were gathered during the course of two previous studies. In each of these studies *S*s spent a total of 17 sessions, distributed over 6 weeks, mastering the tracking task, with each session consisting of 21 1-min. trials.

In the first study (Parker & Fleishman, 1959, 1960) no formal training instructions were administered. Although they were provided knowledge of results *S*s learned the tracking task "on their own" with the single exception that any questions were answered. This group of *S*s will be referred to as Group I.

In the second study (Parker & Fleishman, 1961) 60 *S*s, referred to as Group II, spent an identical period of time mastering the same tracking task. These *S*s were administered a "common sense" training program. This consisted of an initial explanation and demonstration of the tracking device. This was followed by three sessions of practice with an *E* monitoring the entire operation and assisting *S* as required. The remaining 14 sessions consisted of individual practice followed by critiques with each *S* after Sessions 7, 11, and 15. As would be expected, terminal proficiency for the group trained under this program was significantly superior to that of the group which had no formal training.

Retention Testing. Seven groups of 10 *S*s were brought back for retraining following various intervals of no practice. Intervals since training for Group II were 1, 5, 9, and 14 mo. Intervals since training for Group I were 9, 14, and 24 mo. The fact that it was possible to study the 9- and 14-mo. intervals for both groups allows a comparison of retention for the same intervals for two types of original training.

Each retention group was split into two subgroups of 5 *S*s each. One subgroup was retained during four intensive, continuous retraining sessions during the same day. The other subgroup was retrained during four sessions, each scheduled 1 day apart. The purpose of this experimental breakdown was to allow an evaluation of the relative effectiveness of these two retraining schedules where one involved massed and the other distributed practice.

One week following the final retraining session all *S*s were again tested for one additional session. The purpose of this additional testing was to allow a more adequate evaluation of the two types of retraining. This fifth retraining session was included to show whether any differences which might be found occurred only during the retraining program or whether these differences persisted in later performance. If transfer to later performance could be demonstrated, this could be attributed to differential *learning* during the course of retraining rather than to temporary performance factors (e.g., fatigue, inhibition) during the retraining.

Matching of Retention Groups. It will be recalled that the seven retention groups were drawn from two groups of original trainees. One group (Group I) had been trained without benefit of specific guidance while the other group (Group II) had been trained with supplementary instruction and guidance. Accordingly, it was found (Parker & Fleishman, 1961) that Group II was superior in terminal proficiency although the number of practice sessions was identical for each group. For the present retention study an attempt was made to match the different retention samples on the basis of final performance level during original learning. This was done separately for the three retention samples drawn from Group I and for the four retention samples drawn from Group II.

Scores (integrated error) attained by each *S* during the final session of original training were used as a basis for matching. These were converted to standard scores (stanines). An attempt was made to assign a proportionate number from each stanine level to each retention group in order to obtain a normal distribution representative of the original learning population. It soon became apparent that certain Ss needed to fulfill these requirements were not available for retesting. However, this procedure was followed as closely as possible. A preliminary analysis of variance for the first four samples tested indicated that they were not homogeneous. An adjustment was made by eliminating a few Ss whose final scores during the original training were extremely poor. This left a total of 62 Ss in the seven retention samples. Within each of the original learning groups adequate matching was achieved. Analyses of variance performed for each original training group confirmed that the retention samples could be considered comparable (Group I: $F = .22, df = 2/21$; Group II: $F = .09, df = 3/34$).

The comparability of these retention groups becomes especially apparent when one considers the range of *possible* scores from early to late learning.

Results

Magnitude of Retention. A primary concern is the extent to which the developed performance capability deteriorates through time. However, a simple comparison of an S's score following some period of no practice with his final score in initial training will not provide a complete understanding of performance loss. One must have information concerning the course of initial learning and the extensiveness of the training required to develop the skill. . . .

Compared with the original learning of this skill there is little decrement in performance, even for no practice periods of up to 24 mo. There is . . . somewhat more decrement in the 24-mo. group but recovery is rapid even during this first 21-min. retraining session.

Retention and Length of Interval. In order to obtain a more precise description of performance at the beginning of retraining, the results of the first retraining session were plotted on a trial-by-trial (minute-by-minute) basis. For Group I (no formal training) the major part of performance capability was regained during the first 2 or 3 min. of retraining. The 24-mo. group was consistently poorer during this first retraining session than the other two groups. However, even this group was improving to the level of the other groups within this first 21-min. retraining session. A much smaller loss occured for the 9- and 14-mo. intervals and this was regained in just a few minutes. Differences between these latter two groups were negligible.

Group II (formal guidance procedures) showed practically no deterioration without practice. It should be kept in mind that the maximum period without practice for this group was 14 mo. Our findings with this group are consistent with the findings for Group I in finding no differences in retention level for periods of no practice of 9 to 14 mo. The findings with Group II also indicate that the 9- and 14-mo. groups show no greater losses than do the groups with only 1 and 5 mo. of no practice. It is also shown that these groups, which exhibit essentially no forgetting, do not improve much during this first retraining session.

No performance loss as a function of longer intervals of no practice up to 14 mo. was found.

Retention and Original Learning Level. Next an examination was made of the correlation between final performance level at the conclusion of the original learning period and performance level during the first retraining session. For this, an attempt was made to obtain as stable measures of performance as possible. Thus, the *original learning* measure is based upon an average score for the last three original practice sessions, or 44 min. of performance. The *retention score* represents the entire 18 min. which were scored

13

during the first retraining session. (As in previous analyses, the first 3 min. of this session were not scored in order to avoid possible need for warm-up effects.)

The obtained correlations between final level of original learning and performance after different intervals of no practice are exceptionally high (.80 to .98), and all are statistically significant beyond the .01 level. Thus, there is virtually no change in the ordering of Ss in any group with the passage of time without practice. In order to obtain a single estimate of the relationship between retention and original learning level, all these cases were pooled together with scores of 40 other additional Ss. These last 40 Ss were those who learned initially under Group I procedures (no formal training) and who were brought back on a random basis for a single retraining session. Their retention intervals ranged from 9 to 25 mo. For this combined group ($N = 109$), having as it did a wide range of no practice intervals, the zero-order correlation between original learning level and retention score was found to be .80. A partial correlation coefficient between original learning and retention, with the effect of retention interval held constant, was .79. The loss of one point can be attributed to rounding error in the computational process.

The zero-order correlation between retention interval and retention score for this combined sample of 109 Ss was .30; when initial learning is partialed out this drops to .23. This underscores the small amount of variance in the retention score attributable to the retention interval relative to the large amount of variance in retention due to initial learning level.

An important question is whether the effect of initial learning upon retention performance is more important following short periods of no practice as opposed to longer intervals. In other words does the relation between initial learning level and retention level dissipate through time? The correlations offer no evidence in support of this. The relationship between original learning level and retention performance appears to remain relatively high and constant through periods from 1 mo. to 24 mo. of no practice.

Retention and Type of Initial Training. The no-practice intervals of 9 and 14 mo. were common to Groups I and II. The differences between the two retention performance curves at these points reflect differences in the final learning levels of these groups. As described earlier, the differences in final learning level result from two types of initial training procedures. It still remains to be shown if the type of initial training, independent of final learning level, is related to retention performance. An analysis was made to separate the contribution of these two factors.

An analysis was designed to answer the question concerning the importance of type of initial training vs. level of proficiency at the conclusion of initial training, as determiners of performance retention. It was possible to select Ss from Groups I and II who were matched in terms of retention interval (9 or 14 mo.) as well as in terminal proficiency at the conclusion of initial training. When the matching scores (terminal proficiency after initial training) and the mean scores obtained during the first retention session were compared no significant difference was found between scores ($t = .32$, $df = 9$). This indicates that the differences among our Groups I and II retention samples following periods of no practice of 9 and 14 mo. are a function of *level of proficiency* at the end of initial training rather than the *type* of initial training used in this study.

Comparison of Retraining Procedures. Each retention group was split into two subgroups of 5 Ss each. Assignment to a particular group was on the basis of stanine score at the completion of initial training. This was used as a means of making the subgroups approximately comparable in tracking ability. One group was retrained during four 21-min. sessions with 10 min. rest between sessions; the other during four 21-min. sessions scheduled 1 day apart. The two retraining procedures do not result in substantially different performances through the third retraining session, but in the fourth retraining session the distributed practice group appears decidedly superior to the massed practice group.

Apparently, there may be some critical period beyond which performance under massed practice begins to deteriorate. As a means of further evaluating this, the fourth (terminal) session scores for the two retraining procedures were compared statistically. Due to the limited number of cases in each subgroup and the consequent difficulty of matching such scores, an analysis of covariance was conducted which compared fourth session scores while removing the effect of first session scores as a source of variance. In effect, this procedure equates the subgroups statistically and increases the efficiency of the comparison procedure. The results verify the superiority of distributed practice over massed practice as a retraining procedure at the end of four retraining sessions ($F = 10.75$, $df = 1/59$, $P < .01$).

One of the assumptions underlying the use of covariance concerns the homogeneity of within-group regression effect. In this instance it was determined that the two regressions were not homogeneous. This was due to a decrease in the variability of fourth session scores of the distributed practice group as opposed to the massed practice group. To compensate for this, the distributions were transformed by means of a logarithmic transformation and the tests conducted using these scores. The results indicate that the effect of distributed practice, as opposed to massed practice, is both to improve tracking proficiency and to reduce inter-S variability.

Relative Permanence of Retraining Benefit. One week following the final retraining session all Ss were again tested for one additional session. Whereas group performances initially are approximately equal, at the conclusion of the retraining period the distributed practice group is considerably more proficient. However, 1 week later the two groups again are performing at an approximately equal level and this level is closer to that attained by the distributed practice group at the end of retraining than it is to that of the massed practice group. These differences were evaluated statistically; again, an analysis of covariance procedure was used comparing the two groups for the final session with a control on individual variation during the first retraining session. An F of .005 ($df = 1/59$) clearly indicated that during the final session there was no significant difference between the groups. It appears that the differences observed during retraining are not due to differential *learning,* but to temporary factors affecting performance. Thus the same "massed practice, postrest recovery" phenomena are found to occur in *relearning* as has been found repeatedly in studies of original motor learning (see Bilodeau & Bilodeau, 1961).

It is also interesting to note that the performance of both groups during the later session was superior to that attained at the conclusion of the initial training period. Tests were conducted to evaluate this effect. Results indicated a significant improvement for the distributed practice group ($t = 2.57$, $df = 31$, $P = .02$) and similar though not significant improvement for the massed practice group ($t = 1.56$, $df = 29$, $P = .12$). Apparently the five sessions comprising the retraining and the later test trial not only recovered the initial performance capability for these Ss, but produced additional improvement.

Predicting Retention from Ability Measures. Those Ss in Group I had been administered a battery of 44 printed and psychomotor aptitude tests in an earlier study (Parker & Fleishman, 1959, 1960). A subsequent factor analysis of the correlations among these tests identified 15 ability factors, but only 2 of these (Spatial Orientation and Multilimb Coordination) were found related to performance on the tracking task during initial learning. And these two factors, jointly, never contributed more than 25% of the variance in performance at any stage of practice with this task. Nevertheless, it was thought useful to see if measures of these factors were related to performance after periods of *no* practice.

From their loadings on the two factors (see Parker & Fleishman, 1960), the Stick and Rudder Orientation (printed) Test and the Rudder Control (apparatus) Test were chosen to represent the Spatial Orientation and Multilimb Coordination factors, respectively. Correlations between these tests and performance during the first retention session were computed based on an N of 69 (the Group I Ss plus the 40 Ss brought back for a single session of retention testing). These zero-order correlations with retention performance were .21 for the Spatial test and .18 for the Coordination test; these coefficients are significant at the .10 but not the .05 level of confidence. To hold the effects of initial learning level and retention interval constant, second-order partial correlations were computed. With these factors partialed out the Spatial test correlated .21 and the Multilimb Coordination test correlated .20 with performance in the retention session. Again these coefficients are significant only at the .10 level, not at the .05 level, for second-order partials.

Thus, for this particular skill, a negligible to insignificant portion of retention performance is attributable to Ss' abilities as measured prior to initial learning. This is true when retention is defined in terms of performance after no practice, as well as when this performance is residualized with respect to initial learning level and retention interval.

Performance on this task during early stages of *initial* learning was shown to be uncorrelated with performance during late stages of initial learning (e.g., as late as Trial 8 the correlation with Trial 50 was only .13); however, practice sessions late in original learning correlated .70 with each other (Parker & Fleishman, 1960). The communality of the final initial learning trial attributable to independently measured ability factors was only .24. Taken together, these findings suggested that proficiency at the end of training was mainly a function of specific habits and skills acquired during the 6 wk. of practice with the task and only to a small extent a function of Ss' abilities prior to his experience with this task.

The present findings indicate this is also true of *retention* performance after prolonged periods of no practice. This is especially apparent when we recall the high correlations (in the .80s and .90s) between proficiency at the conclusion of training and retention performance, relative to the negligible correlations of retention with the independent ability measures.

Summary

Two groups of Ss were given extended training on a highly complex tracking task. Practice extended over 17 sessions distributed over 6 weeks. The two groups differed only in the amount of verbal guidance provided in initial training. Within each group, subgroups of Ss matched for final proficiency were retested following various no-practice intervals of up to 24 mo. These retention samples were further divided into two subgroups, each of which were given four additional retraining sessions; in one group this relearning practice was massed in 1 day and for the other group it was distributed over 4 days. One week following the retraining all Ss were retested as a means of evaluating the persistence of the effects of these two relearning schedules.

1. The retention of proficiency in a complex, continuous control, perceptual-

motor skill is extremely high, even for no-practice intervals up to 24 mo. For *S*s trained initially to high levels of proficiency (Group II), virtually no loss was observed for periods up to 14 mo. What small losses did occur were recovered in the first few minutes of relearning. With 24 mo. of no practice, rapid recovery still occurred during the first 20 min. of relearning.

2. Variations in retention interval from 1 to 14 mo. are shown to be unrelated to retention performance, even during the first 1 min. of relearning. The function has zero slope until the loss in performance shown by the 24-mo. retention group.

3. The most important factor in retention is the *level* of proficiency achieved by the *S*s during initial learning. This effect is shown to be just as important following long and short periods of no practice.

4. The *type* of initial training (amount of verbal guidance) is unrelated to retention performance when proficiency level after original learning is held constant.

5. Retraining administered under conditions of distributed practice proved to be superior to that administered under mass practice based upon a measure of performance during the final retraining session. However, on retesting 1 week later no difference was noted between the two retraining procedures. Thus, in terms of *transfer* to later performance there was no "permanent" disadvantage in massed retraining. Furthermore, both groups had improved beyond their original learning levels.

6. Predictions of individual differences in retention from independent ability measures were negligible. Retention appears more a function of specific task habits acquired than of *S*s' ability traits developed prior to training.

References

AMMONS, R. B., FARR, R. G., BLOCH, E., NEUMANN, E., DEY, M., MARION, R., & AMMONS, C. H. Long-term retention of perceptual-motor skills. *J. exp. Psychol.,* 1958, 55, 318-328.

BATTIG, W. F., NAGEL, E. H., VOSS, J. F., & BROGDEN, W. J. Transfer and retention of bidimensional compensatory tracking after extended practice. *Amer. J. Psychol.,* 1957, 70, 75-80.

BELL, H. M. Retention of pursuit rotor skill after one year. *J. exp. Psychol.,* 1950, 40, 648-649.

BILODEAU, E. A., & BILODEAU, I. McD. Motor skill learning. *Annu. Rev. Psychol.,* 1961, 12, 243-280.

FLEISHMAN, E. A. Abilities and the learning of psychomotor skills. In P. H. Dubois, W. H. Manning, and C. J. Spies (Eds.), *Factor analysis and related techniques in the study of learning.* St. Louis: Washington University, 1959.

FLEISHMAN, E. A. The description and prediction of perceptual-motor skill learning. In R. Glaser (Ed.), *Training research and education.* Pittsburgh: Univer. Pittsburgh Press, 1962.

GAGNÉ, R. M., & FLEISHMAN, E. A. *Psychology and human performance.* New York: Holt, 1959.

JAHNKE, J. C. Retention in motor learning as a function of amount of practice and rest. *J. exp. Psychol.,* 1958, 55, 270-273.

JONES, E. I., & BILODEAU, E. A. Retention and relearning of a complex perceptual-motor skill after ten months of no practice. *HumRRO res. Bull.,* 1953, No. 53-15.

LEAVITT, H. J., & SCHLOSBERG, H. The retention of verbal and of motor skills. *J. exp. Psychol.,* 1944, 34, 404-417.

MENGELKOCH, R. F., ADAMS, J. A. & GAINER, C. A. The forgetting of instrument flying skills as a function of the level of initial proficiency. *USN Train. Dev. Cent. tech. Rep.,* 1958, No. 71-16-18.

PARKER, J. F., & FLEISHMAN, E. A. Prediction of advanced levels of proficiency in a complex tracking task. *USAF WADC tech. Rep.,* 1959, No. 59-255.

PARKER, J. F., & FLEISHMAN, E. A. Ability factors and component performance measures as predictors of complex tracking behavior. *Psychol. Monogr.*, 1960, 74(16, Whole No. 503).

PARKER, J. F., & FLEISHMAN, E. A. Use of analytical information concerning task requirements to increase the effectiveness of skill training. *J. appl. Psychol.*, 1961, 45, 295-302.

REYNOLDS, B., & BILODEAU, I. McD. Acquisition and retention of three psychomotor tests as a function of distribution of practice during acquisition. *J. exp. Psychol.*, 1952, 44, 19-26.

PART 9

SOCIAL INFLUENCE

*Passive and Active Interactions of Others
with the Performer*

Broadly interpreted, social factors permeate most if not all of learning. We learn how to compete against and cooperate with others, and these are often not exclusive features in any given situation. We experience performing skills in front of a group. From an experimental point of view, though, relatively pure or non-confounded data from social situations have posed a hardship to collect. Thus, common sense and personal experience constitute a good portion of our knowledge of the social influence on human performance.

With advances in research techniques and theory, a greater interest is being shown in designing experiments in this area. Research findings comparing individual with small group performance (dyads, triads, or quads) in cooperative ventures usually indicate the value of social situations that increase motivation and encourage information sharing. Competitive conditions usually lead to better performance outcomes than non-competitive conditions. The prediction of team performance from individual proficiency can be relatively poor under some conditions and reasonably high under others. Performance in front of a passive or an active audience can be positively or negatively affected. Two extremely important variables that must be considered in this case are the skill level of the learner (stage of practice) and task complexity (possible number of competing responses). Social facilitation theory, explained briefly in Martens' article, describes performance probabilities under stress.

In most of the experimentation in motor learning the subject is removed from reality; that is, the setting and the task are usually contrived and artificial. This procedure is followed to isolate variables of concern and to eliminate possible confounding variables. Since activity pursuits and proficiency attained in real-life tasks are to some degree dependent upon peer and culture influence, cooperative and competitive ventures, and social interactions, the conclusions reached in many laboratory studies have limited appeal. Valid behavioral information appears when consistency in observations occurs not only in isolated circumstances but in social settings as well.

Interestingly enough, even the unintentional influence of the experimenter on the subject in traditional laboratory studies can be quite dramatic. Social scientists indicate that even under the most controlled conditions, experimenter bias, attitudes, sex, color, anxiety, and the like will conceivably affect the performance of the subject. Therefore, social interactions may be present when they are not supposed to be. The readings that follow reflect some deliberately developed social situations and shed light on performance expectations.

Chapter 14

SOCIAL FACILITATION AND TEAM
AND INDIVIDUAL PERFORMANCES

Individual vs. Social Performance on Two Perceptual-Motor Tasks*

CLYDE E. NOBLE, JAMES E. FUCHS,
DONALD P. ROBEL, AND RIDGELY W. CHAMBERS

INSTRUCTIONAL situations can be manifested by learners (a) practicing alone or (b) practicing within small subgroups. Proponents of either technique may be found. In the reading that follows, this problem is investigated, along with possible differential effects on dissimilar tasks, and sex distinctions in performance. In industry and education the desirability of forming small working groups to foster motivation, reinforcement, and reciprocal information-sharing is being researched. Perhaps the performer's personality is yet another variable that might influence better output alone or in a group context.

In research on human skill acquisition it is sometimes noted[6] (pp.25–30), [7] (pp.476–487) that Ss working alone perform differently from Ss working in a group of two or more. Other studies, e.g.,[2,6] have reported no differences. Aside from the methodological value of determining for a given apparatus whether size of the group affects proficiency, there are two contradictory hypotheses which might be applied to such situations.

The first, which may be called the hypothesis of social competition, states that a Social (non-partitioned) group will perform at a higher level of skill than an Individual (partitioned) group. Presumably, facilitation would be due to increased motivation arising from S's observation of and effort to surpass his neighbors. This prediction is consistent with experiments on interpersonal rivalry.[5,7]

* Reprinted with permission of author and publisher: Noble, C. E., Fuchs, J. E., Robel, D. P. and Chambers, R. W. Individual vs. social performance on two perceptual-motor tasks. PERCEPTUAL AND MOTOR SKILLS, 1958, 8, 131-134.

The second, an hypothesis of differential stimulus variability, implies exactly the opposite result; namely, that the Individual group will be more proficient and less variable than the Social group. This expectation follows from the fact that S's visual field is more constant when alone or isolated, whereas in a group his tendency to watch the behavior of his competitors should produce more variable stimulation from trial to trial. Theories as diverse as those of Guthrie[3] and Hull[4] would favor this hypothesis.

An important qualification is that the nature of the learning task may influence the amount and direction of performance differences. The behavioral requirements of intermittent selective responding vs. those of continuous eye-hand coordination suggest distinctive combinations of variables. Proficiency on a discriminative speed task, for instance, might be more sensitive to motivational factors than to stimulus changes. But environmental distractions should have a greater decremental effect on pursuit skills, as reported in a prior study.[8] (p.66) Since little knowledge exists of how task factors interact with experimental variables in this area, it was thought desirable to investigate two representative kinds of perceptual-motor apparatus using the same Ss and similar partitioning operations.

Method

Apparatus. The *discrimination* task (DR) consisted of 4 units of the Discrimination Reaction Time Test, Model D2, described elsewhere.[6] The DR units were arranged in the 4-square pattern illustrated by Melton.[6] (p.28) S's task was to snap 1 of 4 toggle switches in response to the simultaneous lighting of a red and a green signal lamp. The position of the red lamp with respect to the green determined which of the 4 switches was correct. Reinforcement was provided by the offset of a white lamp, and S's reaction time was cumulated on a .001-min. clock. A trial was a single 3-sec. presentation, with a 1-sec. average rest between stimulus patterns. Scores were recorded in blocks of 20 trials. The inter-block interval was 40 sec. except between Blocks 4 and 5 when it was increased to 100 sec. in order for E to reset the stepping switch to the first pattern.

The *pursuit* task (RP) consisted of 4 units of the Rotary Pursuit Test, Model B2, also arranged as above.[6] (p.27) S's task was to keep a hinged stylus in contact with a metal target disc having a diameter of .75 in. as it moved horizontally through a circular clockwise path at 60 rpm. Time on target was cumulated on a .01-sec. clock. A trial was 20 sec. work and 10 sec. rest, although actual trial duration measured 20.05 sec. Scores were recorded in blocks of 5 trials. The inter-block interval was 60 sec.

Subjects. Ss were 116 M.S.U. undergraduate psychology students, naive to both tasks, including 69 men and 47 women whose ages ranged from 18 to 37 ($M = 20.9$ yr.). Ss were divided into 2 experimental groups (Individual and Social) of 58 each, and a given S practiced under the same conditions on both tasks.

Procedure. All Ss received 8 blocks of practice on the two apparatus: 160 3-sec. trials on DR followed by 40 20-sec. trials on RP. Instructions were appropriately modified from Melton.[6] DR practice was preceded by 10 demonstration trials, RP practice by none. Ss took the same relative spatial positions in moving from DR to RP.

The first block of trials on either task conformed to the standard (Social) procedure.[6] Performance on Block 1 thus served as a basis for matching the groups for initial ability. Rectangular masonite screens, placed between the members of each subgroup of Individual Ss during the rest interval preceding Block 2, isolated S visually from his partners. Individual Ss were tested in subgroups of 2 to 4 at a time, but the Social subgroups always contained 4 Ss since the maximum amount of personal interaction was desired.

Two Es were trained to treat both groups exactly alike except for the experimental factor, and Ss were assigned by subgroups to the two conditions on each apparatus in a counterbalanced order.

Results and Discussion

Discrimination Reaction. The two groups were well matched for means and variance on Block 1. A t-test of the mean difference gave a ratio of .08, which for 114 df is not significant. With the introduction of the opaque screens, however, the Individual group was slower by a fairly constant amount during Blocks 2 to 8.

A 7×2 analysis of variance was performed on the speed scores. The main effects of the number of practice blocks (N) were significant $(F = 164.28; df = 6/684; p < .001)$, and the conditions of practice (C) were significant $(F = 5.98; df = 1/114; p < .025)$, but the $N \times C$ interaction was not $(F = 1.05; df = 6/684; p > .20)$. Support is thus found for the hypothesis of social-competition but not for the stimulus variability hypothesis, at least as far as DR is concerned. Facilitation is apparently a non-multiplicative effect for there is no evidence of differential trends.

As sex differences in perceptual-motor learning are often observed,[5] a comparison of male and female proficiency on Block 1 is in order. The mean speed score for men was 2.73; that for women 2.48. With 114 df, the t of 2.33 is significant at the 2% level. Inspection of graphs for these Ss indicated that the margin of superiority of the male Ss did not diminish with practice in either the Individual or the Social group.

To find out whether social competition interacts with individual differences in ability, two further analyses were made. The highest and lowest scoring 20 Ss in each experimental group during Blocks 2 to 8 were selected so that Ss were also matched on Block 1. Tests of the mean difference in initial speed between Individual and Social Ss within the High and Low ability groups gave t-ratios of .21 and .00, which are not significant $(df = 18; p > .20)$. Subsequent 7×2 analyses of variance revealed parallel trends over Blocks 2 to 8. For the High ability group, the N effect is significant $(F = 38.17; df = 6/108; p < .001)$, and also the C effect $(F = 4.77; df = 1/18; p < .05)$, but there is no significant interaction $(F = .53; df = 6/108)$. Likewise, for the Low ability group the N effect is significant $(F = 26.46; df = 6/108; p < .001)$, and also the C effect $(F = 10.00; df = 1/18; p < .01)$, but again there is no significant interaction $(F = 1.62; df = 6/108)$. The significant facilitation of DR proficiency under social competition, therefore, is independent of ability level.

Rotary Pursuit. The acquisition curves, expressed as the mean per-cent-time-on-target for each block $(R\%)$, revealed little difference attributable to the independent variable, C. The two groups were comparable on Block 1 $(t = .07; df = 114)$ and remained about the same until Block 8. Mean scores began at 18% and rose to 64% after 800 sec. of distributed practice.

A 7×2 analysis of variance showed a significant N effect $(F = 518.89; df = 6/684; p < .001)$, but no significant C effect $(F = .13; df = 1/114)$ or $N \times C$ interaction $(F = .54; df = 6/684)$. There is no support for either hypothesis in the RP data, suggesting that pursuit skill is unaffected by the number of Ss in a group.

An ability analysis of RP was considered unnecessary,[8] (pp.66-67) but the sex differences reported by others[1,5] (p.555) were confirmed. The mean time on target during Block 1 for men was 21.77 sec.; that for women 13.88 sec.

($t = 3.91$; $df = 114$; $p < .01$). As in the case of DR, the greater proficiency of male Ss on RP continued with practice. Finally, it may be noted that the product-moment correlation between scores on the two tasks for Block 1 was only .13, which is not significantly greater than zero.

Summary

This experiment employed two representative perceptual-motor tasks to determine the influence of individual versus social conditions of practice upon the acquisition of skill. One hundred and sixteen Ss received extended training first on the Discrimination Reaction Time Test, then on the Rotary Pursuit Test. Following an initial period of practice under standard (Social) conditions, half the Ss were visually isolated from each other for the remaining trials. This (Individual) group suffered a significant and uniform decrement in performance on the discrimination task, but showed no relative change in behavior on the pursuit task. The facilitation in discriminative speed appeared to be an additive effect due to social competition, and it was independent of initial level of ability. Men performed better than women on both tasks, but the difference was unaffected by amount of training. Since the same Ss practiced on the two apparatus under analogous conditions, it is suggested that the motivational role of social competition in perceptual-motor learning is contingent upon as yet unanalyzed task factors.

References

1. AMMONS, R. B., ALPRIN, S. I., & AMMONS, C. H. Rotary pursuit performance as related to sex and age of pre-adult subjects. *J. exp. Psychol.*, 1955, 49, 127-133.
2. BILODEAU, E. A. Acquisition of skill on the Rudder Control Test with various forms of social competition. *USAF, Hum. Resour. Res. Cent. Res. Note, P&MS*, 1951, No. 51-6.
3. GUTHRIE, E. R. *The psychology of learning.* (Rev. ed.) New York: Harper, 1952.
4. HULL, C. L. *Principles of behavior.* New York: Appleton-Century-Crofts, 1943.
5. McGEOCH, J. A., & IRION, A. L. *The psychology of human learning.* (2nd ed.) New York: Longmans, Green, 1952.
6. MELTON, A. W. (Ed.) *Apparatus tests.* AAF Aviation Psychology Program Research Report No. 4. Washington, D. C.: U. S. Gov't Printing Office, 1947.
7. MURPHY, G., MURPHY, L. B., & NEWCOMB, T. M. *Experimental social psychology.* (Rev. ed.) New York: Harper, 1937.
8. NOBLE, C. E. An attempt to manipulate incentive-motivation in a continuous tracking task. *Percept. Mot. Skills*, 1955, 5, 65-69.

Effect of An Audience on Learning and Performance of a Complex Motor Skill*

RAINER MARTENS

SOCIAL situations are varied. In this article by Martens, the subjects are required to learn and perform a motor task in front of a passive audience. There is no deliberate interaction between people, for Martens is inter-

* From the *Journal of Personality and Social Psychology*, 1969, *12*, 252-260. Reprinted with permission of the author and the American Psychological Association.

ested in discovering the effects the mere presence of others will have on the learner. Do learners become more motivated in the presence of others, and if so, are the effects manifested throughout the practice trials? Or, are differences between early and late practice observable? Furthermore, the resting anxiety level of the subject is investigated as it interacts with audience effects. Martens bridges theories and research nicely, and presents an ample discussion of his findings in the context of related published literature.

Renewed interest in social facilitation research has been stimulated by Zajonc's (1965) explanation of previously conflicting findings. Social facilitation research examines the consequences upon individual behavior arising from the presence of passive spectators or from coactors. Early findings revealed that simple motor responses are particularly susceptible to social facilitation effects. Triplett (1897) noted increased performance when subjects wound a fishing reel or rode a bicycle in the presence of passive spectators. Later research supported Triplett's observation (Allport, 1920; Dashiell, 1930; Gates, 1924; Travis, 1925) while other investigations have found negative audience effects (Ekdahl, 1929; Pessin, 1933; Pessin & Husband, 1933; Wapner & Alper, 1952).

Zajonc (1965), noting the ambiguities in social facilitation research, attempted to explain these contradictions by distinguishing between learning and performance. He proposed that the emission of well-learned responses is facilitated by the presence of passive spectators, while the acquisition of new responses is impaired. Furthermore, using drive theory concepts, Zajonc suggested that the presence of others increases the arousal level of individuals[1] which increases the individual's generalized drive state, resulting in the emission of dominant responses. Therefore, according to drive theory, during the early stages of learning a complex task the wrong responses are dominant and strong; that is, they have the greatest probability of occurrence. But after the individual has mastered the task, correct responses are more likely to be dominant.

Recent investigations of audience effects using verbal tasks have found evidence consistent with the proposition that an audience enhances the emission of dominant responses (Cottrell, Rittle, & Wack, 1967; Zajonc & Sales, 1966). Cottrell and his co-workers (1967) tested the hypothesis that the presence of an audience affects the quality of individual learning by increasing generalized drive level. The hypothesis was confirmed when using a competitional and noncompetitional paired-associates list. Additional evidence in support of Zajonc's theory has been reported by Ganzer (1968), who found that subjects learning a verbal task in the presence of an audience did less well than subjects who learned alone. Cottrell, Wack, Sekerak, and Rittle (1968) also found that the presence of an audience with audience status enhanced the emission of dominant responses, but the mere presence of other individuals without audience status did not.

Recently Ganzer (1968) related the personality construct of anxiety to social facilitation research. Zajonc's theory of social facilitation does not consider the individual differences in personality when learning and performing before an audience. Ganzer, using the Test Anxiety scale, reported that the presence of an audience was detrimental to high anxiety (HA) and

---

[1] Zajonc (1965) cites the research of Mason and Brady (1964) and Thiessen (1964) as suggestive evidence that the presence of others is a source of arousal.

medium anxiety (MA) women, but not to low anxiety (LA) women when learning a list of nonsense syllables. Cox (1966, 1968), in a series of six experiments, consistently demonstrated a significant interaction between observer presence and test anxiety on a marble-dropping task. The presence of passive observers increased response rate in LA boys and decreased response rate in HA boys.

Previous social facilitation research has examined the effect of an audience on verbal learning tasks and simple motor tasks, but has not investigated the effect of an audience on learning and performance of a complex motor task. The purpose of the present study, therefore, was to investigate the following questions when learning and performing a complex motor task: (*a*) Does an audience affect individual behavior in a manner consistent with social facilitation theory? (*b*) What is the relationship between a general measure of anxiety such as the Taylor (1953) Manifest Anxiety (*MA*) scale and the presence of an audience? (*c*) Is the relationship between the *MA* scale and performance consistent with drive theory predictions?

In addition, the present study determined if groups differed in palmar sweating in the presence of an audience when compared to groups performing alone. Predictions formulated from social facilitation theory and drive theory assume that an audience increases the arousal level of individuals. The possibility of negative results made it highly desirable to measure this intervening variable. When the hypotheses have not been confirmed by the data, assurance is needed that the conditions necessary for testing the hypotheses were in fact created.

Since any psychological event must have a neurological correlate, it seems natural to attempt to measure physiological responses which may be among the concomitants, for example, autonomic arousal. Presumably an intervening process of tension buildup should be accompanied by some autonomic discharge. If it can be demonstrated that the end effects predicted by the theory were preceded by differential states of arousal due to the presence or absence of an audience, a more convincing case for the hypotheses can be established.

A popular area of arousal research has been the palmar sweating phenomenon which has usually been measured indirectly by the galvanic skin response (GSR). Recently Johnson and Dabbs (1967) have outlined a more simple and direct measure of sweating in the palmar region. This method involves counting the number of palmar sweat glands active in a fingertip. Because of its unobtrusiveness, the palmar sweat print method seemed especially suitable for indicating arousal resulting from the presence of others.

Method

Subjects. The MA scale was administered to 519 male undergraduate students ranging in age from 18 to 24. All left-handed subjects were eliminated from the sample due to the task requirements. Selected for participation in the study were 48 students scoring in the top 11% and 48 students scoring in the bottom 11% of the distribution.

Apparatus. The coincident timer, which requires finishing a response simultaneously with an external transient event, was designed and constructed by Schmidt (1967) and Hubbard. This complex task requires a preliminary motion to accelerate a cursor in such a way that the cursor arrives simultaneously at the point where the object is to be struck (coincident point). A target moved on a belt toward the subject at 4.25 feet per second. With his right hand the subject moved the cursor that slid on a trackway perpendicular to the target movement so that the pointer "hit" the moving target.

Several modifications were made to the coincident timer to facilitate its use in the present experiment. A 4.5-inch-long rubber cam was fastened to the underside of the belt and a microswitch was located so the leading edge of the cam closed the switch when the target reached a point precisely 51 inches from the coincident point. This microswitch, when closed, started the milli-second timer. Another microswitch was located adjacent to the track so that the cursor triggered the microswitch and stopped the timer when the pointer passed through the center of the belt. The interval from where the cam started the timer to the coincident point was precisely 1 second. The subject's error was scored in milliseconds deviation from a direct hit.

Palmar Sweat Prints. The palmar sweat print technique, developed by Sutarman and Thomson (1952) and recently described by Johnson and Dabbs (1967), was used to detect changes in autonomic arousal due to the presence of an audience. The method involves counting the number of palmar sweat glands active in a fingertip. Harrison and MacKinnon (1966) have derived a Palmar Sweat Index (PSI) from Sutarman and Thomson's method. The PSI is defined as the number of glands secreting sweat in a 3-millimeter-square area around the central whorl of a fingertip. The solution which forms a plastic mold was applied to the third finger, left hand.

Procedure. As subjects arrived at the laboratory, they were isolated and two sweat prints were taken. When the subject entered the laboratory the task was explained and demonstrated. Subjects learning the task in the alone condi-tion (only the experimenter present) began the experiment immediately. The subject was given knowledge of results after each trial in milliseconds. The subject initially received 15 trials or enough to attain the learning criterion, whichever came later. The criterion was a total score for three consecutive trials of 90 milliseconds or less.

After instructions, individuals learning in the audience treatments were confronted with 10 undergraduate males who were unknown to them. The audience members had been carefully briefed as to their role as passive spectators. Observers were seated in a semicircle around the apparatus in clear view of the subject. Once the audience was seated the experimental procedure was identical to that followed for subjects in the alone condition.

When the learning criterion had been attained the subject proceeded to the performance phase receiving 10 trials. Subjects in the learn-alone-perform-alone treatment and in the learn-audience-perform-audience treatment continued the experiment without change. Subjects in the learn-alone-perform-audience treat-ment were introduced to the audience by the procedure described for the learning phase. Subjects in the learn-audience-perform-alone treatment per-formed the 10 trials in absence of any spectators.

Sweat prints were taken for only one-half of the subjects in each cell because of the increased time required for taking the prints. Basal sweat prints were taken 5 and 12 minutes after arrival at the laboratory, while the remainder of the prints were taken after every fifth trial of the experiment.

Design. The present study was divided into a learning phase and a per-formance phase. A 2 × 2 × 3 factorial design with repeated measures on the last factor was used for the learning phase. The levels for each factor of the learning phase were HA and LA subjects, learning the task alone and in the presence of an audience, and three blocks of five trials. For the perfor-mance phase a 2 × 2 × 2 × 2 factorial design with repeated measures on the last factor was used. The first two factors were the same as those in the learning phase (anxiety and conditions of learning). The two levels of the third factor were the performance of the subjects alone and in the presence of an audience. The repeated-measures factor consisted of two blocks of five trials each.

The subjects were assigned randomly to the treatment factor (conditions of learning) and assigned to the organismic factor (anxiety) on the basis of their *MA* scale score. Twenty-four subjects in each cell of the learning phase received a minimum of 15 trials or until the learning criterion was attained, whichever came later. In the performance phase, 12 subjects in each treatment of the learning phase performed alone, while 12 subjects performed in the presence of an audience.

Measurement. Learning and performance scores were placed into successive blocks of five trials. Arithmetic error was analyzed—the interval between the arrival of the target and the movement at the coincident point with positive error late and negative error early. Intravariance, which indicates within-subject consistency, was computed as the variance of each subject's scores about the subject's mean score for blocks of five trials. Rapidity with which the task was learned was determined by the number of trials required to attain the learning criterion. The effect of treatments on palmar sweating was determined by calculating the difference between the mean of the two basal prints from each successive print.

Results

Learning Phase. The Anxiety × Conditions of Learning × Blocks (2 × 2 × 3) analysis of variance was computed for arithmetic error and arithmetic error intravariance. Mean responses for Blocks 1–3 for all treatments were early and error was reduced considerably after Block 1. The anxiety main effect was nonsignificant for arithmetic error, but a significant Anxiety × Blocks interaction was obtained. HA subjects responded with slightly greater error than LA subjects for Block 1. By Block 3, however, HA subjects committed significantly ($F = 3.67$, $df = 2/184$, $p < .05$) less error (-57 milliseconds) than LA subjects (-71 milliseconds). The analysis of intravariance variance for arithmetic error revealed no significant differences for the anxiety factor.

The significant conditions of learning factor indicated that subjects in the presence of an audience made significantly greater error (-103 milliseconds) than subjects in the alone treatment (-69 milliseconds) when averaged over the anxiety and blocks factors. A significant Conditions of Learning × Blocks interaction was also found. The F test on the simple main effects found a significant increase in error by subjects learning in the presence of an audience for Block 1 ($F = 41.41$, $df = 2/184$, $p < .01$), Block 2 ($F = 21.67$, $df = 2/184$, $p < .01$), and Block 3 ($F = 10.80$, $df = 2/184$, $p < .01$). The effect of an audience was greatest during the initial learning trials, with a significant, but decreasing, difference with continued practice.

The analysis of intravariance variance found the conditions of learning factor and the Conditions of Learning × Blocks interaction to be significant. Further analysis of the interaction indicated that the pattern of consistency of the responses in the two learning conditions also depended upon the amount of practice. The subjects learning alone were significantly ($F = 19.99$, $df = 2/184$, $p < .01$) more consistent (55 milliseconds) than the subjects learning in the presence of an audience (87 milliseconds) for Block 1. No significant difference, however, was found for Block 2 or 3.

The Anxiety × Conditions of Learning (2 × 2) analysis of variance was computed using the total number of trials to criterion as the score. Both the anxiety and conditions of learning factors were significant, but not independent of each other, as the Anxiety × Conditions of Learning interaction was also significant. Post hoc analysis (Winer, 1962, p. 238) indicated no significant difference between HA and LA subjects when learning alone ($F = .03$, $df = 1/92$, ns). When learning in the presence of an audience, however, LA subjects required significantly ($F = 8.75$, $df = 1/92$, $p < .01$) more trials (19.6) than HA subjects (14.0).

   Performance Phase. Significant effects of treatments were determined by an Anxiety × Conditions of Learning × Conditions of Performance × Blocks (2 × 2 × 2 × 2) analysis of variance for arithmetic error and arithmetic error intravariance. The significant anxiety factor indicated that HA subjects performed significantly better (−42 milliseconds) than LA subjects (−52 milliseconds) when averaged over the conditions of learning and conditions of performance factors. Furthermore, HA subjects had a significantly lower (35 milliseconds) mean intravariance than LA subjects (44 milliseconds).

   The analysis of arithmetic error variance revealed that the conditions of performance factor was also significant. When averaged over the anxiety and conditions of learning factor, subjects performing in the presence of passive spectators did significantly better (−36 milliseconds) than subjects who performed alone (−59 milliseconds). The conditions of performance factor and the Conditions of Performance × Blocks interaction was significant for the analysis of intravariance variance for arithmetic error. Further analysis revealed no significant difference between subjects performing alone or in the presence of an audience for Block 1, but for Block 2 a significant difference ($F = 15.36$, $df = 1/88$, $p < .01$) was obtained. Subjects in the alone treatment displayed greater inconsistency than subjects performing before an audience for the second block of five trials.

   The conditions of learning factor was not significant, indicating that the mode of learning had no effect on the subjects' subsequent performance of the task. The blocks factor was not significant, nor were any of the interactions for the analysis of arithmetic error variance.

   Palmar Sweat Index (PSI). The analysis of variance for the learning phase revealed that subjects learning the task in the presence of an audience had a significantly ($F = 136.68$, $df = 1/132$, $p < .01$) greater PSI increase than subjects learning alone when averaged over the anxiety and prints factors. The PSI increase for subjects learning in the presence of an audience was 6.6, whereas those learning alone had a PSI increase of 7.4 active sweat glands. The anxiety factor was nonsignificant ($F = .40$ $df = 1/132$, ns), indicating little difference between LA and HA subjects in PSI increase.

   The analysis of sweat print variance for the performance phase also showed no significant difference ($F = .79$, $df = 1/40$, ns) between HA and LA subjects. The significant conditions of learning factor ($F = 13.15$, $df = 1/40$, $p < .01$), and the Conditions of Learning × Prints interaction ($F = 11.21$, $df = 1/40$, $p < .01$), indicated that the increased PSI in the performance phase depended upon the mode of learning the task. The significant conditions of performance factor ($F = 5.57$, $df = 1/40$, $p < .05$) and the Conditions of Performance × Prints interaction ($F = 4.19$, $df = 1/40$, $p < .05$) indicated that subjects performing in the presence of an audience had a greater PSI increase than subjects performing alone, especially for Print 1.

   The significant Conditions of Learning × Conditions of Performance × Prints interaction ($F = 5.85$, $df = 1/40$, $p < .05$) made the significant Conditions of Performance × Prints interaction dependent upon the conditions of learning factor. Analysis of the three-factor interaction indicated that subjects who learned the task before an audience had a greater PSI increase in the performance phase than subjects who learned alone. Furthermore, subjects in the learn-audience—perform-audience treatment had the greatest PSI increase, while subjects in the learn-alone—perform-alone treatment had the lowest. The increased arousal of subjects in the learn-audience treatment was carried over into Block 1 of the performance phase for both treatments of the conditions of performance factor. The increased PSI decreased after Block 1 when performing alone, but continued at the same high level when performing in the presence of an audience.

Discussion

Cottrell and his associates (1967, 1968), Ganzer (1968), and Zajonc and Sales (1966) have all reported audience effects on verbal tasks that are consistent with social facilitation theory. The results of the present investigation also supported social facilitation theory when learning and performing a complex motor task. Subjects acquiring a new response in the presence of a passive audience committed more error, had less within-subject consistency, and required significantly more trials to learn coincident timing than subjects learning alone. As subjects continued to practice and learning occurred, the means of the alone and audience treatments converged as expected. Once the task had been well learned, individuals in the presence of an audience performed better than individuals performing alone. Not only were performance scores better, but subjects performing in the presence of an audience were more consistent in their responses.

Palmar sweat print results provided evidence in support of the assumption that the presence of others is a source of arousal. Results clearly indicated that significant increases occurred in the PSI when learning and performing a complex motor task in the presence of passive spectators. By providing evidence that the intervening variable of arousal level varied in a manner consistent with social facilitation theory predictions, considerable reliability was added to the significant findings of the learning and performance scores. The effectiveness of the palmar sweat print technique in the present investigation suggests its usefulness for future research on social behavior.

In order to evaluate the significance of the relationship between audience presence, anxiety, and performance it was necessary to hypothesize when the correct response became dominant. Following the procedures of other learning experiments, a Treatment × Trials (4 × 15) analysis of variance was computed which indicated that significant decreases ($F = 27.85$, $df = 14/1,288$, $p < .01$) in error occurred over the initial 15 trials. A modified Newman-Keuls test showed that for each treatment significant differences between pairs of trials ceased after Trial 3. Examination of the learning curve, however, reveals that small improvements continued to occur between Trials 10–15. Consequently, for purposes of the present study the Newman-Keuls test, which is completely arbitrary, may have been too stringent. Assuming that the correct response became dominant when the majority of learning was completed, it was estimated that the correct response became dominant between Trials 10–15.

In determining the relationship between anxiety and audience presence, results of the trials to criterion data indicated that HA subjects learned the task significantly sooner than LA subjects in the presence of an audience, but no difference was found when learning alone. This is not consistent with the results of Cox (1966, 1968) and Ganzer (1968), who found that the presence of an audience was more detrimental for HA subjects than for LA subjects when learning. Results of the arithmetic error data failed to show a significant relationship between anxiety and audience presence when learning or performing.

The failure to find arithmetic error results consistent with the trials to criterion results weakens the significance of the Anxiety $\times$ Conditions of Learning interaction. Furthermore, comparison of the learning curve to the trials to criterion data suggests that the skill was acquired quite rapidly and considerably sooner than the attainment of the learning criterion. Therefore, it is suggested that the criterion may have been so difficult that it better reflected a composite measure of learning and performance. Consequently, the criterion score was a confounded measure which rendered the significant Anxiety $\times$ Conditions of Learning interaction tenuous.

Failure to find consistent results between the studies of Cox (1966, 1968) and Ganzer (1968) and the present investigation appears to be the result of procedural differences. The major differences were in the anxiety scales and tasks employed. The present study used a complex motor task, while Cox used a simple marble-dropping task, and Ganzer used a verbal learning task. Both Cox and Ganzer used test anxiety scales while the present study used the MA scale. Other minor procedural differences also contrasted these studies. Cox used boys as subjects, while Ganzer tested women and the observer was behind a one-way mirror. Perhaps, as Wapner and Alper (1952) found, an unseen audience represents greater threat than an audience which is seen. Any or all of these factors could account for the difference in results.

The results of the Anxiety $\times$ Audience Presence interaction are not consistent with previous research. Therefore, it is concluded that a more generalized anxiety scale such as the MA scale does not interact with the presence of an audience to produce differences in learning and performance on a complex motor task. Certainly, additional research is needed to clarify the relationship between anxiety and audience presence when different anxiety scales and task variables are used.

Independent of the audience factor, significant anxiety differences were found in the present study. Results showed that HA subjects committed less error than LA subjects for the last five trials of the learning phase and all trials of the performance phase. If subjects were still learning the skill during the last five trials of the learning phase, these results would be inconsistent with drive theory predictions. However, as has been indicated, the correct response appears to have become dominant within the first 15 trials. According to Spence and Spence (1966), in a learning situation which is sufficiently competitive and the correct response is the most probable response, HA subjects are expected to be superior. Therefore, these results are consistent with drive theory once the task has been well learned.

No significant difference was found between HA and LA subjects for the first 10 trials. According to drive theory, LA subjects should be significantly better than HA subjects during the initial trials of learning a complex motor task. The failure to find a significant difference probably occurred because the skill was acquired so rapidly. It should be noted that these results in no way reflected a test of drive theory, but only determined if drive theory predictions were applicable to a complex motor task. To test drive theory it is necessary to hypothesize about the degree of intratask competition, which is not possible with a complex motor task.

Finally, according to drive theory, differences between HA and LA subjects should be maximized when subjects are placed in an arousing condition. Consequently, it was expected that HA subjects would have a larger increase in palmar sweat gland activity than LA subjects, especially in the presence of an audience. The results, however, indicated no significant difference between the two anxiety levels when either alone or in the presence of an audience. The failure to find significant differences between HA and LA subjects for the PSI increase was not completely unexpected. Most anxiety research has not found any significant differences in physiological responses between subjects who are extreme on the *MA* scale (Beam, 1955; Berry & Martin, 1957; Raphelson, 1957).

References

ALLPORT, F. H. The influence of the group upon association and thought. *Journal of Experimental Psychology*, 1920, 3, 159-182.

BEAM, J. C. Serial learning and conditioning under real-life stress. *Journal of Abnormal and Social Psychology*, 1955, 51, 543-551.

BERRY, J. E., & MARTIN, B. GSR reactivity as a function of anxiety, instructions, and sex. *Journal of Abnormal and Social Psychology*, 1957, 54, 9-12.

COTTRELL, N. B., RITTLE, R. H., & WACK, D. L. The presence of an audience and list type (competitional or noncompetitional) as joint determinants of performance in paired-associates learning. *Journal of Personality*, 1967, 35, 425-434.

COTTRELL, N. B., WACK, D. L., SEKERAK, G. J., & RITTLE, R. H. Social facilitation of dominant responses by the presence of an audience and the mere presence of others. *Journal of Personality and Social Psychology*, 1968, 9, 245-250.

COX, F. N. Some effects of test anxiety and presence or absence of other persons on boys' performance on a repetitive motor task. *Journal of Experimental Child Psychology*, 1966, 3, 100-112.

COX, F. N. Some relationships between test anxiety, presence or absence of male persons, and boys' performance on a repetitive motor task. *Journal of Experimental Child Psychology*, 1968, 3, 1-12.

DASHIELL, J. F. An experimental analysis of some group effects. *Journal of Abnormal and Social Psychology*, 1930, 25, 190-199.

EKDAHL, A. G. Effect of attitude on free word association-time. *Genetic Psychology Monograph*, 1929, 5, 153-338.

GANZER, V. J. Effects of audience presence and test anxiety on learning and retention in a serial learning situation. *Journal of Personality and Social Psychology*, 1968, 8, 194-199.

GATES, G. S. The effect of an audience upon performance. *Journal of Abnormal and Social Psychology*, 1924, 18, 334-342.

HARRISON, J., & MACKINNON, P. C. B. Physiological role of the adrenal medulla in the palmar anihidrotic response to stress. *Journal of Applied Physiology*, 1966, 21, 88-92.

JOHNSON, J. E., & DABBS, J. M. Enumeration of active sweat glands: A simple physiological indicator of psychological changes. *Nursing Research*, 1967, 16, 273-276.

MASON, J. W., & BRADY, J. V. The sensitivity of psycho-endocrine system to social and physical environment. In P. H. Leiderman & D. Shapiro (Eds.), *Psychobiological approaches to social behavior*. Stanford: Stanford University Press, 1964.

PESSIN, J. The comparative effects of social and mechanical stimulation on memorizing. *American Journal of Psychology*, 1933, 45, 263-270.

PESSIN, J., & HUSBAND, R. W. Effects of social stimulation on human maze learning. *Journal of Abnormal and Social Psychology*, 1933, 28, 148-154.

RAPHELSON, A. C. The relationships among imaginative, direct verbal, and physiological measures of anxiety in an achievement situation. *Journal of Abnormal and Social Psychology*, 1957, 54, 13-18.

SCHMIDT, R. A. Motor factors in coincident timing. Unpublished doctoral dissertation, University of Illinois, 1967.

SPENCE, J. T., & SPENCE, K. W. The motivational components of manifest anxiety: Drive and drive stimuli. In C. D. Spielberger (Ed.), *Anxiety and behavior*. New York: Academic Press, 1966.

SUTARMAN, & THOMSON, M. L. A new technique for enumerating active sweat glands in man. *Journal of Physiology* (London), 1952, 117, 510P.

TAYLOR, J. A. A personality scale of manifest anxiety. *Journal of Abnormal and Social Psychology*, 1953, 48, 285-290.

THIESSEN, D. D. Population density, mouse genotype, and endocrine function in behavior. *Journal of Comparative Physiological Psychology*, 1964, 57, 412-416.

TRAVIS, L. E. The effect of a small audience upon eye-hand coordination. *Journal of Abnormal and Social Psychology,* 1925, 20, 142-146.

TRIPLETT, N. The dynamogenic factors in pacemaking and competition. *American Journal of Psychology.* 1897, 9, 507-533.

WAPNER, S., & ALPER, T. G. The effect of an audience on behavior in a choice situation. *Journal of Abnormal and Social Psychology,* 1952, 47, 222-229.

WINER, B. J. *Statistical principles in experimental design.* New York: McGraw-Hill, 1962.

ZAJONC, R. B. Social facilitation. *Science,* 1965, 149, 269-274.

ZAJONC, R. B., & SALES, S. M. Social facilitation of dominant and subordinate responses. *Journal of Experimental Social Psychology,* 1966, 2, 160-168.

Group Performance in a Manual Dexterity Task*

ANDREW L. COMREY

IT is not at all unusual to think of an individual performance score as being very much related to group performance. Military and industrial aptitude and achievement tests usually measure the person in an alone condition, yet many times he is called upon to work as part of a crew, team, or other small group in a cooperative venture. In physical education, students are given isolated skills tests which presumably will indicate performance in a team venture. The degree of accuracy of this prediction is analyzed by Comrey from observations of the performance of industrial tasks. Also, in a paired performance, output is examined as it is affected by averaging individual scores or high and low performance scores. The author investigates a troublesome issue and draws implications for such situations when they exist.

The research to be reported in this article was designed to provide some information on the following questions: (1) how well might the performance of a pair of individuals on a manual dexterity task be predicted from a knowledge of the individual manual dexterity scores of the two persons making up the group; and (2) does the relative level of group performance seem to be more closely associated with the lower or the higher of the individual performers.

Experimental Procedure

Each "group" studied in this research consisted of two men. One hundred and thirty volunteers were recruited about equally from undergraduate and graduate students to make up 65 groups. No attempt was made to control the placement of individuals into groups. Some pairs were composed of friends,

* From the *Journal of Applied Psychology,* 1953, 37, 207-210. Reprinted with permission of the author and the American Psychological Association.

but in the majority of cases the individuals were either unknown to each other or were only casually acquainted.

The subjects in each pair were brought into a well lighted and ventilated experimental room and seated across from each other at a table of approximately office-desk proportions. The experimenter was seated at the far end of this table. In front of each subject was a Purdue Pegboard Test, the two boards touching each other at the ends containing the peg cups. The standard instructions for the Purdue Pegboard, Assembly Task were read to the subjects. Following this, six standard trials were taken, the "Assembly" scores being recorded after each trial for each subject individually. Each subject was able to see how well the other person was doing in comparison with his own performance.

Following the completion of six trials of individual performance, one of the pegboards was removed and the other was placed between the two subjects, the long direction of the board perpendicular to the axis through the subjects, and the cups away from the experimenter. The following instructions were read by the experimenter:

"In the second part of the experiment, you will work on the same type of task except that you will work together rather than individually. First (*subject A—on E's left*) will pick up a peg and place it in the first hole of the row nearest you. Then (*subject B—on E's right*) will pick up a washer and place it over the pin. Then (*subject A*) will pick up a collar and place it over the washer. Then (*subject B*) will pick up a washer and place it over the collar, completing the first assembly. At the same time, (*subject B*) will pick up a peg with the other hand and place it in the *second* hole of the row nearest him. Then (*subject A*) will place on a washer, (*subject B*) will put on the collar, and finally (*subject A*) will place on the final washer, picking up a peg at the same time with the other hand and placing it in the hole diagonally across from the assembly being completed. Thus, the assemblies zigzag down the board, each person's assignment alternating on each successive assembly. Now do a few assemblies for practice."

When it was clear that the subjects understood the nature of the group task, six trials of one minute each were taken, scores being recorded for each trial. Scoring was the same as for the individual assembly task. This completed the experimental session, usually taking 25 to 30 minutes. In reading the instructions for the group task, the subject's name was inserted in the appropriate space, italicized in the text given above.

Treatment of the Data

The statistical analysis of the data proceeded in the following steps:

(1) For each person, individual assembly scores on trials three and five were added together and scores on trials four and six were added together. These "split-half" scores were used to obtain reliability estimates and also were added to give a total individual performance score. The same procedure was followed for the "group" scores.

(2) The members of each pair were designated as "high" or "low," respectively, on the basis of their total individual performance scores computed in (1) above. The person of the pair with the higher total was automatically classified as "high" and his partner was classified as "low." Many individuals in the "low" classification had higher scores than some persons in the "high" classification. This apparently arbitrary method of dividing subjects was adopted because one objective of the experiment was to determine whether the lower or the higher of the two individual performers of a pair would have a greater influence on their group effort. Common sense might suggest that the pair could do no better than the poorer man, in a normative sense.

Table 1

Summary of Results

Score	M	σ	r_{11}	High	Low	Group	Beta Weight
High	186	16.5	.90	1.00	.52	.56	.35
Low	173	16.8	.92	.52	1.00	.59	.41
Group	178	19.2	.87	.56	.59	1.00	
		R = .66			$R^2 = .44$		

(3) Pearson product-moment correlations were computed between the "split-half" scores in the "high" and "low" categories and also for the "group" performances. Thus, the 65 persons in the "low" category each had two half scores. These scores were correlated and the correlation corrected for doubled length by the Spearman-Brown prophecy formula to obtain a reliability estimate for total individual performance scores in the "low" category. The same procedure was followed for those persons in the "high" classification and for the pairs of individuals involved in the "group" performance.

(4) Pearson correlations were computed between "high" and "low" individual performances, between "high" individual and "group" performances, and between "low" individual and "group" performances. These correlation coefficients were corrected for attenuation in both variables involved, using the estimates of reliability obtained in (3) above. The correlations so obtained were treated as estimates of the values which might be expected between the given variables had the measures involved been entirely free of errors of measurement.

(5) A coefficient of multiple correlation between "group" performance and the respective "high" and "low" individual performances was computed, using the coefficients of correlation corrected for attenuation, as obtained in (4) above. The multiple correlation was computed using correlations corrected for attenuation because it was desired to have an estimate of the maximum amount of variance which could be predicted under ideal conditions, i.e., with errors of measurement absent. The idea was to gain some indication of how much variance might be attributable to certain additional unknown variables.

(6) Beta weights for the "high" and "low" scores, respectively, were computed for the regression equation to predict "group" performance scores.

Results

The results of the statistical analysis have been summarized in Table 1. Inspection of the scatter plots revealed no indication of curvilinear regressions, although the plot between "high" and "low" scores had a restriction due to the fact that the "low" score of a pair could not be greater than the "high" score.[1] In the first column of Table 1 are listed the total score categories, "high," "low," and "group," standing, respectively, for those total performances as described in the previous section. The means and standard deviations of the three sets of scores are given in the second and third columns, respectively.

---

[1] To determine the effect of this artificial restriction, 65 pairs of two-digit numbers were taken from a table of random numbers, placing arbitrarily the higher of the two numbers in the first group and the lower of the two in the second group. The resulting Pearson correlation was .56.

These are based on the totals of the last four of six trials. This procedure was decided upon in advance to obtain more stabilized results. In the fourth column are given the reliability estimates as obtained by the procedure described in (3) of the last section. The next three columns of Table 1 give the inter-correlations of the total score variables, corrected for attenuation. The steps were described in (4) of the section on treatment of the data. The last column contains the beta weights for predicting "group" performance from "high" and "low" individual performances. The multiple correlation, R, and R^2, as described in (5) of the last section, are given in the bottom row of the table.

Discussion

Information pertaining to the first question in this research is given by the multiple correlation coefficient between "high" and "low" scores and the "group" score. The square of that coefficient indicates that 44 per cent of the variance in an errorless measure of group performance could be predicted from a linear combination of perfectly reliable "high" and "low" individual scores. The percentage which can be predicted by fallible measures would be less.

Three possible explanations of this result will be given. First, the task itself may actually be significantly different in its nature from the individual assembly task. It was necessary for the subjects to alternate operations on succeeding assemblies when working together, which was not the case in individual operations. In future work, a redesigned individual task will be used which requires the subject to interchange the sequence of hand movements on alternate assemblies. This should make the operations in the individual task more like those in the group task.

Even though the previously mentioned difference in the individual and "group" tasks were eliminated, this would by no means indicate that the "group" task would then be the same to the participating persons as their individual tasks. The two tasks are probably different to each individual not only because of an intrinsic difference in the sequence or character of the operations but also because the group situation brings in new elements requiring the utilization of different abilities. The person must anticipate the moves of his partner to achieve a smooth performance. In short, it is suggested that there may be a group of abilities possessed to different degrees by different individuals which determine in part how well they will perform in certain group situations. These new abilities may be independent of those which determine the performance of the same operations in the same sequence by the individual as a single performer.

A third possible explanation of these results lies in the hypothesis of inter-actions among individuals. It may be that some or even all subjects will work more effectively with some individuals than with others. Under this hypothesis, variations in group performance may be substantially influenced by the extent to which persons are paired who will work best together.

The second objective of the experiment was to determine if the lower indi-vidual performer of a pair influenced the group performance more than the higher individual performer. This question may be answered by an examina-tion of the correlations of the "low" and "high" scores with the "group" scores. The correlations, corrected for attenuation, were .53 and .50, respec-tively. The difference in effect on group performance by the "high" and "low" pair members is so slight as to be of no practical consequence. Thus, group performance here seems to be a function of the average of the two individual scores. Under these conditions, for a given group of workers, there would seem to be little to gain by trying to pair off the high ones and the low ones, expecting thereby to get more over-all production from the group as a whole. This conclusion naturally presumes a similar type of prediction situation and the lack of further information beyond that which was available here.

The same statistical treatment was also given to the data from the first two trials. Reliabilities were somewhat lower, .76, .82, and .74 for the "high," "low," and "group" scores, respectively. Intercorrelations among these scores, corrected for attenuation as before, were "low-high," .53, "low-group," .67, and "high-group," .58. R^2 was .51. Thus, during the practice trials, the "low" men influenced the group performance slightly more than they did in later trials. Also, during these trials, the group scores were more highly related to the individual performance scores than during the test trials, as shown by the higher R^2. The stabilized performance results probably have the greater practical value, however.

Summary

Sixty-five pairs of volunteer male university students were given six trials on the Purdue Pegboard, Assembly Task, and six trials on the Assembly Task with the two members of each pair working together on the same assemblies rather than individually on separate boards. The members of each pair were divided on the basis of the total of the last four individual trials, Assembly Task, into "high" and "low" categories. Reliabilities were determined for "high," "low," and "group" performances, using alternate trials and correcting for doubled length. Correlations of the "high" and "low" performances with each other were computed and corrected for attenuation. The multiple correlation and regression weights were obtained for predicting "group" performance from "high" and "low" individual performances.

The results showed that less than half the group performance variance could be predicted from a knowledge of the individual performances, even with the effect of errors removed. It is suggested that manifest differences between the "individual" and "group" tests, interactions among individuals, and a constellation of abilities in the general area of cooperation may account for the variance not predicted by perfectly reliable individual performance scores.

The level of group performance was only slightly more dependent on the "low" individual performances. For all practical purposes equal weights could be used for "high" and "low" scores in predicting "group" performance.

Two practical implications of the results of this experiment are as follows. First, in industrial situations where two or more individuals must cooperate on a given task, it must not be assumed that individual performances on a similar type of task will account for most of the variation in group performance. Secondly, for a given group of persons there seems to be little point in taking the trouble to pair them on individual ability in a related type of individual task since group performance seems to be dependent on the approximate average of their individual scores rather than the high or low individual performance.

BIOCHEMISTRY AND NEUROPHYSIOLOGY OF LEARNING

Inside the Organism

A major complaint registered against psychologists studying behavior in general and motor learning in particular has been the apparent neglect of neurological, physiological, and chemical evidence. Behavior can best be explained when all scientists studying the same phenomena interact and incorporate their efforts in a unifying manner. Unfortunately, for the most part, neurophysiologists have gone their own way; psychologists theirs. Part 10 contains summaries and research efforts demonstrating the state of our knowledge at the present time in the biochemical, neurological, and physiological bases of learning.

Chemical breakthroughs are of very recent vintage. Neurophysiologists have examined (a) portions of the brain responsible for particular functions, (b) reflex arcs, (c) nerve pathways, and (d) synapses. Changes that might occur in one of the mechanisms or in a combination of them concomitantly with learning are observed, forming the basis of theoretical evidence. Much of the information on the nature of the learning process has been derived from lower forms of organisms, for obvious reasons. Electrode implantation; cell extirpation; transfer of chemical substances such as RNA from trained to nontrained organisms; and drug application represent some of the ways learning effects and determinants of performance have been studied.

Aspects of the learning process can be adequately explained biochemically, and there appears to be little doubt now that RNA plays a major role. Neurophysiological learning theories embrace (a) the idea of reverberating circuits and paths of least resistance for certain impulses; (b) short, intermediate, and long-term memory processes; (c) synaptic changes, e.g., enlargement due to constant usage; (d) reflex arc formations; (e) brain or cellular locations for control; and other possibilities. Theories are varied due to the incomplete state of our knowledge, and implications are drawn primarily from suggestive data. Nevertheless, as in the case of biochemistry, great advancements in neurophysiological research in the past decade have provided us with a better understanding of learning mechanisms and the learning process itself.

It is extremely difficult to select but a few readings from the many sources in this area. The many "classic" articles from the efforts of Lashley, Penfield, Luria, and others, as well as the latest developments and theoretical advancements, have swelled the available literature. Hopefully, a balanced representation of theory and research findings, of biochemistry and neurophysiology, is attained here. The reader is encouraged to examine some of the many references provided in the summary articles.

Chapter 15

BRAIN FUNCTIONING

*The Physiology of Motor Learning**

F. A. HELLEBRANDT

A review of extensive research and theory evidences that a number of similar processes and mechanisms are involved in any kind of learning and behavior. Then again, a given type of learning, e.g., motor learning, requires certain unique considerations. Hellebrandt synthesizes and summarizes research dealing with the physiological aspects of motor learning. Note the emphasis on the analysis of movement; pattern, reflexes, and specific responses. In contrast, the English scholars have emphasized the importance of sensory mechanisms and feedback information as regulators of purposeful movement. Hellebrandt handles her assignment well in presenting the evidence and pointing out unresolved issues in the late 1950's.

Introductory Remarks

The literature in the field of motor learning is surprisingly extensive. It provides the interested reader with a seemingly limitless reservoir of useful information that flows across many different areas of human knowledge. Among the latter may be listed the various branches of psychology, embryology, neurophysiology, clinical neurology, orthopaedic surgery, kinesiology, and physical education. As yet no one has attempted to integrate the total evidence in a single definitive review. Whether the mind of one person can encompass the wealth of material available, and assess it critically, is a question yet to be answered.

My own interest in the subject of motor learning began in 1930 when I reviewed Coghill's classical work, *Anatomy and the Problem of Behavior,* at a seminar of the Department of Physiology at the University of Wisconsin. In the years that followed the recollection of Coghill's concepts remained undimmed, forming an ever-present frame of reference for a succession of

* From Cerebral Palsy Review, 1958, *19,* 9–14. Reprinted with permission of the author and publisher, Institute of Logopedics, Inc.

clinical and laboratory experiences. The publication of Coghill's London Lectures did, in effect, mark the beginning of a new multi-disciplinary area of investigative effort. Weiss has suggested that this be called *Genetic Neurology*. Almost 25 years elapsed before time and circumstance permitted the systematic accumulation of available source materials. That bibliography now contains approximately 1000 references. If all major leads were followed and important collateral paths pursued the literature would stand at about 2500 titles with at least one tenth of the whole classifiable as basic to a reasonably sound and comprehensive understanding of the subject.

The discussion to be presented is of necessity still incomplete. It is a progress report or a preview, a tentative summing up, strongly biased, as is inevitable, by the character of the research done in the disability evaluation laboratories of the Medical College of Virginia and the Research and Educational Hospitals of the University of Illinois. Although that research was designed to elucidate problems related to the rehabilitation of the disabled, much of the experimental work was done on normal subjects. The data throw light, therefore, on the mobilization of the physiological resources of normal men participating in sport and physical education activities. The selfsame mechanisms operate when the handicapped individual extends the performance of some prescribed rehabilitation task to the limits of his restricted capacity. Indeed, the biological responses evoked in the two situations may be virtually indistinguishable.

Movements Not Muscles are Represented in the Cortex

This aphorism, oft repeated, has lost meaning because of its familiarity. Its implications are increasingly challenging, however, as more is learned about the reflex and volitional control of movement.

If muscles participate in more than one movement, as most do, they must be represented diffusely in the cortex. Presumably different centers connect via internuncial neurons with groups of peripherally disposed motor units. The work of Seyffarth and of Denny-Brown has shown that motor units are activated in a definite sequence which varies with the movement elicited. As the severity of the effort increases, those involved primarily in one movement may be recruited to assist in the performance of others. During elbow flexion, for instance, certain motor units of the biceps brachii only appear at very high tension, whereas the same units go into action at the slightest provocation during supination. Reviewing this work Darcus suggests that the limited field of neurons excited at the onset of contraction widens concentrically as the effort augments. Eventually it overlaps neighboring fields, evoking a concurrent excitation of neurons primarily concerned in other movements by the same and by functionally related muscles.

Gellhorn and Hyde have shown that the size and configuration of the area of cortical representation of an extremity are influenced significantly by the proprioceptive inflow from the limb. Neurons destined to activate the motor units of a given muscle may be quite scattered. One might postulate that those concerned with the action of a particular muscle as a prime mover may be relatively concentrated and of low threshold. Others lie far removed from the primary focus, in association with low threshold neurons destined for other but related muscles. It would follow from such an hypothesis that the full complement of motor units present in any muscle can be activated volitionally only in association with other muscles attached to the same or continuous anatomical segments. Perhaps, as we shall see, an all-out effort may even mobilize more remote parts of the same and/or opposite side in the resultant movement-complex.

The Prefiguration of Movement Responses

Gellhorn has shown that supra-threshold cortical stimulation evokes patterned action in which several anatomical parts may participate. These responses are similar to the total synergies seen so commonly in the clinic. They are perfectly integrated. They range in complexity from agonist-antagonist cocontractions about a single joint to modifications in the functioning of muscles which are distributed so extensively as to change the total adjustmental design of the body and its appendages. We have had a particular interest in those associated with spontaneous variations in the positioning of the head and neck during heavy resistance exercise. Our own studies and innumerable clues in the literature suggest that the reflexes evoked under similar conditions are extraordinarily consistent. Indeed, they are so repetitive as to warrant designating them patterned movements. If all the muscles in a synergy operate under a common governing force, as Seyffarth suggests, the fundamental unit of action may be thought of as a total response in which agonists and antagonists, synergists and fixators participate in balanced and harmonious activity. Partial patterns emerge secondarily, by virtue of special training, but remain forever yoked to the integrated primitive total response.

The concept being outlined is an important one of obvious utility in the rehabilitation of the disabled. If movements are represented in the cortex in their total complexity a muscle may be made to function as a synergist or fixator when it cannot be used as a prime mover. Partridge has shown that a muscle may be so strengthened through systematic participation in a patterned response that it can be emancipated eventually from the total synergy and made to act once again in its capacity as a prime mover.

The complexity of the picture being drawn increases many-fold when the concept of proprioceptive facilitation is added to it. Gellhorn and his associates have demonstrated that the sensory feed-back coming from muscles, tendons and joints greatly affects movement patterns. Central excitations have a tendency to flow always into stretched muscles. Thus, every change in body positioning alters the configuration of the next succeeding efferent response. It affects not only the muscle stretched, but all functionally related muscle groups as well. This means that a change in the responsiveness of one component of a movement-complex spreads autonomously to the other constituents.

Proprioceptive impulses not only increase the excitability of the motor cortex but affect the reflex activity of the cord as well. Electromyographic studies suggest that the myotatic reflex activates striated muscles in functional patterns similar to those elicited by cortical stimulation. The reflex arising in a single muscle excites not only this muscle and its synergists at the same joint, but also those synergists which act on neighboring parts and form, with the stretched muscle, a functional association of ancient origin and obvious utility. The reflex linkage may be so strong that greater activity is evoked by impulses arising proprioceptively in other components of the synergy than by autogenous proprioceptive stimulation. This is of practical importance in muscle re-education and probably also affects the way in which skills are acquired by the normal individual.

Automation or the Emancipation of
Voluntary Acts from Conscious Control

Nielsen believes that willed movements which are new and unfamiliar always demand cerebration. They are performed at first with more or less conscious attention to the details of their execution. Once mastered, they operate automatically. Conscious introspection at this stage may even disrupt the nicety of an established pattern. After an act has become automatic, says Nielsen, it is less well performed if it must first be considered and analyzed.

Nielsen's description of the learning of a planned act such as the tying of a square knot is instructive. The first step calls for appreciation of the relative positions of each part of the rope. This requires inspection and analysis, to wit, cerebration. Vision then guides the moving parts. Kinesthesia is aroused by the act itself. A lasting trace or engram is left in the wake of repeated usage. Eventually a square knot can be tied with little or no thought. Feel is now sufficient. The learner can tie a square knot without looking or with the eyes shut. He can even tie a square knot without any memory of having done so. As Sherrington would say, consciousness is no longer adjunct to the act. This means that as an act becomes automatic the area of the cortex which initially serves in planning it becomes unnecessary to its execution. If automaticity is lost as a result of disease, the patient must re-plan the simplest acts and the results are as crude as his first attempts at initial learning.

A major component of the material from which a learned movement is built is the incessantly varying sensory input. To this must be added what Penfield calls "the guidance of memory and the conclusions of reason." No one knows for certain the seat of that integration which precedes willed movement. This is the so-called mind-brain problem which has puzzled biologists and philosophers for many decades.

Sperry argues that the primary business of the brain is the governing of overt behavior. Since overt behavior consists of no more nor less than patterns of muscular contraction, it follows that the principal function of the nervous system is the coordinated innervation of the musculature. The entire output of our thinking machine consists of nothing but patterns of motor coordination, says Sperry. It yields nothing but motor adjustment. This view will be recognized as the reverse of the one subscribed to by our British colleagues, who would have us believe that the motor cortex is not importantly involved in willed movements. The great pyramidal system has been de-throned by Walshe, Gooddy, and Bartlett, and reduced to a humbler status than that held formerly. To this Twitchell has added his voice. The pyramidal system initiates nothing of itself, they say. It is no more than a way-station in the stream of outgoing volitional impulses, an internuncial path interposed between the integrative system and the final common path over which effector impulses flow to selectively patterned constellations of motor units. The sensory input is the great initiator and moulder of muscular responses, for willed movements are activated by controlling cortical afferent patterns of excitation. But none of this solves the mind-brain enigma. Interposed between the sensory input and the motor outflow is the integrative center. Nielsen localizes it in the posterior association area of Flechsig. But various ablation and sectioning experiments in animals and man suggest that integration does not reside in the cortex. Penfield therefore places it in a biencephalic brain-stem position, and calls this hypothetical seat of the mind-brain union the centrencephalic system.

Penfield conceives the outflow of the centrencephalic system as one arriving in already patterned form at the motor area of both hemispheres. If the cortex is damaged, the system can still operate on a limited but useful plan embracing the activation of primitive subcortical motor mechanisms. There is much of interest in this scheme which is deduced from a large series of human cortical ablations resorted to for the surgical treatment of focal epilepsy. It postulates a mechanism which insures integrated participation of the machine as a whole. Much of value may be learned by closer examination of the behavior pattern in toto, and less fixation of attention on the movement of the presenting part which is only a fraction of the neuromuscular response evoked.

Spinal Cord Mechanisms and their Operation

The outflow from the lower motor centers is a double one now known as the large and the small nerve systems because of the difference in the diameter of the fibers leaving the cord by the anterior roots. The large fibers innervate only the main muscle fibers responsible for the contractions which activate the bony levers for the production of movement. The muscle fibers are grouped into so-called motor units. All of the one hundred or more diffusely scattered muscle fibers of the motor unit shorten synchronously and to their maximal extent or not at all.

The small nerves, or gamma fibers, innervate the sparse intrafusal muscle fibers of the spindle. These are assembled in closely grouped clusters of six or eight fibers. They are considerably modified and bound together by a connective tissue capsule. The polar regions of the intrafusal fibers are muscular and contractile. Barker has shown that the equatorial zone is occupied by a nuclear bag which is packed with .04 or more nuclei. Around this the annulospiral ending winds itself. This is the primary stretch-afferent, or the nuclear bag afferent. When the small nerve fibers stimulate the intrafusal muscle fibers, they contract, stretch the spindle, and evoke a barrage of impulses from the annulospiral ending. These travel by way of large, rapidly transmitting afferent fibers, which form a monosynaptic loop, excitatory to the large motor fibers of the muscle concerned and also its associated synergists. This is a fast, facilitatory servo designed to adjust the level of muscular activity to the magnitude of the stress. Granit believes gamma impulses lead off at the onset of cortically induced movements. These then facilitate selected anterior horn cells which evoke the responses in the motor units which induce the movements willed. Excitation of the main motoneuron pool appears, therefore, to be dependent on the inflow from the spindle afferents, and the level of their activity is set by the gamma system, which, according to Granit and Kaada, is under cerebral control. Thus the small nerve innervation of skeleton muscles mediates the impulses which initiate and drive muscular contraction, especially that concerned with postural adjustments. Rapid movements are activated via the direct route utilizing the large anterior horn cells. Granit, Holmgren and Merton believe the adjustment of activity between the two modes of excitation is a function of the cerebellum. This acts as a neural switch which directs impulses originating in cortical or subcortical motor centers into the large or small nerve route.

Classified as a proprioceptor, the annulospiral feed-back operates preeminently on the cord level where it can in no way be introspected, and hence does not contribute to kinesthesia. Some proprioceptive circuits travel up the cord to the cerebellum, which also contributes to the reflex control of movement.

The muscle spindle also contains one or sometimes two flowerspray endings. These are located in the myotube region which is the transitional area of the intrafusal muscle fiber just before the fibril passes through the nuclear bag. This proprioceptive receptor has a higher threshold than the annulospiral ending. It takes stretch of higher intensity to elicit a response. The impulses evoked travel over smaller and hence slower circuits than those subserving the annulospiral flow. There is some evidence suggesting that they pass on to the somesthetic cortex and hence may reach consciousness. The richness of the alternate circuits discussed previously suggests that the motor moron, who cares nothing about his muscle sense or is incapable of bringing it to awareness, is still protected in the execution of physical skills by a compassionate Mother Nature.

Both the primary and secondary spindle afferents are facilitatory servo-mechanisms. They augment the functional capacity of the motor units from which they arise as well as those synergically associated muscles. Inhibitory mechanisms also exist. They too are built-in devices, giving the muscle an extraordinarily rich autogenetic control. One is the system subserved by the Golgi end-organs. Their presence has long been recognized in at least one region, at the point where the main muscle fibers come together to form the tendons and aponeuroses by which muscles are attached to their bony levers. More recently Golgi end-organs also have been described at the point where the small modified intrafusal fibers of the muscle spindles attach, usually to extrafusal muscle fibers. Newer knowledge of some significance attaches to the function served by such an arrangement of Golgi receptors. The spindle is an excitatory afferent. The Golgi end-organs are inhibitory afferents. Thus the structural linkage of the two gives the muscle a perfect means of auto-nomous self-regulation. Facilitatory reflexes vie with inhibitory reflexes and the level of activity manifest is the resultant of the balanced activity of the two. It would appear that the small nerve fibers which activate the annulospiral and flowerspray endings of the muscle spindle do not have a completely free hand. Should they increase tension of the intrafusal muscle fibers to too high a level, and send too many facilitatory impulses tumbling over the servo loop, the Golgi end-organs can dampen the reactivity of the mechanisms involved.

Adequate as the Golgi system seems, still another autogenous cord level controlling device exists. The large nerve fibers innervating the motor units send a recurrent axon collateral back into the cord. These fibers synapse with Renshaw cells which are small internuncials closely associated with the moto-neuron pool of the anterior horn. They fire at exceedingly high rates and are inhibitory in function. The backfire affects not only the given muscle but also its synergists. This means that outgoing impulses traveling in large nerve fibers inhibit, if not their own, adjacent ventral horn cells. Thus the small Renshaw internuncial cells serve as a kind of commutator which switches excitation to inhibition. Granit believes that the Renshaw negative feed-back stabilizes the output frequency of anterior horn cells to the values adapted for driving muscular tissue. It is a damping device which keeps the brakes on the anterior horn cells. They operate always with the inhibitory controls applied.

The post-war rapid development of electronics and the production of pre-cision tools of extreme sensitivity are the two events which made possible the sudden significant enlargement of our information about muscle receptors and how they function. Proprioception is now considered to be one of the most highly developed senses, exceeded in complexity only by the receptors of the eye and the ear. Among the best recent reviews are the works of Barker, Tiegs, Granit, and Eccles.

Less is known about the sensory inflow from the joints but this story is also unfolding due to the effects of Boyd, Gardner, Andrew and others. Proximal sensitivity exceeds distal. The shoulder may be forty times as sensi-tive as a joint of the finger. Presumably two receptors are involved. The pacinian corpuscles are rapidly adapting. They respond with a burst of action potentials during movement but cease to discharge when new positions are reached. The capsules of the joints are also supplied with spray-type endings called Ruffini corpuscles. These are slowly adapting and discharge indefinitely with a frequency characteristic for each position assumed.

I have dwelt thus exhaustively on the organization of the proprioceptive system because much has been added to our store of knowledge in recent years. Feed-back from the muscles, tendons and joints appears to be a cunningly devised and exceedingly complex mechanism, a large share of which operates at levels below consciousness. Not only has automation come to industry. We now know that the machinery of the living body is equipped with its own servomechanisms. Its operation proceeds to a large extent without placing the slightest demand on the cerebral cortex. Innumerable mechanisms exist which are beyond the reach of the most astute physical therapist or teacher of physical education. Perhaps what we need most are techniques of motor learning that free the subcortical motor mechanisms from an oppressive domination of a stressed cortex. Starting from scratch, decorticated as it were, primitively integrated, we might then explore the wonders of that inherent, ancestral movement repertoire and use it as Nature intended before encephalization produced its present degree of tension and inhibition.

Levels of Control

Motor mechanisms operate normally under several categories of control. It is generally conceded that higher levels tend to exercise domination over lower levels. Yet many neuromuscular operations proceed in an orderly and integrated way without interference by the highest centers. They can, however, be modified at will. We also know that oft-repeated volitional acts sink to levels of operation which proceed with little or no awareness. They become submerged through the office of little understood mechanisms. They can be brought to the surface of the mind again and again and made to re-engage the attention. Similarly wholly involuntary or reflex movements may be brought under subjection to the will. Sherrington has said that when we know how the mind makes itself felt on the running of the reflex machinery we will have gone a long way toward understanding the basis of motor learning.

Our own work has been concerned primarily with the functional usefulness of certain automatic reactions. These emerge sufficiently under stress to be studied. They are either frankly dynamogenic devices, that is, they expedite work output when the machine begins to fail, or they contribute to the automatic training of symmetrical parts which takes place without direct practice and is known as the phenomenon of cross-education. They have one characteristic in common, an expanding pattern of operation which must greatly augment the sensory feed-back. The irradiation associated with extreme stress is so widespread that a willed movement limited to a single appendicular joint may evoke action potentials in muscles located in all four extremities, the head and neck, and the trunk. These seem to us to be orderly and wholly integrated total patterns of response. Observing them we get the impression that they are the obligatory concomitants of very severe stress, and the only way in which the highest threshold motor units of the muscle subjected to direct training can be activated. These are the motor units held in reserve and called upon when truly maximal effort is demanded—when you rush into a burning house and perform some phenomenal feat of strength, or when you break the record of the 4-minute mile, or swing your paralyzed legs across a street in the time-span of the green light that gives you the right of way.

The evolution of the expanding patterns characteristic of the response to physical stress deserves attentive and meticulous study. Here we see primitive compensatory mechanisms of ancient origin coming to the surface in ways designed to reinforce functional capacity. If we understood these better, we might gain new insight into the mechanisms underlying coordination.

Theories of Motor Learning

The theories of motor learning number at least three. No informed and understanding student can help but be impressed by the galaxy of built-in mechanisms with which we are endowed. These are the reflex responses which operate at spinal cord and sub-cortical levels. They are, as Sherrington taught, ancient, stable, certain, invariable, and stereotyped. Easily elicited, they run their course with a machine-like fatality once they have been evoked. Consciousness is not adjunct to their operation. They cannot be introspected. But they exist and must account for a substantial proportion of all of our daily neuromuscular activities.

Weiss proposes, on the basis of 30 years of experimental effort, that the fundamental patterns of coordination arise by self-differentiation within the nervous system prior to and irrespective of experience in their use. They form a repertoire of movement patterns which is pre-experiential in origin. The contemporary machine deserves no credit for these built-in skills. Weiss believes that every muscle has a distinctive constitutional specificity and that the nerves supplying the muscle acquire specific differentials of their own which match and centrally represent those of the muscles. Muscles transform nerves and modulate centers, thus elaborating patterns of coordination in what Weiss calls the myotypic code. There is a large and interesting literature on this subject. It is referred to also as the resonance phenomenon, and it explains in part why the "scores" of the movement repertoire are so repeatable in certain of their dimensions whether or not there has been an opportunity to practice them. Presumably they are full-blown when the maturation of the central nervous system is completed.

For more than 25 years controversy has centered about the primacy of the reflex versus the primacy of an integrated total organization in embryological motor development. These concepts are associated with the names of Windle and of Coghill respectively. The literature on this subject runs into hundreds of papers. The heuristic concept presupposes that isolated reflexes, complete in themselves, are combined bit by bit into more and ever more complex chains and other circuits. Trial-and-error combinations of fragments lead to the development of serviceable constellations further modulated by practice and experience. Partial patterns may be disengaged at will, and re-engaged if desired, but each fragment is complete and autonomous in itself.

Much muscle training in physical therapy has been of this type. It begins with simple normal movements, approached as though instigated by the isolated contraction of some prime mover. Purity of movement has been the ideal, and many a physical therapist has visualized this as the achievement of the particular muscle to which treatment was being directed. There has been much careful suppression of overflow, presumably because overflow is something indicative of decadence in coordination. Simple normal range movements have been added one to another like building blocks used to erect increasingly complex combinations of movement. There is much which is admirable in this approach. What is said about its rationale is perhaps more unacceptable than the technique itself, which has an obvious place in the clinic.

The opposite extreme is the holistic approach to motor learning. This contends that living protoplasm is endowed with a primordial dynamic ability to repsond in toto in ways maximally advantageous to the organism as a whole. The whole is forever greater than its parts. It expands progressively, but always as a totally integrated mechanism. The boundless response of the developing organism becomes more circumscribed only with the emergence of inhibition.

Lesser degrees of input are then required to trigger the same effector response and this too, is gradually narrowed as a result of experience and practice. Partial patterns are individuated within the total pattern and acquire varying degrees of discreteness. But they remain forever yoked to the primordial total response. The total system is thus an hierarchy of many smaller systems of various grades of autonomy and subordination, all of which are so related that their local and partial activities cooperate to maintain the integrity of the whole. Parts become integrated with each other because they are integral factors of a primarily integrated whole, and behavior is normal so long as this wholeness is maintained.

Anyone who has participated in sports or observed the muscle re-education of the disabled has seen precise partial patterns of movement revert to total patterning under the exigencies of fatigue or emotional stress. I have already suggested that such expansions of the response, secondary to strong affective states or other stimulation, are never haphazard movements. They are orderly and patterned. They greatly augment the sensory feed-back, and probably serve to automate facilitatory function. Overflow patterns may be manifestations of a stress too great to be coped with by discretely individuated partial patterns, but they are in no sense grossly disrupted skills.

Some Unsolved Problems

Recent studies of the performance of older workers in industry have turned up one surprising fact related to the thesis being developed. Motor goals are reached in many ways. The same task evokes a variety of responses. The same end-result may be achieved in an apparently infinite variety of ways. Rarely if ever are motor units of different muscles activated in exactly the same spatio-temporal pattern. When a task is learned a memory engram is supposedly laid down, but there is no constant use of the same combination of muscles. Rather, muscles are used in different ways to achieve the same result time and again. If the customary sequence of movements employed is impossible, another is used. Nature endows all organ systems with large margins of safety. The industrial studies of Welford and his associates suggest that as long as the goal has been particularized and as long as a sensory channel is available for estimating the extent to which the objective of the movement has been reached, the cerebrum will use any movements that it can command in an effort to reduce the gap between purpose and fulfillment. As the skill of older workers deteriorates, output may remain quite unchanged because the experienced performer autonomously finds new ways of accomplishing the same task. Anyone who has worked with the disabled knows the fantastic facility with which trick movements are learned. Through their use we witness, time and again, seemingly impossible motor achievement.

Welford and his associates have speculated extensively on the biological significance of this interesting behavior. They believe that such an operational plan automatically spreads the metabolic load over a greater mass of tissue. In this way fatigue is avoided, or its effects are mitigated to an appreciable degree. Denny-Brown has discussed the same point in his writings on electromyography. A normal man "eases the burden of fatigue by changing the nature of the contraction"; that is, he evokes a response in some new constellation of motor units capable of attaining the same objective when the first lot has fatigued. This appears to us to be exactly what occurs when stress becomes intolerable. The exercising subject is able to continue only if spontaneous irradiation patterns are permitted to run their course unhampered. If nicety of technique or purity of movement is the objective, functional capacity may be cut far short of the levels attainable through utilization of spontaneous, primitive, deep-seated facilitatory synergies.

Recently we had an opportunity to observe a severely disabled quadruplegic athetoid patient of reasonable intelligence perform certain sport skills. The extraordinary thing about these cinematographic and electromyographic studies was not how the normal subject differed from the pathological, or vice versa, but how easily the eye could catch the basic similarities in the underlying movement patterns. There are many ways in which the same goal can be reached, and man unconsciously picks and chooses among the gamut of those available, easing the burden of fatigue, as Denny-Brown said, and thus extending the range and sensitivity of his movement vocabulary. The physical therapist, shop foreman, physical educator or coach may wish to impose upon the human subject some precise and specific technique of movement, but an infinitely wise living machine, drawing upon the experience of centuries, makes its own autonomous adjustments. Instead of suppressing these, we would do well to study them. Thus we might learn, perhaps, some of Nature's secrets.

Much has been written about methods of expediting motor learning, especially in the psychological literature. Psychical factors loom large as Bartlett and Gooddy have indicated. No one denies this. Bartlett believes it is more important to know *what* is to be done, than *how* to do it. Presumably he is willing to relegate the *how* to an experienced and well integrated neuromuscular machine, perfected through the ages. It is Bartlett who denies that it is practice which makes perfect. Only practice the results of which are known makes perfect.

The British school has placed great stress on the neglected sensory side of purposive motor behavior. Gooddy believes we learn patterns of sensation, not patterns of movement. Thus the sensory inflow is the initiator and molder of all movement. Feed-back mechanisms operate incessantly, without interruption. The degree to which visual and auditory cues modify movement has never been studied adequately. We have not begun to think in neurophysiological terms about the mechanisms underlying many of the things a good teacher does intuitively to achieve selected neuromuscular objectives. We might enhance the efficacy of our techniques of application if we understood them better.

Twitchell has shown that a limb deprived of sensation is more impaired than one suffering the residual effects of a rolandic cortical ablation. And yet, if the skin sensation of a portion of the palm of the hand is allowed to remain intact, the exteroceptive feed-back from that spared fragment of the whole is sufficient to integrate purposive movements of the total extremity. This may explain why hand positioning is the key to the whole intricate complex of a golf swing. Recent work by Hagbarth suggests that exteroceptive skin sensation alone is capable of evoking reflex movements similar to those elicited by cortical stimulation.

Sherrington more than any one else has emphasized the importance of proprioception. Since movement begins and ends in posture, he postulates that the resident sensations emanating from the part in its resting state may be more important than those associated with movement per se. We have never given this proper attention in our analysis of muscular activities. Usually we think only of the moving part.

Much work was done during the war on many aspects of motor learning, especially those important to the operation of aircraft. This material, which is gradually being assimilated in the literature, is full of suggestive findings. Bartlett has discussed the fact that key cues only rise to awareness in the execution of certain skills, and that the bulk of what is happening proceeds at levels below consciousness. He even suggests that the less we know about this background of postural adjustment and associated movement, the better. When it obtrudes in consciousness, performance deteriorates. These are new ideas, antithetic in a sense to those proposed by the neurophysiologist. Perhaps the kinesthetic acuity we should strive for is not enhanced general body awareness, but rather, a more sharply defined and specific sensitivity to what is happening in those key maneuvers upon which the success or failure of a complex movement pattern may depend.

The biomechanical approach to movement study is a vital step in any program of total understanding. It has been given more attention than the neurophysiological approach. What the normal human being does in the execution of a given skill must be dissected and analyzed in biomechanical terms. I would only remind the biophysicists that behind the angles of projection measured so meticulously are patterns of innervation and servomechanisms of the greatest interest. Behind those variations in the velocity of a moving part are living muscles. It is the contraction of muscles which develops the power to move the parts, and the functional capacity of muscles may be augmented by overload training. We must look behind the physical findings and ferret out the mechanisms which produce them. One side of the story without cognizance of the other gives a distorted picture, at least to the unwary and inexperienced observer.

Some of the references in the bibliography appended are easy reading. Others stretch the limits of the understanding of the trained and disciplined mind. In physical medicine we say a disabled man must rehabilitate himself. The student of motor learning must likewise seek out for himself those parts of the recorded history of this subject which are meaningful to him. I have stressed what seems important only to me, as of this moment, and that has been colored by a particular experience. Many topics remain yet to be studied.

Bibliography

Andrew, B. L.: "The sensory innervation of the medial ligament of the knee joint," *J. Physiol.*, 123:241-250, February, 1954.

Barker, D.: "The innervation of the muscle-spindle," *Quart. J. Microscopical Science,* 89:143-186, June, 1948.

Bartlett, F. C.: "The measurement of human skill," *Brit. Med. J.*, 1:835-838, June 14, 1947; 877-880, June 21, 1947.

Boyd, I. A.: "The histological structure of the receptors in the knee-joint of the cat correlated with their physiological response," *J. Physiol.*, 124:476-488, June, 1954.

Boyd, I. A., and T. D. M. Roberts: "Proprioceptive discharges from stretch-receptors in the knee-joint of the cat," *J. Physiol.*, 122:38-58, July, 1953.

Coghill, G. E.: *ANATOMY AND THE PROBLEM OF BEHAVIOUR,* University Press, Cambridge, 1929.

Coghill, G. E.: "The early development of behavior in Amblystoma and in man," *Arch. Neurol. Psychiat.*, 21:989-1009, May, 1929.

Coghill, G. E.: "The neuro-embryologic study of behavior: principles, perspective and aim," *Science,* 78:131-138, Aug. 18, 1933.

Darcus, H. D.: "Discussion on an evaluation of the methods of increasing muscle strength," *Proc. Roy. Soc. Med.*, 49:999-1008, December, 1956.

Denny-Brown, D.: "Interpretation of the electromyogram," *Arch. Neurol. Psychiat.*, 61:99-128, February, 1949.

Eccles, John Carew: *THE NEUROPHYSIOLOGICAL BASIS OF MIND,* The Clarendon Press, Oxford, 1953.

Eccles, John Carew: *THE PHYSIOLOGY OF NERVE CELLS*, The Johns Hopkins Press, Baltimore, 1957.

Eldred, E., R. Granit, and P. A. Merton: "Supraspinal control of the muscle spindles and its significance," *J. Physiol.*, 122:498-523, December, 1953.

Gardner, Ernest: "Physiology of moveable joints," *Physiol. Rev.*, 30:127-176, April, 1950.

Gellhorn, Ernst: "Patterns of muscular activity in man", *Arch. Phys. Med.*, 28: 568-574, September, 1947.

Gellhorn, Ernst: "The influence of alterations in posture of the limbs on cortically induced movements," *Brain*, 71:26-33, March, 1948.

Gellhorn, E.: "Proprioception and the motor cortex," *Brain*, 72:35-62, March, 1949.

Gellhorn, Ernst: *PHYSIOLOGICAL FOUNDATIONS OF NEUROLOGY AND PSYCHIATRY*, The University of Minnesota Press, Minneapolis, 1953.

Gellhorn, E., and J. Hyde: "Influence of proprioception on map of cortical responses," *J. Physiol.*, 122:371-385, November, 1953.

Gooddy, William: "Sensation and volition," *Brain*, 72:312-339, September, 1949.

Granit, R., and B. A. Kaada: "Influence of stimulation of central nervous structures on muscle spindles in cat," *Acta Physiol., Scand.*, 27:130-160, 1952.

Granit, Ragnar: *RECEPTORS AND SENSORY PERCEPTION*, Yale University Press, New Haven, 1955.

Granit, Ragnar, B. Holmgren, and P. A. Merton: "The two routes for excitation of muscle and their subservience to the cerebellum," *J. Physiol.*, 130:213-224, October, 1955.

Hagbarth, K. E.: "Excitatory and inhibitory skin areas for flexor and extensor motoneurones," *Acta Physiol. Scand.*, 26: Suppl. 94, 1952.

Hellebrandt, F. A., Annie M. Parrish, and Sara Jane Houtz: "Cross education, the influence of unilateral exercise on the contralateral limb," *Arch. Physical Med.*, 28:76-85, February, 1947.

Hellebrandt, F. A., Sara Jane Houtz, and A. Mary Krikorian: "Influence of bi-manual exercise on unilateral work capacity," *J. Applied Physiol.*, 2:446-452, February, 1950.

Hellebrandt, F. A.: "Cross education, ipsilateral and contralateral effects of uni-manual training," *J. Applied Physiol.*, 4:136-144, August, 1951.

Hellebrandt, F. A., Sara Jane Houtz, and Robert N. Eubank: "Influence of alternate and reciprocal exercise on work capacity," *Arch. Physical Med.*, 32:766-776, December, 1951.

Hellebrandt, F. A., Sara Jane Houtz, Donald E. Hockman, and Miriam J. Partridge: "Physiological effects of simultaneous static and dynamic exercise," *Am. J. Physical Med.*, 35:106-117, April, 1956.

Hellebrandt, F. A., Sara Jane Houtz, Miriam J. Partridge, and C. Etta Walters: "Tonic neck reflexes in exercise of stress in man," *Am. J. Physical Med.*, 35: 144-159, June, 1956.

Herrick, C. Judson: *GEORGE ELLETT COGHILL*, The University of Chicago Press, Chicago, 1949.

Nielsen, J. M.: "Ideational motor plan. Role of the parieto-occipital region in planned acts," *J. Nervous Mental Disease*, 108:361-366, November, 1948.

Partridge, Miriam J.: "Electromyographic demonstration of facilitation," *Phys. Therapy Rev.*, 34:227-233, May, 1954.

Penfield, Wilder: "Mechanisms of voluntary movement," *Brain*, 77:1-17 March, 1954.

Seyffarth, H.: "The behavior of motor units in voluntary contraction," Skrifter Norske Videnskaps-Akademi, Oslo, Matematisk-Naturvid. Klasse, 5:1-63, 1940.

Sherrington, Sir Charles: *THE INTEGRATIVE ACTION OF THE NERVOUS SYSTEM*, Second edition, Yale University Press, New Haven, 1947.

Sperry, R. W.: "Neurology and the mind-brain problem," *Am. Scientist*, 40:291-312, April, 1952.

Tiegs, O. W.: "Innervation of voluntary muscle," *Physiol. Rev.*, 33:90-144, January, 1953.

Twitchell, Thomas Evans: "Sensory factors in purposive movement," *J. Neuro-physiol.*, 17:239-252, May, 1954.

Walshe, F. M. R.: *CRITICAL STUDIES IN NEUROLOGY,* The Williams and Wilkins Company, Baltimore, 1948.

Weiss, Paul: "Self-differentiation of the basic patterns of coordination," *Comp. Psychol. Monographs,* Vol. 17, Number 4, Serial Number 88, September, 1941.

Weiss, Paul: *GENETIC NEUROLOGY,* The University of Chicago Press, Chicago, 1950.

Weiss, Paul: "Nervous System (Neurogenesis)," Chap. I, Sec. VII, Willier, Benjamin H., Paul A. Weiss, and Viktor Hamburger: *ANALYSIS OF DEVELOPMENT,* W. B. Saunders Company, Philadelphia, 1955.

Welford, A. T.: *SKILLS AND AGE,* Oxford University Press, London, 1951.

Windle, William Frederick: *PHYSIOLOGY OF THE FETUS,* W. B. Saunders Company, Philadelphia, 1940.

Windle, William F.: "Genesis of somatic motor function in mammalian embryos: A synthesizing article," *Physiol. Zool.,* 17:247-260, July, 1944.

Neural Basis of Memory*

J. ANTHONY DEUTSCH

REVIEWS of literature are interesting and informative, but the development and formulation of a particular theory makes for provocative reading. The student of learning theory can appraise and evaluate the criteria used for its basis as well as its potential significance in contributing to existing knowledge, furthering research, modifying existing theories, and changing instructional methodologies. Deutsch presents data that support the learning theory of a physical change in a synapse which increases transmission efficiency. Working with drugs and rats, the author reaches some conclusions and raises further questions. Various drugs are effectively used to determine the role of the synapse in learning and memory.

At present the physiological basis of learning is unknown. We know that time alters the stability of memory, and this alteration presumably reflects in some way the underlying physical process. Many theories have been advanced to explain these changes, but only recently have discoveries been made that permit us to test the validity of the theories.

An old but still influential theory, put forward by an Italian physiologist, E. Tanzi in 1893, postulates that the passage of nerve impulses causes some kind of physical change in the connections between nerve cells. The connections between the nerve cells, or neurons, are called synapses. While it is possible to show in the laboratory that the *functioning* of synapses can be affected by excessive use or disuse, these experiments do not show that changes occur in actual *learning*. A different kind of evidence is needed to show this, and I shall describe how such evidence has been obtained in some of my recent research.

We know that whatever changes produce the physical basis of memory, at

* Reprinted from PSYCHOLOGY TODAY MAGAZINE, May, 1968. Copyright © Communications/Research/Machines, Inc.

least some of them must occur relatively slowly. Remarkable evidence for this comes from everyday accidents. For example, a person who has struck his head violently in an automobile accident may suffer from retrograde amnesia. He may be unable to remember what happened during the week before the accident, but he is able to remember what happened two weeks, two months or two years before. The gap in memory covers a continuous stretch of time, with one end anchored to the time of the accident. As memories return, those most distant in time always return first.

This indicates that as a memory gets older it becomes more difficult to dislodge. So the physical change that underlies memory must alter slowly with time. If this change is an alteration in the *sensitivity* of a synapse, then it should be possible to show this by the use of drugs.

To understand how this can be done, we must briefly sketch what happens at a synapse when a message is transmitted from one nerve cell to another. The synapse is a microscopic gap (a few hundred angstroms, or less than a millionth of an inch) between adjacent neurons. Inside the neuron itself, a message is transmitted as an electrical impulse or disturbance. When this traveling electrical impulse reaches the synaptic region, it triggers the release of a chemical substance from vesicles at the end of the nerve cell. This chemical transmitter then travels across the narrow synaptic cleft to the receiving nerve cell. The chemical transmitter fits into certain sites on the second nerve cell as a key fits into a lock, mainly because the transmitter molecules have a specific size and shape.

The transmitter, it is believed, depolarizes the membrane of the receptor cell and initiates a new electrical impulse in the second neuron. The electrical impulse then travels along the neuron to the next synapse, triggering the release of a chemical transmitter, and so on.

There are many different types of synapses in the brain, and they may use different kinds of transmitters, such as acetylcholine or norepinephrine (a chemical related to adrenalin). One of the best understood synapses uses acetylcholine (ACh) as the transmitter. ACh is present in relatively high concentration throughout the central nervous system. One of the strange things about this transmitter is that when too much of it accumulates on the synaptic part of the receptor cell, the transfer of messages across that synapse is blocked. To prevent a breakdown in transmission across the synapse, ACh must be inactivated as soon as it has performed its function. This is accomplished by an enzyme called acetylcholinesterase (AChE), which rapidly destroys ACh after it has been ejected.

There are two classes of drugs that interfere with synaptic activity, each in a distinctive way. One kind acts directly on the receptor nerve cells, while the other interferes with the destruction of the transmitter. The first kind is called the anticholinergic drugs, or blocking agents. These drugs fit into the same sites on the receptor nerve cells as does ACh. However, although these blocking agents fit into the same sites, they do not initiate an electrical impulse in the second neuron. In addition, these blocking agents are not rapidly destroyed by the enzyme AChE. This means that the drugs can put parts of receptor cells out of action. The larger the dose of a blocking agent, the more sites are inactivated. The effect of the blocking agent, then, is to subtract from the effectiveness of the transmitter ACh.

A number of blocking agents are found in plants. Scopolamine is found in henbane, whose effects were known to the ancient Greeks. In high doses, scopolamine is a nerve poison: it completely stops transmission across synapses. In lower doses it simply reduces the amount of transmission and can be used medicinally to relieve such disorders as stomach cramps. Atropine, another blocking agent, is found in the deadly nightshade or belladonna plant. In low doses, it is used to relieve muscular spasms and to dilate the pupil of the eye.

Drugs of the second kind that affect transmission across the synapse are the anticholinesterases, or inhibitors of the enzyme AChE. Since the function of AChE is to destroy the transmitter chemical ACh, inactivation of AChE will lead to an accumulation of ACh at the receiving sites of the synapse. As indicated previously, accumulation of too much transmitter at the receptor will block the synapse.

Another interesting effect of inhibitor drugs occurs when a neuron ejects too little transmitter to trigger an electrical impulse in the receptor cell. With the addition of the enzyme inhibitor, the transmitter is destroyed less rapidly and the amount of transmitter at the receptor cell builds up until it triggers an electrical impulse in that nerve cell.

This boosting effect is used in the medical treatment of myasthenia gravis, a disorder marked by progressive weakening of the muscles. A patient with this disorder may be unable to move, even though there is nothing physically wrong with his nerves or his muscles. The muscular weakness is caused by the release of too little ACh at the junction between nerve endings and muscles. By inactivating the enzyme that destroys the transmitter, enough of the transmitter can build up at the receptor sites to initiate muscle contraction, and paralysis disappears. However, the dose of the inhibitor drug is critical. If the dose is too large, too much of the transmitter will pile up at the receptor sites, causing a block, and paralysis will return.

We therefore have drugs that enable us to track changes in the efficiency of transmission across a synapse. Blocking agents, or anticholinergics, can completely stop transmission when relatively small amounts of transmitter are released. Yet this same dose of a blocking agent should not interfere with transmission when the amount of transmitter is high. On the other hand, addition of drugs that inhibit the action of the enzyme AChE, which destroys the transmitter, should not hinder transmission when levels of the transmitter are low. In fact, enzyme inhibitors may even improve transmission in this situation. But when the level of transmitter is high, the same dose of inhibitor should block transmission because of the excessive build-up of transmitter at the receptor sites.

Another way of looking at this is to suppose that learning causes changes in the *sensitivity* of the receptor cell rather than changes in the amount of transmitter released. In some respects, this is a more attractive explanation, but we will follow both interpretations in our guided tour of some of my laboratory experiments to discover the physical basis of learning.

In one set of experiments, I studied the effect of drugs on learning in rats: a rat is placed in a maze on a mildly electrified grid. To escape from the electrical shock, the rat must choose whether to run into a lit alley or into a dark alley. If it runs into the lit alley it escapes the shock. If it runs into the dark alley, the shock continues. It takes about 30 trials for a rat to learn to choose the lit alley. In these studies, learning is defined as the ability to make 10 correct decisions in a row.

After a number of rats have passed the learning test, they are put back into their cages. The rats are divided into several groups. Some are injected with a drug half an hour after the learning trials, others after one day, three days, seven days, or 14 days. A control group does not receive any drugs. Although the rats receive their drug treatment at various times after learning, they all are tested at the same time interval after the drug injection.

It should be noted that the drug doses used in the experiments cause no apparent change in the rats' ability to learn. Groups of rats injected with the drug will later perform as well as untreated rats in learning tests.

When rats are injected with an inhibitor drug, such as diisopropyl fluoro-phosphate (DFP) or physostigmine, which inactivates the AChE enzyme that destroys the ACh transmitter in synapses, some interesting changes in memory occur.

Rats injected with the drug half an hour after the learning trials forget only a little. They take more trials to relearn the maze than rats from the control group, but require far fewer trials to learn than rats that have never been trained.

When rats are injected with the inhibitor drug one and three days after training, they show perfect retention of learning. But rats treated with the drug seven and 14 days after training lose their memory of the training almost completely. A control group of rats not drug injected still remembers to choose the lit alley after seven or 14 days.

We might conclude that the inhibitor drug causes premature forgetting. However, this is too hasty a conclusion. If we retest undrugged rats four weeks after they have learned to run the maze, we find that they have forgotten which path to take. But if we then inject them with an inhibitor drug in the same dose as previously caused forgetting, the rats regain their memory almost perfectly. In this case, the injected drug could be called a "memory improver."

We know that the injected drug prevents the enzyme AChE in the synapse from destroying the chemical transmitter after it has been ejected. From these experiments, we can draw the following conclusions. After one day, the amount of transmitter released in the synapse is relatively small (or we could say that the sensitivity of the receptor cell is low). At three days, the amount is still low, since injection of an enzyme inhibitor does not cause a pile-up of enough transmitter at the receptor sites to block the synapse. But at seven days, the amount of transmitter (or sensitivity of the receptor) rises and remains high even at 14 days. Injection of the drug causes a pile-up of trans-mitter at the receptor and blocks the synapse. After four weeks, the level of transmitter (or sensitivity of the receptor) has dropped to such a low point that the rat has forgotten the learned task. Injection of the drug, however, enables the small amount of transmitter still present to become effective and the rat regains its memory.

These conclusions can be cross-checked by repeating the experiments, this time with blocking agents—drugs that fit into the same sites on the receptor cell as the ACh transmitter. A blocking agent such as scopolamine should abolish memory where we have concluded that synaptic transmission is weak, and leave recall unaffected in cases where we suppose that transmission is high.

In repeating the experiment with scopolamine, we found that memory is unaffected by a drug injection half an hour after learning. But a drug injection one or three days later completely knocks out memory of what was learned. This is what we would predict on the basis of our previous conclusion, that the synaptic transmission level is low at one or three days after learning. At seven and 14 days, injection of scopolamine does not affect memory. This also confirms our interpretation that transmission is strong at seven and 14 days.

We can check our conclusion that synaptic transmission gradually improves during the week after learning without the use of drugs. Rats are given only a small number of learning trials in a maze so that correct choices are only partially learned. The rats are divided into several groups. Each group is given a different waiting period—one day, three days, five days, etc.—before it is brought back to the maze. In this session, rats are allowed to learn the task completely, and we count the number of trials they need to do so. We find, interestingly enough, that the rats who wait seven days before the second session learn with a much smaller number of trials than rats who are tested after one day or three days. This suggests that there is spontaneous strengthening of memory in rats a week after learning.

If our theory is right, one of the things we can expect is that drug-induced disappearance of memory will be temporary. The action of the drug on the synapse should last only as long as the drug is present. And a number of experiments do show that memory returns when the effect of the drug wears off. There is also evidence that the inhibitor drugs, or anticholinesterases, do not completely inactivate the enzyme AChE in the dose strengths used in our experiments. It is likely that only a portion of the enzyme is inactivated and that the destruction of ACh transmitter is not halted but simply slowed down. If this is so, then the spacing of trials after the injection of the inhibitor should affect the degree of amnesia. If the trials are spaced farther apart, more transmitter should be destroyed between trials. Since too much transmitter at the receptor causes the block in the synapse, increased spacing of a well-learned task should improve recall. And, indeed, it turns out that this is what happens. In tests of drug-injected rats seven days after the learning session, when the trials are spaced 25 seconds apart, the rats exhibit almost amnesia. When the trials are set 50 seconds apart, the rats remember their learned task.

From the results of our experiments, it looks as if learning changes a synapse's ability to transmit messages. Our experiments consisted of a large number of trials, and each learning trial could have affected a different set of synapses. On the other hand, each trial could have affected the same set of synapses over and over again. We cannot observe changes in the synapses directly, even with an electron microscope. A typical synapse may measure as little as one millionth of an inch in size. There are millions of neurons in the nervous system and each neuron may have thousands of synapses on it. In the synaptic region, the neurons are intricately intertwined, much like a mass of spaghetti. Detecting changes made by a single learning task is almost impossible. A major difficulty is finding a way to observe the same set of synapses before and after learning—a task similar to finding a needle in a haystack, except that in this case we are trying to find a specific piece of hay.

Fortunately, we can again use drugs to determine whether learning affects the same set of synapses or a different set of synapses on each learning trial. If each trial increases the transmission across the same set of synapses, then the larger the number of learning trials (the more learned the habit), the greater the susceptibility of that learning to inhibitor blocking. Also, if the same set of synapses is affected by learning, then a small number of learning trials should produce weak transmissions and therefore memory will improve with injection of the inhibitor drugs.

On the other hand, if each learning trial simply changes another set of synapses until enough synapses are altered to ensure correct performance, then the number of trials should not alter the susceptibility of the learned habit to blocking by an inhibitor drug. Each synapse will be altered in an all-or-nothing fashion, and each should be equally susceptible to the drug.

To test these two ideas, we trained three groups of rats. One group received 30 training trials, the second 70 trials, and the third 110 trials. The rats with only 30 trials could be considered undertrained. In their last 10 trials, they chose the correct path only two out of three times. Five days later, half of the rats in each group were given a dose of diisopropyl fluorophosphate, a drug that inhibits the AChE enzyme. The undertrained group injected with the drug performed very much better than their undertrained counterparts who were not given the drug. In their first 10 trials, the drug-treated rats performed almost perfectly. Drugged and undrugged rats from the group with 70 trials performed identically. Overtrained rats (110 trials) injected with the drug, however, performed much worse than their undrugged counterparts, and even worse than the undertrained rats that had been drugged.

In other words, a well-learned habit is blocked by injection of this drug, whereas recall of a poorly learned habit is improved. This indicates that the same set of synapses is stimulated more and more with each learning trial.

To show that the results had nothing to do with the *number* of trials but rather were concerned with the degree of learning, we performed another experiment in which the number of learning trials was the same for all rats. This was done by taking advantage of the rat's propensity to learn more quickly when the light in the safe alley of the maze is very bright. Groups of rats were given the same number of trials, but variations in the brightness of the light in the safe alley led to very different rates of learning. The group with a dim light had learned very little at the end of 30 trials, while a group with a very bright light had learned to make the right choice almost every time. Injection of the inhibitor drug produced the same results: the group with the well-learned habit forgot, the group with the poorly-learned habit performed better.

This seems to confirm that the same set of synapses is affected as learning of the same task progresses. The same synapses are stimulated more and more with each trial. As a result of this stimulation, the synapse becomes gradually more efficient at passing messages. This increase in efficiency occurs without any apparent need for practice or repetition of the learned responses.

Our evidence supports the theory that the physical change underlying learning is the increase of transmission efficiency in a synapse. But our experiments do not provide enough information to decide whether the increased efficiency is caused by increased sensitivity in the receptor or increased amounts of transmitter in the synapse.

We can, however, set up an experiment that will identify the correct explanation. There is a class of drugs that mimics the transmitter action of acetylcholine. One of these drugs is carbachol (carbaminoylcholine), a very close chemical relative of ACh. Carbachol is strongly resistant to destruction by the AChE enzyme. When injected in low doses, carbachol acts together with ACh to excite the receptor nerve. Higher doses of carbachol will block memory. Results of research to date indicate that injections of carbachol will improve new memories but block older ones. When the amount of transmitter is small, the injected carbachol teams up with it to improve memory. When the memory is one week old, if we assume that the amount of transmitter increases, then it is hard to explain why the same dose of carbachol results in a blocked synapse. It is unlikely that the increased amount of transmitter would cause the block, because the transmitter would be destroyed at the normal rate by the AChE enzyme. A more likely explanation is that the receptor becomes more sensitive (requires less transmitter to become activated) and that the carbachol blocks synaptic transmission because it alone can now keep the sensitized receptor nerve cell depolarized, which prevents initiation of new electrical impulses in that neuron.

So, although we have good evidence that learning improves transmission across synapses that use ACh as a transmitter, the evidence that this improvement is caused by an increase in the sensitivity of the receptor is much more tentative.

These findings suggest that some human memory disorders may be due to a lowered efficiency in transmission across synapses, particularly those using ACh as the transmitter. If this proves to be the case, some memory disorders may be improved with relatively simple drugs. But in spite of the effect of our drugs on the memory of rats, we have discovered no memory pill. While one day such a drug might be developed, it is not likely to be one of those used in our research. All these drugs are potent poisons; their effects are mixed— they improve some memories while blocking others—and their effects are transitory. Seekers for a pill to end practice and study forever will have to look elsewhere.

DNA and RNA as Memory Molecules*

JOHN GAITO

HISTORICALLY, neurophysiologists and psychologists have been best known for their efforts in establishing theoretical frameworks concerned with the nature of learning. Although biochemists have entered the "game" relatively late, today they represent the most exciting research, with implications for understanding the learning process. Gaito reviews research concerning changes in DNA and RNA molecules resulting from stimulating an organism. Learning and memory may be associated with changes in molecular structure, and Gaito speculates on such possibilities. Although he does not come to any real conclusions (remember, this article was published during the earlier developments in the biochemistry of learning), his clear, concise analyses of numerous articles and his concluding remarks certainly place the research in needed perspective. Investigations since that time have attempted to resolve some of the problems raised by Gaito.

As long as man has been capable of speculating about himself and the universe, probably one of the most perplexing problems which has plagued him has been that of explaining the mechanism whereby the physical energies of the external world are transformed by the organism into representative processes to symbolize experiential events during learning. This problem has confounded philosophers and scientists for many centuries (e.g., see Boring, 1950). Even though some progress has been attained, many answers still elude the scientist.

Biological approaches which have been concerned with the problem of learning and memory have been either of a neurological or biochemical nature. Examples of the neurological approach include Lashley (1929), Köhler (1940), and Hebb (1949). The biochemical treatment is illustrated by Rosenzweig, Krech, and Bennett (1960) and Overton (1959).

This paper[1] will be concerned with another biochemical approach, but at

* From *Psychological Review*, 1963, *70*, 471-480. Reprinted with permission of the author and the American Psychological Association.

[1] Throughout this paper the following abbreviations will be used: DNA (deoxyribonucleic acid), RNA (ribonucleic acid), A (adenine), T (thymine), G (guanine), C (cytosine), U (uracil), and RNase (ribonuclease).

a more molecular level than that of Rosenzweig and his associates and Overton. Such an approach is not a novel one. A number of people have expressed the idea that memory involves a molecular change in certain tissue, e.g., Halstead (1951), Katz and Halstead (1950), Pauling and Weiss during the Hixon Symposium (Jeffress, 1951), Gerard (1960), and Schmitt (1962). In a recent book on the nature of chemical bonding, Pauling (1960) concludes with

> I believe that thinking, both conscious and unconscious, and short-term memory involve electromagnetic phenomena in the brain, interacting with the molecular (material) patterns of long-term memory, obtained from inheritance or experience . . . [p. 570].

In a previous paper (Gaito, 1961), a possible mechanism for the memory function resulting from learning was suggested. This involved a change at one or more loci in DNA, RNA, or amino acid molecules. These ideas were wholly speculative when first presented. However, some exciting research has been conducted in the last few years which is pertinent to the possible involvement of DNA or RNA in memory functions. We would like to consider these data.

Interrelationship of DNA, RNA, and Amino Acids

The interaction of DNA, RNA, and amino acids in protein synthesis has been described frequently (Hurwitz & Furth, 1962; Ochoa, 1962; Rich, 1962). The basic information (genetic code) in DNA is transmitted to RNA in the nucleus. The two-stranded DNA molecule divides; one of these strands then forms a hybrid two-stranded molecule with messenger RNA which forms as a complement of DNA. Thus if the one strand of DNA has the linear sequence ATTGC . . ., messenger RNA would consist of UAACG. . . .

Messenger RNA supervises the joining of amino acids to form proteins in or on the ribosomes of the cytoplasm. The transfer of RNA from nucleus to cytoplasm can be demonstrated by radiographic techniques. In the synthesis of protein, an RNA of 50 to 100 base units (soluble or transfer RNA) gathers an amino acid and attaches itself to its appropriate site on messenger RNA. There are supposed to be different soluble RNA's for each amino acid. Each soluble RNA terminates in the sequence CCA at one end. Thus many soluble RNA's with their associated amino acids line up on messenger RNA and the amino acids become attached to form the specified protein.

A coding procedure of a minimum of three nucleotides for each amino acid has been considered to be most plausible (Crick, 1962; Crick, Barnett, Brenner, & Watts-Tobin, 1961; Rich, 1962). Crick (1962) suggested that:

> The message is read in nonoverlapping groups from a fixed point . . . . in groups of a fixed size that is probably three, although multiples of three are not completely ruled out . . . . There is very little nonsense in the code. Most triplets appear to allow the gene to function and therefore probably represent an amino acid. Thus in general more than one triplet will stand for each amino acid [p. 74].

Matthaei, Jones, Martin, and Nirenberg (1962) have developed tentative codes for most of the 20 amino acids by using synthetic polyribonucleotides to synthesize protein. For example, UUU represents phenylalanine; two C's and one U, proline; etc. The code is degenerate, i.e., more than one triplet can code a single amino acid. For example, two U's and a C or a G is considered the code for leucine.

Even though the trinucleotide coding is most accepted, other coding procedures have been suggested. Roberts (1962) indicated that a doublet code would eliminate degeneracy aspects. In this code a G with a C represents alanine; G and U, valine; etc. However, this coding procedure results in ambiguities, e.g., AA codes lysine and methionine.

An interesting "Book Model" of coding and genetic information transfer has been proposed by Platt (1962). He uses the analogy of a complex instruction manual in which "information" is linearly arranged in "words" that are "read out" sequentially in time. He relates in a clever fashion the various aspects of books and printing procedures to the DNA, RNA, and amino acid interaction.

DNA as a Potential Memory Molecule

In that it has been firmly established that the linear sequence of bases in DNA constitutes the genetic code, it is reasonable to expect that the linear sequence in neural DNA or RNA should provide an experiential or memory code. A main requirement of this expectation is that the nucleic acids need be labile because it is necessary for the molecule to be capable of being changed. However, the molecule should not be overly labile or memory would be changing drastically and make for chaotic behavior.

Of the two nucleic acids, DNA is the least labile. The average DNA content appears to be relatively stable even during marked physiological alterations of cells (Alfert, 1957). White, Handler, Smith, and Stetten (1959), after reviewing the work of a number of investigators, concluded that DNA was formed to an appreciable extent only during active mitosis by a cell.

Base analogues have been used frequently in the DNA of bacteriophages to produce base changes (Sinsheimer, 1960). For example, 5-bromouracil and 2-aminopurine are presumed to act to bring about the replacement of the A-T pairs by G-C ones, and vice versa. These agents also bring about a reversion of these changes. Freese (1961) has indicated that low pH, ethyl ethane sulfonate and other agents will cause transitions from one pair to the other.

Benzer (1961) has made a detailed examination of a small portion of the genetic map of bacteriophage T4, a portion which controls the ability of the phage to grow in *E. coli*. He indicated that A-T pairs are held much less strongly than are G-C pairs, which suggests that in mutation the A-T pairs ("hot spots") will be more subject to substitution. There are two hydrogen bonds for A-T pairs but three for G-C. He stated that A-T pairing would change to A-G and thence to G-C.

Thus DNA is a stable molecule altered only by mutagenic agents. This fact appears to obviate its acting as a memory mechanism; however, we should not discount it completely for several reasons. First, most of the DNA which has been investigated has been from nonneural tissue. It is possible that the stability of DNA in nerve cells is different than it is in other cells and neural DNA may be more conducive to modification.

Some attention has been devoted to the gross DNA content of neural tissue. One study, by Mandel, Harth, and Borkowski (1961), has indicated that the highest DNA content was in the grey and white matter of the cerebellum, and in the olfactory bulb. The lowest amounts were found in the spinal bulb, the mesencephalon, and the thalamus. Moderate amounts were in the white and grey matter of the cerebrum, the hypothalamus, the hippocampus, and the corpus striatum. The amount of DNA indicates the richness of the different areas in nuclei. Vladimirov, Barnov, Pevzner, and Tsyn-Yan (1961) reported that the amount of DNA was the same in the motor, visual, and auditory areas in Layer 2 of cat cortex. Under hypoxic conditions a significant decrease occurred in the motor and visual areas but not in the auditory area.

Other research indicates a moderate degree of lability in neural DNA.

Koenig (1958), using radioactivity tracing techniques, obtained results which suggested greater DNA lability in the central nervous system tissue and related tissue than has generally been assumed. The results indicated a slow, but definite, turnover of DNA in nondividing cells of the brain and the walls of cerebrospinal blood vessels.

Another aspect which obviates excluding DNA as a potential memory mechanism is that several types of DNA have been reported. Swift (1962) concluded from his studies on DNA in species of flies that there are two types of DNA: one which is constant from cell to cell and another varying in particular cell types at particular stages of ontogeny. Likewise, Bendich, Russell, and Brown (1953) found two types of DNA in growing rat tissue. Thus, the varying DNA might be involved in memory functions.

In any event, the stability of the DNA molecule does not necessarily preclude its operating as a source for memory changes. In fact its stability would appear to be an argument in its favor. The experiential code requires great stability. If memory were maintained by molecules which were too labile, it would change rapidly, causing chaotic behavior.

RNA as a Potential Memory Molecule

Information concerning the possibility of RNA playing a role in memory appears to be more encouraging to some individuals because of its great lability. RNA varies from cell to cell and is very active metabolically (Ris, 1957). Sinsheimer (1960) reported that the amount of RNA in the salivary gland of Drosophilia drops rapidly during the early stage of differentiation whereas the amount of DNA increases, and changes in the overall nucleotide composition of RNA of Chlorella cells occur during starvation. LeBaron (1959) indicated that other cytochemical research provides evidence for increased activity of cellular RNA and proteins. He concluded that

> There is certainly ample evidence for the active turnover of various lipide, protein and nucleic acid structural constituents, and the possibility exists that there is some alteration of this turnover on stimulation [p. 597].

Nitrous acid has been used as a mutagen with tobacco mosaic virus RNA to bring about base changes.[2] This reagent substitutes hydroxyl groups (OH) for amino groups (NH_2). Strauss (1960) has indicated that nitrous acid reacts with nucleic acids containing adenine, guanine, and cytosine and converts them to the corresponding hydroxyl compounds, hypoxanthine, xanthine, and uracil. These results imply that the reaction of nitrous acid with nucleic acids produces base analogues which result in mutation upon the duplication of genetic material. Tsugita and Fraenkel-Conrat (1960) have shown that nitrous acid alters the composition of RNA of tobacco mosaic virus and that the resulting protein of the mutant differed from the parent strain, with three amino acids being replaced by three others (proline, aspartic acid, and threonine by leucine, alanine, and serine).

The RNA content of brain tissue has been studied by Mandel and his associates (1961). They reported that the highest RNA content was in the olfactory bulb, the grey matter of the brain cortex, and the cerebellum, the hypothalamus, and the hippocampus. Lower amounts were found in the corpus striatum, the thalamus, and the white matter of the cerebrum and the cerebellum. The lowest figures occurred in the mesencephalon and the spinal bulb. The greatest RNA turnover was found in the olfactory bulb, the hypothalamus, and the grey matter of the brain cortex and the hippocampus.

---

[2] In some organisms, e.g., tobacco mosaic virus, polio virus, and influenza virus, no DNA is present. In this case RNA appears to be the hereditary material.

More pertinent to the relationship between RNA and memory is the work of Hydén and a number of other investigators. Hydén (1959) has demonstrated that RNA is produced in the nerve cells at a rate which follows neuronal activity. He believed that the nerve cell fulfills its function under a steady and rapidly changing production of proteins, with the RNA as an activator and governing molecule. He hypothesized that memory involves a change in the sequence of bases in the RNA molecule; this change occurs when one or more bases are exchanged with the surrounding cytoplasmic materials. Hydén reported that individuals with certain psychic disorders have smaller amounts of RNA and proteins in ganglion cells of the central nervous system than do normal individuals (cited by Davidson, 1960). Administration of malononitrile to these individuals increased the content of these substances. Egyhazi and Hydén (1961) indicated that the malononitrile action was due to the formation of a dimer of malononitrile, tricyano-amino-propene. They reported that small amounts of this latter compound caused a remarkable increase in the amounts of proteins and RNA in the cell and modified the base composition of the RNA with guanine increasing by almost 300%.

Hydén (1961) reported that the RNA content of the nerve cell ranks with the highest of all cells in the body. He showed that in man the RNA content of the motor nerve cells in the spinal cord increases from the third year of life to age 40, remains constant to about 60, and then declines rapidly thereafter. He found that if an animal is deprived of stimulation in one of the sensory systems, e.g., in vision or hearing, the neurons in that system do not develop biochemically. The structure appeared normal but the nerve cell was impoverished in both RNA and proteins.

Riesen (1958), in discussing his work on light deprivation, referred to Brattgard's findings that the content of RNA and proteins decreases in retinal ganglion cells with prolonged light deprivation. He thought that RNA and protein were so highly susceptible to recent prior stimulation as to obviate their being considered as a mechanism for durable memory. Instead he reasoned that they might be important for immediate memory. Pertinent to this thought is the work of Geiger, Yamasoki, and Lyons (1956). These individuals stimulated the brain cortex of cats and found a change of RNA in the stimulated areas which was reversible in minutes.

Likewise, Morrell (1961) has shown gross changes in RNA of nerve cells in a cellular learning-like situation. He stimulated a portion of the cortex with alumina cream. The corresponding tissue of the opposite hemisphere showed activity during this stimulation. At first the activity in the opposite hemisphere appeared only when the stimulated cortex was active. Soon the tissue in the nonstimulated area showed excitation spontaneously even when it was isolated from the stimulated hemisphere by cutting its connections. Biochemical analysis of the neurons in the isolated tissue showed a change in the RNA content.

The above results have been pertinent to sensory stimulation experiments. However, several experiments have been concerned with memory functions. Indirect support for the RNA modification hypothesis is provided by the results of Cameron and Solyom (1961) and Cameron, Solyom, Sved, and Wainrib (1962).[3] They found that administration of RNA (but not DNA)

[3] Unpublished manuscript, 1962, entitled "Effects of Intravenous Administration of Ribonucleic Acid upon Failure of Memory for Recent Events in Presenile and Aged Individuals" by D. E. Cameron, L. Solyom, S. Sved, and B. Wainrib. Obtainable at Royal Victoria Hospital, Montreal, Canada.

to individuals with presenile, arteriosclerotic, and senile syndromes (with some degree of memory impairment) brought about memory improvement. These changes involved almost total retention in some cases. When the RNA was discontinued later, memory relapses occurred. One might possibly explain these results as not involving memory per se but as due to the supplying of nutritional material which has decreased in amount with increased age (see Hydén, 1959).

Kreps has also reported an altered RNA turnover on conditioning (cited by Gerard, 1960).

An interesting experiment by Corning and John (1961) is also pertinent. Using a classical conditioning procedure, pairing light with shock, they conditioned a number of flatworms and then transected them into head and tail sections. Previous experimentation had indicated that heads would regenerate new tails, tails would regenerate new heads, and both would retain some "memory" of the avoidance situation. Corning and John thought that RNA might play a role in the transmission of an acquired structural configuration from the trained to the regenerating tissues. Thus they reasoned that if the trained portions were regenerated in the presence of RNase, the enzyme would affect the altered RNA structure, producing some animals with a naive head (regenerated portion) and trained tails and others with trained heads and naive tails (regenerate). They stated that the head region would probably be dominant and thus the trained head animals should show more retention. Their results indicated that heads regenerated in RNase retained the memory as well as did head and tail sections regenerating in pond water. However, the tails regenerating in RNase performed randomly. The authors suggested that the RNase did not affect intact tissue and maintained that the results are compatible with the assumption that RNA is a memory mechanism.

The idea that changes in the linear sequence of bases in RNA constitute the experiential code has been offered independently by a number of individuals. However, Dingman and Sporn (1961) suggested that changes in the helical structure and overall configuration, as well as sequence changes, could be the basis for memory. They performed two experiments with radioactive 8-azaguanine injections in rats which were pertinent to the RNA hypothesis. 8-Azaguanine was used as an inhibitor of RNA because this base analogue had been shown to be an inhibitor of enzyme synthesis in bacteria. In both experiments paper chromatographic procedures indicated that the base analogue had been incorporated into the RNA of the brain. In neither experiment was there any significant difference between experimental and control animals in average time to run the maze, suggesting that 8-azaguanine had no adverse effect on the motor ability of the animals. However, in one experiment the experimental animals had a significantly greater mean number of errors than did the controls on all 15 trials in the learning of a maze. In another experiment concerned with retention of a maze pattern (tested by a single trial after learning a maze), experimental animals did not differ significantly from control animals. The experimental animals had a greater mean number of errors than did the control animals. There were only eight animals used in each group (as compared with 14 and 15 in the learning experiment); thus it is possible that if n had been larger in the retention experiment, the results would have indicated that 8-azaguanine adversely affects both learning and retention of maze patterns in rats.

Based on their results Dingman and Sporn maintained that RNA may be directly involved in learning but not in retention. However, they admitted that their results did not necessarily indicate that RNA metabolism was intimately linked with the formation of memory traces in the brain because 8-azaguanine might have interfered with metabolic processes which affected RNA indirectly.

Most of the above studies in which RNA changes were reported do not exclude the possibility that the basic changes were effected in DNA which then brought about changes in RNA. However, the results of Cameron and his associates[4] and of Corning and John (1961) appear to argue against the involvement of DNA in memory. Yet, as indicated above, the Cameron work may be more relevant to nutritional needs than to memory. The ingested RNA would be degraded into the constituents (bases, sugars, and phosphates) by enzymatic action before incorporation into individual cells. These portions might increase the pool from which RNA constituents are drawn and, thereby, tend to improve the overall condition of older individuals who have less RNA available (Hydén, 1961). Information relative to this possibility might be obtained by using both young and aged subjects (some having memory deficits whereas others would have no memory impairment) and experimental tasks varying in the degree of memory involvement.

Furthermore, there are possible methodological deficiencies in these studies. In the Cameron studies there is no indication that measures were taken to prevent bias from affecting the improvement ratings of each of the subjects in all the experiments. The ratings were based on performance on several tasks, supplemented by the patient and his relatives. As is well known, results of drug studies such as this can be greatly affected by the attitudes and expectations of the patient and hospital personnel if double blind procedures are not employed. However, in one of the two experiments reported by Cameron and Solyom (1961), double blind procedures were used and some improvement was reported. On one objective test in this experiment, the Wechsler Memory Test, scores of the Placebo and RNA groups did not differ significantly.

In the Corning and John experiment a qualitative analysis of the data suggests that RNase may have sensitized the planaria such that one would expect that head animals reared in RNase would show a greater number of responses to light than would tail animals reared in this enzyme. One would expect such results because the head region contains the light receptors and the head portion of the head animals would be in the RNase for the total regeneration period whereas the head region of the tail animals would be exposed to the influence of the RNase only during the latter portion of the period.

Thus, the hypothesis that alterations occur in RNA molecules during learning situations may appear to have a brighter future than the same conjecture relative to the DNA molecule. However, even though the experimental results tend not to negate the involvement of RNA in memory, its extreme metabolic lability raises some doubt as to how stable memory can be handled by an overly reactive molecule. Thus Riesen's suggestion that RNA subserves an immediate memory function may be entirely appropriate and require that another molecular mechanism be postulated for maintaining permanent memory.

An important problem arises in regard to the above studies on RNA. These studies have been concerned with total RNA. Such RNA is a combination of a number of RNA's in the cell. There is a chromosomal RNA, two RNA fractions in the nucleolus (one of which is messenger RNA), nucleoplasmic RNA, and soluble and ribosomal RNA in the cytoplasm. Thus there are at least six RNA fractions, one of which may be a memory molecule. Assuming that one is important in memory functions, information relative to total RNA

[4] See footnote 3.

is worthless in that it confounds irrelevant and relevant RNA. The important question is, "Which RNA is memory RNA?" Messenger RNA might appear to be a suitable candidate for this role; however, some individuals believe that messenger RNA is too labile. In one of his recent publications, Hydén has suggested chromosomal RNA (Hydén & Egyhazi, 1962).

Investigators are just beginning to consider the different RNA fractions. The content of cytoplasmic RNA of Layer 2 in cat cortex was higher in the motor area than in the visual or auditory cortices (Vladimirov, et al., 1961). The amount in the auditory area was the lowest of the three. Under hypoxia significant decreases occurred in the motor and visual areas.

Hydén and Egyhazi (1962) exposed young rats to a situation in which they had to learn to balance on a wire to reach a platform where food was located. They found that the cytoplasmic RNA of Deiters cells from the vestibular nucleus did not differ from that of controls unstimulated or from functional controls who were rotated to produce vestibular stimulation. In nuclear RNA, there were significant differences in base ratios. In the experimental group there was a greater amount of A and lesser amounts of U than in the other two groups. The authors maintained that the results indicated the change of RNA bases during learning. However, the base changes appear to be related to sensory stimulation rather than to learning. The sensory-motor activity of balancing on the wire to reach the platform provides stimulation for the cells in the vestibular system in the medulla but one would expect that any changes representing the learning aspects of the activity would be found at a higher level in the brain.

This paper has been concerned with the site and mechanism of the memory trace. The problem of reactivation of this molecular trace is an important related point but is a real mystery (Schmitt, 1962). Assuming that one of the nucleic acids is a memory molecule, there is some suggestion that a protein might function as a regulator molecule, making available or unavailable the memory code. Huang and Bonner (1962) found with pea embryo chromatin that when the histone fraction of DNA was removed, the rate of RNA synthesis increased fivefold. Huang and Bonner concluded that the function of histone was to bind DNA and block the transfer of information from DNA. Such regulatory action might be relevant to the reactivation problem.

Leslie (1961) has considered histone as having other functions. He suggested that histone stabilizes RNA so as to prevent any modification of the latter; histones separated from their RNA site were presumed capable of transforming other unprotected RNA molecules of different base compositions.

These results may be relevant to memory formation also. Even though there is a tendency to relate memory to base changes in DNA or RNA, it is possible that the nucleic acids are not altered during memory events. One might suggest that during stimulation the configuration of the histones is modified so as to make available the potential inherent in the nucleic acids. This modification would alter the nucleic acid-histone complex and would represent the symbolic representation of the experimental event.

Conclusions

Based on the above discussion, what can one conclude? There are three points we believe are suggested.

1. There is no *conclusive direct evidence* to indicate that either of the nucleic acids is the memory molecule. Such suggestions have been of an inferential nature. However, in that DNA provides a genetic code via the linear sequence of bases, it is plausible to expect that DNA or RNA provides an experiential code in the same way. The results on sensory stimulation

and memory are consistent with this expectation for RNA but do not directly show the involvement of the nucleic acids in memory events.

2. The indirect evidence for RNA as the experiential code is no stronger than it is for DNA. More attention has been devoted to RNA than to DNA. This is probably due to the great stability of DNA and to the fact that it is the genetic code. Thus DNA should not be excluded as the memory molecule even though investigators prefer RNA.

3. If RNA is the memory molecule, which RNA is it? Furthermore, what is the exact mechanism? The linear sequence of purines and pyrimidines appears to be the most plausible mechanism in that these sequences provide the basis for genetic coding in DNA. However, the suggestions of Dingman and Sporn (1961) that the helical structure and overall configuration are other possible mechanisms should be seriously considered.

Thus, there is definite evidence to indicate that some gross changes in DNA and RNA can occur during stimulation. However, no one has directly detected a change of submolecular structure in either DNA or RNA such as discussed above; all the evidence for changes are of indirect nature. The hypothesizing about nucleic acids still remains in the realm of speculation. The validity of these hypotheses must await further research by biochemists, psychologists, neurophysiologists, and others of related areas.

DNA is more homogeneous than is RNA and should be easier to evaluate. We believe that a plan of research should begin with an evaluation of DNA. Such a program of research is under way at Kansas State University using the facilities of the Psychology Department and the Bacteriology Department. C. W. Dingman[5] of the National Institutes of Health is also concerned with the role of DNA (and protein complex) in memory. A number of other psychologists and biological science teams are attacking the problem of the role of RNA. Exciting research results such as presented by molecular biologists in the last decade should be provided during the next decade by psychologists and other biological scientists.

References

ALFERT, M. Some cytochemical contributions to genetic chemistry. In W. P. McElroy & B. Glass (Eds.), *The chemical basis of heredity*. Baltimore: Johns Hopkins Univer. Press, 1957.

BENDICH, A., RUSSELL, P. J., & BROWN, G. B. On the heterogeneity of the deoxyribonucleic acids. *J. biol. Chem.*, 1953, 203, 305–318.

BENZER, S. On the topography of the genetic fine structure. *Proc. Nat. Acad. Sci.*, 1961, 47, 403–415.

BORING, E. G. *A history of experimental psychology*. New York: Appleton-Century-Crofts, 1950.

CAMERON, D. E., & SOLYOM, L. Effects of ribonucleic acid on memory. *Geriatrics*, 1961, 16, 74-81.

CORNING, W. C., & JOHN, E. R. Effect of ribonuclease on retention of conditioned response in regenerated planarians. *Science*, 1961, 134, 1363–1365.

CRICK, F. H. C. The genetic code. *Scient. American*, 1962, 207, (4), 66–74.

CRICK, F. H. C., BARNETT, L., BRENNER, S., & WATTS-TOBIN, R. J. General nature of the genetic code for proteins. *Nature*, 1961, 192, 1227–1232.

DAVIDSON, J. M. *The biochemistry of the nucleic acids*. New York: Wiley, 1960.

DINGMAN, W., & SPORN, M. B. The incorporation of 8-azaguanine into rat brain RNA and its effect on maze-learning by the rat: an inquiry into the biochemical bases of memory. *J. psychiat. Res.*, 1961, 1, 1–11.

EGYHAZI, E., & HYDÉN, H. Experimentally induced changes in the base composition of the ribonucleic acids of isolated nerve cells and their oligodendroglial cells. *J. biophys. biochem. Cytol.*, 1961, 10, 403–410.

[5] C. W. Dingman, personal communication, 1962.

FREESE, A. B. Transitions and transversions induced by depurinating agents. *Proc. Nat. Acad. Sci.*, 1961, 47, 540–545.

GAITO, J. A biochemical approach to learning and memory. *Psychol. Rev.*, 1961, 68, 288–292.

GEIGER, A., YAMASOKI, S., & LYONS, R. Changes in nitrogenous components of brain produced by stimulation of short duration. *Amer. J. Physiol.*, 1956, 184, 239–243.

GERARD, R. W. Neurophysiology: an integration (molecules, neurons, and behavior). In J. Field (Ed.), *Handbook of physiology-neurophysiology*. Vol. 3. Baltimore: Williams & Wilkins, 1960.

HALSTEAD, W. C. Brain and intelligence. In L. A. Jeffress (Ed.), *Cerebral mechanisms in behavior*. New York: Wiley, 1951.

HEBB, D. O. *The organization of behavior*. New York: Wiley, 1949.

HUANG, R. C., & BONNER, J. Histone, a suppressor of chromosomal RNA synthesis. *Proc. Nat. Acad. Sci.*, 1962, 48, 1216–1222.

HURWITZ, J., & FURTH, J. J. Messenger RNA. *Scient. American*, 1962, 206 (2), 41–49.

HYDÉN, H. Biochemical changes in glial cells and nerve cells at varying activity. In, *Proceedings of the Fourth International Congress on Biochemistry: Biochemistry of the central nervous system*. Vol. 3. London: Pergamon, 1959.

HYDÉN, H. Satellite cells in the nervous system. *Scient. American*, 1961, 205 (6), 62–70.

HYDÉN, H., & EGYHAZI, E. Nuclear RNA changes of nerve cells during a learning experiment in rats. *Proc. Nat. Acad. Sci.*, 1962, 48, 1366–1373.

JEFFRESS, L. A. (Ed.) *Cerebral mechanisms in behavior*. New York: Wiley, 1951.

KATZ, J. J., & HALSTEAD, W. C. Protein organization and mental function. *Comp. psychol. Monogr.*, 1950, 20 (103), 1–38.

KOENIG, H. Uptake of adenine-8-C^{14} and orotic-6-C^{14} acid into nuclear DNA of nondividing cells in the adult feline neuraxis. *J. biophys. biochem. Cytol.*, 1958, 4, 664–666.

KÖHLER, W. *Dynamics in psychology*. New York: Liveright, 1940.

LASHLEY, K. S. *Brain mechanisms and intelligence*. Chicago: Univer. Chicago Press, 1929.

LeBARON, F. N. Neurochemistry. In J. M. Luck, F. W. Allen, & G. MacKinney (Eds.), *Annual review of biochemistry*. Palo Alto, Calif.: Annual Reviews, 1959.

LESLIE, I. Biochemistry of heredity: A general hypothesis. *Nature*, 1961, 189, 260–268.

MANDEL, P., HARTH, S., & BORKOWSKI, T. Metabolism of the nucleic acids in various zones of the brain. In S. S. Kety & J. Elkes (Eds.), *Regional neurochemistry*. New York: Pergamon, 1961.

MATTHAEI, J. H., JONES, O. W., MARTIN, R. G., & NIRENBERG, M. W. Characteristics and composition of RNA coding units. *Proc. Nat. Acad. Sci.*, 1962, 48, 666–667.

MORRELL, F. Electrophysiological contributions to the neural basis of learning. *Physiol. Rev.*, 1961, 41, 443–494.

OCHOA, S. Enzymatic mechanisms in the transmission of genetic information. In M. Kasha & B. Pullman (Eds.), *Horizons in biochemistry*. New York: Academic Press, 1962.

OVERTON, R. K. *Thought and action: A physiological approach*. New York: Random House, 1959.

PAULING, L. *The nature of the chemical bond*. Ithaca: Cornell Univer. Press, 1960.

PLATT, J. R. A "book model" of genetic information transfer in cells and tissues. In M. Kasha & B. Pullman (Eds.), *Horizons in biochemistry*. New York: Academic Press, 1962.

RICH, A. On the problems of evolution and biochemical information transfer. In M. Kasha & B. Pullman (Eds.), *Horizons in biochemistry*. New York: Academic Press, 1962.

RIESEN, A. H. Plasticity of behavior: psychological aspects. In H. F. Harlow & C. N. Woolsey (Eds.), *Biological and biochemical bases of behavior.* Madison: Univer. Wisconsin Press, 1958.

RIS, H. Chromosome structure. In W. D. McElroy & B. Glass (Eds.), *The chemical basis of heredity.* Baltimore: Johns Hopkins Univer. Press, 1957.

ROBERTS, R. B. Further implications of the doublet code. *Proc. Nat. Acad. Sci.,* 1962, 48, 1245–1250.

ROSENZWEIG, M. R., KRECH, D., & BENNETT, E. L. A search for relations between brain chemistry and behavior. *Psychol. Bull.,* 1960, 57, 476–492.

SCHMITT, F. Psychophysics considered at the molecular and submolecular levels. In M. Kasha & B. Pullman (Eds.), *Horizons in biochemistry.* New York: Academic Press, 1962.

*The Chemistry of Learning**

DAVID KRECH

IT is now evident that several chemical changes occur within the organism as learning occurs. Processes affected, experimental designs, and research findings are reported by Krech. He speculates that "in the not too distant future [education] may well be talking about enzyme-assisted instruction, protein memory consolidators, and antibiotic memory repellers." He states conclusively that "we already have available a fairly extensive class of drugs which can facilitate learning and memory in animals . . . [but] different drugs work differentially for . . . different individuals, different intellectual tasks, and different learning components." This optimism is shared by many others concerned with the learning process.

American educators now talk a great deal about the innovative hardware of education, 8 mm cartridge-loading projectors, microtransparencies, and other devices. In the not too distant future they may well be talking about enzyme-assisted instruction, protein memory consolidators, antibiotic memory repellers, and the chemistry of the brain. Although the psychologists' learning theories derived from the study of maze-running rats or target-pecking pigeons have failed to provide insights into the education of children, it is unlikely that what is now being discovered by the psychologist, chemist, and neurophysiologist about rat-brain chemistry can deviate widely from what we will eventually discover about the chemistry of the human brain.

Most adults who are not senile can repeat a series of seven numbers—8, 4, 8, 8, 3, 9, 9—immediately after the series is read. If, however, they are asked to repeat these numbers thirty minutes later, most will fail. In the first instance, we are dealing with the immediate memory span; in the second, with long-term memory. These basic behavioral observations lie behind what is called the two-stage memory storage process theory.

According to a common variant of these notions, immediately after every

* From *Saturday Review,* January 20, 1968, 48–50, *68.* Reprinted with permission of the author and publisher. Copyright 1968 Saturday Review, Inc.

learning trial—indeed, after every experience—a short-lived electrochemical process is established in the brain. This process, so goes the assumption, is the physiological mechanism which carries the short-term memory. Within a few seconds or minutes, however, this process decays and disappears; but before doing so, if all systems are go, the short-term electrochemical process triggers a second series of events in the brain. This second process is chemical in nature and involves, primarily, the production of new proteins and the induction of higher enzymatic activity levels in the brain cells. This process is more enduring and serves as the physiological substrate of our long-term memory.

It would follow that one approach to testing our theory would be to provide a subject with some experience or other, then interrupt the short-term electrochemical process immediately—before it has had an opportunity to establish the long-term process. If this were done, our subject should never develop a long-term memory for that experience.

At the Albert Einstein Medical School in New York, Dr. Murray Jarvik has devised a "step-down" procedure based on the fact that when a rat is placed on a small platform a few inches above the floor, the rat will step down onto the floor within a few seconds. The rat will do this consistently, day after day. Suppose that on one day the floor is electrified, and stepping onto it produces a painful shock. When the rat is afterward put back on the platform—even twenty-four hours later—it will not budge from the platform but will remain there until the experimenter gets tired and calls the experiment quits. The rat has thus demonstrated that he has a long-term memory for that painful experience.

If we now take another rat, but this time *interfere* with his short-term memory process *immediately after* he has stepped onto the electrified floor, the rat should show no evidence of having experienced a shock when tested the next day, since we have not given his short-term electrochemical memory process an opportunity to initiate the long-term protein-enzymatic process. To interrupt the short-term process, Jarvik passes a mild electric current across the brain of the animal. The current is not strong enough to cause irreparable harm to the brain cells, but it does result in a very high level of activation of the neurons in the brain, thus disrupting the short-term electrochemical memory process. If this treatment follows closely enough after the animal's first experience with the foot shock, and we test the rat a day later the rat acts as if there were no memory for yesterday's event; the rat jauntily and promptly steps down from the platform with no apparent expectation of shock.

When a long time-interval is interposed between the first foot shock and the electric-current (through the brain) treatment, the rat *does* remember the foot shock, and it remains on the platform when tested the next day. This, again, is what we should have expected from our theory. The short-term electrochemical process has now had time to set up the long-term chemical memory process before it was disrupted.

Some well known effects of accidental human head injury seem to parallel these findings. Injuries which produce a temporary loss of consciousness (but no permanent damage to brain tissue) can cause the patient to experience a "gap" in his memory for the events just preceding the accident. This retrograde amnesia can be understood on the assumption that the events immediately prior to the accident were still being carried by the short-term memory processes at the time of the injury, and their disruption by the injury was sufficient to prevent the induction of the long-term processes. The patient asks "Where am I?" not only because he does not recognize the hospital, but also because he cannot remember how he became injured.

Work conducted by Dr. Bernard Agranoff at the University of Michigan

Medical School supports the hypothesis that the synthesis of new brain proteins is crucial for the establishment of the long-term memory process. He argues that if we could prevent the formation of new proteins in the brain, then—although the short-term electrochemical memory process is not interfered with—the long-term memory process could never become established.

Much of Agranoff's work has been done with goldfish. The fish is placed in one end of a small rectangular tank, which is divided into two halves by a barrier which extends from the bottom to just below the surface of the water. When a light is turned on, the fish must swim across the barrier into the other side of the tank within twenty seconds—otherwise he receives an electric shock. This training is continued for several trials until the animal learns to swim quickly to the other side when the light is turned on. Most goldfish learn this shock-avoidance task quite easily and remember it for many days. Immediately before—and in some experiments, immediately after—training, Agranoff injects the antibiotic puromycin into the goldfish's brain. (Puromycin is a protein inhibitor and prevents the formation of new proteins in the brain's neurons.) After injection, Agranoff finds that the goldfish are not impaired in their acquisition of the shock-avoidance task, but, when tested a day or so later, they show almost no retention for the task.

These results mean that the short-term memory process (which helps the animal remember from one trial to the next and thus permits him to learn in the first place) is not dependent upon the formation of new proteins, but that the long-term process (which helps the animal remember from one day to the next and thus permits him to retain what he had learned) is dependent upon the production of new proteins. Again, as in the instance of Jarvik's rats, if the puromycin injection comes more than an hour after learning, it has no effect on later memory—the long-term memory process presumably has already been established and the inhibition of protein synthesis can now no longer affect memory. In this antibiotic, therefore, we have our first chemical long-term memory preventative. (Almost identical findings have been reported by other workers in other laboratories working with such animals as mice and rats, which are far removed from the goldfish.)

Thus far I have been talking about disrupting or preventing the formation of memory. Now we will accentuate the positive. Dr. James L. McGaugh of the University of California at Riverside has argued that injections of central nervous system stimulants such as strychnine, picrotoxin, or metrazol should enhance, fortify, or extend the activity of the short-term electrochemical memory processes and thus increase the probability that they will be successful in initiating long-term memory processes. From this it follows that the injection of CNS stimulants immediately before or after training should improve learning performance. That is precisely what McGaugh found—together with several additional results which have important implications for our concerns today.

In one of McGaugh's most revealing experiments, eight groups of mice from two different hereditary backgrounds were given the problem of learning a simple maze. Immediately after completing their learning trials, four groups from each strain were injected with a different dosage of metrazol—from none to five, 10, and 20 milligrams per kilogram of body weight. First, it was apparent that there are hereditary differences in learning ability—a relatively bright strain and a relatively dull one. Secondly, by properly dosing the animals with metrazol, the learning performance increased appreciably. Under the optimal dosage, the metrazol animals showed about a 40 per cent improvement in learning ability over their untreated brothers. The improvement under metrazol was so great, in fact, that the dull animals, when treated with 10 milligrams, did slightly better than their untreated but hereditarily superior colleagues.

In metrazol we not only have a chemical facilitator of learning, but one which acts as the "Great Equalizer" among hereditarily different groups. As the dosage was increased for the dull mice from none to five to 10 milligrams their performance improved. Beyond the 10-milligram point for the dull mice, however, and beyond the five-milligram point for the bright mice, increased strength of the metrazol solution resulted in a deterioration in learning. We can draw two morals from this last finding. First, the optimal dosage of chemical learning facilitators will vary greatly with the individual taking the drug (there is, in other words, an interaction between heredity and drugs); second, there is a limit to the intellectual power of even a hopped-up Southern Californian Super Mouse!

We already have available a fairly extensive class of drugs which can facilitate learning and memory in animals. A closer examination of McGaugh's results and the work of others, however, also suggests that these drugs do not work in a monolithic manner on something called "learning" or "memory." In some instances, the drugs seem to act on "attentiveness"; in some, on the ability to vary one's attacks on a problem; in some, on persistence; in some, on long-term memory. Different drugs work differentially for different strains, different individuals, different intellectual tasks, and different learning components.

Do all of these results mean that we will soon be able to substitute a pharmacopoeia of drugs for our various school-enrichment and innovative educational programs, and that most educators will soon be technologically unemployed— or will have to retool and turn in their schoolmaster's gown for a pharmacist's jacket? The answer is no—as our Berkeley experiments on the influence of education and training on brain anatomy and chemistry suggest. This research is the work of four—Dr. E. L. Bennett, biochemist; Dr. Marian Diamond, anatomist; Dr. M. R. Rosenzweig, psychologist; and myself—together, of course, with the help of graduate students, technicians, and, above all, government money.

Our work, started some fifteen years ago, was guided by the same general theory which has guided more recent work, but our research strategy and tactics were quite different. Instead of interfering physiologically or chemically with the animal to determine the effects of such intervention upon memory storage (as did Jarvik, Agranoff, and McGaugh), we had taken the obverse question and, working with only normal animals, sought to determine the *effects* of memory storage on the chemistry and anatomy of the brain.

Our argument was this: If the establishment of long-term memory processes involves increased activity of brain enzymes, then animals which have been required to do a great deal of learning and remembering should end up with brains enzymatically different from those of animals which have not been so challenged by environment. This should be especially true for the enzymes involved in trans-synaptic neural activity. Further, since such neural activity would make demands on brain-cell action and metabolism, one might also expect to find various morphological differences between the brains of rats brought up in psychologically stimulating and psychologically pallid environments.

I describe briefly one of our standard experiments. At weaning age, one rat from each of a dozen pairs of male twins is chosen by lot to be placed in an educationally active and innovative environment, while its twin brother is placed in as unstimulating an environment as we can contrive. All twelve educationally enriched rats live together in one large, wire-mesh cage in a well lighted, noisy, and busy laboratory. The cage is equipped with ladders, running wheels, and other "creative" rat toys. For thirty minutes each day, the rats are taken out of their cages and allowed to explore new territory. As the rats grow older they are given various learning tasks to master, for which they are rewarded with bits of sugar. This stimulating educational and training program is continued for eighty days.

While these animals are enjoying their rich intellectual environment, each impoverished animal lives out his life in solitary confinement, in a small cage situated in a dimly lit and quiet room. He is rarely handled by his keeper and never invited to explore new environments, to solve problems, or join in games with other rats. Both groups of rats, however, have unlimited access to the same standard food throughout the experiment. At age of 105 days, the rats are sacrificed, their brains dissected out and analyzed morphologically and chemically.

This standard experiment, repeated dozens of times, indicates that as the fortunate rat lives out his life in the educationally enriched condition, the bulk of his cortex expands and grows deeper and heavier than that of his culturally deprived brother. Part of this increase in cortical mass is accounted for by an increase in the number of glia cells (specialized brain cells which play vital functions in the nutrition of the neurons and, perhaps, also in laying down permanent memory traces); part of it by an increase in the size of the neuronal cell bodies and their nuclei; and part by an increase in the diameters of the blood vessels supplying the cortex. Our postulated chemical changes also occur. The enriched brain shows more acetylocholinesterase (the enzyme involved in the trans-synaptic conduction of neural impulses) and cholinesterase (the enzyme found primarily in the glia cells).

Finally, in another series of experiments we have demonstrated that these structural and chemical changes are the signs of a "good" brain. That is, we have shown that either through early rat-type Head Start programs or through selective breeding programs, we can increase the weight and density of the rat's cortex and its acetylocholinesterase and cholinesterase activity levels. And when we do—by either method—we have created superior problem-solving animals.

What does all of this mean? It means that the effects of the psychological and educational environment are not restricted to something called the "mental" realm. Permitting the young rat to grow up in an educationally and experi-entially inadequate and unstimulating environment creates an animal with a relatively deteriorated brain—a brain with a thin and light cortex, lowered blood supply, diminished enzymatic activities, smaller neuronal cell bodies, and fewer glia cells. A lack of adequate educational fare for the young animal —no matter how large the food supply or how good the family—and a lack of adequate psychological enrichment results in palpable, measurable, deteriora-tive changes in the brain's chemistry and anatomy.

Returning to McGaugh's results, we find that whether, and to what, extent, this or that drug will improve the animal's learning ability will depend, of course, on what the drug does to the rat's brain chemistry. And what it does to the rat's brain chemistry will depend upon the status of the chemistry in the brain to begin with. And what the status of the brain's chemistry is to begin with reflects the rat's early psychological and educational environment. Whether, and to what extent, this or that drug will improve the animal's attention, or memory, or learning ability, therefore, will depend upon the animal's past experiences. I am not talking about interaction between "mental" factors on the one hand and "chemical" compounds on the other. I am talking, rather, about interactions between chemical factors introduced into the brain by the biochemist's injection or pills, and chemical factors induced in the brain by the educator's stimulating or impoverishing environment. The biochemist's work can be only half effective without the educator's help.

What kind of educational environment can best develop the brain chemically and morphologically? What kind of stimulation makes for an enriched environment? What educational experiences can potentiate the effects of the biochemist's drugs? We don't know. The biochemist doesn't know. It is at this point that I see a whole new area of collaboration in basic research between the educator, the psychologist, and the neurobiochemist—essentially, a research program which combines the Agranoff and McGaugh techniques with our Berkeley approach. Given the start that has already been made in the animal laboratory, an intensive program of research—with animals and with children —which seeks to spell out the interrelations between chemical and educational influences on brain and memory can pay off handsomely. This need not wait for the future. We know enough now to get started.

Both the biochemist and the teacher of the future will combine their skills and insights for the educational and intellectual development of the child. Tommy needs a bit more of an immediate memory stimulator; Jack could do with a chemical attention-span stretcher; Rachel needs an anticholinesterase to slow down her mental processes; Joan, some puromycin—she remembers too many details, and gets lost.

To be sure, all our data thus far come from the brains of goldfish and rodents. But is anyone so certain that the chemistry of the brain of a rat (which, after all, is a fairly complex mammal) is so different from that of the brain of a human being that he dare neglect this challenge—or even gamble— when the stakes are so high?

PART 11

PSYCHOLOGICAL THEORIES OF MOTOR LEARNING AND SKILL ACQUISITION

Explanation and Prediction

Theories attempt to synthesize the facts, to organize and unify the existing knowledge on a particular matter. In helping us to explain and to predict the occurrence of phenomena, they should be invaluable. In reality, however, learning theory has played a questionable role in generating research and modifying instructional and learning approaches.

In the beginning of the nineteenth century, very broad theories were formulated to explain all of learning. As the years progressed, it became apparent to many that either these theories were (a) too general to have meaningful consequences; (b) research support for such theories was generally insufficient; and (c) the different forms of learning might require alternate models instead of all-encompassing theories. There are yet some scholars today, B. F. Skinner, for example, who feel that the incomplete stage of our knowledge suggests that the time is not ripe to talk in terms of a theory of learning. Many more "facts" are needed.

Then again, when dealing with human behavior, most investigators realize that truisms can never exist the way they can and do in the natural sciences. Good theory provides an adequate framework with which to deal with a wide range of research findings. Reasonably acceptable ones exist in the study of behavior. There is a trend to absorb aspects of classical Behaviorism theory and Gestalt theory into some of the popular learning models today, thus making them more applicable and thereby acceptable for certain forms of learning instead of learning in general. New ways have also been proposed to examine the learning process. Theories or models developed for motor learning and skilled performance include traditional S-R designs, the engineering systems approach, cybernetics applications, and information processing foundations. Even within the psychomotor domain, theories or models have been advanced for specific learning and performance phenomena; e.g., retention, transfer (the generality versus specificity problem), task-to-task differences in response orientation and control required, and man's ability in task component performance.

The formulation of psychological theories specifically related to motor skills has only recently generated considerable interest. Poulton, Fitts, Henry, Adams, and Welford are probably best known for their efforts in the 1950's and 1960's. More recently, Posner, Keele, and Pew have attempted to extend Fitts' work and treat many of the problems with which he was concerned. In earlier years, such as in the 1940's, Hull's S-R general behavioral models suggested guidelines for those interested in motor skills. A number of notable scholars (see Wasserman's article) were involved at that time. Today, it appears that engineering and mathematical psychologists are among those generating the most meaningful theories dealing with skilled performance.

Educational psychologists and educators in various disciplines such as physical education, the performing arts, special education, and industrial technology see much potential value in Skinner's operant conditioning model for molding behavior. Reinforcement techniques, programed learning, and the shaping of behavior have appeal to many individuals. Others like the drill conditioning approach. Regardless of theoretical position, however, there is still a long way to go before scholars stop discussing theories and instead, make a major impact on instructional methods used in the school systems, industry, the military, and recreational programs.

Chapter 16

SKILLED PERFORMANCE, INFORMATION PROCESSING, AND MOTOR LEARNING

*A Unifying Theoretical Approach to Motor Learning**

HILTON N. WASSERMAN

WHEN Behaviorism and the various offshoot schools were in their prime, learning was usually described in S-R terminology. At one time, Clark Hull influenced many psychologists in theory and research, and the review article of Wasserman shows the application to practice and motor learning as viewed in 1952. Reactive inhibition and conditioned inhibition were postulated by Hull to have detrimental effects on learning and performance. Wasserman has attempted to organize some of the existing theories encompassing practice and fit them into Hull's model. Warm-up effects and interval rest periods are the major concern. Although Hull's theories are still applied to motor learning, more appealing are popular theories currently being offered.

Introduction

Within the last fifteen years there has developed an extensive literature in the field of motor learning. A great many of the investigations have been undertaken in order to formulate a "new" theory of motor learning, while others have been designed to test one or more of the already existing theories. As a result of the differing theoretical orientations and the frequency of apparently divergent experimental results, it was almost inevitable that there would develop an increasingly insistent need for a theoretical approach to the problem that would be generally applicable to a wide range of studies.

* From *Psychological Review*, 1952, *59*, 278-284. Reprinted with permission of the author and the American Psychological Association.

An attempt will be made in this paper to indicate a possible way in which a recent theoretical approach may be employed to explain and thereby give added meaning to the results of several investigations which are quite divergent when considered in terms of their respective original theoretical explanations. This attempt is being made here in the interest of a more generalized theory of learning. However, it should be emphasized that the interpretations to be offered in this paper should be taken as suggestive of further research, and not as a final formulation.

The present theory is based upon Hull's[7] Performance Inhibition Theory and the more recent extension of this theory advanced by Kimble,[10] some of whose formulations have been substantiated and extended by Wasserman.[16] Kimble's[10] modification of Hull's theory may be summarized as follows:

The total inhibitory potential is made up of two elementary components, reactive inhibition (I_R) and conditioned inhibition $(_sI_R)$. Reactive inhibition is a drive state similar to pain avoidance. It builds up as a positive function of the amount of work involved in the response in question, and dissipates during a rest interval. In massed practice, I_R is not allowed to dissipate, and therefore the need for rest increases as greater amounts of I_R accumulate. When resting occurs, I_R dissipates and this serves as drive reduction or reinforcement. Because of this reinforcement, the response of resting will become conditioned to whatever stimuli are present in the learning situation. This resting tendency is then a habit, and is called conditioned inhibition.

Starting with this basic part of Hull's theory, Kimble[10] hypothesized that with continuous practice the accumulation of a certain amount of I_R will produce an automatic resting response, thus resulting in the dissipation of I_R before a formal rest interval is introduced. Once I_R is reduced below the critical point, work is resumed and continues until the critical level of I_R is reached again. Thus, a kind of equilibrium is established which results in the maintenance of I_R at, or slightly below the critical level. It should be noted that motivation is of crucial importance in this process, and should it decrease during learning, the critical level of I_R will drop somewhat.

Kimble further hypothesized that the development of $_sI_R$ does not begin until a threshold amount of I_R has accumulated. That is, no $_sI_R$ should be present very early in learning.

Finally, Kimble hypothesized that any condition which tends to reduce the critical amount of I_R will increase the amount of resting, and therefore, the rate of development of $_sI_R$. Thus, if motivation should decrease late in learning (as often occurs with some activities), the rate of development of $_sI_R$ should increase late in learning.

The results of two studies by Kimble[10,11] substantiated these three hypotheses, and another study by Wasserman,[16] which dealt with the factor of motivation more explicitly, also confirmed these points and indicated that high motivation serves to raise the critical level of I_R necessary to produce the automatic resting response.

With this brief description of the present theory in mind, it will now be worthwhile to survey some of the existing theoretical approaches to the study of motor learning in order to make some critical comparisons.

Existing Theories

A recent article by Ammons[1] may be used as a point of departure in this survey. Ammons offers a theoretical formulation, the constructs of which are very similar to those of Hull even though different symbols are utilized. However, of more interest here is Ammons' review of the extent to which existing theories can account for the observed characteristics of a motor learning curve *after the introduction of a rest*. These characteristics are as follows:

(1) An abrupt rise in the curve.
(2) A gradual flattening out of the curve.
(3) Resumption of the pre-rest curve of gradual improvement.
(4) Permanent difference in performance level.

Ammons summarizes the adequacy of each of five different theories to account for these observed characteristics. The theories dealt with are as follows: (a) The Primary and Secondary Growth Theory of Snoddy; (b) The Maturation Hypothesis of Dore and Hilgard; (c) The Learning and Work Factor Theory of Dore and Hilgard; (d) The Interference and Warming Up Effect Theory of Bell; and (e) The Performance Inhibition Theory of Hull.

Hull's Performance Inhibition Theory. Though Ammons deals with Hull's theory last, it will be more advantageous here to deal with it first since the present theoretical approach is directly based upon it.

Of all the characteristics of the post-rest motor learning curve which were listed above, the last one (permanent difference in performance level) is the most difficult to explain. In fact, of all the theories reviewed by Ammons[1] and in the present survey, only Hull's inhibition theory can account for the permanent difference produced by the introduction of a rest interval. According to this theory, this permanent decrement which is characteristic of massed learning as compared with spaced learning is attributed to the greater amount of conditioned inhibition which is built up with massing. Since $_sI_R$ is a habit and does not dissipate with time, its effects are relatively permanent, thus, the superiority of spaced learning is understandable.

Ammons states that Hull's theory does not directly account for the first three characteristics of the post-rest motor learning curve. However, these characteristics may be explained in terms of the present extension of Hull's theory as follows:

(1) The abrupt rise is understandable in terms of the dissipation of I_R during the rest interval.

(2) The gradual flattening out might be understandable in terms of the building up again of inhibitory potential, and the influence of the warming-up effect. The latter is a decrement brought about by the loss of certain perceptual-motor adjustments during the rest interval. This decrement often does not show up immediately after rest because of the greater opposite effect of the dissipation of I_R which occurred during the rest interval.

(3) The resumption of the pre-test curve of gradual improvement might be explained by utilizing some additional concepts of Hull's theory. As noted above, a kind of equilibrium is set up which maintains I_R at, or slightly below the critical point. It is conceivable that with continuing motivation and reinforcement, the reaction potential ($_sE_R$) will be greater than the total inhibitory potential (I_R), and thus, the effective reaction potential ($_s\bar{E}_R$) will be large enough to produce gradual improvement ($_s\bar{E}_R = (_sE_R - I_R)$).[7, (p.284)] In addition, it has been found by Ammons[2] and Irion[9] that the warming-up effect reaches a maximum after the first few trials following rest, and then levels off. In other words, after the first few post-rest trials, there is a reinstatement of set to perform the task. Thus, with continuing motivation and reinforcement the characteristic gradual improvement is understandable in terms of the concepts of effective reaction potential and reinstatement of set.

Snoddy's Growth Theory. According to Snoddy,[13] there are two opposed processes in mental growth. One of these he calls primary growth and the other secondary growth. Primary growth occurs early in learning, is relatively stable (resists loss with time), and is a positive function of the number of repetitions and the amount of time interpolated between trials. As the amount of interpolated time increases indefinitely, the amount of primary growth will increase indefinitely.

Secondary growth occurs later in learning, is relatively unstable (is lost over a long period of time), and is a positive function of the amount of primary growth and a negative function of the length of interpolated time. Secondary growth is at a maximum when the interpolated time is zero, that is to say, when practice is massed.

In order to test this theory, Humphreys[8] performed an experiment with the pursuit rotor, and found that the greater gains early in learning occurred *between* practice periods (after a forty-eight hour rest), while in the later stages of learning the gains were made *during* the practice periods.

Similarly, Travis,[14] utilizing six-minute work periods separated by intervals of three and seven days with rotary pursuit learning, found that gains *between* practice periods were confined to the early stages of learning.

The results of both of these experiments tend to support Snoddy's theory. However, another experiment conducted by Travis[15] yielded results inconsistent with it. Using the pursuit-oscillator with rest intervals ranging from five minutes to 120 hours, Travis found that, contrary to the theory, learning (primary growth) was not increasingly better as the length of interpolated time increased. The optimum rest was twenty minutes, and in addition, the shortest rest (five minutes) resulted in better learning than the three longest intervals (48, 72, and 120 hours). According to Snoddy's theory of primary growth, the longest rest interval should have been the most beneficial.

A basic difficulty with the theory is the way in which Snoddy attempts to explain observed decrements in performance. The explanation is in terms of interference between the two growth processes. The nature of this interference is not at all adequately elaborated.

It seems possible to explain all of these results in terms of the present inhibition theory. Decrements in performance are most easily explained in terms of the accumulation of inhibitory potential. In addition, the gains *between* practice periods are adequately explained in terms of the dissipation of reactive inhibition during the rest interval. The fact that Humphreys and Travis found the gains that occurred between practice periods (after a rest) to be confined largely to the early stages of learning is also understandable without need of Snoddy's theory. Reactive inhibition is built up rapidly and reaches the critical level quite early in learning. However, late in learning, when motivation decreases, more resting occurs during learning and this critical level will tend to decrease. Hence, later in learning less gains are made *between* practice periods because there is less reactive inhibition present to dissipate when a formal rest interval is introduced. This observation that increases after rest are not as great late in learning as they are early in learning has been confirmed by several more recent studies.[2,9,10]

Furthermore, it should be noted that when a rest is introduced, almost all the reactive inhibition is dissipated during the first few minutes of rest (with pursuit rotor learning). In fact, Ammons[2] found that there is probably no further decrease in reactive inhibition after about twenty minutes of rest. However, Humphreys used 48-hour intervals and Travis used three and seven day intervals. Under these conditions, if any increase at all is found after the interval, it would be expected in the early stages of learning when motivational factors are at a maximum, and such factors as warming-up effect and retroactive inhibition are outweighed by the beneficial effects of the dissipation of reactive inhibition. Thus, the effect of the dissipation of reactive inhibition is indicated by a gain in score after rest early in learning, while late in learning the beneficial effect of the dissipation of reactive inhibition *may* be outweighed by such influences as loss of set (warming-up effect), and retroactive inhibition, the effects of which may be enhanced by a drop in motivation which often occurs later in learning with this type of task.

The results of Travis' second experiment[15] are also in agreement with the present theory. Several studies have shown that the longest rest interval is usually not the most advantageous. It has been found by Ammons[2] and Kimble and Horenstein[12] that the rate of dissipation of reactive inhibition is a negatively accelerated function of the length of interpolated rest.

The Maturation Hypothesis of Dore and Hilgard. Dore and Hilgard,[4] utilizing one-minute trials and three different rest intervals (1, 3, and 11 minutes) with rotary pursuit learning, found that the eleven-minute rest was the best, and that the three-minute rest was better than the one-minute rest. Dore and Hilgard attributed the superiority of the greater spacing to growth (maturation) which occurs *between* the practice periods, and which is related to the amount of stimulation provided *during* the practice periods. Thus, according to this view, the obtained scores are a "function of time rather than amount of practice (granted the necessary minimum)."[4] (p.258)

However, according to Dore and Hilgard, the maturation hypothesis ". . . can be shown to be necessary only if well-known processes describing increments and decrements between trials are found to be quantitatively insufficient to account for the changes which occur."[4] (p.259) Actually, their results are completely understandable in terms of the present theory. The superiority of the greater spacing is produced not by growth during rest, but by the dissipation of reactive inhibition during rest. The score is not a function of time alone, but is related to the amount of reinforcement, the amount of work involved, and the length of the interpolated rest.

The Learning and Work Factor Theory of Dore and Hilgard. In an attempt to test Snoddy's theory, Dore and Hilgard[5] performed an experiment using the pursuit rotor which forms the basis of this additional theory. They hypothesized that if Snoddy is correct, with two equated groups having an equal number of trials distributed differently over the same total time, the group having decreasing lengths of interpolated rest (initial spacing and later relative massing) should be superior to the group having increasing lengths of rest (initial massing and later spacing). That is to say, initial spacing should be superior to initial massing if Snoddy's theory is correct.

However, Dore and Hilgard found the exact opposite to be true in their experiment, and as a result concluded that Snoddy's theory was inadequate. To account for their results, Dore and Hilgard formulated the learning and work factor theory according to which the learning factors produce improvement within practice (acquisition) and loss with non-practice (forgetting), while the work factors produce loss within practice (work decrement) and improvement with non-practice (recovery with rest).

It appears that this theory really does not conflict seriously with the present inhibition theory, and may be looked upon as an early and incomplete formulation of the latter. Instead of the learning factor concept Hull's system utilizes such constructs as habit strength and reaction potential, and instead of the work factor concept Hull's theory utilizes the concept of inhibitory potential. Also, the learning factor concept of Dore and Hilgard may imply a disuse theory of forgetting (loss with non-practice). If this is so, it represents a criticism to which the present inhibition theory is not subject.

Bell's Theory of Interference and Warming Up Effect. Another study specifically designed to test Snoddy's mental growth hypothesis is that of Bell.[3]

Utilizing the pursuit rotor, Bell introduced rests of one minute, ten minutes, six hours, twenty-four hours, or thirty hours early in learning (after trial 5) and late in learning (after trial 15). He found the optimum rest interval to be ten minutes, and further, that the one-minute rest was inferior to the much longer ones (6, 24, and 30) hours) when introduced early in learning, but superior to them when introduced late in learning.

Concluding that Snoddy's theory is inadequate, Bell formulated his theory, according to which interference and warming-up effects operate *throughout* the learning process, but with differential effect at different stages. By interference is meant a kind of inhibition or conflict between incorrect and correct responses, this conflict often being observed as an obvious strain and lack of relaxation. Interference is greatest at the beginning of learning and gradually diminishes as learning progresses. On the other hand, during the first few trials, the warming-up effect increases rapidly and then remains fairly constant throughout the remainder of learning. The effect of rest is to remove interference, but to necessitate warming-up. Large gains are produced by a rest early in learning because the amount of interference removed is greater than the warming-up effect. However, late in learning there is a loss after rest because the warming-up effect becomes greater than the amount of interference removed.

Again, these empirical findings appear to be adequately understandable in terms of the present inhibition theory which has room for Bell's warming-up effect, but which eliminates several of the difficulties inherent in his theory. The superiority of the ten-minute rest is understandable in terms of the negatively accelerated relationship between the dissipation of reactive inhibition and the length of interpolated rest. The finding that a one-minute rest becomes superior to much longer intervals when introduced late in learning coincides with the results of Humphreys' and Travis' experiments which were cited above. Late in learning, when there is relatively less reactive inhibition available to be dissipated during a formal rest interval (because of more resting *during* learning and therefore, more dissipation of reactive inhibition *during* learning), the introduction of a long interval of time will be less beneficial than early in learning because of the greater influence of such factors as the warming-up effect and retroactive inhibition. This is essentially substantiated by the findings of Hilgard and Smith.[6] Using the pursuit rotor, they found a longer rest (3 minutes) to be superior early in learning and a shorter rest (1 minute) to be superior late in learning, while an extremely short rest (20 seconds) was always inferior to the one-minute rest. Also, they found decrements *between* daily sessions (24 hour interval) to occur only in the later stages of learning.

Finally, it should be noted that Bell's concept of interference seems to assume a differential forgetting theory of forgetting. That is, it seems necessary to explain the removal of interference during rest in terms of the more rapid forgetting of the incorrect responses. *If* the forgetting is attributed to disuse over the interval of time (this point is not specifically dealt with by Bell), Bell's theory is subject to the usual criticisms leveled against a disuse theory.

Summary

This paper represents an attempt to reconcile the apparently divergent results of several studies, each concerned with the problems common to the motor learning situation, but each oriented towards a specific theoretical approach to these problems. It has been shown that not only are these studies explainable in terms of an extension of Hull's Performance Inhibition Theory, but that this approach leads to a consistency and unity in theory for which it is worthwhile to strive. The present theory is not being advanced as the last word, but rather as suggestive in nature and a stimulus for further research in the interest of a more generalized learning theory.

References

1. AMMONS, R. B. Acquisition of motor skill: I. Quantitative analysis and theoretical formulation. *Psychol. Rev.,* 1947, 54, 263–281.
2. ———. Acquisition of motor skill: II. Rotary pursuit performance with continuous practice before and after a single rest. *J. exp. Psychol.,* 1947, 37, 393–411.
3. BELL, H. M. Rest pauses in motor learning as related to Snoddy's Hypothesis of Mental Growth. *Psychol. Monogr.,* 1942, 54, No. 243.
4. DORE, L. R. & HILGARD, E. R. Spaced practice and the maturation hypothesis. *J. Psychol.,* 1937, 4, 245–259.
5. ———. Spaced practice as a test of Snoddy's two processes of mental growth. *J. exp. Psychol.,* 1938, 23, 359–374.
6. HILGARD, E. R., & SMITH, M. B. Distributed practice in motor learning: Score changes within and between daily sessions. *J. exp. Psychol.,* 1942, 30, 136–146.
7. HULL, C. L. *Principles of behavior.* New York: D. Appleton-Century, 1943.
8. HUMPHREYS, L. G. The factor of time in pursuit rotor learning. *J. Psychol.,* 1937, 3, 429–436.
9. IRION, A. L. Reminiscence in pursuit rotor learning as a function of rest and amount of pre-rest practice. *J. exp. Psychol.,* 1949, 39, 492–499.
10. KIMBLE, G. A. An experimental test of a two-factor theory of inhibition. *J. exp. Psychol.,* 1949, 39, 15–23.
11. ———. Performance and reminiscence in motor learning as a function of the degree of distribution of practice. *J. exp. Psychol.,* 1949, 39, 500–510.
12. ———, & HORENSTEIN, B. R. Reminiscence in motor learning as a function of length of interpolated rest. *J. exp. Psychol.,* 1948, 38, 239–244.
13. SNODDY, G. S. *Evidence for two opposed processes in mental growth.* Lancaster: Science Press, 1935.
14. TRAVIS, R. C. Practice and rest periods in motor learning. *J. Psychol.,* 1937, 3, 183–187.
15. ———. The effect of length of rest period in motor learning. *J. Psychol.,* 1937, 3, 189–194.
16. WASSERMAN, H. N. The effect of motivation and amount of pre-rest practice upon inhibitory potential in motor learning. *J. exp. Psychol.,* 1951, 42, 162–172.

Increased Response Latency for Complicated Movements and A "Memory Drum" Theory of Neuromotor Reaction*

FRANKLIN M. HENRY AND DONALD E. ROGERS

PHYSICAL educators are usually known for their applied interests and work. One exception is Franklin Henry, and in the reading that follows,

* From *The Research Quarterly,* 1960, *31,* 448–458. Abridged and reprinted with permission of the authors and the American Association for Health, Physical Education, and Recreation.

he, along with Rogers, incorporates research data on reaction time to theorize how movement patterns are "stored" and emitted. More importantly, Henry strongly supports his contention for task specificity over task generality; that movement patterns learned are unique for each given task. His graduate students during the past number of years, through experimental approaches, have usually upheld a theory of task specificity. Specific related data dealing with reaction time and movement time are also presented in the article.

The time required for a muscle to begin to respond to direct stimulation is about .015 sec. A simple reflex response such as the eye wink is made in .04 sec., while the reflex to a blow on the patellar tendon requires about .08 sec. The simplest voluntary response to a stimulus (simple RT) requires .15 sec. under the most favorable circumstances; .20 to .25 sec. may be considered more typical. When complications such as discrimination between several stimuli and/or choice between several possible movements are introduced (disjunctive RT), the required time increases and may be as long as .50 sec. It should be noted the RT "is not the time occupied in the execution of a response; rather, it is the time required to get the overt response started."[10]

Theoretical Considerations

Early experimental psychologists considered RT to be a measure of the cumulated time required for a series of mental processes, including stimulus perception and the willing of the movement. This concept was gradually discarded during the period 1873-1893 in favor of the idea that the stimulus simply triggered off a prepared reflex, the voluntary mental phase of the process being limited to the preparation, i.e., the development of a state of readiness to make a specific planned movement. This is essentially the same as the modern view. A reaction cannot be broken up into a series of successive mental and motor acts. The response is a total reaction in which perception of the stimulus runs concurrently with the motor response, with much of the perceptive process and all the overt movement occurring after the reaction, i.e., following the true RT, which is defined as the latent period between the stimulus and the first beginning of physical movement. Woodworth has traced the historical development of these ideas in considerable detail.[9]

While the traditional prepared reflex theory of RT may be accepted in its general aspects, the present writer proposes considerable modification designed to recognize current knowledge of the neuromotor system and its control by the cephalic nervous centers. There is no reflex in the modern physiological use of the term, since a reflex must be nonwillful and not voluntary. There is probably not more than a minimal involvement of the cerebral cortex in the RT response, because the neuromotor coordination centers and pathways are chiefly cerebellar or subcortical without cortical termination.[8] Perhaps in consequence of the neuroanatomy, neuromotor perception is extremely poor, although neuromotor coordination or kinesthetic adjustment (with the absence of perceptual awareness) is exceptionally well developed in humans.[4]

Performance of acts of skill (even though relatively simple) may be assumed to involve neuromotor memory. This may be operationally defined as improved neuromotor coordination and more effective response, the improvement being the result of experience and practice, possibly accumulated over a period of many years. An implication of the neuroanatomy of the system as outlined above is that such memory must be different from ideational or perceptual memory, since conscious imagery is indefinite and largely excluded.

Nevertheless, a rich store of unconscious motor memory is available for the performance of acts of neuromotor skill. Added to this are innate neuromotor coordinations that are important in motor acts. The tapping of the store may be thought of broadly as a memory storage drum phenomena, to use the analogy of the electronic computer. The neural pattern for a specific and well-coordinated motor act is controlled by a stored program that is used to direct the neuromotor details of its performance. In the absence of an available stored program, an unlearned complicated task is carried out under conscious control, in an awkward, step-by-step, poorly coordinated manner.

Voluntary consideration of a particular movement that has already been learned, and is to be accomplished at maximum speed, occurs during the classical foreperiod (an interval of readiness while the subject is attentively waiting for the reaction-causing stimulus). Such consideration may involve visual imagery of the specific intended movement, but it is chiefly the development of a strong intent to start that movement in immediate response to the stimulus. It is not concerned (and indeed cannot be) with the actual formation of the already learned or structured specific program that will guide the released outburst of neural impulses through the proper centers, subcenters, and nerve channels so that it will produce the intended movement. The crucial willful act in the simple reaction is the release of the outburst of neural impulses that will result in the movement. Normally this act is voluntary and intentional rather than reflex, although in special circumstances it may become almost reflex. The term release is used advisedly; impulses are already present in the cephalic nervous system in the form of brain waves and afferent neural discharges from various sources and are directed and channeled rather than created. This is another point of distinction between a voluntary reaction and a simple automatic stimulus-response reflex.

The above concepts can lead to a number of testable predictions in the area of motor coordination. Keeping in mind that the programing of the movement can constitute only a part of the total latency (because synaptic conduction in and of itself requires time) it might, for example, be expected that a minor program change for a simple movement would be easy to accomplish, whereas a long or rather complicated program should be difficult to change after it starts organizing the channels. Various implications of the theory will be examined in subsequent articles.

Problem Investigated

One of these implications, which will be investigated in the present study, is the theoretical requirement that there should be a longer reaction latency for a complicated movement than for a simpler movement. This is because a more comprehensive program, i.e., a larger amount of stored information, will be needed, and thus the neural impulses will require more time for coordination and direction into the eventual motor neurons and muscles.

The voluntary decision to make a movement when the stimulus occurs is thought to cause a state of readiness to respond to (and be triggered by) the stimulus. During this foreperiod, there is some amount of preliminary neuromotor response. It is known that some premovement tension may develop in the muscles that are to make the overt response, but such tension is sometimes absent and sometimes of an inappropriate nature.[9] Action potentials, however, reveal fairly consistent foreperiod excitation of both the reacting and noninvolved muscles. It is argued here that this may indicate alertness rather than implicit or partial reaction.[10] Whether this interpretation is correct or not, it seems obvious that when the movement is complicated and requires considerable skill, it is not possible for the tension during the foreperiod to be related to more than the very first phase of the overt movement. Moreover, a complicated movement necessarily involves several muscle groups and several specific areas of neuromotor coordination centers; more extensive use of learned and stored neuromotor patterns is surely required to initiate the overt motor action in this case. Thus it may be hypothesized that with richer and more complicated patterns involved, a longer latent time for the more complicated circulation of neural impulses through the coordination centers is inevitable. The situation is probably analogous to (but not identical with) the events, whatever they are, that cause greater response latency when there is a choice of movement in the reaction.[9]

The hypothesis can be tested experimentally by observing the simple RT required for the initiation of movements that vary from simple to complex. Note that there can be a simple RT for a complex movement. If the situation for a particular response involves no discrimination as between two or more stimuli, and no choice (at the time of reaction) between which of two or more movements is to be made, the RT is simple, regardless of the complexity of the movement itself.

Review of Literature

While there has apparently been no investigation which approached the problem from the point of view stated above, there have been, over the years, a few researches that are pertinent. The first was a study by Freeman in 1907, which reported that in drawing geometric figures such as a straight line, a circle, and a pentagon, the RT became longer as the figure increased in complexity.[3] In explanation, it was contended that the cause was antagonistic muscular tensions originating from anticipation of the necessary movement reversals. Unfortunately, the data were secured on only four individuals, so although the results are statistically inconclusive, they are in the anticipated direction.

On the other hand, Fitts[2] stated in 1951 that "the latent time is independent of the rate, extent or direction of the specific movement required by the stimulus," basing his interpretation on the 1949 experiment of Brown and Slater-Hammel,[1] although he cites some other references that are less directly related. It may be noted that the experiment in question involved only the variation of the length or direction of a simple movement; complexity was not studied.

Several reports from our laboratory[6] have included data on the RT for movements that differ in complexity. Unfortunately, with respect to the present issue, the experimental designs were oriented to the problems that were being investigated; no attempt was made to control or balance out the practice effect. The most recent of these was by Mendryk,[7] who used two movements that differed considerably in length and slightly in complexity. In subjects of three age groups (N = 50 in each), the RT's were .002, .004 and .009 sec. faster for the longer and more complex movement. However, each subject had been given 50 trials with the short movement and 30 practice trials with the longer movement before the tabled values for the latter were recorded, so there may have been a considerable practice effect acting to decrease the RT and thus occlude the complexity effect.

Mendryk has made available to the writer his data for the last 20 trials with the short movement and the first 20 trials with the subsequent longer and more complex movement, which makes possible a comparison involving less of the practice effect. In his 12-year-old group the RT for the longer movement is

.004 sec. slower than for the short movement (t = 1.2), in the 22-year-old group it is .009 sec. slower (t = 3.8), and in the 48-year-old group it is .006 sec. slower (t = 2.2). Thus while the effect is small, and not completely controlled as to practice, it is in the anticipated direction and is statistically significant for the two adult groups.

Methodology

Apparatus and Movements.   A reaction key was mounted at the forward end of the flat foundation board of the instrument. This was a sensitive key; the weight of the subject's finger was sufficient to keep it closed. At the back end of the board an upright supported a red warning light at eye level. A silent control switch was operated by the experimenter out of sight of the subject. When it was turned to its first position, the warning light came on. After a lapse of 1 to 4 sec. (in chance order), the switch was turned to the second position, which sounded the stimulus going and simultaneously started the RT chronoscope. When being tested with Movement A, the subject simply lifted his finger a few millimeters, which permitted the reaction key to open and stopped the chronoscope.

Movement B was more complicated. A tennis ball hung by a string which placed it about 15 cm. above the reaction key and 30 cm. further back, away from the subject. In response to the stimulus signal, he reached forward to grasp the ball. When the ball was touched, the upper support end of the string pulled out of a switch clip, thus freeing the ball to permit a follow-through. A second chronoscope, which also connected to the reaction key, recorded movement time (MT). It stopped when the string pulled out of the switch clip.

Movement C was somewhat more complicated; it included a series of movements and reversals. A second tennis ball (C), also supported by a string and clip, was hung 30 cm. to the right of ball B. In response to the stimulus, the subject moved his hand from the key, reaching forward and upward to strike ball C with the back of the hand, then reversed direction to go forward and downward, touching a dummy push button on the baseboard to the left of the reaction key, and finally reversed again to go upward and forward, striking down ball B. This two-ball apparatus was illustrated in an earlier publication from this laboratory,[5] which listed references to detailed descriptions of the device. It should be mentioned that the circuits included provision for using an auditory stimulus (an electric gong), and this was used in the present study.

Experimental Design.   There were two experiments. In the first, designated Experiment I, there was continuous rotation of conditions, trial-by-trial, with Movement A required for the first trial, B for the second, C for the third, A for the fourth, and so on. Before each trial, the subject was reminded as to which movement was to be made; moreover, he could see from the way the apparatus was set up that there were no balls, or one, or two, to be hit. Fifteen practice trials were given, followed by 30 trials (10 for each movement) which were used for the statistical analysis. While this design offered the advantage of very exact balancing out of possible practice and fatigue effects, there was a remote possibility that even though the instructions were carefully given, and the nature of the required movement for a particular trial was obvious, some cases may have occurred in which there might have been some element of choice of movement.

Experiment II involved one practice trial with Movement A, followed by 10 trials with that movement. After a brief rest, a practice trial was given on B, followed by 10 trials with that movement. After another rest, one practice trial was given on C, followed by 10 trials with that movement. A third of the subjects followed the A-B-C sequence, another third the sequence B-C-A, and the final third the sequence C-A-B. Each person had 30 trials (10 on each movement) in addition to the practice before each series of ten. All subjects used in Experiment II were well practiced in the movements, since they had gone through Experiment I approximately one week earlier.

Subjects. Group 1 consisted of 30 undergraduate college men. Group 2 was composed of 30 undergraduate college women. In each group approximately half were physical education majors. These groups were tested only under the conditions of Experiment I. Group 3 consisted of 20 young men ranging in age from 19 to 35 years (average 24), and included college students, high school teachers, and others. Group 4 was made up of 20 eighth grade boys, age 11 or 12, and Group 5 was composed of 20 fourth grade boys, age 8 or 9. Not one of these 120 individuals was (or could be) selected in any way, either intentionally or unintentionally, with respect to the possibility that he would do better with one of the movements than with another one. In other words, the samples are completely unbiased with respect to the variable under consideration, which is the RT for Movement A compared with B or C.

Results and Discussion

Reaction Time vs. Complexity. The data of Table 1 show that all groups react more slowly as the movement becomes more complex. The reaction preceding Movement B is about 20 percent slower, on the average, than the RT for A, and the reaction preceding Movement C is about 7 percent slower than the RT for B. Even though the groups are relatively small, the differences between the RT's are without question statistically significant in each, as may be seen by the t-ratios in Table 1. Moreover, the differences are approximately as large and significant under the conditions of Experiment II as under the conditions of Experiment I.

Since the findings are positive in each of five groups of subjects that differ in age and sex, and are positive under both the experimental conditions, the evidence seems adequate to claim that the hypothesis of slower RT for

TABLE 1.—MEAN REACTION TIMES OF THE VARIOUS GROUPS

Group	Movement A		Movement B		B-A	Movement C		C-B
	M (sec.)	σ	M (sec)	σ	t^a	M (sec)	σ	t^a
1(I) Men	.163	.018	.195	.026	8.6	.204	.031	2.9
2(I) Women	.174	.027	.205	.026	8.3	.219	.034	3.8
3(I) Age 24	.158	.025	.197	.034	9.4	.213	.034	5.3
4(I) Age 12	.178	.023	.214	.035	8.1	.226	.033	3.4
5(I) Age 8	.238	.038	.275	.042	8.4	.295	.026	4.9
3(II) Age 24	.144	.019	.186	.031	10.1	.199	.032	3.4
4(II) Age 12	.159	.015	.201	.031	7.5	.214	.033	3.8
5(II) Age 8	.214	.031	.253	.024	7.0	.270	.039	4.0

[a] A t-ratio of 1.70 is significant at the 5 percent level for Groups 1 and 2 (N = 30), while 1.73 is required for Groups 3, 4, and 5 (N = 20). The statistical hypothesis is single-tailed, since the direction of the differences is predicted by the experimental, i.e., alternative, hypothesis. It will be noted that all of the t-ratios are significant and quite large; the smallest is 2.9.

movements of increased complexity, based on the memory drum theory of reaction latency, has been confirmed. It should be emphasized that the simple movement was very simple indeed. Furthermore, the amount of movement required to actuate the reaction key was only a fraction of a millimeter; in other words, the RT did not involve movement in the ordinary meaning of the word. (Some experiments that have purported to measure RT have actually included considerable amounts of movement). The additional serial elements and reversals of direction in Movement C, as compared with B, caused only about a third as much change in RT as did the type and amount of complexity difference of B as compared with A.

The determination of the crucial elements of the complexity effect, and of just how much of a change in complexity is required to produce a noticeable change in RT, will require further investigation. It seems reasonable to expect that increased movement complexity occurring early in a movement will have a much greater influence on RT than if the complexity appears late in a movement that was simple in its early phases. Whether increased demand for accuracy and precision of movement and increased involvement of feedback will slow RT as implicitly predicted by the theory, are among the important questions that remain to be answered. . . .

Summary and Conclusions

Following a consideration of prevailing concepts of reaction time and modern knowledge of the operation of the neuromotor nervous system, a theory has been developed which places heavy reliance on nonperceptive use of motor memory in voluntary acts involving motor coordination. Innate and particularly learned neuromotor coordination patterns are conceived of as stored, becoming accessible for use in controlling the act by a memory drum mechanism that requires increasing time for its operation as the motor act becomes more complex.

To test the hypothesis that the simple reaction time becomes lengthened with increased movement complexity, data were secured on 120 individuals, including both sexes and (in the case of males) three age groups. Sixty of the subjects were tested with two experimental procedures in order to improve the adequacy of the control conditions. Three types of movement varying in complexity were used; both reaction time and movement time were measured.

The data were also examined with respect to several problems secondary to the main study. These included the influence of age and sex on net movement time, and the amount of generality and specificity of individual differences in speed of arm movement ability.

Results of the statistical analysis of the data seem to justify the following conclusions:

1. Under controlled conditions, simple reaction time becomes longer when the type of movement which follows the reaction is varied from very simple to relatively complex. Further increase in complexity produces additional slowing, but to a lessened degree. . . .

4. Individual differences in speed of arm movement ability are predominately specific to the type of movement that is made; there is only a relatively small amount of general ability to move the arm rapidly.

References

1. BROWN, J. S., and SLATER-HAMMEL, A. T. "Discrete Movements in the Horizontal Plane as a Function of their Direction and Extent." *Journal of Experimental Psychology* 38:84-95; 1949.

2. FITTS, P. M. "Engineering Psychology and Equipment Design." *Handbook of Experimental Psychology*. (Edited by S. S. Stevens.) New York: J. Wiley and Sons, Inc., 1951.

3. FREEMAN, F. N. "Preliminary Experiments on Writing Reactions." *Psychological Monographs* 8(34):301-333; 1907.

4. HENRY, F. M. "Dynamic Kinesthetic Perception and Adjustment." *Research Quarterly* 24:176-187; May 1953.

5. HOWELL, M. L. "Influence of Emotional Tension on Speed of Reaction and Movement." *Research Quarterly* 24:22-32; March 1953.

6. LOTTER, W. S. "Interrelationships among Reaction Times and Speeds of Movement in Different Limbs." *Research Quarterly* 31:147-155; May 1960.

7. MENDRYK, S. "Reaction Time, Movement Time, and Task Specificity Relationships at Ages 12, 22, and 48 Years." *Research Quarterly* 31:156-162; May 1960.

8. WENGER, M. A.; JONES, F. N.; and JONES, M. H. *Physiological Psychology*. New York: H. Holt and Company, 1956.

9. WOODWORTH, R. S. *Experimental Psychology*. New York: H. Holt and Company, 1938.

10. WOODWORTH, R. S., and SCHLOSBERG, HAROLD. *Experimental Psychology*. Revised edition. New York: H. Holt and Company, 1954.

Cybernetic Foundations of Physical Behavioral Science*

KARL U. SMITH

A currently popular approach in studying man's behavior is offered by cyberneticians. Importance is placed on control processes in man and in equipment. Feedback from present performance is the operational system which controls and modifies further activity. Smith has written extensively for many years on the application of cybernetic principles to behavior, and in this particular article (a portion of which is presented here) he emphasizes motor behavior. Smith proposes that traditional Behaviorism (S-R) theories are for the most part irrelevant to real-life skills, and that his theoretical approach is much more appropriate and meaningful. The reader can judge for himself, especially if he compares Gagné's material to Smith's writings.

This paper formulates a theory of human factors design in physical behavioral science and describes a program of experimental feedback research which establishes a beginning foundation for this field. We consider physical behavioral science to encompass especially the areas of work physiology and psychology, physical fitness training, physical education, sports medicine and psychology, athletics and athletic design, physical medicine, physical therapy and rehabilitation, and the behavioral sectors of the performing arts. Our view is that traditional psychology has failed completely in providing a rational

* From *Quest*, 1968, Monograph VIII, 26-82. Abridged and reprinted with permission of the author and publisher.

theoretical basis and a critical research methodology for this field of behavior science, but that new ideas, concepts and techniques of feedback research can be employed to define its groundworks and structure.[8]

The terms, cybernetic and cybernetics, have come into fairly common use in recent years, but mean different things to different people.[1,10] Our own use refers specifically to *behavioral cybernetics,* a set of ideas about the organization and control of behavior. A cybernetic theory of behavior is one that interprets activity as a closed-loop feedback-controlled process rather than as a series of discrete stimulus-response units. Cybernetic analyses describe, vary, and conceptualize behavior in terms of its feedback characteristics.

In closed-loop behavior, feedback refers to the sensory effects controlled and generated by response. A behaving individual is never at rest, but engages continually in dynamic activity which is self-generating in that motor responses produce sensory feedback effects which induce and direct subsequent responses. Athletic skills, as well as other types of behavior, are described cybernetically as continuous closed-circuit interactions between motor performance and the sensory effects generated by movement.

A feedback concept of physical or motor skill incorporates specific assumptions about the mechanisms involved. We assume that feedback mechanisms provide self-regulated stimulation through dynamic movement and that both muscular and receptor activity are regulated continuously by means of closed-loop control of sensory input. We assume that movements are integrated according to the temporal and spatial patterns of controlling feedback signals. We assume further that specialized feedback mechanisms exist by means of which internal organic processes of respiration, circulation, and energy conversion are regulated by dynamic skeletal activity. Experimental cybernetic analyses are designed to test hypotheses derived from these assumptions.

Cybernetic Theory in Physical Behavioral Science

Experimental cybernetics is a new science of behavior, learning, and educational design based on the study of feedback mechanisms and their control of performance and learning. . . . The behaving organism is seen not as a passive respondent called into action by chance environmental stimuli, but as a dynamic system which continuously generates activity for feedback control, guidance, and integration of behavior in stimulus selection, environmental control, and physiological regulation. Different specialized movements of the behaving system function to maintain the metabolism and sensitivity of receptor cells, to orient the receptors and the body in relation to gravity and to specific loci in space, and to regulate and manipulate stimuli and the sources of stimuli in the environment.

The primary objective of behavioral cybernetics is to clarify the feedback characteristics of motorsensory systems related to physical skills and physical fitness. This consists of applying feedback methods of behavioral research to study of different phenomena of physical behavioral science. The methodology consists of breaking into the feedback loop of an activity-in-progress and varying and/or perturbing some property of the feedback signal in order to study the effect on performance and learning. We have used a number of different kinds of closed-loop systems of this nature for cybernetic research, including electronic, magnetic-tape, optical, television, and hybrid computer systems. By such means, we have studied both the feedback-control functions of motor performance and the factors determining learning of motor skill.

The general methodology has been diagramed elsewhere, suggesting some of the experimental techniques which have been devised to study the main motor systems of the human body and some of their related organic functions.

Each of the set-ups introduces a specialized instrumental segment into the sensory-feedback loop which is used by the subject in order to control a specific performance. For example, a prism before the subject's eyes is a means of varying visual feedback. In the television or video set-up, the subject controls his manual movements by means of visual feedback generated by his own movements, but the feedback signals are transmitted to his eyes by means of television. He watches his performance in a television monitor. In a set-up involving hearing instead of sight, the auditory feedback of speech is delivered to the subject's ears by means of a tape-recorder playback unit. In all cases, the controlling feedback signals are transmitted to the subject indirectly via the experimental instrument. This arrangement permits experimental manipulation of the feedback signals and analysis of the resulting effects on performance and learning.

Over the past fifteen years, cybernetic methods have created a new approach to all sectors of learning science, training, rehabilitation and therapeutic exercise. The results of cybernetic research show clearly that human learning is defined specifically by the closed-loop, sensory effects of movements— that is, by the dynamic feedback characteristics of performance—rather than by chance or extrinsic open-loop associations or reinforcements. Cybernetic research shows that learning involves continuous, closed-loop, motor-sensory control of response and is not based on discrete and intermittent open-loop S-R events. Learning occurs as a direct result of dynamic response and is not an indirect function of the association of events. It requires self-generation of directed, space-organized activity and is not a passive effect of chance contiguity. It requires immediate sensory feedback, not a poorly defined, flexible, temporal relationship between stimuli and responses. It is cumulative and nonreversible, and establishes memory records which have predictive potential in defining future performance relative to systematic space-time variations.

The Feedback Basis of Control of Human Motions. One of the primary tasks of physical behavioral science is to clarify the mechanisms of control of different patterns of human motion—i.e., posture, transport movements, locomotion, manual behavior, head motion, eye-movements, tool using, and overt social behavior. Using the feedback methods of experimental analysis described above, we have studied all of the main motion systems of the human body as forms of closed-loop, controlled tracking behavior.[4,5,6,9] The results of this research have indicated that different motion mechanisms are all feedback controlled as multidimensional response and multisensory systems, that they are organized primarily as space-organized movement mechanisms, that their timing and rhythms are determined by their real-time, closed-loop properties, and that in learning they are feedback yoked and integrated with internal organic processes. Findings concerning the spatial aspects of feedback control of movement represent the most significant results of the research which has been done and will be described first.

The experimental cybernetic doctrine of motion which we propose as a basis of physical behavioral science rests on three principles of spatial feedback control of motion, namely, that: (one) motions are multidimensional or composed of postural, transport and manipulative movement components; (two) the postural and bilateral transport components of motion serve as built-in, coordinate reference mechanisms to guide articulated movements in relation to body position; (three) these different components of motion are controlled and integrated by the brain as neurogeometric systems.

The principle of multidimensional control of body motion . . . suggests that massive postural motion serves to regulate movements of the body in the

vertical plane in relation to the effects of gravity. Bilateral transport movements govern the head, eyes, and limbs in the horizontal planes of the body.
These two movement systems combine to form a self-contained coordinate
directional reference mechanism which enables the individual to guide his
movements in relation to environmental stimuli while he also directs more
refined movements in relation to changes in his body position.

   . . . The individual continually generates movements in order to displace
sensory input spatially and thus to guide further movement. The brain senses
this displacement and thereby directs subsequent response.

The principle of spatial guidance of motion also applies to integration of
postural, transport and articulated movements. . . . The exteroceptive feedback
of an executed motion may be angularly displaced, inverted or reversed. In
this case, the brain detects differences between the geometric orientation of
the pattern of stimuli as sensed by the eye and that from the kinesthetic and
postural sensory effects of movement. These neurogeometric differences between the coordinate body sensing and the exteroceptive input determine the
degree of integration possible in the motion and the rate at which the motion
can be learned.

We can summarize these two feedback principles of directional guidance
and integration of multidimensional components of motion in this way. Move-
ment-produced sensory feedback can be displaced not only in specific directions
but in relative orientation. That is to say, sensory feedback patterns can be
inverted, reversed, inverted and reversed, rotated, or displaced in other ways.
Such displacements occur normally due to unusual relative positions of parts
of the body. They also are an inevitable aspect of using tools and machines or
the instrumental devices of athletics and sports. Unusual space displacements
of feedback produce the perceptual distortions resulting from some kinds of
injuries or from wearing visual or auditory aids.

According to the neurogeometric hypothesis, when feedback displacements
occur beyond a normal range, a breakdown range occurs in which performance deteriorates and the demands for extensive learning are increased. The
extent of the disturbance is a function of the magnitude of the displacement
beyond the breakdown threshold. . . .

Principles of Human Factors Design in Physical Training

The cybernetic approach to control and guidance of motion creates a first
practice-related theory of human factors design in the applied sectors of physical behavioral science. By *practice-related theory,* we mean a set of concepts
that can be used for exact specification of the features of the behavioral,
instrumental, and social feedback operations utilized in training, education or
therapy. The expression, *human factors design,* refers to the space and time
characteristics of feedback control of motion which can be related to training
operations, techniques, and the instruments and machines used for training.
Heretofore, learning theory in psychology and education has been unsuccessful in formulating meaningful theories of human factors design in education
and physical behavioral science because such theory consists of unproven
mass-action dogma based on generalities of reward and punishment in animal
learning, which cannot be translated into exact specifications of training
techniques and instrumentation at the human level.

Specific Motions as Control Systems. In addition to the concepts of spatial
and neurogeometric guidance and regulation of motion, a second set of principles of physical behavioral design is that specific motions, such as those of
locomotion, hand-arm movement, head-eye tracking, speech and related
processes of tool-using, athletic and artistic performance, are best understood

as control systems. In functioning as closed-loop mechanisms, given sectors of the body are guided by self-generated stimulus feedback patterns. The body does not respond to chance external stimuli, but to feedback stimuli generated and regulated by specialized movements. Each movement creates directional space displacements in the feedback patterns, which are detected by nerve cells and used to control the form and timing of further motions. Postural and bilateral transport movements act to provide a neurogeometric feedback map of the state of the body with reference to gravity and ongoing dynamic movement, against which environmentally related articulated movements are continually adjusted. Different motion systems of locomotion, arm-hand response, and head-eye tracking are specialized both spatially and temporally in relation to these built-in, yoked body tracking systems, as well as in relation to the specific environmental stimuli which are tracked.

An example based on understanding locomotion will illustrate this principle of specialization of integrated body and environmental control in motion. Human locomotion represents distinctive levels of postural, transport, and articulated movement, in which each level of response functions to define particular aspects and dimensions of sensory feedback for supporting the body, for driving the legs in striding action, and for articulating and guiding placement of the foot in the step. Besides their basic dynamic functions in body support and travel, the postural and transport movements reference directional control of the contact movements of the sole of the foot, thus creating the balancing activities of the toes, ball, and heel of the foot in articulating both postural and transport action in relation to guided stepping.

The multidimensional components and levels of feedback control of locomotion are all focalized in the guided stepping action of the foot, so that all components of gait are reflected in the operational contact action of the sole of the foot with the substrate. Therefore, each level of sensory feedback control not only generates proprioceptive, visual and auditory signals significant for governing the motion, but also produces distinctive panoramic patterns of cutaneous, proprioceptive and visual input in terms of which the locomotor pattern is continually adjusted and corrected in relation to the characteristics of the terrain.

The different patterns of locomotion—i.e., walking, running, skipping, hopping, stair climbing, etc.—consist of dynamic differentiation of particular components, levels, and modes of cybernetic regulation in imparting distinctive spatial and temporal dimensions of action to the different component movements. The coordinate bilateral actions of the two legs and feet, which act in different parallel, complementary, compensatory, and opposing ways in feedback interactions with one another, are most important in defining the temporal and spatial dimensions of the patterns of locomotion. For example, the stride time of each leg is almost identical in walking and running, whereas the contact time of both feet with the substrate is zero for running and about 0.17 second for walking. Comparable differences in spatial displacements of feedback control also occur in the two forms of locomotion.

More than a decade of cybernetic research on gait has suggested to us that all of the temporal and spatial dimensions of locomotion are feedback regulated, and that different gait patterns are integrated, multiloop, closed-circuit patterns which combine postural, stride, and step guidance in distinctive ways.[7,9] The methods used in such research have combined electronic behavior-sensing devices for measuring stride and step movements and for controlling tactual, auditory and visual feedback related to these movements. Studies of inversion and reversal of the visual feedback of locomotor patterns have been carried out by requiring subjects to wear prisms that invert or reverse the visual feedback of gait motions. More recently, hybrid computer methods have been devised for analysis of the effects of feedback delay and displacement of postural activity and postural control at the end of a step. The results of all of these studies have confirmed the validity of ideas of gait patterns as specialized feedback mechanisms.

Manual motion also is best conceived as a cybernetic control mechanism in which different movement components of yoked body tracking and environmental control have been differentiated. In addition to general levels of postural, transport and articulated action characteristic of gait, the hand-arm system has been evolved to perform specialized apposed motions of the thumb and fingers as well as many specialized interactive movements of the fingers. The hand-arm system thus acts generally as a five or six-stage multiloop feedback control circuit, in which focal governing of sensory feedback can be directed to the hand as a unit, to the interaction of thumb and fingers, or to the patterned movements of the fingers of one or both hands.

Besides the processes of spatial displacement of feedback and of focal control of closed-loop action by different component movements, the most important differential factor in governing unimanual and bimanual motion is the distinctive properties of tactual and visual feedback related to this system. Tactual control of feedback of all levels of hand motions is exquisitely refined and fast, and makes possible more or less independent control of the two hands as well as of different fingers. In contrast, visual feedback regulation must be focalized on one level of hand, thumb-finger, or finger articulation of one hand, and cannot encompass effective simultaneous focal control of different movements at the same time. All movement integration of the hands and arms depends on the differential roles of tactual and visual feedback.

The division of labor between the two hands and between components of each hand provides the basis of the highly flexible potential of manual motion in performing compensatory, complementary and apposing movements of the two hands and arms, the thumb and fingers, and the different fingers in the functional activities of grasping, holding, manipulating, turning, pressing, throwing, rubbing, pawing and tool using. The spatial and temporal dimensions of these different functional motions represent specific patterning of movement components in effecting hand-arm operations in relation to particular objects, tools, and materials.

The comprehension of the main motion sectors of the body as cybernetic control systems constitutes a base concept of human design for physical education and other sectors of physical behavioral science. Such a concept has been lacking in education heretofore. Training devices, training procedures, therapeutic processes, instructional methods, instrumentation and physical fitness programs can be conceived and tested in terms of design-related theory, which can specify the properties of movement organization and dynamics in both health and injury. For the first time, the educational and training specialist can view human behavior in terms of practice-related theory based on specific concepts of motorsensory mechanisms and their neural control, and avoid the nonsense of mystical probabilistic concepts of reinforcement learning and mental control. The importance of social design in therapy, training, and exercise can be formulated on an objective basis in relation to specific processes of motion and behavioral capacity of the athlete, student, or patient in different patterns of social, instrumental and body tracking.

Continuous Feedback Regulation of Stimulus Selection. Traditional doctrines of psychology and education have never been able to give an account of motor and athletic skills because they contain no meaningful account of perception—the integration of sensory input needed for organized sensing of space, time, and object qualities and quantities. In these patterns of thinking, the active properties of perception, such as alerting behavior, orientation, and vigilance or attention, have never been clarified at all. The cybernetic account of physical behavior is particularly significant for understanding perceptual skills because it is the first doctrine to give a systematic account of how specialized multisensory processes are regulated and integrated in order to produce organized perception.

The term, sensory cybernetics, is used to designate the fact that perception is achieved by means of integrated movement control of receptor function, stimulus selection, and the afferent brain processes underlying alerting, vigilance, and focalizing of receptor action. The principles of sensory cybernetic regulation . . . suggest that different specialized motor activities combine to govern receptor sensitivity, receptor orientation, stimulus energy input, stimulus generation, stimulus pattern formation, modulation of environmental stimulus input and sources of environmental stimulation. All of the dynamic activities in controlling the receptor and stimulus selection go on more or less simultaneously, while activities of the postural system regulate the level of activation of the brain and thus determine alerting reactions and vigilance in perception.

There is extensive evidence today for all of the detailed assumptions and the general concept of sensory cybernetics . . . Different lines of research have shown that dynamic movement is essential to maintain sensitivity of the eye.[2,3] Numerous studies of our own on yoked vision, in which the optic targets are chained in closed feedback loops to eye movements and other body motions, have proved consistently that visual perception and tracking are optimally accurate when the eye tracks self-regulated targets. Other studies on space and time displacement of vision and other avenues of sensory input have indicated that when the intrinsic space and time properties between movement and different modes of stimulus selection are varied, the organization of both perception and motion is disturbed. . . .

Physical Educational Training Design

Specifications for advances in design of training procedures, teaching and coaching practices, and training devices or physical education and rehabilitative practice can be based on concepts of yoked instrumental, social, and psychophysiological tracking. These specifications can be indicated as a summary of the details of this paper. All of the specialized optical, electronic, electromechanical, television, videotape, and real-time, hybrid computer methods which have been developed and described in this report can be used with minor modifications as starting cybernetic instrumentational designs and procedures of training in education and as new feedback methods of diagnosis and therapy in rehabilitative science. The central principle of design of all such methods is that the critical stimuli and sources of stimulation which the student, athlete, or patient should learn must be locked to movement as body-yoked targets for dynamic tracking.

Many specialists in education and psychology have assumed that education reached the zenith of its design with the delineation of Hullian (1945) and Skinnerian (1953) learning doctrines and the buttressing of these views by psychoanalytic, statistical, and informational engineering (Shannon, 1951) elaboration. According to the proponents of current reinforcement dogma, all that needs to be done now is to discover how this grab-bag of conventional thinking and its statistical refinements can be applied to teaching machines, computer-controlled educational systems, and instrumental and social skills. Our adventures into experimental cybernetic research on learning have given us a somewhat different idea about past learning theory, its methodology, and the significance of its applications to educational design.

This idea is that past learning doctrine is, in fact, a mass-action vehicle for distributing ignorance about psychophysiological regulation and for promoting crude research methodology in psychology and education. Rather than creating a zenith for educational design, reinforcement dogma gives us a record of what not to do in trying to understand psychophysiological and motion integration in the human system. Fortunately, good alternatives now exist to following the generalities of reward and punishment psychology and physiology. Therefore, we can relegate reinforcement, conditioning, and associative theory to the historically interesting false archives of man's doings and proceed to understand his educational designs in terms of their evolution and basis as feedback-controlled adaptations and systems. This is the primary meaning of a behavioral approach to cybernetics—i.e., to comprehend and deal with learning in terms of the principles of systems analysis of the interactions between movements, motions, and environmental situations.

References

1. Ashby, W. R. *Cybernetics.* New York: John Wiley and Sons, 1963.
2. Ditchburn, D. W. "Vision with a Stabilized Retinal Image." *Nature,* 170:36-37, 1952.
3. Riggs, L. A., F. Rattiff, J. Cornsweet and T. N. Cornsweet. "The Disappearance of Steadily Fixated Visual Test Objects." *J. Opt. Soc. Amer.,* 45:495-501, 1953.
4. Smith, K. U. *Delayed Sensory Feedback and Behavior.* Philadelphia: W. B. Saunders Co., 1962.
5. ———. "Behavior Organization and Work." Madison, Wis.: College Printing, 1965.
6. ———, J. Gould and L. Wargo. "Sensory Feedback Analysis of Visual Behavior: A New Theoretical-Experimental Foundation of Physiological Optics." *Amer. J. Optom.,* 40:365-417, 1963.
7. ———, C. McDermid and F. Shideman. "Analysis of the Temporal Components of Human Gait." *Amer. J. Phys. Med.,* 39:142-151, 1960.
8. ——— and M. F. Smith. *Cybernetic Principles of Learning and Educational Design.* New York: Holt, Rinehart and Winston, 1966.
9. ——— and W. M. Smith. *Perception and Motion: An Analysis of Space-Structure Behavior.* Philadelphia: W. B. Saunders Co., 1962.
10. Wiener, N. *Cybernetics.* New York: John Wiley and Sons, 1948.

Chaining: Motor*

ROBERT M. GAGNÉ

EDUCATIONAL psychologists are concerned with general learning theory and its immediate application to educational practice. Behaviorism theory, especially as expressed by Thorndike, has had a tremendous impact on classroom teachings. Gagné, a noted contributor to many scholarly causes, believes that there are different "types" of learning as represented by that which is to be learned. Much of his work represents concepts related to

* From Chapter 4, from THE CONDITIONS OF LEARNING by Robert M. Gagné. Copyright © 1965 by Holt, Rinehart and Winston, Inc. Reprinted by permission of Holt, Rinehart and Winston, Inc.

the Behaviorism school of thought. With regard to learning types, Gagné refers to Signal Learnings as Type I, Stimulus Response Learning as Type II, and Chaining as Type III. He postulates additional types, but for our purposes an examination of Type III will suffice, for he relates it to motor activity.

The chaining of behavior is a frequent and widely occurring event within the sphere of learning. The acquiring of chains typically takes place with some rapidity, and often seems a very simple occurrence. But chains are of varying length; they may be as short as the act involved in pushing a light button, or as long as the recitation of "The Rime of the Ancient Mariner." And so naturally they vary in the rapidity with which they are learned.

By chaining is meant the connection of a set of individual $Ss \rightarrow R$'s in a sequence. There are sequences that are made up of motor responses, like that of turning on a television set or a washing machine. There are also sequences that are entirely verbal, like the greeting "How have you been?" or the pledge of allegiance to the flag. Here we will deal with both these varieties of chaining, which have much in common with each other. . . . The main emphasis will be one of describing chaining as a phenomenon, and identifying the conditions under which it occurs. For the acquisition of sequences that are nonverbal, the word *chaining* will be used, whereas the subvariety involving verbal behavior will be referred to as acquiring *verbal chains* or *verbal associates*.

Chaining (Type 3)

When one says to a novice driver, "Now start the engine," one is asking for the execution of a learned chain of $Ss \rightarrow R$ connections. If the training has been successful, what will take place is the reinstatement of a sequence something like this S ("Start the engine") $\rightarrow R$ (looking forward and to the rear) . . . S (sight of clear road) $\rightarrow R$ (testing for gear in neutral) . . . S (gear in neutral) $\rightarrow R$ (turning key to activate starter) . . . S (sound of motor catching) $\rightarrow R$ (release of key) . . . S (key released) $\rightarrow R$ (depressing accelerator). Each of the individual acts in the chain is something that the learner knows how to do. The trick is to get them done in the proper order.

Guthrie tells the story of a young girl who had acquired the habit of dropping her coat on the floor when she entered the house. Being annoyed with this practice, her mother had many times scolded her daughter and required her to go back and pick up the coat. But this was quite ineffective in overcoming the unwanted behavior. The mother, however, discovered an effective procedure: she made the girl go out of the house again with her coat on, then come in and hang it up properly. This illustration shows the importance of correct sequencing of the events in a chain. The original chain that was troubling the mother was: enter house $\rightarrow$ drop coat $\rightarrow$ see mother $\rightarrow$ mother says, "Pick up coat" $\rightarrow$ pick up coat $\rightarrow$ hang up coat. But what had to be established was a shorter chain with quite a different sequence, namely: enter house $\rightarrow$ keep coat on $\rightarrow$ approach closet $\rightarrow$ hang up coat. The mother displayed some most useful wisdom when she realized that the second chain could not be learned by simply adding links to the first one. What was necessary was the institution of the desired chain with correct links from start to finish.

The Phenomenon of Chaining

Unlocking a door with a key provides another simple example of a learned chain that can be used here for analysis. Of course, the assumption needs to be made that such a chain has not yet been learned, as may be true for a child. Descriptively, what must be learned is a sequence like the following: Having the key in his hand, and facing the lock, the child first checks to see that the key is right side up. Then he inserts it into the lock until the stop is reached, turns it until another stop is reached, and pushes the door open. Obviously, each of the individual acts ($Ss \rightarrow R$'s) of this sequence must be performed correctly, and in the proper order, or the performance of opening the door will be unsuccessful. If the key is not right side up, it cannot be inserted; if the insertion is not complete, it cannot be turned; and so on. The point is, the chain as a chain *cannot be learned unless the individual is capable of performing the individual links.*

Assuming that the individual $Ss \rightarrow R$'s that make up the chain have been previously mastered, it would appear a fairly simple matter to learn the chain. In this example, what is acquired may be represented as follows:

$$Ss \longrightarrow R \quad \sim \quad Ss \longrightarrow R \quad \sim$$
key positioning key up inserting key
$$Ss \longrightarrow R \quad \sim \quad Ss \longrightarrow R$$
key in turning key push
key turned door

The opening of the door constitutes a consummatory act, providing reinforcement for the final link and also for the entire chain.

If one were to undertake to set up conditions in which this chain were to be acquired by a human adult who did not know how to do it, it is of interest to note that *verbal instructions* would be used to guide the sequencing. Most probably, one would say something like this: "First hold the key so that the serrated edge points upward, with the point facing the lock. Then push the key into the lock as far as it will go. Now turn the key in the clockwise direction as far as it will go. Now push the door."

What is the function of such instructions? Evidently their most important purpose is to provide *external cues* for the selection of exactly the right links for the chain. Since the learner is capable of inserting the key into the lock in several different ways, an additional external cue may increase the probability that he reinstates the correct response and rejects others. In order to begin the learning, therefore, there must be a situation like this:

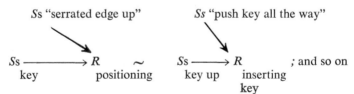

The verbal cues provided by the instructions become, for the verbally competent individual, stimuli that ensure the occurrence of the correct positioning response, or the correct inserting response, rather than an incorrect one. On the second trial they may be quite unnecessary.

Verbal instructions may be self-administered. Some writers have proposed that verbal instructions provided by the individual himself become a part of the chain being learned. This was the suggestion made by William James in his famous chapter on habit. As James pointed out, if self-generated verbal cues are an initial part of the chain that is acquired, they must later *drop out,* since it is evident that the "reeling off" of a well-established chain leaves no time for these verbal responses to occur. However, it is here proposed that verbal instructions, whatever their origin, are simply accompaniments to the initial establishment of a chain, and not a part of the chain at all. They are provided on an initial trial or two in order to ensure that the correct links get reinstated. After that they may simply become unnecessary because the stimuli from one link of the chain provide a suitable stimulus for the occurrence of the next link. One does not have to account for the "dropping out" of self-instructions; it is sufficient to realize that they are not necessary to successful execution of the chain. They are part of the conditions of learning but not a part of what is learned.

But what about learners who may not be able to respond to verbal cues, like animals or very young children? The essential problem is the same: a means must be found of providing external cues during the initial learning trial so that the correct links will be reinstated. If an animal has acquired a set of $Ss \rightarrow R$'s that are to be linked together, this can be done by introducing the external stimuli that have been connected with each link at exactly the proper time in the sequence. Later on, it is possible to eliminate these additional external cues and still have the chain performed satisfactorily. And so too with a very young child. One can imagine "guiding" the production of correct links by suitable cues, even when the individual may not be able to respond properly to such an instruction as "serrated edge." The additional stimuli used for this purpose might include pictures (for example, of a key in the proper position), and gestures (for example, a pushing motion of the instructor's hand). Again, these additional cues would no longer be needed once the chain had been learned.

There are many varieties of chains, and sometimes more than a single trial is required to learn them. This is particularly true when the stimuli of one link are difficult to distinguish from the stimuli of another. Under such circumstances, the learner may tend to reinstate a link out of sequence, and thus be unsuccessful with the chain as a whole. This tends to be the situation in a *maze,* whether one is dealing with animals or with men (using a finger maze). When the learner arrives at a certain point in a maze, it may feel and look almost like some other point, and yet require a different response. Yet when the stimuli controlling each link are made distinctive, such a sequence is not at all difficult to learn. Animals can learn fairly long chains quite rapidly, so long as the stimuli for each new link are readily distinguishable (that is, so long as they have been previously discriminated). Gilbert, for example, describes an easily learnable chain for a rat composed of the following acts: pull light cord . . . turn light on $\rightarrow$ press lever . . . buzzer sounds $\rightarrow$ approach pan . . . obtain food pellet. Human beings learning a finger maze typically make use of additional external cues, such as self-generated verbal instructions ("First right, then left, then left again," and so on), to increase the distinctiveness of the links.

Much experimental study has been devoted to maze learning in animals. Originally, the maze was chosen because it was "hard enough"; in other words, because it contained difficult link discriminations, and therefore required a number of repetitions for its mastery. The study of maze learning tended to obscure the fact that chains, under optimal conditions, are easy to learn. The learning of mazes appeared to be a gradual process primarily because animals were spending their time learning to discriminate the links that composed them (type 2 learning). Maze learning provides an excellent illustration of the fact that one can, if one wishes, get the learner to undertake two kinds of learning at once, in this case, $Ss \rightarrow R$ learning and chaining. But the results of such a mixture are not easy to interpret.

The Conditions for Chaining

The conditions necessary to bring about the variety of learning called chaining can now be described more formally. There are, as usual, some conditions that exist within the learner, and others that may be externally determined.

Conditions within the Learner. Of utmost importance to the acquiring of chains is the requirement that each individual stimulus-response connection be *previously learned.* One cannot expect a chain like opening a door with a key to be learned in an optimal way unless the learner is already able to carry out the $Ss \rightarrow R$'s that constitute the links. He must be able to (1) identify the key's upright position; (2) insert it into the lock fully; (3) turn it clockwise fully; and (4) push the door open. If a novice (a child, perhaps) complains that he cannot do it after being shown how, one immediately suspects that he has not fully mastered one of these links. Similarly, the chain learned in starting the motor of a car requires the previous learning of the individual links. Failure to learn on a single occasion usually indicates that one or more links have not been previously learned (pressing the accelerator as soon as the motor "takes hold" is an example).

If one could make sure that each individual link were fully learned, the additional external cues required could be reduced to an absolute minimum. But to be *fully* learned each link must have as a portion of its discriminated stimulus some kinesthetic feedback from the just-preceding response. For example, the key is not only seen to be inserted fully, it also "feels" right, and this "feel" becomes a part of the stimulus for the next link in the chain. Because it is difficult to ensure that all the stimulation for each link has been fully discriminated, additional external cues are added. But the fastest learning of chains occurs when the necessity for these additional cues is at a minimum; and this happens when the individual links have been individually well learned.

Conditions in the Situation. Several conditions in the situation are important to chain learning.

1. Assuming that the links are known, the main condition for the establishment of a chain is getting the learner to *reinstate them* one after the other *in the proper order.* Two different approaches to this sequencing are possible:

    a. One can begin with the terminal act and work backward, as Gilbert suggests. This ensures that the link one is trying to connect at any given point in the chain will always be introduced in the correct order. Beginning with link 4, one first connects link 3 by waiting for the occurrence of this link and then immediately following it with link 4 (the act leading to reinforcement); then one observes the occurrence of link 2, and follows it with links 3 and 4; and so on. This "progressive part" method, it may be noted, follows the procedure for type 2 learning *for each successive link.*

    b. A *prompting* method may be used, in which additional external cues are employed to ensure the reinstatement of the links in the proper order, beginning from the start of the chain. This is the method illustrated by the example previously given, using verbal instructions as "prompts."

It is evident that both these methods work. Whether or not one is more effective than the other, in some or all circumstances, is a question on which insufficient evidence is currently available.

2. A second condition is the familiar one of *contiguity.* The individual links in the chain must be executed in close time succession if the chain is to be

established. The smoothly executed chain pertaining to unlocking a door, for example, requires that the insertion of the key be followed by turning it to the right. Some of the stimuli for the second of these links arise out of the responses made in the first. Should there be a delay between these two links, the stimuli for the second connection will not be like those of the performance aimed for, and under these circumstances the chain may be learned with difficulty. This does not mean, of course, that it is not possible to learn chains that have delays deliberately built into them. Such instances may certainly be acquired; for example, one learns to delay until the coin has dropped fully into a slot machine before operating the lever.

3. A third condition relates to the *repetition* variable. Presumably, if all other conditions were fully met, repetition would be unnecessary. The chain would tend to form itself on the first occasion. Practically speaking, however, it is difficult to ensure that all the conditions are fully met. The individual links may be only partially learned, or the prompting may be not fully effective, or some delays may creep into the execution of the chain. Given these practical circumstances, repetition of the sequence has the function of "smoothing out" the rough spots, and some practice is almost always desirable for this reason.

Another function of repetition is the prevention of forgetting. Since errors do tend to occur, and are more likely the longer the chain, a means must be provided for practicing each link in its proper order. This effect of repetition becomes much more evident in the recall of verbal chains, which are typically subject to greater interference than are motor ones, ... To the extent that the links have been forged accurately and are connected precisely in the proper order, the need for practice will be reduced. Practice is used to permit the extinction of residual incorrect connections, rather than to establish new ones.

4. Finally, there is the condition of *reinforcement* present in the learning of chains. The terminal link must lead to a satisfying state of affairs—the food pellet is obtained, the engine starts, the door opens. The occurrence of some terminal satisfaction appears to be essential to the establishment of chains. If the reinforcement is omitted, extinction of the final link occurs, and the chain as a whole then disappears. It has been found that the reinforcement needs to be immediate in order for chain learning to occur most readily. The introduction of a delay in reinforcement markedly increases the difficulty of learning.

Other Phenomena of Chaining

Since chains are made up of stimulus-response connections, it is natural that one can see various phenomena of these $Ss \rightarrow R$'s exhibiting themselves in chain learning.

Extinction. The unlearning of a chain may be brought about in the same manner as that of a stimulus-response connection, namely, by omitting the reinforcement. When this is done, the terminal connection first disappears, followed in short order by the rest of the chain. This method is sometimes employed to remove undesirable habits. For example, the rather elaborate chain connected with smoking cigarettes (removing the pack from pocket, taking out a cigarette, tapping it, inserting in the mouth, striking a match, and so on) may presumably be destroyed if the terminal act of inhaling smoke becomes nonreinforcing, as when a substance generating an unpleasant taste is placed in the tobacco. It has even been suggested that such nonreinforcement might be brought about simply by removing from the smoke its resins, tars, nicotine, and its heat; but this procedure awaits verification.

Generalization. Any or all of the $Ss \rightarrow R$ links of a chain may exhibit stimulus generalization. The opening of a particular lock with a particular key naturally may be expected to generalize to a stimulus situation that includes a lock and key of somewhat different but similar appearance. Of course, should the second lock look the same but work differently, as in requiring a counterclockwise rather than a clockwise turn, the learner will be in trouble. In order to solve the problem, he will at the very least need to learn two different chains containing two comparable $Ss \rightarrow R$ links that are discriminated from each other, perhaps on the basis of the appearance of the keys. A still higher level of generalizing may be provided by the learning of a concept, in accordance with still other conditions. . . .

Discrimination. As has been emphasized throughout this section, the individual $Ss \rightarrow R$'s in a chain are discriminated entities. The more precise this discrimination is, the better they are for the purpose of chaining. Frequently for practical reasons, pains must be taken to establish special discriminations in one or more links, in order that some recurring confusion may be overcome. Such might be the case, for example, with the two different locks just described. The sequence required to start the engine of one automobile is usually different in some respects from that of another automobile. Here again, the individual who operates both cars may need to undertake special discrimination learning for some particular $Ss \rightarrow R$ in the chain (for example, the one that includes the response for releasing the starter switch).

Forgetting. Motor sequences of the sort described tend to be retained well for long periods of time. Presumably, individual links in chains are subject to differential forgetting. Not a great deal of systematic evidence is available regarding this phenomenon, however. The forgetting of a link in the middle of a chain may, of course, disrupt the entire chain in such a manner that the individual has the impression of having lost the whole. But it is also known that motor chains like those involved in swimming, skating, or bicycling can be recovered in a short time. Once a forgotten link is restored, the entire chain may reappear in its totality. This kind of experience is often reported by instrumentalists who try to reinstate the lengthy chains that make up a long-unpracticed musical exercise.

The Uses of Chains

Although of widespread occurrence among the human being's activities, chains are of essentially humble nature. In the early grades of school, a number of important chainlike skills must be learned. Buttoning, fastening, tying, using a pencil, erasing, using scissors, and many others fall into this category. At a slightly more complex level are the chains involved in printing and writing, which are of considerable importance as components of more elaborate activities to be acquired in the school. Throwing balls, catching balls, kicking balls, and many other fundamental sorts of athletic skills are also acquired as chains in the early years of the individual's life.

In later years of school, there are varieties of additional chains to be learned. Sometimes, these take the form of *procedures,* complex and lengthy chains that often incorporate simpler chains as components. The student may learn in science courses to carry out weighing procedures, liquid-pouring procedures, and many kinds of measurement procedures. Later still, he may learn to adjust and use a variety of scientific instruments, like microscopes, voltmeters, centrifuges—each of them requiring the learning of procedural chains. The vocational student is likely to have to learn a large number of procedures as basic tasks of the occupation he plans to enter. The student of art may learn procedures such as "brush techniques"; the student of music the complex procedures of playing an instrument.

In accordance with the definition used here, chains are nonverbal, although, to be sure, their learning may be facilitated by verbal cues. They cannot therefore be considered to constitute a central part of the school curriculum. But it would obviously be a mistake to call them unimportant as educational objectives. Certain motor skills and procedures are basic to competence as a scholar and even to wholeness as an adjustable adult person. Motor skills, common or uncommon, are an essential part of the process of self-fulfillment, whether they be a part of the activities of golfing, musicianship, artistic creation, or some other human activity.

Information Theory in the Understanding of Skills*

HARRY KAY

IN a "classic" article published in 1956, George A. Miller helped to popularize a newly developed probability approach to the study of behavior: information theory. In this theory, inputs and outputs are compared with the intent of determining an individual's "channel capacity." *How much* matter can a person process at one time? And *how well* can he process it? Much of the research concerns verbal material or the processing of and distinguishing among tones, hues, and other sensory stimuli associated with a particular sense modality. Kay attempts to relate theory and research to skilled performance. His optimism about the role this theory can play in understanding performance as well as helping to suggest more effective training techniques commensurate with present abilities is shared by others. Those concerned with motor skills would naturally want to improve the capacity of man to handle material, to make him more efficient.

There are so many ramifications to our subject that I am making no attempt to present the now familiar 'overview' of the field. I have arbitrarily selected one or two issues which seem to me important: there are many others. When a developed method of analysing data is taken over from another discipline it not only allows certain measures to be taken, but somewhat inevitably it carries with it the suggestion as to what is worth measuring. I want to consider how information theory has influenced our thinking about skills, and for this purpose I propose (1) to illustrate what it has to say about (a) perceiving and (b) responding in skilled behaviour—or if you prefer it, input and output—and then (2) to examine how this research accords with other findings in the field.

I am limiting my remarks to Shannon's measure of information, which concentrates on the probabilities of events. It is a measure of the *amount* of information, technically the negative logarithm of the probability that an event will occur. Less technically it is a measure of *uncertainty,* the less likely an

* From *Occupational Psychology*, 1957, *31*, 218-224. Reprinted with permission of the author and publisher.

event, the greater being the information it carries. Where two events are equally possible we need one bit (binary unit) of information to decide between them. In fact, appropriately enough one bit of information is what is given to the new mother when she is told the baby is a boy or a girl. When we are discussing a measure of *transmitted information* this is the familiar statistic of the correlation between input and output (cf. G. A. Miller, 1956).

I am not entering into technical discussion as to 'what is information measurement?' or the admissibility of concepts such as 'entropy' and 'channel capacity'. But let it be said at the beginning it is the information theorists themselves who are now most critical of their measures; it is they who have pointed out that there is hardly any situation where amounts of information 'will be the ultimate criterion of performance' (Quastler, 1955); it is they who are skeptical that amount of information does not adequately cope with the problem of discriminability (Crossman, 1955). Nevertheless in many situations information theory may be rightly claimed to provide 'a very good intermediate criterion'.

Let us first consider the position of previous research on skills, say up to 1940. In this field, as in so many psychological areas, we were not short of data. The psychology of human behaviour is often embarrassed by having too much material. What is required is guidance as to what is worth knowing, in other words, some theoretical framework. Without this the psychologist is in danger of collecting either the obvious because he can't miss it or the oddity for its eccentricity. In skills traditional research had been primarily interested in the response. We have to go back to Woodworth's monograph (1899) to find him deploring the lack of interest in the response. Woodworth won his point, and interest in the response was maintained. Of course the response side of a skill is impressive. You can't ignore the K.O. in a boxing match. However, the response is only half the skill and is not enough if we are to understand performance.

When the psychologist began thinking in terms of communication theory he had to consider an external environment generating the signal and recording the response, whilst between them was the human operator providing *the communication channel*. Thus weight was placed on both stimulus and response. This has led to research in which the input side of skills has been carefully analysed. This has coincided in post-war psychology with a marked emphasis upon perceptual learning, etc., which has also played its part, but information theory has notably contributed to this trend in emphasising perception in skills.

In one of Shannon's studies (1951) his subjects were trying to guess the next letter in a sequence of letters which had been selected from English prose passages. The subject was given the $n-1$ letters and then guessed at the nth letter. The game can be played in several ways: *e.g.,* a subject can continue to guess until he is right, and he can be given different numbers of preceding letters. Shannon obtained the following results (see G. A. Miller, 1954):

$(n-1)$	1	2	3	4	5	9	14	99
Per cent. Redundancy	15	25	35	33	45	48	48	68

Thus 15 per cent of the information conveyed by a letter is also contained in the letter immediately preceding it, 25 per cent in the two preceding letters, and when we have 99 preceding letters well over half of the information in the next letter is redundant.

We may compare this situation with the case of someone trying to estimate the future position of a moving object, say a car or the trajectory of a ball, from a limited observation of its initial stages. If we throw a ball for a young child to catch he is invariably too late in positioning his hands and lets the ball hit him on the chest. We say he doesn't anticipate the flight of the ball; he doesn't know where it will go but only where it is. Let us imagine the situation is such that our adult subject's head is fixed and he can only observe the trajectory of the ball by successive fixations. Thus we have the trajectory divided into a series of segments, which we might think of as events *a, b, c,* and so on. An individual, through his experience of watching how objects travel in space, learns about the probable order and temporal relations of these events. Thus given events *a, b, c,* he predicts the future position; and the skilled person is the one who can predict accurately on the fewest possible initial events. Once this is achieved the remaining events in the series are redundant, or at the most confirmatory. So much for the popular dictum about 'keeping your eye on the ball'.

From this kind of example it can be seen that we are clarifying the meaning of such sayings as the skilled man having 'all the time in the world' and the 'need to anticipate'. The skilled man can appreciate some events more quickly than the unskilled because they are less uncertain for him: they carry more information. And when we turn to events which do not necessarily occur in an invariant sequence we have examples where the skilled performer on a quick appraisal of present events is trying to predict on a probability basis future contingencies. Information theory is not the only statistic to handle this kind of situation but it does it competently enough.

So far we have discussed only the input arising from the *external* environment. But the operator is handling information from a second source, an internal source. This input arises from his own musculature as he carries out a skill. It is clear that the practised operator learns to recognise such signals; they are in fact a form of *knowledge of results* and I should like to consider briefly this aspect of an old psychological topic. It would seem that in manual skills the operator is always receiving signals which give him some knowledge of performance. Knowledge of results is not something which the scientist has ingeniously introduced into the skill, it is something intrinsic to it, and what the trainer aims to achieve when he gives knowledge of results is to add something to those signals which the trainee will normally receive. Knowledge of results will then be *augmented feedback* for the operator.

This may take several forms, according to the task and the progress of the operator. In the early stages of learning knowledge of results may serve as directional indicators, identifying difficult signals for the trainee. Some of our experiments with pressure controls bring out that there may arise a most interesting conflict. The trainee may rely too much on the additional indicator, say a light confirming when the correct response is being made. He performs excellently when it is there but he is attending exclusively to the extra indicator and not to the *intrinsic* signal. This gives the trainee better performance during training but a consequent poorer performance once the knowledge of results is withdrawn. This is what R. B. Miller (1953) has called 'action feedback' as against 'learning feedback' where the trainee's performance may not be so spectacular but he is attending to and learning the intrinsic signals of the skill. Our findings would suggest that this is a complex situation, from which we can make as yet no generalisations. But the problem seems to hinge on the relationship between the two incoming streams of information, the internal input arising from the muscular response and the external signal from some imposed criterion. The respective roles of these signals would seem to vary during the course of practice and with the ease or difficulty of the response itself.

So far then we have put the emphasis on the perceptual side of skills and observed that the ability to receive information is the secret of many skilled actions. Ostensibly we witness an economy and uniformity of action but its basis is the expert's ability to handle both the incoming signals from the external and from his own musculature.

We now turn to the measurement of the motor output in skills. It is the case that to date there has been comparatively little measurement of motor output, but there seems no reason in principle why this is so, though it may be difficult. An outstanding example is Fitts' (1954) attempt to measure the information of the action in a simple pin-assembly task. We have carried out assembly experiments similar to those of Fitts, where the apparatus consisted of a row of 8 pins spaced 1½ inches apart. Parallel to this row and 8 inches from it was a second row of 8 holders into which the pins had to be placed. Electrical contact was made when a subject grasped the pin at the end point and when he touched the holder with the pin as he positioned it. Thus we were able to take contact measures of the four elements, grasp, movement loaded, position and movement empty. We also photographed the operation, enabling us to compare the contact and photographic methods of timing.

Fitts had expressed his measure of task difficulty (Id) as follows:

$$Id = - \log_2 \frac{Ws}{2A}$$

where Ws was the position tolerance expressed as the difference in inches between the diameters of the pin and the hole and 2A was twice the amplitude of the movement. By expressing the index of difficulty (Id) over the observed times he obtained a performance index (Ip) in terms of 'bits'

$$Ip = \frac{Id}{t}$$

When we come to use such formulae it is soon apparent that their terms are by no means cut and dried. We might question whether the tolerance is satisfactorily stated in terms of the difference between the diameters of the aperture and the pin, or the rationale of taking *twice* the amplitude as the denominator. Yet using these measures several interesting features emerge. It is clear that the movement times over much of the major part of the arc—15/16ths, in fact—are constant in spite of varying tolerances at the end points. This we might expect if the time for a movement is determined by the amount of information which has to be transmitted in accomplishing the action. Movement time would be proportional to information load. This being so, we should be able to calculate the information involved in the position elements at the varying tolerances and see how far the predicted values square with the observed data. The results suggest that we have a primary movement which is made to an area of about 2 inches diameter, centered upon the actual target. Having reached this target area the secondary movement begins. This agreed well enough with the calculated values which would predict that the tolerance of the primary movement should correspond to twice the apparent amplitude of the secondary movement. We would say that analysis of this kind has shed light upon the older problem of primary and secondary movements in assembly tasks and given us some basis for examining the difficulties which arise in these kinds of responses.

Turning to our present research, we are continuing this measurement of the motor output in some reaction time studies. The attempts of Hick (1952) and Hyman (1953) and Crossman (1953) to measure the information when the number of possible stimuli were varied were outstandingly successful. We are now investigating how far we can make some measurement in reaction time studies where we are using *graded* responses and varying the required tolerances for a particular response pressure. If we are successful we should be able to predict any increases in the reaction times on the basis of the increased information which is being transmitted in the responses.

I have tried to suggest that information theory has provided an elegant measure of both input and output in skilled performance and has enabled us to appreciate more realistically the interdependency within a skill. The human operator is regarded as a limited capacity channel transmitting signals which come both from an external display and from internal sources. We consider such signals as events, and an operator is particularly concerned with learning when and where they are likely to occur. By so doing he materially simplifies the perceptual side of his task, for by appreciating the redundancy of some events an operator can receive the same total information from fewer events. The approach deliberately emphasises the perceptual side of skills. One of the main difficulties facing a trainee is often a complex stream of signals occurring so rapidly that it appears wellnigh impossible to distinguish one from the other. The suggestion is that the operator learns that he does not have to pay equal attention to all signals but that some are more significant than others.

But I should now like to take a broader view of the problem in evaluating whether information theory is contributing to an understanding of skills. Today we have many so-called physiological and mathematical models in psychology. There is no point in hopping on to a 'bandwaggon' just because it is creating more dust than another. But on the other hand it is paltry to disdain an approach because it is or has been fashionable. Equally the psychologist in this country is so ready to accept ideas from other disciplines whilst remaining abnormally sensitive of those in his own subject that we might well be suspicious of information theory.

For myself I find this approach is exciting because of the light which it has shed on many older problems and because the results accord well with those from other fields. We now have a whole series of studies which are converging and which do enable us to build up a fairly convincing picture of the kind of system which the skilled operator represents. Where we are dealing with a situation involving perception of stimulus, cortical transmission and motor response, as in the research on single and serial reaction times we have sound evidence of the intermittency or discontinuity of the operator (Davis, 1956, 1957). Here we have the characteristic not only of single channel transmission but of transmission where there is limited channel capacity. The work on binaural stimulation, particularly Broadbent's (1954) ingenious and comic set-up of sending at the same time one message to one ear and a different message to the other ear suggests the same conclusion—as a system we receive one signal and have to 'store' a second, for the two signals delivered simultaneously are received successively. When we turn to neurological considerations we find Adrian (1954, pp. 239-40) considering the same problem from his stimulation of the auditory nerve of the cat: some messages are selected, some are 'blocked' temporarily.

If, then, these are basic limitations of an organism, it would have to find some means of 'getting round' or overcoming such constraints and the things which we call skillful would be mainly those examples where the operator achieved this; that is, overcame the apparent basic limitations. In fact we find this is so: anticipation, timing, etc., are the everyday hallmarks of a skill for the 'man in the street'. And even psychologists have long been familiar with the idea that perception is 'of probable things' (James); or, to put it in its modern dress, of shifting the information load by making certain events redundant and processing only key items.

This then seems to me to be something more than providing us with familiar statistics with which to cope with familiar probabilities. So far we have considered how perceptual difficulty increases when events carry an increasing information load. I should like in conclusion to suggest that the future may well find us studying complex situations in which many signals are *correlated* with each other, and where the organism perceives by a rapid analysis of what is and is not *redundant* in the messages from the various senses. Where events are not correlated we know the organism handles them successively, as in the reaction time and auditory examples we have just noted. But where events are correlated I think it is true to say we don't as yet know what happens.

The everyday world as we know it is one in which we receive complex stimulation from several different modalities, as exemplified in the old problems of the stone 'looking hard' or the fire 'looking hot.' When we examine the information from one modality we find for example that movements of the retinal image may have to be co-ordinated with the activity of the ocular-motor system and with postural adjustments. The sum total of this co-ordinated activity is for us to see a stable world and on the grounds of economy it is tempting to believe that the organism learns to correlate signals from these various sources and to assess their redundancy. Given a novel situation, as in the case of the drunken man, some of the information is distorted with the result that the remainder does not match with it and the environment is no longer stable. As learning seems to play a large part in achieving this stability, it is possible that the visual world of the baby may well be more buzzing and confusing than James imagined: it may in fact be less stable. But whatever that may be it would seem a useful suggestion that the organism will quickly match and drop redundant signals. The complex and correlated stimulation is typical of the world around us and appreciation of its redundancy would seem to be the most economical and likely way for the human system to handle the situation. And of course, it is the everyday responses of life which are taken for granted, but which are the basic skills of living.

References

ADRIAN, E. D. (1954). The physiological basis of perception, in *Brain Mechanism and Consciousness*. Edited by Delafresnaye, Oxford: Blackwell.

ANNETT, J. and KAY, H. (1956). 'Skilled performance.' *Occup. Psychol.* 30, 112-117.

ANNETT, J. and KAY, H. (1957). Knowledge of results and 'skilled performance'. *Occup. Psychol.* 31, 69-79.

BROADBENT, D. E. (1954). The role of auditory localisation in attention and memory span. *J. exp. Psychol.*, 47, 191-196.

CROSSMAN, E. R. F. W. (1953). Entropy and choice-time: the effect of frequence unbalance on choice response. *Quart. J. exp. Psychol.* 5, 41-51.

CROSSMAN, E. R. F. W. (1955). The measurement of discriminability. *Quart. J. exp. Psychol.* 7, 176-195.

DAVIS, R. (1956). The limits of the "psychological refractory period." *Quart. J. exp. Psychol.* 8, 24-38.

DAVIS R. (1957). The human operator as a single channel information system. *Quart. J. exp. Psychol.* 9, 119-129.

FITTS, P. M. (1954). The information capacity of the human motor system in controlling the amplitude of movement. *J. exp. Psychol.* 47, 381-391.

HICK, W. E. (1952). On the rate of gain of information. *Quart. J. exp. Psychol.*
4, 11-26.
HYMAN, R. (1953). Stimulus information as a determinant of reaction time. *J. exp.
Psychol.* 45, 188-196.
MILLER, G. A. (1954). Communication, in *Annual Review of Psychology,* Volume 5.
MILLER, G. A. (1956). The magical number seven, plus or minus two. *Psychol. Rev.*
63, 81-97.
MILLER, R. B. (1953). *Handbook on Training and Training Equipment Design.*
W.A.D.C.
QUASTLER, H. (1955). *Information Theory in Psychology.* Illinois: Free Press.
SHANNON, C. E. (1951). The redundancy of English, in *Cybernetics.* New York:
Josiah Macey, Junior, Foundation.
WOODWORTH, R. S. (1899). The accuracy of voluntary movement. *Psychol. Rev.
Monograph.*

Components of Skilled Performance*

MICHAEL I. POSNER

ALONG with industrial revolutions and rapid advancements occurring in computer development, mathematic and information theory, and communications models, research and theory dealing with learning reflect terminology and direction in the engineering and mathematical psychologists' "bag." The determination of the channel capacity and abilities of the human organism presents an interesting if not overwhelming challenge. Posner attempts to synthesize research that might relate to man's ability to process information. Mechanisms involved in attention and memory, error reduction, and maximal information (bits) transmission from moment to moment are discussed. The preceding reading by Kay should serve as good background material for this article. It is recommended that the beginning students read the books of C. E. Shannon and W. Weaver, G. A. Miller, F. Attneave, F. H. George, A. T. Welford, and N. Wiener, as a basis for understanding communication theory, cybernetics, information processing theory, and Posner's translations of research to skilled motor performance.

Since its inception, experimental psychology has been engaged in the task of describing the various component functions man performs in doing skilled tasks. Of particular interest has been the quantitative exploration of the limits of man's performance in each component function. Pioneer investigations were concerned with how fast a man can begin a response, how much he can see at a single glance, how much time is required for discrimination, and how much of what he sees is retained after a single exposure.[1] More recently the same questions have been raised in a more general approach to the study of performance limitations in human beings,[2,3] which has included investigation

* From *Science,* 1966, *152,* 1712-1718. Abridged and reprinted with permission of the author and publisher. Copyright 1966 by the American Association for the Advancement of Science.

not only of individual components but also of the interactions between components. This approach was called human performance theory by the late Paul Fitts, who did much to develop it in this country.

Under the influence of developments in communications engineering and computer science, recent studies in experimental psychology have employed much of the logic and language and some of the mathematics of information and communication theory. These influences are apparent in studies concerning the maximum rate of information transmission in human beings, limitation in the capacity for discriminating sensory information, the capacity of visual and auditory short-term memory stores, and the trade-off between speed and accuracy of responses;[2,4] all these studies incorporate the older interest in the limitations of man's capacities within the newer analytic framework. Occasionally the number and complexity of component functions, particularly in studies of intellectual performance, are so great that the psychologist turns to computer simulation as a technique for exploring the interaction of these functions.[5] More typically, and with much the same goal, investigators have used traditional laboratory methods to measure the components of skill and to understand their interactions.

This article is concerned with the limitations of attention and memory in the performance of skills. Prior to the birth of experimental psychology, philosophers discussed limitations in the span of attention (the number of items to which a man could attend simultaneously) and in the memory span (the number of items a man could report after a single presentation).[6] The experimental analysis of these limitations was among the earliest undertaken by psychologists. This article begins with recent efforts to determine a channel capacity for man in simple tasks of information transmission. Although no general limitation to man's rate of processing information has been found, results of such experiments lead to techniques by which the amount of attention required can be controlled by varying the processing demands of the task. In the second section, I discuss use of these techniques to demonstrate that the rate of loss of information from a short-term memory system depends upon the processing capacity (attention) available during a brief period after presentation of the stimulus. In later sections I build upon this analysis to discuss the phenomena of interference and imagery within this general framework. In the final section reference is made to some applications of these principles in the study of familiar skills.

Information Processing Rates

The rate at which man can perform repetitive responses is limited. Such diverse movements as tapping the finger, moving the eyes, or saying short words can be made no more often than about ten times per second.[1] Moreover, the limitation appears to be of the central nervous system rather than of the muscles themselves.[7] It had been known since the 1880's that the time required for making a response in a simple key-pressing task increases logarithmically as the number of alternative stimulus-response combinations is varied from one through ten.[8] With the advent of information measures,[9] it was quickly shown that in many situations reaction time is a linear function of the information transmitted.[10] Some investigators hoped to find a maximum rate (channel capacity) at which man can transmit information, which would permit quantitative analysis of human attention.

In reaction time studies the number of possible stimulus-response combinations is varied and the subject responds as quickly as possible to the particular stimulus presented on a given trial by making the response appropriate to that stimulus. The linear relation between information and time is apparent in the resultant performance curve, but the slopes vary markedly with different stimulus and response codes. Tasks may require transformation from a symbolic to a spatial code—for example, from an arabic number to pressing a key, or from a spatial array of lights to a spoken digit. These codes, which had been used in the earliest studies, give steep slopes and are called incompatible. Other tasks may represent spatial stimulus and response codes, but in different planes. The stimulus lights are presented in the vertical plane, while the keys are in the horizontal plane. The absolute speed is greater than for the first group of tasks and the slopes are somewhat reduced. A third group of tasks represents either symbolic stimulus and response or spatial stimulus and response codes within the same plane. An example is a situation in which the subject's hands rest upon vibrators. Another example is when a subject has to press keys in response to lights, after being given 6 months practice at the task.

These data indicate that the rate of information processing in human beings varies sharply with practice and with different stimulus and response codes. Moreover, tasks such as naming words and pressing vibrating keys[11] show no increase in reaction time with increasing amounts of information, while other tasks which show an increase as information varies from 1 to 3 bits do not show an increase above this value.[12] For these reasons, the concept of a finite maximum capacity for information transmission in tasks of this type is not acceptable. These findings do not mean that such a capacity cannot be found under more restricted conditions, such as for tasks in which a particular alphabet is used, or for movements of a particular type. In fact, Quastler and Wulff[13] have shown that such capacities can be found for tasks like typing and playing music, while Fitts[14] has demonstrated the usefulness of this concept for tasks which involve linear movements of varying required accuracy.

Transformations

The speed with which man can respond to a stimulus reflects the difficulty of the processing which relates input and output information. What are the ways in which stimulus input can be converted to response output? In detail, there are as many ways as there are different tasks which man performs. However, in terms of the informational requirements of the tasks, three logical categories can be distinguished. Some tasks may require the subject to conserve information from input to output. Regardless of whether the task involves an energy or a spatial transformation, if it is to be performed without error the input information must be preserved. It is clear, however, that man is more than just an information-transmitting channel. He can act as a source of new information not present in a given stimulus, or he can decrease information, not merely through the making of errors but also through a recoding which is a reflection of the stimulus information in a condensed output.[15] Here I am not concerned with tasks in which man is required to elaborate upon the input information. I consider tasks, such as addition and classification, which involve information reduction.

How can the difficulty of transforming input to output be analyzed for information-conserving tasks? With the amount of transmission held constant, the degree of compatibility between stimulus and response codes is the variable used to compare the difficulty of transformation processes. Several methods of measuring compatibility have been suggested.[16] One involves ratings or preferential choices (population stereotypes) collected from a sample of subjects, which indicate what response is most natural for a particular stimulus code. Another method is that of comparing the absolute level, or, more usually, the slopes of curves. Estimates of stimulus-response compatibility are usually obtained from a population of relatively unpracticed subjects.[17] However, initial differences between tasks in their degree of stimulus-response compatibility continue to affect performance after many weeks of training.[16] It is possible, therefore, to use relative stimulus-response compatibility as a means of comparing the difficulty of the processing or transformation involved in different tasks. If stimulus-response compatibility is defined in terms of the rate at which information can be transmitted, it may then be used to predict other aspects of information processing, like the ability of subjects to perform two tasks simultaneously.

For information-reduction tasks, a more direct analysis of transformation size is possible, although it is not known how general this will prove to be in predicting the relative difficulty of tasks. For reduction tasks the input information minus the output information provides a direct and objective measure of the size of the transformation. In order to make such a measure reasonable, it is necessary to restrict consideration to tasks which do not allow selection from among stimulus elements, but which require the individual to process all the input in making his response. For example, in adding, the sum represents less information than the components represent, but each digit must be processed in computing the sum. Tasks of this type are said to involve condensation.

Several years ago I tested the hypothesis that the amount of information reduction is related to the difficulty of the transformation for a restricted set of tasks.[15] The tasks all involved the same 48-bit input, consisting of eight numbers. Groups of subjects were required either to record the stimuli or to operate upon them by means of a number of information-reducing tasks. The tasks chosen were such that the output information varied from 48 down to 7.7 bits, no aspect of the input could be ignored in producing a correct response, and the component operations involved were relatively familiar. The tasks included a recording task; alternate recording and summing of the digits of a given number; a partial addition task in which successive pairs of numbers were added together; a 2-bit classification task in which the numbers were classified into four categories—high-odd, low-odd, and so on; and a 1-bit classification task where high and odd or low and even formed one category and high and even or low and odd, the other.

Since these tasks could not be compared directly because the errors were so different, each task was performed at speeds varying from input of one number every four seconds to input of one number per second. The rate of decline in performance with increased speed was calculated for each task. When this rate was plotted against the amount of information reduction required by the task, the relations were found to be linear. That is, as the amount of required information reduction increased, the effectiveness of speed in reducing performance also increased in a regular fashion. For this set of tasks the size of the transformation, as measured by the amount of information reduction, is related to the difficulty, or the amount of processing the task requires. Just as in the case of information-conserving tasks, the relationship between information reduction and difficulty is attenuated as practice on the tasks continues, but the differences do not seem to disappear, at least not with modest levels of practice. For this set of tasks, then, a quantitative analysis of transformation size has been obtained and shown to be closely related to task difficulty.

When man performs an easy task he is able to attend to other aspects of the environment at the same time. Walking, for example, causes little or no interference with speech. As the difficulty of a task increases, it demands more of man's limited attention, and the spare capacity available for dealing with other signals is reduced. Such a limited processing capacity is not identical to a channel capacity in the information-theory sense, since it depends upon the type of transformation process involved. Moreover, this limitation cannot be viewed as static; rather, it changes with the level of practice. For example, when one is learning to ice-skate, it may be difficult to converse at the same time. When one becomes proficient at skating, normal conversation can return. However, a task which is difficult initially will generally continue to demand more attention, even after many weeks of practice, than one which is not.

These anecdotal observations are confirmed by experiment. The amount of practice on a reaction-time task has been shown to affect the degree of interference observed when the subject attempts to do mental arithmetic while performing the reaction-time task. Practice is effective, however, only when the signals in the reaction-time task are regular, so that the subject can learn to anticipate them.[18] It has also been shown[19] that when the stimulus-response codes were highly compatible, the reaction-time task caused little interference with mental arithmetic. The compatible primary task was pressing the finger upon a vibrating key. However, an incompatible primary task of pressing the key under the corresponding finger of the hand opposite the vibrator caused much more interference with the performance of mental arithmetic.

Transformation Size and Retention

In the preceding section it was stated that the ability to perform a second task simultaneously with the primary task depends, in part, upon the stimulus-response compatibility of the primary task. Thus, the level of stimulus-response compatibility can be used to control the spare processing capacity which the subject has available for dealing with new information. Similarly, the amount of required information reduction in the numerical tasks described above may be related to the capacity available for processing new information. This hypothesis could be tested directly by requiring the subject to process new incoming information while performing tasks requiring varying degrees of information reduction. No tests of this type have been made, to my knowledge, but an important consequence of the hypothesis has been tested.

Most skilled tasks involve a combination of transformation of new input and retention of previously presented information. Reading a book, listening to a lecture, or driving an automobile are examples. In these tasks, what is the relation between memory of previous input and attention to incoming stimuli?

Studies of short-term memory suggest the nature of this relation. In 1959 Peterson and Peterson[20] asked subjects to remember three letters while counting backward from a three-digit number for a variable time. They found a dramatic loss in correct recalls as the time increased from 3 to 18 seconds. This result, along with many other studies, shows that forgetting can be rapid when the subject's attention is controlled. If the notion of a processing capacity is accepted, then the degree of available capacity ought to be related to the rate of forgetting. . . .

These results are not very surprising. We all know that having our attention distracted after we have looked up a phone number may cause us to forget the number. The important point here is that the degree of distraction, or of attention given the intervening task, can be manipulated, and that this degree of distraction is systematically related to the amount of forgetting. If man is considered to have limited capacity for processing information, these studies indicate that whatever sustains the memory trace during the first few seconds after presentation requires a portion of that capacity. This process has often been called rehearsal. Rehearsal, as the term is used here, is not identical with covert speech and may vary in strength depending upon the processing capacity available to it. It is perfectly reasonable to talk about rehearsal of non-verbal as well as verbal material. Whether all forms of retention require central processing capacity, and hence rehearsal, can only be determined empirically. Presumably, traces differ in the amount of rehearsal required before the establishment of a memory which does not depend upon continued availability of processing capacity. While these conclusions are based upon studies of human subjects, they are in qualitative accord with results obtained in animal studies of "consolidation processes" in memory.

Role of Interference

Is loss of information from short-term store an inevitable consequence when rehearsal is controlled? The answer from both everyday experience and experiment is clearly no. Some items are retained despite deep and prolonged distraction. Of course, the amount of forgetting depends upon a variety of things besides rehearsal. In one study[21] it was shown that, on the very first trial of a memory experiment like those discussed above, there is little or no loss in retention over 18 seconds of counting backward. It is not until the subjects have had two or three trials that prevention of rehearsal causes a rapid fall-off in performance. Moreover, it has been shown that if a subject is switched to a new type of material after a number of trials, on the first trial after the switch the probability of error is greatly reduced.[22] These studies indicate the importance of the number of stored items and the similarity of the stored items to each other in determining the level of retention.

In order to understand the interaction of attention and memory in skilled tasks, one must know when a given level of rehearsal prevention is likely to result in forgetting. The experiments discussed below were conducted in an effort to describe how the number of stored items and their similarity to a new item affects the rate of forgetting the new item. Two different views are possible, depending upon whether traces of individual items do or do not remain independent during the retention interval. Perhaps they remain independent and stored material competes with the item to be recalled only at the time of recall. That is, at the moment of recall the subject searches his memory and selects the item that is strongest at that time. According to this "trace comparison" view, traces do not interact during the interval but, because of differential changes in the strength of the traces over time, errors occur due to competition during recall. In contrast, there is the "acid bath" view: competing items do not remain independent, but similar items inter-mingle during the retention interval and destroy the information contained in the trace. The simplest "acid bath" model would be one in which the effectiveness of competing items (interference) depends only upon time and the similarity between the stored traces. [The analogy with an acid bath is this: if an object sat in an infinite acid bath, the absolute magnitude of the effects of the acid (interference) would not be reduced by an operation (rehearsal) which added to the size of the object.] On the other hand, any "trace comparison" view predicts that, as rehearsal is reduced, competition among traces at recall must increase. Thus these views lead to quite different predictions about the result of controlling attention during the retention interval; while both models suggest that rehearsal will improve retention, the trace comparison view suggests that it will also diminish interference effects, while the acid bath view does not.

In a series of experiments we systematically manipulated the similarity among stored items by using populations of letters of either high or low

Table 1.   Effectiveness of Interference as a Function
of Difficulty of the Interpolated Task (Addition or
Classification) for All Time Intervals*

Time Interval (sec.)	Effectiveness of Interference	
	Addition	Classification
0	3.6	4.9
5	14.7	14.5
10	12.6	11.8
20	20	15

* Effectiveness of interference is given in terms of the difference in percentage of recall errors for low acoustic confusion and high acoustic confusion.

acoustic similarity.[23] Acoustic similarity has been shown by others to exert important influence upon recall scores.[24] In connection with each letter population we used two interpolated tasks requiring different degrees of information reduction, addition and classification, which had been shown to control rehearsal differentially. Groups of subjects were tested with one of the letter populations but with both types of interpolated tasks and with delay intervals of 0, 5, 10, and 20 seconds.

All the main effects of similarity of items and difficulty of interpolated task were significant and in the expected direction. Both high similarity of items and high difficulty of task increased forgetting. What is crucial is the effectiveness of interference, as measured by the difference in recall errors between items of low and of high similarity at the two levels of interpolated-task difficulty. These effects are shown in Table 1 in terms of percentages of letters incorrectly recalled, averaged across two independent experiments, for each time interval.

The results, which are confirmed by statistical analysis and which hold up in both studies, are quite simple. The effectiveness of interference was never greater under the high-difficulty task than under the low-difficulty task, as the trace-comparison view would require. Moreover, the values for the two tasks are closely related to the interval of time the items have been in store, though the interference effects remain roughly constant after the first 5 seconds. These data provide some support for a view of the "acid bath" type.

The "acid bath" view is closely related both to the decay theory and the interference theory of short-term memory. Moreover, related models have been suggested by a number of recent findings.[25] The "acid bath" view implies the following concerning the behavior of items stored in short-term memory. Stored items tend to lose precision of information over time. Such effects may be eliminated when full processing capacity is available for rehearsal. However, when opportunity for rehearsal is reduced, the rate at which precision is lost is a function of the number and similarity of items which have been stored in short-term memory. Thus, the rate of decay is a function of the amount of interference among items. Interference itself is a function both of the amount of "acid" (the number of stored items) and its "concentration" (the similarity of the stored items). That the number of items is important in determining the rate of forgetting is clear from the limitation of the memory span. As the number of items which are stored increases, the effectiveness of a period of free rehearsal in preventing loss during a subsequent task is reduced. Our study[23] shows remarkably similar effects of item similarity when it is manipulated by acoustic pattern. When items are similar the rate of loss of information for a fixed number of items is increased and the effectiveness of rehearsal tends to be reduced.

Since many language skills demand the continuous intake, storage, and recall of information, such skills provide nearly optimum conditions for the occurrence of forgetting. The intake of new items tends to block rehearsal, while the competition from earlier items leads to a rapid loss in precision. Because of the rapid loss of stored information in such situations, memory limitations are basic to the information processing analysis of many skills.

Imagery

One of the limitations of the evidence presented so far is that only retention of materials such as letters, digits, and words which are easily stored in verbal form has been discussed. Many skills involve the retention of patterns of visual or kinesthetic information which may not be easily or completely encoded in words. The typed letters *A* and *a* are usually given an identical verbal coding, but it is possible that retention of their visual difference may still remain. Several recent studies[26] of perceptual-motor skills have suggested that nonverbal information concerning the distance, form, and location of prior movements must be stored between successive trials. This type of storage of nonverbal material is usually called imagery. Evidence[27] has indicated that such information is lost over time, but relatively little is known about the details of short-term retention of these materials.

Studies currently in progress in our laboratory are directed toward the incorporation of imagery within a general information-processing framework. Two different tasks are being studied. At present we know that these two memory situations give strikingly different results, but we are not completely sure why this is so.

In the first task the subject must recall the location of a point at one of 12 positions along a 180-millimeter line. He is given about 1 second in which to view the position of a circle on the line, and after a variable delay he must indicate the location of the circle's center on an identical unmarked line. Since similar results are obtained whether or not the subject moves his hand to the original target, it is clear that in this task the subject must rely upon visual information.

In the second task the subject moves a lever one of 12 distances from a starting position to a finish peg. He must then reproduce this distance in a second box in which the lever starts at a new position. Since he cannot see his hand in either box, his only source of information is kinesthetic.

In each task, two major independent variables are considered. First, the length of time between exposure and recall is varied, in the range from 0 to 30 seconds. Second, the difficulty of the interpolated information transformations is varied. In two experiments there were four groups of 12 subjects each. Each subject was assigned one interpolated task. During the experiment each subject reproduced the 12 distances four times, each time with a different delay interval.

The second task was kinesthetic. The basic pattern, confirmed by statistical analysis and by subsequent replication, indicates that the mean error or reproduction increases regularly with delay. This is true even when the subject has no task to perform during the interval. Moreover, there are no significant differences in the curves for various interpolated tasks: forgetting is not significantly more rapid under the classification condition than under the resting condition. Both the loss of accuracy over time in the resting condition and the lack of differences in the curves for various interpolated tasks distinguish these results from those of the verbal tasks studied previously. Retention seems not to depend upon the central processing capacity available during the retention interval.

The results for the first, or visual task, are quite different. In this task, with the resting condition there is no forgetting at all. Moreover, the curve for the recording condition, in which the subject must deal with as many digits as he deals with under the other conditions, shows little evidence of forgetting over time. In two separate studies, comparison of the results for the 0-second and 20-second intervals for the recording condition indicates that half the subjects show increasing error over the interval and half show decreasing error. However, under the classification condition, every subject shows an increase in error. Moreover, the interpolated tasks order themselves in the same way, from the standpoint of difficulty, as in the previous verbal studies. For this task, forgetting is clearly a function of the processing capacity available during the interval.

The most obvious explanation of the difference in results for the two tasks is the explanation that subjects are using numbers for retaining information in the visual but not in the kinesthetic task. A detailed analysis of the data argues against this explanation. The introspective reports of the subjects obtained after the experiment indicate in all conditions the use of crude verbal labels, such as left or right of center, and so on. However, this use of imprecise verbal labels cannot account for the extreme accuracy found, particularly in the visual task. Even if the subjects were assigning numbers accurately to the nearest inch, they could not, by this means, achieve the accuracy of reproduction that is obtained. Only one or two subjects reported use of labels as precise as this, and they showed no evidence of superior performance. Moreover, there was no indication of the large errors which would be expected if subjects were forgetting verbal labels. Analysis of the median errors, in which the effects of a few large errors would tend to be eliminated, indicates the same results for means. Some verbalization undoubtedly is involved, but it seems to be equally extensive in the two situations—visual and kinesthetic—and not sufficient to account for the observed accuracy of reproduction.

If the differences in results for the two tasks do not lie in the degree of verbalization, why does the retention of information in the visual task seem to depend upon available processing capacity while in the kinesthetic task it does not? At present our work is directed toward finding the answer to this question. It may lie in fundamental characteristics of the two modalities, or it may lie in other differences between the two tasks, such as the requirement for retaining a location fixed in space as compared with the requirement for retaining a distance which must be integrated over time.

The results obtained thus far indicate support for the view that some memory tasks involve retention of information in nonverbal form and that such information is subject to forgetting which can be measured over time. The results also indicate that these tasks may differ from each other and from verbal tasks in the extent to which they are affected by control of the subject's central processing capacity. These effects are not due to differences in the initial level of accuracy of retention. In fact our present work indicates that, when measured in similar situations, the initial accuracy of retention for the two modalities is rather similar, but the crucial differences discussed above remain. Since it is possible to measure the amount of information generated by the reproduced responses after each delay interval, it is possible to make direct comparisons of the informational capacity and decay characteristics of various memory systems.

Applications

Human performance theory has for its goal the analysis of skills. The capacities of attention and memory which are explored in this article play an important role in many types of performance. In order to illustrate this viewpoint, in the space remaining I review a few examples of the application of techniques developed in the experimental laboratory to the analysis of familiar tasks.

Shephard and Sheenan[28] have shown the usefulness of data on man's limited memory span to the design of optimum systems for the storage and retrieval of numbers of the type used in telephone dialing. In a proposed system they seek to minimize storage time for the high-information portions of the number by allowing the familiar prefix code to be dialed last. This simple procedure cut errors by 50 percent.

Another common task which has been studied involves the measurement of performance during automobile driving as a function of road, traffic, and vehicle conditions. Normally it is difficult to make such comparisons because the details of the skill shift with the independent variable. Brown and Poulton[29] approach this problem by adding a simple numerical task to the primary skill and observing changes in the capacity available for processing the numerical information. The amount of spare capacity shows predictable changes as the driving task demands more of the subject's attention.

At a more complex level, recent efforts have been made to analyze the processes of induction in terms of informational transformations and memory. In several studies it has been found that the amount of information to be absorbed on a given trial affects the ability of subjects to make full use of incoming evidence. Studies of this type have led to proposals for systems of decision-making in which machines are used to relieve man of memory load and other limitations which affect his ability to combine information over time.[30]

References and Notes

1. R. S. Woodworth, *Experimental Psychology* (Holt, New York, 1938).
2. P. M. Fitts, in *Categories of Human Learning*, A. W. Melton, Ed. (Academic Press, New York, 1964).
3. D. E. Broadbent, *Perception and Communication* (Pergamon, London, 1958).
4. F. Attneave, *Applications of Information Theory to Psychology* (Holt, New York, 1959).
5. W. R. Reitman, *Science* 144, 1192 (1964).
6. W. Hamilton, in R. S. Woodworth, *Experimental Psychology* (Holt, New York, 1938), p. 685; A. Blankenship, *Psychol. Bull.* 35, 1 (1938).
7. W. O. Fenn, *J. Appl. Phys.* 9, 165 (1938).
8. J. Merkel, *Phil. Studies* 2, 73 (1885).
9. C. E. Shannon, *Bell System Tech. J.* 27, 379 (1948); *ibid.*, p. 623.
10. W. E. Hick, *Quart. J. Exp. Psychol.* 4, 11 (1952).
11. J. R. Pierce and J. E. Karlin, *Bell System Tech. J.* 36, 497 (1957); J. A. Leonard, *Quart. J. Exp. Psychol.* 11, 76 (1959).
12. R. Seibel, *J. Exp. Psychol.* 66, 215 (1963).
13. H. Quastler and V. J. Wulff, *Control Systems Lab. Rept. No. 62* (Univ. of Illinois, Chicago, 1955).
14. P. M. Fitts and J. R. Peterson, *J. Exp. Psychol.* 67, 103 (1964).
15. M. I. Posner, *Psychol. Rev.* 71, 491 (1964).
16. P. M. Fitts, *IBM Res. Rept. RC-109* (1955).
17. R. Davis, N. Moray, A. Treisman, *Quart. J. Exp. Psychol.* 13, 78 (1961).
18. H. P. Bahrick, M. Noble, P. M. Fitts, *J. Exp. Psychol.* 48, 298 (1954).
19. D. E. Broadbent, *Acta Psychologia* 23, 325 (1964).
20. L. R. Peterson and M. J. Peterson, *J. Exp. Psychol.* 58, 193 (1959).

21. G. Keppel and B. J. Underwood, *J. Verbal Learning Verbal Behavior* 1, 153 (1962).
22. D. D. Wickens, D. G. Born, C. K. Allen, *ibid.* 2, 440 (1963).
23. M. I. Posner and A. Konick, *J. Exp. Psychol.*, 72, 221 (1966).
24. R. Conrad, *Brit. J. Psychol.* 55, 75 (1964).
25. L. R. Peterson and A. Gentile, *J. Exp. Psychol.* 70, 473 (1965); W. Wickelgren, *J. Verbal Learning Verbal Behavior* 4, 55 (1965).
26. L. R. Boulter, *Can. J. Psychol.* 18, 281 (1964); J. A. Adams and S. Dijkstra, *J. Exp. Psychol.*, 71, 314 (1966); E. C. Poulton, *Ergonomics* 6, 117 (1963).
27. E. A. Bilodeau and C. M. Levy, *Psychol. Rev.* 71, 27 (1964).
28. R. N. Shephard and M. Sheenan, *Perceptual Motor Skills* 21, 262 (1965).
29. I. D. Brown and E. C. Poulton, *Ergonomics* 5, 35 (1961).
30. W. Edwards, *Human Factors* 4, 59 (1962); M. I. Posner, *Brit. J. Psychol.* 56, 197 (1965).

DATE DE RETOUR

UM-5